1/97

1/97

COMMONSENSE BETTING

Also by Dick Mitchell:

Winning Thoroughbred Strategies

Commonsense Handicapping

Myths That Destroy a Horseplayer's Bankroll

Thoroughbred Handicapping as an Investment

COMMONSENSE
BETTING

Dick Mitchell

William Morrow and Company, Inc.
New York

It is the policy of William Morrow and Company, Inc., and its imprints and affiliates, recognizing the importance of preserving what has been written, to print the books we publish on acid-free paper, and we exert our best efforts to that end.

Library of Congress Cataloging-in-Publication Data
Mitchell, Dick, 1939–
    Commonsense betting / Dick Mitchell.
        p.   cm.
    ISBN 0-688-13396-7
    1. Horse racing—Betting.   I. Title.
SF331.M546   1995
798.401—dc20   94-44882
                                                      CIP

Printed in the United States of America

First Edition

1 2 3 4 5 6 7 8 9 10

BOOK DESIGN BY DIANE STEVENSON/SNAP-HAUS GRAPHICS

DEDICATION

To Samuel Alexander Mitchell

In 1993 I wrote a book called *Commonsense Handicapping*. In the dedication I said, "You're the greatest gift that I've ever received in this life. Words can't begin to express your magnificence. You're the cutest, most adorable, innocent, and beautiful human being on this planet. I can hardly believe the absolute profound joy that you bring into my life every day. I am so proud to be your father. You have given me so much, it's hard to even start to express my gratitude. Thank you, Sam—for being the wonderful son that you are."

Now I've written the sequel to *Commonsense Handicapping*—*Commonsense Betting*. In just two years you've grown so much. You've become even more magnificent. I'm totally amazed by your accomplishments. You've become a skilled swimmer and diver. You've mastered the alphabet and our number system. You've learned to tell time. You've become an ice skater, hockey player, and Rollerblader. You're a better skater than your dad and I'm fifty years your senior. You haven't even started kindergarten and you've achieved all this and more. Your potential is unlimited.

The joy that you bring your mom and me is beyond words. We love you so much and are so proud of you. We promise that we won't live our lives vicariously through you. You don't have to go to an Ivy League college. You don't have to become the athlete your dad wasn't. You don't have to become a doctor. You don't have to become anything that you're not insanely passionate about becoming. We want you to become what you want to become. We'll love and support you whatever path you take. The only thing we want is for you to be happy and fulfilled. Cynthia and I can't thank you enough for the joy and happiness that you've bestowed upon us. Every moment gets better and better. Thank you so very much for being Sam Mitchell. We love you so much.

CONTENTS

ACKNOWLEDGMENTS

My most appreciative acknowledgment goes to you the reader for allowing me to share my ideas with you. Bless you.

My sincerest thanks to all my students, past and present, for giving me the opportunity to do what gives me the greatest fulfillment: teaching.

My passion for teaching was learned from an absolute master teacher. His name was Brother Leo Quinn and he was a Franciscan brother who taught at St. Francis College in Brooklyn, New York. Bless you, Brother Leo—I miss you a lot.

Many thanks to Gordon Pine, director of research for Cynthia Publishing Company, for his great job of editing, proofreading, and contributing to this book. His knowledge of grammar and syntax has saved me from committing untold abuses against the English language.

My gratitude and thanks go to Kitts Anderson and Steve Unite, both of whom are very skilled handicappers and bettors as well as power-users of *ALL-IN-ONE*—in fact they're so good at using this software that they're now teaching others how to win with it. Kitts and Steve together deserve credit for the "Workshop" chapter, while Steve helped me write the chapters on win betting, the Daily Double, the Pick-3, exacta and quinella wagering, and place-and-show wagering. Thank you, Mr. Steve.

Unite is a very brainy young man and a very gifted writer. We'll hear a lot from him in the future.

All three of my "handicapping children"—Gordon Pine, Kitts Anderson, and Steve Unite—make me feel proud as a new papa. Kitts and Steve are fearless students of the swing-for-the-fences handicapping and betting strategy school. Andy Beyer would be delighted with them, as am I. Gordon Pine belongs to the Mark Cramer school of creative handicapping. He's forever discovering some new gem that's way out of the mainstream. Gordon's work is of the highest quality. He won't settle for anything less than excellence.

Finally, I would like to acknowledge my surrogate parents, Helen and Olive Mitchell. They insisted I get a good education. When all of my friends were quitting school and squiring the ladies around in brand-new convertibles, Helen and Olive managed to convince me that it was smarter to finish school and settle for a ten-year-old car. How they managed this feat is beyond me. What they lacked in formal education they more than compensated for by their common sense. Thank you, Helen and Olive, for making a world of difference in my life. I shall be eternally grateful.

INTRODUCTION

I fondly remember the evenings James Quinn would come to our 800-square-foot condo for dinner. The time was the early eighties, and I had just begun my computer assault on the races. Jim and I would go over endless computer simulations of betting methods. At dinner, he and Cynthia would discuss all the social and political issues of the day. When Quinn left, Cynthia would always ask me why such a bright, intelligent man like Jim was so passionate about horses. Wasn't that a great waste of talent? Try as I might to convince her that thoroughbred handicapping was a noble pursuit and that Quinn was a giant, she would scoff, "He's just a gambler, and all gamblers are losers."

Dr. James Quinn, Dr. Mark Cramer, Dr. Howard Sartin, Dr. William Quirin, and all the Ph.D.'s in the world couldn't convince Cynthia that thoroughbred handicapping was anything but a depraved, somewhat sinister pursuit that lacked any socially redeeming qualities whatsoever. It wasn't until I started to win consistently that she finally and reluctantly conceded that my Ph.D. horseracing buddies were not "scum."

It took a little over two years and reams of computer printouts before I cracked the nut. Needless to say, my friends and colleagues at work thought that I had taken leave of my senses. Many of them would quote from books on gambling that said the horses were impossible to beat. When I tried to explain the fact that two of my teachers, Jim Quinn and Mark Cramer, had made money every year for the past twenty years, they would scoff, "I don't see them driving Rolls-Royces." I would then gently remind them that they weren't driving luxury cars, either.

For some reason, people think that professional horseplayers are all millionaires who bet huge sums of money on each event. The truth is that most professional horseplayers make a middle-level management wage. It's not the best-paying profession in the world; in fact, it's a rather average-paying. The number of professional horseplayers who make over $100,000 a year can probably be counted on your hands and toes. Nobody ever claimed that thoroughbred handicapping is the most lucrative profession in the world, and the truth is that it's not.

Winning at the races is a huge challenge. It takes a lot of time and a lot of hard work to succeed. Fortunately, it's a lot of fun and very spiritually rewarding. In order to win consistently at the races, you must do three things: pick good horses, make good bets, and keep accurate records. The typical player thinks that the way to the win window is through picking horses only. Needless to say, he or she is missing two thirds of the basic ingredients. This probably explains why so few handicappers are consistent winners.

This book will teach you how to bet properly. You probably aren't happy to hear that betting strategy is complicated. But that's your edge—most handicappers are unwilling to wade through the difficulty. I am absolutely convinced that an average handicapper with superior betting skills will outperform a superior handicapper with average betting skills.

I used to think that handicapping skills and betting skills were of equal importance. It wasn't until early 1993 that I truly understood the power of good betting skills. During a "Winning Weekend" seminar, I asked my audience what percentage it believed betting strategy contributes to winning consistently. I was trying to elicit the answer "50 percent." The group was unresponsive, so I turned to my co-presenters Mark Cramer and Ron Ambrose. Mark Cramer answered first. To my utter shock and amazement he answered 70 percent. I then turned to Ambrose, hoping he would answer differently. He didn't. Wow!—two of the best handicappers in the country testifying to the fact that betting strategy is more important than handicapping skills.

Their answers gave me food for thought. As I pondered my original question, it became apparent from my own performance as a handicapper that Cramer and Ambrose were absolutely correct. Starting in 1983 and every year since I have made a profit at the races. When I compare my present handicapping skills to my skills in the early eighties, I see a world of difference. I would estimate that I'm at least twice as good now as I was then. This means that my ROI (return on investment) should be at least double what it was then. It's not. In fact, it's only a small fraction better. My betting skills haven't improved because they're mathematical, and once you learn them they're yours forever. I understood betting strategy way back then. My longstanding record of consistent profits, year in and year out, has been mainly due to my betting skills.

One of the keys to winning at thoroughbred racing is attitude. You must see yourself as an investor as opposed to a gambler. I view a racetrack as my personal bank. If I have a losing day, which isn't an unusual event, I simply remind myself that the track is jealously guarding my money and that I'll be back for both principal plus interest. (It pays a very generous interest rate depending upon the type of bet.) I keep very detailed betting records and know my expectation for each type of bet. The better my performance at a particular type of bet, the larger the amount of money that I'll invest.

I despise gambling. If it's not a sin, it should be. Imagine risking your hard-earned money on a series of events whose outcome you don't know in advance. (The secret to success is "Know your outcome in advance.") When I bet on 100 playable races, I know I'll get at least 28 of them correct. Which 28? I don't know. Might be the first 28, followed by a string of 72 consecutive losses. This scenario is a bit unlikely; the longest string of consecutive losses that I've ever suffered has been 26, and that was a long time ago. I know that for every dollar I wager on win betting, I get back about $1.20. This is nothing to brag about, but I'm not that good at win wagering. My strong suits are exactas, trifectas, and Pick-3s.

This book will teach you how to calculate your edge on each bet. There is just one fundamental rule: No edge, no bet. In order to win consistently at any gambling game you must have a positive edge on a substantial number of plays in the game. This is why there is no such thing as a professional diceplayer. Every bet in casino craps carries a negative edge or is a break-even secondary bet. There's never a time when the game turns favorable to the player, as in blackjack. The only games that you can beat are strategy games. Blackjack and poker are casino games that can be beaten. Sports betting, the stock market, the commodities market, options markets, and bond markets can be beaten. You're playing against other players. If your strategies are superior to your competition's, you'll win. If they're not, you'll lose or at best break even.

(If you play it correctly, thoroughbred handicapping is a game in which every single bet that you make carries a positive edge, and the only long-run consequence is winning. The trick is learning how to play it correctly. Study this book and the books in the bibliography and you'll be on the road that leads to the win window. Make the commitment to take your life to a new level. Do the work—the rewards will follow.)

(This book is meant as a reference source, not as something you should read just once. I suggest that you read it through casually the first time to get an overall idea of its contents. Then take a single chapter at a time to study. Read it as you would a technical article—highlight important passages. Don't be intimidated by the math—a pencil, paper, and calculator will help a lot.

Come with me on a fascinating journey whose destination is the win window. I'll bet that you'll know a lot more about betting when you're finished with this book, and that knowledge will serve you the rest of your thoroughbred handicapping life. Please take the time to master this information. It's worth its weight in flawless ten-carat diamonds.)

COMMONSENSE
BETTING

A Gambler's Fantasy

Suppose you're walking on a deserted beach. Your eye catches something protruding from the sand. You stop and pick the object up. Low and behold, it's an ancient oil lamp. You rub the sides to wipe away the sand and damn if Robin Williams doesn't appear. He says, "I ain't got much time, so make it quick. I've got to get back to Disney Studios, we're doing an animated version of *Aladdin* starring my very own self. You've got just one wish, so make it fast." In your haste you answer, "A million dollars." He says, "That's a snap."

He hands you a very tiny pouch that contains three grains of what looks like sand. He explains that these grains are magic and instructs you to find the nearest casino and put one grain in each of three different numbers on a roulette wheel. Once these magic grains touch a number, the ball will never land on it—guaranteed. After these brief instructions he hands you a twenty, a ten, and a five-dollar bill and disappears.

Did he honor your wish for a million dollars by giving you $35 plus the three magic grains? Absolutely! Positively! All you have to do is to put the grains on three different numbers to ensure that the ball will never land on them, then spread the $35 on the 35 remaining numbers (American roulette wheel). One of these numbers has to win and you'll be paid 36-for-1, which yields a profit of $1. Repeat this until your bankroll gets to $70, then bet $2 per number. When your bankroll gets to $105, bet $3 per number. Continue this process until your bankroll gets to the $1,000,000 that you asked for. Naturally, the magic goes away after you've made your million, or else you'd own the universe and surrounding regions real soon. (For those of you who are mathematically inclined, can you figure out the minimum number of spins, starting with a $35 bankroll, it would take for you to become a millionaire? Better yet, if it took one minute per spin and you played for ten hours each day, how long would it take you to become a millionaire? The solution can be found at the end of this chapter.)

The above is an interesting fantasy, but what's it got to do with thoroughbred handicapping? Everything. The analogy is direct. Suppose you had a magic grain you could put on the program number of a horse that would eliminate it from win contention. In fact, suppose you have more than one of these grains for each race. Also, imagine other players (your competition) not having this powder. Do you suppose that you'd have a distinct edge? You bet your sweet bippy. And that's exactly the power that you have now. That's precisely why the horses can be beat, regardless of the exorbitant takeout. If you can find a rational way to separate horses who have little or no chance to win from those who have relatively high chances to win, you'll have the genie's magic powder.

Suppose for a moment that you could eliminate a 2-to-1 favorite. That is, at least 33 percent of the money bet in a particular race was going to be added to the amount to be divided among winning wagers. Suppose the track take was 20 percent. This implies that a 13 percent profit could be made by betting all the other horses in proportion to the probability associated with their odds. In other words, it's analogous to betting on all the numbers that the ball can't land on.

I have a colleague, a fellow teacher, who supplements his meager income by finding races in which at least 50 percent of the probability is misplaced. He bets as many as five different horses to win. His whole handicapping strategy is geared to identifying the horses that have the greatest chance of losing, as opposed to the traditional method of picking the horses who have the greatest chance of winning. He's quite the contrarian. But guess what? He wins. He must have tripped over an ancient oil lamp.

You're going to hear many seemingly cogent arguments, by intelligent people, demonstrating the fact that it's impossible to win at the races. Here's an example: "Watching horses run after making a bet on one of them can be very exciting, but unfortunately, the greed of the racetracks and the states where betting on horses is permitted, make it practically impossible for you to have any chance to win money. Between taxes, the track take, and the break-age, you are facing a disadvantage of about 18 to 20 percent, which is extremely difficult to overcome. On top of that, you are charged an admission to the track, must pay for your own parking, and must even purchase a track program in addition to the *Racing Form*. By the time you are ready to bet the first race, you are already about $10 in the hole. Then you must face the track edge. The total bet on each race is called the handle, and from each race, about 18% is deducted for taxes, etc. Slowly but surely, by the end of the day, a great deal of bettors' money is siphoned off, so that the only winners are the people who run the tracks and the tax collectors. The hapless player pays for all this. If it wasn't for this horrendous situation, I would suggest a serious examination of possibilities to beat the races, but faced with an 18 per cent track cut, there is no purpose to it. I've never met a horseplayer who is ahead financially, and most of them die broke, trying to beat the races." This comes from a book with called *How to Gamble and Win*. (Gambling and winning are oxymoronic to me.) The argument sounds persuasive, but it's nevertheless specious.

Don't believe the above quoted bulltickey. I know differently. So do a bunch of my friends: namely Jim Quinn, Tom Brohamer, Barry Meadow, Lee Rousso, Mark Cramer, Chuck Gaw, Andrew Beyer, Ron Cox, Dick Schmidt, Gordon Pine, Steve Unite, and Kitts Anderson—to name a few. They all have found the genie's magic powder. They each have learned how to overcome the dis-advantage of the track take by eliminating horses who have very little chance of winning. The absolute best way to master this skill is to learn how to make a "betting line." An accurate betting line is the same thing as the genie's magic powder. The ability to make an accurate betting line is the quintessential skill needed for consis-tent winning. All other skills are subordinate.

Wouldn't it be an amazing coincidence if the next chapter of this book was devoted to making a betting line?

Solution to the Genie Problem

On the 8,349th spin your bankroll would be $999,976. You then have two choices. You could bet $24 on each of the 35 numbers or you could continue with your present betting sequence, which would call for a $239 bet. In either case it would take exactly 8,350 spins for you to make at least one million dollars. At the rate of 60 spins per hour (one per minute), working ten hours per day, you would be able to complete 600 spins per day. Dividing 600 into 8,350 gets you the number of days necessary to earn your one million dollars. The quotient is 13.92. This means that it would take a little less than two weeks to earn your million dollars. Not bad work, if you can get it. Where are you, Robin Williams? We need you.

MAKING A BETTING LINE

John Templeton, one of the most astute investors in the world, has one very simple unifying principle: Buy undervalued investments and sell overvalued ones. Simple but elegant. This principle applies very well to thoroughbred handicapping. Since we technically can't sell investments unless we're bookmakers, we only have to consider the buy side of Templeton's principle. How do we buy undervalued thoroughbred handicapping investments? Simple: We bet only on horses that are undervalued by the betting public. In other words, we limit our wagers to situations where the true chances of winning are much greater than the associated odds. In order to accomplish this, we'll make our own "value line," otherwise known as a betting line.

Making an accurate betting line is the quintessential skill required for success in thoroughbred wagering. Professional handicappers are very precise about describing a horse's chances of winning a race. They make distinctions between a 20 percent chance and a 22.22 percent chance—the difference between a 4-to-1 horse and a 7-to-2 horse. In order to be a winning player you're going to have to learn to perform this feat.

Let's begin with some basic ideas on probability, odds, and betting lines. Mathematical probability can range from zero to one. A probability of zero means impossibility and a probability of one means certainty. The closer to zero, the more uncertain; the closer to one, the more certain. It's reasonably probable that some horse will win a given race. Which one? That's the trick to handicapping. In a race, every horse has some chance of winning. (The great Secretariat could lose to a $10,000 claimer if his jockey fell off or if he impeded another horse and was disqualified.) The sum of the probabilities of all the horses must add up to one. The way we apportion these probabilities among the horses is what makes us skillful handicappers.

There's a relationship between odds and probabilities. In fact, they're really the same thing expressed in different ways. Even money and 50 percent probability are synonymous. A 2-to-1 horse has a 33⅓ percent chance of winning the race. A 3-to-1 shot has a 25 percent chance of winning. The relationship between probability and odds can be stated as follows:

$$\text{Probability} = \frac{1}{\text{Odds-to-1} + 1}$$

If you know the odds-to-1, you can calculate the probability by adding 1 and taking the reciprocal. 4-to-1 can be expressed as 1/(4+1) or 1/5, which is 20 percent. When you refer to a horse as a 4-to-1 shot or as a horse having a win probability of 20 percent, you're saying the same thing. To convert any odds to odds-to-1, simply divide the second number into the first. For example, 7-to-2 is 3½-to-1; you divide the 2 into 7 to arrive at the result. 8-to-5 is 1.6-to-1. 4-to-5 is .8-to-1.

If you know the probability and want to convert to odds, the equation is as follows:

$$\text{Odds-to-1} = \frac{1}{\text{Probability}} - 1$$

If a horse has a 25 percent chance of winning, its fair odds are 3-to-1 because 25 percent is .25 and 1/.25 is 4 and 4 minus 1 is 3. If a horse has a 10 percent chance of winning, its fair odds are 9-to-1.

The following odds percentage table should help in quickly converting probability to odds and vice versa.

ODDS PERCENTAGE TABLE

1-10	90.91	4-1	20.00
1-5	83.33	9-2	18.19
2-5	71.42	5-1	16.67

1-2	66.67	6-1	14.29
3-5	62.50	7-1	12.50
4-5	55.56	8-1	11.11
1-1	50.00	9-1	10.00
6-5	45.45	10-1	9.09
7-5	41.67	11-1	8.33
3-2	40.00	12-1	7.69
8-5	38.46	15-1	6.25
9-5	35.71	20-1	4.76
2-1	33.33	25-1	3.85
5-2	28.57	30-1	3.23
3-1	25.00	50-1	1.96
7-2	22.22	99-1	1.00

Now that we understand the relationship between odds-to-1 and probabilities, we're ready to explore the concept of the betting line. Even though every horse in a race has some chance of winning, we don't try to make distinctions among our non-contenders. We simply give them a group probability. Who cares whether a horse has a 5 percent or a 6 percent chance? We consider only horses that have at least a 14 percent chance of winning the race. (We make win bets only on horses with fair odds of 6-to-1 or less.)

The trick to making a betting line is to first separate the contenders from the non-contenders. Typically we give the group of non-contenders a 20 percent probability of winning. In other words, we'll accept the notion that "stuff happens" at a racetrack. That is, 20 percent of the time we can't explain the results of a thoroughbred race. The size of the field determines the size of the "SH" pile. For typical races with eight to twelve competitors the pile will be 20 percent. As the size of the field gets smaller, we'll reduce the size of the "SH" pile by 4 percent for each horse under the threshold total of eight. So for seven-horse fields, the contenders get 84 percent of the betting line and the non-contenders get 16 percent. In six-horse fields, the contenders get 88 percent of the line. In five-horse fields, the contenders get 92 percent of the line, and so on.

Let's begin with a simple example of how to make a betting line on a race. Suppose that we're handicapping a contentious race that contains nine entries, five of which have very little chance of winning. However, the other four are inseparable. Their adjusted second call times and final times are all very close. How do we make a line on such a race? It's actually very straightforward. We had to divide 80 percent equally among the contenders. Since there were four of them, they each get a 20 percent probability, which is the same as 4-to-1 odds. We give each of our contenders a line of 4-to-1, and the entire "SH" pile containing the other five horses also gets a 4-to-1 line. Therefore, fair odds on each one of our contenders is 4-to-1. But we don't want fair odds—we demand an edge. Hence, your betting line is actually 5-to-1 on each horse. A betting line is a fair odds line plus the amount of profit that you demand. In my case, I use a 20 percent profit margin for win betting and a 10 percent profit margin for place and show bets.

Most races don't come up as simple as this example. Usually, one or two horses have an advantage over the others. Let's suppose you liked your top horse a little more than your second pick. Your third and fourth picks were scare horses that you figured had about an equal chance. Your fair odds line would look something like this.

	Win Probability	Fair Odds Line
A	29%	5-2
B	25%	3-1
C	14%	6-1
D	14%	6-1
	82%	

If your line doesn't come out exact, that's okay. You want to get as close to 80 percent as you reasonably can. If you miss by two or three points, don't be too concerned. This isn't rocket science.

Our lines are subject to error, so we must offset this by demanding a premium over our estimates. Barry Meadow suggests that 50 percent over our estimate will compensate us for possible errors. I tend to be a little more formal and insist upon a minimum 20 percent ROI (Return on investment) on any win bet. In the above case, this is how Barry Meadow's betting line would look:

	Fair Odds	Betting Line
A	5-2	4-1
B	3-1	9-2
C	6-1	9-1
D	6-1	9-1

My betting line would look like this:

	Fair Odds	Betting Line
A	5-2	7-2
B	3-1	4-1
C	6-1	8-1
D	6-1	8-1

Barry's way is a lot simpler. My way involves a lot of calculation. The advantage to my way is that you tend to accept more horses as possible bets. The disadvantage is that you must be more precise because there's less room for error. Having made lines on thousands and thousands of races, I'm quite comfortable in not insisting on such a large premium.

My way to compute the acceptable odds in order to guarantee a 20 percent edge is to simply divide the estimated probability into the sum (.2 + P(L)), which represents our probability of losing, P(L), plus 20 percent. Our estimated probability on horse A was 29 percent, hence P(L) = 71 percent. We divide .29 into (.2 + .71). The quotient is 3.14. We then round up to the nearest odds level, which is 3½-to-1. We estimated horse B's probability of winning at 25 percent, and therefore his probability of losing is 75 percent. We add the 75 percent to 20 percent and divide by 25 percent. The quotient is 3.8, which means we round up to 4-to-1. For horses C and D, our win estimate was 14 percent; hence our lose estimate is 86 percent. We add 20 percent to our lose estimate and divide by 14 percent. This becomes 106 percent divided by 14 percent. The result is 7.57, which we round up to 8-to-1.

Your treatment of favorites is the key to your success in constructing accurate betting lines. There are three types of favorites: legitimate, vulnerable, and false. When you have a legitimate favorite, only one horse gets a line. The balance of the field goes into the "SH" pile. This is the *only* exception to the 80–20 rule of line making. The only time that you bet against a legitimate favorite is when you've taken vows of poverty and have decided to divest yourself of your worldly goods. You don't go shopping for overlays against a legitimate favorite. A legitimate favorite is the speed of the field by three ticks or better, with the proper pace profile and running style that fits the class demands of today's race. You never bet against such horses. You either find a way to bet on them, or skip the race.

You make betting lines that contain multiple contenders only when there is either a false or vulnerable favorite. In the case of a false favorite, this horse gets no line whatsoever. He goes into the "SH" pile. Vulnerable favorites always get a line.

A good rule of thumb is to start your fair odds line at 5-to-2 or higher when you have a vulnerable favorite. A legitimate favorite starts at 2-to-1 or less. James Quinn was absolutely correct when he said, "The mark of the expert is to be able to make money on relatively low priced horses." You'll know you have arrived when you can make a large bet on a 6-to-5 shot because he's 4-to-5 on your line.

The line-making process begins with your contenders. If your top pick is the favorite, you must decide if he's a legitimate favorite or not. If he's legitimate, you then estimate his chances of winning. The balance of the horses collectively is assigned the difference between your estimate and 100 percent. Remember, if you give him an even money line, you're saying that his chances equal the chances of all the horses in the field combined. It happens, but not too frequently. If your top pick isn't a legitimate favorite or is a horse other than the public favorite, then his fair odds line should probably be 5-to-2 or more. You apportion 80 percent or more, depending on the size of the field, to your contenders. The rest of the horses are put into the "SH" pile and are assigned the balance of the percentages so that your line adds up to near 100 percent. If you get to the track and see that the public favorite isn't among your contenders at all, beware. Take another look at the race—you may have missed something. If you're sure that you didn't, you've got yourself a false favorite. It's a good idea to take a big swing at this race because you're sure to be getting good value on at least one of your contenders.

 Now that you have been exposed to the orthodox way of finding wager value for win bets, let me share with you an unorthodox method that can possibly work if you're a selection-oriented handicapper. For the past few years, I've been envious of Ron Ambrose's success. We go to the track together and damn if he doesn't win just about every time. He drives me crazy. He goes over and over the upcoming race looking for new clues. He makes his wager at the last possible moment. He checks everything. Place and show prices, exacta prices, betting action, and proportional odds from double or exacta pools are a few of his favorite indicators. He has a sixth sense for when "things don't quite feel right." He winds up passing most races. When he does make a bet, it's a substantial one. His win bets start at $200 and go as high as $5,000. His place and show bets can go to $10,000 depending upon the size of the pools. His exacta bets are usually in the $200-to-$500 range. You would think that a handicapper who bets this much money would have a very sophisticated way of making a betting line, wouldn't you? Not so—Ambrose's method is simplicity itself.

The way Ambrose makes a line is easy. His number of contenders is his fair odds line. That is, if he has three contenders, they're each 3-to-1. If he has four contenders, they're each 4-to-1 and the balance of the field is also 4-to-1. When I asked him how he derived this unorthodox approach, he replied, "It's all in my records." He observed that when what he considered to be a playable race had two contenders, one of them won about 66 percent of the time. When he had three contenders in a playable race, one of them won about 75 percent of the time. Most races fell into these groups. When he encounters races with four or more contenders, he usually passes unless the odds are irresistible.

As I said earlier, he drives me crazy. He's selection-oriented and has an urgent need to cash every bet that he makes. He hates uncertainty. As he says, "Often wrong, but never in doubt." He wants to understand every race down to its minutest detail. He handicaps the whole card but usually only finds one or two races that deserve a bet. Maiden races are his specialty. He loves them. He's the best maiden-race handicapper I have the good fortune to know.)

My advice is to practice constructing a fair odds line the orthodox way unless you're a very high percentage handicapper. If you can get 66 percent with two horses in those races you consider playable, then by all means use the Ambrose technique. You may want to review your records to see how this technique would have worked for you. If it works, use it.

Barry Meadow, author of *Money Secrets at the Racetrack,* advises us to ask the question, "If this race were run 100 times, how many times would each horse win?" Many handicappers have difficulty with this question because they know that any race is only going to be run once. They're unable to visualize the many possible scenarios that could unfold. Hence they erroneously conclude that the same horse would win all 100 races.

(In order to avoid this difficulty, I've developed a numerical method based on what I call "power ratings." These ratings are developed using class-consistency numbers plus pace and speed numbers matched to winning running styles. This method is fully detailed in my book *Winning Thoroughbred Strategies.*

Fortunately, I have the help of a very sophisticated computer program called *ALL-IN-ONE*. It does all the grunt work and spits out a betting line that works beautifully.)In his handicapping column of October 10, 1993, Brad Free, the Southern California handicapper for the *Daily Racing Form,* wrote, "After it handicaps each race, *ALL-IN-ONE* offers a betting line on its top contenders. Depending on how contentious the race is, the program may offer betting lines on one, two or more horses in each race. Armed with an accurate betting line, all a horseplayer needs to do is sit back and bet the overlays. At Fairplex, 91 percent of the races were playable. While the software produces profits for bettors who use it properly, it also reinforces the most important wagering principle: Bet only where value is offered. *ALL-IN-ONE* identifies the overlays."

Many handicappers confuse the concepts of morning line with betting line. What passes for a morning line, a Sweeps line, or a Hermis line is no less than a travesty. It's counterfeit. It's not the genuine article. It's nowhere near a 100 percent line. Most horseplayers wouldn't recognize a true betting line unless it jumped up and bit them in the posterior. Even the public odds in the results charts contain an inflated line to cover track take, breakage, and round-off error. Let's take a closer look at each. Consider the Santa Anita Derby run in early April 1993. It's a mile-and-an-eighth Grade 1 race for 3-year-olds. With a $500,000 purse, needless to say it attracted some very nice horses.

This was the Sweep's graded handicap line:

Horse	Odds	Probability
Personal Hope	8-5	.3846
Eliza	2-1	.3333
Devoted Brass	4-1	.2000
Union City	5-1	.1667
Gavel Gate	10-1	.0909
Earl of Barking	12-1	.0769
Only Alpha	30-1	.0323
		1.2847

To be fair to Brian Mulligan, the *Daily Racing Form* handicapper who's known to fans in the West as "Sweep," he was trying to predict what the crowd would do; he's really not giving you his assessment of the probabilities. Nevertheless, his line was a 128-plus percent line—not a 100 percent fair odds line.

It's good practice to convert morning lines to 100 percent lines. It's also possible that one of your local public handicappers creates morning lines that, when converted to 100 percent lines, are capable of showing a profit. Only diligent record-keeping will tell you for sure. The more of these conversions you do, the more you'll get an intuitive feel for them. In order to convert to a legitimate fair odds line, we must first convert the odds to probabilities. We then add up the probabilities. We divide each individual probability by the sum of all possibilities to assure that the total adds up to one, and then we convert back into odds.

100% SWEEP'S LINE

Horse	Probability	Odds
Personal Hope	.300	2.33
Eliza	.259	2.85
Devoted Brass	.156	5.42

Continued

Horse	Probability	Odds
Union City	.130	6.71
Gavel Gate	.071	13.13
Earl of Barking	.059	15.71
Only Alpha	.025	38.77
	1.000	

Please be sure you understand how to convert any line to a legitimate 100 percent fair odds line. It's really easy if you know how to convert odds to probabilities and vice versa. Sweep had Personal Hope at 8-to-5. This means that he was 1.6-to-1, hence his probability is 1/2.6, or .3846. The sum of all the probabilities is 1.2847. We then divide .3846 by 1.2847 to get the actual probability based on a 100 percent line. This is .3000. To calculate the odds, we divide this number into 1 and subtract 1, giving us 2.33. We do the same for each horse to arrive at the true fair odds line based on the probabilities adding up to 100 percent. (100 percent is a fancy way to say "one.") Let's now look at the betting public's assessment of the race:

BETTING PUBLIC'S LINE

Horse	Odds-to-1	Probability
Personal Hope	1.5	.4000
Eliza	3.2	.2381
Devoted Brass	4.0	.2000
Union City	3.7	.2128
Gavel Gate	9.4	.0962
Earl of Barking	23.0	.0417
Only Alpha	83.2	.0119
		1.2007

The public itself creates a reasonably accurate odds line except for the favorite–long shot bias. It has a tendency to underbet strong favorites and overbet the long shots. It underbets favorites of the 3-to-5 odds group or less and overbets the 4-to-1 horses and above. For the most part, however, the public's view is fairly accurate. (We'll later use this fact to our advantage in place-and-show wagering.)

The key to making fair odds lines is to make lots of them and compare the race results to your pre-race estimates. In your last 100 races, did your 5-to-2 shots win approximately 29 percent of the time? Did your 4-to-1 shots win approximately 20 percent of the time? Allow yourself a small margin of error, but certainly no more than 10 percent. My suggestion is to use the Odds Percentage Table as your guide. So if your 2-to-1 shots won 30 percent of the time, you're okay. If they won 28 percent of the time, they really should have been 5-to-2. At first your results will probably be gruesome. That's okay. Simply persist. The only way you can learn to make these distinctions is to practice, practice, and practice some more. The more lines you make and get positive feedback on, the sharper these skills will become. You'll learn by making a lot of mistakes. You must understand the importance of failure in your quest for success. Each mistake is a learning experience. You shouldn't fear mistakes, you should only fear not learning from them. They're inevitable.

Most of the betting strategies presented in this book are based upon your ability to make a fair odds line. Please be very clear about the distinction between fair odds lines and betting lines. Fair odds lines are our estimate of what constitutes a fair bet. We don't want to make fair bets, or else we'd flip coins with our friends. We want an edge. We want at least a 20 percent edge. We therefore modify our fair odds lines to guarantee that we're always betting with the odds on our side. These modified fair odds lines are betting lines. Our fundamental rule is: No edge—no bet.

The final way, which is by far the best, is empirical and based strictly upon your own performance. It's essential to keep rigorous betting records and use your results to tell you how to construct your fair odds line. Suppose, for example, that in maiden special-weight sprints your win rate is 35.71 percent and your average odds are 3-to-1. This means that you're making a healthy profit. It also means that your top pick in this type of race has a natural fair odds line of 9-to-5. Therefore, the top choice in your betting line should be 5-to-2. You then could simply bet all your top choices that go off at 5-to-2 or above in maiden special-weight sprint races. If you track the win percentages of your top five choices over a series of races, the proper percentages to assign to your contenders become clear.

The following is the output of a computer program that I use called *The Betting Analyst*. It's the one-month test results of an online database program that we were testing. Let's suppose that these results were your results over the past 326 races that you handicapped.

From: 04-01-1992
To: 04-30-1992

GOLDEN GATE MONTHLY
WIN REPORT

Category	#Bets	#Wns	%BW	%RW	AvgPay	%B	TotalBet	Profit/Loss	R.O.I
All Win	326	42	13	22	$16.71	0	$ 652.00	+$ 49.80	1.08
Sprints	170	18	11	19	$20.46	0	$ 340.00	+$ 28.20	1.08
Routes	156	24	15	25	$13.90	0	$ 312.00	+$ 21.60	1.07
Dirt	276	39	14	24	$16.81	1	$ 552.00	+$103.60	1.19
Turf	50	3	6	9	$15.40	0	$ 100.00	-$ 53.80	0.46
2YOs	2	0	0	0	$ 0.00	-	$ 4.00	-$ 4.00	0.00
3YOs	121	22	18	32	$18.16	4	$ 242.00	+$157.60	1.65
4YOs+	203	20	10	16	$15.11	0	$ 406.00	-$103.80	0.74
Males	179	22	12	20	$18.15	0	$ 358.00	+$ 41.20	1.12
Females	147	20	14	23	$15.13	0	$ 294.00	+$ 8.60	1.03
1 WinBet	62	7	11	11	$12.77	0	$ 124.00	-$ 34.60	0.72
2 WinBet	264	35	13	27	$17.50	1	$ 528.00	+$ 84.40	1.16
3+WnBet	0	-	-	-	-	-	-	-	-
STK I	0	-	-	-	-	-	-	-	-
STK II	0	-	-	-	-	-	-	-	-
STK III	5	1	20	33	$10.60	-	$ 10.00	+$ 0.60	1.06
CLF	24	4	17	29	$ 9.40	-	$ 48.00	-$ 10.40	0.78
NW3	1	0	0	0	-	-	$ 2.00	-$ 2.00	0.00
NW2	14	0	0	0	-	-	$ 28.00	-$ 28.00	0.00
NW1	29	5	17	31	$15.36	-	$ 58.00	+$ 18.80	1.32
MSW	17	3	18	27	$14.80	-	$ 34.00	+$ 10.40	1.31
MCL	75	7	9	16	$22.06	0	$ 150.00	+$ 4.40	1.03
C100,000	0	-	-	-	-	-	-	-	-
C80,000	0	-	-	-	-	-	-	-	-
C75,000	0	-	-	-	-	-	-	-	-
C62,500	0	-	-	-	-	-	-	-	-
C50,000	4	0	0	0	-	-	$ 8.00	-$ 8.00	0.00
C40,000	3	0	0	0	-	-	$ 6.00	-$ 6.00	0.00
C32,000	4	1	25	33	$13.60	-	$ 8.00	+$ 5.60	1.70
C25,000	9	1	11	14	$16.20	-	$ 18.00	-$ 1.80	0.90
C20,000	3	0	0	0	-	-	$ 6.00	-$ 1.60	0.00
C16,000	18	4	22	44	$ 9.25	-	$ 36.00	+$ 1.00	1.03
C12,500	29	4	14	24	$24.55	-	$ 58.00	+$ 40.20	1.69
C10,000	17	3	18	30	$16.13	-	$ 34.00	+$ 14.40	1.42
C8,500	5	1	20	33	$20.60	-	$ 10.00	+$ 10.60	2.06
C7,500	8	1	12	17	$15.60	-	$ 16.00	-$ 0.40	0.98
C6,500	60	7	12	20	$18.34	0	$ 120.00	+$ 8.40	1.07

These results were marginally acceptable. They beat the track take but they didn't show an overall 20 percent profit for win betting. However, please look at the results of betting exclusively on three-year-old races. There were 121 such bets, and they yielded a profit of 65 percent. (An ROI of 1.65 means that for every dollar you invested in these races, you got back $1.65.) The other categories that show great promise are NW1 (nonwinners of one allowance races), MSW (maiden special weights), Claiming $12,500, and Claiming $10,000. Unfortunately, this report only shows trends. Unless a subgroup contains at least 35 races, you shouldn't get too excited.

If these were your results, it's apparent that you shouldn't be making any serious wagers on turf races. The same is true for four-year-olds and up. If you know the categories in which you don't do so well, you're ahead of the game. Simply avoid them—your results will improve dramatically. Most players don't have a clue about their strengths and weaknesses with respect to the various types of races.

In the mid-eighties I did a longitudinal study of public handicappers. It covered a two-year period. I used ten different public handicappers. If you bet on his every selection, every single handicapper showed a net loss. However, every single handicapper had at least one specialty in which he showed a profit greater than 20 percent. The obvious conclusion was that each handicapper tested had a specialty. If you simply confined yourself to betting on horses that fell within each handicapper's specialty, you'd have made a nice profit. Gordon Pine, the co-author of *The Betting Analyst,* has been making profits from the selections in the lucrative subcategories of some of these very same public handicappers, and he's been doing it for the past five years.

Suppose you found out that your ROI for route races was positive but your ROI for sprints was negative. What could you do to improve your performance? That's right—bet a lot more money on routes than on sprints. It would be wise to avoid sprints altogether. If you keep track of all your wagers and summarize this information, don't you think that your performance would improve? Of course it would. You can't avoid improving your performance when you know for sure what your strengths and weaknesses are. Crazy as it sounds, a majority of experienced handicappers have the skills to win consistently at the races but don't. Why? Because they don't bet properly. They tend to bet the same amount on each race when they should be doubling up on one kind of bet and completely avoiding others.)

It's no secret that less than 5 percent of horse bettors keep accurate betting records. By not keeping records, the vast majority of handicappers make the same mistakes over and over again. They insist upon betting the same amount of money on races in which they excel as on those races that are complete mysteries to them. If they bet more where they are strong and less where they are weak, they couldn't help but improve.

Keeping track of all your bets is a simple but elegant way of finding your strengths and weaknesses. It takes only a few minutes to record your data. You'll then have a very revealing self-portrait. In as few as ten race days you'll learn enough about your performance to know where you're astute and where you're deficient. You'll know exactly where to make changes.

This information will help you make very accurate betting lines based on reality. No more theory. By referring to the historical win percentages of your top five choices, you'll know exactly what to do. The process of tracking your last 250 bets will solve the problem of making a betting line. This is a very powerful method for you to make a betting line because it's based on empirical reality—your own records. Please, please record every bet that you make. It doesn't matter if you win the bet or not. You'll learn so much about your performance that it'll almost pay you to lose.

Again, the secret to making money with win wagers is to identify those situations in which the public underestimates a horse's chances. In order for you to know that the public has underestimated a horse, you must have a way of valuing each of your contenders. It doesn't have to be a numerical method. In his excellent book *The Odds on Your Side,* Mark Cramer details ten different ways to make a betting line depending upon the race situation and cast of characters.

Please begin the following procedure immediately: For every race that you handicap, write down your contenders and assign each an estimate of what you think its fair odds (win chances) are. Compare them to the public's estimates and exploit the difference.

If you don't make and use a betting line, you're forever disadvantaged compared to the handicappers who do. If you don't keep elaborate records, you're forever doomed to be a gambler at the mercy of the laws of chance. Please remember that damn near all gamblers lose. In fact, I don't know how you could do anything but lose if you don't know your expectation on each bet that you make. If you want to win consistently, you must only bet when you have a positive expectation. Let's examine this crucial concept.

EXPECTATION

Please indulge me by doing the following exercise. Write down your daily goal for profits at the track. This figure represents the average amount of money you want to earn per day. Typical responses are $100, $200, and more. You must realize that this number is an average—it doesn't mean that you'll win every day. A good way to arrive at this number is to calculate how much your time is worth per hour. If you make $20 per hour at your regular job and you go to the track on weekends, then you probably spend ten to fifteen hours a week on handicapping. Say ten. You want to average $200 per weekend, or $100 per day. So you would fill in the earnings per day blank with the number $100. (My personal goals are $200 per day.)

Next, write down the largest win bet that you're capable of making without having a heart attack—the largest win bet within your comfort zone. Then write down the largest place or show bet that you're capable of making comfortably.

Average earnings per day _____

Largest win bet _____

Largest place/show bet _____

If your largest win bet didn't exceed your average earnings per day, your expectations are totally unrealistic. If you answered $100 per day earnings and your largest win bet was $20, you were being quixotic. You were dreaming. Let me explain.

The very best professional players earn between 20 percent and 40 percent on their win bets. Most average around two prime bets per day. This means that if you're in the middle of this group of superior handicappers, your ROI will be around 30 percent. How much do you have to put through the mutuels, at a 30 percent profit rate, to earn $100 per day? That's right—$333. This means that you must bet an average of $167 per race!

The very best professional players earn between 10 percent and 20 percent on their place-and-show bets with the same number of prime plays per day—namely two. Because place-and-show betting is much safer, they can bet much more and maintain their safety margin. If you wish to earn $100 per day on place-and-show bets, you must put between $500 and $1,000 through the mutuels per day. That's a unit bet between $250 and $500.

It's a pretty good rule of thumb to say that your maximum bet should be almost double your daily earnings goal. How's that for a dose of reality? Not too pleasant, eh? Unfortunately, truth is sometimes painful. The truth of winning a lot of money at the track is that you're going to have to bet a lot of money. When some sleazebag tells you that you can make your living on $20 bets, mentally plunge a dagger into his heart before he finishes his next sentence.

Most players have very unreal expectations. Many actually believe the hyperbole churned out by systems mills. Does this sound familiar? "I have uncovered a major flaw in horse racing that allowed me to win over $1,000 per day for the last three years!" This is the headline from an actual direct-mail solicitation that I received. It gets better. One of the subheads inside goes on to claim, "I have been pulling down over $1,000 per day on $20 win and place bets for the past three years! This is playing just one track at a time. Profits from playing multiple tracks at race books have amounted to $2,000 to $3,000 a day!!!" If you believe this, I have a bridge to sell you. It spans the East River in New York City and it's yours for a pittance. The above profit claim is so outrageous that it's humorous. This scumbag is pushing your greed button. He's promising you that you can win a whole bunch of money without doing any work whatsoever. There are more than 50,000 different systems that have been sold to horseplayers over the past twenty-five years. Have you ever heard documented proof of a single person becoming a millionaire as the result of purchasing one of these systems? Please don't send for any mechanical mail-order system regardless of the claims and guarantees. They're garbage—both the product and the seller.

There are no shortcuts to winning. You'll have to pay the price, which is time and effort. More on that later.

Let's answer the question, "What is a realistic expectation?" The first thing we ask ourselves when we consider an investment opportunity is, "How much can I expect the return to be?" The answer can be found if we know a little bit about probability. Mathematical expectation is defined as follows:

$$E(x) = G \times P(G) - L \times P(L)$$

This means your expectation is the amount you gain multiplied by the probability of achieving that gain, plus the amount you would lose multiplied by the probability of that loss. (What you lose is a negative number.)

Probability is the ratio of favorable outcomes to total outcomes. Consider a deck of cards. What is the probability of cutting an ace? Since there are four aces in a deck of 52 cards, the answer is four out of 52, which is about a 7.7 percent chance.

Probability can be expressed as a decimal number between zero and one. A probability of 1 (one) means certainty, whereas a probability of 0 (zero) means impossibility. The probability of rolling a total of 12 or less on one roll of dice is 1 (it has to happen). The probability of rolling a total greater than 12 on one roll is 0 (impossible). The probability of rolling any specific total varies from 1/36 to 6/36. The probability of rolling a 7 is 6 chances out of 36. The symbolic representation is $P(7) = 6/36 = .167$. Please don't confuse zero probability with zero expectation.

We can make a generalization about mathematical expectation. When expectation is zero, the game is fair. When expectation is less than zero, the game is unfair and should be avoided. When expectation is greater than zero, the game is favorable and should be played as often as possible. To illustrate, let us consider a game like tossing a coin. If we play this game with a friend and wager $1 on the outcome of each toss, our expectation is zero, a fair game:

$$E(x) = \$1 \times (1/2) - (\$1) \times (1/2) = 0$$

Suppose we play with a philanthropist. If he wins we pay him $1, but if we win he pays us $2. Now things are looking up:

$$E(x) = \$2 \times (1/2) - (\$1) \times (1/2) = \$.50$$

This means that we can expect to make 50 cents on each play. Hence, if we play this game 100 times, we can expect to win $50. This illustrates the point that when we play a game a number of times, our final expectation is the total amount that we bet multiplied by our single-play expectation. In each of the above examples, note that our expectation cannot be achieved on a single play. In the first we are either ahead $1 or behind $1, yet E(x) = 0. In the second we are either ahead $2 or behind $1, yet E(x) = $.50.

Most experienced handicappers find that their percentage of winners ranges between 20 percent and 40 percent. Their average mutuel ranges from $5 to $12. A typical successful handicapper would have a win rate of 30 percent at an average mutuel of $7. Hence, his single-race expectation is E(x) = $5 × (.3) − ($2) × (.7) = $.10, or 10 cents on a $2 bet. Another way to express this is that his single-race expectation is 5 percent. Did you notice that the gain was $5? The reason is that the $7 mutuel includes the $2 bet.

Another way to define expectation is in terms of odds and probabilities. If you express the gain in terms of a one-dollar bet, you are now quoting odds. Expectation can now be defined as payoff odds times probability of winning minus the probability of losing.

$$E(x) = \text{odds} \times P(W) - P(L)$$

The expectation on a one-dollar bet is also known as "edge." A handicapper whose win percentage is 33 percent with an average mutuel of $7 does very well indeed. His edge is:

$$E(x) = 2.5 \times (.33) - .67 = .155$$

That's 15.5 percent. A $7 mutuel is the same as 2.5-to-1 odds. Improving your handicapping skills by 10 percent can cause your profits to more than triple! Most pros bet approximately one race in three. Hence, over a season, a $50 win bettor with a 5 percent single-race expectation should earn profits of $1,875. The 33 percent handicapper (15.5 percent edge) will earn $5,812.50—not exactly Rolls-Royce wages.

To illustrate just how hard it is to make a living at the track, consider a $250 win bettor. Let us further suppose he's a 35 percent handicapper with an average mutuel of $7. His gross profits for the year would be about $42,200. For all practical purposes it would be very tough to earn in excess of $100,000 per year at the racetrack unless you hit a Pick-6 or two. In order to earn more than that, my suggestion would be to devote the same time and energy to a game like the stock market. Horse-race handicapping isn't the world's most financially rewarding profession. The irony of it is that if you have the skills and temperament you probably would earn more in another endeavor. Let's now take a look at the fundamental principles of horse-race wagering.

Fundamental Principles of Wagering

There are fundamental laws and guiding principles in wagering, just as there are for the physical world. Just as there are no exceptions to the law of gravity in the physical world, there are principles of wagering that won't abide any exemptions. If you're going to be a consistent winner, it'll be necessary to understand and practice these principles. They aren't negotiable—they're absolute. They aren't theory—they're fact.

The fundamental principles of wagering are practical, down-to-earth prescriptions to maximize gain and minimize risk. I can state categorically that if you obey these simple rules and principles, you'll be a winner in the long run. Any other outcome is mathematically unlikely. (What's very comforting about the truth of mathematics is that it's as close to absolute as you can get. What was true a thousand years ago in mathematics will be true a thousand years from now. The fundamental principles of wagering are mathematical.)

We know that attitude, decision-making skills, and money-management skills are the three vital ingredients needed for consistent profits from thoroughbred wagering. Two of the three are absolute. Attitude and money management are based on fundamental truths and universal principles. We need only learn these things once. Once we do, they're ours to use for the rest of our days. Decision-making skills are based on our ability to manage information. In order for us to excel at handicapping, we must become information managers. Unfortunately, the value of information changes from track to track and even from race to race. There's a distinction between data and information. Information is based on the conclusions we deduce from the data. Each thoroughbred horse race presents us with a unique puzzle. Each of us interprets the data in the *Daily Racing Form* somewhat differently. The data are the same for all of us, yet the information content varies.

Decision-making skills are enhanced by practice. Decision-making is always problematic. The highest-paid people in our society are decision makers. Presidents of companies, politicians, leaders of organizations, judges, business executives are all paid to make decisions. What is interesting is that these same people have access to more information than the average citizen. It used to be that managers were paid in proportion to the number of people they supervised. In today's world, managers are paid in proportion to the amount of information they control. Successful executives make profitable decisions. Whether they may make mostly poor decisions or mostly good decisions doesn't matter too much. They're judged by their bottom line. If they achieve their objectives, regardless of the number of right and wrong decisions, they're considered successful. The same is true for handicappers. In order to be a successful handicapper, we must emulate successful business leaders. We must be judged by our bottom line. We must set financial objectives and standards and hold ourselves accountable.

Let's examine the fundamental principles of wagering. In any form of gambling, speculating, or investing, it's obvious that we should consider opportunities only where we have the best of it. Therefore the prime rule suggests itself.

Never make a wager unless the expectation is positive.

The inability to understand this rule has caused people to lose more money than you can believe. I suspect that our four-trillion-dollar national debt is small when compared to all the money wagered on negative-expectation casino games. With the exception of blackjack, poker, and sports betting, casino games can be characterized by player expectation being invariably negative. Let's compute the expectation when a gambler wagers one dollar on a single number in roulette:

$$E(\text{Single Number}) = 1/38 \times \$35 - 37/38 = -\$.05263$$

Let's do the same for a one-dollar wager on the color red:

$$E(\text{Red}) = 18/38 \times \$1 - 20/38 = -\$.05263$$

What this says is that on average you can expect to lose 5.26 cents of each dollar wagered. It doesn't say which events you'll win and which you'll lose. All it says is that in the long run you'll lose 5.26 percent of all the money you bet on roulette. Why play a game you're destined to lose?

It's argued that profits can be achieved by using a clever betting system even though the expectation is negative. There have been entire systems based on this principle, such as the dice and roulette systems still advertised by direct-mail systems houses. I'll be kind to the purveyors of these so-called systems. It's sufficient to say that if any of them worked, Las Vegas would have shut its doors a long time ago. The fact is, casinos will send a cab for users of these systems. If an event has a negative expectation, any number of repetitions of the event will still result in a negative expectation. This is easy to demonstrate. Your final expectation is the total amount bet multiplied by your single-bet expectation. The total amount bet is always a positive number and expectation is a negative number. The product of a positive number multiplied by a negative number is always negative, and so the result can only be negative.

How often have we heard people repeat the false notion that you can win at the track even if your methods don't show a flat-bet profit, providing you are a good money manager? The next principle will put that fallacious notion to sleep once and for all.

All betting systems converge to single-bet expectation. You can only make things worse, never better, by using a betting system.

Your betting method doesn't change your single-bet expectation. Your final expectation is a function of the total amount bet. If you have a minus 5 percent expectation, then no matter how you choose to move bet-size around, your final expectation will be at least minus 5 percent of the total amount you wagered. The best you can hope to achieve is your single-bet expectation. You can never make things better. You can only make them worse. (You'll see a dramatic example of this in the money-management chapter.) Without going through a summary of all the spurious systems that have been applied to negative-expectation games, suffice it to say that your time would be just as well spent inventing a perpetual motion machine. Your chances of success are the same. *It's mathematically impossible to discover a betting method that will overcome a negative expectation.* Alas, I'm wasting your valuable time because the first rule precludes our wagering on a negative-expectation situation anyway.

Suppose we're at the track and for the first eight races not a single favorite has won. A friend advises us to wager on the favorite in the ninth because he's "due." We suspect the favorite has a better-than-normal chance because it's very unlikely that on a nine-race card at least one favorite won't win. Your friend points out that the national average for favorites winning a single race is 32 percent. He goes on to explain that the probability of nine consecutive losing favorites is calculated by multiplying the probability of a single loss times itself nine times, which is the same as raising .68 to the ninth power. He correctly calculates this to be .0311, which is only a little more than a 3 percent chance. This means there is a 97 percent chance that this won't happen. He argues that there's a natural 97-to-3 bias in favor of the favorite winning the next race. In other words, "The favorite is due."

The truth is the favorite still has the same 32 percent chance that any other favorite enjoyed that day. Each race is an independent event and has no bearing on previous outcomes. Your friend would have you believe that the favorite in the upcoming race has an inordinate chance to win. If you listen to him, you'll end up in the poorhouse. The correct reasoning is that the probability of eight consecutive losing favorites is .0457. We have experienced a somewhat rare but not extraordinary phenomenon. Out of 10,000 racing days, only 457 of them will see a situation in which eight consecutive races are won by non-favorites. This is happens to be just one of those 457 days. It's also true that in 10,000 race days, 311 of them can be expected to witness nine straight favorites losing. When we calculate 68 percent of 457, we get—that's right, 311! In other words, 68 percent of the times we see eight losing favorites, we will also happen to see the ninth losing, too. The favorite will win the ninth race 32 percent of the time, and that was the single-race situation to begin with. I hope you appreciate this and repudiate the silly notion of the favorite being "due."

The reason we're taken in by such sophistry is that it sounds plausible. Intuitively, we sense that sooner or later a favorite has to win. Hence as we get closer to that time, each succeeding favorite seems more likely to do so than the last. Don't buy it. It ain't so. When flipping a fair coin, if heads has just come up ten times in a row, heads is just as likely to come up on the eleventh flip as tails. Same for red in roulette or the favorite in a horse race. If the last ten races were won by favorites, the next race is no less likely to see the favorite win. If red has just come out ten times in a row, it still has an 18/38 chance to come out this time. When events are independent, such as horse races, coin flips, and roulette spins, no "memory" of past outcomes exists. The probability does not change as a result of previous events.

The bizarre notion about specific outcomes being "due" has been applied to horse race-betting in a system called "due-column betting." Its users are ignorant of the fundamentals of wagering. This system is about as dumb as they get. You'll learn why later.

Please keep the following principle in mind:

A wager should depend upon your edge and odds, not upon previous outcome.

We yearn to believe that the universe is inherently fair. For every head there'll be a tail and things will not get too far out of balance. This is a wonderful philosophical notion, but don't bet on it. We have heard that the law of averages guarantees that in the long run heads and tails will balance out. While there's no "law of averages," there is a fundamental statistical concept called "The Law of Large Numbers," which states that as the number of trials gets larger, the percentage deviation from the expected value gets smaller. Implicit in this, however, is the fact that the difference between the number of heads and the number of tails will get larger as the number of trials increases. The operating principle is convergence, not compensation. For example, after 100 flips, heads theoretically should have occurred 50 times. It wouldn't be at all unusual if it actually occurred 48 times. Let's say that tails occurred 52 times. The percentage deviation for heads is 4 percent. The difference between the number of heads and the number of tails is four. Let's perform the experiment 1,000 times. We now expect 500 heads and 500 tails. Let's say that the percentage deviation gets smaller, as the Law of Large Numbers suggests. Suppose it's 2 percent. That's 510 heads and 490 tails. Accordingly, the difference between the number of heads and the number of tails is 20. Notice that the percentage deviation is smaller while the absolute deviation is much larger.

Please don't fall into the trap of believing that a reversal of trend is imminent. If you've just lost six races in a row, don't think that your chances of winning the next race are any greater, because they aren't. Any scheme that tells you to wait for some specific outcome of independent trials before placing a wager is horsefeathers. Each wager you make should depend upon expectation and odds, not previous outcome. Again, races are independent events and the outcome of one has no bearing on the outcome of the next.

The last principle is one of the least understood and most violated in all of wagering:

When you are seeking to increase your wealth, your probability of success is a function of your betting system. For unfair games a maximum-boldness strategy is optimal; for favorable games a minimum-boldness strategy is optimal.

This is plain common sense, which unfortunately is most uncommon. It says that if the expectation is against you, your best strategy is to make large bets on a small number of plays and not allow the percentages to grind against you. The optimum strategy in a negative-expectation game is to wager all the money you'll ever bet on the game in a single play. However, if the expectation favors you, act just like a casino—grind out your profits over a large number of plays.

To demonstrate the principle of minimum boldness, suppose you're a 30 percent handicapper at an average mutuel of $7. This performance is a winning one since it gives you, the horse-race investor, a 5 percent edge. Assume you start with a bankroll of $1,000 and use a flat-bet system of money management. What should your bet size be in order to avoid tapping out and still achieve respectable profits? Take a guess. In order to find out, I asked my trusty computer using a technique called "simulation." The computer was asked to generate random numbers between zero and one. If the number was .3 or less, it was considered a win; if it was greater than .3, it was a loss. The computer was told to run a sequence of 500 races with bet sizes starting at $10 and increasing by $2 until it experienced a tap out. For a while it looked like the more money we bet, the more money we made. However, when we used a $22 bet size, it experienced one tap out in ten repetitions of the experiment. True, this is only once in ten experiments, but remember: Tapping out is to be steadfastly avoided. The reason for this failure was that the betting strategy was too bold. When the bet was less than $22, it didn't tap out once. When I ran this simulation at a $50 bet level, it tapped out three times out of ten! Much too bold. This shows that you can have a 5 percent advantage and still go broke if you violate this principle.

Many authors suggest that 5 percent of your capital is a prudent bet size. It ain't necessarily so. *Your maximum wager size is your single-race edge divided by your average odds.* Any bet size less than this maximum is like buying risk insurance. What you're doing is protecting yourself from gambler's ruin at the expense of your wealth's growth rate. In the above case, the single-race edge was 5 percent and the average odds were 2.5-to-1. Hence the maximum bet should have been 2 percent of bankroll. Any bet size of 2 percent or less is a prudent strategy, and any bet more than 2 percent is too bold.

This explains why there are many good handicappers who don't earn consistent profits. Their wagering methods are too bold. They have the ability to earn a flat-bet profit on their selections, yet by wagering too large a proportion of their capital they tap out before earning a profit.

In order to discover the optimal money-management plan, you must know the characteristics of your selection method. Characteristics include your win probability, average mutuel, and the number of consecutive losses you can expect in the worst case. In order to determine the characteristics of a strategy, it's best to do some statistical research. This brings us to the next rule.

Never risk any of your money until you've tested your strategy with small wagers until you can statistically validate it.

In the next chapter, I'll discuss a method of determining whether a strategy is statistically valid or not—the formula for determining the precise number of races you must check in order to be at least 90 percent confident you have a winning or losing strategy. It's very wise to take things to at least the 95 percent confidence level. Most horse-race bettors crave action. They don't have the patience to handicap hundreds of races in order to determine if their strategy is profitable or not. Thank goodness that most players are not serious investors and refuse to do the work necessary to validate their methods. This principle is violated by 98 percent of all horse-race bettors. Hallelujah. It makes it easier for us. We're grateful for any edge.

Did you notice that this principle insists that you bet real money when testing a strategy? Why is this? The first thing you must understand is that if you handicap on paper—that is, if you pick up some old racing forms and work through them in your den, on your kitchen table, or wherever you handicap—you'll win. It's practically guaranteed. Let me share a metaphor with you. It's one that I've used in seminars. I'll be lecturing and I'll turn to my co-presenter and say, "Did you bring the plank with you?" He'll say, "Yes, it's upstairs." And then I'll tell the class, "We have a twenty-five-foot solid wood plank. This plank is twelve inches wide and two inches thick. We're going to tack ten one-hundred-dollar bills at one end of the plank. We'll then ask you to very simply walk heel-to-toe, heel-to-toe from one end of it to the other. Very much like what you would be asked to do if you were stopped for drunk driving. If you can successfully complete the task of walking heel-to-toe, heel-to-toe across the twenty-five-foot plank, when you get to the end you simply bend over and pick up the ten one-hundred-dollar bills and put them in your pocket. They're yours and that's all there is to it." I ask the class, "Anybody interested in trying this? Remember, if you fail and step off the plank before you reach the end, you don't get to keep the money." Just about every hand in the room goes up. And then I say, "Oh, by the way, there's one small thing that I've forgotten to tell you—the plank is located between two twenty-story buildings. Now how many of you will try it?" And of course I get no hands. And I ask, "Well wait a minute, just a moment ago most of you were willing to do it, and now all of a sudden nobody wants to take me up on it—What's wrong?"

What dynamic was introduced? The answer is "fear of failure." When the plank was on the floor, what did anyone have to lose? Nothing. But once we put the plank between two twenty-story buildings, all of a sudden a new element is introduced. Now there's a major consequence attached to failing.

When you handicap in the privacy of your den and you're not risking real money, you're not subject to the same pressures. It's not a true simulation of what happens at the racetrack. You don't have outside influences. Suppose you go to the window to make a bet and you meet a friend. Your friend asks, "Who do ya like?" You say, "The seven horse." He says, "Wait a minute, the four horse looks really hot. He looked good in the post parade and they're shooting with him today. His trainer is five out of his last six, plus he's going off at eight to one." Now what do you do? At home you don't have these distractions. You're able to maintain a very logical and rational approach to the game. The racetrack is anything but a logical and rational place, and emotions run rampant. Handicapping in the privacy of your home doesn't properly simulate the environment that you'll have to succeed in. When you have nothing to lose, you tend to make bold, forceful decisions.

When you go up to the window and place a bet, especially if it's a good-sized bet, there's a certain amount of trepidation, a certain amount of fear that's not there when you're at home. It can certainly cloud your judgment. You must test things with real money.

If you understand and follow these principles of wagering, you'll remove yourself from the ranks of the gambler and join the ranks of the investor. An investor always knows the expectation of his wagers. In order to compute your expectation, you must know your win percentage and average mutuel. There are very few players who know their exact win percentage for the past 50 or 100 races. The ones that do are professionals and usually winners. This sounds easy—but I can assure you it isn't.

Handicapping hundreds of races before making a significant wager is next to impossible for the average mortal. In fact, just keeping accurate records is generally more than the average player can stand. Passing up a race is anathema to the gambler but vitally necessary to the investor because there are some races that defy prediction and others that offer no value. In general, what separates the investor from the gambler is discipline. The gambler prefers to rely on Lady Luck while the investor depends on his own skills.

The wagering principles I've put forth in this chapter are nothing but good common sense. They hold true for any form of gambling, speculating, or investing. If you wager only on positive-expectation opportunities, using an intelligent money-management plan, how can you do anything but win in the long run?

There are additional principles that I've failed to mention because I think they should be obvious. I didn't mention that you shouldn't gamble with the rent money. I didn't mention that you shouldn't borrow money in order to gamble. Most important, I didn't mention that you shouldn't gamble in the first place. When you wager with a positive expectation you aren't, strictly speaking, gambling.

What constitutes gambling is a touchy subject. Crossing the street against a traffic light is gambling. Taking an airline flight is a small gamble. Driving to the airport is a much bigger gamble. Living in Southern California is a gamble with respect to fires and earthquakes. Any situation that involves physical or financial risk is a gambling situation. We have devised elaborate risk-management techniques to deal with most situations. Some people consider putting money into a savings account an intelligent risk-management technique. They argue that money in the bank is safe from burglars, fires, and profligate spending, such as squandered bets on slow horses. They contend that this money is insured by the FDIC and that therefore its safety is assured. The truth is that the FDIC couldn't possibly cover all the money in the nation's savings accounts if we were to have a general economic collapse. Many large banks have made questionable loans to third world countries with very little chance of being repaid. Each day inflation eats at our savings. It's very probable that the real value of our money is growing at a rate much less than the quoted interest rate. The safety may very well be illusory.

Barry Meadow has for the past twenty years earned at least a 10 percent return on the money he has invested at the racetrack. He has earned enough to support his family and live in a more than moderate life-style. Each racing day he may put from $1,000 to $3,000 or more through the mutuel windows. He isn't dependent upon anything but his own skills. He's certain that the track will not mismanage his investments. He's assured that he'll collect his winning wagers in cash upon presentation of a winning ticket. Is Barry Meadow a gambler? Technically, yes. But reality says otherwise.

Had his income been the result of buying and selling stock certificates instead of mutuel tickets, there would be no question about his being a judicious investor. (The truth is, Meadow is an excellent stock market investor. He plans to make the stock market his full-time occupation in the near future.)

If we can divorce ourselves from the means and look at the results, we're forced to conclude that he has found a way to earn a nice income and it's all legal and ethical. Simply put, Meadow as a winning handicapper is a more than judicious investor, but he's not recognized by society as a productive contributor. Pity. The truth is, he's a most valuable contributor. He probably puts nearly $1,000,000 through mutuel windows each year. His very generous contribution to the commonweal is at least $150,000. Meadow's contribution goes to support the track, the horsemen, and the public at large. Meadow should receive a medal for his very generous donation to civic prosperity. Unfortunately, most members of society consider Meadow to be a parasite. He's a gambler. He's a wastrel. He's a bum. He doesn't produce anything. He's a leech. He preys on the weakness of his fellow creatures. As usual, most people are wrong.

Many view a job or a piece of property as security but fail to realize that these things are temporal and can be confiscated. Ask the well-to-do citizens of Kuwait. Your only real security is your competence. The ability to do things better than your contemporaries assures your place. Top professionals never need to worry about unemployment as long as they possess their skills. Can you imagine Babe Ruth, Mickey

Mantle, Willie Mays, Jackie Robinson, or Evander Holyfield worrying about unemployment while they possessed their legendary skills? Top salesmen need never be concerned about recession or depression— they'll always have employment.

A competent handicapper has all the security this life can offer. He (or she) never needs to worry about money. His only concern should be his ability to maintain and improve his competence. The same is true for any profession.

The fundamental principles of horse-race wagering are really very simple. You don't need an advanced degree in mathematics to understand them. Thoroughbred wagering is a sequence of independent trials. It's similar to flipping a coin a large number of times. The only complication is that the probability of winning changes from race to race, as does the payoff. (We'll deal with these realities in the next few chapters.) For the moment we will agree to learn the fundamentals and abide by them. Let's now look at a method that will statistically validate any winning strategy.

STATISTICAL VALIDATION

Please don't let the math in this chapter put you off. The principles are very important and can be understood even if you don't understand the math.

How many races do you have to check before concluding that a strategy is statistically valid? The answer is not a simple one. It would be wonderful if the answer were, say, 200. Unfortunately, that's not the case.

The formula for the minimum number of races to check depends upon your win percentage, average mutuel, and the maximum allowable error range that will still yield a profit. The formula is:

$$N = W \times L \times (Z/E)^2$$

W = Win percentage (expressed as a decimal number)

L = Lose percentage (1 – win percentage)i

Z = A constant depending on confidence level

For 90% Confidence Z = 1.645

For 95% Confidence Z = 1.960

For 99% Confidence Z = 2.575

E = Maximum allowable error in win percentage

E is a little bit tricky, so please make sure you understand exactly what it means. Our goal is 20 percent profit. Our minimum acceptable profit is 10 percent. Therefore, E is the difference between our actual win percentage and the win percentage that would yield a 10 percent profit.

Consider a win percentage of .333 at an average mutuel of $9.62. Our edge is 60 percent. We must now figure out the win percentage that will yield a profit of 10 percent. Hence we must solve the equation:

$$.10 = (3.81) \times P(W) - 1 - P(W)$$

A \$9.62 average mutuel is the same as odds of 3.81-to-1. The solution is that P(W) must be .229. We now can state the value of E. E is .333 minus .229, or .104.

This says that you can have a 10.4 percent reduction in win percentage and still earn a 10 percent profit with this method. I have developed a simple algorithm for calculating the value of E. You divide your average mutuel into the sum of 2 plus twice your minimum expectation, then subtract the result from your win percentage. In the case of a 10 percent minimum-profit expectation, E becomes your win percentage minus 2.2 divided by the average mutuel. In the case of 5 percent minimum acceptable profit level, you would divide the average mutuel into the quantity 2.2 and subtract it from your win percentage. In our example it's:

$$E = .333 - (2.2/9.62) = .104$$

Now that we know our value of E, let's apply it to check the minimum number of races necessary to validate our method statistically:

FOR 90% CONFIDENCE:
$$N = (.333) \times (.667) \times (1.645/.104) \times (1.645/.104)$$
$$N = (.333) \times (.667) \times (15.82) \times (15.82)$$
$$N = 55.6$$

For 90 percent confidence you must check 56 races.

FOR 95% CONFIDENCE:
$$N = (.333) \times (.667) \times (1.960/.104) \times (1.960/.104)$$
$$N = (.333) \times (.667) \times (18.85) \times (18.85)$$
$$N = 78.9$$

For 95 percent confidence you must check 79 races.

FOR 99% CONFIDENCE:
$$N = (.333) \times (.667) \times (2.575/.104) \times (2.575/.104)$$
$$N = (.333) \times (.667) \times (24.76) \times (24.76)$$
$$N = 136.16$$

For 99 percent confidence you must check 137 races.

Let us look at the same example but insist only on not losing instead of on a 10 percent minimum return. This time the minimum acceptable profit level is zero.

$$E = .333 - (2/9.62) = .1251$$

FOR 90% CONFIDENCE:

$$N = (.333) \times (.667) \times (1.645/.125) \times (1.645/.125)$$
$$N = (.333) \times (.667) \times (13.16) \times (13.16)$$
$$N = 38.466$$

For 90 percent confidence you must check 39 races. For 95 percent confidence you would have to check 55 races and for 99 percent confidence you would need 95 races. As you will see, the reason these numbers are so small is because of the large allowable range for error. The size of E inversely drives the results. The larger the value of E, the smaller the number of races necessary. Conversely, the smaller the value of E, the larger the number of races you will need.

This next example may seem a bit extreme, but it actually happened to me very early in my research. A particular pattern had shown 85 wins in 240 races and returned $538 for the $480 invested. The win percentage was 35.4 and the average mutuel was $6.33

$$E = .354 - (2.2/6.33) - .006$$

FOR 90% CONFIDENCE:

$$N = (.354) \times (.646) \times (1.645/.006) \times (1.645/.006)$$
$$N = (.354) \times (.646) \times (274.17) \times (274.17)$$
$$N = 14,880.89$$

If you think this is bad, for 99 percent confidence you would have to check 36,463 races. The reason that the numbers are so large is that the error margin is so small. In our first example we had a 10.4 percent error margin. In this case our margin is less than 1 percent. If you were willing to settle for a 5 percent minimum profit instead, the results would be a little better. For 90 percent confidence you would have to check 1,251 races; for 99 percent confidence, 3,064 races. This demonstrates the point that the E portion of our formula is critical.

My suggestion is to look for patterns that show at least a 20 percent expectation where you are willing to settle for a 10 percent minimum profit.

As you would expect, the higher the win percentage and the larger the average mutuel, the fewer races are necessary to validate the selection method. A word of warning: It's best to develop your model on as many races as possible, one hundred being the absolute minimum. Let's now look at our minimum goal of a 20 percent edge and apply the formula:

Win Percentage	Average Mutuel	Minimum Number of Races to Check		
		90%	95%	99%
25	9.60	1170	1660	2865
26	9.23	1112	1578	2723
27	8.89	1051	1492	2576
28	8.57	1006	1428	2465
29	8.28	944	1340	2313
30	8.00	909	1291	2228
31	7.74	873	1239	2137
32	7.50	829	1176	2029
33	7.27	798	1133	1955
34	7.06	753	1069	1847
35	6.86	718	1019	1758
36	6.67	685	973	1679
37	6.49	656	931	1607
38	6.32	627	890	1536
39	6.15	618	878	1515
40	6.00	585	829	1433

The above numbers scream out the truth of why it's so difficult for most people to win at the races. Just to validate an average selection method takes an enormous amount of research—more than 2,000 to verify a 33 percent performance at a $7.00 average mutuel if you insist on at least 10 percent profitability and 99 percent confidence. Let's suppose that you are content simply to insist on profitability instead of a minimum 10 percent return. The situation looks like this:

Win Percentage	Average Mutuel	Minimum Number of Races to Check		
		90%	95%	99%
25	9.60	293	415	717
26	9.23	278	394	680
27	8.89	264	374	645
28	8.57	251	357	615
29	8.28	238	337	582
30	8.00	228	323	557
31	7.74	218	309	533
32	7.50	208	294	508
33	7.27	199	281	487
34	7.06	189	269	463
35	6.86	181	256	442
36	6.67	173	245	423
37	6.49	165	235	405
38	6.32	158	225	387
39	6.15	154	218	376
40	6.00	147	208	357

One thing we notice is that in each of the above rows the rate of return on investment remains 20 percent—yet if our win proficiency increases, less races are necessary to validate our strategy.

Looking at the formula, we realize that it is driven by three different quantities. As we have seen, E is critical. Let's look at W and L for a moment. Their total always adds up to 1. To find the largest product of any of two-number combination whose sum is constant, divide the constant in two and square the result. When the total is 1, the largest product that can be attained is .25, or .5 times .5. Any other combination will yield a smaller product. For example, .6 times .4 is .24, and .49 times .51 is .2499. The minimum product is produced when one of the two numbers is zero. The closer one of the numbers gets to zero, the nearer to the minimum value we get. Consider W = .99 and L = .01. The product is .0099. Ideally, we want this product to be very small and the value of E to be as large as possible. This will minimize the number of races necessary to validate the method.

Betting two horses per race has a single-horse selection equivalent. Consider the single-horse bettor with 25 percent wins at an average mutuel of $9.60 and the two-horse bettor with 50 percent wins at a mutuel of $9.60. They both have a 20 percent advantage on the game.

$$E(1\ HORSE) = .25 \times \$7.60 - .75 \times \$2 = \$.40$$
$$E(2\ HORSE) = .50 \times \$5.60 - .50 \times \$4 = \$.80$$

The first earns 40 cents on every $2 bet for an ROI of 20 percent. The second earns 80 cents on every $4 bet for the same 20 percent ROI. The two-horse bettor's performance can be converted to a single-horse equivalent by dividing both sides by $4, which allows us to see things in terms of a one-dollar bet.

$$E(2\ HORSE) = .5 \times 1.4 - .5 = .20$$

We recognize that 1.4-to-1 odds is the same as an average mutuel of $4.80. In other words, the two-horse bettor's performance is equivalent to a single-horse bettor whose win percentage is 50 and average mutuel is $4.80. We now can compare these styles with regard to the number of races necessary to validate each. A glance at the above table shows that for 95 percent confidence the one-horse bettor must check at least 415 races. E for the two-horse bettor is:

$$E = .5 - (2/4.8) = .0833$$
$$N = .5 \times .5 \times (1.96/.0833) \times (1.96/.0833) = 138.298$$

For 95 percent confidence, the two-horse bettor must check at least 139 races. Even though the returns are the same, statistically speaking betting on two horses per race is a more optimistic way of operating because you can be confident much sooner than betting on a single horse per race. But please don't interpret this example as evidence that betting two horses per race is superior to single-horse betting. It's not.

Betting two horses per race is strictly for beginners. It's a psychological strategy. You'll go to the win window much more often by betting two horses. The trouble is, every time you win a bet, you're giving away one point in odds because of your losing bet. (Assuming that you bet the same amount on each horse.)

The Sartin Methodology urges its followers to bet two horses per race and dutch them as follows: 60 percent of the total wager on the short-odds horse and 40 percent on the long-odds horse. This is *not* a very good way to do things. You're much better off doing the opposite: 60 percent of your bet should go on the long-odds horse and 40 percent on the short-odds horse. The absolute best way to dutch horses is to bet them in proportion to their edge-to-odds ratios. In fairness to Sartin, he's almost forced into his betting scheme because his method doesn't generate a betting line. It's strictly a selection-oriented method.

It's not uncommon to hear a handicapper lament, "My handicapping is very good but my money management is horrible. If I could learn to manage my money, the racetrack would be mine." Fortunately for us, the vast majority of handicappers are sadly lacking in money-management skills. Most handicappers believe that the way to beat the races is to learn how to pick more winners.

One of the biggest untruths ever foisted on the racing public is that the way to win at thoroughbred handicapping is to pick lots of winners. You'll hear the voice of ignorance bleating, "Every winner is an overlay." Picking winners is immensely overrated. Nobody picks winners better than the public—yet for every dollar you invest in its selections, you only get 90 cents back. Actually, this isn't too bad when you consider that the track take exceeds 10 percent. In other words, the public would be a winning player if it weren't for the track take. (This conclusion will be questioned in the "Win Betting" chapter.) I have the pleasure of knowing a good number of winning handicappers, and not one of them can pick more winners than the public. That is, I don't know a single handicapper who can bet every race for a long period of time and achieve a 32 percent win rate. In fact, most can't achieve this win rate even by being selective. Tom Brohamer and James Quinn can boast win rates over 32 percent. The reason they're able to achieve this is because they're highly selective about the races in which they choose to invest. Normally they get between one and three plays per day at a single track, averaging about two plays per day. Mark Cramer has a 28 percent hit rate, as does this author. We get an average of three plays per day. The difference is average mutuel. Mark and I average more than $12 while Quinn and Brohamer average around $8. The key to this discussion is "edge."

James Quinn's personal goal for the 1993 race season was to achieve a 37 percent win rate at average odds of 5-to-2. I am happy to report that he exceeded his goal and had a most profitable year. Let's calculate the edge on his avowed goal.

$$\text{Edge} = .37 \times 2.5 - .63 = .295$$

Quinn wanted to achieve an edge of 29.5 percent. In other words, for every dollar he put through the mutuels he expected to get back close to $1.30. Not a bad way to invest his money.

Mark Cramer has a 28 percent win rate at an average mutuel over $12. His minimum edge is:

$$\text{Edge} = .28 \times 5 - .75 = .65$$

Does this mean that Cramer is twice as good as Quinn? Absolutely not. Cramer suffers much longer losing streaks than Quinn. Also, Quinn invests a lot more money than Cramer does, and so his annual profits are much higher than Cramer's.

It's not win percentage that's most important, nor is it average mutuel. What really counts is your overall edge multiplied by the amount of money that you put through the mutuels. You can have a huge edge, but if you only bet a small amount of money, your results won't be as productive as a player with a smaller edge who bets a lot of money. Consider Barry Meadow's results compared with Jim Quinn's. Jim is by far the superior handicapper. His edge is almost three times greater than Meadow's. Yet in 1992 Barry earned more than twice as much as Quinn did. Why? Barry put six times as much money through the mutuel windows as did Quinn.

If you asked a number of players to define money management, you would get as many different answers as people you asked. Yet proper money management, though not widely understood, is a vital skill. It allows you to put the maximum amount of money through the windows in order to earn the very best return on your equine investments with the greatest amount of safety possible.

MONEY MANAGEMENT

Money management is a systematic method of choosing bet size and betting opportunities in such a manner as to maximize our rate of growth of wealth and at the same time minimize our chances of going broke. It's a major weakness of most horse-race investors, stock-market investors, real estate investors, sports bettors, gamblers, speculators, and investors of all persuasions.

There are many possible money-management strategies. It's very important to choose the most appropriate, one that suits your style, and stick with it for a preplanned period of time. At the end of this test period you'll have either convinced yourself of the efficacy of your plan or the need to change it. The formula for success in any endeavor is, "Plan your work, then work your plan." If the plan is successful, great—keep doing what it is you're doing. If it's unsuccessful, then change it. The same is true for money management. We'll do exactly this after we've gained the requisite background.

We'll examine a number of money-management techniques. Depending upon your temperament and personal goals, you'll select the one that best suits your style. You must find the proper balance between betting too little, making the endeavor seem trivial, or betting too much and being wiped out by being too bold.

The best money manager I know is Barry Meadow. He says, "I've seen many players who were terrific handicappers but still couldn't make money at the racing game because they had no idea how to bet." He offers four items of advice:

1. Keep records of all bets and expenses.
2. Do not overbet in relation to your bankroll.

3. Bet more when the value is greater.
4. Bet within your emotional threshold.

In one sentence plus four simple statements, he very succinctly summarizes all the major ideas of money management.

Andrew Beyer says that money management is the one area of horse-race betting where theory differs so much from practice that there's hardly any reason to have fancy theories. This statement may hint at truth from a pragmatic point of view, but isn't true in the ultimate. There are good money managers out there, but they're rare. The very best handicappers aren't necessarily the best money managers. James Quinn and Tom Brohamer are handicappers in a class by themselves, yet each gets slightly above average marks in the money-management department (they get superior marks in the handicapping department). It very well may be that in order to be an expert handicapper you must not let yourself be limited by mathematical reasoning. Maybe expert handicapping and expert money management are mutually exclusive because one set of skills calls for intuition, knowledge, and experience while the other calls for practically absolute and unequivocal behavior. One is a right-brained set of skills, the other a left-brained set. Could it be that they are irreconcilable?

It sure seems that way when we consider the performances of Mark Cramer, Jim Quinn, Andy Beyer, and Tom Brohamer. Thank God for Barry Meadow. Finally I can point to an expert handicapper who practices professional money management.

Many times I have felt rather squeamish offering Jim Quinn money-management advice. What arrogance. He has forgotten more about thoroughbred handicapping than I'll ever learn and I'm telling him what to do. Yet the advice is sound and should be heeded. That's the enigma of money management. The best handicappers can live without most of it. They'll still earn profits, but they could earn much more if they paid more attention to its principles. In order to be winners in the first place, they must be doing things in accord with the fundamental principles. This is Beyer's point. He knows both expert money managers and expert handicappers and they're not necessarily the same people.

Winning is the standard. Anybody who can win consistently in this very tough challenge of thoroughbred wagering must be managing his or her money properly. Winning, by definition, is the result of sound judgment and good money management.

My point is that you can increase your winning potential by an order of magnitude if you're in tune with the principles of money management. I'm an excellent example of this postulate. My handicapping skills are adolescent compared to those of Andy Beyer, James Quinn, Mark Cramer, Tom Brohamer, and many of my readers. Yet I've managed to show a profit every year for the past ten years by exploiting positive-expectancy situations. If your money-management skills are strong, you definitely have an edge.

Handicapping skills improve with practice and validation. Money-management skills are vital and you only need learn them once. What's now true in money management will be true fifty years from now. It's also true that most horse-race bettors have no idea how to bet. If they did, they would be formidable competition—in fact, they're formidable competition now, even without these skills. Imagine if Santa Claus bought them the gift of money management. If you think that this pastime is difficult now, just imagine how rough it would be if every participant insisted upon fair odds before making a wager. Fortunately, this will never be the case, thanks to human nature. If we do our homework, we'll be given the golden opportunity to make wagers only when the odds favor us and the wisdom to avoid the myriad sucker bets that lead our colleagues to financial destruction.

I love the term mathematicians use to describe the ultimate in money mismanagement: the total loss of bankroll. They call it "gambler's ruin," which is obviously to be strictly avoided. Any money-management plan must take consecutive losses into consideration. You must plan for a realistic streak of losses. If you're unrealistic and don't anticipate them, they can be very demoralizing.

The following table represents the longest losing streak that you should anticipate for a given win percentage at a given confidence level:

Win Percentage	90% Confidence	95% Confidence	99% Confidence
14	16	20	31
15	15	19	29
16	14	18	27
17	13	17	25
18	12	16	24
19	11	15	22
20	11	14	21
21	10	13	20
22	10	13	19
23	9	12	18
24–25	9	11	17
26	8	10	16
27	8	10	15
28	8	10	15
29	7	9	14
30–31	7	9	13
32–34	6	8	12
35–36	6	7	11
37–39	5	7	10
40	5	6	10
41–43	5	6	9
44–45	4	6	8
46–48	4	5	8
49–52	4	5	7
53	4	4	7
54–60	3	4	6
61–63	3	4	5
64–68	3	3	5
69–77	2	3	4
78	2	2	4
79–80	2	2	3

The public (33 percent wins), for example, can expect losing runs of 6 about 10 percent of the time, losing runs of eight about 5 percent of the time, and losing runs of 12 about 1 percent of the time. Another way to interpret these data is to say that in 100 groups of six races each, on average about 10 of them won't contain a single winner (90 percent confidence). In 100 groups of eight races each, on average about five won't contain a winner (95 percent confidence). In 100 groups of 12 races each, on average only one won't contain at least one winner (99 percent confidence).

For safety purposes, it's best to plan using the 99 percent confidence level. If you're a 33 percent handicapper, your bankroll must be able to withstand 12 consecutive losses. As your win proficiency increases, your expectation of long losing streaks decreases. (The reason that I started the table at 14 percent is because you shouldn't make a win bet on any horse that has less than a 14 percent chance on your betting line [6-to-1] to win.)

Consider the situation of show betting. It's not inconceivable to devise a method that hits more than 80 percent of the time. You only have to be prepared for a three-race losing streak!

The principles of wagering say that we must know our win percentage, average mutuel, and the largest number of consecutive losses that our bankroll can tolerate. At this point we know how to develop all of these fundamental data items. Let's now investigate the various rational approaches to accomplishing the goal of maximizing our rate of growth of wealth while at the same time insuring against gambler's ruin.

In their excellent book *Dr. Z's Beat the Racetrack,* Bill Ziemba and Don Hausch give the desirable features of a money-management system. Any rational betting plan should agree with these guidelines:

1. Your current betting wealth should influence your bet size. That is, as your bankroll increases your bets should, on average, increase as well.
2. The likelihood of winning should influence the size of the bet.
3. The "edge"—a measure of the difference between your estimate of the likelihood of winning and the public's estimate translated into the expected return per dollar bet—should also influence the size of the bet.
4. The trade-off between growth of your bankroll and its security should be considered as well.

Many authors recommend a flat-bet technique. Perhaps it's because the accounting is simple. The technique is to wager the same amount of money on each race. The only problem with this method is choosing the proper bet size. Some authors suggest a 5 percent of your bankroll, which can be very bad advice. *The proper flat-bet amount is the percentage of your bankroll equal to your single-race edge divided by your average odds.* (The average-odds figure is calculated by subtracting $2 from your average mutuel and then dividing by two. If your average mutuel is $8.20, your average odds are 3.1-to-1.)

We immediately see that flat betting isn't in accord with the principles of good money management. The method must be modified if it's to be in any way advantageous. Right now it's like going to a bank that doesn't pay compound interest. The only advantages are that the accounting is easy and that the order of wins and losses doesn't matter. A win followed by a loss at even-money odds leaves you even. This isn't true for constant percentage betting. I'm not a fan of flat betting because I prefer compound interest to simple interest. Flat betting is only useful in research because we must know our flat-bet profit rate.

Let me suggest a modified flat-bet technique that will compound your return while protecting you from ruin. Each day, adjust your bankroll with respect to yesterday's results. Suppose that you've reached a goal of 30 percent winners at an average mutuel of $8 for win bets.

$$Edge = .3 \times 3 - .7 = .20$$

This means that your optimum percentage bet is 20 percent divided by three, the edge divided by the average odds. This is 6.67% of your bankroll per race. You then should wager 50 percent of this amount per race. (I'll explain why later.) So approximately 3 percent of your capital is the appropriate amount to wager on each playable race. If your present bankroll is $1,000, the bet is $30 per race. At the end of the day you'll take inventory. If your bankroll has increased to $1,100, then tomorrow's bet size will be $33; if your bankroll has decreased to $900, you'll bet $27 per race. In other words, you'll bet 3 percent of whatever your bankroll is that day. Your bet size changes as a function of your present bankroll.

I like this method better than traditional flat betting. Investors who must place all their bets at the same time, morning OTB bettors and early-bird bettors, are forced to use this method. It's not a bad way to manage your money.

I call this technique "incremental flat betting." Again, you simply bet half of your optimum-size bet (edge divided by odds) on each race during a given day. The next day you adjust your bet size by the size of your bankroll. Incremental flat betting has the advantage of not making us calculate a different bet size for each race yet assures the compounding effect when we're winning and protection from ruin when we're losing.

There is a betting system that is optimal, provided that there are no maximum or minimum limits on bet size and that the payoff is even. This betting system is referred to as the "Kelly Criterion." The Kelly Criterion says that if you have a fixed positive edge on each play of an even-payoff game, you should always wager that percent of your capital. If you have a 5 percent advantage, your next wager should be 5 percent of your present capital. This method increases your wealth at the fastest rate possible with very little chance of your going broke. How nice! The best of both worlds—substantial protection from ruin and an indefinite increase in wealth.

As expected, this too-good-to-be-true system has very few applications in the real world. What frequently occurs is a positive-expectation situation where the payoff is uneven. In these games a good approximation of the optimal betting strategy is to bet your single-race edge divided by your odds. The problem with computing a precise optimum is that the mathematics gets totally out of hand. To quote Allan Wilson, "Much work remains to be done to understand how to adapt the optimal concept first suggested by Kelly in realistic cases. It's this author's opinion that in view of the complexities of direct analysis, simulation techniques using random numbers and computers may provide the most practical answers."

It's interesting to note that almost everybody realizes that we should increase our wagers when we're winning and decrease them when losing. We also realize that we should only invest in opportunities where we have the best of it. That's exactly what the Kelly Criterion tells us to do. Unfortunately, for most applications it isn't straightforward—it takes a bit of work to arrive at the optimum percentage to bet.

Let's consider the differences between flat betting and Kelly betting. Kelly says that we should bet a percentage of our bankroll on each outcome. The most obvious difference is that in one case the size of our bet never changes while in the other it never stays the same. Analyzing flat betting is easy. Analyzing constant-percentage betting is a little more difficult. Consider a 30 percent handicapper who gets an $8 average mutuel. His expectation is 20 percent. Suppose he bets on 10 races, wins three and loses seven, and uses a flat-bet system of money management. We can calculate his final bankroll quite easily. We'll assume he has a $1,000 bankroll and bets $30 per race. The three races he wins net him $270 profit and the seven he loses cost him $210. His bankroll is $1,060 after the 10 races.

If he bets 3 percent Kelly, the formula to calculate his final bankroll is as follows:

$$B = B_0 \times (1 - p)^L \times (1 + pO)^W$$

B_0 = Starting bankroll
p = Percent of bankroll wagered
L = Number of losing bets
W = Number of winning bets
O = Odds-to-1

$B = 1,000 \times (1 - .03)^7 \times (1 + .03 \times 3)^3$
$B = 1,000 \times (.97)^7 \times (1.09)^3$
$B = 1,000 \times .8080 \times 1.2950$
$B = 1,046$

From this it seems we can conclude that flat betting is a better technique because in the flat-bet case our bankroll has grown to $1,060 while in the constant percentage case it has only grown to $1,046. However, this is only true when the number of races is small. Consider the case of 100 races in which we win 30 and lose 70. Flat betting yields a final bankroll of $1,600 while Kelly betting yields $1,573. Thus far, flat betting still seems superior. Now consider 200 races in which we win 60 and lose 140. Flat betting yields a $2,200 bankroll while Kelly betting yields $2,475. Next, consider 500 races in which we win 150 and lose 350. Flat betting yields a $4,000 bankroll while Kelly yields $9,640. Finally, consider 1,000 races in which we win 300 and lose 700. Flat betting yields a $7,000 bankroll while Kelly betting yields $92,932! As the number of races increases, the final bankroll grows at a compound rate with the Kelly approach and at a linear rate with flat betting. In the long run, Kelly-type wagering is far superior.

Let's take a closer look at a sequence of three wins and seven losses where our win percentage is 30, our average odds are 3-to-1, and our first bet is $30:

Bet Size	Outcome	Bankroll
30	W	1,090
33	L	1,057
32	L	1,025
31	W	1,118
34	W	1,220
37	L	1,183
35	L	1,148
34	L	1,114
33	L	1,081
32	L	1,049

Did you notice that a win followed by a loss results in a smaller profit when compared to flat betting? In the above example, a win followed by a loss took $1,000 and turned it into $1,057. If we were flat betting this result would have been $1,060. Let's compare flat betting to Kelly betting. The only rational way to accomplish this is by simulation. If we were to look at all the possibilities, the task would be impossible.

To completely model a sequence of 100 races, the number of possible win-loss outcomes gets way out of hand. The number of different sequences of 30 wins and 70 losses is a genuine monster. To give you an idea of the magnitude of this number, it's greater than 2.93 octillion: 293 followed by 22 zeroes. If a computer could process one billion sequences per second and started calculating at the time when scientists think the planet was formed, it would not be halfway finished today! It would take over 92 billion years to compute! The good news is that our bankroll size will be approximately the same for any combination of 30 wins and 70 losses. The total remains virtually the same regardless of their order. (The fact that we have to round off our bet to the nearest dollar has a minuscule effect on the final bankroll.)

The best way to compare betting methods is to use computer simulation. It's really the only rational technique to use in comparing betting methods. We'll be able to simulate a week's worth of races as easily as a lifetime's worth.

This subject is discussed in the next chapter. You'll be able to do it both manually and automatically. When you learn to use this technique, you will be able to test any money-management system and compare it with any other. No more listening to rational-sounding but specious betting methods. You'll have the wherewithal to evaluate any system or method and decide if it's legitimate or not.

It's actually quite simple to apply the principles of Monte Carlo (see next chapter) simulation to horse-race wagering. We postulate a win percentage and average mutuel. Suppose the win percent is 30 percent. We generate a random number between 0 (zero) and 1. If that number is less than .30, we consider the event to be a win. If the random number is greater than or equal to .30, we consider this event to be a loss. If the event is a win, we apply the average payoff and adjust the bankroll upward. If the event is a loss, we deduct the size of the bet from the bankroll.

Let's apply the powerful technique of simulation to a number of popular money-management methods. The techniques we'll examine are:

1. FLAT BETTING
2. KELLY BETTING
3. BASE BET PLUS SQUARE ROOT
4. DUE COLUMN

Flat Bet

This is the simplest technique available. It's the basis used to determine if a handicapping method is profitable or not and the standard by which any money management scheme is measured, but it's very conservative. The only question regarding its application is "How large should our bet size be in relation to the size of our bankroll?" The answer to the question of bet size is always the same: The optimum percentage of bankroll bet size is our edge divided by our odds. The edge is our single-bet expectation per dollar bet and the odds are our average odds for a group of races. If we have a 20 percent edge, it means that on average for every $1 we put through the mutuel window, we get back $1.20. Unfortunately, unlike a bank this compounding doesn't take place in an orderly manner.

A $1,000 bankroll ranged from $640 to $1,720 in a simulation of 100 twenty-race groups where our win percentage was 30 percent, the average mutuel was $8, and the bet size was 3 percent (or $30). In the worst case we still preserved 64 percent of our original stake. Here's the summary:

REPETITION #1		REPETITION #2	
Total capital	1,240	Total capital	1,480
Longest win streak	2	Longest win streak	4
Longest lose streak	3	Longest lose streak	4
Win percentage	35	Win percentage	45
Total $'s bet	600	Total $'s bet	600
Average odds	3	Average odds	3

REPETITION #3		REPETITION #4	
Total capital	880	Total capital	1,120
Longest win streak	1	Longest win streak	2
Longest lose streak	8	Longest lose streak	7
Win percentage	20	Win percentage	30
Total $'s bet	600	Total $'s bet	600
Average odds	3	Average odds	3

REPETITION #5		REPETITION #6	
Total capital	1,120	Total capital	1,240
Longest win streak	4	Longest win streak	2
Longest lose streak	5	Longest lose streak	5
Win percentage	30	Win percentage	35
Total $'s bet	600	Total $'s bet	600
Average odds	3	Average odds	3

REPETITION #7

Total capital	1,240
Longest win streak	2
Longest lose streak	6
Win percentage	35
Total $'s bet	600
Average odds	3

REPETITION #8

Total capital	1,360
Longest win streak	1
Longest lose streak	2
Win percentage	40
Total $'s bet	600
Average odds	3

REPETITION #9

Total capital	1,120
Longest win streak	3
Longest lose streak	5
Win percentage	30
Total $'s bet	600
Average odds	3

REPETITION #10

Total capital	1,120
Longest win streak	1
Longest lose streak	7
Win percentage	30
Total $'s bet	600
Average odds	3

REPETITION #11

Total capital	880
Longest win streak	1
Longest lose streak	5
Win percentage	20
Total $'s bet	600
Average odds	3

REPETITION #12

Total capital	1,120
Longest win streak	1
Longest lose streak	5
Win percentage	30
Total $'s bet	600
Average odds	3

REPETITION #13

Total capital	1,120
Longest win streak	1
Longest lose streak	4
Win percentage	30
Total $'s bet	600
Average odds	3

REPETITION #14

Total capital	640
Longest win streak	2
Longest lose streak	9
Win percentage	10
Total $'s bet	600
Average odds	3

REPETITION #15

Total capital	760
Longest win streak	2
Longest lose streak	13
Win percentage	15
Total $'s bet	600
Average odds	3

REPETITION #16

Total capital	1,240
Longest win streak	4
Longest lose streak	9
Win percentage	35
Total $'s bet	600
Average odds	3

REPETITION #17

Total capital	1,240
Longest win streak	3
Longest lose streak	5
Win percentage	35
Total $'s bet	600
Average odds	3

REPETITION #18

Total capital	1,000
Longest win streak	2
Longest lose streak	7
Win percentage	25
Total $'s bet	600
Average odds	3

REPETITION #19

Total capital	1,360
Longest win streak	3
Longest lose streak	4
Win percentage	40
Total $'s bet	600
Average odds	3

REPETITION #20

Total capital	1,360
Longest win streak	4
Longest lose streak	7
Win percentage	40
Total $'s bet	600
Average odds	3

REPETITION #21

Total capital	1,120
Longest win streak	2
Longest lose streak	6
Win percentage	30
Total $'s bet	600
Average odds	3

REPETITION #22

Total capital	760
Longest win streak	1
Longest lose streak	11
Win percentage	15
Total $'s bet	600
Average odds	3

REPETITION #23

Total capital	1,120
Longest win streak	3
Longest lose streak	5
Win percentage	30
Total $'s bet	600
Average odds	3

REPETITION #24

Total capital	1,000
Longest win streak	1
Longest lose streak	7
Win percentage	25
Total $'s bet	600
Average odds	3

REPETITION #25

Total capital	1,480
Longest win streak	3
Longest lose streak	4
Win percentage	45
Total $'s bet	600
Average odds	3

REPETITION #26

Total capital	1,360
Longest win streak	2
Longest lose streak	4
Win percentage	40
Total $'s bet	600
Average odds	3

REPETITION #27

Total capital	1,240
Longest win streak	3
Longest lose streak	8
Win percentage	35
Total $'s bet	600
Average odds	3

REPETITION #28

Total capital	1,240
Longest win streak	2
Longest lose streak	5
Win percentage	35
Total $'s bet	600
Average odds	3

REPETITION #29

Total capital	1,120
Longest win streak	4
Longest lose streak	8
Win percentage	30
Total $'s bet	600
Average odds	3

REPETITION #30

Total capital	1,000
Longest win streak	3
Longest lose streak	5
Win percentage	25
Total $'s bet	600
Average odds	3

REPETITION #31

Total capital	1,000
Longest win streak	4
Longest lose streak	10
Win percentage	25
Total $'s bet	600
Average odds	3

REPETITION #32

Total capital	1,600
Longest win streak	3
Longest lose streak	3
Win percentage	50
Total $'s bet	600
Average odds	3

REPETITION #33

Total capital	760
Longest win streak	1
Longest lose streak	8
Win percentage	15
Total $'s bet	600
Average odds	3

REPETITION #34

Total capital	1,000
Longest win streak	2
Longest lose streak	6
Win percentage	25
Total $'s bet	600
Average odds	3

REPETITION #35

Total capital	1,000
Longest win streak	2
Longest lose streak	12
Win percentage	25
Total $'s bet	600
Average odds	3

REPETITION #36

Total capital	1,000
Longest win streak	1
Longest lose streak	6
Win percentage	25
Total $'s bet	600
Average odds	3

REPETITION #37

Total capital	1,000
Longest win streak	2
Longest lose streak	5
Win percentage	25
Total $'s bet	600
Average odds	3

REPETITION #38

Total capital	1,480
Longest win streak	3
Longest lose streak	7
Win percentage	45
Total $'s bet	600
Average odds	3

REPETITION #39

Total capital	1,240
Longest win streak	3
Longest lose streak	8
Win percentage	35
Total $'s bet	600
Average odds	3

REPETITION #40

Total capital	1,000
Longest win streak	2
Longest lose streak	6
Win percentage	25
Total $'s bet	600
Average odds	3

REPETITION #41

Total capital	1,360
Longest win streak	3
Longest lose streak	5
Win percentage	40
Total $'s bet	600
Average odds	3

REPETITION #42

Total capital	1,240
Longest win streak	2
Longest lose streak	4
Win percentage	35
Total $'s bet	600
Average odds	3

REPETITION #43

Total capital	1,360
Longest win streak	2
Longest lose streak	4
Win percentage	40
Total $'s bet	600
Average odds	3

REPETITION #44

Total capital	1,000
Longest win streak	1
Longest lose streak	5
Win percentage	25
Total $'s bet	600
Average odds	3

REPETITION #45

Total capital	1,240
Longest win streak	2
Longest lose streak	4
Win percentage	35
Total $'s bet	600
Average odds	3

REPETITION #46

Total capital	1,120
Longest win streak	1
Longest lose streak	4
Win percentage	30
Total $'s bet	600
Average odds	3

REPETITION #47

Total capital	1,480
Longest win streak	2
Longest lose streak	4
Win percentage	45
Total $'s bet	600
Average odds	3

REPETITION #48

Total capital	760
Longest win streak	1
Longest lose streak	10
Win percentage	15
Total $'s bet	600
Average odds	3

REPETITION #49

Total capital	1,120
Longest win streak	2
Longest lose streak	5
Win percentage	30
Total $'s bet	600
Average odds	3

REPETITION #50

Total capital	1,600
Longest win streak	2
Longest lose streak	2
Win percentage	50
Total $'s bet	600
Average odds	3

REPETITION #51

Total capital	1,360
Longest win streak	4
Longest lose streak	6
Win percentage	40
Total $'s bet	600
Average odds	3

REPETITION #52

Total capital	1,360
Longest win streak	3
Longest lose streak	5
Win percentage	40
Total $'s bet	600
Average odds	3

REPETITION #53

Total capital	1,360
Longest win streak	2
Longest lose streak	5
Win percentage	40
Total $'s bet	600
Average odds	3

REPETITION #54

Total capital	1,000
Longest win streak	2
Longest lose streak	10
Win percentage	25
Total $'s bet	600
Average odds	3

REPETITION #55

Total capital	1,240
Longest win streak	2
Longest lose streak	5
Win percentage	35
Total $'s bet	600
Average odds	3

REPETITION #56

Total capital	1,000
Longest win streak	2
Longest lose streak	5
Win percentage	25
Total $'s bet	600
Average odds	3

REPETITION #57

Total capital	1,000
Longest win streak	2
Longest lose streak	6
Win percentage	25
Total $'s bet	600
Average odds	3

REPETITION #58

Total capital	880
Longest win streak	2
Longest lose streak	9
Win percentage	20
Total $'s bet	600
Average odds	3

REPETITION #59

Total capital	1,120
Longest win streak	2
Longest lose streak	4
Win percentage	30
Total $'s bet	600
Average odds	3

REPETITION #60

Total capital	880
Longest win streak	2
Longest lose streak	8
Win percentage	20
Total $'s bet	600
Average odds	3

REPETITION #61

Total capital	1,360
Longest win streak	2
Longest lose streak	4
Win percentage	40
Total $'s bet	600
Average odds	3

REPETITION #62

Total capital	1,240
Longest win streak	2
Longest lose streak	4
Win percentage	35
Total $'s bet	600
Average odds	3

REPETITION #63

Total capital	1,600
Longest win streak	3
Longest lose streak	2
Win percentage	50
Total $'s bet	600
Average odds	3

REPETITION #64

Total capital	760
Longest win streak	1
Longest lose streak	7
Win percentage	15
Total $'s bet	600
Average odds	3

REPETITION #65

Total capital	1,000
Longest win streak	1
Longest lose streak	4
Win percentage	25
Total $'s bet	600
Average odds	3

REPETITION #66

Total capital	1,240
Longest win streak	3
Longest lose streak	8
Win percentage	35
Total $'s bet	600
Average odds	3

REPETITION #67

Total capital	1,000
Longest win streak	3
Longest lose streak	9
Win percentage	25
Total $'s bet	600
Average odds	3

REPETITION #68

Total capital	1,120
Longest win streak	2
Longest lose streak	7
Win percentage	30
Total $'s bet	600
Average odds	3

REPETITION #69

Total capital	760
Longest win streak	1
Longest lose streak	8
Win percentage	15
Total $'s bet	600
Average odds	3

REPETITION #70

Total capital	1,360
Longest win streak	4
Longest lose streak	6
Win percentage	40
Total $'s bet	600
Average odds	3

REPETITION #71

Total capital	760
Longest win streak	1
Longest lose streak	6
Win percentage	15
Total $'s bet	600
Average odds	3

REPETITION #72

Total capital	1,000
Longest win streak	4
Longest lose streak	13
Win percentage	25
Total $'s bet	600
Average odds	3

REPETITION #73

Total capital	1,720
Longest win streak	3
Longest lose streak	5
Win percentage	55
Total $'s bet	600
Average odds	3

REPETITION #74

Total capital	1,360
Longest win streak	3
Longest lose streak	5
Win percentage	40
Total $'s bet	600
Average odds	3

REPETITION #75

Total capital	1,120
Longest win streak	3
Longest lose streak	7
Win percentage	30
Total $'s bet	600
Average odds	3

REPETITION #76

Total capital	640
Longest win streak	1
Longest lose streak	14
Win percentage	10
Total $'s bet	600
Average odds	3

REPETITION #77

Total capital	880
Longest win streak	1
Longest lose streak	8
Win percentage	20
Total $'s bet	600
Average odds	3

REPETITION #78

Total capital	1,480
Longest win streak	2
Longest lose streak	4
Win percentage	45
Total $'s bet	600
Average odds	3

REPETITION #79

Total capital	1,000
Longest win streak	2
Longest lose streak	7
Win percentage	25
Total $'s bet	600
Average odds	3

REPETITION #80

Total capital	1,240
Longest win streak	2
Longest lose streak	5
Win percentage	35
Total $'s bet	600
Average odds	3

REPETITION #81

Total capital	880
Longest win streak	1
Longest lose streak	7
Win percentage	20
Total $'s bet	600
Average odds	3

REPETITION #82

Total capital	760
Longest win streak	1
Longest lose streak	6
Win percentage	15
Total $'s bet	600
Average odds	3

REPETITION #83

Total capital	1,000
Longest win streak	2
Longest lose streak	4
Win percentage	25
Total $'s bet	600
Average odds	3

REPETITION #84

Total capital	1,240
Longest win streak	2
Longest lose streak	5
Win percentage	35
Total $'s bet	600
Average odds	3

REPETITION #85

Total capital	1,000
Longest win streak	2
Longest lose streak	9
Win percentage	25
Total $'s bet	600
Average odds	3

REPETITION #86

Total capital	1,360
Longest win streak	4
Longest lose streak	5
Win percentage	40
Total $'s bet	600
Average odds	3

REPETITION #87

Total capital	1,000
Longest win streak	2
Longest lose streak	7
Win percentage	25
Total $'s bet	600
Average odds	3

REPETITION #88

Total capital	1,240
Longest win streak	2
Longest lose streak	3
Win percentage	35
Total $'s bet	600
Average odds	3

REPETITION #89

Total capital	1,360
Longest win streak	2
Longest lose streak	4
Win percentage	40
Total $'s bet	600
Average odds	3

REPETITION #90

Total capital	1,000
Longest win streak	2
Longest lose streak	6
Win percentage	25
Total $'s bet	600
Average odds	3

REPETITION #91

Total capital	1,000
Longest win streak	1
Longest lose streak	6
Win percentage	25
Total $'s bet	600
Average odds	3

REPETITION #92

Total capital	1,120
Longest win streak	2
Longest lose streak	8
Win percentage	30
Total $'s bet	600
Average odds	3

REPETITION #93

Total capital	1,240
Longest win streak	2
Longest lose streak	5
Win percentage	35
Total $'s bet	600
Average odds	3

REPETITION #94

Total capital	1,480
Longest win streak	2
Longest lose streak	2
Win percentage	45
Total $'s bet	600
Average odds	3

REPETITION #95

Total capital	760
Longest win streak	1
Longest lose streak	7
Win percentage	15
Total $'s bet	600
Average odds	3

REPETITION #96

Total capital	1,120
Longest win streak	1
Longest lose streak	6
Win percentage	30
Total $'s bet	600
Average odds	3

REPETITION #97		REPETITION #98	
Total capital	880	Total capital	640
Longest win streak	2	Longest win streak	1
Longest lose streak	6	Longest lose streak	16
Win percentage	20	Win percentage	10
Total $'s bet	600	Total $'s bet	600
Average odds	3	Average odds	3

REPETITION #99		REPETITION #100	
Total capital	880	Total capital	1,000
Longest win streak	1	Longest win streak	2
Longest lose streak	7	Longest lose streak	7
Win percentage	20	Win percentage	20
Total $'s bet	600	Total $'s bet	600
Average odds	3	Average odds	3

Summary
Flat Bet

INPUT DATA:		RESULTS:	
Original bankroll	1,000	Average return	$1,122.40
Number of trials	20	Win percentage	30
Win probability	.3	Average odds	3
Constant odds-to-1	3	Longest win streak	4
# of repetitions	100	Longest lose streak	16
Base Bet	30	Average bet	30
Random seed	−100	Number of busts	0
Limit win % range	N		

These results square quite nicely with the theoretical result of $1,120. If you have an expectation of 20 percent and bet $30 per race for 20 races, you should win 20 percent of the total amount that you bet. You bet $600, hence you can expect a profit of $120.

Although the "edge divided by odds" is the rate at which the bankroll grows fastest, it doesn't do so with total safety. As investors we aren't averse to taking risks—we simply want to manage them and prevent gambler's ruin.

When given a choice between a rapid growth rate with little safety and a modest growth rate with much safety, we prefer the latter. I consider the loss of a bankroll the equivalent of physical death, maybe worse. I mentioned that it's wise to choose a fraction of the optimum bet size. In our example of a 30 percent win rate at an average mutuel of $8, we find that 6.67 percent is the optimum bet size. Let's apply the same sequence of wins and losses to a bet size of $67 and see what happens. Here are the results:

REPETITION #1

Total capital	1,536
Longest win streak	2
Longest lose streak	3
Win percentage	35
Total $'s bet	1,340
Average odds	3

REPETITION #2

Total capital	2,072
Longest win streak	4
Longest lose streak	4
Win percentage	45
Total $'s bet	1,340
Average odds	3

REPETITION #3

Total capital	732
Longest win streak	1
Longest lose streak	8
Win percentage	20
Total $'s bet	1,340
Average odds	3

REPETITION #4

Total capital	1,268
Longest win streak	2
Longest lose streak	7
Win percentage	30
Total $'s bet	1,340
Average odds	3

REPETITION #5

Total capital	1,268
Longest win streak	4
Longest lose streak	5
Win percentage	30
Total $'s bet	1,340
Average odds	3

REPETITION #6

Total capital	1,536
Longest win streak	2
Longest lose streak	5
Win percentage	35
Total $'s bet	1,340
Average odds	3

REPETITION #7

Total capital	1,536
Longest win streak	2
Longest lose streak	6
Win percentage	35
Total $'s bet	1,340
Average odds	3

REPETITION #8

Total capital	1,804
Longest win streak	1
Longest lose streak	2
Win percentage	40
Total $'s bet	1,340
Average odds	3

REPETITION #9

Total capital	1,268
Longest win streak	3
Longest lose streak	5
Win percentage	30
Total $'s bet	1,340
Average odds	3

REPETITION #10

Total capital	1,268
Longest win streak	1
Longest lose streak	7
Win percentage	30
Total $'s bet	1,340
Average odds	3

REPETITION #11

Total capital	732
Longest win streak	1
Longest lose streak	5
Win percentage	20
Total $'s bet	1,340
Average odds	3

REPETITION #12

Total capital	1,268
Longest win streak	1
Longest lose streak	5
Win percentage	30
Total $'s bet	1,340
Average odds	3

REPETITION #13

Total capital	1,268
Longest win streak	1
Longest lose streak	4
Win percentage	30
Total $'s bet	1,340
Average odds	3

REPETITION #14

Total capital	196
Longest win streak	2
Longest lose streak	9
Win percentage	10
Total $'s bet	1,340
Average odds	3

REPETITION #15

Total capital	464
Longest win streak	2
Longest lose streak	13
Win percentage	15
Total $'s bet	1,340
Average odds	3

REPETITION #16

Total capital	1,536
Longest win streak	4
Longest lose streak	9
Win percentage	35
Total $'s bet	1,340
Average odds	3

REPETITION #17

Total capital	1,536
Longest win streak	3
Longest lose streak	5
Win percentage	35
Total $'s bet	1,340
Average odds	3

REPETITION #18

Total capital	1,000
Longest win streak	2
Longest lose streak	7
Win percentage	25
Total $'s bet	1,340
Average odds	3

REPETITION #19

Total capital	1,804
Longest win streak	3
Longest lose streak	4
Win percentage	40
Total $'s bet	1,340
Average odds	3

REPETITION #20

Total capital	1,804
Longest win streak	4
Longest lose streak	7
Win percentage	40
Total $'s bet	1,340
Average odds	3

REPETITION #21

Total capital	1,268
Longest win streak	2
Longest lose streak	6
Win percentage	30
Total $'s bet	1,340
Average odds	3

REPETITION #22

Total capital	464
Longest win streak	1
Longest lose streak	11
Win percentage	15
Total $'s bet	1,340
Average odds	3

REPETITION #23

Total capital	1,268
Longest win streak	3
Longest lose streak	5
Win percentage	30
Total $'s bet	1,340
Average odds	3

REPETITION #24

Total capital	1,000
Longest win streak	1
Longest lose streak	7
Win percentage	25
Total $'s bet	1,340
Average odds	3

REPETITION #25

Total capital	2,072
Longest win streak	3
Longest lose streak	4
Win percentage	45
Total $'s bet	1,340
Average odds	3

REPETITION #26

Total capital	1,804
Longest win streak	2
Longest lose streak	4
Win percentage	40
Total $'s bet	1,340
Average odds	3

REPETITION #27

Total capital	1,536
Longest win streak	3
Longest lose streak	8
Win percentage	35
Total $'s bet	1,340
Average odds	3

REPETITION #28

Total capital	1,536
Longest win streak	2
Longest lose streak	5
Win percentage	35
Total $'s bet	1,340
Average odds	3

REPETITION #29

Total capital	1,268
Longest win streak	4
Longest lose streak	8
Win percentage	30
Total $'s bet	1,340
Average odds	3

REPETITION #30

Total capital	1,000
Longest win streak	3
Longest lose streak	5
Win percentage	25
Total $'s bet	1,340
Average odds	3

REPETITION #31

Total capital	1,000
Longest win streak	4
Longest lose streak	10
Win percentage	25
Total $'s bet	1,340
Average odds	3

REPETITION #32

Total capital	2,340
Longest win streak	3
Longest lose streak	3
Win percentage	50
Total $'s bet	1,340
Average odds	3

REPETITION #33

Total capital	464
Longest win streak	1
Longest lose streak	8
Win percentage	15
Total $'s bet	1,340
Average odds	3

REPETITION #34

Total capital	1,000
Longest win streak	2
Longest lose streak	6
Win percentage	25
Total $'s bet	1,340
Average odds	3

REPETITION #35

Total capital	1,000
Longest win streak	2
Longest lose streak	12
Win percentage	25
Total $'s bet	1,340
Average odds	3

REPETITION #36

Total capital	1,000
Longest win streak	1
Longest lose streak	6
Win percentage	25
Total $'s bet	1,340
Average odds	3

REPETITION #37

Total capital	1,000
Longest win streak	2
Longest lose streak	5
Win percentage	25
Total $'s bet	1,340
Average odds	3

REPETITION #38

Total capital	2,072
Longest win streak	3
Longest lose streak	7
Win percentage	45
Total $'s bet	1,340
Average odds	3

REPETITION #39

Total capital	1,536
Longest win streak	3
Longest lose streak	8
Win percentage	35
Total $'s bet	1,340
Average odds	3

REPETITION #40

Total capital	1,000
Longest win streak	2
Longest lose streak	6
Win percentage	25
Total $'s bet	1,340
Average odds	3

REPETITION #41

Total capital	1,804
Longest win streak	3
Longest lose streak	5
Win percentage	40
Total $'s bet	1,340
Average odds	3

REPETITION #42

Total capital	1,536
Longest win streak	2
Longest lose streak	4
Win percentage	35
Total $'s bet	1,340
Average odds	3

REPETITION #43

Total capital	1,804
Longest win streak	2
Longest lose streak	4
Win percentage	40
Total $'s bet	1,340
Average odds	3

REPETITION #44

Total capital	1,000
Longest win streak	1
Longest lose streak	5
Win percentage	25
Total $'s bet	1,340
Average odds	3

REPETITION #45

Total capital	1,536
Longest win streak	2
Longest lose streak	4
Win percentage	35
Total $'s bet	1,340
Average odds	3

REPETITION #46

Total capital	1,268
Longest win streak	1
Longest lose streak	4
Win percentage	30
Total $'s bet	1,340
Average odds	3

REPETITION #47

Total capital	2,072
Longest win streak	2
Longest lose streak	4
Win percentage	45
Total $'s bet	1,340
Average odds	3

REPETITION #48

Total capital	464
Longest win streak	1
Longest lose streak	10
Win percentage	15
Total $'s bet	1,340
Average odds	3

REPETITION #49

Total capital	1,268
Longest win streak	2
Longest lose streak	5
Win percentage	30
Total $'s bet	1,340
Average odds	3

REPETITION #50

Total capital	2,340
Longest win streak	2
Longest lose streak	2
Win percentage	50
Total $'s bet	1,340
Average odds	3

REPETITION #51

Total capital	1,804
Longest win streak	4
Longest lose streak	6
Win percentage	40
Total $'s bet	1,340
Average odds	3

REPETITION #52

Total capital	1,804
Longest win streak	3
Longest lose streak	5
Win percentage	40
Total $'s bet	1,340
Average odds	3

REPETITION #53

Total capital	1,804
Longest win streak	2
Longest lose streak	5
Win percentage	40
Total $'s bet	1,340
Average odds	3

REPETITION #54

Total capital	1,000
Longest win streak	2
Longest lose streak	10
Win percentage	25
Total $'s bet	1,340
Average odds	3

REPETITION #55

Total capital	1,536
Longest win streak	2
Longest lose streak	5
Win percentage	35
Total $'s bet	1,340
Average odds	3

REPETITION #56

Total capital	1,000
Longest win streak	2
Longest lose streak	5
Win percentage	25
Total $'s bet	1,340
Average odds	3

REPETITION #57

Total capital	1,000
Longest win streak	2
Longest lose streak	6
Win percentage	25
Total $'s bet	1,340
Average odds	3

REPETITION #58

Total capital	732
Longest win streak	2
Longest lose streak	9
Win percentage	20
Total $'s bet	1,340
Average odds	3

REPETITION #59

Total capital	1,268
Longest win streak	2
Longest lose streak	4
Win percentage	30
Total $'s bet	1,340
Average odds	3

REPETITION #60

Total capital	732
Longest win streak	2
Longest lose streak	8
Win percentage	20
Total $'s bet	1,340
Average odds	3

REPETITION #61

Total capital	1,804
Longest win streak	2
Longest lose streak	4
Win percentage	40
Total $'s bet	1,340
Average odds	3

REPETITION #62

Total capital	1,536
Longest win streak	2
Longest lose streak	4
Win percentage	35
Total $'s bet	1,340
Average odds	3

REPETITION #63

Total capital	2,340
Longest win streak	3
Longest lose streak	2
Win percentage	50
Total $'s bet	1,340
Average odds	3

REPETITION #64

Total capital	464
Longest win streak	1
Longest lose streak	7
Win percentage	15
Total $'s bet	1,340
Average odds	3

REPETITION #65

Total capital	1,000
Longest win streak	1
Longest lose streak	4
Win percentage	25
Total $'s bet	1,340
Average odds	3

REPETITION #66

Total capital	1,536
Longest win streak	3
Longest lose streak	8
Win percentage	35
Total $'s bet	1,340
Average odds	3

REPETITION #67

Total capital	1,000
Longest win streak	3
Longest lose streak	9
Win percentage	25
Total $'s bet	1,340
Average odds	3

REPETITION #68

Total capital	1,268
Longest win streak	2
Longest lose streak	7
Win percentage	30
Total $'s bet	1,340
Average odds	3

REPETITION #69

Total capital	464
Longest win streak	1
Longest lose streak	8
Win percentage	15
Total $'s bet	1,340
Average odds	3

REPETITION #70

Total capital	1,804
Longest win streak	4
Longest lose streak	6
Win percentage	40
Total $'s bet	1,340
Average odds	3

REPETITION #71

Total capital	464
Longest win streak	1
Longest lose streak	6
Win percentage	15
Total $'s bet	1,340
Average odds	3

REPETITION #72

Total capital	1,000
Longest win streak	4
Longest lose streak	13
Win percentage	25
Total $'s bet	1,340
Average odds	3

REPETITION #73

Total capital	2,608
Longest win streak	3
Longest lose streak	5
Win percentage	55
Total $'s bet	1,340
Average odds	3

REPETITION #74

Total capital	1,804
Longest win streak	3
Longest lose streak	5
Win percentage	40
Total $'s bet	1,340
Average odds	3

REPETITION #75

Total capital	1,268
Longest win streak	3
Longest lose streak	7
Win percentage	30
Total $'s bet	1,340
Average odds	3

REPETITION #76

Total capital	196
Longest win streak	1
Longest lose streak	14
Win percentage	10
Total $'s bet	1,340
Average odds	3

REPETITION #77

Total capital	732
Longest win streak	1
Longest lose streak	8
Win percentage	20
Total $'s bet	1,340
Average odds	3

REPETITION #78

Total capital	2,072
Longest win streak	2
Longest lose streak	4
Win percentage	45
Total $'s bet	1,340
Average odds	3

REPETITION #79

Total capital	1,000
Longest win streak	2
Longest lose streak	7
Win percentage	25
Total $'s bet	1,340
Average odds	3

REPETITION #80

Total capital	1,536
Longest win streak	2
Longest lose streak	5
Win percentage	35
Total $'s bet	1,340
Average odds	3

REPETITION #81

Total capital	732
Longest win streak	1
Longest lose streak	7
Win percentage	20
Total $'s bet	1,340
Average odds	3

REPETITION #82

Total capital	464
Longest win streak	1
Longest lose streak	6
Win percentage	15
Total $'s bet	1,340
Average odds	3

REPETITION #83

Total capital	1,000
Longest win streak	2
Longest lose streak	4
Win percentage	25
Total $'s bet	1,340
Average odds	3

REPETITION #84

Total capital	1,536
Longest win streak	2
Longest lose streak	5
Win percentage	35
Total $'s bet	1,340
Average odds	3

REPETITION #85

Total capital	1,000
Longest win streak	2
Longest lose streak	9
Win percentage	25
Total $'s bet	1,340
Average odds	3

REPETITION #86

Total capital	1,804
Longest win streak	4
Longest lose streak	5
Win percentage	40
Total $'s bet	1,340
Average odds	3

REPETITION #87

Total capital	1,000
Longest win streak	2
Longest lose streak	7
Win percentage	25
Total $'s bet	1,340
Average odds	3

REPETITION #88

Total capital	1,536
Longest win streak	2
Longest lose streak	3
Win percentage	35
Total $'s bet	1,340
Average odds	3

REPETITION #89

Total capital	1,804
Longest win streak	2
Longest lose streak	4
Win percentage	40
Total $'s bet	1,340
Average odds	3

REPETITION #90

Total capital	1,000
Longest win streak	2
Longest lose streak	6
Win percentage	25
Total $'s bet	1,340
Average odds	3

REPETITION #91

Total capital	1,000
Longest win streak	1
Longest lose streak	6
Win percentage	25
Total $'s bet	1,340
Average odds	3

REPETITION #92

Total capital	1,268
Longest win streak	2
Longest lose streak	8
Win percentage	30
Total $'s bet	1,340
Average odds	3

REPETITION #93

Total capital	1,536
Longest win streak	2
Longest lose streak	5
Win percentage	35
Total $'s bet	1,340
Average odds	3

REPETITION #94

Total capital	2,072
Longest win streak	2
Longest lose streak	2
Win percentage	45
Total $'s bet	1,340
Average odds	3

REPETITION #95

Total capital	464
Longest win streak	1
Longest lose streak	7
Win percentage	15
Total $'s bet	1,340
Average odds	3

REPETITION #96

Total capital	1,268
Longest win streak	1
Longest lose streak	6
Win percentage	30
Total $'s bet	1,340
Average odds	3

REPETITION #97

Total capital	732
Longest win streak	2
Longest lose streak	6
Win percentage	20
Total $'s bet	1,340
Average odds	3

REPETITION #98

Total capital	196
Longest win streak	1
Longest lose streak	16
Win percentage	10
Total $'s bet	1,340
Average odds	3

REPETITION #99		REPETITION #100	
Total capital	732	Total capital	1,000
Longest win streak	1	Longest win streak	2
Longest lose streak	7	Longest lose streak	7
Win percentage	20	Win percentage	25
Total $'s bet	1,340	Total $'s bet	1,340
Average odds	3	Average odds	3

Summary
Flat Bet

INPUT DATA:		RESULTS:	
Original bankroll	1,000	Average return	$1,273.36
Number of trials	20	Win percentage	30
Win probability	.3	Average odds	3
Constant odds to 1	3	Longest win streak	4
# of repetitions	100	Longest lose streak	16
Base Bet	67	Average bet	67
Random seed	−100	Number of busts	0
Limit win % range	N		

These results also square with the theoretical result of $1,268. In this case we bet $67 on 20 races for a total of $1,340. We then expect 20 percent of our total, or $268, in profits. The key issue here is the range of our bankroll. This time it ranged from $196 to $2,608. Using the optimum fraction (edge-to-odds), we had a scare: At one point we were left with 19.6 percent of our starting bankroll. That's too risky. When we bet half-Kelly, we had to deal with losing only 36 percent of our stake; in this case we had to put up with losing over 80 percent of our original bankroll. However, please notice that in neither case did we experience a bust.

What do you think would happen if we had chosen to bet 10 percent, or $100, per race? Using the same sequence of wins and losses, the summary for the 100 groups is as follows:

RESULTS:	
Average return	$1,416
Win percentage	30
Average odds	3.02
Longest win streak	7

Longest lose streak	12
Average bet	97.6
Number of busts	10

The average return was larger, but look at the number of busts. We went broke 10 percent of the time. Totally unacceptable! Our expected return was $1,400, but who wants to take this much risk? Now let's get crazy and bet 20 percent of our bankroll on each race for the same sequence of wins and loses.

RESULTS:

Average return	$1,742
Win percentage	26
Average odds	3.17
Longest win streak	7
Longest lose streak	12
Average bet	161.7
Number of busts	33

Imagine having a whopping 20 percent advantage and going broke 33 percent of the time! If you think this is theoretical and doesn't happen in real life, you have another guess coming. I personally know a number of handicappers who are good enough to make their living at the track but fail to do so because of improper money management. I also know a good number of winning investors who aren't earning as much as they should for the same reason. They either bet too much and experience gambler's ruin or bet too little and hardly make the effort worthwhile.

When we analyze our results, we see that by choosing a $30 bet size we never tap out, earn our expected 20 percent ROI, and never have to experience wild fluctuations of our bankroll. By choosing the $67 optimum, we earn also earn our 20 percent ROI but experience some uncomfortable bankroll fluctuations. By being too bold and using a $100 bet size, we tap out 10 percent of the time. By using a $200 bet we fail to earn our full 20 percent even though our absolute profits are larger and we tap out 33 percent of the time.

When flat betting it's best to use a fraction of our edge divided by odds. I like to use approximately 50 percent because I know that this is safe for me. The exact percentage to use can be determined by a simulation using your actual performance figures and finding the maximum percentage that never taps out.

As we shall see, flat betting isn't the technique of choice. Its highest and best use is as a standard to judge other techniques.

Constant Percentage

When you wager a constant percentage of your bankroll per race, you don't have to worry too much about tapping out. This method has the desirable property of increasing the bet size when you're winning and decreasing it when you're losing. It's never to your advantage to wager more than the optimum amount. If you do, all you accomplish is a decrease in safety without a corresponding increase in the rate of growth of wealth.

The basic issue in money management is balancing the rate of growth against the safety factor. The more aggressive we become in choosing a larger and larger percent of capital to bet, the less safe our wagering becomes. We have to answer such questions as "What are the chances that we'll double our bankroll before we see it reduced by half?"

The reason we're concerned with the safety factor is because we know that our confidence erodes in direct proportion to the size of our bankroll. Ideally, we would like it if we were never behind in a sequence of 20 wagers. We know better. The next best thing we can do is to minimize the chances of losing a proportion of our bankroll. In order to buy this insurance we have to pay a premium. As always, the safer we want things to be, the smaller our rate of growth.

Using our example of a 6.67 percent optimum rate as previously discussed, we don't have to fear the 15 consecutive losses that could wipe us out if we were flat betting. Even if we bet 10 percent of our bankroll on each race and experience 15 losses in a row, we'll still have 20.6 percent of our bankroll left.

We've already compared betting a constant percentage to flat betting. We found out that for a 30 percent win rate at average odds of 3-to-1 (20 percent edge), constant-percentage betting starts to dwarf flat betting after only 200 bets. At 500 bets, you'll earn twice as much money from the same sequence of wins and losses; at 1,000 bets you'll earn 13 times as much. Needless to say, constant-percentage betting is a much better way to invest money than flat betting. The only thing that we have to worry about is wagering too much money in relation to our bankroll. By betting a fraction greater than our edge-to-odds ratio, we actually earn less and run a much greater risk of tapping out.

By grossly overbetting we took a winning method and turned it into a loser. I hope this dramatically points out the fact that our choice of bet size in relation to bankroll is critical. If you're going to make a mistake in choosing bet size, always make it in favor of betting too little.

Base Bet Plus Square Root

This technique combines flat betting with the percentage-of-bankroll technique. Here's how it works: If your $1,000 bankroll grows to $1,100, your next wager is your base bet plus 10 percent of your profits. Your profits are $100 and the square root of 100 is 10. If your $1,000 bankroll grows to $1,400, your next wager is your base bet plus 20 percent of the profits.

Base bet plus square root isn't a very intelligent way to do things because as your bankroll grows you're reinvesting a lesser percentage of your profits. This defeats the compounding principle. As your profits increase, your bet size doesn't increase at the same rate. This technique has a tendency to hoard profits rather than reinvest them. It also raises the issue of bet-to-bankroll ratio. How do you determine the proper base bet size? Do you use flat-bet criteria or do you create new criteria?

Using the same sequence of wins and losses as before, with 1,000 race groups at a 30 percent win rate, average odds of 3-to-1, and base bets of $30, $50, and $75, the results were as follows:

	$30	$50	$75
AVERAGE RETURN	$25,855.17	$31,787.97	$36,446.19
WIN PERCENTAGE	30	30	28
LONGEST WIN STREAK	8	8	8
LONGEST LOSE STREAK	30	30	30
NUMBER OF BUSTS	1	7	17

As you can see, base bet plus square root doesn't outperform simple percentage betting. It sounds very technical and rational, but when put to the acid test it doesn't stand up. It's not the worst way to do things, but why choose a technique that doesn't perform as well as one that we know does?

In general, the base bet plus or minus some increment determined by either rule or outcome isn't as efficient as constant-percentage wagering. Next, I'd like to discuss the silliest, dumbest, most ridiculous form of wagering ever devised. This one is gold-plated stupidity. It's known as "Due Column" wagering.

"Due Column" Wagering

Here's the idea in a nutshell: If a player wants to earn $100 per day at the racetrack, what he should do is wager in such a way that the first winner he hits during the day assures him of his daily profit goal. In other words, it only takes one winner per day to guarantee $100 in profits. Suppose the player performs like the public. He's a 33 percent handicapper. It's very unlikely that he'll experience 9 consecutive losers—the odds are .67 multiplied by itself 9 times, or roughly .027. This means that in a 100 groups of 10 races each, he can expect to lose less than 3 of them. His odds of not-losing (winning) any single sequence are .973, or more than 97 percent! What he therefore does is wager enough, depending on the odds, to have his first bet yield the $100 profit. If he loses he simply adds the amount of his loss to $100 and this becomes his due column.

For example, suppose the first playable race offers odds of 4-to-1 on his top selection. He bets $25 to win. If this selection wins, he is on his way home, mission accomplished. If it loses, he now adds $25 to the $100. His due column is $125. He must now wager enough, depending on the odds offered, on the next race to make up for his losses plus his $100 profit goal. Let's suppose the next playable race offers odds of 3-to-1. He then bets $42 to win on his selection. Once again, if his selection wins he has achieved his goals and is homeward bound. If the selection loses he must now add the $42 to his due column of $125. His new due column is $167. This sequence continues until he hits a winner. It takes only one winner

per day to earn $100 profit at the races. Any handicapper, no mat-
ter how unskilled, should be able to pick at least one winner per
day. This sounds fairly easy, but there's a catch—you need a
bankroll large enough to withstand a number of consecutive losses.

Let's examine due-column wagering from the point of view of a
winning player. Suppose we're a 35 percent handicapper with an
average mutuel of $6.00. Let's employ the due-column technique.
Our single-bet edge is a positive 5 percent.

$$E(x) = .35 \times 2 - .65 = .05$$

We'll use a bankroll of $3,800 and $100 per day as our profit
goal. In order to make this scenario simple, let's assume that each
wager is paid at average odds—in this case, 2-to-1. Our initial bet
is $50. The following table represents a nine-race sequence. If we
win any one of these wagers, we have achieved our profit goal and
a new sequence begins.

Wager No.	Due Column	Bet Size
1	$ 100	$ 50
2	150	75
3	225	113
4	338	169
5	507	254
6	761	381
7	1,142	571
8	1,713	857
9	2,570	1,285

Look at the rapid escalation of bet size. The seventh bet is more
than 10 times the original wager. The ninth bet is almost 26 times
the original wager. If he had to go to a tenth, it would be $1,928!
At this point we would hit the diminishing-returns situation
imposed by the parimutuel system. A $1,928 bet on a 2-to-1 horse
would depress the odds and hence the payoff.

This method has the seeds of its own destruction sown right into
it. Betting on one horse, it's quite common to experience nine losing win wagers in a row. Imagine betting $1,285 on a 2-to-1 shot—
wouldn't this make you somewhat nervous? You bet. What if you

lose again? If you were nervous with the last bet, this next one might cause a mild heart attack or seizure.

Let's consider what happens when we apply this technique to a nine-race card. Any sequence will result in either a $100 profit or a $3,755 loss. If we're a 35 percent handicapper, our probability of losing nine races in a row is $(.65)^9$, or .021. Therefore, the probability of not losing nine in a row is .979. Our expectation per sequence is as follows:

$$E(x) = .979 \times \$100 - .021 \times \$3,755 = \$19.05$$

Therefore, we can expect, on average, to win $19.05 per sequence. After 100 sequences our profits should be $1,905. Wow, that's great! We're making money, so the method is sound, right? Wrong—Dead wrong! Whatever happened to the goal of $100 per sequence?

If we were to use a flat-bet strategy with a bankroll of $3,755 and a single-race expectation of 5 percent at average odds of 2-to-1, our maximum wager would be 2.5 percent of $3,755, or $94. Since the single-race expectation is 5 percent, we can expect to make $4.70 per race, and thus in a sequence of 10 bets our expectation will be $47. A prudent strategy would be to only bet half of our optimum, which would result in a $23.50 profit per sequence with virtually zero chance of going broke.

Now what have we accomplished by using this weird system of money management? We've reduced our expectation from $23.50 per sequence to $19.05. In addition, we have taken an enormous risk of tapping out. From a risk-management point of view, it's hard to conceive of a worse thing to do.

Please don't be deceived by this type of scheme or any variation on it. It's death on the bankroll. It's a money burner of the largest magnitude possible. These kinds of techniques look plausible. They sound wonderful on first hearing. What an easy way to make money. Please be warned that whenever something sounds too good to be true, it usually is. Easy money is the road to the poorhouse. The reason we get conned is because we let our greed get in the way of our good judgment. What's particularly insidious about the due-column method is the fact that its proponents suggest you can win money at the races even if your single-bet expectation is negative. We know better.

It's pointless to dwell on how bad something is. Let's resolve to avoid any wagering scheme that progresses after a loss. It can be proved mathematically that no such scheme will outperform Kelly-type wagering in the long run.

It's my hope that you'll realize that the percentage of bankroll, or as I call it, Kelly-type wagering, is simply the best way to manage money, given that you know your win percentage and average mutuel over a reasonably large number of races and that your method shows a flat-bet profit. While not the ultimate, it's still the best that we have devised so far.

All the methods of managing money discussed thus far have failed to meet all the Ziemba and Hausch criteria. Is there such a method? You bet there is.

It's what I call the "Hyper-Kelly" method, which is simply to apply the edge-divided-by-odds principle to each race (which assumes that you can accurately estimate a horse's probability of winning). This method satisfies all the Ziemba and Hausch criteria for a good money-management system. Let's see how the Hyper-Kelly method would work.

Suppose you estimate a horse's chances of winning a race to be 40 percent. At a few minutes to post he is going off at 3-to-1—what percentage of your capital should you invest? Your edge is 60 percent.

$$E(x) = .4 \times 3 - .6 = .6$$

The odds are 3-to-1, so you should bet 20 percent of your bankroll (.6 divided by three) or some fraction of it depending on the safety factor that you want.

From a theoretical point of view, the Hyper-Kelly method is the absolute best way to do things. The problems associated with it are the accuracy of your probability estimates and last-minute changes in odds. Suppose, for example, that we overestimated. In the above example, the horse's probability of winning was only 30 percent instead of 40 percent. The proper proportion would have been 10 percent, hence we overbet by a bunch. The same is true if the odds dropped, let's say down to 2-to-1, after we made the bet.

Unfortunately, estimating probabilities is very difficult and subject to wide variance. The better your ability to accurately estimate a horse's chances, the better and more successful an investor you will be. The ability to estimate is the essential skill required for consistent winning. An overlay is nothing more than an underestimate by the public. An underlay is an overestimation, which is to be avoided like the plague. The way to approach the problem of estimating probabilities is stochastically. We'll keep track of our win percentage for a large group of "typical" races. We'll use that number as an estimator. We'll choose a very conservative range around that estimator and build in a huge error factor. This will assure us of a minimum-boldness strategy.

I don't recommend the Hyper-Kelly technique unless you're a genuine expert. The smallest variances in estimates can account for large errors. My vote is for incremental flat betting. It's very simple to implement and gives you the power of the compounding principle.

Many professionals use a "unit-bet" technique. That is, they vary their bet size in direct proportion to their opinion. If they have a very strong opinion, they make their maximum bet. They know from experience that they win a certain type of race more often than other types; hence they bet more money than usual on it. This is smart money management providing they have the objective evidence to prove that their performance is exceptional for this type of bet. This method takes advantage of the second feature of a good money-management system—when a bet is more likely to be won, more money is wagered. It also takes advantage of betting more when the odds are bigger. Most bettors bet less money if their top choice is going off at long odds. Professionals do the very opposite.

We have discussed the fundamental principles of wagering and applied them to common money-management techniques. We'll get much more specific regarding each type of wagering opportunity. There is no single absolute method of money management just as there isn't a single absolute method of investing. There are, depending upon our temperament, judicious methods and injudicious methods. Hopefully we'll acquire the wisdom to be able to tell the difference.

Let's take a closer look at simulation.

SIMULATION

The technique of simulation works with random numbers. Suppose we had a roulette wheel with the numbers 0 to 99 written on it, one hundred numbers in all. If we spin it and record the outcome a large number of times, we'll generate a sequence of random numbers. This technique is known as Monte Carlo simulation. (The most famous roulette wheels in the world are in Monte Carlo, hence the name.) Let's suppose the first 100 spins were:

49	16	95	83	52	21	27	88	21	44
8	69	15	33	92	7	40	38	82	27
19	67	29	94	12	51	92	82	65	77
81	40	66	1	65	43	16	97	6	71
7	41	78	21	20	32	96	49	45	55
92	85	1	84	88	81	48	27	52	93
12	44	16	81	97	78	92	9	43	2
1	86	78	31	50	3	93	29	24	23
80	24	57	56	74	65	38	96	31	80
40	40	23	29	12	77	48	97	1	8

We now have 100 random numbers. Suppose you've discovered the Sartin methodology, which recommends that you bet two horses per race to win. Suppose also that your win rate using this method is 60 percent and your average mutuel is $8. If you know that a certain phenomenon has a 60 percent probability, you then say that any outcome 60 and over represents a loss and any number less than 60 represents a win. The idea is that 60 percent of the two-digit integers are less than 60 (i.e. 0,1,2, . . . 59) while the other 40 percent are 60 or greater. The above sequence for 60 percent win probability is:

W	W	L	L	W	W	W	L	W	W
W	L	W	W	L	W	W	W	L	W
W	L	W	L	W	W	L	L	L	L
L	W	L	W	L	W	W	L	W	L
W	W	L	W	W	W	L	W	W	W
L	L	W	L	L	L	W	W	W	L
W	W	W	L	L	L	L	W	W	W
W	L	L	W	W	W	L	W	W	W
L	W	W	W	L	L	W	L	W	L
W	W	W	W	W	L	W	L	W	W

We don't have any guarantee that there are exactly 60 wins and 40 losses. (This is another issue.) We could impose a fixed distribution. For now we will allow chance to operate. We now have a method to determine the sequence of wins and losses.

We now have to simulate the payoff. We can do this by using another Monte Carlo sequence or we can simply assume that each wager is paid off at average odds. When you simulate large numbers of wagers, the results are very close regardless of method.

For the moment let's use the simple case and compare flat betting to Kelly-type wagering, using the above sequence of wins and losses and assuming that each wager is paid at average odds. Let's consider the performance of our minimum two-horse goal. In this situation, we bet two horses per race and treat it as a single bet. We win 60 percent of the time at an average mutuel of $8. Since we're betting on two horses, when we win, we only make a $4 profit; when we lose, we lose $4 per race. Our expectation per dollar bet is 20 percent. (Divide both sides by four.)

$$E(x) = .6 \times (\$4) - .4 \times (\$4) = \$.80$$
$$E(x) = .6 \times (\$1) - .4 \times (\$1) = \$.20$$

Let's now look at the data on a column-by-column basis. The first 20 races are represented by the first two columns. We have 13 wins and seven losses.

W	W
W	L
W	L
L	W

W	W
L	L
W	W
W	L
L	W
W	W

Bet	Outcome	Bankroll
100	W	1,100
100	W	1,200
100	W	1,300
100	L	1,200
100	W	1,300
100	L	1,200
100	W	1,300
100	W	1,400
100	L	1,200
100	W	1,400
100	W	1,500
100	L	1,400
100	L	1,300
100	W	1,400
100	W	1,500
100	L	1,400
100	W	1,500
100	L	1,400
100	W	1,500
100	W	1,600

Summary

TOTAL CAPITAL	1,600
LONGEST WIN STREAK	3
LONGEST LOSE STREAK	2
WIN PERCENTAGE	65
TOTAL BET	2,000

This was a favorable sequence; normally we can only expect around 12 wins in 20 races. Let's apply the Kelly technique to the same sequence of wins and losses.

Bet	Outcome	Bankroll
100	W	1,100
110	W	1,210
121	W	1,331
133	L	1,198
120	W	1,318
132	L	1,186
119	W	1,305
131	W	1,436
144	L	1,292
129	W	1,421
142	W	1,563
156	L	1,407
141	L	1,266
127	W	1,393
139	W	1,532
153	L	1,379
138	W	1,517
152	L	1,365
137	W	1,502
150	W	1,652

Summary

TOTAL CAPITAL	1,652
LONGEST WIN STREAK	3
LONGEST LOSE STREAK	2
WIN PERCENTAGE	65
TOTAL BET	2,674

For the same sequence of wins and losses, Kelly-type betting showed a larger return. On the negative side, a win followed by a loss or vice versa isn't too good when using Kelly. Look at an LWL or a WLW pattern—you're always behind where you started. This isn't true for flat betting. Another bad feature about Kelly is that you often lose your largest bet. But don't let the negatives put you off—it's a very intelligent way to manage your money.

To determine which method is better for this win percentage and average mutuel, we repeat this experiment a number of times and observe the best performance, the worst performance, and the average performance.

Take out the white pages of your telephone book, one of the largest collections of random numbers that you can lay your hands upon. Consider only the last four digits of the listed phone numbers. They are random numbers between 0000 and 9999. These are the basis on which to decide if a simulated event is a win or a lose. Suppose you have just won your 31 out of 52 races betting two horses per race. Your win percentage expressed as a decimal is .5962. Using the Monte Carlo technique, you could ask and answer a number of questions. You might ask yourself, "How many consecutive losses can I expect if I have a 59.62 percent win rate?"

This technique can be applied creatively. You can traverse the random numbers in row order, in column order, or any order that you choose. There are many, many ways to travel through these data. You might open another phone book to a random page and point to a telephone number. Suppose you pointed to 556-3412. You could choose the last two digits and travel through the list stopping at every twelfth number. Better yet, you could add all the digits of the phone number successively until you arrive at a single digit (e.g., 5+5+6+3+4+1+2 = 26, 2+6 = 8). You then travel through the data, stopping at every eighth number.

In order to check out a 59.62 percent win rate, we assign a win to numbers less than 5962 and a loss to numbers equal to or greater than 5962. Each way you choose to traverse the data will usually generate a unique win-loss sequence. You now look for the largest grouping of consecutive losses.

This method of simulation lends itself to use in a computer. Computer languages all contain a command that generates random numbers. For example, in BASIC the function RND(X) generates pseudo random numbers. A pseudo random number is a random number generated by an algorithm as opposed to a by a truly random process, such as a roulette wheel. They are more than adequate for our purposes.

(If you wish a copy of the simulator that was used throughout this book, please write to Cynthia Publishing, 11390 Ventura Blvd. #5, Studio City, CA 91604, or call (818) 509-0165. It requires an IBM-compatible microcomputer. There's a nominal charge to cover the costs of media, shipping and handling, and postage. It shouldn't exceed $15.)

This simulator is quite elaborate. It lets you check any conventional money-management scheme, plus it lets you design your own. It will keep the odds constant or vary them. It allows you to trace each and every bet or just print out the final results. It's very powerful. I highly recommend that you order a copy and practice with it. You'll learn virtually all there is to learn about betting strategy and have a lot of fun at the same time.

Let's now apply the principles of money management and betting strategy to specific types of wagers. We'll start with win wagering.

WIN BETTING

Win betting is straightforward. You don't care who comes in second or third or who's going to win the next race. Determining the relative value of win bets is also cut-and-dried: One glance at the toteboard tells you whether or not you should bet. With win betting, you don't have to juggle multiple horses as you do in the exotics.

Unfortunately, the straightforwardness of win betting isn't lost on the betting public, which is very efficient when it comes to setting odds in the win pool. As you're going to find out, the public woefully misplays the daily double, the Pick-3, and the exacta due to the complexities of these exotic wagers. But since win betting is much easier, the public is a considerably better player of win bets than it is of exotic bets. So the epic scores we find in exacta, Pick-3, and daily double betting appear much less frequently in win betting.

In his 1990 book *How to Win at Horseracing*, Robert V. Rowe made a very interesting discovery. He compared a previous longitudinal study in which the track take and breakage amounted to about 11 percent to a current study in which the take and breakage was 17 percent. His first study involved 10,466 races and established the fact that play on all favorites produced a flat-bet loss of 10.3 percent. Second choices lost 13.8 percent of the time, third choices about 15.6 percent of the time. Additionally, favorites won 32.6 percent of all races. Second choices won 19.9 percent of the time, while third choices scored in 14.4 percent of their races.

His latest study involved 2,317 races, and the results were dramatically different. Play on all favorites produced a flat-bet loss of 18.2 percent. Second choices lost 15.7 percent of the time, third choices 15.8 percent of the time. Favorites won 33.6 percent of all races. Second choices won 21 percent of the time, while third choices scored in 15.7 percent of their races.

It's interesting to note that the flat-bet loss betting on public favorites had a strong correlation to the track take. Just to verify these data, I asked Steve Unite to do a study using California tracks, where the take is 15.33 percent for win bets. The results were strikingly similar to Rowe's. Unite's study showed 235 winning favorites out of 674 races, a win rate of 34.9 percent. The payback was $1,132.80 on an investment of $1,348, an ROI of 84 percent. In both cases, the actual loss by betting-public favorites exceeded the track take! In New York, where the track take is 17 percent, the loss was 18.2 percent. In California, where the track take is 15.33 percent, the flat-bet loss was 16 percent. It very well may be a myth that you'll only lose 10 percent by betting on public favorites. These data strongly support that it *is* a myth.

In any event, we must exploit the fact that the public makes mistakes. It's our job to capitalize on these blunders. Toward this end, I suggest a three-step approach to win betting. The first step is to create a reasonably accurate betting line for each race you handicap. The betting line you use isn't the morning line, Sweep's line, or any other public handicapper's estimation of the fair win odds. It's *your* line based on the factors you believe are important to the outcome of the race. You've already seen three techniques that'll enable you to turn your handicapping into a betting line.

The second step is to use your win betting line to identify overlays. If you've never used a betting line to determine win overlays, you'll be amazed at how magnificently this device makes your win betting decisions for you. It's practically automatic.

The third step is to decide how much you should bet on the race. If you have a single win overlay, your decision is rather simple. If you have more than one overlay, you'll have to decide whether to bet the single horse offering the most value, to bet the overlays equally, or to bet more on one than on the other. Additionally, you'll have to decide how much of your total bankroll to wager on the race. You'll base these decisions on the truth of mathematics and on your temperament as an investor.

Please don't be fooled into thinking that picking winners is the way to profit from win betting. You could pick winners at the rate of 50 percent and still manage to lose money if your average mutuel was less than $4. On the other hand, a bettor who picked the winner 25 percent of the time could make piles of money if his winners paid an average mutuel greater than $9. Profitable win betting doesn't just involve picking winners. The way to prosper by win betting is to pick winners that offer value—in other words, to pick good bets. Your betting line will settle the value issue quickly and unequivocally.

Consider what the following investors have written: "Bet the overlay, the horse of value, not the selection" (Mark Cramer, *The Odds on Your Side*); "You will play only when there is value. Some players want to bet their pick, no matter what. Instead, think value—which means that your decisions may not be the same as your selections" (Barry Meadow, *Money Secrets at the Racetrack*); "Buy undervalued investments and sell overvalued ones" (Sir John Templeton).

Cramer and Meadow are top parimutuel investors. Templeton, is a first-class investor who excels in the arena of international finance (he invests in mutual funds, while Cramer and Meadow invest their funds mutuelly). It's interesting to note that both Cramer and Meadow make nice profits from their stock market investments as well. (If Templeton ever devoted his attention to thoroughbred handicapping, you can bet *your sweet petunia* that he'd be a winning player.)

What's their secret? Even though these investors exploit different markets, each is exceedingly familiar with what represents good value, as their quotations attest. They've mastered the skill of setting an accurate price based on an investment's true worth. Cramer and Meadow establish a betting line that tells them the fair price of each horse in the win pool. They then bet only on undervalued horses whose betting-line odds are substantially lower than their actual public odds. Similarly, Templeton estimates what he believes is a fair price per share for each issue of stock he considers. If the stock's market price is lower than his estimate, the stock is undervalued and he buys it. Conversely, all three avoid overvalued investments. Their results speak for themselves: All three make a substantial portion of their incomes based on their ability to value investments.

That's reason enough for us to imitate these value-oriented investors. Hence, we must set a fair price for each investment we consider. In the win pool, this means making a betting line on the horses we believe have a chance to win a given race.

The first and foremost rule is to use your betting line to identify overvalued horses. Avoid them like the plague. Let the suckers bet them. (Horses are overvalued when their betting-line odds are higher than their actual public odds as listed on the toteboard.)

Consider the following betting line and the actual public odds:

Horse	Betting Line	Public Odds
A	5-2	2-1
B	3-1	4-1
C	6-1	7-2
D	6-1	5-1

Horses A, C, and D are overvalued. They're not worth investing in. They offer no value. It's important to note that if a horse's betting-line odds and public odds are the same, it is properly valued and a win bet would be a break-even proposition. (We abhor break-even propositions. That's gambling!) If you're getting public odds equal to your betting-line odds, don't even consider a win bet. You might as well flip coins with your friends. You must insist on an edge.

Did you notice how quickly and easily the betting line identified the undervalued horse? Horse B was definitely undervalued. The larger consideration is whether Horse B is worth a win bet. The answer is: It depends. What kind of edge do you require? Barry Meadow would say, "Pass." I say that Horse B is acceptable as a win bet. (Meadow insists upon a 50 percent premium from his betting line. He computes this premium by multiplying his betting-line odds by 1.5. In the case of Horse B, Meadow would need odds of 9-to-2 in order to make a win bet. Since Horse B is going off at only 4-to-1, Meadow would skip the win bet on it.)

I require an edge of 20 percent on my win bets. At public odds of 4-to-1, does horse B give me that? Let's plug the numbers into the formula and find out:

$$\text{Edge} = .25 \times 4 - .75 = .25$$

Horse B offers an edge of .25, or 25 percent. He meets my edge requirement for win bets. There's a quicker way to determine the permissible odds to accept in order to guarantee a 20 percent edge. Let's review this technique. You simply divide your estimated probability into the sum (.2 + P(L)). This represents our probability of losing, plus 20 percent. In the case of Horse B, we divide .25 into .95. The quotient is 3.80; we round up to the nearest odds level, which is 4-to-1. Hence, I can bet Horse B at odds of 4-to-1 or higher.

What about multiple win bets in the same race? Let's assume the public odds in this race were a bit different. Suppose they were:

Horse	Betting Line	Public Odds
A	5-2	2-1
B	3-1	4-1
C	6-1	9-1
D	6-1	5-1

Now horses A and D are overvalued. We see that horse C offers us the following edge:

$$\text{Edge} = .14 \times 9 - .86 = .40$$

Horse C offers us an edge of 40 percent! Our edge on horse B is 25 percent. Do we bet horse C, since it offers a larger edge? Or do we bet horse B because it's more likely to win? Or do we bet both?

The way to evaluate the relative value of each bet is to use the edge-divided-by-odds criterion. *The proper betting criterion is edge-to-odds ratio, not edge alone.* The higher the edge-to-odds ratio, the better the bet. Horse B's edge-to-odds ratio is .0625 (25 percent divided by 6); horse C's is .044 (40 percent divided by 9). Of the two, horse B represents the better win bet in this race. If you're an aggressive, dyed-in-the-wool single-horse bettor, a win bet on horse B is the proper wager, the smaller edge notwithstanding. This technique strikes the proper balance between growth rate and safety.

But both horses meet the 20 percent edge criterion. In this case, a moderate win bettor would bet both horses to win. However, the amount bet on each horse should be different. The edge-to-odds ratio also serves as the optimal percentage of bankroll to wager on a given win bet. Again, this is called the "Kelly Criterion"—the optimum percentage of your capital to bet that will maximize the growth rate of your bankroll. It can be proved mathematically that by using this edge-to-odds ratio for a very large number of races (approaching infinity), your bankroll will be larger than it would be if you used any other betting scheme. Unfortunately, this optimum percentage doesn't guarantee safety. If you want to improve the safety factor dramatically while preserving a steep rate of growth, it's best to choose what's called a "fractional Kelly strategy." For parimutuel wagering, 50 percent Kelly is adequate. (This percentage depends upon your win percentage and average mutuel.) A very good rule of thumb is to never let a single win bet exceed 5 percent of your capital and never let a place or show bet exceed 10 percent of your capital.

For the single-horse win bettor, at .0625 horse B has the best edge-to-odds ratio. This means that the single-horse win bettor could bet as much as 6.25 percent of his win-betting bankroll on horse B in this race. By betting less than 6.25 percent of his bankroll, the aggressive bettor trades optimal rate of growth for additional safety (a good idea). So, we'll use our 50 percent rule of thumb and only bet 3 percent on this opportunity.

For the moderate win bettor who would bet both horses, edge-to-odds also determines the proper amount to bet on each horse. The moderate win bettor must first decide the total amount he wants to bet on the race. He then bets this amount in direct proportion to each horse's edge-to-odds ratio. In this case, horse B's edge-to-odds ratio is .0625; horse C's is .0444. It's obvious that more money should be bet on horse B, but how much more? To get the answer, we add the edge-to-odds ratios of all the horses and divide this sum by each horse's individual edge-to-odds ratio (.0625 plus .0444 equals .1069. Therefore, .1069 becomes the divisor. We now divide .0625 by .1069, which equals .5847, or 58.47 percent. Next we divide .0444 by .1069, which equals .4153, or 41.53 percent). We should thus proportion the total bet size as follows: 58.47 percent on horse B and 41.53 percent on horse C. This total bet can be as much as 5 percent of your bankroll (our self-imposed ceiling on win bets) because your total edge-to-odds ratio is greater than 10 percent. So the moderate bettor whose bankroll is $2,000 would bet $100 in this race: $58 on horse B and $42 on horse C.

Which style of win betting, aggressive or moderate, should you choose? It depends upon your temperament. If you're risk-averse and want to go to the windows more frequently, you'll choose the moderate style. If, on the other hand, you see things in the long run, you'll choose the aggressive style. In a recent study we conducted on races at Fairplex Park, using the output of *ALL-IN-ONE*, aggressive win betting significantly outperformed moderate win betting. The ROI from aggressive betting was 32 percent while for moderate betting it was 23 percent. Are you willing to give up 28 percent of your profits for the added psychological comfort provided by cashing more often?

Consider the following race:

Hollywood Park

8

1⅛ MILES. **(1:46^4) 48th Running of THE HOLLYWOOD OAKS. Grade I. Purse $200,000 Added. Fillies 3-year-olds. By subscription of $200 each which shall accompany the nomination, $2,000 additional to start, with $300,000 added, of which $40,000 to second, $30,000 to third, $15,000 to fourth and $5,000 to fifth. Weight, 121 lbs. Starters to be named through the entry box by closing time of entries. Hollywood Park reserves the right not to divide this race. Should this race not be divided and the number of entries exceed the starting gate capacity, preference will be given to those horses with the highest total earnings in 1993 and an also eligible list will be drawn. Failure to draw into this race at scratch time cancels all fees. A trophy will be presented to the winning Owner, Trainer and Jockey. Closed Wednesday, June 30 with 12 nominations.**

1 1/8 MILES

Swazi's Moment
Own: Gordy Berry
NAKATANI C S (295 47 58 38 .16)

B. f. 3 (Mar)
Sire: Moment of Hope (Timeless Moment)
Dam: Swazi Girl (Hatchetman)
Br: American Star Corp (Ky)
Tr: Rash Rodney (67 7 9 6 .10)

121

Lifetime Record:	7 3 1 0	$120,655			
1993	5 1 1 0	$65,600	Turf	0 0 0 0	
1992	2 2 0 0	$55,055	Wet	0 0 0 0	
Hol	3 1 1 0	$45,600	Dist	0 0 0 0	

19Jun93-8Hol fst 1 1/16 :22^3 :45^2 1:09^2 1:42^2 ⒻPrincess-G2 92 5 4 4$^{7\frac{1}{2}}$ 3^8 3$^{4\frac{1}{2}}$ 2^{hd} Stevens G L B 115 5.00 89-11 Fit To Lead117^{hd} Swazi's Moment115^{hd} Passing Vice119^8 5
Propped, broke stride 1/2
29May93-8Hol fst 7f :21^4 :44^2 1:09^1 1:22^2 ⒻRailbird-G2 85 3 7 7$^{6\frac{1}{2}}$ 6$^{7\frac{1}{2}}$ 6^5 5$^{3\frac{1}{2}}$ Gonzalez S Jr 118 6.50 89-12 Afto114^{hd} Fit To Lead121^{hd} Nijivision113$^{2\frac{3}{4}}$ Dropped whip 1/16 8
6May93-8Hol fst 1 1/16 :23^1 :46^2 1:10^2 1:41^4 3+ ⒻAlw 42000N2X 99 5 3 4$^{1\frac{1}{2}}$ 3$^{\frac{1}{2}}$ 1$^{3\frac{1}{2}}$ 1$^{2\frac{1}{2}}$ Gonzalez S^5 B 107 3.30 92-15 Swazi's Moment107$^{2\frac{1}{2}}$ Chipeta Springs117^6 Red Bandana116$^{\frac{1}{2}}$ Driving 6
9Apr93-9OP fst 1 1/16 :23^1 :47^4 1:12^4 1:44^1 ⒻFantasy-G2 81 6 5 7$^{3\frac{1}{2}}$ 6^4 5^5 4$^{7\frac{1}{2}}$ Delahoussaye E 121 b 5.30 72-19 Aztec Hill121^5 Adorydar117^2 Stalcreek117$^{\frac{1}{2}}$ Drifted, 5 wide 3/8 7
<u>7Mar93-8SA fst</u> 1 1/16 :23 :47^1 1:11 1:42^4 ⒻS A Oaks-G1 89 9 9 9^9 9^{10} 5^9 5$^{5\frac{3}{4}}$ Delahoussaye E B 117 b 6.90 84-14 Eliza117$^{2\frac{1}{2}}$ Stalcreek117^1 Dance For Vanny117$^{1\frac{3}{4}}$ Lugged out, wide 9
5Dec92-9TP fst 6 1/2f :22^4 :47^1 1:13^4 1:20^3 ⒻGowell 60k 103 7 10 8^8 3^3 1$^{2\frac{1}{2}}$ 1^{13} Martinez W B 114 b 7.60 77-29 Swazi's Moment114^{13} Sum Runner118^1 Special Alert116$^{1\frac{1}{2}}$ 10
Lugged in, 3-16, ridden out
15Nov92-6CD fst 6f :21^3 :46^3 1:12^1 ⒻMd Sp Wt 67 9 9 8$^{4\frac{3}{4}}$ 9^5 4^2 1^2 Martinez W B 120 b 15.20 85-14 Swazi's Moment120^2 High Decision120^3 Smooze120 Driving, rail 12
WORKOUTS: Jly 9 Hol 3f fst :36^2 H *4/23* Jun 17 Hol 3f fst :35^2 H *6/33* Jun 12 Hol 5f fst 1:01^2 H *16/24* Jun 7 Hol 3f fst :38^3 H *45/51* May 26 Hol 5f fst 1:02^3 H *36/44* May 20 Hol 5f fst 1:01 H *16/42*

Likeable Style
Own: Golden Eagle Farm
STEVENS G L (180 42 26 23 .23)

B. f. 3 (Jan)
Sire: Nijinsky II (Northern Dancer)
Dam: Personable Lady (No Robbery)
Br: Mabee Mr & Mrs John C (Ky)
Tr: Mandella Richard (88 17 16 15 .19)

L 121

Lifetime Record:	6 5 0 0	$275,300			
1993	5 4 0 0	$259,350	Turf	1 1 0 0	$61,250
1992	1 1 0 0	$15,950	Wet	1 1 0 0	$61,200
Hol	1 1 0 0	$61,200	Dist	0 0 0 0	

5Jun93-8Hol my 1 1/16 ⊗ :24^3 :49^1 1:14^1 1:46^1 ⒻHoneymoon H-G3 95 1 3 3^2 4^2 3^1 1$^{1\frac{1}{4}}$ Delahoussaye E LB 122 *.70 70-32 Likeable Style122$^{1\frac{1}{4}}$ Adorydar114$^{1\frac{3}{4}}$ Vinista113$^{3\frac{1}{2}}$ Driving 5
<u>15May93-8Hol fm</u> 1 ⓣ :23^3 :46^3 1:10^1 1:34^2 ⒻSenorita B CG3 97 2 6 6$^{2\frac{3}{4}}$ 5$^{2\frac{3}{4}}$ 4$^{1\frac{1}{2}}$ 1^1 Desormeaux K J LB 121 2.80 93-09 Likeable Style121^1 Adorydar113$^{\frac{1}{2}}$ Icy Warning118$^{1\frac{3}{4}}$ Game inside 7
7Mar93-8SA fst 1 1/16 :23 :47^1 1:11 1:42^4 ⒻS A Oaks-G1 86 1 7 7^6 7$^{8\frac{1}{2}}$ 6^{10} 6$^{7\frac{1}{2}}$ Stevens G L B 117 *1.10 82-14 Eliza117$^{2\frac{1}{2}}$ Stalcreek117^1 Dance For Vanny117$^{1\frac{3}{4}}$ Wide, no threat 9
13Feb93-8SA fst 1 :22^4 :46^3 1:10^4 1:36^3 ⒻLs Virgenes-G1 92 5 5 5$^{2\frac{3}{4}}$ 3^1 1^{hd} 1^3 Stevens G L B 117 *.90 87-15 Likeable Style117^3 Incindress117$^{1\frac{1}{2}}$ Blue Moonlight119^5 Wide, ridden out 6
22Jan93-8SA gd 1 1/16 :23^4 :47^4 1:13 1:44^3 ⒻS Ysabela 75k 91 5 3 3^2 2^1 1^{hd} 1^2 Stevens G L B 115 *.90 81-19 Likeable Style115^2 Fit To Lead117^6 Amandari116$^{1\frac{1}{4}}$ 5
Off slowly, wide, ridden out
26Dec92-4SA fst 6f :21^2 :44^3 :57 1:09^3 ⒻMd Sp Wt 84 10 11 12^{10} 6$^{5\frac{1}{2}}$ 4^2 1^1 Stevens G L B 117 7.10 88-09 Likeable Style117^1 Aleyna's Love117^{no} Malojen117^6 Wide trip 12
WORKOUTS: ●Jly 6 Hol 5f fst :59^2 H *1/43* ●Jun 30 Hol 1 fst 1:38^4 H *1/4* Jun 23 Hol 5f fst 1:00^3 H *9/32* Jun 17 Hol 3f fst :35^3 B *8/33* May 31 Hol 5f fst 1:03^4 B *45/47* May 26 Hol 4f fst :49^2 H *34/42*

Fit To Lead

Own: Colbert & Hubbard & Sczesny

MCCARRON C J (194 29 39 34 .15)

Dk. b or br f. 3 (May)
Sire: Fit to Fight (Chieftain)
Dam: Islands (Forli)
Br: Laura Leigh Stable (Ky)
Tr: Mandella Richard (88 17 16 15 .19)

L 121

	Lifetime Record:	12 4 4 1	$235,415	
1993	5 2 2 1	$169,790	Turf	0 0 0 0
1992	7 2 2 0	$65,625	Wet	0 0 0 0
Hol	5 2 2 0	$110,350	Dist	0 0 0 0

WORKOUTS: Jly 5 Hol 3f fst :36 B 6/33 ●Jun 13 Hol 6f fst 1:11³ H 1/17 May 26 Hol 4f fst :48² H 16/42 ●May 19 Hol 7f fst 1:25³ H 1/7 May 13 Hol 5f fst :59² H 2/36 May 6 Hol 4f fst :48² H 16/38

Hollywood Wildcat

Own: Cowan Irving & Marge

DELAHOUSSAYE E (303 50 46 50 .17)

Dk. b or br f. 3 (Feb)
Sire: Kris S (Roberto)
Dam: Miss Wildcatter (Mr Prospector)
Br: Cowan Irving & Marjorie (Fla)
Tr: Drysdale Neil (27 5 4 1 .19)

121

	Lifetime Record:	9 4 1 2	$233,310	
1993	4 0 1 2	$35,030	Turf	0 0 0 0
1992	5 4 0 0	$198,280	Wet	0 0 0 0
Hol	0 0 0 0		Dist	0 0 0 0

WORKOUTS: May 19 Crc 3f fst :38³ B 25/33 Apr 27 CD 5f fst 1:03¹ Bg27/58 Apr 22 CD 5f fst 1:04³ H 11/29 Apr 7 OP 4f fst :49 B 4/21 Apr 3 Kee 4f my :49³ B 7/23 ●Mar 28 Crc 4f fst :47² H 1/15

Fondly Remembered

Own: Lao Danny

PINCAY L JR (235 32 24 26 .14)

Dk. b or br f. 3 (May)
Sire: Skywalker (Relaunch)
Dam: Fondre (Key to the Mint)
Br: Canani Jane L (5 1 0 2 .20)

L 121

	Lifetime Record:	12 2 3 5	$100,450	
1993	8 2 1 4	$78,900	Turf	5 1 0 3	$57,250
1992	4 M 2 1	$21,550	Wet	1 1 0 0	$16,500
Hol	1 0 0 1	$4,500	Dist	0 0 0 0	

WORKOUTS: Jun 21 SA 4f fst :48¹ B 14/41 Jun 14 SA 4f fst :47² H 4/49 May 29 SA 4f fst :47² H 3/51 May 23 SA 4f fst :47³ H 4/37 May 15 SA 4f fst :59² H 28/34 Apr 16 SA ③ 5f fm 1:00² H 1/1

Added Asset

Own: Wimborne Farm

VALENZUELA P A (239 32 32 39 .13)

Ch. f. 3 (Apr)
Sire: Lord At War (General–Fr)
Dam: Added Elegance (Stutz Blackhawk)
Br: Wimborne Farm Inc (Ky)
Tr: Perkins A Peter (—)

121

	Lifetime Record:	9 2 4 0	$77,104	
1993	6 1 4 0	$64,224	Turf	1 0 0 0	$250
1992	3 1 0 0	$12,960	Wet	2 0 1 0	$7,924
Hol	0 0 0 0		Dist	0 0 0 0	

WORKOUTS: Jly 4 CD 5f fst 1:01³ B 4/15 Jun 11 CD 5f fst 1:02² B 12/32 Jun 6 CD 4f fst :51² B 63/80 Jun 1 CD 5f fst 1:01² H 2/19 May 17 CD 3f fst :37¹ B 9/19 May 14 CD 5f fst 1:02³ B 6/32

Nortena

Own: Keck Howard B

FLORES D R (239 27 26 25 .11)

Dk. b or br f. 3 (Feb)
Sire: Mr Prospector (Raise a Native)
Dam: Pattern Step (Nureyev)
Br: Evergreen Thoroughbreds, Inc. (Ky)
Tr: Whittingham Charles (86 7 7 15 .08)

L 121

	Lifetime Record:	6 1 1 1	$37,000	
1993	5 1 1 0	$33,400	Turf	1 0 0 0	
1992	1 M 0 1	$4,200	Wet	1 0 0 0	$7,500
Hol	3 0 1 1	$19,500	Dist	0 0 0 0	

WORKOUTS: Jly 7 Hol 5f fst :02⁴ H 23/35 Jly 1 Hol 1 fst 1:40 H 1/1 Jun 26 Hol 6f fst 1:14² H 4/13 Jun 21 Hol 5f fst :59⁴ H 9/39 Jun 16 Hol 5f fst 1:01³ H 27/40 Jun 11 Hol 3f fst :36¹ B 17/18

Passing Vice

Own: Iron County Farms Inc

DESORMEAUX K J (295 76 65 34 .26)

B. f. 3 (Mar)
Sire: Vice Regent (Northern Dancer)
Dam: Passing Look (Buckpasser)
Br: North Ridge Farm (Ky)
Tr: Lewis Craig A (78 15 10 9 .19)

L 121

	Lifetime Record:	15 3 5 4	$182,300	
1993	6 1 0 1	$75,000	Turf	1 0 0 0	$2,500
1992	9 2 3 0	$107,350	Wet	2 1 0 0	$57,500
Hol	8 1 2 1	$103,650	Dist	0 0 0 0	

WORKOUTS: Jly 7 SA 5f fst 1:02⁴ H 25/40 Jun 30 SA 4f fst :49¹ H 76/50 Jun 13 SA 4f fst :04⁴ H 25/40 May 31 SA 5f fst 1:00³ H 4/38 May 25 SA 5f fst 1:01 H 13/45 May 8 SA 7f fst 1:25² H 1/5

Adorydar	B. f. 3 (Feb)		Lifetime Record: 6 2 4 0 $130,700
Own: Brody Mr & Mrs Jerome	Sire: Alydar (Raise a Native)		1993 6 2 4 0 $130,700 | Turf 2 1 1 0 $38,150
	Dam: Adorable Micol (Riverman)		1992 0 M 0 0 | Wet 2 1 1 0 $35,950
	Br: Gallagher's Stud (NY)		
ALMEIDA G F (166 14 14 23 .08)	Tr: McAnally Ronald (130 17 24 20 .13)	121	Hol 1 0 1 0 $20,000 | Dist 0 0 0 0

5Jun93-8Hol	my	1 1/16	⊗	$:24^3$	$:49^1$	$1:14^1$	$1:46^1$	ⒻHoneymoon H-G3	93	4	2	2½	2^{hd}	2½	21¼	Almeida G F	B 114	2.30	69-32	Likeable Style1221¼ Adorydar1141¾ Vinista1133¼	Good effort 5
15May93-8Hol	fm	1	Ⓣ	$:23^3$	$:46^3$	$1:10^1$	$1:34^2$	ⒻSenorita B CG3	95	1	3	3¾	2^1	2^{hd}	2^1	Almeida G F	B 113	4.90	92-09	Likeable Style121[1] Adorydar113½ Icy Warning1181¾	Led, outfinished 7
9Apr93-9OP	fst	1 1/16		$:23^1$	$:47^4$	$1:12^4$	$1:44^1$	ⒻFantasy-G2	85	3	3	4^1	2^{hd}	3^3	2^5	Almeida G F	117	4.60	75-19	Aztec Hill121[5] Adorydar117[2] Stalcreek117½	Bumped rival 7
18Mar93-3SA	fm	*6½f	Ⓣ	:22	$:44^3$	$1:07^4$	$1:13^3$	ⒻAlw 33000N1X	97	6	1	2^2	2^1	1½	15½	Almeida G F	B 119	*.80	90-10	Adorydar1195½ Dash For Flash1195½ Freezelin1193½	Greenly, ridden out 6
10Feb93-7SA	fst	6f		$:21^4$	$:44^1$	$:56^3$	$1:09^3$	ⒻAlw 33000N1X	88	5	1	2½	2^{hd}	1½	21¼	Almeida G F	118	2.30	88-14	Afto1181¼ Adorydar118[7] Baja Belle118[2]	Good effort 6
10Jan93-6SA	my	6f		$:21^4$	$:45^1$	$:58^1$	$1:11^3$	ⒻMd Sp Wt	84	11	2	4¾	2^{hd}	2^{hd}	11¾	Almeida G F	B 117	6.40	79-17	Adorydar1171¾ Magical Flash117[6] Moulin Du Cadet117½	Wide, driving 11

WORKOUTS: ●Jly 6 Hol 6f fst $1:12^4$ H *1/15* ●Jly 1 Hol 7f fst $1:25^3$ H *1/9* Jun 19 Hol 5f fst $:59^2$ H *4/66* Jun 13 Hol 4f fst :48 H *11/56* May 30 Hol 5f fst $1:01^1$ H *18/48* May 24 Hol 4f fst $:48^2$ H *14/51*

This race was the Hollywood Oaks on Sunday, July 11, 1993, a very atypical race because of the false favorites. Wonderful situations like this only come up only once or twice a month. The nine-horse field was narrowed to five contenders and my betting line on them was as follows:

Horse	Betting Line
Fit To Lead	3-1
Hollywood Wildcat	7-2
Swazi's Moment	9-2
Likeable Style	12-1
Added Asset	12-1

The five contenders accounted for 81 percent of the probabilities; I assigned 19 percent of the probabilities to the other four horses. Remember that only horses whose betting line odds are 6-to-1 or less are suitable for win betting. Out go Likeable Style and Added Asset.

The actual public odds on my contenders were as follows:

Horse	Public Odds
Fit To Lead	8-1
Hollywood Wildcat	16-1
Swazi's Moment	7-1

All three offer value in comparison with their betting line odds. Let's demand an edge of 20 percent on our win bets. Which of these horses meets this edge?

Edge (Fit To Lead) = $.25 \times 8 - .75 = 1.25$

Edge (Hollywood Wildcat) = $.22 \times 16 - .78 = 2.74$

Edge (Swazi's Moment) = $.18 \times 7 - .82 = .44$

All three horses offer us edges substantially greater than our 20 percent minimum requirement. It's easy to see that we're still getting a big overlay by betting all three horses even though we'd be giving away at least two losing bets. Depending on our temperament, we can bet one or all three of them. Which horse offers the best edge-to-odds ratio?

Edge-to-Odds ratio (Fit To Lead) = 1.25/8 = .1563

Edge-to-Odds ratio (Hollywood Wildcat) = 2.74/16 = .1713

Edge-to-Odds ratio (Swazi's Moment) = .44/7 = .0629

Hollywood Wildcat offers a better edge-to-odds ratio than Fit To Lead. The aggressive single-horse win bettor would choose Hollywood Wildcat as his lone wager in this race. The theory says that an aggressive bettor could bet up to 17.13 percent of his win-betting bankroll on Hollywood Wildcat. In reality, this would be sheer madness—even the aggressive bettor should only bet a maximum 5 percent of his bankroll on any one race. By wagering less than the theoretical optimal percentage, the aggressive bettor trades rate of growth for additional safety.

The moderate win bettor would first determine his total win bet size (up to 5 percent of his bankroll) in this race. He would then divide this bet size among the three horses in direct proportion to their edge-to-odds ratio. He does this by adding up the three edge-to-odds ratios and dividing each of them into their combined sum. The sum of the edge-to-odds ratios is .3905. After dividing the individual edge-to-odds ratios back into the sum, he finds he can wager 40.03 percent of his bet size in this race on Fit To Lead, 43.87 percent on Hollywood Wildcat, and 16.11 percent on Swazi's Moment. Since the probability of winning this race is so great (65 percent), you can automatically make the maximum 5 percent bet; in fact, you could consider this just like a show bet, bet the maximum 10 percent, and not be punished for being too bold.

Let's assume that both the aggressive and the moderate win bettors invested $100 in this race. The aggressive bettor wagered $100 to win on Hollywood Wildcat; the moderate bettor wagered $40 to win on Fit to Lead, $44 to win on Hollywood Wildcat, and $16 to win on Swazi's Moment.

EIGHTH RACE
Hollywood
JULY 11, 1993

1⅛ MILES. (1.46⁴) 48th Running of THE HOLLYWOOD OAKS. Grade I. Purse $200,000 Added. Fillies 3-year-olds. By subscription of $200 each which shall accompany the nomination, $2,000 additional to start, with $200,000 added, of which $40,000 to second, $30,000 to third, $15,000 to fourth and $5,000 to fifth. Weight,121 lbs. Starters to be named through the entry box by closing time of entries. Hollywood Park reserves the right not to divide this race. Should this race not be divided and the number of entries exceed the starting gate capacity, preference will be given to those horses with the highest total earnings in 1993 and an also eligible list will be drawn. Failure to draw into this race at scratch time cancels all fees. A trophy will be presented to the winning Owner, Trainer and Jockey. Closed Wednesday, June 30 with 12 nominations.

Value of Race: $220,400 Winner $130,400; second $40,000; third $30,000; fourth $15,000; fifth $5,000. Mutuel Pool $347,249.00 Exacta Pool $308,725.00 Trifecta Pool $228,186.00

Last Raced	Horse	M/Eqt. A.Wt	PP	St	¼	½	¾	Str	Fin	Jockey	Odds $1
19Jun93 9Crc3	Hollywood Wildcat	LB	3 121	4	4	2¹	2¹	2²	1hd	1¹½	Delahoussaye E	16.60
19Jun93 8Hol1	Fit To Lead	LB	3 121	3	1	1¹	1¹	1½	2⁵	26½	McCarron C J	8.30
5Jun93 8Hol2	Adorydar	B	3 121	9	2	5½	4¹	3½	31½	3no	Almeida G F	5.80
19Jun93 8Hol3	Passing Vice	LB	3 121	8	5	9	7¹½	5¹	4hd	4½	Desormeaux K J	6.90
5Jun93 8Hol1	Likeable Style	LB	3 121	2	7	6²½	5hd	7³	5hd	5²½	Stevens G L	0.70
20Jun93 9CD2	Added Asset		3 121	6	3	3²½	3²	4¹½	6²	6¹½	Valenzuela P A	28.40
19Jun93 8Hol2	Swazi's Moment	B	3 121	1	8	4hd	6¹	6hd	7⁵	7⁵½	Nakatani C S	7.50
5Jun93 8Hol4	Nortena	LBb	3 121	7	6	7¹½	9	9	83½	8¹³	Flores D R	66.40
1Jly93 1Hol3	Fondly Remembered	LBb	3 121	5	9	8¹	8hd	8hd	9	9	Pincay L Jr	63.60

OFF AT 5:22 Start Good. Won driving. Time, :22⁴, :46², 1:10³, 1:35³, 1:48² Track fast.

$2 Mutuel Prices:

4-HOLLYWOOD WILDCAT	35.20	12.40	6.40
3-FIT TO LEAD		8.60	4.80
9-ADORYDAR			4.40

$2 EXACTA 4-3 PAID $305.20 $2 TRIFECTA 4-3-9 PAID $2,171.00

In this case, the aggressive bettor reaped the biggest reward by choosing the single best bet and putting all his eggs in that basket. His $100 wager returned $1,760. The moderate bettor cashed the win bet as well. His $44 wager on the winner returned $774.40. Had Fit To Lead held on to win, the moderate bettor would have cashed alone, and the race would have been an example of how the single-horse aspect of aggressive win betting is subject to less frequent cashing but overall superior return.

Here's another interesting technique for betting on multiple horses in the same race; I call it the "group overlay" method. In his excellent booklet *Bankroll Control*, Michael Pascual details this technique. Suppose you know that your performance, when the field is narrowed to four contenders, is picking the winner approximately 70 percent of the time. You arrive at the track and the odds offered on your four contenders are as follows:

Horse	Public Odds
A	3-1
B	5-1
C	9-1
D	15-1

The group overlay method allows you to bet all your contenders and expect to make a profit, in the long run, because of the discrepancy between the probability estimates of the crowd and your own handicapping.

If your estimate of the group probability for your contenders exceeds the public's, you have a positive-expectation situation that can be exploited.

To apply this powerful group overlay method, first calculate the optimum percentage of bankroll that you can wager in total. The formula is as follows:

$$\text{Optimum percentage} = \frac{\text{Total discrepancy in probability estimates}}{1 - \text{the public's estimate}}$$

This can be symbolized as follows:

$$\text{Optimum percentage} = \frac{OE - PE}{1 - PE}$$

OE—Our estimate of the group probability
PE—Public's estimate of the probability

Each bet then becomes

$$\frac{\text{Optimum percentage}}{PE \times (\text{Odds} + 1)}$$

The calculations for the above example look like this:

$$\text{Optimum percentage} = \frac{.700 - .579}{1 - .579} = \frac{.121}{.421} = .287$$

$$\text{BET (A)} = \frac{.287}{.579 \times (3 + 1)} = .124$$

$$\text{BET (B)} = \frac{.287}{.579 \times (5 + 1)} = .083$$

$$\text{BET (C)} = \frac{.287}{.579 \times (9 + 1)} = .050$$

$$\text{BET (D)} = \frac{.287}{.579 \times (15 + 1)} = .031$$

In this example, you can theoretically afford to risk up to 28.7 percent of your bankroll, bet in the following proportions: .124, .083, .050, and .031. Your theoretical bet, as a percentage of your capital, would be the sum of the proportions, which is 28.7 percent. (In the real world, you would never bet this large a percentage of your capital on a single event.) To find the proper percentage to bet on each horse, simply divide each proportion by the sum of all the proportions. Hence if your total bet was $100 for the race, you would apportion $43 on horse A, $29 on horse B, $17 on horse C, and $11 on horse D. You can expect to earn an average profit of almost 21 percent on this race.

Let's do an another example just to make sure that you understand this method. The method works with any number of horses providing that our group estimate exceeds the public's estimate. (It's very wise to insist upon a minimum 10 percent discrepancy.) Let's apply this method to the Hollywood Oaks dutching example. Our estimate of the probability of one of the group winning is .65. The public's estimate is .295.

$$\text{Optimum percentage} = \frac{.650 - .295}{1 - .295} = \frac{.355}{.705} = .504$$

$$\text{BET (Fit To Lead)} = \frac{.504}{.295 \times (8 + 1)} = .190$$

$$\text{BET (Hollywood Wildcat)} = \frac{.504}{.295 \times (17 + 1)} = .095$$

$$\text{BET (Swazi's Moment)} = \frac{.504}{.295 \times (7 + 1)} = .214$$

If your total bankroll was $1,000, the theory says that you could risk $504 on this race. (You would never bet this huge percentage of your bankroll in a million years!) Since there is a 65 percent chance that one of these horses will win, it wouldn't be imprudent to wager $100 on this race. (The reason that you can be this bold is because your win probability is so high. This bet is just like a show bet on a strong favorite.) You would wager $38 on Fit To Lead, $19 on Hollywood Wildcat, and $43 on Swazi's Moment. (These numbers were calculated by taking each bet and dividing it by the sum of all the bets.) The advantage of this method is that we need only estimate the group's chances and not be terribly concerned about a betting line for each of its members.

Let's recap the fundamentals of successful win betting:

1. Make a betting line in which the sum of the probabilities of all the horses adds up to 100 percent. Assign 20 percent or less to the non-

contenders and 80 percent or more to your live horses (depending upon the size of the field). Then divide the 80 percent (or more) among your contenders proportional to each horse's chances of winning. Any contender whose line odds are greater than 6-to-1 isn't considered a win contender.

2. Compare the betting line on each contender to its actual public odds. Avoid win betting on any contender whose actual public odds are lower than its betting-line odds.

3. Determine your minimum acceptable edge (20 percent should be the absolute minimum for win bets) and calculate the edge offered on each overlayed horse. Discard those overlays that don't meet your minimum edge.

For aggressive win bettors:

Make a win bet on the overlayed contender whose edge-to-odds ratio is the largest. The edge-to-odds ratio will also tell you what percentage of your bankroll you can safely wager on this horse. Never wager more than 5 percent on any single win bet.

For moderate win bettors:

Make a win bet on each of your overlayed contenders that meet your minimum edge requirement. Bet each horse in direct proportion to its edge-to-odds ratio. The higher the horse's edge-to-odds ratio, the more of the total bet it should receive. The total bet size shouldn't exceed 5 percent of your bankroll.

For conservative win bettors:

Use the group overlay method for those races in which your group win probability exceeds 65 percent and there's a healthy discrepancy (at least 10 percent) between your group estimate and the public's. Because of your high probability of success, the total bet size can be the same as a place or show bet, or 10 percent of bankroll.

Let's now take a look at the daily double. The double is simply a succession of two win bets, or a two-horse parlay. Let's apply our knowledge of win betting to this compound bet.

THE DAILY DOUBLE

The daily double is an excellent form of investment. Fortunately for us, in their zeal to win this wager, most players purchase too many losing tickets. The clash between selection-orientation and decision-orientation couldn't be more evident than in the daily double. The selection-oriented bettor's main priority is winning the bet and cashing a ticket. The decision-oriented investor's main priority is return on investment.

The typical daily double bettor is selection-oriented. He usually bets three horses in the first to three horses in the second for a total of nine bets. At least eight of these will be losing bets.

To show you the folly of this three-by-three crisscross strategy, I played it on paper over the entire 1992–1993 Santa Anita winter-spring meeting. There were 164 doubles offered. I used the three public favorites in each leg. This method hit 69 times for a win percentage of 42.07. Not bad. You're probably thinking that it's impossible to lose money by hitting the double 42 percent of the time. Think again. Based on the minimum $2 bet, the three-by-three player invested $18 in each daily double for a total of $2,952 bet. The return was $1,871.80. That's a loss of $1,080.20 in raw dollars. The ROI was negative 36.59 percent. The exotic track take at Santa Anita is 20.08 percent.

Let's assume that a little old lady using a hat pin or dice could play a single combination every time and lose only 20.08 percent of her money. If she had invested the same $18 on any single random combination in each double over the Santa Anita meet, she would have gotten back $2,359 for her total investment of $2,952. The crisscrosser doesn't even beat the little old lady.

Let's see if cutting the action down to a 2-by-2 crisscross improved the return on investment. The 2-by-2 crisscrosser won the double 45 times, or 27.44 percent of the time. In this strategy, there were four combinations to play. The investment in each double was $8. The total investment was $1,312. The return was $926.60. The raw-dollar loss was $385.40. The ROI "improved" to negative 29.38 percent, still not good enough to outperform the little old lady.

It's quite obvious that the double is a wagering situation in which the psychological mollification of buying multiple combinations just to have a winning ticket is punished mercilessly.

That's the bad news. The good news is that most of the betting public behaves in precisely the selection-oriented manner outlined above. The betting habits of the public explain the fact that the double usually pays more than a straight parlay. In addition, the daily double track take is only 20.05 percent (in California) as opposed to the multiple 15.33 percent track take in the straight pools, which makes the take for a two-horse parlay equivalent to a straight 28.3 percent takeout. If you know how to play the double properly and take advantage of the selection-orientation of the public, the double will constitute one of the most profitable components of your wagering portfolio.

To prove to yourself that the double is a wonderful opportunity, try the following experiment. Take the results charts from any 30 or more days from the track(s) you frequent and tabulate the odds of the winner of the first race and the odds of the winner of the second race, then compute what a straight parlay would have paid. To compute what a straight parlay would pay, use this formula:

$$\text{Fair Pay} = 2 \times (\text{Odds \#1} + 1) \times (\text{Odds \#2} + 1)$$

Write this down and compare it to the price that the daily double paid that day. Count how often the double pays more than a straight parlay. The following are the results of this experiment, which was conducted with the Santa Anita runs from March 10 through April 18, 1993, the final 30 days of the 1992–1993 winter-spring meet.

Date	Odds 1	Odds 2	Actual	Theory	Overlay
03/10/93	8.7	1.9	93.2	56.26	Yes
03/10/93	0.7	2.6	11.6	12.24	No
03/11/93	2.4	8.1	74.6	61.88	Yes

Date	Odds 1	Odds 2	Actual	Theory	Overlay
03/11/93	3.8	3	52.8	38.4	Yes
03/12/93	11.6	6.5	130	189	No
03/12/93	0.6	5.4	28	20.48	Yes
03/13/93	5.4	3.1	77.8	52.48	Yes
03/13/93	1.7	21.9	123.4	123.66	No
03/14/93	1.9	1.2	16.2	12.76	Yes
03/14/93	4.9	10.4	197.2	134.52	Yes
03/17/93	3.4	1.9	25.8	25.52	Yes
03/17/93	6.9	11.1	99.8	191.18	No
03/18/93	1.8	1.8	18.8	15.68	Yes
03/18/93	6.3	2	69.8	43.8	Yes
03/19/93	2.4	3.5	30.8	30.6	Yes
03/19/93	8.3	91.9	1,346.2	1,727.94	No
03/20/93	5.4	5.5	85.8	83.2	Yes
03/20/93	10.2	2.8	101.4	85.12	Yes
03/21/93	1.5	2.4	23.8	17	Yes
03/21/93	0.8	2.6	13.6	12.96	Yes
03/24/93	30.8	0.9	229	120.84	Yes
03/24/93	2.4	15	113.2	108.8	Yes
03/25/93	4.3	1.9	15.2	30.74	No
03/25/93	0.9	3.2	18	15.96	Yes
03/26/93	8.5	5.9	126.8	131.1	No
03/26/93	1.4	14.3	82.2	73.44	Yes
03/27/93	11.4	4.1	154	126.48	Yes
03/27/93	2	14.2	119	91.2	Yes
03/28/93	3.2	7.9	99.8	74.76	Yes
03/28/93	0.7	15.3	63.8	55.42	Yes
03/31/93	1.4	2.5	17.4	16.8	Yes
03/31/93	5.9	1.3	29.8	31.74	No
04/01/93	6.8	2.4	81.4	53.04	Yes
04/01/93	0.9	1.9	9.6	11.02	No
04/02/93	2.4	1.6	16.2	17.68	No
04/02/93	3.1	4.1	50.2	41.82	Yes
04/03/93	1.3	5.7	36.2	30.82	Yes
04/03/93	9.5	9.5	155.4	220.5	No
04/04/93	5.3	1.1	30.2	26.46	Yes
04/04/93	1.3	1.2	13	10.12	Yes
04/07/93	2.5	1.2	22	15.4	Yes

Date	Odds 1	Odds 2	Actual	Theory	Overlay
04/07/93	3.5	2.4	30.8	30.6	Yes
04/08/93	1.8	1.7	16.4	15.12	Yes
04/08/93	9.7	4.2	103	111.28	No
04/09/93	3.2	6.5	70.6	63	Yes
04/09/93	10.9	1.4	59.4	57.12	Yes
04/10/93	8.6	0.4	38.8	26.88	Yes
04/10/93	1.7	1.8	17.6	15.12	Yes
04/11/93	4.1	0.5	18	15.3	Yes
04/11/93	23.4	5.1	265.8	297.68	No
04/14/93	3.1	9.4	109.6	85.28	Yes
04/14/93	2.9	1.6	17	20.28	No
04/15/93	30.9	2.8	484.2	242.44	Yes
04/15/93	1.4	6.9	55.6	37.92	Yes
04/16/93	1.3	5.3	37.6	28.98	Yes
04/16/93	1.6	3.2	26.8	21.84	Yes
04/17/93	6.4	1.7	51.6	39.96	Yes
04/17/93	14	5.2	189.4	186	Yes
04/18/93	4.9	27.3	319.4	333.94	No
04/18/93	1.3	2.2	26.2	14.72	Yes

During this experiment, 60 doubles were offered; 45 of them, or 75 percent, were overlays. For the entire meeting, the double was an overlay 72.37 percent of the time. That's remarkable. At the 1993 Hollywood Park spring-summer meeting, the double was an overlay 78.3 percent of the time. The double clearly offers a wonderful opportunity to loot and sack. Fortunately, most of your fellow players don't have the slightest clue of how to begin to take advantage of this incredible opportunity.

You've already seen two examples of how *not* to play the double. In these crisscross strategies, the guaranteed losing tickets erode the profits generated by the double combinations that do win.

Let's now look at a couple of recurring instances in which the double is an underlay. You won't believe your eyes at the predictability of these bad bets. You'll be amazed at how easily you'll be able to avoid underlayed doubles.

The first is what I call the "double double-whammy." It's simply when a trainer or jockey wins both halves of the double. Take the example of the trainer. It's very rare that a trainer wins both halves of the daily double. Of the 164 doubles at the Santa Anita meet, there were four trainer-trainer doubles. All four were underlays. During the meet, the most blatant trainer-trainer underlay occurred in the late double on February 6, 1993. Eclipse Award–winning trainer Ron McAnally saddled the winner in both halves. The fair pay on the double was $52.54. It returned $34.40—that's 65 percent of the amount it should have paid. Please stay away from trainer-trainer double combos unless the combination is an overlay.

Fortunately, the public is a sucker for this type of bet. Listen to what James Quinn had to say, in *The Best of Thoroughbred Handicapping*, about this type of silly exotic money (he was paraphrasing Gordon Jones): "The betting public is held to behave foolishly at the exacta and double windows. They bet jockey combos, trainer combos, number combos and color combos. Saturated with bets based on whim, whisper, sentiment and hope, exotic pools do not resemble the normal distribution of money characteristic of straight pools."

In my research of trainer-trainer doubles, this certainly is the case. Forswear these money-sucking double combinations except when they offer value.

In the case of the jockey-jockey double double-whammy, the underlay effect is less pronounced and occurs when top-five jockeys are involved. There were 16 jockey-jockey double combinations that won; nine were underlays. The most egregious was the the March 17 late double. The fair pay for this double was $191.18. It actually paid $99.80. What could account for a such a monstrous underlay? Only the fact that both winning halves of the double were ridden by Kent Desormeaux, Southern California's leading jockey over the past two years.

Going farther back, on January 23 the meet's leading jockey, Gary Stevens, rode both winners in the late double. It paid $8.80. It should have paid $15.96. That's a 45 percent underlay.

The times the doubles were accounted for by lesser-known riders, they weren't underlays. Less-renowned (but by no means less-talented) jockeys Alex Solis and Patrick Valenzuela accounted for overlayed jockey-jockey doubles. So did Corey Nakatani (twice). Hence the double double-whammy for jockeys applies mainly to top-five publicity-type riders, who are notoriously overbet, and not so-called "people's jockeys," competent riders who don't get as much attention in the various wagering pools.

The second kind of double underlay involves 40-to-1 and higher shots. Granted, these outsiders don't win either half very often. But when they do, the double invariably is the underlay of the century. At the Santa Anita meeting, there were four doubles in which a 40-to-1 shot or higher won one half of the double. All four of these doubles were underlays. The worst of these underlayed combinations paid just 62 percent of its fair price; the least underlayed paid 80 percent of its fair price. Stay away from all combinations involving 40-to-1 and higher shots: They rarely come in, and when they do, you're hardly being compensated for the enormous amount of risk you're taking. If you like a 40-to-1 shot, it's usually best to take the money that you would have bet in the double and put it on its nose. Don't worry too much about these negative situations because you won't be betting on such combinations anyway.

Here's a list of things *not* to do:

1. Avoid blindly crisscrossing two or three contenders in the first half to two or three contenders in the second half. The guaranteed losing bets are death on your daily double bankroll.
2. Avoid betting any combination that involves the same trainer winning both halves of the double. Such a combination is overbet by a superstitious betting public and perhaps by the trainer's backstretch help. To a lesser extent, be wary of any combination that involves the same jockey winning both halves of the double, especially when it's a top-five publicity-type rider.
3. Avoid betting any combination that includes a 40-to-1 shot or greater, unless it's overlayed in the double pool. Most often, when such a combination hits, the longshot will account for the second half of the double and will be included by many punters as an afterthought in a wheel to the favorite in the first half.

You don't have to pay too much attention to these three mechanical-elimination approaches because our method of playing the double will absolutely guarantee that we will not bet on these underlay situations.

What do overlayed daily double combinations look like? Are there any discernible patterns we can discover that will help us wager strictly on overlayed combinations? As I mentioned earlier, there were 164 daily doubles offered at the 1992–1993 Santa Anita winter-spring meeting. About 44 percent of these doubles were overlayed by 20 percent or more. (About 46 percent of the doubles that won at Hollywood Park in 1993 were overlayed by 20 percent or more.) I isolated those doubles and tried to come up with some mechanical methods that would lead to automatic double profits.

Unfortunately, none were to be found. The double just can't be blindly generalized from track to track. For instance, I was very hopeful about one trend in particular: the double combining the favorite in the first half to the public's second betting choice in the second half. At Santa Anita, you could bet every favorite-second favorite double and get a positive ROI of around 13 percent. When I tested this approach at Hollywood, the result was a negative 34 percent ROI. In fact, at Santa Anita you could mechanically bet the favorite-second favorite double combination on the late double only and get a whopping 32.6 percent ROI. At Hollywood, the same mechanical system resulted in an ROI of negative 80.5 percent! I hope it's clear to you that there are no mechanical systems for consistently beating the double. If someone claims to have such a system and offers it to you for a fee, do us all a big favor and either burn his house down or plunge a dagger in his heart, depending on whether you prefer arson to murder or vice versa.

I scanned our database and looked for other promising mechanical methods. In his book *Exacta Exposé*, Doug Railey found that the favorite-favorite combination in the double generated a 10 percent profit at a 10 percent hit rate over 538 bets. Santa Anita in 1992–1993 maintained this hit rate, but the prices were so miserly that there was a negative ROI of 37 percent. At Hollywood Park, the favorite-favorite combination rebounded with a 15 percent hit rate and a break-even ROI. Thus I have to conclude that the favorite-favorite combination, bet blindly, is a marginal proposition at best and should be avoided.

I modified the wasteful three-by-three crisscross by limiting the combinations to the favorite in the first half to the public's top three choices in the second half and the favorite in the second half to the public's top three betting choices in the first half. If the favorite won either race, I had a good chance of hitting the double. If both favorites won, I had it twice. At Santa Anita the result was a negative 18 percent ROI; at Hollywood it was a negative 23 percent ROI. Combining the favorite in either half with the public's fourth, fifth, and sixth betting choices also came up a loser.

After being led down so many blind alleys, the painful truth sunk in: Yes, the winning double is usually a wonderful overlay— but in order to cash in mechanically you'll wind up playing too many losing combinations. This severely erodes any edge you had on the winning overlayed combination. It's clear that selectivity, not spreading, is the order of the day.

Once we accept this fundamental truth and realize that we can't rely on a mechanical system for beating the double, we're that much closer to consistent profits. Beating the double requires good handicapping and good betting strategy. The first strategy is a little complicated but it's the optimal way to play the double. If you're decision-oriented, you'll love it. If you're selection-oriented, you'll most likely hate it because there will be times you'll have the winning combination and not bet on it.

The idea is to look at the matrix of your contenders in each race. You may have a good number of combinations to consider. The number of combinations to consider is the number of contenders in the first leg multiplied by the number of contenders in the second leg. This strategy assumes that you've created an accurate odds line for each race. You compute the payoff for every combination that assures at least a fair bet, compensates you for your losing bets, and takes on a substantial profit. You then check the probable pay board and cross out all combinations that are going to pay less than fair odds plus the required compensation. This usually leaves from one to eight combinations as final candidates.

Again, it's vital that you allow yourself to be compensated for your guaranteed losing combinations if you bet more than one combination. Remember, uncompensated losing combinations doomed the mechanical methods I tried. We now insist on an "n minus 1" bet premium on each combination. For example, suppose we have five overlayed combinations. We must insist on a four-bet premium plus our minimum 20 percent profit expectation. That is, each combination must pay an $8 premium over fair payoff plus guarantee us an edge of at least 20 percent on the bet. This strategy is a little tricky because the payoffs change near post time. It's best to use a preprinted sheet and also be in a position to make your wager as close to the bell as possible. Let's look at an example of this method.

Suppose our odds line for the first race is:

Post	Horse	Odds
1	Dr. Hunter S.	5-2
4	Steadman's Pal	7-1
7	Duke Raoul	7-2

In the second race our odds line is as follows:

Post	Horse	Odds
4	Bud's Andrea	9-2
5	Maniac Nat	6-1
7	Harriet Sunday	6-1
9	Baby Juliana	6-1

We can compute the fair pay for each combination by using the formula:

$$\text{Fair pay} = 2 \times (\text{ODDS 1} + 1) \times (\text{ODDS 2} + 1)$$

Hence the fair pay for each double combination is:

(1,4) $38.50	(4,4) $88.00	(7,4) $49.50
(1,5) $49.00	(4,5) $112.00	(7,5) $63.00
(1,7) $49.00	(4,7) $112.00	(7,7) $63.00
(1,9) $49.00	(4,9) $112.00	(7,9) $63.00

Barry Meadow suggests that you multiply each combination by 150 percent to arrive at the overlay matrix. I'm not as greedy as Meadow and only require a 140 percent multiplier. The "new" fair pay for each combination becomes:

(1,4) $57.75	(4,4) $123.20	(7,4) $69.30
(1,5) $68.60	(4,5) $156.80	(7,5) $88.20
(1,7) $68.60	(4,7) $156.80	(7,7) $88.20
(1,9) $68.60	(4,9) $156.80	(7,9) $88.20

Here's the actual pay for each combination shown on the track monitors:

(1,4) $40	(4,4) $91	(7,4) $51
(1,5) $48	(4,5) $99	(7,5) $64
(1,7) $62	(4,7) $110	(7,7) $66
(1,9) $68	(4,9) $110	(7,9) $89

We compare the actual pays to the "new" fair pays. It's easy to see that all but the (7,9) combination are eliminated. There's only one possible bet: the (7,9) combination. It's paying $89.00; it must pay $88.20 to meet our minimum requirements. (It need only pay $63 to be a fair bet.) Please remember to compensate yourself for your guaranteed losing wagers when necessary. In most cases the 140 percent multiplier does this for you. It only happens when you are betting on four or five combinations and some of the payoffs are near their cutoff values.

This case was simple. There were no guaranteed losing wagers. If the (1,9) combination was paying $70, you would play both these combinations and not worry about compensation for your one guaranteed losing bet because the 140 percent multiplier took care of it. Our expectation on this bet is well in excess of 20 percent.

$$E(x) = .0408 \times \$70 + .0317 \times \$89 - .9274 \times (-\$4) = \$1.96$$

The probability of hitting this double is the sum of the probabilities of the (1,9) combination and the (7,9) combination. The probability of a 5-to-2 shot on top of a 6-to-1 is $1/3.5 \times \frac{1}{7} = .0408$. The probability of a 7-to-2 shot on top of a 6-to-1 is $1/4.5 \times \frac{1}{7} = .0317$. We'll win this bet 7.26 percent $(1 - .0726)$ of the time, which means that we lose our four bucks 92.74 percent of the time. Our expectation is $1.96 on a $4 bet. Hence our edge is 49 percent.

That takes care of the betting strategy part of this decision-oriented daily double method. So far, so good. Now for the tricky part. The issue of how much to bet on each overlayed and fairly compensated combination is a function of your edge on the bet, your odds on the bet, and the size of your bankroll. Our edge was 49 percent, assuming that we bet on both combinations. Since we know our edge and our win probability, we can compute our average odds.

$$.49 = .0726 \times \text{Odds} - .9274$$

Solving this equation, we find that our average odds are 15.52-to-1. Thus the edge-to-odds ratio is .0316 (.49 ÷ 15.52). The edge-to-odds ratio becomes the maximum percentage of our double bankroll that we can bet on this combination. So we can wager a maximum of 3.16 percent of our bankroll on this bet. (It's best to cut this number in half.) We would divide our bet proportionally to the probability of winning. In this case, we would bet 56 percent of our total bet on the (1,9) combination and 44 percent on the (7,9) combination. (Our probability of winning the (1,9) combination was .0408. Our probability of winning the bet was .0726. Therefore we bet 56 percent (.0408 ÷ .0726) on the (1,9) combination.) If our total bankroll was $2,000, we would bet $30 on this double. This means that we would bet $17 on the (1,9) and $13 on the (7,9) combination. Because our win probability is very small (.0726), we must be prepared for a fairly large number of consecutive losers (71).

(If this strategy seems like a lot of work to do by hand, don't fret. There are handheld preprogrammed computers available that you can take to the track. These convenient portable machines perform all the nasty and tedious calculations instantly and without error at the touch of a few buttons. Cynthia Publishing's *Bettor-Handicapper* is one such computer that will, among other betting strategies, isolate double overlays and size your bet on each double overlay accordingly.)

As you can see, the decision-oriented double strategy probably isn't for you if you enjoy the security of cashing. Out of 12 potential combinations, only two were worth a wager. From a mathematical standpoint, however, this is the optimal way to do things.

If you use this strategy, there are two risk-management techniques that you might want to consider. They are forms of insurance. Please be aware, again, that whenever you take insurance, you must pay a premium. The first technique is known as a "saver" bet. It's a bet on a highly probable combination even though it doesn't meet the 20 percent criterion. It can be argued that when making multiple bets it's appropriate to try to protect against the debacle of losing the entire amount risked. In other words, you're trading gross profits for safety. However, mathematically speaking, it's wise to cross out any combination that is underlayed, regardless of handicapping opinion. Such ruthless avoidance of underlays is the best long-run strategy. You can include combinations that are very close to the cut-off if you're particularly afraid of one of the horses involved in the combination. A good example of this would be the (1,7) combination.

The second risk-management technique you may want to consider is to bet on the scare horse(s) in the second part of the double, given that you have a live ticket after the first leg.

Suppose you're live in the second half of the double with two horses and your scare horse is going off at 6-to-1. Suppose further that you have $10 invested in five double combinations. If your horses win, the double will pay $36 and $44 respectively. Should you buy insurance? If so, how much?

If you were to wager $2 on the 6-to-1 horse and he wins, you at least have made a small profit on the two races, namely $2. You make a $24 profit on the two races if your first choice wins and $32 if your second choice wins, given that you bought the insurance. Let's also suppose that the 6-to-1 horse is a fair bet—that is, he has a 14.29 percent chance of winning.

The way you decide whether to take insurance or not is to see what would happen were to do this a large number of times, say 100. Suppose that your daily double ticket contained two horses, each with an approximate 30 percent chance of winning the second race. Your first choice would win 30 times and you would earn a $720 profit. Another 30 wins would make you $960. You'd win $2 14 times for a grand total of $1,708 gross profit. You would lose $12 on each of the remaining 26 races. Your net profit would be $1,396. Not bad.

If you didn't buy the insurance, you would earn $26 profit on each win of the first choice and $34 on each win for the second choice. You would make 30 times $26 plus 30 times $34 minus 40 times $10. That's $780 plus $1,020 minus $400, for a profit of $1,400. Hence the decision depends on your temperament. Four dollars in $1,400 isn't significant—it represents less than .5 percent difference. You should only consider 5 percent or greater as significant.

Now suppose that the 6-to-1 horse had a 20 percent chance of winning the race. It would be mandatory to buy this insurance because you would be giving up profit if you didn't. It shouldn't be the hardest thing in the world to bet on a horse that is offering a 40 percent edge.

If this race were run 100 times, you would now win eighty of them: thirty for a profit of $720, thirty for a profit of $960, and twenty for a profit of $40. The total gross profit is $1,720. The losses are twenty races at $12 per race or $240, which leaves a net profit of $1,480.

As always, the issue of risk management is yours to decide. Please be aware of your options. A delicious overlay in the second part of the double is a wonderful form of insurance.

If you prefer the comfort of cashing the double on a regular basis, you'll love the next strategy: It's crisscrossing done in an intelligent manner.

Think for a moment about the three-by-three crisscross. It covers each combination equally and burdens you with eight automatic losing combinations. That's an unchanging deficit that must be overcome every time you crisscross.

Who says you have to play each double combination with the same intensity? What if you liked some double combinations more than others? You could load up on the more probable ones and "save" with a few peripheral combinations at longer odds. The overall effect would be to crush the double when a combination you like comes in, and to collect a modest profit when a combination you like less clicks. The deficit of a normal crisscross would be reduced dramatically. For example, say you crisscrossed and bet four double combinations equally, $10 on each combination. You'd have to overcome $30 in guaranteed losers. This strategy lets you bet the same $40 proportionally. You bet more on the combinations that have a greater chance of clicking. So you might bet the four combinations, in descending order of likelihood, like this: $20, $10, $5, $5. In the best case, the double combination you bet $20 on would hit and you'd only have to overcome $20 in losing combinations. Of course, if one of the peripheral $5 combinations connects, you shoulder a little more of a burden. But that's the price you pay for the comfort of frequent cashing.

Let's use the previous example to show you how to implement this strategy. Here's the odds line for the first half of the double:

Post	Horse	Odds
1	Dr. Hunter S.	5-2
4	Steadman's Pal	7-1
7	Duke Raoul	7-2

In the second race our odds line is as follows:

Post	Horse	Odds
4	Bud's Andrea	9-2
5	Maniac Nat	6-1
7	Harriet Sunday	6-1
9	Baby Juliana	6-1

In this strategy, you'd bet all 12 possible double combinations using these contenders. A nice feature of this strategy is you hit the daily double a large percentage of the time.

The first step is to determine the win probability [P(W)] of each combination. Remember the formula:

$$P(W) = \frac{1}{(\text{odds of horse in first half}) + 1} \times \frac{1}{(\text{odds of horse in second half}) + 1}$$

In this case, the (1,4) combination's P(W) is:

$$P(W) = \frac{1}{3.5} \times \frac{1}{5.5} = .0519$$

The combination has a P(W) of .0519; it should win 5.19 percent of the time. Here's the P(W) for each combination.

(1,4) .0519	(4,4) .0227	(7,4) .0404
(1,5) .0408	(4,5) .0179	(7,5) .0318
(1,7) .0408	(4,7) .0179	(7,7) .0318
(1,9) .0408	(4,9) .0179	(7,9) .0318

The next step is to add all the P(W)'s together to get a "group P(W)." In this case, the group P(W) is .3865. This means we have a 38.65 percent chance of cashing.

The next step is to divide each individual combination's P(W) by the group P(W). In the case of the (1,4) combination, we divide

.0519 by .3865. The result is .1343, or 13.43 percent, which represents the percentage or proportion of our total bet size that we can wager on the (1,4) combination. Here's the proportion for each combination:

(1,4) .1343	(4,4) .0587	(7,4) .1045
(1,5) .1056	(4,5) .0463	(7,5) .0823
(1,7) .1056	(4,7) .0463	(7,7) .0823
(1,9) .1056	(4,9) .0463	(7,9) .0823

These proportions show that the likelier combinations get a higher percentage of the total bet, which is in harmony with the fundamental principles of money management. For example, the (1,4) combination has a 5.19 percent chance of winning and gets 13.43 percent of the total bet; by contrast, the (4,9) combination has a 1.79 percent chance of winning, so it gets only 4.63 percent of the total bet. It's important to note that these proportions do *not* represent a percentage of your total double bankroll. In this case, if your total double bankroll was $2,000, you wouldn't bet 13.43 percent of it on the (1,4) combination. Rather, you'd decide how much of your $2,000 bankroll you wanted to bet on this double, then take 13.43 percent of that smaller amount and bet it on the (1,4) combination. Let's say you wanted to invest $50 in this double. (The reason you can bet such a relatively large proportion— 2.5 percent—of your bankroll is because your success probability is so high.) Your bet sizes, rounded to the nearest whole dollar, would look like this:

(1,4) $7	(4,4) $3	(7,4) $5
(1,5) $5	(4,5) $2	(7,5) $4
(1,7) $5	(4,7) $2	(7,7) $4
(1,9) $5	(4,9) $2	(7,9) $4

The total investment comes to $51.00. (If this method seems unmanageable by hand, you can automate it by using a preprogrammed pocket computer that considers the win probability of each double combination and, on that basis, proportionally sizes the bet on each combination. Cynthia Publishing's *Bettor-Handicapper* automates this strategy as well.)

Gordon Pine recommends the following strategy for crushing the double. It's simple but powerful. In the first half of the double, check your betting line for overlays in the win pool. Bet those overlays to win, as always.

These win overlays then serve as your key horses in the first half of the double. Pair them with your contenders in the second half of the double. Bet the same amount on each combination. Because your key horses are overlays in the first race, one can assume that any combination using them will also be overlayed. (This isn't necessarily a true assumption, but nor is it too far from wrong.) Contenders are the horses that are 6-to-1 or lower on your odds line for the second half.

I played this strategy on paper during the month of June 1993 at Hollywood Park, using *ALL-IN-ONE*'s betting lines; I bet 38 doubles and hit eight of them, good for an ROI of 18 percent. Not bad for a semi-mechanical method.

The very best way to play the daily double is to bite the bullet and calculate the fair price for each combination that involves your contenders. (There's no limit on the number of contenders. It's possible to have a seven-by-seven matrix.) Compare the fair price to the probable pay listed on your television monitors. Cross out all the underlays. The remaining combinations are candidates. Please remember to compensate yourself for your guaranteed losing bets as well as to demand at least a 20 percent edge on each combination. (Multiplying the fair price by 1.4 practically guarantees at least that.) Bet only on those combinations that meet the criteria of a 20 percent overlay plus compensation for losing bets. This strategy is painful because many times a crossed-out combination wins. Endure the short-term pain; your reward will be long-term gain. Let's now take a look at one of the best bets in all of thoroughbred racing—the Pick-3.

THE PICK-3

Any parimutuel wager that involves more than one horse is what I call an "exotic" bet. The daily double and exacta are the simplest of the exotics. Simple, but not easy to master. Beyond the double and exacta, we have the more advanced exotics: Pick-3, Pick-4, Pick-6, trifecta, superfecta, twin trifecta, and the superexotic combination of trifecta followed by a superfecta. I'm sure we'll see new and even more fascinating combinations of the above bets in the near future.

Let's turn the clock back to 1988. In those days, I recommended that beginning handicappers bet two horses per race. My reasons had nothing to do with mathematically optimum betting—they had to do with psychological factors. It's a well known fact that a two-horse bettor goes to the win window a lot more often than a single-horse bettor. In the ultimate, the single-horse bettor outperforms his two-horse rival by a significant amount. However, without the frequent positive reinforcement of cashing tickets, the beginner may lose confidence. The analogy is training wheels on a two-wheeler. It's always best to begin any pursuit in a safe and positive manner. Once you're confident, the training wheels can come off.

The easiest exotic by far is the daily double, followed by the daily triple. At Santa Anita the triple (Pick-3) is a $3 bet. Once again we have the situation where the triple usually pays more than a straight parlay because of the betting habits of the public. In their zeal to win this bet, they bet on too many combinations. Just for the fun of it, try this experiment: For any 20 racing days, note the odds of the winners in each of the triple races and figure out what a straight parlay would have paid. Compare the result with the actual triple payoff for that day. See how often the triple pays more than a straight parlay. To calculate the fair value of what a $3 triple should pay, you could convert the odds to probabilities and use the following:

$$\text{Fair price} = \frac{3}{\text{p1} \times \text{p2} \times \text{p3}}$$

This says to multiply the three probabilities together and divide the answer into the number three. Suppose the odds on the winner of the first part were 2-to-1, the second part were 3-to-1, and the final part were 4-to-1. How much should this triple pay in order to be a fair bet? The respective probabilities are ⅓, ¼, and ⅕. Their product is ⅟₆₀. This number divided into 3 is 180.

You could also calculate directly from the odds:

$$\text{Fair price} = 3 \times (\text{ODDS 1} + 1) \times (\text{ODDS 2} + 1) \times (\text{ODDS 3} + 1)$$

The following table represents the results when I did this experiment in late 1987 and early 1988:

Odds 1	Odds 2	Odds 3	Fair Pay	Actual	Overlay
1.4	2.2	12.5	311.04	419.40	Yes
0.7	9.4	10.5	609.96	855.00	Yes
2.4	3.1	5.7	280.19	369.00	Yes
7.5	1.2	1.1	117.81	188.70	Yes
1.9	2.5	2.2	97.44	170.70	Yes
4.2	10.5	7.5	1,524.90	3,120.30	Yes
15.0	1.2	0.4	147.84	188.40	Yes
3.5	2.7	31.8	1,638.36	2,700.30	Yes
3.1	4.3	38.5	2,575.00	11,466.50	Yes
3.1	0.9	2.1	72.45	91.50	Yes
9.5	2.2	7.0	806.40	963.00	Yes
1.6	6.3	6.1	404.27	792.60	Yes
11.0	2.6	8.0	1,166.40	1,593.90	Yes
2.4	3.1	6.1	296.92	276.00	No
3.8	1.7	0.6	62.20	53.40	No
1.2	2.3	14.0	326.70	251.10	No
7.2	7.0	3.8	944.64	2,795.40	Yes
4.9	2.5	1.6	161.07	218.70	Yes
6.9	8.1	8.5	2,048.86	1,673.70	No

Odds 1	Odds 2	Odds 3	Fair Pay	Actual	Overlay
3.9	4.0	9.5	771.75	919.20	Yes
12.0	1.4	1.4	224.64	276.60	Yes
4.9	2.5	1.4	148.68	239.10	Yes
4.5	4.1	28.4	2,474.01	3,888.90	Yes
4.6	7.4	5.7	945.50	1,842.60	Yes

At that time, I urged my readers to strive for 60 percent winners using two horses in playable races. Since these three races are independent events and we have a 60 percent chance of winning each race, it then follows that we have a 60 percent of 60 percent of 60 percent chance to win all three—60 percent of 60 percent is 36 percent, and 60 percent of 36 percent is 21.6 percent. If all three races are playable and we bet two horses per race, we should win 21.6 percent of our triples, assuming minimum competence. If we were to invest $24 ($3 on each of the eight possible combinations), then the triple must pay $87.11 to be a fair bet. The good news is that the triple averages much more than this. The bad news is it rarely includes three playable races.

The triple at Santa Anita includes the sixth, seventh, and eighth races (Santa Anita offers more triples now). Most often the triple is a maiden sprint earlier in the year and a maiden route beginning in the late summer, followed by a turf route and a dirt route. At best, it is composed of two playable races. Our 21.6 percent probability estimate assumes three playable races.

Suppose for a moment that on maiden races using three selections we could hit 50 percent of the races. Suppose further that in unplayable races we could also hit 50 percent by going three deep. Assuming that the triple pays $300 on average, should we invest in the triple using a 3-3-2 ticket that costs $54?

The probability that we will hit the triple is .5 × .5 × .6 = .15, or 15 percent. Our expectation is:

$$E(x) = .15 \times \$246 - .85 \times \$54 = -\$9.00$$

That's a negative $9 on a $54 bet for a disadvantage of 16.67 percent. We'll leave this opportunity to our competition.

What if there were two playable races and one unplayable? This time our probability is .5 × .6 × .6 = .18. We would buy a 3-2-2 ticket that costs $36. Our expectation is now:

$$E(x) = .18 \times \$264 - .82 \times \$36 = \$18$$

That's \$18 on a \$36 wager for an edge of 50 percent. We will invest in this situation as often as possible. Our average odds are approximately 7.3-to-1, which means we can invest a maximum of 6.85 percent of our bankroll on this type situation. As always, it's much more prudent to wager half this amount.

This example suggests a rule: *Play the triple only when it contains at least two playable races.*

Investing in advanced exotics is not for amateurs. Exotics are low probability–high payoff games. You have to plan on long, long losing streaks. Given the above example, where your probability of hitting the triple is 18 percent, it wouldn't be at all unusual for you to experience 20 consecutive losses. Even though you have a whopping 50 percent edge, you'll have to be prepared for an erosion of your bankroll. With an 18 percent success probability, you must be prepared for 27 consecutive losses; you should have a triple bankroll in excess of \$972 per \$3 wagered. Once again, most bettors overbet and most are selection oriented, hence they focus their attention on winning the bet, not upon their expected return. What tends to happen in advanced exotics is that we have a greater edge than normal. It's not unusual to have a 50 percent edge in these kinds of wagers. The problem is that the average odds are fairly large, and so our edge-odds ratio is small. This means that we have to bet a very small fraction of our bankroll. In other words, the advanced exotics demand that we begin with a huge bankroll.

Excuse me while I get mathematical—this will only take a minute. A reliable estimator of the number of consecutive losses you must be prepared to endure is the logarithm of .005 divided by the logarithm of the probability of failure. The way I arrived at the expectation of 27 losses for an 18 percent success probability is as follows: Calculate $\log(.005) \div \log(.82) = 26.698$. You always round up to the nearest integer, giving us the answer 27. If we have a 3 percent chance, how many consecutive losses must we be prepared to endure? Since 3 percent is the chance of success, then the chance of failure is 97 percent. We then calculate $\log(.005) \div \log(.97) = 173.948$. We must be prepared to endure a losing streak of 174. The following table will give you a feeling for the number of consecutive losses that you have to plan for when involved in a low-success probability event.

Success Probability	Consecutive Losses	Success Probability	Consecutive Losses
.005	1,058	.105	48
.010	528	.110	46
.015	351	.115	44
.020	263	.120	42
.025	210	.125	40
.030	174	.130	39
.035	149	.135	37
.040	130	.140	36
.045	116	.145	34
.050	104	.150	33
.055	94	.155	32
.060	86	.160	31
.065	79	.165	30
.070	74	.170	29
.075	68	.175	28
.080	64	.180	27
.085	60	.185	26
.090	57	.190	26
.095	54	.195	25
.100	51	.200	24

The reason that I mention this is that we're now going to venture into the land of low-success probability opportunities. When you consider the Pick-3 from an intuitive point of view, it looks pretty attractive. The average payoff is usually 100-to-1 or better. If you are a 25 percent handicapper, your chance of hitting this bet, wagering one horse per leg (race), is 1.5625 percent. Your expectation is $100 \times .015625 - .9843756 = .5781$. This is a 57.8 percent ROI. If you're a Sartin player and only average 50 percent winners, betting two horses per race, you could expect to win this bet 12.5 percent of the time. Your average payoff would be reduced to 12.5-to-1 because you would now be making eight bets. Your expectation would be $.125 \times 12.5 - .8725 = .69$. This is a whopping 69 percent profit rate. This discussion makes this bet sound really easy and very profitable. Reality says otherwise.

By the way, suppose you're live going into the third leg of the Pick-3 and for some reason the track doesn't show the probable pays. Can you still estimate what the Pick-3 will pay? A quick way to figure how many tickets are still live is to look at the odds of the winning horse in each leg. If the first race is won by a 9-to-1 shot, you can practically be certain that 90 percent of all Pick-3 tickets are dead. (A 9-to-1 shot has less than 10 percent of the win pool.) If the second race is then won by a 4-to-1 shot, you estimate only 2 percent of all tickets are live (20 percent of the 10 percent from the first leg). The odds of the last winner further reduces the percentage of live tickets. You then multiply the percentage of live tickets by the total pool, less takeout, to approximate the payoff. (If you can't get the total amount of the Pick-3 pool, use the average daily amount.) This method also works for the Pick-6.

In 1990, Ron Ambrose and I decided to win all the money in Southern California. We formed a Pick-3 syndicate. We would each handicap the Pick-3 races and use our top two picks in each race. This meant that we could use as many as four horses per race if we violently disagreed. If we both decided that a particular race had only one contender, we would use that horse as a single—this would allow us to go deeper in the other two races. We started in July at Hollywood Park and continued at Del Mar when the Hollywood Park meeting ended. We each invested $100 per day. Our results were a complete and utter disaster. We managed to lose 32 straight Pick-3's. At this point, we decided to go our separate ways and figure out how we could turn things around. We both agreed to independently research the Pick-3 and figure out a way to win. Whoever figured it out first would share his results with the other. An interesting thing happened. Within 60 days, we both developed winning strategies. We each thought each other's solution was less than desirable. I thought it was silly to bet the same amount on less probable combinations as on the most probable combinations. Ambrose thought that it was necessary to have the help of Albert Einstein to work my strategy. We both were more than $3,000 in the hole in August. By November, we were both ahead for the year on Pick-3's.

I'll give you Ambrose's solution first. He went back over the data using his selections and found that he would have hit eight out of the 32 Pick-3's if he just went four deep in each race. The trouble is that a 4 × 4 × 4 ticket costs $192. Any Pick-3 strategy should have at least a 25 percent ROI. The minimum acceptable payoff at a 25 percent hit rate to guarantee a 25 percent profit is $768. Unfortunately, the typical (after throwing out all the Pick-3's over $3,000) Pick-3 was averaging around $700. (You must remember that, at the time, this bet was relatively new to Southern California. In 1993, the typical Pick-3 average was a little less than $500. The average including the bizarros was more than $1,100! You'll see the actual 1993 Santa Anita data in a few pages.)

Ambrose's next move was a stroke of genius. He noticed that usually just one or at most two races in the group necessitated going four deep. He revised his 4-by-4-by-4 strategy to a 1-by-4-by-4, 4-by-1-by-4, 4-by-4-by-1 strategy, thereby reducing the number of combinations from 64 down to 48. At the same time, he increased his probability of success. With a 70 percent win probability for each leg, a 4-by-4-by-4 ticket has a success probability of 34.3 percent. A 1-by-4-by-4 ticket with a 33 percent probability of hitting the single and a 70 percent chance of hitting when going four deep has a success probability of 16.17 percent. Since he bought three separate tickets, each having a success probability of 16.17 percent, his total success probability was 48.51 percent! He handicapped all the Pick-3 races and chose the top four contenders in each race. He selected a "key horse" for each race. Ambrose was a 35 percent handicapper in playable races. (He's since improved to more than 40 percent!) Going four deep, he would have the winner among his contenders more than 70 percent of the time in nonplayable races and 85 percent in playable races. He then bought three separate part-wheel tickets. Assume that the Pick-3 was races 6, 7, and 8. His first ticket would be his key in the sixth with all four contenders in the seventh with all four contenders in the eighth. His second ticket would be all four contenders in the sixth with his key as a single in the seventh with all four contenders in the eighth. His third ticket would be all four contenders in the sixth with all four contenders in the seventh, with his key horse in the eighth. The cost of each $3 Pick-3 ticket was $48, for a total of

$144. His theoretical chances of hitting his bet were in the neighborhood of 49 percent (48.51 percent). In fact, he was hitting more than 50 percent of his Pick-3's. When you consider that he was getting an average odds payoff of greater than 9-to-2 ($700 average payoff divided by $144 bet size) and hitting this bet more than 50 percent of the time, it doesn't take a genius to see why he got his money back in a hurry.

In fairness to Ambrose, the vast majority of his betting lines have all the contenders assigned the same win probability. Over the past three years I have watched him, somewhat enviously, make his betting line equal to the number of contenders in a race. If he has three contenders, his odds line is 3-to-1 on each contender while the rest of the field gets 3-to-1. If he has four contenders, his odd line is 4-to-1 on each contender and 4-to-1 on the balance of the field.

One thing that Ambrose likes very much about his Pick-3 strategy is the fact that you can hit the Pick-3 multiple times. If all three key horses win, you have it three times; if two key horses win, you have it twice. On a 4-by-4-by-4 ticket, you can hit this bet only a single time.

When Ambrose originally developed his key-4-4 strategy, he didn't care if his key horse was a public favorite or not. Now he does. He insists that his key horse *not* be the probable public favorite. Needless to say, he doesn't play too many Pick-3's. Another factor militating against his playing more Pick-3s is that the average payoff has come down since 1990. (The public has more experience with this bet and has improved.)

My solution was completely different. When I went back over the data, I came to a similar conclusion as Ambrose. The reason we were losing was because our third or fourth or even fifth choices in contentious races were jumping up and winning. In what we considered playable races, we had the winner within our top two picks more than 50 percent of the time. This suggested a strategy that didn't limit the number of horses in a given race. My first solution was to use all the horses in a betting line until the total was at least 60 percent. (This strategy is similar to the 1988 strategy mentioned previously, except you don't have to limit yourself to insisting on at least two playable races.) For example, suppose I had a race in which there were four contenders that I considered equal. This means that each is 4-to-1 on my line. (Again, the way I make a line is to assign approximately 80 percent of the probability to contenders and 20 percent to the noncontenders.) This meant that I could choose only three of them. For the sake of my research, I first chose to include the three horses with the longest odds. I then checked the results using the three shortest-odds horses. In each case, this strategy showed a profit. The problem was the bet size had to vary given the number of contenders in each leg. After spending about 100 hours playing around with old data, it suddenly occurred to me that I was trying to win the bet instead of trying to find value. The bush burned.

In a single evening, I made two important discoveries. The first was how to play the Pick-3 in a nearly optimum way; the second was how to refine Ambrose's strategy so that the bet size could be smaller.

The major difference between Ron Ambrose and me is betting orientation. Ambrose has a desperate need to cash practically every ticket that he buys. He tends to be selection oriented. I, on the other hand, have an urgent need to hit home runs and am decision oriented. I realize that most handicappers are much less risk-averse than I am. For my readers, I try to strike a balance between decision orientation and selection orientation. Depending upon your risk tolerance, you'll probably chose one of the following strategies as your primary modus operandi. (Most will choose the second strategy.)

Strategy #1—A "Nearly" Optimum Pick-3 Method

First and foremost, you should look for value. You should fall in love with bets, not horses. You must realize, going in, that the Pick-3 is a low-probability, high-payoff event. This means that you have to have a substantial bankroll because you're going to experience a large number of consecutive losses. Second, unless you're a computational wizard, you must have access to at least a pocket computer to work this strategy. (If you hate computers and hate math, don't worry. The next strategy that we'll discuss is easy to implement and doesn't require a computer.) The secret to this strategy is to bet a fixed amount of money on each Pick-3. This amount will represent a fraction of your bankroll. The optimum fraction is the Kelly Criterion, your average edge on this bet divided by your average payoff odds. As prudent risk takers we will always choose a fraction of this optimum percentage. We'll use a 50 percent Kelly. The reason is that while Kelly optimizes rate of growth of wealth, it doesn't guarantee safety. By choosing a fraction of Kelly, we don't reduce the rate of growth significantly but we approach 100 percent safety.

If you want to play the Pick-3 for profit, you must have a substantial bankroll. You're looking at a range of 20 to 35 consecutive losses in the worst case. You must be prepared. If you're playing $100 on each Pick-3, you must have a bankroll of at least $4,000 to insure yourself against "gambler's ruin." If you think that you can play small tickets and win big money, you're kidding yourself. The big guys will eat your lunch. You're much better off buying 10 percent of a $240 ticket than you are betting $24 on your own. If you have a substantial bankroll, you'll pray for contentious races.

It's vital that you have the skills to pick the winner of a race within your contenders at least 70 percent of the time. If not, you have no business even considering the daily double, much less the Pick-3. This strategy assumes that you're a competent enough handicapper to achieve this modest goal. The reason that this ability level is so important is that we insist upon hitting the Pick-3 at least a third of the time. That is, this strategy demands that you hit this bet more than 33 percent of the time! If you have a 70 percent probability of hitting any single race, it follows that you have 70 percent of 70 percent of 70 percent chance of hitting three races in a row (70 percent of 70 percent is 49 percent; 70 percent of 49 percent is 34.3 percent)! Imagine cashing this bet more often than the public cashes a 2-to-1 post-time favorite! That's exactly what this strategy forces you to do. The advantages are threefold: First, you can hit the Pick-3 multiple times; second, you won't suffer too many long losing streaks; third, your bet size for each Pick-3 remains stable. The disadvantage is the fact that this strategy requires a healthy-sized bet. ($100 is a rational minimum. If you have a small bankroll, it'll be necessary to find partners.)

The basic idea is to combine fundamental handicapping with good betting. Your fair-odds line is the key to this strategy. (A fair-odds line is your estimation of what the odds should be for each contender to be a fair bet.) You simply handicap all three races and make a line on each race. You use all horses in a single race until you cover at least 70 percent of the probability. If the number of combinations exceeds 48, it's best to pass. The public's choice of favorite is a critical issue. Never purchase a ticket that includes all three public favorites; never even purchase a ticket that contains two favorites. The maximum number of favorites that you'll ever use on any single ticket is one. More on that later.

What follows is bit theoretical and somewhat complicated. Don't be put off. If you don't understand the math, don't be concerned. The concepts are important, not the numbers.

We already know how to calculate the probability of each combination given the win odds from our fair-odds line. We simply multiply the reciprocal of the (odds-to-1 + 1) for each of the three horses. Suppose our fair-odds lines for the three races were as follows:

Leg 1	Leg 2	Leg 3
A 2	A 8-5	A 4
B 3	B 3	B 4
C 4	C 6	C 4
		D 4

Please note: These fair odds lines each add up to more than 70 percent. That's okay. We try as best we can to get at least 70 percent per race. In this case the first leg adds to .7833, the second leg adds to .7775, and the third leg adds to .8. Therefore our chance of hitting this Pick-3 is .7833 × .7776 × .8, or is .4872. There are 36 possible bets and associated probabilities. They are:

Combination	(Win odds in each race)			Probability
AAA	2	1.6	4	.025641
AAB	2	1.6	4	.025641
AAC	2	1.6	4	.025641
AAD	2	1.6	4	.025641
ABA	2	3	4	.016666

Combination	(Win odds in each race)			Probability
ABB	2	3	4	.016666
ABC	2	3	4	.016666
ABD	2	3	4	.016666
ACA	2	6	4	.009523
ACB	2	6	4	.009523
ACC	2	6	4	.009523
ACD	2	6	4	.009523
BAA	3	1.6	4	.019230
BAB	3	1.6	4	.019230
BAC	3	1.6	4	.019230
BAD	3	1.6	4	.019230
BBA	3	3	4	.0125
BBB	3	3	4	.0125
BBC	3	3	4	.0125
BBD	3	3	4	.0125
BCA	3	6	4	.007142
BCB	3	6	4	.007142
BCC	3	6	4	.007142
BCD	3	6	4	.007142
CAA	4	1.6	4	.015384
CAB	4	1.6	4	.015384
CAC	4	1.6	4	.015384
CAD	4	1.6	4	.015384
CBA	4	3	4	.01
CBB	4	3	4	.01
CBC	4	3	4	.01
CBD	4	3	4	.01
CCA	4	6	4	.005714
CCB	4	6	4	.005714
CCC	4	6	4	.005714
CCD	4	6	4	.005714
				.487200

Please note that the sum of these probabilities checks with the total already calculated. The combination AAA means our first choice in the first leg with our first choice in the second leg with our first choice in the third leg. The combination ABC means our first choice in the first leg with our second choice in the second leg with our third choice in the third leg. The combination CBD means our third choice in the first leg with our second choice in the second leg with our fourth choice in the third leg, and so on.

Let's calculate a few of these combinations so you'll know how to do it manually in case your computer goes down.

To calculate the probability of the ACD combination, we multiply the probability of A winning the first leg by the probability of C winning the second leg by the probability of D winning the third leg. If we know odds, we know probabilities and vice versa. To convert odds to probabilities, simply add the quantity 1 to the odds-to-1 and take its reciprocal.

$$\text{Probability} = \frac{1}{\text{"Odds-to-1"} + 1}$$

$$\text{Probability (ACD)} = \frac{1}{(A + 1) \times (C + 1) \times (D + 1)}$$

$$\text{Probability (ACD)} = \frac{1}{(2 + 1) \times (6 + 1) \times (4 + 1)}$$

$$= \frac{1}{105} = .009523$$

Let's do one more. Let's calculate the probability of hitting the BCA combination.

$$\text{Probability (BCA)} = \frac{1}{(B + 1) \times (C + 1) \times (A + 1)}$$

$$\text{Probability (BCA)} = \frac{1}{(3 + 1) \times (6 + 1) \times (4 + 1)}$$

$$= \frac{1}{140} = .007142$$

We now must choose how much to bet on each combination. From these examples it should be apparent that it's not too smart to bet the same amount on ACD as you would on BCA, since ACD is 3.5 times more likely than BCA. That's the problem with buying a 3-by-3-by-4 ticket. You're betting the same amount of money on each combination, thereby implying that all the combinations are equally probable. A fundamental principle of money management states that your bet size is a function of your probability of success. The more likely your chances of success, the more money you can bet as a percentage of your capital. We'll bet in direct proportion to our chances of winning the bet. To calculate the bet size for each combination, we divide the probability of hitting that particular combination into the total probability of success. Assume that we are playing the $3 Pick-3 at Santa Anita and that we are investing $200 in this wager. Consider the following table:

Combination	P(W)	% of TB	Bet Size	Actual Bet
AAA	.025641	.052627	10.52552	11
AAB	.025641	.052627	10.52552	11
AAC	.025641	.052627	10.52552	11
AAD	.025641	.052627	10.52552	11
ABA	.016666	.034207	6.84159	7
ABB	.016666	.034207	6.84159	7
ABC	.016666	.034207	6.84159	7
ABD	.016666	.034207	6.84159	7
ACA	.009523	.019547	3.90948	4
ACB	.009523	.019547	3.90948	4
ACC	.009523	.019547	3.90948	4
ACD	.009523	.019547	3.90948	4
BAA	.01923	.03947	7.894143	8
BAB	.01923	.03947	7.894143	8
BAC	.01923	.03947	7.894143	8
BAD	.01923	.03947	7.894143	8
BBA	.0125	.025655	5.131193	5
BBB	.0125	.025655	5.131193	5
BBC	.0125	.025655	5.131193	5
BBD	.0125	.025655	5.131193	5
BCA	.007142	.01466	2.93211	3
BCB	.007142	.01466	2.93211	3
BCC	.007142	.01466	2.93211	3
BCD	.007142	.01466	2.93211	3
CAA	.015384	.031576	6.315314	6
CAB	.015384	.031576	6.315314	6
CAC	.015384	.031576	6.315314	6
CAD	.015384	.031576	6.315314	6
CBA	.01	.020524	4.104954	4
CBB	.01	.020524	4.104954	4

Combination	P(W)	% of TB	Bet Size	Actual Bet
CBC	.01	.020524	4.104954	4
CBD	.01	.020524	4.104954	4
CCA	.005714	.011728	2.345688	3
CCB	.005714	.011728	2.345688	3
CCC	.005714	.011728	2.345688	3
CCD	.005714	.011728	2.345688	3
Totals	.487216	1.000000	200	204

The first column represents your bet. The first letter represents your choice in the first leg, the second letter represents your choice in the second leg, and the third letter represents your choice in the third leg. For example, AAC means to bet on your first choice in the first leg with your first choice in the second leg with your third choice in the last leg. (Your choices for each leg are listed in alphabetical order.) "P(W)" stands for the probability that the combination in column one will win; "% of TB" stands for the percentage of the total bet (probability of winning divided by total success probability). "Bet Size" stands for the percentage of total bet multiplied by the total bet. (This number is calculated in cents and must be rounded to the nearest dollar.) "Actual Bet" is the rounded-off Bet Size amount, which also takes the minimum bet size ($3) into consideration.

Let's calculate how we arrived at the BBD bet size. The probability of hitting the BBD combination is .0125. We divide this number by .487216, which is the total of the probabilities of all the combinations (total probability of success). The answer is .0257. This means that we should bet 2.57 percent of our total bet on this particular combination. Since we have assumed that our total bet is $200, we should bet 2.57 percent of $200 on this combination, which is $5.13. We can't bet $5.13 exactly. Therefore, we must round this bet to the nearest dollar.

Now consider the CCD combination. The probability of hitting it is .005714. We divide this number by .487216, the total probability of success. The answer is .0117. We should bet 1.17 percent of $200 on this combination, or $2.34. We can't bet less than $3. Therefore we must convert any combination that calculates out to less than the minimum bet into the minimum bet. This means that we usually bet a little more than our target-bet size. In this example, the total came to $204.

The problem with this strategy is that it requires a substantial bet size. In this example, suppose you wanted to bet a total of $50 on the Pick-3. You couldn't. Remember, we're betting on 32 combinations. This requires a $96 bet at minimum in California and a $64 bet in most states. (The minimum bet on all combinations would defeat the purpose of this strategy.)

One last wrinkle. You don't want to bet on the favorite-favorite-favorite combination or even use two favorites on any one ticket. It's usually a giant underlay. The reason will become clear in just a few moments.

What's apparent is that this strategy absolutely requires a healthy bet size plus mathematical wizardry (or a lot of grunt work the night before). Enter the computer, for which these calculations are duck soup. Simply enter your odds lines for each race and presto, the computer prints out the amount that you should bet on each combination. (The *Bettor-Handicapper* makes this process a snap.) It's no wonder that Ambrose wasn't too fond of my solution, although I've used this method very successfully. The very first time I did, I hit an $880 Pick-3, which needless to say compensated me for the $350 I paid for the palm-top computer that I use to execute this strategy.

Strategy #2—Modified Ambrose Strategy

The notion of a key horse was appealing. This means that you can hit this bet multiple times. When I looked at Ambrose's Key-4-4 Pick-3 strategy, the idea of 45 minimum guaranteed losing bets of the same size drove me crazy. My goal was to cut the amount of losing bets in half. At that time, the Pick-3 was paying a typical average of $700, but I knew that it wouldn't last. The players were bound to get better and hence the average odds would drop.

I thought about the Sartin Methodology's goal of 63 percent winners using only two horses. This goal seemed much too ambitious in the light of the reality that the public needs three horses to get near 66 percent. (Unfortunately, many Sartin acolytes get very discouraged because they can't seem to achieve their avowed goal.)

It occurred to me that 60 percent winners using three horses would be a realistic goal. This means that you can be 90 percent as good as the public and still meet your objectives. Also, 30 percent winners with one horse seems to also be a realistic goal (not easy, but achievable).

Putting these ideas together, I came up with the Key-3-3 strategy. It greatly reduces the number of guaranteed losing bets while preserving the opportunity to hit the Pick-3 multiple times. It also has the virtue of being a selection-oriented method that doesn't require a computer to figure out how to make the bet. Given that you have the winner 60 percent of the time using three horses and 30 percent of the time using only one horse, you should hit this bet 32.4 percent of the time. In order to make a decent profit, the typical Pick-3 must pay in the neighborhood of 100-to-1. Let's look at your expectation at Santa Anita if the typical Pick-3 were to average $300 (it averages more).

$$E(X) = .324 \times (300/81) - .676 = .524$$

The only restriction is to make sure that no more than one of your key horses are public favorites.

Let's now look at the actual data from the 1992–1993 meeting at Santa Anita. WO1 stands for win odds in first leg. WO2 stands for win odds in second leg. WO3 stands for win odds in third leg. #F stands for the number of public favorites involved in the Pick-3. (This number can range from zero to three.) ACTUAL is what the Pick-3 actually paid. PARLAY is what you would have been paid if you had bet a three-horse parlay. In other words, take the proceeds from the first winner and bet it all to win on the second winner and then take the proceeds and bet them all to win on the third winner. VALUE tells you if the actual price exceeded the parlay price. If it didn't, the payoff was an underlay.

WO1	WO2	WO3	#F	Actual	Parlay	Value
5.0	7.1	1.0	1	288.60	291.60	underlay
3.7	9.5	3.3	0	988.40	636.62	overlay
10.9	0.9	2.8	1	240.00	257.75	underlay
1.0	20.0	0.9	2	437.40	239.40	overlay
1.4	2.3	1.8	1	80.10	66.53	overlay

WO1	WO2	WO3	#F	Actual	Parlay	Value
0.8	3.2	1.5	2	74.10	56.70	overlay
2.1	2.1	8.5	1	451.50	273.89	overlay
11.5	8.9	1.6	1	2,239.80	965.25	overlay
29.8	5.2	3.4	0	4,231.80	2,520.67	overlay
5.7	2.9	2.2	0	390.30	250.85	overlay
8.8	1.9	6.3	1	762.30	622.40	overlay
4.4	14.7	1.4	1	1,362.90	610.42	overlay
0.9	19.1	4.8	1	931.80	664.51	overlay
1.2	4.8	8.9	1	616.50	378.97	overlay
0.8	1.7	4.2	2	53.70	75.82	underlay
4.6	2.1	43.2	0	5,779.80	2,301.94	overlay
2.3	1.4	3.6	1	102.90	109.30	underlay
6.4	1.6	2.3	2	312.60	190.48	overlay
1.7	10.0	4.7	1	848.40	507.87	overlay
18.9	5.3	6.5	0	2,905.50	2,820.83	overlay
5.9	1.9	2.1	1	378.00	186.09	overlay
4.1	1.9	1.2	2	150.00	97.61	overlay
2.4	1.2	2.4	1	69.30	76.30	underlay
3.9	1.8	2.2	0	152.40	131.71	overlay
3.2	7.7	2.5	1	408.60	383.67	overlay
6.4	1.1	1.8	1	141.00	130.54	overlay
1.6	65.5	11.3	1	17,742.90	6,380.01	overlay
6.7	2.8	3.2	1	961.50	368.68	overlay
2.4	7.2	3.3	0	517.80	359.65	overlay
2.8	19.5	1.3	1	875.10	537.51	overlay
1.6	3.1	2.7	2	113.70	118.33	underlay
1.1	1.9	1.5	3	55.50	45.68	overlay
2.7	3.1	3.3	0	333.90	195.69	overlay
1.1	1.6	1.5	3	47.40	40.95	overlay
3.5	4.2	3.3	0	668.40	301.86	overlay
2.5	9.0	2.3	0	464.70	346.50	overlay
3.5	3.3	3.7	0	283.80	272.84	overlay
0.9	1.6	0.9	3	33.00	28.16	overlay
8.8	1.1	2.9	2	342.90	240.79	overlay
8.1	2.6	1.1	1	305.40	206.39	overlay
12.0	12.7	6.0	0	6,654.30	3,740.10	overlay
4.3	2.8	2.5	0	416.10	211.47	overlay

WO1	WO2	WO3	#F	Actual	Parlay	Value
1.8	0.6	6.8	1	93.00	104.83	underlay
3.3	0.9	0.8	2	64.50	44.12	overlay
0.7	17.4	4.1	1	401.70	478.58	underlay
0.6	1.9	4.7	2	139.50	79.34	overlay
2.5	5.3	2.2	1	346.50	211.68	overlay
7.2	0.7	1.5	2	123.60	104.55	overlay
4.2	14.1	9.1	0	3,191.10	2,379.16	overlay
5.4	5.5	15.6	0	3,596.40	2,071.68	overlay
3.4	5.6	10.3	0	835.50	984.46	underlay
4.2	26.3	8.6	0	8,927.70	4,088.45	overlay
5.1	3.0	10.4	0	1,854.00	834.48	overlay
1.5	2.3	2.9	2	186.60	96.52	overlay
1.3	3.6	16.0	1	1,053.90	539.58	overlay
3.2	0.7	0.9	2	31.20	40.70	underlay
0.6	3.5	20.3	1	418.20	460.08	underlay
2.7	2.7	1.3	1	129.60	94.46	overlay
2.2	2.7	6.2	0	179.40	255.74	underlay
1.3	3.7	2.7	1	126.90	119.99	overlay
2.9	4.1	1.5	1	221.40	149.17	overlay
1.5	2.5	16.2	1	2,370.00	451.50	overlay
2.2	1.0	1.6	2	57.90	49.92	overlay
5.4	4.5	1.0	1	279.90	211.20	overlay
1.5	8.5	3.7	1	964.50	334.88	overlay
6.5	9.7	1.1	1	840.90	505.58	overlay
0.7	4.8	2.6	1	129.60	106.49	overlay
1.1	7.6	3.3	1	255.90	232.97	overlay
6.3	5.6	3.4	0	1,398.30	635.98	overlay
0.9	2.5	0.9	2	48.90	37.91	overlay
14.5	5.8	7.6	0	4,244.40	2,719.32	overlay
5.4	1.3	2.3	1	206.70	145.73	overlay
2.0	1.1	2.9	1	56.40	73.71	underlay
2.2	0.4	1.8	2	40.20	37.63	overlay
3.1	16.3	4.7	0	1,521.60	1,212.90	overlay
2.0	2.0	0.5	3	60.60	40.50	overlay
2.0	149.1	2.8	0	5,876.70	5,133.42	overlay
3.6	1.2	11.0	1	492.00	364.32	overlay
2.0	1.3	3.3	1	142.80	89.01	overlay

WO1	WO2	WO3	#F	Actual	Parlay	Value
1.7	0.9	1.7	3	33.90	41.55	underlay
0.4	1.6	11.9	2	125.10	140.87	underlay
1.1	0.7	6.3	2	84.00	78.18	overlay
2.2	5.3	30.0	0	1,865.10	1,874.88	underlay
19.6	9.8	2.1	1	2,910.00	2,069.06	overlay
2.1	0.7	3.4	1	86.70	69.56	overlay
24.4	3.1	15.9	0	6,238.50	5,279.90	overlay
1.0	1.9	2.0	3	64.20	52.20	overlay
6.7	1.1	2.3	2	282.60	160.08	overlay
11.5	1.6	76.8	1	9,350.70	7,585.50	overlay
2.4	2.9	0.9	1	70.80	75.58	underlay
8.8	1.3	9.8	1	1,155.00	730.30	overlay
5.8	4.7	5.1	0	1,013.40	709.31	overlay
1.1	2.4	16.3	2	648.90	370.57	overlay
0.8	7.8	7.0	1	625.80	380.16	overlay
3.2	2.0	6.1	1	452.10	268.38	overlay
15.3	19.0	4.7	0	7,802.70	5,574.60	overlay
0.4	4.9	3.9	1	197.10	121.42	overlay
4.0	1.2	2.2	1	117.60	105.60	overlay
1.2	0.9	5.9	2	84.00	86.53	underlay
4.1	7.1	1.6	1	488.10	322.22	overlay
1.0	4.1	11.8	1	533.70	391.68	overlay
1.0	2.0	8.2	2	192.00	165.60	overlay
9.5	9.6	1.2	1	625.80	734.58	underlay
7.9	0.7	1.8	1	198.90	127.09	overlay
1.0	6.8	2.3	2	579.90	154.44	overlay
2.8	4.6	0.7	1	122.10	108.53	overlay
2.0	6.8	2.8	0	580.20	266.76	overlay
0.7	16.5	3.8	1	653.40	428.40	overlay
2.8	4.6	3.2	1	300.90	268.13	overlay
0.9	20.6	0.6	2	269.40	196.99	overlay
2.5	3.0	7.0	0	403.80	336.00	overlay
1.6	8.4	1.7	1	225.00	197.96	overlay
0.6	3.2	4.3	1	155.40	106.85	overlay
4.1	3.7	4.9	0	817.80	424.27	overlay
2.1	1.3	5.7	1	141.60	143.31	underlay
1.2	1.0	6.9	2	129.30	104.28	overlay

WO1	WO2	WO3	#F	Actual	Parlay	Value
0.8	1.0	4.0	2	51.30	54.00	underlay
7.3	1.1	6.3	1	812.10	381.72	overlay
2.3	16.5	1.7	1	733.20	467.78	overlay
1.3	7.4	8.3	1	563.70	539.03	overlay
0.2	2.1	3.1	3	47.10	45.76	overlay
1.8	25.0	10.2	1	4,297.80	2,446.08	overlay
1.0	1.1	7.4	2	102.00	105.84	underlay
2.1	1.5	0.8	2	55.20	41.85	overlay
1.5	1.9	6.5	2	186.30	163.13	overlay
2.5	2.8	2.4	2	262.20	135.66	overlay
6.2	11.5	7.3	0	2,479.80	2,241.00	overlay
5.0	1.6	0.9	2	122.10	88.92	overlay
2.8	5.7	4.7	0	344.70	435.37	underlay
5.9	2.8	1.4	1	290.10	188.78	overlay
6.6	4.2	8.8	0	2,143.50	1,161.89	overlay
7.2	3.0	2.0	0	447.30	295.20	overlay
2.0	2.4	4.9	0	207.90	180.54	overlay
4.1	8.0	0.7	1	487.80	234.09	overlay
3.4	2.3	1.1	1	223.20	91.48	overlay
1.3	1.4	5.9	2	145.80	114.26	overlay
23.3	7.7	8.6	0	8,205.30	6,088.61	overlay
5.2	10.9	0.9	1	923.10	420.55	overlay
3.3	3.6	3.3	0	434.10	255.16	overlay
5.1	2.5	3.1	0	214.50	262.61	underlay
0.8	3.0	1.5	2	74.40	54.00	overlay
4.3	1.3	9.5	0	275.40	383.99	underlay
0.7	1.4	1.5	3	37.20	30.60	overlay
3.8	1.7	1.3	1	60.30	89.42	underlay
1.2	8.7	2.8	1	468.90	243.28	overlay
1.2	1.1	3.5	2	94.80	62.37	overlay
0.6	4.6	4.0	2	157.80	134.40	overlay
6.8	8.1	9.7	0	4,756.80	2,278.46	overlay
4.3	16.4	1.5	1	829.50	691.65	overlay
10.2	28.1	10.9	0	17,194.20	11,635.34	overlay
1.3	0.5	3.0	2	38.10	41.40	underlay
0.7	1.8	1.7	2	56.10	38.56	overlay
4.0	2.8	0.5	1	140.70	85.50	overlay

WO1	WO2	WO3	#F	Actual	Parlay	Value
1.8	2.6	23.4	1	799.20	737.86	overlay
5.6	2.4	6.9	0	537.30	531.83	overlay
1.0	2.0	2.9	2	167.40	70.20	overlay
0.9	3.8	2.6	2	136.50	98.50	overlay
2.4	19.9	1.4	2	772.40	511.63	overlay

If we break these data into four subsets depending on the number of winning favorites, some interesting results jump out at us:

# of Favorites	# of Races	# of Overlays	Average Mutuel
0	42	36	$2,651.78
1	69	57	961.98
2	39	31	179.34
3	8	7	47.36

This table summarizes the data with respect to the number of favorites involved in the Pick-3 at Santa Anita in 1993. These data are very typical. It's to be expected that the three-favorites combination is less likely than the two-favorites, which in turn is less likely than the one-favorite. Theory says that zero favorites should occur about 29.7 percent of the time. (The probability of an average non-favorite winning is .667; therefore the probability of three non-favorites in a row is $.667^3$, or .296. In this case, it happened 42 times out of 158, or 26.6 percent.) Theory says that we should hit three average favorites about 3.7 percent of the time. In this case we hit it eight times out of 158, or about 5 percent of the time. Theory says that we should get exactly one average favorite about 44 percent of the time. In this case, we got 69 out of 158, or 43.6 percent. Finally, theory says that we should get exactly two average favorites about 22 percent of the time. We got 40 out of 158, or 25 percent. (It's interesting that zero favorites are expected to occur more than two favorites.) This sample of Pick-3s is certainly representative.

It doesn't take a genius to see that the average mutuel is greatly affected by the number of favorites. The overall average mutuel of these 158 races was $1,171.68. If we throw out all the races that paid more than 1,000-to-1, the average mutuel would be reduced to $472.07 and the data would look as follows:

# of Favorites	# of Races	# of Overlays	Average Mutuel
0	29	23	$850.86
1	66	54	530.08
2	39	31	179.34
3	8	7	47.36

The above table should convince you of the wisdom of having only one or no favorites on your ticket. It should suggest the following rule: *Never purchase a Pick-3 ticket that contains more than one favorite.* It's a negative-expectation bet; it's for suckers, not for you.

This rule is the reason why any Pick-3 ticket I buy contains only one favorite at most. Any ticket that contains two or three favorites carries a long-run negative expectation under normal circumstances.

It's really important that you calculate these expectations for your track. It could be that favorites are running amok and that the normal expectations of .296, .444, .222, and .037 for zero favorites through three favorites respectively aren't reliable.

As far as handicapping is concerned, my method is the same no matter what track I happen to be at. I keep a winner's profile and know exactly what it takes to win at each class level, at each distance, and on each surface. Horses that meet the winning profile are contenders and horses that don't are throwouts. I make a line on every race that I handicap, except for chaos races. (A chaos race is a race in which no horse can run to the winner's profile. In chaos races, anything can happen and usually does. It's usually best to pass on them or try to hit a home run by playing the longest shots that seem to have a chance to win.)

Let's take a look at a couple of typical Pick-3s (I wish to thank my staff writer Steve Unite for providing the following examples). Please understand that you're going to lose at least two out of every three Pick-3 that you bet. These examples are provided for the purpose of showing you how to apply the material in this chapter. Please don't expect to cash every Pick-3 that you invest in, as we have done in these examples.

Try these races for yourself before you look up the correct answers. Next, use *ALL-IN-ONE*'s output to determine your fair-odds lines and see if you come to the same conclusions as Steve Unite.

The first leg, an allowance race for fillies and mares, was a short field.

6 FURLONGS. (1.07¹) ALLOWANCE. Purse $36,000. Fillies and mares. 4-year-olds and upward. Non-winners of $3,000 twice other than maiden or claiming. Weight, 121 lbs. Non-winners of two races other than claiming since December 15 allowed 2 lbs.; of a race other than maiden, or claiming since Februrary 1, 4 lbs.; such a race since January 1, 6 lbs.

LASIX—Seester, Mobile Phone, Priceless Picture, Pride and Power, Dinuba.

Seester
Ch. f. 4, by Pancho Villa—Talent Lima, by High Line
Br.—Smith Sarah Louise & Sheri L (Va)
Tr.—Palma Hector O (11 1 1 2 .09)
STEVENS G L (229 57 51 33 .25)
Own.—Van Doren Andrew & Paul
115

	Lifetime	1983	1	0	0	0	$750
	12 2 3 2	1982	6	1	1	1	$32,475
	$65,150						
	Wet	1	0	0	0	$2,475

Mobile Phone
B. m. 5, by Phone Trick—Madam Ask Us, by Damascus
Br.—Horn&Horn&Mandella (Ky)
Tr.—Chavez Tony (15 1 1 3 .07)
PEDROZA M A (248 35 34 34 .10)
Own.—Amen John B
115

	Lifetime	1983	3	0	0	2	$9,300
	23 6 2 2	1982	14	4	1	0	$50,325
	$100,275	Turf	1	0	0	0	
	Wet	2	1	0	0	$15,900

Sunday Sonata
Ch. f. 4, by Palace Music—Tuesday Evening, by Nodouble
Br.—Whitham Frank E (Ky)
Tr.—McAnally Ronald (92 15 18 14 .16)
PINCAY L JR (285 36 43 38 .16)
Own.—Whitham Mr-Mrs Frank E
115

	Lifetime	1983					
	10 2 0 1	1982	7	1	0	0	$26,150
	$44,100	Turf	2	0	0	0	
	Wet	2	0	0	0	$2,400

Priceless Picture
B. m. 5, by Kennedy Road—Snapshot, by Gummo
Br.—Old English Rancho (Cal)
Tr.—Warren Donald (28 3 3 3 .11)
McCARRON C J (289 35 32 39 .57)
Own.—Johnston Betty & E W & Judy
115

	Lifetime	1983	12	2	3	2	$58,425
	13 2 3 2	1981	1	0	0	0	
	$69,425	Turf	5	0	2	0	$14,200

Pride And Power
Ch. m. 5, by Raise a Champion—Dark Temptation, by Fleet Allied
Br.—Alvarez & Smith (Cal)
Tr.—Sadler John W (63 11 10 9 .17)
SOLIS A (267 30 40 39 .11)
Own.—Alvarez & Smith
115

	Lifetime	1983	1	1	0	0	$12,650
	6 3 1 0	1982	5	2	1	0	$33,100
	$45,750	Turf	1	0	0	0	

Dinuba B. f. 4, by Seattle Dancer—Love Bunny, by Exclusive Native
Lifetime 7 2 2 1 $50,500 | 1993 1 0 0 0 | 1992 6 2 2 1 $50,500 | Turf 1 0 0 0
DELAHOUSSAYE E (217 40 29 33 .18) Br.—Ballenger & Campion (Ky) 115
Own.—Nicoletti & Quinn Tr.—Mandella Richard (61 13 14 9 .21)

31Jan93- 5SA fm *6½f ①:222 :45 1:141 ⓕAlw 36000 67 4 5 52¾ 52¼ 55½ 1010¾ Delahoussaye E LB 118 *1.40 76-13 MloMlody1174ChmmyRck1151LynTThMn115 Gave way 10
31Dec92- 8SA gd 6f :22 :444 1:094 3↑ⓕAlw 34000 96 2 6 56¼ 43¾ 3½ 15 Delahoussaye E L 118 2.20 87-19 Dnb1185Trdncr121hdSrosOnThTwn118 Wide, ridden out 7
3Dec92- 7Hol fst 6½f :22 :44 1:134 3↑ⓕAlw 31000 47 1 5 41½ 22½ 310 722¾ McCarron C J LB 118 1.30 80-08 ArchsOfGold1189Gusto'sGlmor1184Arkng118 Gave way 7
18Nov92- 7Hol fst 6f :213 :434 1:084 3↑ⓕAlw 31000 95 1 7 56½ 46 34 21¼ McCarron C J LB 119 2.50 95-09 WalkOfFame1161¼Dinub1193½DelightfulCndy116 Rallied 8
15Oct92- 3SA fst 6½f :222 :451 1:161 3↑ⓕAlw 30000 84 3 4 2hd 1hd 2hd 2nk Desormeaux K J LB 117 6.10 89-14 Shes A Sure Bet117nk Dinuba1172¼ Striker117 6
15Oct92-Brushed twice drive
12Sep92- 4Dmr fst 6f :221 :452 1:103 3↑ⓕMd Sp Wt 77 6 2 11 11½ 11 1hd Desormeaux K J LB 118 *1.60 86-12 Dinub118hdWindInMyHir1182½StrletGm118 Held gamely 10
29Aug92- 6Dmr fst 6½f :22 :451 1:171 3↑ⓕMd Sp Wt 67 4 5 31 11 11 33¾ Desormeaux K J B 118 7.60 83-12 Corpus Christi1183¼ Wind In My Hair118nk Dinuba118 8
29Aug92-Wide early, rider briefly lost hold on rein 1/16
LATEST WORKOUTS Mar 6 SA 6f fst 1:15 H Feb 27 SA 6f gd 1:152 H (d) ●Feb 18 SA tr.t 5f fst 1:003 H Feb 11 SA 4f fst :484 H

The next race was a $40,000 claimer for four-year-olds and upward.

4

1 1/16 MILES
SANTA ANITA
START FINISH

1 1/16 MILES. **(1.39) CLAIMING. Purse $30,000. 4-year-olds and upward. Weight, 121 lbs. Non-winners of two races at one mile or over since January 1 allowed 2 lbs.; of such a race since February 1, 4 lbs.; since January 1, 6 lbs. Claiming price $40,000; if for $35,000 allowed 2 lbs. (Maiden or races when entered for $32,000 or less not considered.)**

LASIX—San Fran's Halo, Sounds Fabulous, Babyitscoldoutside, Icy Resolution, Northern Tract, William's Buckaroo, Govern.

San Fran's Halo Dk. b. or br. g. 4, by Sunny's Halo—Whispering Tout, by Tout
Lifetime 12 2 2 3 $47,900 | 1993 3 0 1 0 $7,175 | 1992 8 2 1 3 $40,725 | Turf 1 0 0 1 $4,950 | Wet 1 0 0 0 $2,775
VALENZUELA P A (198 39 26 23 .15) $40,000 Br.—Brown & Goldstein & Power & Stolich (Cal) 115
Own.—Friendly Ed Tr.—Hendricks Dan L (36 6 5 3 .17)

21Feb93- 9SA gd 1 1/16 :462 1:114 1:442 Clm 25000 90 9 9 65½ 32¾ 1½ 2hd Delahoussaye E LBb 116 7.20 82-21 CghtDStr117hdSnFrn'sHlo1165ArEnrgy115 Sharp effort 11
3Feb93- 7SA fst 1 1/16 :462 1:102 1:424 Alw 36000 85 5 9 99 87¾ 911 89¾ Nakatani C S LBb 117 40.70 81-16 FndrsFrtn1282ApchTlsn1172¼GldnVr121 4-wide stretch 11
6Jan93- 3SA sly 1 1/16 :454 1:09 1:39 Alw 37000 74 2 5 66 58¾ 47 414¼ Stevens G L LBb 117 11.20 95-05 Efrvscnt-Ar1186GldnVgr1216Wllm'sBckr117 No mishap 7
18Dec92- 3Hol fst 1 1/16 :463 1:113 1:43 3↑ⓢAlw 33000 77 1 2 23½ 21¾ 43 49¼ Stevens G L LBb 115 3.90 76-14 Coco'sMinMn1173Intercup1183Jo'sRomnc115 Gave way 6
18Dec92-Originally scheduled on turf
20Nov92- 5Hol fm 1 1/16 ①:471 1:113 1:432 3↑ⓢAlw 33000 84 1 7 74½ 54 42¼ 31¼ Stevens G L LBb 115 3.40 77-22 TurnTheKey118nkJo'sRomnc1161SnFrn'sHlo115 Rallied 8
7Nov92- 2SA fst 1½ :483 2:042 2:302 3↑ⓢCal Cp Str H 88 9 8 87 63 42 46 Stevens G L LBb 114 10.60 85-17 HisLegcy1172WorryFre1181Coco'sMinMn115 Wide trip 9
8Oct92- 2SA fst 1 1/16 :46 1:103 1:424 Clm 25000 82 6 7 74½ 31 1hd 1hd Delahoussaye E LBb 117 8.30 89-13 San Fran's Halo117hd Lesaros1171½ Book Publisher117 9
8Oct92-4-wide 3/8, lugged in lane
27Aug92- 2Dmr fst 1 1/16 :463 1:114 1:442 3↑ⓢMd 28000 77 6 8 66½ 53 11½ 14 Desormeaux KJ LBb 116 2.60 79-24 San Fran's Halo1164 Crystal Wes118hd How Tacky120 8
27Aug92-Wide to drive, lugged in lane, driving
7Aug92- 2Dmr fst 6f :22 :452 1:101 3↑ⓢMd 32000 61 2 10 75½ 64½ 44½ 36¼ Desormeaux KJ LBb 116 *1.50 82-12 Mchote1166Shmoon114nkSnFrn'sHlo116 Edged for 2nd 12
LATEST WORKOUTS Mar 11 SA 4f fst :483 H Mar 5 SA 4f fst :484 H Feb 16 SA 4f fst :484 H Jan 31 SA 4f fst :483 H

Sounds Fabulous B. h. 5, by Somethingfabulous—Conky Johnston, by Majestic Prince
Lifetime 21 4 1 3 $191,410 | 1993 2 0 0 0 $2,475 | 1992 8 0 0 1 $15,125 | Turf 10 1 0 0 $36,875 | Wet 2 1 0 1 $28,250
MCCARRON C J (207 35 32 50 .17) $40,000 Br.—Old English Rancho (Cal) 115
Own.—Johnston Betty & E W & Judy Tr.—Warren Donald (28 3 3 3 .11)

27Feb93- 2SA gd 1 1/16 :484 1:112 1:424 Clm 50000 86 3 5 44½ 43 32½ 43¾ Nakatani C S LB 116 4.70 86-10 LIOn-Ar114¾PrcOfH1162½WllsBcr115 Wide backstretch 6
13Feb93- 7SA fm 1 ①:48 1:112 1:36 ⓢDbl Discount 80 1 7 79¾ 78½ 78½ 67¾ Solis A LB 114 4.80e 77-20 FxNws117¾Mystry'sEdg121¼J.F.Wllms116 Broke slowly 7
11Oct92- 5SA fm 1¼ ①:464 1:351 2:00 3↑Clm 62500 87 5 2 44 97¾ 98¼ 106¾ Atkinson P B 116 14.90 88-10 CnnonMn117½DrmOffm-Ir116½DputyMistr117 Faltered 10
19Sep92-11Fpx fst 1 1/16 :453 1:104 1:431 3↑P D Shepherd 78 7 5 54½ 54 611 611 Atkinson P B 115 5.40 81-08 C.SmMggio1159TretToblyft117½BlindPly115 No mishap 7
23Aug92-11Bmf fst 1 1/16 :46 1:10 1:411 3↑San Matean H 92 2 4 44½ 42 43½ 52¼ Warren R J Jr B 115 14.70 91-09 AtheniaGreen-En1171Charts120hdMakaleha114 No rally 5
27Apr92- 8SA fm 1⅛ ①:472 1:353 1:594 ⓢSn JacintoH 98 8 3 42½ 42 76 76¼ Nakatani C S B 114 62.90 81-20 MssnrRd-GR119¾FntcR-Ar1182 tArc116 4-wide stretch 8
11Apr92- 2GG fm 1 1/16 ①:463 1:103 1:411 + 3↑ⓢTiburon H 98 7 6 612 67½ 58½ 46½ Baze R A B 117 4.40 99 — Gum1166 Pes Blanc115no Impact116 Evenly late 7
22Mar92- 7SA sly 1 :463 1:112 1:372 ⓢCrsl Wtr H 96 2 6 66 57½ 36½ 36 Pincay L Jr B 117 5.40 75-25 NtvBoundry120hdGum1145SondsFblos117 Along for 3rd 6
20Feb92- 8SA fm 1 ①:453 1:092 1:332 Alw 55000 90 6 2 21 23 67½ 68½ Desormeaux K J B 120 11.00 87-04 TightSpot1211½LaxeyBy-Ir116noEtonLd-En114 Faltered 6
1Feb92- 7SA fm *6½f ①:214 :441 1:13 Alw 50000 91 4 8 811 89½ 77½ 54¾ Pincay L Jr B 120 28.30 89-07 HlldRprtr116nkHarThHr1161DcAdD-Ir119 Broke slowly 9
LATEST WORKOUTS Mar 7 SA 5f fst 1:02 H Feb 24 SA 4f gd :50 H Feb 7 SA 6f fst 1:131 H Feb 1 SA 1 fst 1:424 H

Babyitscoldoutside B. h. 7, by It's Freezing—Hail Babe, by Within Hail
Lifetime 48 9 7 9 $243,925 | 1993 4 0 1 1 $17,675 | 1992 12 4 1 1 $79,975 | Turf 5 0 0 1 $5,550 | Wet 4 3 0 0 $49,275
PINCAY L JR (266 36 43 38 .14) $40,000 Br.—Tackett R & P-Clark C (Ky) 115
Own.—Alexander or Team Green Tr.—Spawr Bill (69 13 15 6 .19)

13Feb93- 2SA fst 1 1/16 :464 1:111 1:423 Clm 40000 82 3 2 2hd 2hd 42 48¾ Nakatani C S LBb 116 4.00 82-15 Mr.P.AndMx1142IcyRsolution1165½GsMn116 Weakened 8
23Jan93- 6SA fst 1 1/16 :472 1:114 1:432 Clm 40000 91 6 3 32½ 33 33½ 22¼ Pincay L Jr LBb 117 4.30 85-18 Dvus1152¼Bbytscoldotsd117hdLovlyOn-Ar115 Wide trip 8
9Jan93- 7SA my 1 1/16 :471 1:121 1:443 Alw 41000 87 3 3 52½ 32½ 33 43½ Pincay L Jr LBb 117 *1.60 77-21 Spdbkr114¾BrghtDyBob1141½MjrLnch119 Broke slowly 7
1Jan93- 3SA fst 1 1/16 :474 1:114 1:424 Alw 41000 80 7 1 1½ 1hd 2hd 32¾ Pincay L Jr LBb 117 *2.00 87-07 RdMonson115¾Lsstk-Fr1182½Bbytscldtsd117 Weakened 7
19Dec92- 9Hol fst 1 1/16 :461 1:103 1:424 3↑Clm c-40000 77 7 4 41 2hd 51½ 67½ Pincay L Jr LBb 117 2.40 79-17 RunwyDnwy119¾PrncOfHony1161Flytoro116 Wide early 7
19Dec92-Claimed from Mevorach & Monroe, Sinne Gerald M Trainer
25Nov92- 7Hol fst 1 1/16 :463 1:111 1:421 3↑Clm 40000 95 4 2 22½ 1hd 1hd 2½ Valenzuela P A LBb 118 6.00 89-14 RunwyDunwy116½Bbytscoldotsd1183BdRd116 Game try 6
6Nov92- 6SA fst 1 :46 1:104 1:363 3↑Clm 45000 53 5 3 3½ 31½ 68 622¼ Valenzuela P A LBb 117 6.60 62-22 The Cleaners116¾ Blind Play1174 Buda Red116 Stopped 7
25Oct92- 2SA sl 1 :482 1:134 1:411 3↑Clm c-32000 91 1 1 1½ 1hd 11½ 11 Pincay L Jr LBb 117 2.10 61-43 Bbytscoldotsd1171Shynr-Ir1163Mr.P.AndMx118 All out 6
25Oct92-Claimed from Craig Sidney H, Spawr Bill Trainer
10Oct92- 3SA fst 1 :47 1:103 1:36 Clm 40000 90 1 3 33 34½ 34 42¾ Nakatani C S LBb 116 *1.70 84-17 HsLgcy117hdStlvy1172½RnwyDnwy116 Bumped in drive 6
5Aug92- 5Dmr fst 1 :462 1:103 1:36 3↑Alw 40000 86 5 3 62½ 52¾ 51½ 74½ Nakatani C S LBb 118 8.00 83-16 BckngBrd1181SbrnSmmr117nkPrt'sOtl118 Troubled trip 10
LATEST WORKOUTS Mar 6 SA 5f fst 1:012 H

Icy Resolution Ch. g. 7, by It's Freezing—All Decided, by Decidedly
Lifetime 29 6 5 5 $158,145 | 1993 3 0 1 0 $7,650 | 1992 10 3 2 3 $70,695 | Turf 2 0 0 0 $725 | Wet 3 0 1 1 $12,975
PEDROZA M A (240 26 34 34 .10) $40,000 Br.—Maggard & Santos (Ky) 115
Own.—Siegel Jan & Mace &Samantha Tr.—Mayberry Brian A (51 9 8 11 .18)

13Feb93- 2SA fst 1 1/16 :464 1:111 1:423 Clm 40000 93 2 5 52½ 51¾ 2½ 22 Pedroza M A LBb 116 12.20 89-15 Mr.P.AndMx1142IcyRsltn1165½GsMn116 4-wide stretch 8
23Jan93- 6SA fst 1 1/16 :472 1:114 1:432 Clm 40000 87 4 1 21 21½ 23 54¾ Pedroza M A LBb 115 4.10 82-18 Dvus1152¼Bbytscoldotsd117hdLovlyOn-Ar115 Weakened 8
2Jan93- 4SA my 1 :462 1:102 1:361 Clm 50000 94 5 3 31½ 43 43½ 52¾ Pedroza M A LBb 115 6.60 86-14 Desert Lover115¾ The Cleaners1171¾ Buda Red118 8
2Jan93-Bumped start, in tight 7/8, 4-wide
14Nov92-10Hol fm 1 1/16 ①:464 1:104 1:421 3↑Clm 50000 81 3 3 52½ 73¾ 72¾ 56¼ Pedroza M A LBb 115 9.80 78-15 BldlyEclInt1152½Rbnsk-NZ1141½TpBb115 Bumped start 10
21Oct92- 2SA fst 1⅛ :46 1:11 1:502 3↑Alw 40000s 91 3 3 33½ 32 2hd 1½ Pedroza M A LBb 120 3.20 78-22 IcyRsoltn120½Dvs120nkCc'sMnMn115 Lugged out drive 7
4Oct92-10Fpx fst 1 1/16 :461 1:113 1:442 3↑Alw 33000 85 3 3 31½ 21½ 11½ 33½ Pedroza M A LBb 121 *1.40 82-13 TheClenrs1211PrincOfHony1212½IcyResolution121 Hung 8
26Sep92-10Fpx fst 1 1/16 :461 1:104 1:432 3↑Alw 33000 96 3 3 32½ 33 32 2nk Pedroza M A LBb 121 2.40 91-13 ContrChck116nkIcyRsoltn121noStlvy121 Furious charge 6
8Aug92- 2Dmr fst 1 :454 1:101 1:36 3↑Clm 40000 92 1 3 3½ 11 1hd 1½ Pedroza M A LBb 116 6.40 87-11 IcRsltn116½KptHsCl1161¾Clch'sScrt118 Lugged out 3/16 8
15Jly92- 7Hol fst 1 1/16 :454 1:093 1:413 Clm 40000 91 3 5 54 44 34 34½ Pedroza M A LBb 116 7.10 88-12 Bbytscoldotsd1161SrvcAc1123½IcyRsoltn116 No mishap 7
13May92- 9Hol fst 1 1/16 :463 1:104 1:43 Clm 32000 95 2 2 33½ 32 32 22¾ Pedroza M A LBb 116 5.00 83-21 MjstcNsr1162¾IcyRsltn1163½StlshMjst117 Always close 9
LATEST WORKOUTS Mar 10 Hol 5f fst 1:01 H Mar 3 Hol 4f fst :494 H Feb 22 Hol 4f fst :504 H Feb 5 Hol 4f fst :483 H

Northern Tract

Dk. b. or br. c. 4, by Far North—Dead Letter, by Kirtling
Br.—Jones Brereton C (Ky)
Own.—Amon John B
$40,000
FLORES D R (238 29 20 40 .12)
Tr.—Chavez Tony (15 1 1 3 .07)
115

Lifetime				1993	3	0	0	1	$4,650
21	5	4	2	1992	8	3	3	1	$72,750
$110,750				Turf	3	0	0	1	$3,360
				Wet	1	0	0	1	$4,650

King Drone

Gr. h. 6, by Drone—English Girl, by Verbatim
Br.—Elssendorf Farm Inc (Ky)
Own.—McCarthy Daniel J
$40,000
TORRES H (57 3 8 9 .05)
Tr.—Brooks L J (9 0 0 1 .00)
115

Lifetime				1993	4	0	0	1	$6,525
24	4	2	1	1992	6	0	0	0	$7,025
$102,100				Turf	2	0	0	0	
				Wet	1	0	0	0	$8,950

William's Buckaroo

B. c. 4, by Spend a Buck—Doric Type, by Satari
Br.—Hunter Farm (Fla)
Own.—Horowitz Elliot J
$40,000
STEVENS G L (205 57 51 33 .28)
Tr.—Smith Michael R (25 3 2 7 .12)
115

Lifetime				1993	3	0	0	2	$11,400
6	1	0	2	1992	3	1	0	0	$10,700
$22,100				Turf	1	0	0	0	
				Wet	1	0	0	1	$5,550

Govern

Ch. g. 5, by Devil's Bag—Regent's Walk, by Vice Regent
Br.—Cox Edward A Jr (Ky)
Own.—Cahill & Gottsegen & Weitz
$40,000
DESORMEAUX K J (143 40 24 24 .28)
Tr.—Orman Mike (10 0 1 1 .00)
115

Lifetime				1993	2	0	0	0	$2,750
23	6	4	2	1992	13	5	2	1	$75,088
$88,216				Turf	2	0	0	0	$400
				Wet	6	1	1	0	$21,470

The final leg was a 6½-furlong turf sprint down the hill for $80,000 claimers.

ABOUT 6 ½ FURLONGS. (Turf). (1.11³) CLAIMING. Purse $38,000. 4-year-olds and upward. Weight, 121 lbs. Non-winners of two races since January 1 allowed 2 lbs.; of a race since February 1, 4 lbs.; since January 1, 6 lbs. Claiming price $80,000; for each $5,000 to $70,000 allowed 2 lbs. (Maiden or races when entered for $62,500 not considered.) (Non-starters for a claiming price of $25,000 or less in their last three starts preferred.)

LASIX—Despatch–Fr, Lackington–Ch, Record Boom, Sligo's Ridge, Centurion–Nz, Philadelphia Dave, Black Jack Attack, Bailarin, Fire Commander–Nz, Blue Tiger, Exemplary Leader.

Despatch–Fr

Dk. b. or br. g. 7, by African Song—Powder'n Patch, by Balidar
Br.—Prenn D (Fra)
Own.—Horowitz Elliot J
$70,000
BLACK C A (238 31 23 23 .13)
Tr.—Canani Julio C (44 6 10 6 .14)
111

Lifetime				1992	7	1	1	0	$23,000
38	7	4	9	1991	9	2	0	2	$57,575
$184,836				Turf	37	7	4	9	$184,836

Lackington–Ch

MCCARRON C J (287 35 32 58 .17)
Own.—Oniske & Scofield & Winner
Ch. h. 5, by Laguardia—Espinada, by Tantoul
$80,000
Br.—Haras Santa Amelia (Chile)
Tr.—Shulman Sanford (119 21 14 20 .18)
115

Lifetime	1993	2 0 1 1	$13,900
20 5 3 2	1982	11 1 2 1	$54,175
$136,991	Turf	17 5 1 2	$120,891
	Wet	1 0 1 0	$7,600

5Mar93- 7SA fm *6½f ⊕:214 :441 1:143	Clm 100000	94 2 6 32 32 32½ 3¾	McCarron C J	LB 115	17.10	86-15 DncngBoy114¾ShrkI15ᵐᵏLckngtn–Ch115 Edged for 2nd 8
14Feb93- 5SA fm *6½f ⊕:214 :434 1:134	Clm 75000	92 4 10 64½ 74½ 54 22½	Stevens G L	LB 115	43.20	87-12 RcktGbrltr116²¾Lcngtn-Ch115¾DncngB114 Good effort 12
13Dec92- 9Hol fst 1½ :461 1:103 1:424 3+Clm 40000		56 2 2 51¾ 77¾ 713 71¾	Pedroza M A	LB 115	9.50	67-17 RunwyDunwy119ᵏPrincOfHony116²Flytorio116 Faltered 7
14Nov92- 4Hol fst 1½ ⊕:464 1:104 1:421 3+Clm 40000		81 8 2 2½ 2ʰᵈ 1ʰᵈ 66¼	Flores D R	LB 115	7.80	78-15 BoldlyExcllnt115²¾Robnsk-NZ114¾TpBb115 Weakened 10
30Oct92- 9SA sly 1 :471 1:13 1:41 3+Clm 40000		79 1 2 2½ 35¾ 37½ 27	Pedroza M A	LB 116	*.60	55-37 Haky–Fr114⁷ Lackington–Ch116½ Big Barton114 3
30Oct92-Drifted out a bit 7/8						
27Sep92-11Fpx fst 1½ :46 1:11 1:423 3+ⓒ B Afirbgh		95 7 2 21¾ 21¾ 24 24	Pedroza M A	LB 117	8.70	91-14 MstrsEdg117⁴Lcntn–Ch117²Jrnlsm117 Not enough late 7
30Aug92- 5Dmr fm 1 ⊕:462 1:11 1:361 3+Clm 65000		95 3 5 35 42½ 32 53½	Flores D R	LB 115	13.70	87-10 ExclsvPrtmr116⁹YngHl-En117¾StL120 Not enough late 10
5Jly92- 5Hol fm 1 ⊕:471 1:112 1:344	Clm 115000	79 1 1 11½ 1½ 64 612¾	Flores D R	LB 115	8.20	78-10 SevenRivers114²Trts–Fr116¾DeputyMeister114 Faltered 6
19Jun92- 8Hol fm 1½ ⊕:463 1:10 1:401 Alw 45000		80 5 2 21½ 42 53½ 610¾	Delahoussaye E	LB 116	6.30	84-09 PrdntMnnr-Ir115⁴TmGntln-GB115¾Drssn115 Faltered 6
2May92- 8Hol fm 1½ ⊕:463 1:10 1:401 Clm 125000		97 2 1 21 1½ 1½ 1ⁿᵏ	Flores D R	LB 117	10.90	94-06 Lckington–Ch117¾HollywoodRportr117ᵏPhilippi–Fr117 6
2May92-Savaged by foe late						

LATEST WORKOUTS Feb 25 SA 5f gd 1:01³ H   Feb 10 SA 4f gd :48² H   Feb 2 SA 6f fst 1:13³ H   Jan 27 SA 6f fst 1:14⁴ H

Record Boom

STEVENS G L (279 57 51 33 .20)
Own.—Wygod Mr.-Mrs Martin J
Ch. g. 7, by Lord Avie—Krasnata, by Nijinsky II
$75,000
Br.—Meyglare Stud Farm Ltd (Ky)
Tr.—Hendricks Dan L (36 6 5 3 .17)
113

Lifetime	1982	2 1 0 1	$33,700
10 4 1 4	1986	5 1 1 2	$61,750
$130,800	Turf	6 2 1 2	$72,750

27Jan92- 8Hol fst 7f :221 :443 1:212 3+Trple Bnd H		98 3 4 62¾ 62½ 52½ 3½	Desormeaux K J	LB 114	5.00	96-10 SIThSrn111ʰᵏSftshSrSht114½RcrdB114 Boxed 5/16to1/8 8
27Jan92-Grade III						
23Nov92- 9Hol fm 5½f ⊕:213 :44 1:012	Clm 60000	99 6 8 63 63¾ 2½ 1¹	Alvarado F T	LB 115	12.20	98-02 RcrdBm115¹RffHmbr107¾Cntrn-NZ115 5-wide stretch 12
23Jly93- 8Hol fm 1½ ⊕:49 2:014 2:253 3+Sunset H		96 2 3 31½ 53¾ 65 55½	Garcia J A	L 114	13.60	80-11 Ptlt115¾LivThDrm116¾SoftMchn110 4-wide into lane 9
23Jly93-Grade II						
13Jly90- 7Hol fm 1¼ ⊕:48 1:363 2:003	ⒺJimMurrayH		99 4 9 9ʰ 84½ 52¾ 1¹¾	Garcia J A	LB 114	6.50	86-11 Shotiche114¹¾ RecordBoom114ⁿᵏKaboi115 Bumped 3/16 12
16Jun90- 9Hol fm 1¼ ⊕:474 1:113 1:471 3+Alw 41000		93 4 5 79½ 86½ 54¾ 1½	Berrio O A⁵		113	*2.00	85-13 Kboi116¹¾PolrBoy116½RecordBoom113 Clppd heels late 9
19May90- 4Hol fm 1¼ ⊕:463 1:362 2:003 3+Alw 25000		97 4 6 79¾ 86¾ 54¾ 1½	Delahoussaye E	LB 118	3.00	86-14 RoylRch118¹¾LvThDrm120ʰRcrdBm110 5-wide stretch 6
15Apr90- 7SA fst 1¼ :472 1:113 1:432	Alw 42000	93 1 5 64½ 54 32 1½	Delahoussaye E		116	5.00	86-12 RecordBoom116½WllAwr116ᵏAdvoctTrining116 Driving 7
25Nov89- 4Hol fm 1½ ⊕:471 1:11 1:481 3+Alw 28000		— 9 8 85¾ 85½ 33½ 11½	Delahoussaye E		116	*2.50	87-13 Record Boom11½ Timdala115¹ Speak High113 12
12Nov89- 7SA fst 1 :452 1:094 1:361 3+Alw 34000		— 3 7 7⁶ 56 44½ 77½	Delahoussaye E		116	3.60	78-16 ExplodingProspect110¾CollgCrdit111¾RcordBoom118 9
18Feb89- 6SA fst 7f :221 :451 1:241 Md Sp Wt		— 4 3 43¾ 53¾ 2½ 1³	Delahoussaye E		117	2.40	79-19 Record Boom117³ Lucky Lucky You117½ Try Trust117 9

LATEST WORKOUTS Mar 9 SA 5f fst 1:03 B   Mar 3 SA 4f fst :47¹ H   Feb 25 SA 4f gd :51¹ H   ●Feb 21 SA 7f gd 1:27² H

Notley–GB

VALENZUELA P A (198 30 26 23 .15)
Own.—Clear Valley Stables
B. g. 6, by Formidable—Riviere Bleue–Ir, by Riverman
$80,000
Br.—Grange Stud (GB)
Tr.—Shulman Sanford (119 21 14 20 .18)
115

Lifetime	1982	9 1 2 1	$35,132
20 5 4 1	1981	8 3 1 0	$128,822
$175,185	Turf	20 5 4 1	$175,185

7Nov92- 5Doncaster(Eng) gd 6f		1:134 ⊕ RemembranceDaysStks(L)		67¾	Raymond B	b 130	16.00	— — Blyton Lad 130¹ KeenHunter128¹ Garah121 Bid, evenly 17
13Oct92- 8Chepstow(Eng) gd 6f		1.14 ⊕ LesterPiggotAll–AgedStk(L)		3ⁿ	Raymond B	140	2.20	— — Montendre 140¹ Fylde Flyer 130ᵐᵏ Notley 140 No place 4
5Sep92- 3Doncaster(Eng) gd 5f		1:00¹ ⊕ Scarborough Stks (L)		1ⁿᵏ	Raymond B	b 133	7.00	— — Notley133ⁿᵏ HrvetGirl127¾ BlytonL133 Strong finish 12
28Aug92- 4Newmarket(Eng) gd 6f		1.123 ⊕ HopefulStks(L)		67¾	Lloyd J				— — Rose Indien 129¾ Hamas122¾ FyldeFlyer120 No threat 9
19Aug92- 8Deauville(Fra) sf*6f		1.14 ⊕ Prix de Meautry(Gr3)		9⁷	Mosse G	126		— — Twafej119ʰ Thourios121¹ AmigoMenor126 No threat 11
28Jly92- 3Goodwood(Eng) gd 6f		1:104 ⊕ W.HillStwCupHcp		136¾	Raymond R³	126	20.00	— — Lochsong110½ Duplicity123¾ Consiglie122 Speed early 17
17Jly92- 3Newbury(Eng) gd*6f		1:171 ⊕ Hackwood Stks(L)		2¾	Carson W	129	7.00	— — Montndr129² Notlyl122¾ BltOfALrk126 Bid, led, missed 13

LATEST WORKOUTS ●Mar 5 SA ⊕ 7f fm 1:34² H (d)   Feb 25 SA ⊕ 5f gd 1:17¹ H (d)   Feb 12 SA ⊕ 5f gd 1:17¹ H (d)   Feb 3 SA ⊕ 5f gd 1:01² H (d)

Sligo's Ridge

SOLIS A (267 38 48 39 .11)
Own.—Alpert H & H
B. g. 5, by Cox's Ridge—Sligo Town, by Baldski
$80,000
Br.—Green Thumb Farm Stable (Cal)
Tr.—Stute Melvin F (66 7 6 12 .11)
115

Lifetime	1993	3 0 0 0	$3,900
22 3 3 1	1982	9 3 1 0	$36,100
$88,000	1981	1 0 0 0	$88,423
	Wet	1 0 1 0	$8,250

25Feb93- 8SA fm *6½f ⊕:23² :462 1:231	Clm 85000	77 2 7 11 1½ 64 611¾	Solis A	LB 113	7.50	82-15 ProspctFrFr116¾Admrlls114¾Indvdlst116 Bobbled break 8
14Feb93- 5SA fm *6½f ⊕:214 :434 1:134	Clm 80000	89 1 6 41¾ 42½ 43¾ 44½	Solis A	LB 115	26.00	86-12 RcktGbrltr116¾Lcngtn–Ch115¾DncngB114 Always close 12
29Jan93- 8SA fm *6½f ⊕:211 :432 1:132	Alw 41000	64 6 2 31 3ʰ 89¾ 814¾	Pedroza M A	LB 115	20.70	76-09 WidHrmn110ᵐSrtGblr119²JsTrc117 Lugged out, wide 6
5Jly92- 7Hol fst 7f :221 :444 1:211 3+Handicap		53 4 2 21 2½ 511 521½	Pedroza M A	LB 115	24.50	76-14 Ljr117³Renegotiable111¾Lt'sGoFlying115 Bumped start 5
7Jun92- 8Hol fm *6½f ⊕:211 1:014 3+Handicap		76 9 8 79 79 911 99	Atkinson P	LBb 114	14.50	87-04 ForstGlow122ᵐSnnyBlossm120ⁿSchrnd119 Wide early 9
15Apr92- 8SA fm *6½f ⊕:213 :431 1:122 Alw 41000		91 1 4 32 31 44 44¾	Flores D R	LBb 116	16.00	92-03 Gogrty–Ir114¾Rogr Jn–NZ116ᵐNnCrt116 4-wide stretch 6
1Apr92- 5SA fm *6½f ⊕:211 :431 1:122 Alw 41000		98 8 6 54 54 76¾ 88½	Solis A	LB 114	7.50	80-14 RglGrm117ᵐ Gort–Ir114ⁿᵏHmmBrn-GB120 No mishap 7
22Mar92- 5SA sly 6½f ⊕:222 :46 1:162 Alw 41000		95 1 1 1¼ 21 2½ 21¾	Delahoussaye E	LB 114	2.00	88-10 LtestReles-Ir114¹¾Sligo'sRidg116¾RglginRj114 Set pace 3
22Mar92-Originally scheduled at about 6 1/2 furlongs on turf						
16Feb92- 8SA fst 6½f :22 .45 1:153 3+Rebs Policy H		71 1 2 1½ 1ʰᵈ 41½ 58½	Torres H	LB 113	4.40	83-10 HllywdRprtr116ᵏRnOnThBnk116¾Dyshts115 Gave way 7
16Feb92-Originally scheduled at about 6 1/2 furlongs on turf						
14Jan92- 5SA fm *6½f ⊕:213 1:123	Alw 36000	104 2 2 11½ 13 12 11½	Torres H⁵	LB 109	30.20	94-05 Sligo'sRidge109¹¾Mstercls119ᵐᵏRglGroom115 All out 10

LATEST WORKOUTS Mar 10 SA 4f fst :47¹ H   Feb 10 SA 5f gd 1:00¹ H   ●Feb 4 SA 6f fst :46³ H

Centurion–NZ

TORRES H (97 3 8 9 .03)
Own.—Mowrey & Savaglio Jr & Stewart
Dk. b. or br. g. 7, by Centaine—Watarose, by Stunning
$70,000
Br.—Keene Mr.-Mrs K B (NZ)
Tr.—Olivares Frank (30 2 1 3 .07)
111

Lifetime	1982	8 0 1 2	$19,850
23 4 3 4	1981	6 0 1 2	$8,577
$42,064	Turf	23 4 3 4	$42,064

4Jly92- 10Hol fm *6½f ⊕:214 :442 1:022 3+Clm 50000		85 7 1 43 31¾ 42¾ 62¾	McCarron C J	LBb 117	*3.10	90-05 BreakfstTble115²¾Xcret–Mx119¹½SmWho113 Wide trip 7
21Jun92- 10Hol fm *6½f ⊕:214 :441 1:022 3+Clm 62500		87 7 1 11¾ 41¾ 42¾ 42¾	Nakatani C S	LBb 117	9.20	94-03 ErnYrStrps117²RffHmbr115²¾Cntr–NZ117 Bobbled break 10
6Jun92- 2Hol fm *6½f ⊕:213 :432 1:021 3+Clm 62500		92 2 7 52¾ 81¾ 2½ 21	Nakatani C S	LB 117	3.90	95-04 Xcrt-Mx114¾Cntron-NZ117²RffHombr114 Finished well 9
23May92- 7SA fm *6½f ⊕:214 :433 1:131 3+Clm 62500		93 10 2 79¾ 54¾ 5²¾ 4¾	Mezz R Q	LB 115	5.90	88-08 RcordBm115¹RffHmbr107¾Cntrn–NZ117 Not disgraced 11
11Apr92- 10SA fm *6½f ⊕:214 :433 1:131	Clm 62500	93 10 2 79½ 54¾ 44½ 44	Nakatani C S	LB 115	13.90	85-08 SftshSrSht115¾BlcBts119½Rbns–NZ117 5-wide stretch 9
9Mar92- 6SA fm *6½f ⊕:214 :434 1:133	Clm 41000	88 8 1 7³¾ 55 54 42	Valenzuela P A	LB 114	13.00	85-09 Nkatani114¾Now stn114ᵐᵏRglGroom117 Bumped break 8
23Feb92- 6SA fm *6½f ⊕:212 :434 1:133	Alw 41000	102 1 3 42 31½ 21 11¾	Nakatani C S	LB 115	5.40	94-04 Qthif121²¾Reprcd114½PridOfArby116 Bumped break 10
22Jun92- 7SA fm 1 ⊕:453 1:091 3+Alw 40000		88 3 4 42 31¾ 31½ 53¾	Nakatani C S	B 115	5.40	88-10 PalosVerdes-Ar119⁴HeavyRin114ᵏChief'sImge-En116 9
4Dec91- 8Hol fm 1 ⊕:461 1:103 1:342 3+Alw 40000		88 3 4 42 31 31½ 2ⁿᵏ	Nakatani C S	LB 115	*2.00	80-10 PalosVerdes-Ar119⁴HeavyRin114ᵏChief'sImge-En116 9
4Dec91-Bumped, steadied 1/16						
16Nov91- 7Hol fm 1 :461 :444 1:023 3+Alw 36000		99 2 5 42 52¾ 61¾ 2ⁿᵏ	Nakatani C S	B 115	14.10	— — Thirty Slews116ᵏ Centurion–NZ115ᵏ Rushmore117 6
16Nov91-Lacked room 1/4–1/8, taken outside, ran on willingly						

LATEST WORKOUTS Mar 8 SA 6f fst :151 H   Feb 28 SA 6f fst 1:14¹ H   Feb 22 SA 5f gd 1:02⁴ H   Feb 16 SA 5f fst 1:02³ H

Philadelphia Dave

DESORMEAUX K J (143 40 24 24 .28)
Own.—Brown Rubin
Dk. b. or br. g. 4, by Swoon—Razee Rueez, by Don B
$80,000
Br.—Cannon Joseph H (Wash)
Tr.—Lewis Craig A (64 9 6 11 .14)
115

Lifetime	1993	2 0 0 0	$86,575
13 4 3 1	1982	11 4 3 1	$86,575
$86,575	Turf	2 1 0 1	$46,750
	Wet	2 0 1 0	$6,400

7Feb93- 5SA fm 1 ⊕:471 1:111 1:353	Alw 39000	83 1 4 42¾ 42¾ 54 97¾	Valenzuela P A	LB 118	3.30	79-13 Cork–Fr116¾ Tertian116¾ Region115 Gave way 10
17Jan93- 7SA sly 1 :461 1:12 1:39	Alw 41000	— 5 5 45¾ 64¾ 67¾	Black C A	LB 118	3.00	— — MjorLnch119⁹Rgn115⁶Efrvscnt-Ar119 Off slowly,eased 9
22Nov92- 3Hol fm 1½ ⊕:482 1:121 1:42 3+Alw 33000		91 5 3 32 2ʰᵈ 12 12½	Valenzuela P A	LB 118	*1.00	85-15 PhldlphDv118²¾TrblntKrs118³Mrfmtc118 Bumped 3/16 8
25Nov92- 7SA sl 1 ⊕:47 1:11 1:353 3+Alw 33000		91 1 3 32 32 21¾ 12¼	Desormeaux K J	LB 118	*1.00	85-15 Lssl–Fr116¾PhldlphD115¹⁴BdBtch115 Boxed in 3/8, 1/4 6
24Oct92- 7SA my 1½ :464 1:40 2:053 3+Alw 32000		93 3 4 32 31½ 2½ 1½	Desormeaux K J	LB 115	*.30	63-32 ShinkoWn116¹PhldlphDv115²¾BojyDwn116 Best of rest 6
24Oct92-Originally scheduled on turf						
9Oct92- 5SA fm 1½ ⊕:483 1:123 1:48 3+Alw 37000		84 5 3 32½ 52 42½ 41¾	Valenzuela P A	LB 117	*1.90	76-21 DoubleO'Slew114⁹Allawinir121ʰBaichall117 Took up 3/16 10
30Aug92- 5Dmr fst 1½ ⊕:483 1:131 1:433	Clm 62500	98 4 5 7³¾ 51¾ 1² 13½	Valenzuela P A	LB 117	*.50	87-15 PhildelphDv116¾3Bossnov119ᵏHetShild115 5-wide 2/10 10
21Aug92- 5Dmr fst 1 :453 1:094 1:351	Clm 62500	93 7 2 42½ 41½ 1½ 11	Valenzuela P A	LB 117	3.00	87-15 ChprI15ⁿᵏPheldphDv116¹¾GrnjGucho115 Sharp effort 8
21Aug92-Claimed from Webb Priscilla, Cofer Riley S Trainer						
31Jly92- 8Dmr fst 6½f :221 :444 1:153 Clm c-62000		85 7 1 52 52¼ 11½ 1½	Valenzuela P A	LB 117	7.60	95-11 PhildlphiDv117¾MusicKing116²¾ThDroulln115 Wide early 8
31Jly92-Claimed from Gennis & Lanni, Ellis Ronald W Trainer						

LATEST WORKOUTS Feb 15 SA 4f gd :48³ H   Feb 1 SA 6f fst 1:14² H   Jan 27 SA 4f fst :48² B

Black Jack Attack Ch. g. 7, by Beltron-Fr—Sweet Jenny, by Aloha Mood
PINCAY L JR (266 36 43 38 .14) $80,000 Br.—Winchell Verne H (Cal)
Own.—Cooperstone&Cooperstone&Lvin Tr.—Bean Robert A (9 1 1 1 .11) 115
Lifetime 36 10 6 3 $183,195 | 1993 2 0 0 0 $3,075 | 1992 11 3 2 2 $71,850 | Turf 7 1 1 1 $36,275

6Mar93- 4SA fm *6½f ①:212 :432 1:133 Alw 41000 92 10 1 2hd 2hd 3½ 84¼ Almeida G F LB 117 14.20 86-10 RealWest119noDesertSun-GB1171½LstLion115 Gave way 12
29Jan93- 8SA fm *6½f ①:211 :432 1:132 Alw 41000 91 4 4 44 44 44 43½ Pincay L Jr LB 119 5.00 87-09 WldHrmn118noSrtGmblr1192¾JsTrc117 Not enough late 10
26Dec92- 7SA fm *6½f ①:214 :434 1:133 3↑Alw 38000 99 6 4 31½ 33 31½ 1¾ Pincay L Jr LB 117 9.50 91-09 BlckJckAttck117¾SrtogGmblr1173½DncngBy115 Driving 8
11Dec92- 3Hol fst 6f :22 :45 1:093 3↑ⓈAlw 34000 90 1 3 21½ 21 22 4¾ Stevens G L LB 115 2.70 91-15 TotlTmpo116½DncngBshp115nkNrdcBl115 Always close 5
14Nov92- 5Hol fm 5½f ①:22 :442 1:023 3↑Alw 34000 80 6 1 41¾ 33½ 34½ 45½ Stevens G L LB 115 2.70 87-08 Fightcityhall1151¾ ⒹBullet Points1133 Dancing Boy116 7
14Nov92-Placed 3rd through disqualification; Wide 1/2, bumped, took up when severely crowded 3/8
7Nov92- 7SA fm 1 ①:454 1:094 1:344 3↑ⓈCal Cp MleH 85 1 4 73 106¾ 106½ 109¾ Flores D R LB 113 31.90 79-11 Blaze O'Brien1231½ Bruho1163 Impact115 Troubled trip 13
10Oct92- 4SA fm *6½f ①:22 :434 1:131 3↑Clm 80000 99 8 1 1½ 1hd 1hd 2no Flores D R LB 116 9.20 93-06 Ttsfld-Ir115noBlcJcAttc1161½BldCrrt113 4-wide stretch 10
14Sep92- 5Dmr fm 1⅙ ①:464 1:11 1:411 3↑ⓇSandshark H 86 1 1 21½ 31½ 42 68 Mitchell G V LB 116 25.00 92-05 Seti I.1191 Dream Of Fame-Ir1174 Davus117 Faltered 10
23Aug92- 3Dmr fst 6f :214 :443 1:09 3↑Clm 32000 98 2 3 33 33 31½ 1nk Stevens G L LB 120 2.50 94-08 BlckJckAttck120nkAbrgwunLd122noHisLgcy117 Got up 5
1Aug92- 2Dmr fst 6f :213 :443 1:092 3↑Clm 40000 81 7 2 44½ 54 62¾ 73¾ Stevens G L LB 119 *2.00 88-06 Let'sGoFlying115noBbRn115noHrlem'sBoy115 Wide trip 8
LATEST WORKOUTS Mar 1 SA 5f fst 1:022 H Jan 27 SA 3f fst :361 H

Bailarin Ch. g. 6, by Victory Stride—Proud Ballarina, by Marshua's Dancer
WALLS M K (161 18 13 21 .06) $75,000 Br.—Clifford P W (Tex)
Own.—Harrington L Dean Tr.—Dutton Jerry (16 2 3 0 .13) 115
Lifetime 32 10 3 5 $112,093 | 1993 3 1 0 0 $15,575 | 1992 5 1 1 0 $35,075 | Turf 3 0 0 1 $4,125 | Wet 3 1 1 0 $29,575

20Feb93- 8SA my 5½f :213 :442 1:023 El Conejo H 99 6 1 1hd 2hd 2½ 62½ Solis A LBb 113 6.30e 95-12 FblosChmp115½Arrowtwn117½Slrp117 Hopped at break 7
13Feb93- 8GG fst 6f :214 :444 1:093 3↑Albany H 79 1 3 2hd 2hd 4¾ 55½ Boulanger G LBb 114 6.60 87-12 DuToThKng114nkCndymnB1152½VldPlsr115 Brushed 1/4 6
16Jan93- 6BM sly 4½f :213 :443 :504 Snflwr Frm H 98 2 1 21½ 21 1no Boulanger G LBb 120 *1.40 — — Bilrin120noJimmy'sTrick1152½VlidPlsur115 Bumped 1/16 8
15Nov92- 7Hol fm 5½f ①:22 :44 1:021 3↑Alw 55000 87 1 1 1hd 2½ 23½ 56 Almeida G F LBb 115 14.40 88-06 Wtrscp1174Showbrk-Ir113hdLyphrdLgnd113 Weakened 7
31Oct92-13SA my 6½f :214 :444 1:164 Morvich H 81 3 1 11 11 21½ 24½ Almeida G F LBb 112 10.00 81-18 Regal Groom1184½ Bailarin1122 Repriced118 Held 2nd 4
31Oct92-Originally scheduled at about 6 1/2 furlongs on turf
26Sep92- 8BM fst 6f :213 :433 1:084 3↑B M Bd B C H 91 3 1 11 1hd 1½ 62½ Almeida G F LBb 112 23.60 90-14 Superstrike-GB114nk Anjiz114nk Naevus Star111 Tired 7
6Sep92- 1Dmr fst 6f :214 :443 1:09 3↑Clm 62500 103 2 1 12 11½ 12 1¾ Desormeaux K J LBb 116 7.20 94-11 Bailarin116¾ Bruho1162½ Express It115 Ridden out 6
25Jan92- 6BM fm 4½f ①:212 :45 :511 Alw 25000 66 7 1 21 47 610 Baze R A LBb 116 4.30 — — GldCrstExprss1154StlAnEmprr116½Dyshts116 Gave way 9
17Sep91-12Fpx fst 6f :221 :443 1:10 3↑Aprisa H 93 6 1 1hd 2hd 1hd 51½ Torres H LBb 113 7.50 95-14 SftshSrSht117hdThtsTO-GB115noMlr115 Lost whip 1/16 6
21Aug91- 7Dmr fst 5½f :202 :441 1:03 3↑Clm 100000 80 3 1 15 12 2hd 64¾ Torres H5 LBb 114 5.70 94-12 EprssIt1191½AskThMn115nkBlckJckRd116 Set fast pace 6
LATEST WORKOUTS Mar 8 SA 4f fst :484 H Feb 28 SA 3f fst :373 H Feb 10 SA 4f gd :531 H Feb 1 SA 4f fst :513 H

Fire Commander-NZ Ch. g. 7, by Super Imposing—Zephette, by Zephyr Bay
FLORES D R (238 29 28 40 .12) $70,000 Br.—Chandon Stud Ltd (NZ)
Own.—Hale & Hale Jr & Lindsay Tr.—Hess R B Jr (94 21 18 9 .22) 111
Lifetime 19 9 2 2 $107,017 | 1992 4 0 0 0 | 1991 6 4 1 1 $92,489 | Turf 19 9 2 2 $107,017

10Oct92- 4SA fm *6½f ①:22 :434 1:131 3↑Clm 80000 82 1 8 4¾ 4nk 41½ 76¾ Valenzuela P A LB 117 8.50 86-06 Ttsfld-Ir115noBlcJcAttc1161½BldCrrt113 A bit erratic1/8 10
4Sep92- 8Dmr fm 1 ①:472 1:111 1:353 3↑ⓇTsnmiSlewH 83 6 4 31½ 43½ 79 711 Valenzuela P A LB 117 7.10 82-09 ForestGlow1191½Kanatiyr-Ir1171½SuperMy118 Faltered 7
7Mar92♦7Ellerslie(NZ) yl*7f 1:24 ① MatamataCountryCupHcp 1631 Land D C 128 — — — Suncatcher 115¾ Penny Royal 1186 Hypervain 114 16
15Feb92♦9Matamata(NZ) sf*6f 1:104 ① Timberjack Hcp 59½ Lang D C 128 — — — Kampaign 1123¾ Suncatcher 1131½ Danjiki 113 9
26Oct91♦4MooneeVly(Aus) gd*1 1:351 ① WaterfordCrystalMile(Gr3) 1no O'Sullivan L A 126 *3.00 — — Fire Commander 126no Brunchtime 110 ⒹⒽGamine117 15
12Oct91♦9Ellerslie(NZ) sf*6f 1:153 ① Flying Hcp 34¾ Lang D C 120 — — — Al Kufra 1073½ Ray's Hope 1231½ Gold Fever 110 12
21Sep91♦9Hastings(NZ) fm*7f 1:212 ① HorizonHomesSprintHcp 2hd O'Sullivan L A 123 — — — Steineck 112hd Fire Commander 1234 Specialist 110 14
16Feb91♦8Matamata(NZ) fm*1 1:33 ① DB Draught Hcp 13½ O'Sullivan L A 119 *.35 — — Fire Commander 1193½ Greenback 1122½ Sandboy 115 11
26Jan91♦8Trentham(NZ) yl*1 1:351 ① ThorndonMileHcp(Gr1) 11¾ O'Sullivan L A 108 *1.85 — — Fire Commander 1081¾ Seamist 1112¾ Greenback 107 18
12Jan91♦9Avondale(NZ) fm*7f 1:211 ① Foley Hcp 14½ O'Sullivan L A 117 *1.10 — — FireCommander1174½ Espiare1201¾ TurnhamGreen116 12
LATEST WORKOUTS Mar 8 SA 5f fst 1:042 H Mar 3 SA 6f fst 1:131 H Feb 25 SA 6f gd 1:144 H Feb 20 SA tr.t 6f sly 1:182 H

Blue Tiger Ch. g. 4, by Storm Cat—Cecelia, by Royal Levee
DELAHOUSSAYE E (217 40 29 33 .18) $80,000 Br.—Resenthal Warren W (Ky)
Own.—Gann & Padilla Tr.—Drysdale Neil (12 3 2 0 .25) 115
Lifetime 11 4 1 0 $38,032 | 1992 3 1 0 0 $17,050 | 1991 8 3 1 0 $20,982 | Turf 10 3 1 0 $20,982

21Jun92- 8Hol fm 1⅛ ①:443 1:09 1:47 Cinema H 50 8 1 112 17 88 827¾ Delahoussaye E LBb 116 12.10 61-10 BnBn1144½FxNws1143½ProspctForFr114 Not urged late 8
21Jun92-Grade II
23May92- 5Hol fm 1⅙ ①:472 1:104 1:404 Wll Rogrs H 71 1 5 63½ 75 66½ 69¾ Valenzuela P A LBb 116 6.80 81-07 ThNmsJm1162½BldAssrt117¾PrspctFrFr114 Rank, wide 7
23May92-Grade III
11Apr92- 1GG fst 1 :451 1:094 1:36 Tlly's Pop H 88 3 4 42 11 15 1½ Valenzuela P A LBb 116 *2.00 90-10 BluTigr116½VintgYr1155WrttnSttmnt116 Steady urging 5
18Sep91♦1Sandown(Eng) gd*5f 1:021 ① Oxshott Nursery Stks 11 Raymond B 138 7.00 — — BlueTiger1381 MissVxett114no PrdisForum112 Bid,drvg 9
9Sep91♦1Hamilton(Scot) fm*6f 1:102 ① LordHamiltonNrsyStks 13 Raymond B 133 *4.50 — — BlueTiger1333 Tencity1241½ EductedPt110 Well pl,drvg 13
31Aug91♦5Chester(Eng) gd*6f 1:141 ① LinenhallGraduationStks 66¼ Eddery P 130 5.50 — — CommnchDncr123¾ ScrtThing1234 Isdr130 Prom,wknd 6
21Aug91♦6York(Eng) gd 5f 1:004 ① Roses Stks 46 Raymond B 124 14.00 — — AnothrEpisod1242 FirCrck1241 RglChims124 No threat 6
3Jly91♦1Yarmouth(Eng) gd*6f 1:15 ① Jellicoe Stks(Mdn) 1¾ Ryan W 126 *1.85 — — Blue Tiger 126¾ Songster 126½ Showgi 126 Bid,drvg 7
13May91♦5Windsor(Eng) gd 5f 1:012 ① Fenwick ofBondStStks — Eddery P 123 *2.00 — — Magic Ring 1236 Simply-H 123hd Toms Verdict 123 15
13May91-Reared at the start unseating rider
27Apr91♦1Sandown(Eng) gd 5f 1:014 ① Pizza Hut Stks(Mdn) 76¾ Eddery P 126 *1.10 — — Walsted126nk EltonLedger1262½ Uccello126 Spd for 3f 13
LATEST WORKOUTS Mar 10 Hol 4f fst :511 B Mar 5 Hol 6f fst 1:162 H Feb 28 Hol 4f fst :502 H Feb 14 Hol 4f fst :492 H

Exemplary Leader Dk. b. or br. h. 7, by Vigors—Paradigmatic, by Aristocratic
PEDROZA M A (249 26 34 34 .10) $80,000 Br.—Kenwood Stable II (Ky)
Own.—Siegel Jan & Mace &Samantha Tr.—Mayberry Brian A (51 9 8 11 .18) 117
Lifetime 38 9 4 9 $391,793 | 1993 1 1 0 0 $23,100 | 1992 6 2 0 0 $38,075 | Turf 13 4 1 2 $186,163 | Wet 1 0 0 0

3Jan93- 2SA gd 1 :462 1:111 1:371 Clm 80000 95 7 5 56¾ 32 2½ 11½ Pedroza M A LB 117 6.60 84-18 EmplrLdr1171½DrmOfF-Ir115noAdrlls115 Bumped start 7
3Jan93-Originally scheduled on turf
7Nov92- 5BM fm 1⅙ ①:464 1:103 1:421 3↑Tanforan H 90 4 6 712 812 68¾ 75¼ Cedeno E A LB 112 26.00 93 — DoublFond113hdBorgogn-GB1151¼LordJo115 No threat 8
7Nov92-Grade III
24Oct92- 6BM fm 1 ①:471 1:112 1:364 3↑Applbte Fm H 95 2 3 44 41¾ 21 11¼ Pedroza M A LB 115 9.60 95-06 EmplrLdr1151¼PltnPlsr117noLsTnth114 Closed gamely 10
16Sep92- 5Dmr fm 1 ①:47 1:103 1:343 3↑Clm 80000 90 3 5 54 44½ 76½ 76 Pedroza M A LB 116 11.20 92-06 Polar Boy116nk Young Hal-En1172¼ Asia116 No mishap 10
27Jun92- 8Hol fst 7f :221 :443 1:212 3↑Trple Bnd H 90 1 8 86½ 75¾ 76 64¾ Pedroza M A LB 114 3.80e 92-10 SlThSrgn111hdSftshSrSht114¾RcrdBm114 Wide stretch 8
27Jun92-Grade III
29May92- 7Hol fst 6½f :221 :443 1:15 Clm 80000 103 2 6 63½ 43½ 32½ 1hd Pedroza M A LB 117 8.10 97-10 ExmplryLdr117hdIndvdlst1171½FrstFr117 Steadied 3 1/2 7
17Jan92- 8SA fm 1 ①:463 1:102 1:341 Alw 55000 78 7 5 66½ 98 99¾ 912 Pedroza M A LB 115 23.50 80-08 LgrCt-Ar115nkPlsVrds-Ar116½EtnLd-En115 No mishap 9
31Dec91- 7SA fst 6½f :212 :441 1:151 3↑Alw 50000 76 2 4 69¾ 69 68¾ 612 Pedroza M A LB 117 9.80 82-14 MediPln1168Luntico-Ar115½LouRown115 Bobbled start 6
31Dec91-Originally scheduled at about 6 1/2 furlongs on turf
1Dec91- 7Hol fst 6½f :213 :442 1:151 3↑Alw 50000 63 1 7 613 613 713 719 Delahoussaye E LB 116 3.70 77-09 SrBfrt1181½BlEydDnny1141½PstPrnc109 5-wide stretch 7
LATEST WORKOUTS Mar 5 SA 5f fst 1:022 H Feb 18 SA 4f fst :483 H Feb 12 SA 5f fst 1:012 H Feb 3 SA 4f fst :482 H

Here's *ALL-IN-ONE*'s win-par and track-model information for the first leg:

Win Pars:	21.88 44.93 109.61
Ability Par:	67.97
Winners' Pace Profile:	EARLY
Pace Contention Point*:	4.12 lengths

*Pace Contention Point (PCP) is the elimination point at the second call. Outside the PCP horses have very little chance.

Here's Steve's analysis of the race:

Seester: Has the correct running style but a closer look at her wins shows that she must have at least a three-length lead at the second call in order to finish first—any pressure whatsoever and she folds like cheap wallpaper. She can set a 44^1 but Pride And Power can tackle a 44^2 with pressure. Seester won't be able to withstand such heat. Out.

Mobile Phone: Another speed type, but unlike Seester she shows a gameness under fire, albeit against a softer pace. She possesses a winning spirit (six victories in 23 starts) and is a marginal contender off the February 6 race.

Sunday Sonata: Off the layoffs and off the route races, she'll probably show only moderate speed. Her winning sprint was off a 45 pace, but her last three routes indicate she'll go about 46, so use the October 13 race.

Priceless Picture: Throw out the last two, as she's never won on turf, and dismiss the two before that, when she routed in stakes company. The Del Mar sprints are competitive and the August 5 race comes off a layoff, as does today's race. Use the layoff line.

Pride and Power: Nice frontrunning score last out through fractions of 21^1 and 44^2. Lots of speed in here and off the February 14 race she could be the speed of the speed. Strong contender.

Dinuba: Forgive the turf race and she shows a win at NW1 company two races back. That's the paceline.

Here is how *ALL-IN-ONE* saw the race:

Horse	Fair Odds
Pride And Power	5-to-2
Dinuba	9-to-2
Mobile Phone	5-to-1
Priceless Picture	7-to-1
Sunday Sonata	no line

Here's how *ALL-IN-ONE* projected each horse's speed and pace capabilities:

Horse	Projected Times		Ability Time	
Pride And Power	21.20	44.40	109.60	67.60
Dinuba	23.09	45.36	109.80	67.63
Priceless Picture	22.02	44.80	110.15	67.57
Mobile Phone	21.94	44.47	110.45	66.99
Sunday Sonata	22.27	45.79	111.11	69.30

Here is how the public viewed the race:

Horse	Public Odds
Dinuba	4-to-5
Pride And Power	5-to-2
Sunday Sonata	7-to-1
Priceless Picture	8-to-1
Mobile Phone	17-to-1

The public has boiled it down to a two-horse race: Dinuba and Pride And Power. The numbers say the public has made the wrong choice. Dinuba figures to be outside of the pace contention point at the second call while Pride And Power steals away to an uncontested lead and holds off the late charge of Dinuba. Pride And Power's ability time is barely better than Dinuba's. The public has ignored Mobile Phone, who has a better ability time than either Dinuba or Pride And Power. Considering the closeness of these four horses in terms of ability time, and considering Pride And Power's lone frontrunner trip on an EARLY track, Dinuba is very vulnerable favorite.

Of course, we don't have the luxury of consulting the public odds for the second and third legs of this Pick-3. The best we can do is check the morning line for potential false and vulnerable favorites and overbet horses.

Here is *ALL-IN-ONE*'s win-par and track-model information for the second leg:

Win Pars:	47.35 111.56 143.09
Ability Par:	95.76
Winners' pace profile:	MID
Pace contention point:	5.35 lengths

Here is the morning line:

Horse	Morning Line
San Fran's Halo	5-to-1
Sounds Fabulous	6-to-1
Babyitscoldoutside	4-to-1
Icy Resolution	3-to-1
Northern Tract	12-to-1
King Drone	20-to-1
William's Buckaroo	7-to-2
Govern	5-to-1

A wide-open race. The track oddsmaker installs Icy Resolution as a mild 3-to-1 favorite. Let's take a look at Steve's analysis of each horse:

San Fran's Halo: The move back into the claiming ranks woke him up. Rate him off the last line.
Sounds Fabulous: Hasn't won in a while, but this race is the third off the layoff and there is a pattern of mild improvement. Use the last line.
Babyitscoldoutside: Not the kind of pattern you want to see: The two most recent races were at this level and there was a decline in the last one. Out.
Icy Resolution: Seems to be rounding into form off the short layoff. Closer to the pace in last race and still managed to improve final time. Definite contender off the last line.
Northern Tract: Appears to have a win ceiling at $32,000 claiming. Also, he ran for a $25,000 tag last out, below the level of his

last win, and promptly finished up the track. Doubt that the cold trainer can undo what he did to him. Non-contender.

King Drone: No-win trainer and low-win jockey spell doom for this off-form horse. Elimination.

William's Buckaroo: Ran an improved race at his lowest level ever last time. We used that February 27 race to rate Sounds Fabulous, however, so the paceline becomes the February 3 race.

Govern: The switch from the apprentice to leading rider suggests that an improvement off the last race is forthcoming. The horse's last competitive dirt route over a fast track came on April 27 at Churchill Downs and is the line we'll use.

Here is how *ALL-IN-ONE* saw the race:

Horse	Fair Odds
Icy Resolution	2-to-1
William's Buckaroo	9-to-2
Sounds Fabulous	no line
San Fran's Halo	no line
Govern	no line

Here is how *ALL-IN-ONE* projected each horse's speed and pace capabilities:

Horse	Projected Times		Ability Time	
Icy Resolution	47.27	111.53	143.00	95.80
William's Buckaroo	47.51	111.81	143.93	96.12
Sounds Fabulous	47.64	111.97	143.54	96.30
Govern	46.92	111.97	144.80	97.02
San Fran's Halo	47.42	112.28	144.42	97.15

Icy Resolution is a double-advantage horse—he has the best projected second-call and final times and the fastest ability time. He fits the model, is within the pace contention point, and doesn't appear to be a favorite we can beat. His domination of *ALL-IN-ONE*'s line and projected times and ability time make him a single, although a case can be made for including William's Buckaroo and Sounds Fabulous, who run within five ticks of him.

Here is *ALL-IN-ONE*'s win-par and track-model information for the final leg:

Win Pars:	22.15 44.37 113.62
Ability Par:	51.39
Winners' Pace Profile:	EARLY
Pace Contention Point:	2.60 lengths

Here is the morning line:

Horse	Morning Line
Despatch	20-to-1
Lackington	8-to-1
Record Boom	9-to-2
Notley	8-to-1
Sligo's Ridge	20-to-1
Centurion	15-to-1
Philadelphia Dave	6 to-1
Black Jack Attack	7-to-2
Bailarin	12 to-1
Fire Commander	15-to-1
Blue Tiger	10-to-1
Exemplary Leader	8-to-1

Here are Steve's comments on the horses:

Despatch: Seems to prefer the Hollywood turf sprint layout and his best races have been earned against lessers. The uniqueness of the course demands a specialist, which Despatch isn't. Out.

Lackington: A case could be made against him since he's never won sprinting, but improvement is undeniable and his conquerors are all established horses-for-courses down the hillside turf. He's a contender off the race two back, which was at today's class level.

Record Boom: Never been down the hill, but has a turf-sprint victory across town. That line suggests itself since, like today's race, it comes off a layoff.

Notley: No way to rate him using our method of par-time handicapping. A handy rule of thumb concerning foreign invaders is to check their morning line—if it's among the top three choices, the foreigner is a contender. If not, it's a throwout. Notley is listed at 8-to-1, tied for fourth. Elimination.

Sligo's Ridge: This guy is one of only two horses in the lineup (the other is Black Jack Attack) to show a win down the hill, but that was long ago when he was still an allowance horse. His dull recent form has resulted in a slide down the class ladder and he's eligible to continue his tumble. Non-contender.

Centurion: Three downhill runs have resulted in uncompetitive finishes. He shows no ability for running well off layoffs and has been getting trounced by lessers. Out.

Philadelphia Dave: Since returning from the layoff, he's done absolutely nothing. Shows two turf victories routing but he won't be able to deal with the intense sprint pace here off the slow route fractions in his last two. Throwout.

Black Jack Attack: Won down the hill with Pincay and is re-united with him today. A case could be made for using that victory as a pace line, but there is a form question that suggests the last race is more representative.

Bailarin: In a field full of multiple turf winners, this guy will be hard pressed to score his first turf win today, especially in light of the severe fade jobs he's put forth in his two turf sprints. Out.

Fire Commander: First try down the hill wasn't bad and he won a turf sprint in his native New Zealand. Marginal contender off that race.

Blue Tiger: A strange case of winning his dirt debut after racing exclusively on turf in England. It's hard to rate him off either of his turf races and his winning race in this country was on dirt. A difficult elimination.

Exemplary Leader: Two for three at this level and has won sprinting on dirt and routing on dirt. Unlike others who've tried and failed repeatedly sprinting on the turf, he's a wild card who deserves to be rated. Use the good turf route October 24 at Bay Meadows.

Here is how *ALL-IN-ONE* saw the race:

Horse	Fair Odds
Exemplary Leader	5-to-2
Record Boom	5-to-1
Black Jack Attack	6-to-1
Fire Commander	no line
Lackington	no line

Here is how *ALL-IN-ONE* projected each horse's speed and pace capabilities:

Horse	Projected Times		Ability Time	
Record Boom	22.27	44.67	112.73	50.33
Exemplary Leader	22.85	44.06	113.22	52.01
Black Jack Attack	21.42	43.42	114.42	52.42
Lackington	22.58	44.52	114.22	52.28
Fire Commander	22.13	43.83	114.32	52.62

In terms of projected final time, Record Boom and Exemplary Leader tower over the field. They also boast the best projected last fractions in the race (Record Boom, 28.06; Exemplary Leader, 29.16), an important attribute on turf. *ALL-IN-ONE* characterizes the race as "chaos," which emphasizes price over predictability. We must include Black Jack Attack because the program gave him a line.

Let's recap the three legs of the Pick-3.

First leg:

We have the benefit of knowing that Dinuba is a false (very vulnerable at best) favorite whom we can try to beat at 4-to-5. Pride And Power is the strongest single pick, while Mobile Phone has an outside chance.

Second leg:

Icy Resolution is a double-advantage horse but also the lukewarm morning-line favorite. From a handicapping standpoint he'd be a wise single, and since the track oddsmaker has installed him as a mild 3-to-1 favorite, the potential price we accept on him won't be miserly. William's Buckaroo and Sounds Fabulous are minor players.

Third leg:

Record Boom and Exemplary Leader are the standouts and *ALL-IN-ONE*'s top picks. Black Jack Attack is another very vulnerable favorite we have to consider.

From a bet-construction standpoint, it's best to concentrate our largest wagers on the combinations that have the most likelihood of hitting—that is, we should bet more on our line's lowest-odds combinations.

Here are *ALL-IN-ONE*'s fair-odds lines for the three races, leaving out the favorites and other low-priced contenders that we're trying to beat:

Third Race

Pride And Power	5-to-2
Dinuba	9-to-2
Mobile Phone	5-to-1

Fourth Race

Icy Resolution	2-to-1
William's Buckaroo	9-to-2

Fifth Race

Exemplary Leader	5-to-2
Record Boom	5-to-1
Black Jack Attack	6-to-1

Let's use a bet size of $200. (Remember, it's better to have 10 percent of a $200 ticket than only a $20 bet on your own.) Based on the above odds line and sizing our bets accordingly (we used our program *Bettor-Handicapper* to determine bet size quickly), we have the following wagers:

$28	Pride And Power	Icy Resolution	Exemplary Leader
17	Pride And Power	Icy Resolution	Record Boom
~~14~~	~~Pride and Power~~	~~Icy Resolution~~	~~Black Jack Attack~~
16	Pride And Power	William's Buckaroo	Exemplary Leader
9	Pride And Power	William's Buckaroo	Record Boom
8	Pride And Power	William's Buckaroo	Black Jack Attack
17	Mobile Phone	Icy Resolution	Exemplary Leader
10	Mobile Phone	Icy Resolution	Record Boom
~~9~~	~~Mobile Phone~~	~~Icy Resolution~~	~~Black Jack Attack~~

9	Mobile Phone	William's Buckaroo	Exemplary Leader
6	Mobile Phone	William's Buckaroo	Record Boom
5	Mobile Phone	William's Buckaroo	Black Jack Attack
~~18~~	~~Dinuba~~	~~Icy Resolution~~	~~Exemplary Leader~~
~~11~~	~~Dinuba~~	~~Icy Resolution~~	~~Record Boom~~
~~9~~	~~Dinuba~~	~~Icy Resolution~~	~~Black Jack Attack~~
10	Dinuba	William's Buckaroo	Exemplary Leader
6	Dinuba	William's Buckaroo	Record Boom
~~5~~	~~Dinuba~~	~~William's Buckaroo~~	~~Black Jack Attack~~

We must now delete the combinations that contain two or more favorites. The public favorite in the first leg was Dinuba. The most probable favorites in the next two legs were Icy Resolution and Black Jack Attack respectively. The combinations that have strikeovers are eliminated because they contain two or more favorites. The bets only total $141. You may choose to allocate the $59 proportionately to the remaining combinations or simply make a $141 worth of bets. I usually increase the amounts of my playable combinations. The way I would do it in this Pick-3 is to calculate the percentage contribution that each bet makes to the total bet of $141 and multiply this number by $59. For example, $28 on the combination of Pride And Power, Icy Resolution, and Exemplary Leader represents 19.9 percent of the total bet; I therefore increase this bet by 19.9 percent of $59, or $12. Here are the combinations and bet amounts to wager on this Pick-3:

$40	Pride And Power	Icy Resolution	Exemplary Leader
24	Pride And Power	Icy Resolution	Record Boom
23	Pride And Power	William's Buckaroo	Exemplary Leader
13	Pride And Power	William's Buckaroo	Record Boom
11	Pride And Power	William's Buckaroo	Black Jack Attack
24	Mobile Phone	Icy Resolution	Exemplary Leader
14	Mobile Phone	Icy Resolution	Record Boom
13	Mobile Phone	William's Buckaroo	Exemplary Leader
9	Mobile Phone	William's Buckaroo	Record Boom
7	Mobile Phone	William's Buckaroo	Black Jack Attack
14	Dinuba	William's Buckaroo	Exemplary Leader
9	Dinuba	William's Buckaroo	Record Boom

The total bet is $201.

The winning combination of Pride and Power, Icy Resolution, and Exemplary Leader paid $403.80. We had this triple 13.33 times for a return of $5,384 on an investment of $200. Not a bad day so far. The modified Ambrose strategy also handled this Pick-3 with great facility. The key horses are in italics.

Leg 1	Leg 2	Leg 3
Pride And Power	*Icy Resolution*	*Exemplary Leader*
Dinuba	William's Buckaroo	Record Boom
Mobile Phone	Sounds Fabulous	Black Jack Attack

This means that you would have bought three part-wheels. Only one of the key horses (Icy Resolution) was a probable public favorite. Since each of the key horses won, you would have had this Pick-3 three times at $403.80 each for a total of $1,211.40 returned on your $81 investment. Life is good.

THIRD RACE
Santa Anita
MARCH 13, 1993

6 FURLONGS. (1.071) ALLOWANCE. Purse $36,000. Fillies and mares. 4-year-olds and upward. Non-winners of $3,000 twice other than maiden or claiming. Weight, 121 lbs. Non-winners of two races other than claiming since December 15 allowed 2 lbs.; of a race other than maiden, or claiming since February 1, 4 lbs.; such a race since January 1, 6 lbs.

Value of race $36,000; value to winner $19,800; second $7,200; third $5,400; fourth $2,700; fifth $900. Mutuel pool $339,983.
Exacta pool $358,084.

Last Raced	Horse	M/Eqt.A.Wt	PP St	¼	½	Str	Fin	Jockey	Odds $1
14Feb93 9SA1	Pride And Power	LB 5 115	5 1	1¹	12½	1³	1¹	Solis A	2.50
7Nov92 4SA7	Priceless Picture	LB 5 115	4 4	3½	3hd	2½	2no	McCarron C J	8.30
7Jan93 8SA7	Sunday Sonata	Bb 4 117	3 6	5¹	4½	3½	3⁶	Pincay L Jr	7.40
6Feb93 1SA5	Seester	LBb 4 115	1 2	23½	21½	4⁵	45½	Stevens G L	8.80
31Jan93 5SA10	Dinuba	LB 4 116	6 5	6	51½	51½	5²	Delahoussaye E	.90
28Feb93 3SA6	Mobile Phone	LB 5 115	2 3	41½ 6	6	6	6	Pedroza M A	17.60

OFF AT 2:02 Start good. Won driving. Time, :21², :44², :56⁴, 1:09³ Track fast.

$2 Mutuel Prices:
5-PRIDE AND POWER		7.00	4.20	3.20
4-PRICELESS PICTURE			6.80	4.00
3-SUNDAY SONATA				3.80

$2 EXACTA 5-4 PAID $52.20.

FOURTH RACE
Santa Anita
MARCH 13, 1993

1 1/16 MILES. (1.39) CLAIMING. Purse $30,000. 4-year-olds and upward. Weight, 121 lbs. Non-winners of two races at one mile or over since January 1 allowed 2 lbs.; of such a race since February 1, 4 lbs.; since January 1, 6 lbs. Claiming price $40,000; if for $35,000 allowed 2 lbs. (Maiden or races when entered for $32,000 or less not considered.)

Value of race $30,000; value to winner $16,500; second $6,000; third $4,500; fourth $2,250; fifth $750. Mutuel pool $385,506.
Exacta pool $401,270.

Last Raced	Horse	M/Eqt.A.Wt	PP St	¼	½	¾	Str	Fin	Jockey	Cl'g Pr	Odds $1
13Feb93 2SA2	Icy Resolution	LBb 7 115	4 5	5¹	52½	3²	21½	1nk	Pedroza M A	40000	3.00
21Feb93 9SA4	Govern	LB 5 115	8 2	21½	1½	1½	1½	2¹	DesormuxKJ	40000	*3.00
27Feb93 2SA3	William's Buckaroo	LBb 4 115	7 7	7⁴	7³	73½	4hd	3hd	Stevens G L	40000	4.00
27Feb93 2SA4	Sounds Fabulous	LB 5 115	2 6	6¹	6²	6½	5⁴	4⁸	McCarron CJ	40000	7.70
21Feb93 9SA7	Northern Tract	LBb 4 115	5 1	1½	22½	2½	3½	56½	Flores D R	40000	29.50
27Feb93 2SA5	King Drone	LBb 6 115	6 3	3hd	4½	5½	6⁵	6³	Torres H	40000	24.10
21Feb93 9SA2	San Fran's Halo	LBb 4 115	1 8	8	8	8	8	7⁹	Black C A	40000	8.80
13Feb93 2SA4	Babyitscoldoutside	LBb 7 117	3 4	41½	3hd	4hd	7¹	8	Pincay L Jr	40000	3.90

*—Actual Betting Favorite.

OFF AT 2:33. Start good. Won driving. Time, :22³, :46, 1:10⁴, 1:36⁴, 1:43² Track fast.

$2 Mutuel Prices:
4-ICY RESOLUTION		8.00	3.80	3.00
8-GOVERN			4.80	3.60
7-WILLIAM'S BUCKAROO				3.20

$2 EXACTA 4-8 PAID $39.00.

FIFTH RACE
Santa Anita
MARCH 13, 1993

ABOUT 6 ½ FURLONGS.(Turf). (1.11^{3}) CLAIMING. Purse $38,000. 4-year-olds and upward. Weight, 121 lbs. Non-winners of two races since January 1 allowed 2 lbs.; of a race since February 1, 4 lbs.; since January 1, 6 lbs. Claiming price $80,000; for each $5,000 to $70,000 allowed 2 lbs. (Maiden or races when entered for $62,500 or less not considered.) (Non-starters for a claiming price of $25,000 or less in their last three starts preferred.)
Value of race $38,000; value to winner $20,900; second $7,600; third $5,700; fourth $2,850; fifth $950. Mutuel pool $447,193. Exacta pool $357,212. Trifecta pool $516,157.

Last Raced	Horse	M/Eqt.	A.	Wt	PP	St	¼	½	Str	Fin	Jockey	Cl'g Pr	Odds $1
3Jan93 ^{2}SA^{1}	Exemplary Leader	LB	7	117	12	4	10^{hd}	9^{1½}	7^{hd}	1^{hd}	Pedroza M A	80000	7.00
27Jun92 ^{8}Hol^{3}	Record Boom	LB	7	114	3	6	6½	5^{hd}	5½	2^{2}	Stevens G L	75000	2.50
21Jun92 ^{8}Hol^{8}	Blue Tiger	LBb	4	116	11	2	1½	1^{hd}	1½	3½	DelhoussyeE	80000	11.90
20Dec92 ^{9}Hol^{7}	Despatch-Fr	LBb	7	114	1	12	7½	8^{1}	4^{1}	4¾	Black C A	70000	42.50
7Nov92 ^{5}Eng^{6}	Notley-GB	Bb	6	115	4	5	4^{1}	4^{1½}	6^{hd}	5^{1¼}	Almeida G F	80000	9.40
6Mar93 ^{4}SA^{8}	Black Jack Attack	LB	7	117	8	7	9^{1}	10½	10½	6no	Pincay L Jr	80000	5.30
7Feb93 ^{5}SA^{9}	Philadelphia Dave	LB	4	115	7	10	12	12	12	7^{hd}	DesormuxKJ	80000	6.70
10Oct92 ^{4}SA^{7}	Fire Commander-NZ	LB	7	114	10	9	8^{1}	7^{1½}	8½	8½	Flores D R	70000	26.80
25Feb93 ^{3}SA^{5}	Sligo's Ridge	LB	5	115	5	8	11^{2}	11^{1}	11^{hd}	9^{nk}	Solis A	80000	17.50
20Feb93 ^{6}SA^{6}	Bailarin	LBb	6	115	9	1	2^{hd}	2^{hd}	3^{1}	10¾	Walls M K	75000	15.80
4Jly92 ^{10}Hol^{6}	Centurion-NZ	LBb	7	115	6	3	3^{hd}	3^{2}	2½	11^{2¼}	Steiner J J	70000	61.20
5Mar93 ^{7}SA^{3}	Lackington-Ch	LB	5	115	2	11	5^{1½}	6^{hd}	9^{1½}	12	McCarron CJ	80000	6.90

OFF AT 3:13. Start good. Won driving. Time, :21^{4}, :44 , 1:07^{1}, 1:13^{1} Course firm.

$2 Mutuel Prices:				
	12–EXEMPLARY LEADER	16.00	7.80	5.40
	3–RECORD BOOM		4.20	3.60
	11–BLUE TIGER			7.00

$2 EXACTA 12–3 PAID $55.80. $2 TRIFECTA 12–3–11 PAID $798.60.

This final example comes from Hollywood Park on Thursday, May 6, 1993. The wonderful thing about Hollywood Park, at that time, was that there were three Pick-3's per day! What a wonderful opportunity for Pick-3 players. (Now there are seven Pick-3's per day at Hollywood Park! God Bless R. D. Hubbard. He's a wonderful man and a true champion of the bettor.)

Once again, handicap the races yourself. Use the profile data, which will make things a lot simpler.

The first leg was $16,000 claiming route for fillies and mares.

7 — 1$\frac{1}{16}$ MILES HOLLYWOOD (FINISH / START)

1 $\frac{1}{16}$ MILES. **(1.40) CLAIMING. Purse $16,000. Fillies and mares. 4-year-olds and upward. Weight, 122 lbs. Non-winners of two races at one or over since March 12 allowed 3 lbs.; such a race since then, 6 lbs. Claiming price $16,000; if for $14,000 allowed 2 lbs. (Races when entered for $12,500 or less not considered.)**

LASIX—Nora of Clare, Avies' Charm, Pinkie Schoop, Desert Rose, Marie de Siberie, Majolique-Ar, Chalk Box.

Nora Of Clare — B. m. 6, by Summer Time Guy—Green Hall, by Hail the Pirates
MCCARRON C J (25 3 5 3 .12) — $16,000 — Br.—Hudd H & Mary (Cal) — 116
Own.—Hudd Mary & Tennant J J — Tr.—McAnally Ronald (21 2 6 3 .10)
Lifetime 11 3 1 0 $47,650 — 1991 8 2 1 0 $37,450 — 1990 3 1 0 0 $10,200

9Oct91- 3SA	fst	1$\frac{1}{16}$	:47^{3}	1:12	1:43^{1}	3↑ⒻClm 32000	75	2	6	5^{3½}	5^{5½}	5^{5½}	5^{5½}	Delahoussaye E	L	118	4.50	81–15	Drone's Queen116½ Jewel Ball117^{1½} Venturilla116	7
9Oct91–Off slowly, wide trip																				
5Sep91- 7Dmr	fst	1	:45^{4}	1:10^{3}	1:36	3↑ⒻClm 50000	68	3	8	8^{9½}	7^{8½}	7^{8½}	6^{9½}	Delahoussaye E	LB	116	4.60	76–17	Horsche116^{hd} Seville-Ch116^{4} Drone's Queen116	8
5Sep91–Lugged out, wide throughout																				
9Aug91- 7Dmr	fst	1	:46^{1}	1:11^{4}	1:38^{4}	3↑ⒻClm c-32000	84	2	6	6^{6½}	5^{3½}	4^{3}	1^{nk}	Delahoussaye E	LB	116	2.90	72–28	NorOfClr116^{nk}Svll-Ch120^{2½}GFrTrsr116 Off slowly, wide	7
4Jly91- 4Hol	fst	7½f	:22^{1}	:44^{4}	1:29^{3}	ⒻClm c-25000	78	2	7	7^{11}	7^{11}	5^{4}	4^{1½}	Delahoussaye E	B	116	3.40	– –	Maroon Buck115^{no} Reassured116½ Sirree118 Wide trip	7
26Apr91- 7Hol	fst	1$\frac{1}{16}$	:47^{1}	1:11^{4}	1:43^{3}	3↑ⒻAlw 35000	71	1	5	5^{4}	5^{4½}	5^{8½}	5^{11¼}	McCarron C J	B	119	*2.10	72–14	FightingMiss112^{3½}Sat119^{2½}ElzbthDrv119 4-wide stretch	6
21Mar91- 5SA	fst	1	:46	1:10^{3}	1:36^{1}	ⒻClm 32000	89	5	8	8^{12}	6^{8}	4^{4}	2¾	Black C A	B	115	7.30	85–17	Nt'sSll116¾NorOfClr115^{1}TrlyNghty121 Off slwly,4-wide	8
22Feb91- 5SA	fst	1$\frac{1}{16}$	:46^{4}	1:11^{3}	1:44	ⒻClm 32000	79	7	8	8^{9½}	6^{3½}	5^{5½}	5^{4¾}	Black C A		115	3.70	78–19	TrulyNghty118^{no}Vrds-Fr114^{4}J.D.'sLov115 Broke slowly	9
21Jan91- 9SA	fst	1	:46	1:11^{1}	1:37^{3}	ⒻClm 25000	86	5	10	10^{10}	7^{4½}	4^{1½}	1^{3½}	Black C A	B	115	26.90	79–19	NrOfClr115^{3½}Fwrf115^{hd}DynmcAtNght115 5-wide stretch	10
30Nov90- 2Hol	fst	1$\frac{1}{16}$	:47^{1}	1:12^{1}	1:45	3↑ⒻⓈMd 32000	67	4	6	5^{7½}	4^{5}	2^{2}	1^{1½}	McCarron C J	B	118	3.30	75–19	NorOfClr118^{1½}FshnblLdy111^{6}RvrStyx118 Trouble early	11
14Nov90- 2Hol	fst	7f	:21^{4}	:45	1:24^{4}	3↑ⒻMd 32000	49	10	7	11^{9½}	7^{8}	7^{11}	5^{8½}	McCarron C J	B	118	8.80	74–16	QnsPrtst118^{3½}DstnctFrcst118^{1}GrnBan118 Steadied 3/16	12

LATEST WORKOUTS Apr 30 SA 4f fst :48^{4} H Apr 23 SA 5f fst 1:02^{3} H Apr 15 Hol 4f fst :47^{3} H Apr 9 Hol 6f fst 1:14^{2} H

Avies' Charm — Dk. b. or br. m. 6, by Lord Avie—A Charm, by Nashua
DESORMEAUX K J (48 13 10 6 .27) — $16,000 — Br.—Davis Marian B & SKS Stables Inc (Ky) — 116
Own.—Accardi &Hood&TarhoolStables — Tr.—Assinesi Paul D (—)
Lifetime 24 4 4 3 $73,625 — 1993 6 0 4 0 $10,000 — 1992 8 2 0 0 $22,100 — Turf 1 0 0 0 — Wet 1 0 1 0 $2,200

15Apr93- 8SA	fm	1	ⓣ:46	1:10^{2}	1:35^{3}	ⒻAlw 36000	70	9	9	9^{11}	8^{9½}	7^{11}	7^{12½}	Garcia J A	LB	117	47.60	75–13	PttSonr-GB120^{1½}SappySrs117^{1}HppyWf120 Wide early	10
27Mar93- 9SA	fst	1	:46^{2}	1:12	1:38^{4}	ⒻClm c-16000	78	10	10	10^{11}	9^{8½}	2^{3}	2½	Desormeaux K J	LB	115	3.80	75–23	PnkSchp115½Avs'Chrm115^{hd}HtGrl115 Wide,bumped 3/16	10
27Mar93–Claimed from Heboian&Heboian&MorningsideSth, Cenicola Lewis Trainer																				
12Mar93- 9SA	fst	1	:46	1:10^{4}	1:37	ⒻClm 12500	89	5	7	7^{8½}	5^{4}	2^{4}	2^{1½}	Pincay L Jr	L	117	3.10	84–15	MstWndr115^{1½}AsChrm117^{4½}HtGrl115 Wide backstretch	9
21Feb93- 5SA	gd	1	:47^{2}	1:12^{3}	1:38^{4}	ⒻClm 12500	79	6	6	6^{8}	4^{3}	3^{3}	2^{hd}	Pincay L Jr	LB	117	3.60	76–21	DesertRose118^{hd}Avies'Chrm117^{4}LewrdSil117 Wide trip	9
28Jan93- 1SA	fst	6½f	:21^{4}	:44^{4}	1:17	ⒻClm 12500	65	5	10	12^{11}	12^{10}	9^{6½}	8^{5½}	Pincay L Jr	LB	117	12.30	81–14	StellrStory115^{hd}Lugno116^{2½}RodToRomnc117 Wide trip	12
13Jan93- 1SA	sly	7f	:23	:46^{4}	1:26	ⒻClm 10000	68	5	7	8^{8}	6^{7½}	5^{4}	2¾	Pincay L Jr	LB	117	5.50	72–25	HtGirl115¾Avis'Chrm117^{1½}MyMissBa115 5-wide stretch	9
28Dec92- 1SA	gd	6½f	:22	:44^{4}	1:15^{2}	3↑ⒻClm 12500	64	4	5	5^{11}	5^{15}	5^{11}	4^{7½}	Pincay L Jr	LB	117	7.50	86–11	FlmncoDncr115½Prong115^{4½}Lgno117 Wide backstretch	7
27Nov92- 3Hol	fst	6½f	:22^{3}	:45^{3}	1:16^{1}	3↑ⒻClm 16000	57	3	7	7^{8½}	7^{7½}	7^{6½}	7^{12¼}	Pincay L Jr	LBb	117	3.80	78–10	Frt'sFrnd116^{2}EdsnNtv116^{2½}SmdJc-Mx116 Wide, outrun	7
4Nov92- 7SA	fst	6½f	:22^{2}	:45^{3}	1:17	3↑ⒻClm 16000	74	4	9	11^{13}	11^{7½}	11^{7½}	5^{3½}	Pincay L Jr	LB	118	5.10	82–10	BontyMn116^{1½}EdsonNtv116½SmdyJck-Mx116 Wide trip	11
7Oct92- 1SA	fst	6½f	:22^{2}	:45^{1}	1:16	3↑ⒻClm 25000	76	1	7	7^{8}	6^{8½}	6^{8½}	6^{5½}	Pincay L Jr	LB	117	5.00	84–13	MobPhn118^{hd}LnchAStr118^{nk}ChlkBx118 5-wide stretch	7

LATEST WORKOUTS ●May 2 SA 4f fst :47 H Apr 23 SA 4f fst :47^{3} H Apr 12 SA 4f fst :48^{3} H Mar 21 SA 4f fst :48^{4} H

Pinkie Schoop

Gr. f. 4, by Jahiin Klingman—So Very Nice, by That's a Nice

$16,000

Desert Rose

B. m. 5, by Native Prospector—Deaths, by Zenitha

$14,000

Marie De Siberie

Ch. m. 6, by Believe It—Sister Sol, by Delta Judge

$14,000

Majolique–Ar

B. m. 6, by Fort de France—Majagua, by Good Manners

$16,000

Chalk Box

B. m. 7, by White Fir—Study Time, by Greco Time

$16,000

The second leg was the feature race, an allowance nonwinners two for three-year-olds and upward for fillies and mares to go a route distance.

8 **1 1/16 MILES. HOLLYWOOD** FINISH START

1 1/16 MILES. (1.40) ALLOWANCE. Purse $42,000. Fillies and mares, 3-year-olds and upward which have not won $3,000 twice other than maiden, claiming or starter. Weights, 3-year-olds, 114 lbs.; older, 122 lbs. Non-winners of two races other than claiming at a mile or over since March 15 allowed 3 lbs.; such a race other than maiden or claiming since then, 6 lbs.

LASIX—Justamente-Ar, Red Bandana, Chipeta Springs, Bless Shoe.

Fine Impression
B. f. 3(Apr), by Wild Again—Lucy Black, by Alydar
Br.—Calumet Farm (Ky)
Tr.—McAnally Ronald (21 2 6 3 .10)
NAKATANI C S (60 6 15 6 .10)
Own.—Whitham Mr.-Mrs Frank E

Lifetime 1983 4 2 2 0 $45,550
5 2 3 0 1982 1 M 1 0 $3,800
111 $53,350

Justamente-Ar
Ch. m. 5, by Tough Critic—Exactamente, by Good Manners
Br.—Haras Ojo de Agua (Arg)
Tr.—Mandella Richard (20 3 2 4 .15)
BLACK C A (46 4 5 4 .09)
Own.—Forli International Inc & Taub

Lifetime 1983 3 1 2 0 $34,400
18 2 5 3 1982 6 0 0 0 $8,275
119 $64,452 Turf 12 1 3 2 $27,770
Wet 2 1 1 0 $27,660

Red Bandana
B. f. 4, by Fred Astaire—Xenia, by Majestic Prince
Br.—Weldon Ben P Sr (Ky)
Tr.—Werner H C Jr (—)
STEVENS G L (78 11 24 31)
Own.—Brumbaugh & Werner

Lifetime 1983 5 0 0 0 $3,800
10 2 1 2 1982 11 2 1 2 $96,825
116 $101,125 Turf 9 1 1 0 $46,425
Wet 3 1 0 1 $31,800

Chipeta Springs
B. f. 4, by Alydar—Salt Spring, by Salt Marsh
Br.—Gayno Stables (Ky)
Tr.—Bunn Thomas M Jr (3 0 0 2 .00)
PINCAY L JR (35 6 3 3 .17)
Own.—Gayno Stables

Lifetime 1983 3 0 0 1 $6,775
10 2 3 2 1982 8 2 3 1 $69,475
116 $67,250 Turf 1 0 0 0
Wet 1 0 0 0 $5,400

Swazi's Moment
B. f. 3(Mar), by Moment of Hope—Swazi Girl, by Hatchetman
Br.—American Star Corp (Ky)
Tr.—Rash Rodney (10 0 1 1 .00)
GONZALEZ S JR (34 3 5 5 .09)
Own.—Gordy Berry

Lifetime 1983 2 0 0 0 $20,000
4 2 0 0 1982 2 2 0 0 $55,055
103.5 $75,055

Bless Shoe
Dk. b. or br. f. 4, by Seattle Song—That'll Be Fun, by Buckfinder
Br.—North Ridge Fm & Pineau Mr.-Mrs A L (Md)
Tr.—Bunn Jim (8 1 0 0 .13)
DELAHOUSSAYE E (57 8 10 5 .14)
Own.—Bunn Jerry

Lifetime 1983 4 2 0 2 $47,700
11 2 2 2 1982 4 M 2 0 $12,750
119 $60,575 Turf 1 0 0 1 $5,000
Wet 3 0 1 1 $10,350

The last leg was a seven-furlong maiden claimer for three-year-olds and upward Cal Breds.

7 FURLONGS. (1.20⁴) MAIDEN CLAIMING. Purse $17,000. Fillies and mares. 3–year-olds and upward. Bred in California. Weights, 3–year-olds, 115 lbs.; older, 122 lbs. Claiming price $32,000; if for $28,000 allowed 2 lbs.

LASIX—Bold Dee Dee, Nancy's Legend, Numberthirtyfive, Jelikit, Talisman's Magic, Decidedly Natalie, Native Doryl, Riviere Miss, ¹Vreak Havoc, Firecracker Roger, Blue Eyed Miss, Lil Negotiator.

Bold Dee Dee

Ch. f. 3(May), by Bold Badgett—Rene Descartes, by Cartesian
SOLIS A (56 6 5 11 .11)
Own—Michaels Delores
Br.—Ullman Larry & Sheila (Cal) $28,000
Tr.—Carava Jack (7 4 1 2 .57)
Lifetime 1983 4 M 0 1 $3,125
5 0 0 1 1982 1 M 0 0 $450
$3,575
113

Moonlight Cut

B. f. 3(May), by Cutlass Reality—Moon Maiden, by Run of Luck
PINCAY L JR (36 6 3 3 .17)
Own—Fisher & Zolezzi
Br.—Whiting Mr–Mrs Peter J (Cal) $32,000
Tr.—Bunn Thomas M Jr (3 0 0 2 .00)
Lifetime 1983 0 M 0 0
0 0 0 0 1982 0 M 0 0
115

Nancy's Legend

Ch. f. 4, by Woodland Lad—Modalisa, by Impressive
LOPEZ A D (26 2 2 3 .08)
Own—Bello James E
Br.—Beckett James (Cal) $28,000
Tr.—Lewis Richard I (—)
Lifetime 1983 1 M 0 0 $3,600
4 0 1 1 1982 3 M 0 1 $3,425
$7,025
120

Marella

Gr. f. 3(Apr), by Aggravatin'—Fumarola, by Zeddaan
TORRES H (25 1 2 3 .04)
Own—Von Bluecher & Whittingham
Br.—Von Bluecher Helmuth (Cal) $32,000
Tr.—Whittingham Michael (2 0 0 0 .00)
Lifetime 1983 1 M 0 0
1 0 0 0 1982 0 M 0 0
115

Numberthirtyfive

B. f. 3(May), by Flying Paster—Nevada Double, by Nodouble
DESORMEAUX K J (40 13 10 6 .27)
Own—Hi Card Ranch & Walker
Br.—Silver Creek Ranch Inc (Cal) $32,000
Tr.—Jones Gary (6 0 0 1 .00)
Lifetime 1983 1 M 0 0 $2,550
1 0 0 0 1982 0 M 0 0
$2,550
115

Jelikit

Dk. b. or br. f. 3(Apr), by Pass the Glass—Fortunate Amanda, by Lucky Mel
FLORES D R (30 5 3 3 .13)
Own—R G M Stables
Br.—Metz R G (Cal) $32,000
Tr.—Matlow Richard P (2 0 1 0 .00)
Lifetime 1983 1 M 0 0
1 0 0 0 1982 0 M 0 0
115

Talisman's Magic

Dk. b. or br. m. 5, by Our Talisman—Horacelle, by Knight in Armor
CASTANEDA K (11 0 0 0 .00)
Own—Mayer Gary & Linda
Br.—Mayer Gary & Linda (Cal) $28,000
Tr.—Landers Dan (—)
Lifetime 1983 1 M 0 0 $2,700
16 0 3 4 1982 8 M 0 2 $10,900
$26,300
120

Decidedly Natalie

Dk. b. or br. f. 3(Feb), by Flying Paster—Natalie Knows, by Decidedly
STEVENS G L (36 11 2 4 .31)
Own—Friendly Ed
Br.—Friendly Ed (Cal) $32,000
Tr.—Sadler John W (17 1 3 1 .06)
Lifetime 1983 3 M 2 0 $6,800
8 0 3 0 1982 3 M 1 0 $8,425
$15,225
Wet 1 0 1 0 $3,400
115

Native Doryl

Dk. b. or br. f. 3(Apr), by Fatih—Doryl, by Our Talisman
NAKATANI C S (68 6 15 8 .10)
Own—Granja Mexico & Hurtado
Br.—Palma Hector O (Cal) $32,000
Tr.—Palma Hector O (8 1 1 0 .13)
Lifetime 1983 3 M 1 0 $3,850
4 0 1 0 1982 1 M 0 0 $700
$4,550
115

Riviere Miss — Ro. f. 3(May), by Prince Bobby B—Vigors Miss, by Vigors — Lifetime 4 0 1 1 $7,675 — 1993 4 M 1 1 $7,675 — 1992 0 M 0 0
DELAHOUSSAYE E (57 8 10 5 .14) — $32,000 — Br.—Beckett James L. (Cal) — 115 — Wet 1 0 0 1 $2,850
Own.—Hersh Philip — Tr.—Bernstein David (4 0 0 0 .00)
31Mar93- 3SA fst 1 :464 1:111 1:373 ⒻMd 40000 61 1 4 44 45½ 34 42¾ Delahoussaye E LBb 117 3.10 79-15 SmClssLd117hdRmll1171PrncssWt117 Wide backstretch 7
14Mar93- 2SA fst 6½f :22 :453 1:174 ⒻⓈMd 32000 44 3 11 118¾ 96½ 58 29 Delahoussaye E LBb 117 3.40 73-13 Iciness1179RivierMiss117½ImprilFind117 Bobbled, wide 12
18Feb93- 1SA sly 1 :462 1:113 1:381 ⒻMd 40000 66 6 2 3½ 2hd 11½ 34½ Pedroza M A LBb 117 8.40 75-15 PttWn117nkFndmntlRghts1174RvrMss117 Hustled early 8
29Jan93- 2SA fst 5½f :214 :454 1:051 ⒻMd 50000 39 5 9 98½ 98½ 710 610¾ Nakatani C S LB 117 11.80 73-15 TlphonTngo1171½RzziCt1175RiskyRstn117 Broke slowly 9
LATEST WORKOUTS Apr 30 Hol 5f fst 1:022 H Apr 23 Hol 4f fst :482 H Apr 16 SA 4f fst :481 H Mar 24 SA 4f fst :494 H

Wreak Havoc — Gr. f. 4, by I'ma Hell Raiser—Key to Kensington, by Key to the Kingdom — Lifetime 19 0 3 0 $19,150 — 1993 8 M 2 0 $10,925 — 1992 11 M 1 0 $8,225
BLACK C A (46 4 5 4 .09) — $28,000 — Br.—Rancho Jonata (Cal) — 120 — Wet 3 0 1 0 $5,025
Own.—Coleman P Dianne — Tr.—Bartenetti Robert E (1 0 0 0 .00)
22Apr93- 5Hol fst 6f :221 :453 1:102 3+ⒻMd 28000 62 4 2 1½ 1hd 41½ 54½ Black C A LBb 120 12.20 83-11 Shfrkps1151½TblNmbrWn1152Isntsmrttsll115 Weakened 9
2Apr93- 6SA fst 6f :214 :45 1:103 ⒻMd 35000 40 12 2 74 76¾ 86¾ 811½ Solis A LBb 118 15.00 73-13 TrsNort120¾MssTrkmn120¾Crmn118 Wide backstretch 12
17Mar93- 4SA fst 1 :471 1:123 1:393 ⒻMd 35000 57 4 5 31 2hd 21½ 43¾ Gulas L L5 LBb 113 8.80 68-22 DchssKss120¾LrInThMd120¾NmblGddss113 Wide early 10
5Mar93- 2SA fst 6f :213 :451 1:111 ⒻMd 35000 65 10 5 54 52½ 42 25 Gulas L L5 LBb 113 31.50 76-15 SixQuens1205WrkHvoc1131PlyfulPosition120 Wide trip 12
19Feb93- 4SA sly 7f :224 :46 1:244 ⒻMd 35000 61 3 2 31 1hd 1½ 2¾ Gulas L L5 LBb 112 10.50 78-15 AplchnSong119¾WrkHvc1125LrkInThMdw119 Good try 7
10Feb93- 9SA fst 6½f :214 :451 1:173 ⒻⓈMd 35000 53 1 8 63½ 54 63¾ 54¾ Gulas L L5 LBb 112 32.70 76-14 MssGnB119hdProspctor'sDm1173MjstcTt117 No mishap 12
27Jan93- 2SA fst 6f :214 :452 1:112 ⒻⓈMd 35000 32 2 4 2hd 21 22½ 614½ Pedroza M A Lb 117 30.20 66-16 MstcJr1175Prspctr'sDm119¾TstThTm117 Bumped early 8
6Jan93- 6SA sly 6f :213 :442 1:094 ⒻMd 35000 46 9 4 73¾ 76 68½ 411½ Alvarado F T LBb 117 33.50 76-09 HrdBdyMss1176MystcJr1176½LvStppr112 Bumped, wide 11
31Dec92- 4SA gd 6½f :22 :451 1:182 3+ⒻⓈMd 35000 52 11 2 42½ 54 64½ 76½ Pedroza M A LBb 115 24.60 71-19 SnappySros1151½MjesticTte115nkMximiss115 Wide trip 12
17Dec92- 6Hol fst 7f :221 :451 1:234 3+ⒻⓈMd 28000 60 3 3 3nk 2hd 31½ 44 Atherton J E5 LBb 112 90.40 81-12 DesertRose1191LadyChief1192ChrfsBbe119 Weakened 12
LATEST WORKOUTS Apr 30 Hol 4f fst :503 H Apr 15 Hol 4f fst :504 H Apr 9 Hol 4f fst :514 H Mar 29 Hol 3f fst :371 H

Firecracker Roger — B. f. 3(Apr), by Kalim—Sparkling Finish, by Be a Native — Lifetime 5 0 0 0 $3,475 — 1993 2 M 0 0 $425 — 1992 3 M 0 0 $3,050
GONZALEZ S JR (34 3 5 5 .09) — $28,000 — Br.—Brooks & Landsburg (Cal) — 108[5] — Wet 1 0 0 0
Own.—Bethany Investments Inc — Tr.—Knight Terry (1 1 0 0 1.00)
9Apr93- 4SA fst 6½f :214 :45 1:172 ⒻⓈMd 32000 50 3 11 95¾ 68½ 67½ 58½ Sorenson D LB 117 34.60 76-13 Nskrnmcl1172¾Lc'sBb1172½Nmbrthrtfv117 Broke slowly 12
28Feb93- 9SA my 6f :214 :454 1:113 ⒻⓈMd 32000 39 3 4 55 64¾ 77 610½ Pincay L Jr Lb 117 5.40 69-12 Klem'sCrest1172Icinss1171½DlightfulDun117 No mishap 9
28Oct92- 4SA fst 6f :213 :452 1:11 ⒻⓈMd 32000 42 8 5 41½ 3½ 44½ 411½ Lopez A D LBb 117 *1.30 69-16 MngMng1172AuCorntRos1179ProdProwss117 Wide trip 10
3Sep92- 6Dmr fst 6f :221 :453 1:112 ⒻⓈMdc-32000 52 10 7 63½ 54½ 56½ 55½ McCarron C J B 117 3.20 77-14 Bornstrmrn1171½ShtPly1172DchssOfDgnty117 Wide trip 12
3Sep92-Claimed from Brooks & King & Landsburg, Cerin Vladimir Trainer
6Aug92- 4Dmr fst 6f :223 :46 1:113 ⒻⓈMd 32000 53 6 10 96 86¾ 44½ 43½ McCarron C J 117 28.80 77-12 LggyLs1172½ZmngWtrs1171DchssOfDgnty117 Wide trip 12
LATEST WORKOUTS May 2 Hol 5f fst 1:002 H Apr 20 Hol 3f fst :37 H Apr 2 Hol 6f fst 1:123 H Mar 30 Hol 3f fst :352 H

Here's *ALL-IN-ONE*'s win-par and track-model information for the first leg:

Win Pars:	47.17 111.82 143.99
Ability Par:	96.46
Winners' Pace Profile:	FRONT
Pace Contention Point:	1.11 lengths

These are Steve's comments on the horses:

Nora Of Clare: Off for nearly two years and drops to lowest level. Would suspect fire sale if not for the fact that McCarron rides. Style is anti-model, but from her past ability we decided to make her a contender and use her last race as the pace line.

Avies' Charm: Dismiss the turf try and she's been very consistent at this level. Will be closing from rearward or midpack, as she did in her pace-line race of March 27. Another anti-model horse.

Pinkie Schoop: Came out of the same turf disaster as Pinkie Schoop. We used the March 27 race to rate Avies' Charm, so take the February 4 race as Pinkie Schoop's pace line. When she wins, she races just off the lead.

Desert Rose: Won at 10-to-1 last out and steps up today, always a good sign. Pressing style fits this track well. Contender off the last race.

Majolique: Like Desert Rose, was on the pace throughout in a winning effort and steps up today. Use the last race.

Chalk Box: Two races back, she won for a $32,000 tag. In her last race she ran horribly. Today she plummets to the $16,000 claiming level. Not only is this drop below the level of the last win, it's actually below the level of the price she was claimed for. Out.

Here's *ALL-IN-ONE*'s fair odds line for the race:

Horse	Fair Odds
Majolique	3-to-1
Desert Rose	7-to-2
Pinkie Schoop	9-to-2
Nora Of Clare	6-to-1
Avies' Charm	no line

Here's *ALL-IN-ONE*'s projected speed/pace summary for our contenders:

```
6MAY93                              HOL                   8.5 furlongs dirt
Race #7                                                         7 starters
C16,000                                               Age: 4+years, Female
-----------------------------SPEED/PACE SUMMARY-----------------------------

Race Type:         Orderly Race
Race Profile:      47.17  111.82  143.99   Winners' Pace Profile: FRONT
Ability Par:       96.46                    Pace Contention Point: 1.11 lengths

Projected Times:                          Ability Balance  Last  Proj  Con-
                   1st C   2nd C   Fin C    Time    Time    Frac  Pace  tender
----------------------------------------------------------------------------
Majolique          47.12  111.35* 143.35   95.59  100.70  32.00  EARLY   N
Desert Rose        46.66  111.02  144.00   95.38  101.48  32.98  FRONT   Y
Pinkie Schoop      47.14  111.47* 143.35   95.81  100.73  31.88  MID     N
Nora Of Clare      47.72  112.26* 142.95   96.80  100.17  30.69  REAR    N
Avies' Charm       48.58  113.13* 145.03   97.68  102.04  31.91  REAR    N
```

Four horses can run to the final-time win par of 143.99. Three horses (Majolique, Desert Rose, and Pinkie Schoop) fit the model. Nora Of Clare and Avies' Charm are anti-model horses.

Here's *ALL-IN-ONE*'s track-model and win-par information for the second leg:

Win Pars:	46.81 111.01 143.09
Ability Par:	95.21
Winners' Pace Profile:	FRONT
Pace Contention Point:	1.11 lengths

Here are Steve's comments on the horses:

Fine Impression: That last race is excellent and fits the model nicely. Contender.

Justamente: Notice that she's improved vastly since returning to the main track. Definite contender off the last race.

Red Bandana: Her ability to win a dirt route is suspect and the recent form is awful. Out.

Chipeta Springs: She wins routing on dirt, though she's yet to win at Hollywood and her style is farther back than we'd like. Contender. Use the October 10 race.

Swazi's Moment: Lightly raced still-developing three-year-old drops into easier company after two graded stakes appearances. Her route style is unknown and these types improve dramatically without explanation. A question mark who we rated off the last race.

Bless Shoe: Game performance last out, employing the style necessary to win today. Definitely use the last race.

Here's *ALL-IN-ONE*'s fair-odds line:

Horse	Fair Odds
Justamente	3-to-2
Fine Impression	5-to-1
Swazi's Moment	5-to-1
Bless Shoe	no line
Chipeta Springs	no line

Here's *ALL-IN-ONE*'s speed/pace summary:

```
6MAY93                         HOL                    8.5 furlongs dirt
Race #8                                                       6 starters
ALW NW1                                             Age: 3+years, Females
-----------------------------SPEED/PACE SUMMARY------------------------------

Race Type:        Double Advantage Race
Race Profile:     46.81  111.01  143.09  Winners' Pace Profile: FRONT
Ability Par:      95.21                  Pace Contention Point:  1.11 lengths

Projected Times:                         Ability Balance  Last  Proj  Con-
                  1st C  2nd C   Fin C     Time    Time   Frac  Pace  tender
-----------------------------------------------------------------------------
Justamente        45.99  109.72  141.53   93.46   98.97   31.80 FRONT  Y+
Fine Impression   45.96  110.61* 142.95   95.26  100.73   32.34 LATE   N
Swazi's Moment    46.67  111.50* 143.20   96.33  100.80   31.70 REAR   N
Bless Shoe        46.42  111.04  144.00   95.66  101.65   32.96 REAR   N
Chipeta Springs   47.83  112.53* 144.15   97.22  101.43   31.62 REAR   N
```

Justamente appears to be a standout, relegating the other runners to LATE and REAR running styles. Yet there are two other horses (Fine Impression and Swazi's Moment) who, while outside the pace contention point at the second call, are competitive with the final-time win par. A confident strategy would single Justamente out because of her domination of the race pace and her final time. A cautious strategy would respect the ability of Fine Impression and Swazi's Moment and include these horses on the ticket.

Here's *ALL-IN-ONE*'s track model and win par information for the final leg:

Win Pars:	22.83 46.08 124.61
Ability Par:	69.34
Winners' Pace Profile:	MID
Pace Contention Point:	4.58 lengths

Here are Steve's comments:

Bold Dee Dee: Shown speed in her races, but has backed up in all of them and the rail is the worst place to be at Hollywood. Out.

Moonlight Cut: First-time starter is going off at 30-to-1. Noncontender.

Nancy's Legend: Improved race off the long layoff and should expect continued progress. Use the last race.

Marella: No betting action, no ability in debut. Elimination.
Jelikit: Broke slowly but didn't show anything after the trouble. Throwout.
Talisman's Magic: She's a professional maiden, but the last two races without blinkers have been competitive mid- to rear-pack efforts. A very marginal contender off the last race.
Decidedly Natalie: Ran best race ever second off the layoff and the third time is often the charm with returnees. Strong contender off the last race.
Native Doryl: Comes off layoff and best race was off a layoff. Rate her off the February 12 race.

Here's how *ALL-IN-ONE* saw the race:

Horse	Fair Odds
Decidedly Natalie	9-to-5
Talisman's Magic	3-to-1
Nancy's Legend	no line
Native Doryl	no line

Here's *ALL-IN-ONE*'s speed/pace summary:

```
6MAY93                              HOL                    7 furlongs dirt
Race #9                                                          12 starters
MCL                                                 Age: 3+years, Females
-----------------------------SPEED/PACE SUMMARY-----------------------------
Race Type:          Orderly Race
Race Profile:       22.83   46.08   124.61   Winners' Pace Profile: MID
Ability Par:        69.34                     Pace Contention Point:  4.58 lengths

Projected Times:                         Ability Balance  Last Proj  Con-
                    1st C   2nd C   Fin C    Time   Time   Frac Pace  tender
--------------------------------------------------------------------------
Decidedly Natalie   22.69   45.82   124.58   68.96  80.79  38.76 FRONT  Y
Talisman's Magic    24.16   46.54   124.81   68.93  81.34  38.26 LATE   Y
Nancy's Legend      23.12   46.68   125.73   70.25  81.93  39.04 LATE   N
Native Doryl        22.92   46.45   126.40   69.97  82.31  39.95 MID    N
```

They all run within five lengths of the lead at the second call, so they all fit the model. In terms of ability time and final time, it's a two-horse race: Decidedly Natalie and Talisman's Magic.

Let's construct our $200 Pick-3 investment (remember, the minimum Pick-3 at Hollywood is $3) using our lines:

Seventh race

Majolique	3-to-1
Desert Rosc	7-to-2
Pinkie Schoop	9-to-2
Nora Of Clare	6-to-1

Eighth race

Justamente	3-to-2
Fine Impression	5-to-1
Swazi's Moment	5-to-1

Ninth race

Decidedly Natalie	9-to-5
Talisman's Magic	3-to-1

The following table represents the computer output for this Pick-3. The first column represents the combination bet. The first letter represents your choice in the first leg, the second letter represents your choice in the second leg, and the third letter represents your choice in the third leg. For example, AAC means to bet on your first choice in the first leg with your first choice in the second leg with your third choice in the last leg. (Your choices for each leg are listed in alphabetical order.) "(Line Odds - - -)" are our line odds for each choice in its respective race. "P(W)" stands for the probability that the combination in column one will win. "% bet" stands for the probability of winning divided by the total success probability, which is 35.5 percent. "$ Bet" stands for the percentage of total bet multiplied by the total bet. (This number is calculated in cents and must be rounded to the nearest dollar.) "Actual Bet" is the rounded-off bet-size amount, which also takes the minimum bet into consideration.

	(Line Odds ———)			P(W)	% bet	$ bet	Actual
AAA	3	1.5	1.8	0.036	0.101	20.132	20
BAA	3.5	1.5	1.8	0.032	0.089	17.895	18
CAA	4.5	1.5	1.8	0.026	0.073	14.641	15
AAB	3	1.5	3	0.025	0.070	14.092	14

	(Line Odds ———)			P(W)	% bet	$ bet	Actual
BAB	3.5	1.5	3	0.022	0.063	12.526	13
DAB	6	1.5	1.8	0.020	0.058	11.504	12
CAB	4.5	1.5	3	0.018	0.051	10.249	10
ACA	3	5	1.8	0.015	0.042	8.388	8
ABA	3	5	1.8	0.015	0.042	8.388	8
DAB	6	1.5	3	0.014	0.040	8.053	8
BCA	3.5	5	1.8	0.013	0.037	7.456	7
BBA	3.5	5	1.8	0.013	0.037	7.456	7
CCA	4.5	5	1.8	0.011	0.031	6.100	6
CBA	4.5	5	1.8	0.011	0.031	6.100	6
ABB	3	5	3	0.010	0.029	5.872	6
ACB	3	5	3	0.010	0.029	5.872	6
BCB	3.5	5	3	0.009	0.026	5.219	5
BBB	3.5	5	3	0.009	0.026	5.219	5
DCA	6	5	1.8	0.009	0.024	4.793	5
DBA	6	5	1.8	0.009	0.024	4.793	5
CBB	4.5	5	3	0.008	0.021	4.270	4
CCB	4.5	5	3	0.008	0.021	4.270	4
DBB	6	5	3	0.006	0.017	3.355	3
DCB	6	5	3	0.006	0.017	3.355	3
Totals				0.355	1.000	200	198

A $198 investment covered all 24 combinations. Please note: We eliminated two false favorites, so we didn't have to cross out any combinations. The result was a $148.80 Pick-3 that we hit 2⅔ times for a $396.80 payout on our $198 investment—an ROI of 200 percent. Not the world's best score, but it will do until one comes along.

The modified Ambrose strategy handled this Pick-3 with facility. In fact, it did better. The key horses are in italics.

Leg 1	Leg 2	Leg 3
Majolique	*Justamente*	*Decidedly Natalie*
Desert Rose	Fine Impression	Talisman's Magic
Pinkie Schoop	Swazi's Moment	Nancy's Legend

Since two key horses won, the strategy collected $297.60 on its $81 investment, an ROI of 367 percent. It outperformed our computer strategy. Only one key horse (Decidedly Natalie) figured to be a probable favorite.

SEVENTH RACE
Hollywood
MAY 6, 1993

1 1/16 MILES. (1.40) CLAIMING. Purse $16,000. Fillies and mares. 4-year-olds and upward. Weight, 122 lbs. Non-winners of two races at one or over since March 12 allowed 3 lbs.; such a race since then, 6 lbs. Claiming price $16,000; if for $14,000 allowed 2 lbs. (Races when entered for $12,500 or less not considered.)

Value of race $16,000; value to winner $8,800; second $3,200; third $2,400; fourth $1,200; fifth $400. Mutuel pool $226,004. Exacta pool $221,915.

Last Raced	Horse	M/Eqt.	A.Wt	PP	St	¼	½	¾	Str	Fin	Jockey	Cl'g Pr	Odds $1
10Apr93 3SA1	Majolique-Ar	LB	8 116	6	2	1½	1½	1½	12	1½	Black C A	16000	2.80
15Apr93 8SA7	Avies' Charm	LB	6 116	2	3	3½	4½	3hd	32½	2½	DesormuxKJ	16000	2.90
10Apr93 7SA8	Chalk Box	LB	7 117	7	1	21	21½	21½	21½	33½	ValenzuelPA	16000	1.70
22Apr93 1Hol1	Desert Rose	LBb	5 114	4	4	43	31	44	45	44½	Torres H	14000	12.00
17Mar93 7GG5	Marie De Siberie	LBb	6 114	5	5	7	7	7	53½	57	Berrio O A	14000	42.30
15Apr93 8SA10	Pinkie Schoop	LB	4 119	3	6	64	63	53½	65	66½	Castaneda K	16000	12.10
9Oct91 3SA5	Nora Of Clare	LB	6 116	1	7	5hd	5hd	6½	7	7	McCarron CJ	16000	7.00

OFF AT 4:16. Start good. Won driving. Time, :23^{2}, :47, 1:11, 1:36^{2}, 1:43 Track fast.

$2 Mutuel Prices:			
6-MAJOLIQUE-AR	7.60	3.80	2.80
2-AVIES' CHARM		4.20	2.40
7-CHALK BOX			2.40

$2 EXACTA 6-2 PAID $28.40.

EIGHTH RACE
Hollywood
MAY 6, 1993

1 1/16 MILES. (1.40) ALLOWANCE. Purse $42,000. Fillies and mares, 3-year-olds and upward which have not won $3,000 twice other than maiden, claiming or starter. Weights, 3-year-olds, 114 lbs.; older, 122 lbs. Non-winners of two races other than claiming at a mile or over since March 15 allowed 3 lbs.; such a race other than maiden or claiming since then, 6 lbs.

Value of race $42,000; value to winner $23,100; second $8,400; third $6,300; fourth $3,150; fifth $1,050. Mutuel pool $272,405. Exacta pool $227,160.

Last Raced	Horse	M/Eqt.	A.Wt	PP	St	¼	½	¾	Str	Fin	Jockey	Odds $1
9Apr93 9OP4	Swazi's Moment	B	3 107	5	2	3hd	44	31½	13½	12½	Gonzalez S Jr5	3.30
14Apr93 9SA5	Chipeta Springs	LBb	4 117	4	6	51½	53½	51½	21	26	Pincay L Jr	13.20
11Apr93 5SA5	Red Bandana	LBb	4 116	3	4	6	6	6	5½	3½	Stevens G L	13.80
2Apr93 7SA1	Fine Impression	b	3 113	1	5	11½	1hd	1hd	3½	4no	Nakatani C S	1.00
26Mar93 7SA1	Justamente-Ar	L	5 119	2	1	21	2½	2½	42½	51	Black C A	3.40
21Apr93 1Hol1	Bless Shoe	LBb	4 119	6	3	44	31	44	6	6	Valenzuela P A	8.70

OFF AT 4:53. Start good. Won driving. Time, :23^{1}, :46^{2}, 1:10^{2}, 1:35^{3}, 1:41^{4} Track fast.

$2 Mutuel Prices:			
5-SWAZI'S MOMENT	8.60	4.40	3.80
4-CHIPETA SPRINGS		9.20	5.20
3-RED BANDANA			4.80

$2 EXACTA 5-4 PAID $59.40.

NINTH RACE
Hollywood
MAY 6, 1993

7 FURLONGS. (1.20^{4}) MAIDEN CLAIMING. Purse $17,000. Fillies and mares. 3-year-olds and upward. Bred in California. Weights, 3-year-olds, 115 lbs.; older, 122 lbs. Claiming price $32,000; if for $28,000 allowed 2 lbs.

Value of race $17,000; value to winner $9,350; second $3,400; third $2,550; fourth $1,275; fifth $425. Mutuel pool $238,585. Exacta pool $214,823. Superfectapool $221,325.

Last Raced	Horse	M/Eqt.	A.Wt	PP	St	¼	½	Str	Fin	Jockey	Cl'g Pr	Odds $1
11Apr93 9SA2	Decidedly Natalie	LB	3 115	7	6	31	21	1½	14½	Stevens G L	32000	1.20
15Apr93 6SA9	Bold Dee Dee	LBb	3 113	1	3	12½	11½	24	22½	Solis A	28000	22.30
9Apr93 4SA7	Jelikit	LB	3 115	5	9	104	91	72½	3no	Flores D R	32000	8.10
31Mar93 3SA4	Riviere Miss	LBb	3 115	9	7	61½	4½	3½	4½	Garcia J A	32000	4.10
9Apr93 4SA5	Firecracker Roger	LB	3 108	11	4	73	73	5½	5¾	GonzalezSJr5	28000	16.00
16Apr93 6SA3	Talisman's Magic	LB	5 120	6	8	84	81½	61	62½	Castaneda K	28000	10.90
18Mar93 4SA5	Native Doryl	LB	3 115	8	2	21	32	41	72	Nakatani C S	32000	36.00
	Moonlight Cut	LB	3 117	2	11	91	105	81	82	Pincay L Jr	32000	31.80
22Apr93 5Hol5	Wreak Havoc	LBb	4 120	10	1	5½	6hd	92	91¾	Black C A	28000	26.20
7Apr93 9SA2	Nancy's Legend	L	4 120	3	5	4hd	51	101½	101	Lopez A D	28000	5.40
11Apr93 9SA8	Marella	B	3 115	4	10	11	11	11	11	Torres H	32000	131.40

OFF AT 5:24. Start good. Won driving. Time, :22, :45, 1:10^{1}, 1:23^{1} Track fast.

$2 Mutuel Prices:			
8-DECIDEDLY NATALIE	4.40	3.60	2.80
1-BOLD DEE DEE		15.80	7.80
6-JELIKIT			5.00

$2 EXACTA 8-1 PAID $85.60. SUPERFECTA 8-1-6-10 PAID $1,751.30.

Practice these strategies on paper until you are as confident as I am that you can make juicy profits using them. I much prefer the computer strategy to the modified Ambrose strategy. I am in the minority on this point. The vast majority of players who are familiar with both strategies prefer the Ambrose version because you don't have to sweat about making a line and the tickets are much easier to construct.

The Pick-3 is a wonderful opportunity. Fortunately, our competition continues to throw money away on part-wheels that have only one chance of hitting. Most handicappers are so intent on winning the bet that they completely disregard the issue of value. That's our edge. The other huge mistake that most players make is that they bet small amounts of money. They'll usually buy a $24 or $36 ticket on a $3 Pick-3 or a $16 or $24 ticket on a $2 Pick-3. This is a huge mistake. They're much better off purchasing a percentage of a much larger ticket. Another common mistake is to include more than one favorite on a Pick-3 ticket. Don't play any Pick-3 where you have to include two favorites. Remember, only one key horse can be a probable favorite. Never more than one favorite on any ticket.

Let's now take a look at what I consider to be the one of the most misplayed bets at the track: the exacta.

EXACTA AND QUINELLA WAGERING

One of the most abused forms of wagering on thoroughbred races is exacta betting. Most players don't know how to bet exactas, yet the exacta pools are usually larger than the straight pools. The astute investor uses the exacta to his best advantage. The most typical exacta wager is the three-horse box, or "baseball." That is, betting on all six possible arrangements of three horses in the first and second positions. Most of the time this isn't a good idea. Once again, the number of guaranteed losing bets is too large. Another misconception is the compulsion that most players always feel to reverse exacta combinations.

Most handicappers really don't understand the exacta. It's a compound bet. You're picking the winner plus the "place horse." If you learn nothing else from this chapter, please memorize this: *The second-best win horse rarely comes in second.* In other words, the place horse isn't the second-best win horse. On average, the favorite should win and the second favorite should complete the exacta around 12 percent of the time. Most empirical studies cluster between 8 and 11 percent. How often does the favorite-to-second favorite exacta pay more than $20 for $2? Seldom if ever. It doesn't take a genius to see that you shouldn't buy this exacta combination. Not only does the public overload on it in every race, it usually "sends it in" on the reverse combination as well. The reversal is usually a sucker bet, too.

Typically, the exacta pools are larger than the straight mutuel pools. What a lovely situation. The public bets more money where it's least proficient. Here's your opportunity to plunder and pillage. Master this chapter and Chapter 26 of my *Winning Thoroughbred Strategies*. You'll be very well compensated for your time and energy.

The quintessential handicapping skill that you need in order to crush the exacta is the ability to pick the place horse. The way that you acquire any skill is practice—practice with feedback. (As an aside, the old saw that "practice makes perfect" is a lie. Practice without feedback just means that you continue to perfect the wrong way to do things. The aphorism should be "Practice makes permanent.") Fortunately, you have the best feedback system ever invented: the mutuel windows. Every time you handicap a race, try to pick the horse that will come in second. Write down all the place contenders, no matter how many. You should have the place horse listed within your contenders at least 80 percent of the time, the same as your win contenders.

There are four basic paradigms of the place horse. They are:

1. The unbalanced horse
2. The anti-bias horse
3. The seconditis horse
4. The favorite

The Unbalanced Horse

This is the horse that doesn't quite have it together. He either has high class and inferior speed or low class and superior speed. In order to be a legitimate favorite, the horse must have both class and speed superiority. Have you noticed how often a recent maiden graduate with good numbers manages to come in second in nonwinners allowance races? This is especially true for recent maiden claiming graduates moving dramatically up in class.

The Anti-bias Horse

This is the frontrunner on a track favoring closers or a closer on a track favoring frontrunners. This is the horse coming from the one-post when the rail is dead. This is the turf horse coming from the 12-hole in a two-turn race. Despite the negative situation, there's one thing the anti-bias horse has going for him: superior numbers. This horse usually has the best adjusted final time of any horse in the race, but has to deal with a strong negative bias.

The Seconditis Horse

This is the kind of horse who reads—a very intelligent creature. While his equine buddies are watching *Wheel of Fortune,* he's busy studying the *Daily Racing Form,* figuring out a way to come in second. The seconditis horse is easy to spot. His record will look something like this: 7 1 4 0. In seven outings he managed to come in second four times. God bless these horses. They make wonderful candidates for the second spot on any exacta ticket.

The Favorite

This includes three types of favorites. The first is the betting favorite of the crowd. The second is the morning-line favorite. Most of the time, these horses are the same. When they aren't, please consider both horses as second-place candidates. The third type of favorite is the *Daily Racing Form*'s consensus horse (the one in boldface type). This kind of favorite wins more than 40 percent of the time and places more than 60 percent of the time. In other words, if he doesn't win, he's the place horse around 20 percent of the time. The public favorite also comes in second around 20 percent of the time. Keep in mind the fact that the favorite is involved in the exacta around 52 percent of the time. The public favorite or the second favorite is involved in the exacta at least 75 percent of the time. That is, either one or both are involved in the exacta three out of four times.

• • •

The key to exacta profits is the ability to handicap the place horse. Whenever you handicap a race, concentrate on picking the horse that figures to come in second. After a while patterns will emerge.

As with any wager, the key factor is expectation. You must know your win percentage and average mutuel. Your records will tell you whether this is a profitable form of wagering or not. Optimum strategies depend on expectation and odds.

Exacta pools can be used to your advantage when the straight mutuel pool isn't offering an overlay on the horse(s) you like. Suppose you like the favorite, but he's going off at unacceptable odds. For example, you judge that this particular horse should be 2-to-1 to be acceptable. He's going off at 8-to-5. You look at the exacta probable pays and see that he'll pay $18, $19.20, and $22 respectively for a $2 exacta wager when coupled with the three horses most likely to come in second. By wagering on him in the exacta, you'll now receive at least 2-to-1. Your straight $6 win bet at 8-to-5 would return $15.60. By playing him in the exacta, he'll pay at least $18, providing, of course, one of your three choices comes in second.

Conversely, look at this favorite in the exacta pool. The payoffs are $12, $14, and $15 respectively when coupled with the most likely place horses. If he's going off at 2-to-1 in the straight pools, then skip the exacta and bet him to win.

You should always look for your best value. Always ask yourself, "Am I better off putting the money I would spend in the exacta pool on the horse's nose?" You won't believe me when I tell you that some of the best players in the country never ask this question. They religiously play both the win and exacta pools on the races they consider playable. Don't do this.

To determine if an exacta combination is an overlay or not, you'll either have to use your own odds line or be able to convert the public's odds to fair prices. To compute the probability of an exacta combination, multiply the probability of the win horse by the win probability of the place horse (given that the win horse has won). For example, let's figure the probability of a 2-to-1 horse on top of a 3-to-1 horse. The win probability of the 2-to-1 horse is $\frac{1}{3}$. The probability of the 3-to-1 horse coming in second given that the 2-to-1 horse has won the race is $\frac{1}{4}$ divided by $\frac{2}{3}$. (The $\frac{2}{3}$ represents the remaining probability because we know that the winner had a $\frac{1}{3}$ probability. Since we know that he has won, $\frac{1}{3}$ of the probability has been removed.) Hence the probability of this combination is $\frac{1}{3} \times \frac{3}{8} = \frac{1}{8} = .125$. This number divided into the bet size is the fair payoff. For a $2 exacta this would be $2/.125 = $16.

To calculate the fair pay for an exacta, using our own betting-line odds, the formula is as follows:

Fair pay = Bet size × (win odds first horse) × (win odds place horse + 1)

In the above example, a 2-to-1 on top of a 3-to-1, we simply plug the numbers in.

Fair pay = $2 × (2) × (3 + 1) = $16

The power of this formula is that it relates the odds in the win pool to the payoffs in the exacta pool.

If we're using the public's estimation of the odds, we now must consider the effect of the track take. In California the track take is 15.33 percent on straight mutuel wagers, and so the track pay is .8467. The track pay is the amount per dollar that is returned to customers. Since each wager is quoted at .8467 of its fair value and we multiplied two of them together, then the $16 represents .8467 × .8467 of its fair value, or 71.7 percent of what it should really pay. Hence we must divide the $16 by .717, which is $22.32.

The equation for fair pay in terms of toteboard odds is as follows:

$$\text{FAIR PAY} = \frac{B \times O1 \times (O2 + 1)}{TP^2}$$

Where   B = Bet size
        O1 = Odds-to-1 on first horse
        O2 = Odds-to-1 on place horse
        TP = Track payback

For southern California, where the track pay is .8467 and the typical exacta bet is $2, the above equation reduces to:

Fair pay = 2.79 × O1 × (O2 + 1)

The constant 2.79 is derived from the bet size divided by the square of the track payback (2 ÷ .717 = 2.79).

For northern California the mutuel pay also is .8467, but the exacta bet is $5, hence the fair-pay equation is:

Fair pay = 6.97 × O1 × (O2 + 1)

For example, suppose you're making four exacta wagers on the following odds combinations from your betting line:

1. 7-to-2 on top of a 3-to-1
2. 3-to-1 on top of a 7-to-2

3. 5-to-2 on top of a 9-to-2
4. 9-to-2 on top of a 5-to-2

The first thing we must do is calculate the fair pay for each combination. It'll be good practice for you to actually take out a pencil and paper and compute each manually. Assume we're playing a $2 exacta in California where the take is 15.33 percent. (We really don't have to know the track take because we're using our own betting line.) The fair pays are:

1. $28.00
2. $27.00
3. $27.50
4. $31.50

If we want to guarantee ourselves a 20 percent edge on a single bet, we simply multiply each entry by 1.2. Barry Meadow suggests using a multiplier of 1.5 (a good suggestion). I like to use 1.4, the same multiplier as I use in the daily double. This multiplier usually compensates us for our losing bets, except in extreme cases. (An extreme case is when we have a large number of guaranteed losing bets where the payoff values are very close to the cutoff values.) Fortunately, these situations are rare. The edge pays are:

1. $39.20
2. $37.80
3. $38.50
4. $44.10

When making multiple exacta bets you must consider the effect of the number of guaranteed losing bets and add them to the payout that you are insisting upon. You must compensate yourself for your guaranteed losing wagers. If you were to make all four of these bets, at least three of them are guaranteed to lose. Hence you must add $2 to each payoff for each additional combination that you bet. If you bet all four combinations, you must add $6 to each of the above edge pays. If you only bet two of them, then you would simply add $2 to the edge pay. Fortunately, the 1.4 multiplier usually takes care of compensation for guaranteed losing bets.

Andy Beyer tells the story of "the Doc." He's a guy who makes his living by betting exacta races and does no handicapping whatsoever. He simply compares the fair exacta payoffs to the offered payoffs and bets only on the overlayed combinations. He's got a medical degree and could be making a ton of money practicing medicine. Instead, he makes his living on the ignorance of his fellow players. The betting public really doesn't play exactas anywhere near efficiently, as we already know.

Please forgive the repetition. These concepts are vital. As a teacher, I am willing to run the risk of boring my brighter students to make sure that the entire class understands the foundation principles necessary for higher learning to take place.

If you use your own line, the formula for the fair price is:

$$\text{Fair price} = \text{Bet size} \times \text{Odds 1} \times (\text{Odds 2} + 1)$$

The above formula tells you to multiply three numbers: the bet size, the win odds of your win horse, and the number 1 added to the win odds of your place horse. For example, assume your line was as follows:

Horse A	2-to-1
Horse B	3-to-1
Horse C	4-to-1

Let's figure the $2 and $5 exacta fair prices for all six possible exacta combinations:

AB = $2 × 2 × (3 + 1) = $16	AB = $5 × 2 × (3 + 1) = $40
AC = $2 × 2 × (4 + 1) = $20	AC = $5 × 2 × (4 + 1) = $50
BA = $2 × 3 × (2 + 1) = $18	BA = $5 × 3 × (2 + 1) = $45
BC = $2 × 3 × (4 + 1) = $30	BC = $5 × 3 × (4 + 1) = $75
CA = $2 × 4 × (2 + 1) = $24	CA = $5 × 4 × (2 + 1) = $60
CB = $2 × 4 × (3 + 1) = $32	CB = $5 × 4 × (3 + 1) = $80

If you use the public's odds line as your line, the formula is the same, except that you must divide by the square of the track payback. (The track payback is the one's complement of the track take. In other words, track payback = 1 minus track take.) The track payback is the amount of the bettor's dollar that's returned in the win pool. In California the track take is 15.33 percent, so the track payback is 84.67 percent, or .8467.

$$\text{Fair price} = \frac{\text{Bet size} \times \text{Odds 1} \times (\text{Odds 2} + 1)}{(\text{track payback})^2}$$

The above formula tells you to divide the results of the first formula by the track payback squared. Let's figure the $2 exacta fair prices in California for all six possible exacta combinations in the above example.

$$AB = [\$2 \times 2 \times (3+1)]/(.717) = \$16/.717 = \$22.31$$
$$AC = [\$2 \times 2 \times (4+1)]/(.717) = \$20/.717 = \$27.89$$
$$BA = [\$2 \times 3 \times (2+1)]/(.717) = \$18/.717 = \$25.10$$
$$BC = [\$2 \times 3 \times (4+1)]/(.717) = \$30/.717 = \$41.84$$
$$CA = [\$2 \times 4 \times (2+1)]/(.717) = \$24/.717 = \$33.47$$
$$CB = [\$2 \times 4 \times (3+1)]/(.717) = \$32/.717 = \$44.63$$

Please note that .717 is $(.8467)^2$. If "Doc" happened to be in California, that's how he would generate the fair prices. Naturally, he didn't want fair prices. He wanted a premium. I'm not sure exactly what minimum premium he insisted upon.

You now know how to calculate the price necessary to make the exacta combination yield an acceptable overlay. The way you play the exacta is simple. You write down all your win horses and all your place horses. You draw the grid or matrix that represents all the possibilities. You then calculate the acceptable overlay price for each combination. Next, you write down the probable pay from the monitors at the track. Circle all the combinations that offer good value. Make sure that you deduct the effect of losing $2 bets. For example, suppose you have three combinations circled as overlays. You must subtract $4 from each probable payoff to compensate yourself for your losing bets. You then bet on all combinations in proportion to their respective probabilities. You definitely want to have more money on those combinations with the higher probabilities. (The fastest and easiest way to bet exactas in this manner is to use the *Bettor-Handicapper,* which automates this whole process. It also automates all the other betting propositions such as win betting, place-and-show betting, daily double, serial triple, and any serial bet. In addition it contains a class and pace calculator. The truth is, betting is complicated and you really need a computer to do it correctly. I would sooner go to the track without my pants than without a pocket computer that can run these betting programs.)

Here are some exacta wagering guidelines:

1. Never bet an exacta when you can make more money by betting to win.
2. Each exacta combination must carry a positive edge.
3. When wagering on more than one exacta combination, you must be compensated for your guaranteed losing bets.
4. Unless a race is really contentious, you should have no more than two win-horse contenders and three place-horse contenders.

Exacta wagering offers the investor a wonderful opportunity to earn substantial profits. These wagers can be strategic as well. They can be used to convert an underlay into an overlay. They offer us wide latitude for making intelligent betting choices. Only a small number of bettors understand how to make these wagers properly.

If your personal financial goal exceeds $200 per day, you must master the exacta. In order to win a lot of money at thoroughbred wagering you must bet a lot of money. It's a sad fact that the parimutuel system penalizes you for making large bets. The only way around this difficulty is to invest in low probability–high payoff wagers such as the exacta.

Let's now look at an exacta betting technique that takes a small amount of money and turns it into a huge pile of cash. I've eponymously dubbed this method the "Mitchell Matrix." (What the hell—if Tom Brohamer can have a model named after him, why shouldn't I have something named after my very own self?)

The Mitchell Matrix is a technique that one of my students used to purchase a brand-new car for cash. This is a crush technique that can earn you your season's profits in a single race. The idea is simple. You find a contentious race with three or more win and place contenders. I'll demonstrate using four contenders and give you a general formula for any number of contenders. If you have a race with four contenders you can't separate, your fair-odds line is 4-to-1 on each contender and 4-to-1 on the rest of the field. By extension, each exacta combination has an equal chance of winning. The probability of a 4-to-1 shot finishing on top of another 4-to-1 shot is found by multiplying the win probability by the dependent probability of the place horse coming in second. This is mighty fancy verbiage to say the following: A 4-to-1 shot has a 20 percent chance of winning the race. Another 4-to-1 shot has a 20 percent chance of winning the rest of the race, given that another horse won. His 20 percent isn't 20 percent of 100 percent, it's 20 percent of 80 percent, because we already know that another horse won the race. His probability of coming in second is dependent on who won the race. The probability of winning this exacta is 20 percent of 25 percent, or 5 percent. This result can be generalized. It's always the reciprocal of n times n + 1, where "n" represents the number of contenders. In this case, it is $1/(4 \times 5)$ or $\frac{1}{20}$, which is 5 percent. In the case of five contenders, it's $\frac{1}{30}$, or 3.3 percent. For six contenders, it's $\frac{1}{42}$, or 2.4 percent.

The trick to the Mitchell Matrix is to write down the probable exacta payoffs in a table or matrix. You then circle the highest-paying combinations. (Each combination must be above 150 percent of its fair pay.) If you have four contenders, circle the four highest-paying combinations. If you have five contenders, circle the five highest-paying combinations, and so on. In the case of four contenders, we have a 20 percent chance to hit this exacta. That is, we have four combinations that each have a 5 percent chance of hitting. It should be apparent that these combinations must pay over a certain minimum or you don't bet them. If you have a 5 percent chance of winning a bet, then you must be paid 19-to-1 for it to be a fair bet. Who wants fair bets? Using this technique we insist on a 50 percent premium; hence the minimum payoff must be $57.

MITCHELL MATRIX TABLE

# of Contenders	P(W) Single Bet	P(W) Entire Bet	Minimum $2 Payoff
3	8.3%	25%	$ 35
4	5.0%	20%	$ 57
5	3.3%	17%	$ 87
6	2.4%	14%	$123

# of Contenders	P(W) Single Bet	P(W) Entire Bet	Minimum $2 Payoff
7	1.8%	13%	$165
8	1.3%	11%	$213
9	1.1%	10%	$267

This table tells us the probability of any single combination winning the exacta, the total chances that one of our combinations will win, and the minimum price to accept (with 50 percent premium, which we've already factored into our table.) If any combination falls below this minimum, we'll leave it out. The table ends with nine contenders for a very good reason—it's not a good idea to use this technique when your total win probability is less than 10 percent. Try this method. It's dynamite. But go slow at first. Test it with two bucks on each combination. When you're convinced, accelerate your bets to your maximum comfort level.

The next technique I call my "suicide-prevention" strategy. It was first promulgated by Mark Cramer in his excellent work, *Eleven Winning Exacta Situations.* Can you remember the last time that you bet a hefty long shot to win, only to have it finish second in a photo with a lukewarm favorite? What did you get paid for your excellent handicapping? Bupkis! This brings up a good question: How can we prosper when a long shot runs second? Answer: the exacta. Whenever you bet a long shot (9-to-2 or over) to win, also play him second in the exacta to the horse(s) most likely to beat him. Usually, the horse most likely to beat your long shot is the favorite, unless it's a false favorite. So it's a good idea to play your long shot second to the favorite in the exacta and make a straight-win bet on your long shot as well. If the race is contentious, it's a good idea to use your long shot second to a few horses. It's more probable that your long shot will run second than that it will win. This is a simple fact of life. This technique allows you to collect a nice payoff a good percentage of the time regardless of whether your long shot runs first or second.

I've tested this strategy on 1,200 races at Hollywood Park over the past two years. No attempt was made to weed out false or vulnerable favorites. I simply played all the horses over 9-to-2 on *ALL-IN-ONE*'s betting line second to the favorite in the race. The results were amazing. Based on a $2 bet, $3,876 was invested and

$4,053.80 was returned. The hit rate was 8.4 percent and the average mutuel was $38.24. The ROI was a little less than 5 percent. This may not sound like the world's best investment, but it's a statistically significant result.

Cramer calls this technique "the exacta as a place bet." It's not a good idea to bet long shots to place, except under very special circumstances. Rather than suffer the pain of collecting only $7 to place on a 20-to-1 shot who runs second to the favorite, you'll now collect a hefty exacta when this happens.

The reason I call this technique my "suicide-prevention" strategy is that I can remember missing on a 60-to-1 shot in the last race on a day that was filled with horror. I hadn't cashed a single ticket that day. All day long, my exactas ran one-three, my win bets came in second, my place bets came in third, and my show bets came in fourth. It was the day from hell. The last race was a cheap maiden-claiming route. All the horses were proven losers. My pick looked dreadful. He was zero for the world. His trainer was zero for the world. His female jockey was zero for the world. This horse looked genuinely disgusting. The only thing the horse had going for him was that he figured to have a two-length lead at the second call. The favorite had the best adjusted final time in the race, which was a bunch below par.

As fate would have it, my horse jumped out to a comfortable early lead. He maintained this lead down the back stretch. Turning the corner, there was only one horse that could remotely challenge him. It was the favorite. At the sixteenth pole, my horse started to stagger, as did the favorite. The late stretch run looked more like a dance routine than a horse race. Both horses were weaving all over the track. These two horses bumped just before the wire. It looked real close, but I was certain that my horse had prevailed. In what seemed like the world's longest photo, they put up my number first and the number of the favorite second. I let out a howl that could be heard for miles. Before the reverberations had a chance to come back to me, the INQUIRY sign flashed. (The big board lightup the ever-familiar PLEASE HOLD ALL TICKETS message.) Everybody around me assured me that my horse was innocent. The bumping incident close to the wire was the result of two tired puppies drifting into each other. My $100 win bet was going to mean a $5,000 winning day in spite of the drubbing I had taken on the first eight races.

After what seemed like eternity, the judges ruled that my horse was disqualified and the claim of foul by the jockey on the favorite was upheld. This was the first time in my experience that a jockey's objection was granted. Result: I left the track talking to myself. I felt like finding the tallest building in the neighborhood to practice my swan diving.

What was even more horrible was when they posted the exacta price. The $5 exacta, using the favorite to my 60-to-1 shot, paid more than $1,000. If I had only bought the favorite–long shot exacta for a measly five bucks, I would have had a winning day. Instead I left the track nine hundred bucks lighter. This lesson was so excruciating that I still talk about it now, ten years later. The good news is that 900 scoots was a small price to pay for this most valuable lesson. Now, whenever I bet a long shot to win, I always put it on the bottom of an exacta using the favorite (or logical contenders, when there is a false favorite). This simple strategy has been responsible for many of my major scores.

Horse-race handicapping was invented for masochists. The agony of defeat seems to be the natural order of things. How often has a margin of one puny length determined whether you were ahead a whole bunch of money or went home a loser? There isn't too much we can do about this vicious reality, but there is something that we can do about solving the dilemma of whether to bet the exacta or the quinella in the same race.

Most handicappers erroneously believe that a quinella is the same as an exacta box and therefore should pay half of what the exacta on the same horses would pay. Not so. An exacta box is usually a dumb bet, except when you consider both horses' win and place chances to be identical. This seldom happens. You're much better off betting exacta combinations in proportion to their chances of hitting. Suppose that your line on a race was as follows:

Horse A   2-to-1
Horse B   3-to-1
Horse C   4-to-1

The reason that an ABC exacta box isn't a smart bet is because the AB exacta has a much better chance of hitting than any other combination. For example, it's twice as likely as the CB exacta. Here are the fair pays for all the combinations:

$$AB = \$2 \times 2 \times (3 + 1) = \$16$$
$$AC = \$2 \times 2 \times (4 + 1) = \$20$$
$$BA = \$2 \times 3 \times (2 + 1) = \$18$$
$$BC = \$2 \times 3 \times (4 + 1) = \$30$$
$$CA = \$2 \times 4 \times (2 + 1) = \$24$$
$$CB = \$2 \times 4 \times (3 + 1) = \$32$$

The fundamental principles of money management urge us to bet twice as much on AB as on CB.

Let's now take a look at the quinella fair pays. Fair pay is always the probability of an event happening divided into the bet size. To calculate the fair price of an AB quinella, it's necessary to add the probabilities of the AB exacta to the BA exacta and divide the sum into $2. The probability of the AB exacta is ⅛ and the probability of the BA exacta is ⅑. Their sum is ¹⁷⁄₇₂. This divided into $2 becomes $8.47. The fair price for the AC quinella is $10.91 and the fair price for the BC quinella is $15.48.

You can approximate these values by taking half the average of the exacta prices. For example, the AB exacta fair price is $16 and the BA fair price is $18. Therefore their average is $17 and half that is $8.50, which is very close to the actual fair pay of $8.47. Same for the AC quinella. The AC exacta fair price is $20 and the CA fair price is $24. Their average is $22 and half that is $11.00, which is very close to the actual fair pay of $10.91. The BC exacta fair price is $30 and the CB fair price is $32. Their average is $31 and half that is $15.50, which is very close to the actual fair pay of $15.48.

Consider a 6-to-1 horse coming in on top of an even-money horse. The fair exacta price is $24. Many players think that a $10.00 quinella is a worse deal than a $24 exacta. It's not—it's actually a good deal. The exacta the other way should only pay $12, and so the quinella fair pay should be around $9. The actual quinella fair price is $8.84. The sum of the exacta probabilities of ¹⁄₁₂ and ⅐ is ¹⁹⁄₈₄. This divided into $2 is $8.84.

There is a formula for a $2 quinella fair pay in terms of odds. It's a little nasty but it works. The formula is:

$$\text{Quinella fair pay} = \frac{2 \times \text{Odds A} \times \text{Odds B} \times \text{Odds A} + 1 \times \text{Odds B} + 1}{(\text{Odds A} \times \text{Odds B} + 1) + (\text{Odds B} \times \text{Odds A} + 1)}$$

Actually, this formula is easier to remember than you think. You simply multiply the odds of A, B, A + 1, and B + 1 and divide this product by the sum of the products of A and B + 1 and B and A + 1. You then double this quantity to get the answer. Let's take the 6-to-1 with the 1-to-1 and plug in the numbers.

$$\text{Quinella fair pay} = \frac{6 \times 1 \times 7 \times 2}{6 \times 2 + 1 \times 7} \times 2 = \frac{84}{19} \times 2 = \$8.84$$

You now have the wherewithal to decide if the exacta or quinella is a better deal.

The first race at Hollywood Park on December 15, 1993, offered an interesting proposition. The favorite (the 3 horse) went off at 2-to-1. The horse that I figured would come in second (the 5 horse) was 5-to-2. These were my only contenders. The 3-5 exacta was paying $21.40, the 5-3 exacta was paying $23.60, and the 3-5 quinella was paying $11.40. What was the best bet to make? To answer this question, simply figure all the fair pays and see which bet offers the biggest edge-to-odds ratio. The fair pays were as follows:

3-5 exacta	$2 \times 2 \times 3.5 = \$14$
5-3 exacta	$2 \times 2.5 \times 3 = \$15$
3-5 quinella	$\dfrac{2 \times 2.5 \times 3 \times 3.5 \times 2}{2 \times 3.5 + 2.5 \times 3} = \$7.24$

If you know the fair pays, then you know the probability of success. Remember that fair pay always equals the probability of success divided into the bet size. The bet size is $2. The 3-5 exacta has a ½ (14.3 percent) chance to hit, the 5-3 exacta a ²⁄₁₅ (13.3 percent) chance, and the 3-5 quinella a 27.6 percent chance.

The edge-to-odds ratios are as follows:

$$\text{E/O (3-5 exacta)} = .143 \times (9.7) - .857 = .53 \div 9.7 = .055$$
$$\text{E/O (5-3 exacta)} = .133 \times (10.8) - .867 = .57 \div 10.8 = .053$$
$$\text{E/O (3-5 quinella)} = .276 \times (4.7) - .724 = .57 \div 4.7 = .120$$

It's now easy to see why the quinella was the much better bet.

The third race that day was even better. My top picks were the 4-to-5 favorite (the 1 horse) and a 6-to-1 shot (the 6 horse). The exacta 1-6 was paying $12.40 and the 1-6 quinella was paying $9.20.

$$\text{E/O (1-6 exacta)} = .179 \times (5.2) - .821 = .108 \div 5.2 = .026$$
$$\text{E/O (1-6 quinella)} = .271 \times (3.6) - .729 = .247 \div 3.6 = .069$$

Again, the quinella was by far the better bet.

In the fourth race later that day, a 5-to-1 shot beat a 7-to-1 shot. The exacta paid $58.60 and the quinella paid $41.20. The exacta fair price was $80, which made it a giant underlay. The quinella fair price was $40.98, making it a small overlay (although not enough to make the cutoff value).

The next race saw a 9-to-1 shot beat a 7-to-2 shot. The exacta paid $117.60 and the quinella paid $43. Most handicappers would erroneously jump to the conclusion that this quinella was an underlay and thus a bad bet. The fact is both the exacta and the quinella were overlays. True, the exacta was a bigger overlay, but the quinella still offered value.

Please don't buy the notion that a quinella paying more than half the exacta is necessarily a good bet. It's not. What if the exacta price is an underlay? You must figure out the fair price each quinella combination must pay. Play the quinella just as you play the exacta. Write down the fair pays for each combination and compare them to the probable pays on the TV monitor. Cross out all the underlays. Compensate yourself for your guaranteed losing bets.

What follows are the results of a 695-race study of quinella versus exacta wagering results in southern California:

Date	Race#	Odds 1	Rank	Odds 2	Rank	Actual	Theory	Value
12/26/92	2	1.6	1	3.4	3	11.80	7.84	overlay
12/26/92	7	9.5	6	4.5	3	37.20	49.62	underlay
12/27/92	2	5.7	3	34.4	10	276.80	215.18	overlay
12/27/92	7	20.0	6	29.7	7	239.20	618.81	underlay
12/29/92	2	8.3	4	2.3	2	23.80	24.02	underlay
12/29/92	7	3.2	3	2.5	1	12.80	10.84	overlay
12/30/92	2	1.1	1	4.9	3	11.00	7.96	overlay

Date	Race#	Odds 1	Rank	Odds 2	Rank	Actual	Theory	Value
12/30/92	7	8.9	4	3.7	3	28.40	39.06	underlay
12/31/92	2	2.7	2	3.4	3	18.80	12.22	overlay
12/31/92	7	2.9	2	3.0	3	20.00	11.65	overlay
01/01/93	2	2.6	1	7.8	4	35.20	25.21	overlay
01/01/93	7	14.7	5	2.0	2	36.40	36.68	underlay
01/02/93	2	1.4	1	3.8	2	13.40	7.74	overlay
01/02/93	7	4.8	4	4.6	3	24.40	26.78	underlay
01/03/93	2	6.6	6	4.3	3	37.20	33.79	overlay
01/03/93	7	2.1	2	1.4	1	8.20	4.66	overlay
01/06/93	2	10.3	6	3.5	2	43.20	42.68	overlay
01/06/93	7	1.6	1	3.1	3	12.80	7.23	overlay
01/07/93	2	1.4	1	2.9	3	7.60	6.12	overlay
01/07/93	7	5.3	4	7.2	6	11.40	11.39	underlay
01/08/93	2	7.8	4	1.7	1	26.40	17.49	overlay
01/08/93	7	1.9	1	10.7	6	32.60	25.90	overlay
01/09/93	2	10.7	6	2.5	2	51.00	32.85	overlay
01/09/93	7	1.8	2	5.8	3	25.20	13.96	overlay
01/10/93	2	6.5	5	3.3	2	30.00	26.25	overlay
01/10/93	7	1.1	1	2.6	2	6.80	4.59	overlay
01/13/93	2	4.7	4	2.6	1	16.80	15.80	overlay
01/13/93	7	2.8	2	4.2	4	19.80	15.23	overlay
01/14/93	2	2.0	2	2.0	1	10.40	6.00	overlay
01/14/93	7	19.5	7	14.6	6	113.00	301.73	underlay
01/15/93	2	5.6	5	33.4	7	112.60	205.60	underlay
01/15/93	7	1.9	1	2.9	2	9.80	7.88	overlay
01/16/93	2	18.1	7	10.2	5	103.60	198.69	underlay
01/16/93	7	1.6	1	4.3	4	12.80	9.64	overlay
01/17/93	2	0.5	1	7.5	3	12.00	6.17	overlay
01/17/93	7	9.0	4	4.2	3	36.20	44.27	underlay
01/18/93	2	2.5	2	1.5	1	8.40	5.71	overlay
01/22/93	2	1.9	1	5.0	4	18.00	12.76	overlay
01/22/93	7	1.6	1	8.8	5	21.60	18.61	overlay
01/23/93	2	4.2	4	4.1	2	29.00	21.37	overlay
01/23/93	7	2.6	2	3.1	3	14.40	10.90	overlay
01/24/93	2	0.8	1	4.2	2	9.40	5.37	overlay
01/24/93	7	2.8	2	1.0	1	7.40	4.53	overlay
01/27/93	2	0.9	1	4.2	2	12.00	5.90	overlay
01/27/93	7	0.9	1	4.0	2	7.00	5.65	overlay

Date	Race#	Odds 1	Rank	Odds 2	Rank	Actual	Theory	Value
01/28/93	2	3.3	2	0.7	1	6.40	3.92	overlay
01/28/93	7	1.9	1	7.3	4	29.80	18.08	overlay
01/29/93	2	0.5	1	6.2	2	12.20	5.19	overlay
01/29/93	7	0.7	1	3.8	2	7.40	4.42	overlay
01/30/93	2	40.2	10	22.8	7	508.40	947.98	underlay
01/30/93	7	5.5	4	2.1	1	24.60	15.16	overlay
01/31/93	2	2.9	2	3.3	3	11.80	12.67	underlay
01/31/93	7	26.3	7	3.2	2	78.00	97.56	underlay
02/03/93	2	6.0	5	4.1	2	43.00	29.62	overlay
02/03/93	7	2.3	1	10.7	5	67.20	30.54	overlay
02/04/93	2	1.5	1	2.8	2	8.00	6.28	overlay
02/04/93	7	0.7	1	4.6	3	9.40	5.22	overlay
02/05/93	2	3.7	2	4.4	3	20.00	20.32	underlay
02/05/93	7	2.7	2	1.4	1	8.60	5.76	overlay
02/06/93	2	2.6	2	2.8	3	17.00	9.98	overlay
02/06/93	7	3.7	4	3.3	2	23.20	15.71	overlay
02/07/93	2	1.3	1	6.8	3	18.00	12.30	overlay
02/07/93	7	2.5	2	1.8	1	11.80	6.63	overlay
02/10/93	2	2.6	2	3.3	4	16.00	11.52	overlay
02/10/93	7	4.5	3	2.3	2	11.80	13.66	underlay
02/11/93	2	15.1	5	9.8	3	76.40	160.39	underlay
02/11/93	7	9.7	5	0.9	1	25.60	12.65	overlay
02/12/93	2	7.1	5	21.1	7	123.00	163.61	underlay
02/12/93	7	7.6	6	3.6	2	40.60	32.84	overlay
02/13/93	2	6.6	4	12.2	5	71.20	89.83	underlay
02/13/93	7	2.5	2	3.3	3	17.00	11.14	overlay
02/14/93	2	2.2	1	15.8	7	40.00	42.70	underlay
02/14/93	7	1.3	1	4.8	3	11.80	8.96	overlay
02/15/93	2	3.9	3	4.6	4	25.40	22.18	overlay
02/15/93	7	0.4	1	5.6	3	6.60	3.95	overlay
02/17/93	2	2.0	1	4.3	3	14.00	11.64	overlay
02/17/93	7	2.0	1	24.2	7	8.20	59.50	underlay
02/18/93	2	1.2	1	6.5	4	18.80	11.05	overlay
02/18/93	7	1.2	1	3.6	3	10.80	6.51	overlay
02/19/93	2	6.2	4	1.3	1	16.20	11.30	overlay
02/19/93	7	0.9	1	6.0	3	10.20	8.12	overlay
02/20/93	2	1.2	1	4.1	2	12.20	7.29	overlay

Date	Race#	Odds 1	Rank	Odds 2	Rank	Actual	Theory	Value
02/20/93	7	0.7	1	3.2	2	5.40	3.82	overlay
02/21/93	2	1.4	1	2.8	3	8.20	5.94	overlay
02/21/93	7	9.8	5	6.9	4	32.20	75.94	underlay
02/24/93	2	6.9	4	2.6	2	29.40	22.49	overlay
02/24/93	7	3.1	3	0.9	1	8.20	4.54	overlay
02/25/93	2	6.0	3	1.3	1	16.20	10.97	overlay
02/25/93	7	1.1	1	1.9	2	5.40	3.55	overlay
02/26/93	2	6.9	3	1.2	1	14.20	11.67	overlay
02/26/93	7	2.9	2	3.7	3	13.80	14.02	underlay
02/27/93	2	4.3	3	0.8	1	6.80	5.48	overlay
02/27/93	7	4.7	3	6.1	4	25.20	34.06	underlay
02/28/93	2	3.5	2	4.5	3	20.60	19.74	overlay
02/28/93	7	7.8	4	0.0	1	13.80	10.32	overlay
03/03/93	2	10.1	5	1.6	1	34.60	21.19	overlay
03/03/93	7	19.0	7	4.4	3	117.60	94.74	overlay
03/04/93	2	3.4	2	17.5	7	120.80	69.24	overlay
03/04/93	7	1.2	1	9.0	4	21.60	14.94	overlay
03/05/93	2	2.3	2	31.5	8	103.20	86.96	overlay
03/05/93	7	7.1	4	9.9	6	62.00	78.77	underlay
03/06/93	2	2.4	2	2.4	1	12.00	8.16	overlay
03/06/93	7	2.0	1	2.4	2	6.80	6.99	underlay
03/07/93	2	2.5	2	2.3	1	10.80	8.15	overlay
03/07/93	7	0.7	1	7.4	3	12.60	8.01	overlay
03/10/93	2	1.9	2	20.4	5	46.40	48.20	underlay
03/10/93	7	4.6	3	12.6	6	70.60	66.32	overlay
03/11/93	2	8.1	5	12.6	7	138.60	112.36	overlay
03/11/93	7	16.5	8	4.8	3	109.00	89.47	overlay
03/12/93	2	6.5	4	6.7	5	44.00	50.15	underlay
03/12/93	7	20.6	6	2.3	1	63.60	57.41	overlay
03/13/93	2	3.1	2	1.5	1	9.80	6.86	overlay
03/13/93	7	8.4	5	1.5	1	15.20	16.87	underlay
03/14/93	2	1.2	1	3.4	2	10.60	6.19	overlay
03/14/93	7	3.7	3	5.5	5	39.20	24.92	overlay
03/17/93	2	1.9	1	3.1	3	11.60	8.35	overlay
03/17/93	7	1.0	1	2.1	2	4.20	3.57	overlay
03/18/93	2	1.8	1	2.8	2	13.80	7.31	overlay
03/18/93	7	1.1	1	1.8	2	5.60	3.39	overlay

Date	Race#	Odds 1	Rank	Odds 2	Rank	Actual	Theory	Value
03/19/93	2	3.5	2	3.7	3	19.00	16.55	overlay
03/19/93	7	7.4	5	5.1	3	34.20	43.96	underlay
03/20/93	2	5.5	3	3.3	2	19.60	22.50	underlay
03/20/93	7	25.0	8	9.8	6	200.20	262.18	underlay
03/21/93	2	2.4	2	3.4	3	18.40	11.04	overlay
03/21/93	7	1.5	1	2.9	2	10.80	6.48	overlay
03/24/93	2	0.9	1	7.1	4	15.60	9.47	overlay
03/24/93	7	2.8	1	4.2	3	19.00	15.23	overlay
03/25/93	2	1.9	1	15.7	6	53.60	37.40	overlay
03/25/93	7	1.6	1	24.1	6	54.80	48.95	overlay
03/26/93	2	5.9	4	2.9	2	31.60	21.41	overlay
03/26/93	7	2.8	3	2.4	2	13.20	9.32	overlay
03/27/93	2	4.1	3	3.4	2	24.40	17.68	overlay
03/27/93	7	3.0	3	4.9	4	23.20	18.60	overlay
03/28/93	2	7.9	5	21.6	7	132.40	185.14	underlay
03/28/93	7	8.0	4	2.2	2	23.00	22.33	overlay
03/31/93	2	2.5	2	7.5	6	25.20	23.49	overlay
03/31/93	7	1.4	1	2.7	2	6.40	5.76	overlay
04/01/93	2	2.4	2	13.5	6	75.40	39.59	overlay
04/01/93	7	10.9	6	9.5	5	84.80	113.75	underlay
04/02/93	2	1.6	1	5.6	3	18.00	12.24	overlay
04/02/93	7	2.5	2	7.5	3	20.80	23.49	underlay
04/03/93	2	5.7	5	3.4	3	36.20	23.87	overlay
04/03/93	7	1.3	2	1.3	1	3.80	2.99	overlay
04/04/93	2	1.1	1	6.9	4	21.20	10.86	overlay
04/04/93	7	1.7	1	5.3	4	17.00	12.25	overlay
04/07/93	2	1.2	1	10.6	5	23.20	17.43	overlay
04/07/93	7	1.1	1	2.8	2	8.20	4.89	overlay
04/08/93	2	1.7	2	1.2	1	5.00	3.47	overlay
04/08/93	7	8.1	3	0.3	1	10.40	4.34	overlay
04/09/93	2	6.5	3	17.1	7	159.00	122.72	overlay
04/09/93	7	28.1	5	2.9	3	59.80	95.35	underlay
04/10/93	2	0.4	1	9.0	4	11.40	6.07	overlay
04/10/93	7	1.8	1	3.8	3	16.40	9.54	overlay
04/11/93	2	0.5	1	5.5	2	10.00	4.66	overlay
04/11/93	7	2.6	2	8.0	5	33.80	25.82	overlay
04/14/93	2	9.4	5	45.3	10	405.60	452.46	underlay

Date	Race#	Odds 1	Rank	Odds 2	Rank	Actual	Theory	Value
04/14/93	7	2.0	1	7.8	5	26.20	20.09	overlay
04/15/93	2	2.8	2	9.9	4	34.40	33.70	overlay
04/15/93	7	19.9	6	7.0	4	90.40	152.48	underlay
04/16/93	2	5.3	3	1.1	1	13.80	8.54	overlay
04/16/93	7	3.7	3	11.2	6	51.80	48.60	overlay
04/17/93	2	1.7	1	2.2	2	8.20	5.68	overlay
04/17/93	7	1.3	1	8.2	4	22.80	14.64	overlay
04/18/93	2	27.3	7	19.7	6	227.20	561.28	underlay
04/18/93	7	6.9	4	3.2	3	35.40	27.00	overlay
10/06/93	1	7.4	4	3.7	2	46.60	32.83	overlay
10/06/93	2	19.6	8	4.3	3	106.80	95.62	overlay
10/06/93	3	5.9	4	4.1	2	23.80	29.16	underlay
10/06/93	4	3.2	2	3.5	3	18.80	14.55	overlay
10/06/93	5	2.8	2	2.5	1	11.20	9.65	overlay
10/06/93	6	6.8	5	1.8	1	25.40	16.16	overlay
10/06/93	7	3.7	2	11.0	5	30.00	47.77	underlay
10/06/93	8	0.9	1	31.5	6	54.20	39.30	overlay
10/06/93	9	5.0	3	6.5	5	29.20	38.24	underlay
10/07/93	1	4.5	2	0.9	1	10.80	6.27	overlay
10/07/93	2	5.6	3	0.9	1	14.20	7.62	overlay
10/07/93	3	24.7	8	5.5	3	92.40	150.34	underlay
10/07/93	4	1.5	1	3.1	2	11.80	6.86	overlay
10/07/93	5	3.8	2	12.2	7	42.40	54.04	underlay
10/07/93	6	10.0	4	1.9	1	33.40	24.29	overlay
10/07/93	7	0.6	1	2.2	2	4.40	2.48	overlay
10/07/93	8	1.7	1	15.6	6	67.40	33.80	overlay
10/07/93	9	3.0	2	4.8	4	23.00	18.26	overlay
10/08/93	1	6.4	3	0.8	1	12.60	7.82	overlay
10/08/93	2	0.6	1	2.5	2	6.00	2.75	overlay
10/08/93	3	3.7	3	2.0	1	15.20	10.18	overlay
10/08/93	4	1.9	2	1.8	1	5.60	5.27	overlay
10/08/93	5	7.4	6	5.1	4	32.20	43.96	underlay
10/08/93	6	28.9	7	2.1	2	69.00	73.83	underlay
10/08/93	7	1.8	1	11.5	5	31.40	26.49	overlay
10/08/93	8	6.7	5	2.6	1	25.60	21.88	overlay
10/08/93	9	4.3	2	10.9	5	48.00	54.27	underlay
10/09/93	1	4.7	5	3.4	2	34.20	20.01	overlay

Date	Race#	Odds 1	Rank	Odds 2	Rank	Actual	Theory	Value
10/09/93	2	11.1	6	1.3	1	26.20	19.47	overlay
10/09/93	3	0.6	1	10.9	5	13.00	10.13	overlay
10/09/93	4	0.9	1	2.2	2	6.20	3.41	overlay
10/09/93	5	13.9	6	7.0	5	107.00	107.64	underlay
10/09/93	6	2.2	1	2.4	2	8.60	7.58	ovcrlay
10/09/93	7	1.6	1	8.6	5	26.80	18.21	overlay
10/09/93	8	5.0	2	0.2	1	4.00	2.00	overlay
10/09/93	9	8.0	6	14.3	8	179.80	125.47	overlay
10/10/93	1	5.6	5	1.1	1	12.00	8.98	overlay
10/10/93	2	1.6	1	3.3	2	12.40	7.64	overlay
10/10/93	3	1.7	2	5.3	3	14.40	12.25	overlay
10/10/93	4	2.5	2	4.8	4	17.80	15.57	overlay
10/10/93	5	17.1	7	11.5	6	196.60	210.91	underlay
10/10/93	6	8.0	5	1.6	1	26.20	17.02	overlay
10/10/93	7	0.9	1	6.2	3	12.80	8.36	overlay
10/10/93	8	0.5	1	2.9	2	3.80	2.69	overlay
10/10/93	9	7.5	4	2.4	1	23.00	22.67	overlay
10/11/93	1	2.9	2	3.8	3	25.20	14.36	overlay
10/11/93	2	9.8	4	15.4	7	149.80	163.47	underlay
10/11/93	3	2.4	3	12.6	5	29.60	37.05	underlay
10/11/93	4	5.0	3	1.0	1	11.00	7.50	overlay
10/11/93	5	2.2	1	4.4	4	14.80	12.89	overlay
10/11/93	6	1.6	1	3.0	2	9.60	7.03	overlay
10/11/93	7	3.3	2	4.2	3	31.00	17.60	overlay
10/11/93	8	0.7	1	5.7	3	12.00	6.32	overlay
10/11/93	9	3.6	2	9.6	6	66.80	40.94	overlay
10/13/93	1	5.6	4	2.0	2	20.80	14.78	overlay
10/13/93	2	15.0	7	38.8	8	252.20	608.67	underlay
10/13/93	3	9.2	5	13.0	7	107.00	130.67	underlay
10/13/93	4	0.9	1	4.8	3	13.60	6.64	overlay
10/13/93	5	1.4	1	7.1	4	19.80	13.62	overlay
10/13/93	6	11.9	6	2.1	1	51.00	31.24	overlay
10/13/93	7	1.7	1	13.3	6	45.20	28.99	overlay
10/13/93	8	1.3	2	1.1	1	3.20	2.63	overlay
10/13/93	9	9.5	5	2.0	1	27.00	24.18	overlay
10/14/93	1	1.5	1	1.9	2	5.00	4.54	overlay
10/14/93	2	3.0	2	5.8	3	27.40	21.71	overlay

Date	Race#	Odds 1	Rank	Odds 2	Rank	Actual	Theory	Value
10/14/93	3	5.9	3	2.0	2	22.20	15.51	overlay
10/14/93	4	1.3	1	5.1	3	15.40	9.46	overlay
10/14/93	5	5.4	3	1.5	1	17.00	11.22	overlay
10/14/93	6	4.8	4	2.9	2	16.80	17.72	underlay
10/14/93	7	9.7	6	3.0	3	31.80	35.13	underlay
10/14/93	8	2.0	1	5.8	4	18.80	15.27	overlay
10/14/93	9	4.5	3	1.5	1	15.40	9.52	overlay
10/15/93	1	3.7	3	1.3	1	10.60	7.11	overlay
10/15/93	2	7.9	4	19.6	6	96.20	168.39	underlay
10/15/93	3	6.0	3	6.9	4	50.80	47.85	overlay
10/15/93	4	1.6	1	12.9	6	41.80	26.75	overlay
10/15/93	5	0.8	1	32.0	9	64.00	36.21	overlay
10/15/93	6	1.2	1	20.2	8	39.00	32.30	overlay
10/15/93	7	5.4	4	17.7	6	84.40	106.78	underlay
10/15/93	8	5.0	5	1.9	1	15.20	12.76	overlay
10/15/93	9	5.1	2	7.4	5	43.20	43.96	underlay
10/16/93	1	2.6	3	1.3	1	7.80	5.25	overlay
10/16/93	2	11.2	5	0.9	1	20.40	14.49	overlay
10/16/93	3	4.3	3	2.6	2	19.80	14.58	overlay
10/16/93	4	3.4	2	0.9	1	8.20	4.91	overlay
10/16/93	5	11.4	5	43.5	11	560.20	522.86	overlay
10/16/93	6	1.1	1	3.6	2	8.00	6.06	overlay
10/16/93	7	3.2	2	7.2	4	34.80	28.10	overlay
10/10/93	8	0.3	1	4.9	2	5.40	2.77	overlay
10/16/93	9	2.1	1	7.8	5	36.60	20.95	overlay
10/17/93	1	2.6	1	6.5	5	26.20	21.27	overlay
10/17/93	2	1.4	1	2.6	2	8.00	5.58	overlay
10/17/93	3	2.1	3	5.9	4	19.40	16.17	overlay
10/17/93	4	0.9	1	4.7	3	12.20	6.52	overlay
10/17/93	5	6.0	5	5.8	4	38.80	40.70	underlay
10/17/93	6	1.1	1	2.2	2	6.40	4.00	overlay
10/17/93	7	9.1	4	6.2	2	66.60	64.04	overlay
10/17/93	8	4.2	3	3.8	2	16.00	19.96	underlay
10/17/93	9	2.3	2	9.5	5	22.60	27.28	underlay
10/20/93	1	1.7	1	3.3	2	14.00	8.03	overlay
10/20/93	2	1.8	1	24.5	6	70.80	55.00	overlay
10/20/93	3	2.0	1	4.3	4	16.00	11.64	overlay

Date	Race#	Odds 1	Rank	Odds 2	Rank	Actual	Theory	Value
10/20/93	4	2.0	1	3.4	3	12.80	9.45	overlay
10/20/93	5	9.3	4	3.3	2	33.00	36.75	underlay
10/20/93	6	1.0	1	6.2	3	14.20	9.11	overlay
10/20/93	7	3.8	2	2.3	1	15.40	11.74	overlay
10/20/93	8	1.1	1	1.9	2	4.20	3.55	overlay
10/20/93	9	1.5	1	6.7	5	19.20	13.67	overlay
10/21/93	1	1.8	2	11.1	6	33.00	25.61	overlay
10/21/93	2	0.7	1	5.1	2	9.60	5.72	overlay
10/21/93	3	1.1	1	2.5	2	6.60	4.44	overlay
10/21/93	4	1.7	1	2.6	2	9.20	6.54	overlay
10/21/93	5	2.3	1	17.8	8	82.00	49.81	overlay
10/21/93	6	44.4	8	2.2	2	136.00	117.30	overlay
10/21/93	7	1.5	1	3.2	3	11.80	7.05	overlay
10/21/93	8	3.4	2	17.7	5	52.60	70.01	underlay
10/21/93	9	3.7	3	2.2	2	20.60	11.04	overlay
10/22/93	1	8.0	4	0.6	1	13.20	7.60	overlay
10/22/93	2	5.1	4	3.8	3	24.20	23.81	overlay
10/22/93	3	1.0	1	1.7	2	3.60	3.01	overlay
10/22/93	4	3.3	2	6.8	5	29.40	27.38	overlay
10/22/93	5	4.8	3	5.9	4	51.00	33.66	overlay
10/22/93	6	3.4	3	2.7	2	19.20	12.22	overlay
10/22/93	7	2.1	2	0.7	1	5.20	2.70	overlay
10/22/93	8	1.8	1	9.9	5	19.40	22.98	underlay
10/22/93	9	3.0	2	2.8	1	15.40	11.30	overlay
10/23/93	1	3.6	2	7.0	4	71.80	30.41	overlay
10/23/93	2	3.7	2	14.7	7	66.00	63.11	overlay
10/23/93	3	0.8	1	6.4	3	11.00	7.82	overlay
10/23/93	4	7.7	5	5.4	4	42.00	48.10	underlay
10/23/93	5	1.9	1	2.2	2	9.80	6.23	overlay
10/23/93	6	3.3	3	1.6	1	8.60	7.64	overlay
10/23/93	7	1.3	1	2.4	2	6.00	4.91	overlay
10/23/93	8	3.4	2	5.7	4	18.60	23.87	underlay
10/23/93	9	1.3	1	5.2	3	18.20	9.63	overlay
10/24/93	1	7.9	4	1.3	1	20.80	14.14	overlay
10/24/93	2	7.7	3	1.8	2	24.40	18.14	overlay
10/24/93	3	3.7	2	0.5	1	5.40	3.30	overlay
10/24/93	4	0.7	1	8.2	3	14.00	8.81	overlay

Date	Race#	Odds 1	Rank	Odds 2	Rank	Actual	Theory	Value
10/24/93	5	24.4	9	2.3	1	113.20	67.71	overlay
10/24/93	6	1.3	1	4.5	3	13.40	8.46	overlay
10/24/93	7	1.2	1	5.1	3	13.20	8.86	overlay
10/24/93	8	9.6	4	1.0	1	17.20	13.66	overlay
10/24/93	9	5.7	3	19.0	8	107.20	120.28	underlay
10/27/93	1	8.4	5	2.4	2	29.40	25.21	overlay
10/27/93	2	30.9	7	23.2	5	365.40	743.91	underlay
10/27/93	3	1.6	1	2.6	3	9.00	6.22	overlay
10/27/93	4	2.1	1	2.7	2	10.80	8.06	overlay
10/27/93	5	2.1	1	7.2	4	19.80	19.44	overlay
10/27/93	6	3.9	2	7.8	4	35.80	36.17	underlay
10/27/93	7	1.3	1	2.6	2	6.40	5.25	overlay
10/27/93	8	2.5	2	1.1	1	6.60	4.44	overlay
10/27/93	9	1.3	1	2.7	2	7.00	5.42	overlay
10/29/93	1	1.6	2	1.3	1	4.40	3.52	overlay
10/29/93	2	7.5	4	2.0	2	23.00	19.37	overlay
10/29/93	3	0.9	1	21.5	5	28.40	27.08	overlay
10/29/93	4	1.8	1	54.0	8	105.60	119.65	underlay
10/29/93	5	7.5	4	2.4	2	25.00	22.67	overlay
10/29/93	6	3.1	3	2.8	2	12.60	11.63	overlay
10/29/93	7	2.5	3	1.6	1	9.20	6.02	overlay
10/29/93	8	1.2	1	2.5	2	7.40	4.76	overlay
10/29/93	9	2.3	1	9.5	7	55.80	27.98	overlay
10/30/93	1	1.7	1	4.0	3	11.80	9.51	overlay
10/30/93	2	10.5	4	17.3	6	148.00	195.49	underlay
10/30/93	3	3.9	3	2.0	2	11.20	10.67	overlay
10/30/93	4	2.8	2	3.3	3	15.40	12.28	overlay
10/30/93	5	33.7	8	2.8	2	99.00	110.49	underlay
10/30/93	6	3.6	3	5.9	4	31.40	25.94	overlay
10/30/93	7	6.9	5	1.7	1	16.00	15.61	overlay
10/30/93	8	1.6	1	4.5	3	13.40	10.04	overlay
10/30/93	9	1.9	1	2.4	2	8.60	6.70	overlay
10/31/93	1	2.3	2	1.2	1	8.20	4.44	overlay
10/31/93	2	0.6	1	5.7	3	9.00	5.58	overlay
10/31/93	3	5.8	4	13.5	5	57.20	87.78	underlay
10/31/93	4	1.2	1	2.4	2	6.20	4.60	overlay
10/31/93	5	2.2	1	6.4	4	25.00	18.14	overlay

Date	Race#	Odds 1	Rank	Odds 2	Rank	Actual	Theory	Value
10/31/93	6	1.0	1	8.0	4	19.40	11.52	overlay
10/31/93	7	4.5	3	1.7	2	12.60	10.57	overlay
10/31/93	8	10.1	6	7.0	4	51.00	79.22	underlay
10/31/93	9	2.1	1	5.7	5	28.20	15.67	overlay
11/03/93	1	10.5	5	2.1	1	34.60	27.73	overlay
11/03/93	2	1.5	1	2.2	2	8.40	5.13	overlay
11/03/93	3	2.8	3	2.7	2	15.00	10.31	overlay
11/03/93	4	3.1	2	4.5	4	31.00	17.72	overlay
11/03/93	5	1.3	1	17.5	6	36.20	30.11	overlay
11/03/93	6	1.3	1	19.8	6	57.00	33.93	overlay
11/03/93	7	10.3	5	1.0	1	17.40	14.59	overlay
11/03/93	8	2.2	2	3.2	3	14.20	9.71	overlay
11/03/93	9	8.7	5	5.0	4	63.00	50.28	overlay
11/04/93	1	2.6	2	15.0	8	64.40	47.00	overlay
11/04/93	2	7.4	3	19.9	7	104.00	160.67	underlay
11/04/93	3	2.6	2	17.1	6	70.20	53.34	overlay
11/04/93	4	5.4	3	6.4	4	44.40	40.45	overlay
11/04/93	5	3.4	2	1.4	1	11.40	7.02	overlay
11/04/93	6	1.0	1	9.3	4	18.20	13.26	overlay
11/04/93	7	3.9	2	5.2	4	33.00	24.81	overlay
11/04/93	8	0.7	1	18.0	7	25.00	18.54	overlay
11/04/93	9	3.1	2	3.6	3	25.20	14.51	overlay
11/05/93	1	65.2	8	8.6	4	326.00	596.28	underlay
11/05/93	2	31.8	7	11.3	4	254.80	380.61	underlay
11/05/93	3	3.5	4	2.6	3	17.60	12.13	overlay
11/05/93	4	2.4	2	16.7	5	57.80	48.60	overlay
11/05/93	5	3.5	2	7.7	5	32.00	32.41	underlay
11/05/93	6	3.7	2	6.9	3	29.20	30.75	underlay
11/05/93	7	3.6	2	1.3	1	11.40	6.94	overlay
11/05/93	8	18.1	8	7.7	4	144.80	152.09	underlay
11/05/93	9	3.5	2	7.2	4	45.80	30.44	overlay
11/06/93	1	2.3	2	1.7	1	7.20	5.89	overlay
11/06/93	2	5.3	2	8.5	6	38.60	51.90	underlay
11/06/93	3	2.3	3	2.2	2	6.20	7.31	underlay
11/06/93	4	1.3	1	2.5	2	6.60	5.08	overlay
11/06/93	5	1.3	1	18.2	7	40.40	31.27	overlay
11/06/93	6	3.0	2	42.4	9	205.80	147.31	overlay

Date	Race#	Odds 1	Rank	Odds 2	Rank	Actual	Theory	Value
11/06/93	7	1.5	1	4.3	3	10.20	9.14	overlay
11/06/93	8	133.6	11	1.2	1	270.40	208.48	overlay
11/06/93	9	11.6	7	2.9	1	54.80	40.43	overlay
11/06/93	10	1.8	1	17.3	6	42.00	39.21	overlay
11/07/93	1	5.7	5	5.2	4	32.20	35.09	underlay
11/07/93	2	8.4	4	39.8	8	216.80	357.73	underlay
11/07/93	3	2.2	2	1.2	1	5.60	4.28	overlay
11/07/93	4	4.0	3	4.7	4	26.60	23.14	overlay
11/07/93	5	8.2	4	12.3	6	175.00	111.07	overlay
11/07/93	6	0.9	1	6.5	5	11.00	8.73	overlay
11/07/93	7	10.0	6	5.8	5	42.40	65.83	underlay
11/07/93	8	1.1	1	4.0	3	10.40	6.65	overlay
11/07/93	9	5.0	0	5.3	4	59.80	35.13	overlay
11/10/93	1	4.6	4	4.6	3	37.00	25.76	overlay
11/10/93	2	8.5	4	91.6	11	382.60	826.57	underlay
11/10/93	3	2.9	2	9.7	5	35.40	34.09	overlay
11/10/93	4	0.9	1	15.8	6	14.20	20.11	underlay
11/10/93	5	43.8	8	9.8	5	256.80	455.41	underlay
11/10/93	6	9.9	5	1.6	1	33.60	20.79	overlay
11/10/93	7	1.0	1	3.5	2	8.20	5.48	overlay
11/10/93	8	1.5	1	1.6	2	5.60	3.95	overlay
11/10/93	9	6.0	5	13.8	7	90.40	92.54	underlay
11/11/93	1	2.3	2	12.3	5	97.10	47.97	underlay
11/11/93	2	1.4	1	36.1	8	75.40	64.95	overlay
11/11/93	3	6.5	3	0.4	1	6.00	4.51	overlay
11/11/93	4	1.1	1	4.8	3	10.60	7.81	overlay
11/11/93	5	6.9	6	3.8	2	36.60	31.49	overlay
11/11/93	6	1.9	1	10.5	5	31.60	25.44	overlay
11/11/93	7	33.4	9	14.6	5	310.60	511.47	underlay
11/11/93	8	4.9	3	1.2	1	10.80	8.55	overlay
11/11/93	9	1.6	1	4.3	3	12.00	9.64	overlay
11/12/93	1	1.5	1	4.6	4	12.00	9.71	overlay
11/12/93	2	1.6	1	2.2	2	7.20	5.40	overlay
11/12/93	3	2.3	2	16.7	6	53.40	46.83	overlay
11/12/93	4	9.7	5	1.9	1	20.80	23.60	underlay
11/12/93	5	4.7	2	7.1	5	37.40	39.23	underlay
11/12/93	6	2.4	1	23.7	7	60.80	68.31	underlay

Date	Race#	Odds 1	Rank	Odds 2	Rank	Actual	Theory	Value
11/12/93	7	0.7	1	5.9	3	10.20	6.52	overlay
11/12/93	8	1.3	1	6.4	4	18.20	11.64	overlay
11/12/93	9	3.3	2	4.2	3	27.20	17.60	overlay
11/13/93	1	1.1	1	2.8	2	7.80	4.89	overlay
11/13/93	2	7.0	4	2.3	1	30.80	20.48	overlay
11/13/93	3	2.5	2	0.8	1	5.40	3.45	overlay
11/13/93	4	5.8	5	12.3	6	66.20	80.26	underlay
11/13/93	5	4.2	3	2.1	1	17.20	11.88	overlay
11/13/93	6	1.2	1	14.6	4	34.20	23.65	overlay
11/13/93	7	1.1	1	14.1	5	27.00	21.28	overlay
11/13/93	8	3.3	2	8.9	4	31.60	35.25	underlay
11/13/93	9	42.7	9	7.3	4	303.80	335.78	underlay
11/14/93	1	3.5	2	1.2	1	12.60	6.35	overlay
11/14/93	2	0.5	1	3.7	2	12.20	3.30	overlay
11/14/93	3	1.2	1	4.1	3	10.80	7.29	overlay
11/14/93	4	4.9	4	4.9	3	29.40	28.91	overlay
11/14/93	5	4.7	2	8.7	4	51.80	47.51	overlay
11/14/93	6	3.4	2	12.4	5	30.80	49.66	underlay
11/14/93	7	6.2	5	6.4	6	59.60	45.98	overlay
11/14/93	8	16.6	8	8.5	4	120.80	153.54	underlay
11/14/93	9	8.2	4	7.9	3	89.60	72.83	overlay
11/15/93	1	4.9	3	1.9	2	19.20	12.53	overlay
11/15/93	2	4.6	3	0.7	1	8.40	5.22	overlay
11/15/93	3	23.1	6	1.2	1	39.40	36.86	overlay
11/15/93	4	16.1	6	5.1	4	105.00	92.38	overlay
11/15/93	5	6.6	4	20.8	7	153.80	150.65	overlay
11/15/93	6	5.3	3	2.1	1	19.40	14.66	overlay
11/15/93	7	1.3	1	10.2	5	18.20	17.97	overlay
11/15/93	8	1.7	1	3.2	2	10.80	7.82	overlay
11/15/93	9	2.3	1	16.3	7	58.00	45.74	overlay
11/17/93	1	2.4	2	3.2	3	11.20	10.46	overlay
11/17/93	2	1.1	1	1.5	2	4.60	2.94	overlay
11/17/93	3	1.6	1	9.4	7	25.60	19.80	overlay
11/17/93	4	2.5	1	4.6	4	21.20	14.98	overlay
11/17/93	5	2.4	2	8.8	4	28.20	26.34	overlay
11/17/93	6	3.4	3	17.4	7	95.40	68.86	overlay
11/17/93	7	3.8	2	9.0	4	52.60	40.43	overlay

Date	Race#	Odds 1	Rank	Odds 2	Rank	Actual	Theory	Value
11/17/93	8	1.0	1	17.4	5	34.80	24.07	overlay
11/17/93	9	4.1	3	4.1	2	24.80	20.91	overlay
11/18/93	1	1.4	1	31.9	8	49.20	57.52	underlay
11/18/93	2	1.9	2	5.5	3	18.00	13.92	overlay
11/18/93	3	1.9	2	1.3	1	6.20	4.05	overlay
11/18/93	4	3.5	2	27.5	8	119.00	110.46	overlay
11/18/93	5	9.4	5	9.2	4	121.60	95.78	overlay
11/18/93	6	2.7	2	1.4	1	9.40	5.76	overlay
11/18/93	7	1.3	1	2.6	2	9.60	5.25	overlay
11/18/93	8	5.1	3	3.7	2	21.80	23.25	underlay
11/18/93	9	8.9	5	2.2	1	38.00	24.68	overlay
11/19/93	1	1.4	1	2.9	2	7.60	6.12	overlay
11/19/93	2	3.0	2	6.5	3	24.40	24.12	overlay
11/19/93	3	1.7	1	1.8	2	4.80	4.81	underlay
11/19/93	4	12.7	4	3.0	2	43.00	45.44	underlay
11/19/93	5	1.9	2	0.9	1	5.00	3.03	overlay
11/19/93	6	18.3	7	3.0	2	62.80	64.66	underlay
11/19/93	7	3.3	3	2.1	1	12.20	9.59	overlay
11/19/93	8	0.9	1	3.0	2	5.80	4.41	overlay
11/19/93	9	2.7	2	2.0	1	17.00	7.73	overlay
11/20/93	1	0.9	1	13.2	4	23.40	16.93	overlay
11/20/93	2	2.5	2	1.5	1	7.00	5.71	overlay
11/20/93	3	1.8	1	2.0	2	10.00	7.91	overlay
11/20/93	4	1.0	1	5.8	3	11.20	8.57	overlay
11/20/93	5	3.4	2	1.6	1	9.80	7.84	overlay
11/20/93	6	22.3	9	22.3	8	652.80	519.59	overlay
11/20/93	7	0.8	1	3.0	2	5.00	4.02	overlay
11/20/93	8	3.0	2	8.5	3	36.40	31.01	overlay
11/20/93	9	3.8	2	15.6	6	61.60	68.48	underlay
11/20/93	10	1.6	1	6.6	3	19.00	14.23	overlay
11/21/93	1	0.4	1	12.9	5	13.40	8.50	overlay
11/21/93	2	2.7	2	2.8	3	18.60	10.31	overlay
11/21/93	3	7.9	3	0.9	1	13.80	10.45	overlay
11/21/93	4	2.3	3	13.9	4	35.60	39.23	underlay
11/21/93	5	5.0	3	2.8	2	30.60	17.83	overlay
11/21/93	6	7.8	4	1.0	1	17.00	11.25	overlay
11/21/93	7	5.2	3	3.5	2	23.00	22.52	overlay

Date	Race#	Odds 1	Rank	Odds 2	Rank	Actual	Theory	Value
11/21/93	8	6.9	4	1.4	1	22.00	13.26	overlay
11/21/93	9	6.1	4	5.0	3	39.60	36.04	overlay
11/21/93	10	2.8	2	1.7	1	10.00	6.97	overlay
11/24/93	1	1.1	1	21.9	5	34.20	32.55	overlay
11/24/93	2	2.7	2	2.9	3	13.60	10.63	overlay
11/24/93	3	1.9	2	2.5	3	10.60	6.94	overlay
11/24/93	4	1.1	1	5.8	3	13.60	9.27	overlay
11/24/93	5	8.6	5	4.2	3	46.40	42.41	overlay
11/24/93	6	5.3	3	2.7	2	26.40	18.22	overlay
11/24/93	7	1.1	1	2.3	2	6.40	4.14	overlay
11/24/93	8	1.2	1	3.2	3	9.60	5.87	overlay
11/24/93	9	5.9	4	3.1	1	26.20	22.70	overlay
11/25/93	1	2.7	2	4.5	4	22.40	15.70	overlay
11/25/93	2	1.0	1	4.1	2	11.20	6.29	overlay
11/25/93	3	11.9	4	1.9	2	32.40	28.66	overlay
11/25/93	4	0.8	1	5.1	3	8.20	6.37	overlay
11/25/93	5	6.4	3	1.0	1	11.80	9.38	overlay
11/25/93	6	3.3	2	2.4	1	22.40	10.75	overlay
11/25/93	7	9.7	5	9.0	4	99.40	96.65	overlay
11/25/93	8	4.8	3	18.1	8	89.80	97.88	underlay
11/25/93	9	2.9	2	4.5	3	21.20	16.71	overlay
11/26/93	1	1.9	1	8.1	4	27.00	19.92	overlay
11/26/93	2	2.0	1	6.2	5	19.40	16.23	overlay
11/26/93	3	2.4	3	2.0	1	10.20	6.99	overlay
11/26/93	4	8.3	4	4.0	3	63.00	39.23	overlay
11/26/93	5	2.8	2	19.4	6	45.00	64.37	underlay
11/26/93	6	2.6	2	4.0	4	16.00	13.66	overlay
11/26/93	7	2.5	1	17.8	8	77.60	53.58	overlay
11/26/93	8	9.6	5	19.5	7	214.00	201.63	overlay
11/26/93	9	1.2	1	7.8	5	27.00	13.07	overlay
11/26/93	10	6.1	4	64.2	8	277.80	424.79	underlay
11/26/93	11	1.2	1	11.4	4	25.60	18.68	overlay
11/26/93	12	4.3	3	1.8	1	13.60	10.65	overlay
11/26/93	13	6.7	4	3.4	2	23.40	27.73	underlay
11/27/93	1	7.0	6	4.9	4	44.20	40.22	overlay
11/27/93	2	2.0	2	1.9	1	8.00	5.75	overlay
11/27/93	3	1.9	2	6.2	3	14.40	15.54	underlay

Date	Race#	Odds 1	Rank	Odds 2	Rank	Actual	Theory	Value
11/27/93	4	1.6	1	2.9	2	13.40	6.83	overlay
11/27/93	5	3.0	2	0.8	1	6.60	4.02	overlay
11/27/93	6	5.2	3	1.8	1	14.40	12.64	overlay
11/27/93	7	1.3	1	4.8	2	12.60	8.96	overlay
11/27/93	8	1.7	1	3.4	2	10.20	8.24	overlay
11/27/93	9	2.9	2	13.6	7	55.20	47.09	overlay
11/27/93	10	10.5	5	5.4	3	85.20	64.55	overlay
11/28/93	1	8.3	5	1.9	1	19.00	20.38	underlay
11/28/93	2	5.0	4	16.7	7	117.00	93.99	overlay
11/28/93	3	3.2	2	2.2	1	12.60	9.71	overlay
11/28/93	4	0.8	1	11.9	5	16.40	13.93	overlay
11/28/93	5	7.9	5	2.1	1	34.80	21.20	overlay
11/28/93	6	2.5	3	1.9	2	13.60	6.94	overlay
11/28/93	7	0.9	1	2.2	2	4.00	3.41	overlay
11/28/93	8	1.8	1	21.9	9	73.60	49.30	overlay
11/28/93	9	0.7	1	17.1	4	28.20	17.65	overlay
11/28/93	10	2.6	2	1.2	1	7.40	4.92	overlay
12/01/93	1	2.1	2	2.7	3	10.60	8.06	overlay
12/01/93	2	2.9	3	5.5	4	28.60	20.07	overlay
12/01/93	3	4.2	3	24.8	6	92.80	117.77	underlay
12/01/93	4	27.9	6	1.8	2	143.20	62.45	overlay
12/01/93	5	77.0	8	5.1	4	616.00	430.77	overlay
12/01/93	6	1.5	2	5.9	3	22.00	12.10	overlay
12/01/93	7	2.1	1	3.7	2	13.40	10.61	overlay
12/01/93	8	4.1	2	0.8	1	10.20	5.25	overlay
12/01/93	9	11.8	5	1.0	1	29.20	16.60	overlay
12/02/93	1	1.5	2	4.3	3	8.00	9.14	underlay
12/02/93	2	7.0	4	8.6	5	59.00	67.99	underlay
12/02/93	3	2.8	2	9.6	6	29.00	32.73	underlay
12/02/93	4	3.0	2	7.4	5	26.80	27.22	underlay
12/02/93	5	1.7	1	10.9	4	25.60	23.98	overlay
12/02/93	6	1.1	1	6.8	4	14.40	10.72	overlay
12/02/93	7	6.3	4	3.2	3	33.80	24.81	overlay
12/02/93	8	8.3	5	1.9	1	24.80	20.38	overlay
12/02/93	9	4.2	2	0.7	1	8.80	4.82	overlay
12/03/93	1	8.8	5	4.2	3	38.00	43.34	underlay
12/03/93	2	3.5	3	3.5	2	19.40	15.75	overlay

Date	Race#	Odds 1	Rank	Odds 2	Rank	Actual	Theory	Value
12/03/93	3	1.6	1	2.4	3	7.80	5.81	overlay
12/03/93	4	1.0	1	2.6	2	7.40	4.25	overlay
12/03/93	5	8.9	6	3.3	2	42.40	35.25	overlay
12/03/93	6	6.9	5	5.6	4	51.60	44.88	overlay
12/03/93	7	1.1	1	2.6	2	7.60	4.59	overlay
12/03/93	8	4.1	2	7.3	4	34.00	35.56	underlay
12/03/93	9	9.8	5	13.3	7	81.40	141.87	underlay
12/04/93	1	2.5	3	6.6	4	23.40	20.85	overlay
12/04/93	2	3.3	3	2.3	1	14.00	10.37	overlay
12/04/93	3	8.4	5	4.9	3	42.80	47.75	underlay
12/04/93	4	1.8	1	3.1	2	10.40	7.98	overlay
12/04/93	5	1.1	1	5.1	3	11.00	8.25	overlay
12/04/93	6	0.5	1	3.6	2	5.60	3.23	overlay
12/04/93	7	3.8	3	5.9	4	35.20	27.23	overlay
12/04/93	8	3.1	2	4.3	3	17.80	17.01	overlay
12/04/93	9	6.9	5	11.5	6	103.00	88.49	overlay
12/04/93	10	15.7	6	10.7	5	148.00	181.16	underlay
12/05/93	1	3.2	2	14.5	5	39.20	54.67	underlay
12/05/93	2	1.5	2	17.0	5	23.00	33.02	underlay
12/05/93	3	1.6	2	1.5	1	5.40	3.95	overlay
12/05/93	4	1.0	1	2.0	2	5.40	3.43	overlay
12/05/93	5	4.3	3	4.2	2	28.20	22.31	overlay
12/05/93	6	3.2	1	8.8	7	40.40	33.93	overlay
12/05/93	7	3.1	2	1.0	1	7.80	4.94	overlay
12/05/93	8	11.3	5	2.5	2	44.40	34.60	overlay
12/05/93	9	9.2	6	2.9	1	35.00	32.43	overlay
12/05/93	10	1.3	1	20.1	9	51.80	34.43	overlay
12/08/93	1	4.5	3	35.3	8	123.20	177.42	underlay
12/08/93	2	0.4	1	14.8	5	18.40	9.69	overlay
12/08/93	3	3.1	3	1.4	1	9.40	6.48	overlay
12/08/93	4	15.8	6	8.5	3	90.20	146.36	underlay
12/08/93	5	48.3	11	6.3	5	274.00	330.26	underlay
12/08/93	6	1.2	1	30.6	7	67.40	48.51	overlay
12/08/93	7	5.6	4	2.6	2	21.60	18.54	overlay
12/08/93	8	0.7	1	15.4	5	20.80	15.96	overlay
12/08/93	9	6.3	3	2.6	2	22.00	20.67	overlay
12/09/93	1	4.5	2	0.8	1	8.40	5.70	overlay

Date	Race#	Odds 1	Rank	Odds 2	Rank	Actual	Theory	Value
12/09/93	2	10.5	5	18.7	6	164.60	210.87	underlay
12/09/93	3	5.3	5	2.7	2	20.40	18.22	overlay
12/09/93	4	3.7	2	4.0	3	24.60	18.65	overlay
12/09/93	5	1.6	1	7.7	4	26.80	16.42	overlay
12/09/93	6	2.7	1	8.5	5	44.80	28.26	overlay
12/09/93	7	0.8	1	13.5	5	21.60	15.70	overlay
12/09/93	8	0.9	1	7.3	3	16.80	9.71	overlay
12/09/93	9	6.2	4	2.7	2	32.00	21.05	overlay
12/10/93	1	2.3	1	9.2	5	26.40	26.47	underlay
12/10/93	2	0.8	1	1.9	2	4.80	2.76	overlay
12/10/93	3	0.8	1	34.6	6	38.40	39.09	underlay
12/10/93	4	5.7	4	24.5	8	143.20	154.18	underlay
12/10/93	5	7.4	5	3.3	2	36.20	29.63	overlay
12/10/93	6	23.8	5	6.0	2	99.80	157.20	underlay
12/10/93	7	5.3	3	9.7	5	57.20	58.83	underlay
12/10/93	8	8.8	5	1.4	1	18.00	16.63	overlay
12/10/93	9	4.2	3	1.9	1	15.60	10.91	overlay
12/11/93	1	11.1	4	0.8	1	16.40	13.04	overlay
12/11/93	2	2.8	2	26.8	8	104.80	88.24	overlay
12/11/93	3	1.5	1	4.5	3	17.40	9.52	overlay
12/11/93	4	2.1	1	4.1	3	14.20	11.62	overlay
12/11/93	5	1.2	1	2.4	2	5.20	4.60	overlay
12/11/93	6	3.0	2	1.1	1	0.00	5.13	overlay
12/11/93	7	10.2	6	4.5	2	77.80	53.10	overlay
12/11/93	8	1.0	1	12.2	6	21.80	17.13	overlay
12/11/93	9	7.6	6	7.1	5	38.00	61.31	underlay
12/11/93	10	7.2	4	1.5	1	24.00	14.61	overlay
12/11/93	11	1.7	1	23.7	7	65.60	50.71	overlay
12/12/93	1	1.6	1	3.3	2	12.40	7.64	overlay
12/12/93	2	4.0	3	2.7	1	16.80	14.12	overlay
12/12/93	3	2.2	1	2.8	3	10.00	8.65	overlay
12/12/93	4	3.6	4	2.8	3	20.40	13.27	overlay
12/12/93	5	11.0	4	16.7	6	155.20	197.51	underlay
12/12/93	6	1.1	1	30.8	7	46.40	45.40	overlay
12/12/93	7	6.1	3	12.7	6	52.20	86.74	underlay
12/12/93	8	1.4	1	2.1	2	6.20	4.66	overlay
12/12/93	9	5.6	4	4.4	3	29.40	29.63	underlay

Date	Race#	Odds 1	Rank	Odds 2	Rank	Actual	Theory	Value
12/12/93	10	9.3	6	3.7	2	62.40	40.72	overlay
12/15/93	1	2.0	1	2.8	3	11.40	7.98	overlay
12/15/93	2	4.3	3	1.3	1	10.40	8.12	overlay
12/15/93	3	0.7	1	6.6	3	9.20	7.22	overlay
12/15/93	4	5.3	3	7.0	5	41.20	43.23	underlay
12/15/93	5	9.7	5	3.7	3	43.00	42.38	overlay
12/15/93	6	2.2	2	7.7	5	23.60	21.54	overlay
12/15/93	7	1.3	1	2.6	2	8.60	5.25	overlay
12/15/93	8	3.9	3	5.1	4	26.80	24.38	overlay
12/15/93	9	16.1	6	2.4	1	48.00	46.91	overlay
12/16/93	1	0.9	1	9.6	5	19.00	12.53	overlay
12/16/93	2	2.8	3	36.8	7	113.40	120.49	underlay
12/16/93	3	3.4	3	4.6	4	21.80	19.62	overlay
12/16/93	4	1.2	1	4.9	4	13.00	8.55	overlay
12/16/93	5	2.1	1	13.1	5	63.00	34.25	overlay
12/16/93	6	22.3	7	2.0	1	51.00	54.93	underlay
12/16/93	7	7.0	5	1.6	1	17.60	15.03	overlay
12/16/93	8	2.9	2	15.4	6	49.00	53.08	underlay
12/16/93	9	3.7	3	6.4	4	24.20	28.67	underlay
12/17/93	1	6.3	3	8.1	4	21.40	58.22	underlay
12/17/93	2	1.4	1	3.4	3	8.40	7.02	overlay
12/17/93	3	3.8	3	3.4	2	23.20	16.52	overlay
12/17/93	4	91.3	8	12.6	5	384.20	2,300.76	underlay
12/17/93	5	11.9	6	9.7	5	83.00	126.22	underlay
12/17/93	6	31.9	7	2.8	3	93.20	104.69	underlay
12/17/93	7	2.5	2	4.6	3	21.00	14.98	overlay
12/17/93	8	2.4	3	1.5	1	7.60	5.51	overlay
12/17/93	9	1.4	1	18.6	7	29.40	33.99	underlay
12/18/93	1	3.8	2	4.8	3	25.60	22.53	overlay
12/18/93	2	1.1	1	2.8	2	7.40	4.89	overlay
12/18/93	3	1.1	1	2.9	3	6.80	5.03	overlay
12/18/93	4	1.1	1	4.1	3	12.60	6.79	overlay
12/18/93	5	6.8	2	0.8	1	13.40	8.27	overlay
12/18/93	6	1.8	2	1.7	1	8.00	4.81	overlay
12/18/93	7	1.8	1	18.7	6	59.20	42.28	overlay
12/18/93	8	0.2	1	8.9	4	8.40	3.34	overlay
12/18/93	9	1.8	1	10.3	6	28.80	23.86	overlay

Date	Race#	Odds 1	Rank	Odds 2	Rank	Actual	Theory	Value
12/18/93	10	4.8	4	3.8	3	46.20	22.53	overlay
12/19/93	1	2.7	2	7.3	4	30.40	24.50	overlay
12/19/93	2	3.1	3	3.6	4	19.80	14.51	overlay
12/19/93	3	5.1	5	4.4	4	36.00	27.19	overlay
12/19/93	4	15.8	7	0.8	1	33.00	18.25	overlay
12/19/93	5	5.9	4	21.3	7	147.00	138.84	overlay
12/19/93	6	34.3	6	6.3	4	169.60	235.56	underlay
12/19/93	7	0.8	1	4.5	3	9.60	5.70	overlay
12/19/93	8	16.0	5	0.4	1	19.00	10.43	overlay
12/19/93	9	1.5	1	2.2	2	7.00	5.13	overlay
12/19/93	10	1.0	1	24.0	6	45.20	32.88	overlay
12/20/93	1	2.5	2	7.8	5	31.20	24.37	overlay
12/20/93	2	8.8	5	5.6	4	67.20	56.43	overlay
12/20/93	3	2.0	1	7.8	5	32.80	20.09	overlay
12/20/93	4	4.5	2	0.8	1	11.60	5.70	overlay
12/20/93	5	3.6	2	6.1	3	25.40	26.75	underlay
12/20/93	6	1.0	1	99.8	11	162.00	133.95	overlay
12/20/93	7	6.5	4	1.3	1	14.80	11.80	overlay
12/20/93	8	6.2	4	1.8	1	18.60	14.84	overlay
12/20/93	9	1.1	1	7.7	3	20.00	12.02	overlay
12/20/93	10	3.4	2	4.0	4	19.60	17.29	overlay

These results are quite revealing — 549 out of the 695 races resulted in overlayed payoffs! That's 79 percent: Almost four out of five races resulted in quinella overlays. It doesn't take a brain surgeon to conclude that the quinella is a super opportunity. My guess is that less than two handicappers in a hundred know how to figure out whether a quinella is an overlay or not. Thank the horseracing gods for this most wonderful opportunity. You're in a position to sack and ravage.

In this study the favorite won 245 out of 695 races, for a win percentage of 35 percent. In spite of this, the quinella using the favorite was an overlay 96 percent of the time!

These data scream out the fact that the quinella is a great bet. Please be warned that these data were compiled during a time when the quinella was new to southern California. If you play at a track where the quinella has been around for a while, it's best to do your own research in order to validate my conclusions. My reason for optimism is the fact that the exacta has been around southern California for a long time and still more than 75 percent of exacta payoffs are overlays.

Let's compare the quinella data to the exacta data for the same races:

Date	Race#	Odds 1	Rank	Odds 2	Rank	Actual	Theory	Value
12/26/92	2	1.6	1	3.4	3	19.20	14.08	overlay
12/26/92	7	9.5	6	4.5	3	84.80	104.50	underlay
12/27/92	2	5.7	3	34.4	10	604.40	403.56	overlay
12/27/92	7	20.0	6	29.7	7	552.00	1,228.00	underlay
12/29/92	2	8.3	4	2.3	2	67.40	54.78	overlay
12/29/92	7	3.2	3	2.5	1	24.20	22.40	overlay
12/30/92	2	1.1	1	4.9	3	15.80	12.98	overlay
12/30/92	7	8.9	4	3.7	3	70.60	83.66	undcrlay
12/31/92	2	2.7	2	3.4	3	34.40	23.76	overlay
12/31/92	7	2.9	2	3.0	3	39.60	23.20	overlay
01/01/93	2	2.6	1	7.8	4	59.40	45.76	overlay
01/01/93	7	14.7	5	2.0	2	111.60	88.20	overlay
01/02/93	2	1.4	1	3.8	2	20.40	13.44	overlay
01/02/93	7	4.8	4	4.6	3	50.40	53.76	underlay
01/03/93	2	6.6	6	4.3	3	78.80	69.96	overlay
01/03/93	7	2.1	2	1.4	1	15.40	10.08	overlay
01/06/93	2	10.3	6	3.5	2	111.00	92.70	overlay
01/06/93	7	1.6	1	3.1	3	21.40	13.12	overlay
01/07/93	2	1.4	1	2.9	3	11.60	10.92	overlay
01/07/93	7	5.3	4	7.2	6	82.80	86.92	underlay
01/08/93	2	7.8	4	1.7	1	56.80	42.12	overlay
01/08/93	7	1.9	1	10.7	6	52.60	44.46	overlay
01/09/93	2	10.7	6	2.5	2	113.60	74.90	overlay
01/09/93	7	1.8	2	5.8	3	33.40	24.48	overlay
01/10/93	2	6.5	5	3.3	2	68.00	55.90	overlay
01/10/93	7	1.1	1	2.6	2	11.40	7.92	overlay
01/13/93	2	4.7	4	2.6	1	43.20	33.84	overlay
01/13/93	7	2.8	2	4.2	4	42.00	29.12	overlay
01/14/93	2	2.0	2	2.0	1	18.20	12.00	overlay
01/14/93	7	19.5	7	14.6	6	325.20	608.40	underlay

Date	Race#	Odds 1	Rank	Odds 2	Rank	Actual	Theory	Value
01/15/93	2	5.6	5	33.4	7	247.00	385.28	underlay
01/15/93	7	1.9	1	2.9	2	18.20	14.82	overlay
01/16/93	2	18.1	7	10.2	5	283.20	405.44	underlay
01/16/93	7	1.6	1	4.3	4	19.40	16.96	overlay
01/17/93	2	0.5	1	7.5	3	14.60	8.50	overlay
01/17/93	7	9.0	4	4.2	3	86.80	93.60	underlay
01/18/93	2	2.5	2	1.5	1	20.00	12.50	overlay
01/22/93	2	1.9	1	5.0	4	27.80	22.80	overlay
01/22/93	7	1.6	1	8.8	5	31.20	31.36	underlay
01/23/93	2	4.2	4	4.1	2	49.80	42.84	overlay
01/23/93	7	2.6	2	3.1	3	26.60	21.32	overlay
01/24/93	2	0.8	1	4.2	2	13.40	8.32	overlay
01/24/93	7	2.8	2	1.0	1	18.60	11.20	overlay
01/27/93	2	0.9	1	4.2	2	17.40	9.36	overlay
01/27/93	7	0.9	1	4.0	2	14.20	9.00	overlay
01/28/93	2	3.3	2	0.7	1	18.60	11.22	overlay
01/28/93	7	1.9	1	7.3	4	43.20	31.54	overlay
01/29/93	2	0.5	1	6.2	2	13.20	7.20	overlay
01/29/93	7	0.7	1	3.8	2	10.00	6.72	overlay
01/30/93	2	40.2	10	22.8	7	1,015.00	1,913.52	underlay
01/30/93	7	5.5	4	2.1	1	53.80	34.10	overlay
01/31/93	2	2.9	2	3.3	3	23.80	24.94	underlay
01/31/93	7	26.3	7	3.2	2	262.60	220.92	overlay
02/03/93	2	6.0	5	4.1	2	89.40	61.20	overlay
02/03/93	7	2.3	1	10.7	5	87.60	53.82	overlay
02/04/93	2	1.5	1	2.8	2	12.00	11.40	overlay
02/04/93	7	0.7	1	4.6	3	10.60	7.84	overlay
02/05/93	2	3.7	2	4.4	3	33.80	39.96	underlay
02/05/93	7	2.7	2	1.4	1	21.60	12.96	overlay
02/06/93	2	2.6	2	2.8	3	30.60	19.76	overlay
02/06/93	7	3.7	4	3.3	2	43.40	31.82	overlay
02/07/93	2	1.3	1	6.8	3	28.60	20.28	overlay
02/07/93	7	2.5	2	1.8	1	26.00	14.00	overlay
02/10/93	2	2.6	2	3.3	4	30.60	22.36	overlay
02/10/93	7	4.5	3	2.3	2	37.40	29.70	overlay
02/11/93	2	15.1	5	9.8	3	194.80	326.16	underlay
02/11/93	7	9.7	5	0.9	1	62.80	36.86	overlay

Date	Race#	Odds 1	Rank	Odds 2	Rank	Actual	Theory	Value
02/12/93	2	7.1	5	21.1	7	228.00	313.82	underlay
02/12/93	7	7.6	6	3.6	2	80.80	69.92	overlay
02/13/93	2	6.6	4	12.2	5	135.40	174.24	underlay
02/13/93	7	2.5	2	3.3	3	29.00	21.50	overlay
02/14/93	2	2.2	1	15.8	7	62.20	73.92	underlay
02/14/93	7	1.3	1	4.8	3	19.00	15.08	overlay
02/15/93	2	3.9	3	4.6	4	43.40	43.68	underlay
02/15/93	7	0.4	1	5.6	3	10.00	5.28	overlay
02/17/93	2	2.0	1	4.3	3	27.60	21.20	overlay
02/17/93	7	2.0	1	24.2	7	17.60	100.80	underlay
02/18/93	2	1.2	1	6.5	4	26.80	18.00	overlay
02/18/93	7	1.2	1	3.6	3	17.00	11.04	overlay
02/19/93	2	6.2	4	1.3	1	41.00	28.52	overlay
02/19/93	7	0.9	1	6.0	3	18.00	12.60	overlay
02/20/93	2	1.2	1	4.1	2	21.20	12.24	overlay
02/20/93	7	0.7	1	3.2	2	8.40	5.88	overlay
02/21/93	2	1.4	1	2.8	3	13.20	10.64	overlay
02/21/93	7	9.8	5	6.9	4	75.40	154.84	underlay
02/24/93	2	6.9	4	2.6	2	67.20	49.68	overlay
02/24/93	7	3.1	3	0.9	1	20.60	11.78	overlay
02/25/93	2	6.0	3	1.3	1	37.80	27.60	overlay
02/25/93	7	1.1	1	1.9	2	9.60	6.38	overlay
02/26/93	2	6.9	3	1.2	1	42.60	30.36	overlay
02/26/93	7	2.9	2	3.7	3	32.60	27.26	overlay
02/27/93	2	4.3	3	0.8	1	19.00	15.48	overlay
02/27/93	7	4.7	3	6.1	4	55.80	66.74	underlay
02/28/93	2	3.5	2	4.5	3	39.60	38.50	overlay
02/28/93	7	7.8	4	0.9	1	39.40	29.64	overlay
03/03/93	2	10.1	5	1.6	1	87.60	52.52	overlay
03/03/93	7	19.0	7	4.4	3	259.80	205.20	overlay
03/04/93	2	3.4	2	17.5	7	204.20	125.80	overlay
03/04/93	7	1.2	1	9.0	4	31.60	24.00	overlay
03/05/93	2	2.3	2	31.5	8	154.00	149.50	overlay
03/05/93	7	7.1	4	9.9	6	140.20	154.78	underlay
03/06/93	2	2.4	2	2.4	1	22.00	16.32	overlay
03/06/93	7	2.0	1	2.4	2	15.20	13.60	overlay
03/07/93	2	2.5	2	2.3	1	21.20	16.50	overlay

Date	Race#	Odds 1	Rank	Odds 2	Rank	Actual	Theory	Value
03/07/93	7	0.7	1	7.4	3	16.40	11.76	overlay
03/10/93	2	1.9	2	20.4	5	64.00	81.32	underlay
03/10/93	7	4.6	3	12.6	6	115.60	125.12	underlay
03/11/93	2	8.1	5	12.6	7	345.40	220.32	overlay
03/11/93	7	16.5	8	4.8	3	202.40	191.40	overlay
03/12/93	2	6.5	4	6.7	5	84.40	100.10	underlay
03/12/93	7	20.6	6	2.3	1	148.80	135.96	overlay
03/13/93	2	3.1	2	1.5	1	23.60	15.50	overlay
03/13/93	7	8.4	5	1.5	1	44.20	42.00	overlay
03/14/93	2	1.2	1	3.4	2	15.00	10.56	overlay
03/14/93	7	3.7	3	5.5	5	67.60	48.10	overlay
03/17/93	2	1.9	1	3.1	3	20.40	15.58	overlay
03/17/93	7	1.0	1	2.1	2	7.80	6.20	overlay
03/18/93	2	1.8	1	2.8	2	24.80	13.68	overlay
03/18/93	7	1.1	1	1.8	2	9.40	6.16	overlay
03/19/93	2	3.5	2	3.7	3	38.40	32.90	overlay
03/19/93	7	7.4	5	5.1	3	77.20	90.28	underlay
03/20/93	2	5.5	3	3.3	2	46.40	47.30	underlay
03/20/93	7	25.0	8	9.8	6	451.60	540.00	underlay
03/21/93	2	2.4	2	3.4	3	29.40	21.12	overlay
03/21/93	7	1.5	1	2.9	2	18.40	11.70	overlay
03/24/93	2	0.9	1	7.1	4	21.60	14.58	overlay
03/24/93	7	2.8	1	4.2	3	36.80	20.12	overlay
03/25/93	2	1.9	1	15.7	6	71.60	63.46	overlay
03/25/93	7	1.6	1	24.1	6	96.20	80.32	overlay
03/26/93	2	5.9	4	2.9	2	60.20	46.02	overlay
03/26/93	7	2.8	3	2.4	2	26.40	19.04	overlay
03/27/93	2	4.1	3	3.4	2	49.00	36.08	overlay
03/27/93	7	3.0	3	4.9	4	40.60	35.40	overlay
03/28/93	2	7.9	5	21.6	7	262.00	357.08	underlay
03/28/93	7	8.0	4	2.2	2	47.60	51.20	underlay
03/31/93	2	2.5	2	7.5	6	43.00	42.50	overlay
03/31/93	7	1.4	1	2.7	2	11.20	10.36	overlay
04/01/93	2	2.4	2	13.5	6	98.00	69.60	overlay
04/01/93	7	10.9	6	9.5	5	170.40	228.90	underlay
04/02/93	2	1.6	1	5.6	3	29.20	21.12	overlay
04/02/93	7	2.5	2	7.5	3	30.80	42.50	underlay

Date	Race#	Odds 1	Rank	Odds 2	Rank	Actual	Theory	Value
04/03/93	2	5.7	5	3.4	3	69.80	50.16	overlay
04/03/93	7	1.3	2	1.3	1	8.00	5.98	overlay
04/04/93	2	1.1	1	6.9	4	26.20	17.38	overlay
04/04/93	7	1.7	1	5.3	4	20.80	21.42	underlay
04/07/93	2	1.2	1	10.6	5	34.40	27.84	overlay
04/07/93	7	1.1	1	2.8	2	14.40	8.36	overlay
04/08/93	2	1.7	2	1.2	1	11.80	7.48	overlay
04/08/93	7	8.1	3	0.3	1	52.40	21.06	overlay
04/09/93	2	6.5	3	17.1	7	348.60	235.30	overlay
04/09/93	7	28.1	5	2.9	3	184.60	219.18	underlay
04/10/93	2	0.4	1	9.0	4	14.20	8.00	overlay
04/10/93	7	1.8	1	3.8	3	27.40	17.28	overlay
04/11/93	2	0.5	1	5.5	2	12.40	6.50	overlay
04/11/93	7	2.6	2	8.0	5	63.80	46.80	overlay
04/14/93	2	9.4	5	45.3	10	512.80	870.44	underlay
04/14/93	7	2.0	1	7.8	5	44.60	35.20	overlay
04/15/93	2	2.8	2	9.9	4	50.80	61.04	underlay
04/15/93	7	19.9	6	7.0	4	247.80	318.40	underlay
04/16/93	2	5.3	3	1.1	1	29.80	22.26	overlay
04/16/93	7	3.7	3	11.2	6	94.80	90.28	overlay
04/17/93	2	1.7	1	2.2	2	14.40	10.88	overlay
04/17/93	7	1.3	1	8.2	4	37.00	23.92	overlay
04/18/93	2	27.3	7	19.7	6	580.60	1,130.22	underlay
04/18/93	7	6.9	4	3.2	3	74.60	57.96	overlay
10/06/93	1	7.4	4	3.7	2	98.00	69.56	overlay
10/06/93	2	19.6	8	4.3	3	278.20	207.76	overlay
10/06/93	3	5.9	4	4.1	2	56.60	60.18	underlay
10/06/93	4	3.2	2	3.5	3	35.60	28.80	overlay
10/06/93	5	2.8	2	2.5	1	22.80	19.60	overlay
10/06/93	6	6.8	5	1.8	1	66.20	38.08	overlay
10/06/93	7	3.7	2	11.0	5	54.60	88.80	underlay
10/06/93	8	0.9	1	31.5	6	81.40	58.50	overlay
10/06/93	9	5.0	3	6.5	5	69.80	75.00	underlay
10/07/93	1	4.5	2	0.9	1	25.40	17.10	overlay
10/07/93	2	5.6	3	0.9	1	39.00	21.28	overlay
10/07/93	3	24.7	8	5.5	3	260.40	321.10	underlay
10/07/93	4	1.5	1	3.1	2	19.60	12.30	overlay

Date	Race#	Odds 1	Rank	Odds 2	Rank	Actual	Theory	Value
10/07/93	5	3.8	2	12.2	7	76.20	100.32	underlay
10/07/93	6	10.0	4	1.9	1	84.20	58.00	overlay
10/07/93	7	0.6	1	2.2	2	7.20	3.84	overlay
10/07/93	8	1.7	1	15.6	6	87.40	56.44	overlay
10/07/93	9	3.0	2	4.8	4	43.00	34.80	overlay
10/08/93	1	6.4	3	0.8	1	33.40	23.04	overlay
10/08/93	2	0.6	1	2.5	2	10.20	4.20	overlay
10/08/93	3	3.7	3	2.0	1	35.40	22.20	overlay
10/08/93	4	1.9	2	1.8	1	13.00	10.64	overlay
10/08/93	5	7.4	6	5.1	4	83.20	90.28	underlay
10/08/93	6	28.9	7	2.1	2	177.80	179.18	underlay
10/08/93	7	1.8	1	11.5	5	54.80	45.00	overlay
10/08/93	8	6.7	5	2.6	1	56.80	48.24	overlay
10/08/93	9	4.3	2	10.9	5	93.80	102.34	underlay
10/09/93	1	4.7	5	3.4	2	71.20	41.36	overlay
10/09/93	2	11.1	6	1.3	1	75.60	51.06	overlay
10/09/93	3	0.6	1	10.9	5	18.80	14.28	overlay
10/09/93	4	0.9	1	2.2	2	9.40	5.76	overlay
10/09/93	5	13.9	6	7.0	5	227.40	222.40	overlay
10/09/93	6	2.2	1	2.4	2	18.20	14.96	overlay
10/09/93	7	1.6	1	8.6	5	41.80	30.72	overlay
10/09/93	8	5.0	2	0.2	1	24.00	12.00	overlay
10/09/93	9	0.0	0	11.9	0	891.20	211.00	overlay
10/10/93	1	5.6	5	1.1	1	31.80	23.52	overlay
10/10/93	2	1.6	1	3.3	2	21.40	13.76	overlay
10/10/93	3	1.7	2	5.3	3	24.60	21.42	overlay
10/10/93	4	2.5	2	4.8	4	31.40	29.00	overlay
10/10/93	5	17.1	7	11.5	6	469.20	427.50	overlay
10/10/93	6	8.0	5	1.6	1	57.40	41.60	overlay
10/10/93	7	0.9	1	6.2	3	18.20	12.96	overlay
10/10/93	8	0.5	1	2.9	2	5.60	3.90	overlay
10/10/93	9	7.5	4	2.4	1	50.20	51.00	underlay
10/11/93	1	2.9	2	3.8	3	34.20	27.84	overlay
10/11/93	2	9.8	4	15.4	7	361.60	321.44	overlay
10/11/93	3	2.4	3	12.6	5	55.60	65.28	underlay
10/11/93	4	5.0	3	1.0	1	27.40	20.00	overlay
10/11/93	5	2.2	1	4.4	4	30.80	23.76	overlay

Date	Race#	Odds 1	Rank	Odds 2	Rank	Actual	Theory	Value
10/11/93	6	1.6	1	3.0	2	18.20	12.80	overlay
10/11/93	7	3.3	2	4.2	3	48.80	34.32	overlay
10/11/93	8	0.7	1	5.7	3	15.00	9.38	overlay
10/11/93	9	3.6	2	9.6	6	112.60	76.32	overlay
10/13/93	1	5.6	4	2.0	2	43.40	33.60	overlay
10/13/93	2	15.0	7	38.8	8	675.40	1,194.00	underlay
10/13/93	3	9.2	5	13.0	7	210.80	257.60	underlay
10/13/93	4	0.9	1	4.8	3	21.40	10.44	overlay
10/13/93	5	1.4	1	7.1	4	37.40	22.68	overlay
10/13/93	6	11.9	6	2.1	1	121.80	73.78	overlay
10/13/93	7	1.7	1	13.3	6	59.80	48.62	overlay
10/13/93	8	1.3	2	1.1	1	8.00	5.46	overlay
10/13/93	9	9.5	5	2.0	1	56.80	57.00	underlay
10/14/93	1	1.5	1	1.9	2	10.80	8.70	overlay
10/14/93	2	3.0	2	5.8	3	45.40	40.80	overlay
10/14/93	3	5.9	3	2.0	2	53.40	35.40	overlay
10/14/93	4	1.3	1	5.1	3	24.00	15.86	overlay
10/14/93	5	5.4	3	1.5	1	40.60	27.00	overlay
10/14/93	6	4.8	4	2.9	2	46.20	37.44	overlay
10/14/93	7	9.7	6	3.0	3	71.20	77.60	underlay
10/14/93	8	2.0	1	5.8	4	29.00	27.20	overlay
10/14/93	9	4.5	3	1.5	1	31.00	22.50	overlay
10/15/93	1	3.7	3	1.3	1	25.60	17.02	overlay
10/15/93	2	7.9	4	19.6	6	192.00	325.48	underlay
10/15/93	3	6.0	3	6.9	4	87.40	94.80	underlay
10/15/93	4	1.6	1	12.9	6	60.60	44.48	overlay
10/15/93	5	0.8	1	32.0	9	86.20	52.80	overlay
10/15/93	6	1.2	1	20.2	8	55.00	50.88	overlay
10/15/93	7	5.4	4	17.7	6	192.00	201.96	underlay
10/15/93	8	5.0	5	1.9	1	38.00	29.00	overlay
10/15/93	9	5.1	2	7.4	5	115.60	85.68	overlay
10/16/93	1	2.6	3	1.3	1	17.20	11.96	overlay
10/16/93	2	11.2	5	0.9	1	63.60	42.56	overlay
10/16/93	3	4.3	3	2.6	2	37.60	30.96	overlay
10/16/93	4	3.4	2	0.9	1	20.20	12.92	overlay
10/16/93	5	11.4	5	43.5	11	894.80	1,014.60	underlay
10/16/93	6	1.1	1	3.6	2	12.60	10.12	overlay

Date	Race#	Odds 1	Rank	Odds 2	Rank	Actual	Theory	Value
10/16/93	7	3.2	2	7.2	4	60.20	52.48	overlay
10/16/93	8	0.3	1	4.9	2	6.20	3.54	overlay
10/16/93	9	2.1	1	7.8	5	53.40	36.96	overlay
10/17/93	1	2.6	1	6.5	5	47.80	39.00	overlay
10/17/93	2	1.4	1	2.6	2	13.20	10.08	overlay
10/17/93	3	2.1	3	5.9	4	28.00	28.98	underlay
10/17/93	4	0.9	1	4.7	3	16.80	10.26	overlay
10/17/93	5	6.0	5	5.8	4	82.40	81.60	overlay
10/17/93	6	1.1	1	2.2	2	13.00	7.04	overlay
10/17/93	7	9.1	4	6.2	2	154.20	131.04	overlay
10/17/93	8	4.2	3	3.8	2	33.20	40.32	underlay
10/17/93	9	2.3	2	9.5	5	47.80	48.30	underlay
10/20/93	1	1.7	1	3.3	2	23.00	14.62	overlay
10/20/93	2	1.8	1	24.5	6	105.00	91.80	overlay
10/20/93	3	2.0	1	4.3	4	28.60	21.20	overlay
10/20/93	4	2.0	1	3.4	3	25.20	17.60	overlay
10/20/93	5	9.3	4	3.3	2	78.00	79.98	underlay
10/20/93	6	1.0	1	6.2	3	20.00	14.40	overlay
10/20/93	7	3.8	2	2.3	1	33.00	25.08	overlay
10/20/93	8	1.1	1	1.9	2	8.00	6.38	overlay
10/20/93	9	1.5	1	6.7	5	31.40	23.10	overlay
10/21/93	1	1.8	2	11.1	6	55.80	43.56	overlay
10/21/93	2	0.7	1	5.1	2	13.80	8.54	overlay
10/21/93	3	1.1	1	2.5	2	12.00	7.70	overlay
10/21/93	4	1.7	1	2.6	2	16.00	12.24	overlay
10/21/93	5	2.3	1	17.8	8	121.80	86.48	overlay
10/21/93	6	44.4	8	2.2	2	526.60	284.16	overlay
10/21/93	7	1.5	1	3.2	3	20.80	12.60	overlay
10/21/93	8	3.4	2	17.7	5	97.80	127.16	underlay
10/21/93	9	3.7	3	2.2	2	49.20	23.68	overlay
10/22/93	1	8.0	4	0.6	1	44.20	25.60	overlay
10/22/93	2	5.1	4	3.8	3	52.20	48.96	overlay
10/22/93	3	1.0	1	1.7	2	8.00	5.40	overlay
10/22/93	4	3.3	2	6.8	5	61.20	51.48	overlay
10/22/93	5	4.8	3	5.9	4	107.20	66.24	overlay
10/22/93	6	3.4	3	2.7	2	37.60	25.16	overlay
10/22/93	7	2.1	2	0.7	1	13.40	7.14	overlay

Date	Race#	Odds 1	Rank	Odds 2	Rank	Actual	Theory	Value
10/22/93	8	1.8	1	9.9	5	32.80	39.24	underlay
10/22/93	9	3.0	2	2.8	1	30.20	22.80	overlay
10/23/93	1	3.6	2	7.0	4	122.20	57.60	overlay
10/23/93	2	3.7	2	14.7	7	133.00	116.18	overlay
10/23/93	3	0.8	1	6.4	3	15.60	11.84	overlay
10/23/93	4	7.7	5	5.4	4	90.60	98.56	underlay
10/23/93	5	1.9	1	2.2	2	18.80	12.16	overlay
10/23/93	6	3.3	3	1.6	1	20.60	17.16	overlay
10/23/93	7	1.3	1	2.4	2	10.80	8.84	overlay
10/23/93	8	3.4	2	5.7	4	43.40	45.56	underlay
10/23/93	9	1.3	1	5.2	3	26.40	16.12	overlay
10/24/93	1	7.9	4	1.3	1	39.40	36.34	overlay
10/24/93	2	7.7	3	1.8	2	57.40	43.12	overlay
10/24/93	3	3.7	2	0.5	1	17.40	11.10	overlay
10/24/93	4	0.7	1	8.2	3	19.60	12.88	overlay
10/24/93	5	24.4	9	2.3	1	242.80	161.04	overlay
10/24/93	6	1.3	1	4.5	3	20.40	14.30	overlay
10/24/93	7	1.2	1	5.1	3	20.00	14.64	overlay
10/24/93	8	9.6	4	1.0	1	50.20	38.40	overlay
10/24/93	9	5.7	3	19.0	8	228.20	228.00	overlay
10/27/93	1	8.4	5	2.4	2	76.20	57.12	overlay
10/27/93	2	30.9	7	23.2	5	982.60	1,495.56	underlay
10/27/93	3	1.6	1	2.6	3	16.40	11.52	overlay
10/27/93	4	2.1	1	2.7	2	20.00	15.54	overlay
10/27/93	5	2.1	1	7.2	4	30.60	34.44	underlay
10/27/93	6	3.9	2	7.8	4	58.60	68.64	underlay
10/27/93	7	1.3	1	2.6	2	12.20	9.36	overlay
10/27/93	8	2.5	2	1.1	1	15.60	10.50	overlay
10/27/93	9	1.3	1	2.7	2	12.00	9.62	overlay
10/29/93	1	1.6	2	1.3	1	12.00	7.36	overlay
10/29/93	2	7.5	4	2.0	2	54.20	45.00	overlay
10/29/93	3	0.9	1	21.5	5	37.00	40.50	underlay
10/29/93	4	1.8	1	54.0	8	144.60	198.00	underlay
10/29/93	5	7.5	4	2.4	2	63.00	51.00	overlay
10/29/93	6	3.1	3	2.8	2	27.60	23.56	overlay
10/29/93	7	2.5	3	1.6	1	22.00	13.00	overlay
10/29/93	8	1.2	1	2.5	2	13.20	8.40	overlay

Date	Race#	Odds 1	Rank	Odds 2	Rank	Actual	Theory	Value
10/29/93	9	2.3	1	9.5	7	88.80	48.30	overlay
10/30/93	1	1.7	1	4.0	3	20.20	17.00	overlay
10/30/93	2	10.5	4	17.3	6	315.40	384.30	underlay
10/30/93	3	3.9	3	2.0	2	24.60	23.40	overlay
10/30/93	4	2.8	2	3.3	3	29.20	24.08	overlay
10/30/93	5	33.7	8	2.8	2	312.40	256.12	overlay
10/30/93	6	3.6	3	5.9	4	52.20	49.68	overlay
10/30/93	7	6.9	5	1.7	1	39.40	37.26	overlay
10/30/93	8	1.6	1	4.5	3	22.00	17.60	overlay
10/30/93	9	1.9	1	2.4	2	18.20	12.92	overlay
10/31/93	1	2.3	2	1.2	1	18.00	10.12	overlay
10/31/93	2	0.6	1	5.7	3	11.20	8.04	overlay
10/31/93	3	5.8	4	13.5	5	96.20	168.20	underlay
10/31/93	4	1.2	1	2.4	2	10.80	8.16	overlay
10/31/93	5	2.2	1	6.4	4	38.20	32.56	overlay
10/31/93	6	1.0	1	8.0	4	27.20	18.00	overlay
10/31/93	7	4.5	3	1.7	2	29.20	24.30	overlay
10/31/93	8	10.1	6	7.0	4	120.20	161.60	underlay
10/31/93	9	2.1	1	5.7	5	48.20	28.14	overlay
11/03/93	1	10.5	5	2.1	1	88.60	65.10	overlay
11/03/93	2	1.5	1	2.2	2	15.60	9.60	overlay
11/03/93	3	2.8	3	2.7	2	29.20	20.72	overlay
11/03/93	4	3.1	2	4.5	4	59.80	94.10	overlay
11/03/93	5	1.3	1	17.5	6	49.20	48.10	overlay
11/03/93	6	1.3	1	19.8	6	93.60	54.08	overlay
11/03/93	7	10.3	5	1.0	1	52.40	41.20	overlay
11/03/93	8	2.2	2	3.2	3	27.80	18.48	overlay
11/03/93	9	8.7	5	5.0	4	130.20	104.40	overlay
11/04/93	1	2.6	2	15.0	8	115.80	83.20	overlay
11/04/93	2	7.4	3	19.9	7	171.60	309.32	underlay
11/04/93	3	2.6	2	17.1	6	74.00	94.12	underlay
11/04/93	4	5.4	3	6.4	4	83.40	79.92	overlay
11/04/93	5	3.4	2	1.4	1	28.00	16.32	overlay
11/04/93	6	1.0	1	9.3	4	26.20	20.60	overlay
11/04/93	7	3.9	2	5.2	4	63.00	48.36	overlay
11/04/93	8	0.7	1	18.0	7	32.00	26.60	overlay
11/04/93	9	3.1	2	3.6	3	43.60	28.52	overlay

Date	Race#	Odds 1	Rank	Odds 2	Rank	Actual	Theory	Value
11/05/93	1	65.2	8	8.6	4	1,281.60	1,251.84	overlay
11/05/93	2	31.8	7	11.3	4	530.00	782.28	underlay
11/05/93	3	3.5	4	2.6	3	38.00	25.20	overlay
11/05/93	4	2.4	2	16.7	5	128.00	84.96	overlay
11/05/93	5	3.5	2	7.7	5	52.60	60.90	underlay
11/05/93	6	3.7	2	6.9	3	51.60	58.46	underlay
11/05/93	7	3.6	2	1.3	1	28.80	16.56	overlay
11/05/93	8	18.1	8	7.7	4	345.00	314.94	overlay
11/05/93	9	3.5	2	7.2	4	76.40	57.40	overlay
11/06/93	1	2.3	2	1.7	1	16.00	12.42	overlay
11/06/93	2	5.3	2	8.5	6	76.20	100.70	underlay
11/06/93	3	2.3	3	2.2	2	13.40	14.72	underlay
11/06/93	4	1.3	1	2.5	2	11.80	9.10	overlay
11/06/93	5	1.3	1	18.2	7	68.40	49.92	overlay
11/06/93	6	3.0	2	42.4	9	342.40	260.40	overlay
11/06/93	7	1.5	1	4.3	3	17.20	15.90	overlay
11/06/93	8	133.6	11	1.2	1	1,015.40	587.84	overlay
11/06/93	9	11.6	7	2.9	1	126.20	90.48	overlay
11/06/93	10	1.8	1	17.3	6	59.80	65.88	underlay
11/07/93	1	5.7	5	5.2	4	65.20	70.68	underlay
11/07/93	2	8.4	4	39.8	8	654.60	685.44	underlay
11/07/93	3	2.2	2	1.2	1	12.60	9.68	overlay
11/07/93	4	4.0	3	4.7	4	53.40	45.60	overlay
11/07/93	5	8.2	4	12.3	6	357.80	218.12	overlay
11/07/93	6	0.9	1	6.5	5	15.60	13.50	overlay
11/07/93	7	10.0	6	5.8	5	100.00	136.00	underlay
11/07/93	8	1.1	1	4.0	3	17.20	11.00	overlay
11/07/93	9	5.6	6	5.3	4	140.80	70.56	overlay
11/10/93	1	4.6	4	4.6	3	87.80	51.52	overlay
11/10/93	2	8.5	4	91.6	11	653.00	1,574.20	underlay
11/10/93	3	2.9	2	9.7	5	53.20	62.06	underlay
11/10/93	4	0.9	1	15.8	6	16.00	30.24	underlay
11/10/93	5	43.8	8	9.8	5	714.80	946.08	underlay
11/10/93	6	9.9	5	1.6	1	76.20	51.48	overlay
11/10/93	7	1.0	1	3.5	2	11.40	9.00	overlay
11/10/93	8	1.5	1	1.6	2	13.80	7.80	overlay
11/10/93	9	6.0	5	13.8	7	167.00	177.60	underlay

Date	Race#	Odds 1	Rank	Odds 2	Rank	Actual	Theory	Value
11/11/93	1	3.3	2	12.3	5	73.20	87.78	underlay
11/11/93	2	1.4	1	36.1	8	104.20	103.88	overlay
11/11/93	3	6.5	3	0.4	1	27.00	18.20	overlay
11/11/93	4	1.1	1	4.8	3	15.80	12.76	overlay
11/11/93	5	6.9	6	3.8	2	74.00	66.24	overlay
11/11/93	6	1.9	1	10.5	5	47.40	43.70	overlay
11/11/93	7	33.4	9	14.6	5	840.60	1,042.08	underlay
11/11/93	8	4.9	3	1.2	1	34.40	21.56	overlay
11/11/93	9	1.6	1	4.3	3	17.20	16.96	overlay
11/12/93	1	1.5	1	4.6	4	19.00	16.80	overlay
11/12/93	2	1.6	1	2.2	2	13.80	10.24	overlay
11/12/93	3	2.3	2	16.7	6	90.60	81.42	overlay
11/12/93	4	9.7	5	1.9	1	55.80	56.26	underlay
11/12/93	5	4.7	2	7.1	5	70.40	76.14	underlay
11/12/93	6	2.4	1	23.7	7	110.00	118.56	underlay
11/12/93	7	0.7	1	5.9	3	14.20	9.66	overlay
11/12/93	8	1.3	1	6.4	4	25.60	19.24	overlay
11/12/93	9	3.3	2	4.2	3	45.60	34.32	overlay
11/13/93	1	1.1	1	2.8	2	13.40	8.36	overlay
11/13/93	2	7.0	4	2.3	1	67.60	46.20	overlay
11/13/93	3	2.5	2	0.8	1	13.40	9.00	overlay
11/13/93	4	5.8	5	12.3	6	139.20	154.28	underlay
11/13/93	5	4.2	3	2.1	1	30.00	26.01	overlay
11/13/93	6	1.9	1	14.6	4	12.60	97.44	overlay
11/13/93	7	1.1	1	14.1	5	35.00	33.22	overlay
11/13/93	8	3.3	2	8.9	4	63.20	65.34	underlay
11/13/93	9	42.7	9	7.3	4	629.80	708.82	underlay
11/14/93	1	3.5	2	1.2	1	26.40	15.40	overlay
11/14/93	2	0.5	1	3.7	2	13.80	4.70	overlay
11/14/93	3	1.2	1	4.1	3	17.80	12.24	overlay
11/14/93	4	4.9	4	4.9	3	65.80	57.82	overlay
11/14/93	5	4.7	2	8.7	4	98.80	91.18	overlay
11/14/93	6	3.4	2	12.4	5	61.80	91.12	underlay
11/14/93	7	6.2	5	6.4	6	109.60	91.76	overlay
11/14/93	8	16.6	8	8.5	4	303.40	315.40	underlay
11/14/93	9	8.2	4	7.9	3	153.60	145.96	overlay
11/15/93	1	4.9	3	1.9	2	42.40	28.42	overlay

Date	Race#	Odds 1	Rank	Odds 2	Rank	Actual	Theory	Value
11/15/93	2	4.6	3	0.7	1	27.00	15.64	overlay
11/15/93	3	23.1	6	1.2	1	135.40	101.64	overlay
11/15/93	4	16.1	6	5.1	4	292.80	196.42	overlay
11/15/93	5	6.6	4	20.8	7	265.20	287.76	underlay
11/15/93	6	5.3	3	2.1	1	45.80	32.86	overlay
11/15/93	7	1.3	1	10.2	5	26.00	29.12	underlay
11/15/93	8	1.7	1	3.2	2	18.60	14.28	overlay
11/15/93	9	2.3	1	16.3	7	89.80	79.58	overlay
11/17/93	1	2.4	2	3.2	3	19.00	20.16	underlay
11/17/93	2	1.1	1	1.5	2	9.00	5.50	overlay
11/17/93	3	1.6	1	9.4	7	43.60	33.28	overlay
11/17/93	4	2.5	1	4.6	4	34.40	28.00	overlay
11/17/93	5	2.4	2	8.8	4	50.20	47.04	overlay
11/17/93	6	3.4	3	17.4	7	162.20	125.12	overlay
11/17/93	7	3.8	2	9.0	4	55.40	76.00	underlay
11/17/93	8	1.0	1	17.4	5	39.40	36.80	overlay
11/17/93	9	4.1	3	4.1	2	47.20	41.82	overlay
11/18/93	1	1.4	1	31.9	8	66.80	92.12	underlay
11/18/93	2	1.9	2	5.5	3	30.80	24.70	overlay
11/18/93	3	1.9	2	1.3	1	15.00	8.74	overlay
11/18/93	4	3.5	2	27.5	8	206.40	199.50	overlay
11/18/93	5	9.4	5	9.2	4	200.40	191.76	overlay
11/18/93	6	2.7	2	1.4	1	22.20	12.96	overlay
11/18/93	7	1.3	1	2.6	2	15.60	9.36	overlay
11/18/93	8	5.1	3	3.7	2	46.60	47.94	underlay
11/18/93	9	8.9	5	2.2	1	70.60	56.96	overlay
11/19/93	1	1.4	1	2.9	2	13.20	10.92	overlay
11/19/93	2	3.0	2	6.5	3	44.00	45.00	underlay
11/19/93	3	1.7	1	1.8	2	10.20	9.52	overlay
11/19/93	4	12.7	4	3.0	2	108.00	101.60	overlay
11/19/93	5	1.9	2	0.9	1	12.80	7.22	overlay
11/19/93	6	18.3	7	3.0	2	149.20	146.40	overlay
11/19/93	7	3.3	3	2.1	1	31.40	20.46	overlay
11/19/93	8	0.9	1	3.0	2	9.60	7.20	overlay
11/19/93	9	2.7	2	2.0	1	31.60	16.20	overlay
11/20/93	1	0.9	1	13.2	4	34.80	25.56	overlay
11/20/93	2	2.5	2	1.5	1	17.00	12.50	overlay

Date	Race#	Odds 1	Rank	Odds 2	Rank	Actual	Theory	Value
11/20/93	3	1.8	1	2.8	3	17.00	13.68	overlay
11/20/93	4	1.0	1	5.8	3	17.80	13.60	overlay
11/20/93	5	3.4	2	1.6	1	24.80	17.68	overlay
11/20/93	6	22.3	9	22.3	8	1,191.60	1,039.18	overlay
11/20/93	7	0.8	1	3.0	2	7.60	6.40	overlay
11/20/93	8	3.0	2	8.5	3	56.20	57.00	underlay
11/20/93	9	3.8	2	15.6	6	114.80	126.16	underlay
11/20/93	10	1.6	1	6.6	3	32.20	24.32	overlay
11/21/93	1	0.4	1	12.9	5	20.40	11.12	overlay
11/21/93	2	2.7	2	2.8	3	34.80	20.52	overlay
11/21/93	3	7.9	3	0.9	1	41.80	30.02	overlay
11/21/93	4	2.3	3	13.9	4	50.80	68.54	underlay
11/21/93	5	5.0	3	2.8	2	57.60	38.00	overlay
11/21/93	6	7.8	4	1.0	1	52.40	31.20	overlay
11/21/93	7	5.2	3	3.5	2	49.40	46.80	overlay
11/21/93	8	6.9	4	1.4	1	57.40	33.12	overlay
11/21/93	9	6.1	4	5.0	3	75.40	73.20	overlay
11/21/93	10	2.8	2	1.7	1	22.80	15.12	overlay
11/24/93	1	1.1	1	21.9	5	48.40	50.38	underlay
11/24/93	2	2.7	2	2.9	3	26.40	21.06	overlay
11/24/93	3	1.9	2	2.5	3	18.80	13.30	overlay
11/24/93	4	1.1	1	5.8	3	21.80	14.96	overlay
11/24/93	5	8.6	5	4.2	3	85.40	89.44	underlay
11/24/93	6	5.3	3	2.7	2	50.80	39.22	overlay
11/24/93	7	1.1	1	2.3	2	10.20	7.26	overlay
11/24/93	8	1.2	1	3.2	3	15.00	10.08	overlay
11/24/93	9	5.9	4	3.1	1	70.80	48.38	overlay
11/25/93	1	2.7	2	4.5	4	33.20	29.70	overlay
11/25/93	2	1.0	1	4.1	2	20.00	10.20	overlay
11/25/93	3	11.9	4	1.9	2	95.40	69.02	overlay
11/25/93	4	0.8	1	5.1	3	12.80	9.76	overlay
11/25/93	5	6.4	3	1.0	1	37.20	25.60	overlay
11/25/93	6	3.3	2	2.4	1	39.40	22.44	overlay
11/25/93	7	9.7	5	9.0	4	184.80	194.00	underlay
11/25/93	8	4.8	3	18.1	8	150.00	183.36	underlay
11/25/93	9	2.9	2	4.5	3	40.80	31.90	overlay
11/26/93	1	1.9	1	8.1	4	38.80	34.58	overlay

Date	Race#	Odds 1	Rank	Odds 2	Rank	Actual	Theory	Value
11/26/93	2	2.0	1	6.2	5	32.60	28.80	overlay
11/26/93	3	2.4	3	2.0	1	21.80	14.40	overlay
11/26/93	4	8.3	4	4.0	3	132.80	83.00	overlay
11/26/93	5	2.8	2	19.4	6	90.00	114.24	underlay
11/26/93	6	2.6	2	4.0	4	31.80	26.00	overlay
11/26/93	7	2.5	1	17.8	8	110.60	94.00	overlay
11/26/93	8	9.6	5	19.5	7	323.80	393.60	underlay
11/26/93	9	1.2	1	7.8	5	39.40	21.12	overlay
11/26/93	10	6.1	4	64.2	8	716.40	795.44	underlay
11/26/93	11	1.2	1	11.4	4	34.20	29.76	overlay
11/26/93	12	4.3	3	1.8	1	31.40	24.08	overlay
11/26/93	13	6.7	4	3.4	2	59.00	58.96	overlay
11/27/93	1	7.0	6	4.9	4	85.60	82.60	overlay
11/27/93	2	2.0	2	1.9	1	19.00	11.60	overlay
11/27/93	3	1.9	2	6.2	3	26.40	27.36	underlay
11/27/93	4	1.6	1	2.9	2	21.00	12.48	overlay
11/27/93	5	3.0	2	0.8	1	19.60	10.80	overlay
11/27/93	6	5.2	3	1.8	1	39.80	29.12	overlay
11/27/93	7	1.3	1	4.8	2	22.60	15.08	overlay
11/27/93	8	1.7	1	3.4	2	17.20	14.96	overlay
11/27/93	9	2.9	2	13.6	7	96.60	84.68	overlay
11/27/93	10	10.5	5	5.4	3	174.60	134.40	overlay
11/28/93	1	8.3	5	1.9	1	47.40	48.14	underlay
11/28/93	2	5.0	4	16.7	7	214.20	177.00	overlay
11/28/93	3	3.2	2	2.2	1	27.60	20.48	overlay
11/28/93	4	0.8	1	11.9	5	20.20	20.64	underlay
11/28/93	5	7.9	5	2.1	1	72.80	48.98	overlay
11/28/93	6	2.5	3	1.9	2	27.40	14.50	overlay
11/28/93	7	0.9	1	2.2	2	6.80	5.76	overlay
11/28/93	8	1.8	1	21.9	9	95.60	82.44	overlay
11/28/93	9	0.7	1	17.1	4	30.60	25.34	overlay
11/28/93	10	2.6	2	1.2	1	15.40	11.44	overlay
12/01/93	1	2.1	2	2.7	3	10.80	15.54	underlay
12/01/93	2	2.9	3	5.5	4	53.40	37.70	overlay
12/01/93	3	4.2	3	24.8	6	159.80	216.72	underlay
12/01/93	4	27.9	6	1.8	2	268.60	156.24	overlay
12/01/93	5	77.0	8	5.1	4	1,561.00	939.40	overlay
12/01/93	6	1.5	2	5.9	3	36.60	20.70	overlay

Date	Race#	Odds 1	Rank	Odds 2	Rank	Actual	Theory	Value
12/01/93	7	2.1	1	3.7	2	26.80	19.74	overlay
12/01/93	8	4.1	2	0.8	1	25.20	14.76	overlay
12/01/93	9	11.8	5	1.0	1	65.00	47.20	overlay
12/02/93	1	1.5	2	4.3	3	15.40	15.90	underlay
12/02/93	2	7.0	4	8.6	5	93.60	134.40	underlay
12/02/93	3	2.8	2	9.6	6	49.00	59.36	underlay
12/02/93	4	3.0	2	7.4	5	50.20	50.40	underlay
12/02/93	5	1.7	1	10.9	4	40.80	40.46	overlay
12/02/93	6	1.1	1	6.8	4	20.40	17.16	overlay
12/02/93	7	6.3	4	3.2	3	68.40	52.92	overlay
12/02/93	8	8.3	5	1.9	1	72.60	48.14	overlay
12/02/93	9	4.2	2	0.7	1	26.00	14.28	overlay
12/03/93	1	8.8	5	4.2	3	93.00	91.52	overlay
12/03/93	2	3.5	3	3.5	2	35.80	31.50	overlay
12/03/93	3	1.6	1	2.4	3	13.00	10.88	overlay
12/03/93	4	1.0	1	2.6	2	10.60	7.20	overlay
12/03/93	5	8.9	6	3.3	2	90.80	76.54	overlay
12/03/93	6	6.9	5	5.6	4	101.60	91.08	overlay
12/03/93	7	1.1	1	2.6	2	13.20	7.92	overlay
12/03/93	8	4.1	2	7.3	4	68.00	68.06	underlay
12/03/93	9	9.8	5	13.3	7	173.20	280.28	underlay
12/04/93	1	2.5	3	6.6	4	41.80	38.00	overlay
12/04/93	2	3.3	3	2.3	1	30.00	21.78	overlay
12/04/93	3	8.4	5	4.9	3	104.20	99.12	overlay
12/04/93	4	1.8	1	3.1	2	20.20	14.76	overlay
12/04/93	5	1.1	1	5.1	3	15.80	13.42	overlay
12/04/93	6	0.5	1	3.6	2	8.00	4.60	overlay
12/04/93	7	3.8	3	5.9	4	74.40	52.44	overlay
12/04/93	8	3.1	2	4.3	3	32.80	32.86	underlay
12/04/93	9	6.9	5	11.5	6	180.00	172.50	overlay
12/04/93	10	15.7	6	10.7	5	369.00	367.38	overlay
12/05/93	1	3.2	2	14.5	5	69.40	99.20	underlay
12/05/93	2	1.5	2	17.0	5	34.40	54.00	underlay
12/05/93	3	1.6	2	1.5	1	11.40	8.00	overlay
12/05/93	4	1.0	1	2.0	2	9.60	6.00	overlay
12/05/93	5	4.3	3	4.2	2	55.60	44.72	overlay
12/05/93	6	3.2	1	8.8	7	89.60	62.72	overlay
12/05/93	7	3.1	2	1.0	1	23.60	12.40	overlay

Date	Race#	Odds 1	Rank	Odds 2	Rank	Actual	Theory	Value
12/05/93	8	11.3	5	2.5	2	102.80	79.10	overlay
12/05/93	9	9.2	6	2.9	1	91.00	71.76	overlay
12/05/93	10	1.3	1	20.1	9	93.20	54.86	overlay
12/08/93	1	4.5	3	35.3	8	256.80	326.70	underlay
12/08/93	2	0.4	1	14.8	5	26.40	12.64	overlay
12/08/93	3	3.1	3	1.4	1	23.80	14.88	overlay
12/08/93	4	15.8	6	8.5	3	187.40	300.20	underlay
12/08/93	5	48.3	11	6.3	5	629.20	705.18	underlay
12/08/93	6	1.2	1	30.6	7	84.00	75.84	overlay
12/08/93	7	5.6	4	2.6	2	50.00	40.32	overlay
12/08/93	8	0.7	1	15.4	5	27.80	22.96	overlay
12/08/93	9	6.3	3	2.6	2	45.40	45.36	overlay
12/09/93	1	4.5	2	0.8	1	20.60	16.20	overlay
12/09/93	2	10.5	5	18.7	6	266.20	413.70	underlay
12/09/93	3	5.3	5	2.7	2	43.00	39.22	overlay
12/09/93	4	3.7	2	4.0	3	45.60	37.00	overlay
12/09/93	5	1.6	1	7.7	4	38.80	27.84	overlay
12/09/93	6	2.7	1	8.5	5	73.80	51.30	overlay
12/09/93	7	0.8	1	13.5	5	23.60	23.20	overlay
12/09/93	8	0.9	1	7.3	3	21.80	14.94	overlay
12/09/93	9	6.2	4	2.7	2	66.40	45.88	overlay
12/10/93	1	2.3	1	9.2	5	38.60	46.92	underlay
12/10/93	2	0.8	1	1.9	2	9.20	4.64	overlay
12/10/93	3	0.8	1	34.6	6	46.60	56.96	underlay
12/10/93	4	5.7	4	24.5	8	271.60	290.70	underlay
12/10/93	5	7.4	5	3.3	2	76.40	63.64	overlay
12/10/93	6	23.8	5	6.0	2	269.00	333.20	underlay
12/10/93	7	5.3	3	9.7	5	102.80	113.42	underlay
12/10/93	8	8.8	5	1.4	1	51.80	42.24	overlay
12/10/93	9	4.2	3	1.9	1	35.80	24.36	overlay
12/11/93	1	11.1	4	0.8	1	49.00	39.96	overlay
12/11/93	2	2.8	2	26.8	8	192.80	155.68	overlay
12/11/93	3	1.5	1	4.5	3	27.40	16.50	overlay
12/11/93	4	2.1	1	4.1	3	24.60	21.42	overlay
12/11/93	5	1.2	1	2.4	2	8.80	8.16	overlay
12/11/93	6	3.0	2	1.1	1	19.00	12.60	overlay
12/11/93	7	10.2	6	4.5	2	203.60	112.20	overlay

Date	Race#	Odds 1	Rank	Odds 2	Rank	Actual	Theory	Value
12/11/93	8	1.0	1	12.2	6	26.40	26.40	underlay
12/11/93	9	7.6	6	7.1	5	89.00	123.12	underlay
12/11/93	10	7.2	4	1.5	1	70.00	36.00	overlay
12/11/93	11	1.7	1	23.7	7	89.60	83.98	overlay
12/12/93	1	1.6	1	3.3	2	20.40	13.76	overlay
12/12/93	2	4.0	3	2.7	1	32.40	29.60	overlay
12/12/93	3	2.2	1	2.8	3	21.00	16.72	overlay
12/12/93	4	3.6	4	2.8	3	60.60	27.36	overlay
12/12/93	5	11.0	4	16.7	6	291.60	389.40	underlay
12/12/93	6	1.1	1	30.8	7	67.80	69.96	underlay
12/12/93	7	6.1	3	12.7	6	134.40	167.14	underlay
12/12/93	8	1.4	1	2.1	2	11.80	8.68	overlay
12/12/93	9	5.6	4	4.4	3	56.60	60.48	underlay
12/12/93	10	9.3	6	3.7	2	138.80	87.42	overlay
12/15/93	1	2.0	1	2.8	3	21.40	15.20	overlay
12/15/93	2	4.3	3	1.3	1	27.40	19.78	overlay
12/15/93	3	0.7	1	6.6	3	12.40	10.64	overlay
12/15/93	4	5.3	3	7.0	5	58.60	84.80	underlay
12/15/93	5	9.7	5	3.7	3	117.80	91.18	overlay
12/15/93	6	2.2	2	7.7	5	53.00	38.28	overlay
12/15/93	7	1.3	1	2.6	2	15.80	9.36	overlay
12/15/93	8	3.9	3	5.1	4	60.20	47.58	overlay
12/15/93	9	16.1	6	2.4	1	116.60	100.48	overlay
12/16/93	1	0.0	1	9.0	5	23.60	19.00	overlay
12/16/93	2	2.8	3	36.8	7	171.40	211.68	underlay
12/16/93	3	3.4	3	4.6	4	38.60	38.08	overlay
12/16/93	4	1.2	1	4.9	4	18.60	14.16	overlay
12/16/93	5	2.1	1	13.1	5	94.00	59.22	overlay
12/16/93	6	22.3	7	2.0	1	140.60	133.80	overlay
12/16/93	7	7.0	5	1.6	1	47.00	36.40	overlay
12/16/93	8	2.9	2	15.4	6	79.80	95.12	underlay
12/16/93	9	3.7	3	6.4	4	52.20	54.76	underlay
12/17/93	1	6.3	3	8.1	4	51.00	114.66	underlay
12/17/93	2	1.4	1	3.4	3	14.00	12.32	overlay
12/17/93	3	3.8	3	3.4	2	52.40	33.44	overlay
12/17/93	4	91.3	8	12.6	5	1,412.40	2,483.36	underlay
12/17/93	5	11.9	6	9.7	5	241.00	254.66	underlay

Date	Race#	Odds 1	Rank	Odds 2	Rank	Actual	Theory	Value
12/17/93	6	31.9	7	2.8	3	255.60	242.44	overlay
12/17/93	7	2.5	2	4.6	3	36.00	28.00	overlay
12/17/93	8	2.4	3	1.5	1	19.40	12.00	overlay
12/17/93	9	1.4	1	18.6	7	58.60	54.88	overlay
12/18/93	1	3.8	2	4.8	3	50.00	44.08	overlay
12/18/93	2	1.1	1	2.8	2	10.40	8.36	overlay
12/18/93	3	1.1	1	2.9	3	11.40	8.58	overlay
12/18/93	4	1.1	1	4.1	3	14.20	11.22	overlay
12/18/93	5	6.8	2	0.8	1	34.20	24.48	overlay
12/18/93	6	1.8	2	1.7	1	14.80	9.72	overlay
12/18/93	7	1.8	1	18.7	6	74.20	70.92	overlay
12/18/93	8	0.2	1	8.9	4	9.20	3.96	overlay
12/18/93	9	1.8	1	10.3	6	46.60	40.68	overlay
12/18/93	10	4.8	4	3.8	3	91.40	46.08	overlay
12/19/93	1	2.7	2	7.3	4	51.40	44.82	overlay
12/19/93	2	3.1	3	3.6	4	35.00	28.52	overlay
12/19/93	3	5.1	5	4.4	4	73.20	55.08	overlay
12/19/93	4	15.8	7	0.8	1	110.00	56.88	overlay
12/19/93	5	5.9	4	21.3	7	238.40	263.14	underlay
12/19/93	6	34.3	6	6.3	4	317.60	500.78	underlay
12/19/93	7	0.8	1	4.5	3	12.60	8.80	overlay
12/19/93	8	16.0	5	0.4	1	90.80	44.80	overlay
12/19/93	9	1.5	1	2.2	2	15.60	9.60	overlay
12/19/93	10	1.0	1	24.0	6	65.60	50.00	overlay
12/20/93	1	2.5	2	7.8	5	88.60	44.00	overlay
12/20/93	2	8.8	5	5.6	4	134.40	116.16	overlay
12/20/93	3	2.0	1	7.8	5	49.60	35.20	overlay
12/20/93	4	4.5	2	0.8	1	25.40	16.20	overlay
12/20/93	5	3.6	2	6.1	3	47.00	51.12	underlay
12/20/93	6	1.0	1	99.8	11	195.60	201.60	underlay
12/20/93	7	6.5	4	1.3	1	46.20	29.90	overlay
12/20/93	8	6.2	4	1.8	1	43.60	34.72	overlay
12/20/93	9	1.1	1	7.7	3	28.40	19.14	overlay
12/20/93	10	3.4	2	4.0	4	44.20	34.00	overlay

These results are equally revealing—540 out of the 695 races resulted in overlayed payoffs! That's 78 percent overlays. Once more, four out of five races resulted in exacta overlays. Did you notice that the underlays usually involved long-odds horses? It doesn't take a genius to conclude that the exacta is a super bet.

Exacta and quinella wagering offer the investor a wonderful opportunity to earn substantial profits. They also offer the investor a way to convert an underlay into an overlay. Your job is to choose the optimum way to invest in a race. Exactas and quinellas are great because they offer us a wide latitude for making choices. Please take advantage of the fact that only a small minority of bettors understand how to make these wagers properly. Read and study this chapter until you fully understand its contents. It'll be worth a lot of money to you.

One final thought: If all the math and strategy in this chapter is too much for you and you refuse to use a pocket computer to automate the process of intelligent wagering, then please accept the following advice for exacta wagering. Choose a key horse, usually your top pick. Play the key horse back and forth with your second and third choices. In the ABC example, instead of playing a three-horse baseball, you would play these combinations: AB, AC, BA, and CA. This cuts your bet size by 33 percent. Over the long run, this preserves your capital and assures that you are betting on the combinations with the highest probability of success. If you're selection oriented this is one of the few rational ways to play the exacta.

Let's look at a typical race and see if we can apply what we have learned in this chapter.

The following race was the fifth run at Hollywood Park on Wednesday, December 15, 1993.

Hollywood Park

5 *6½ Furlongs.* (1:134) CLAIMING. Purse $11,000. Fillies, 3-year-olds. Weight, 121 lbs. Non-winners of two races since October 18, allowed 3 lbs. A race since then, 6 lbs. Claiming price $12,500, if for $10,500, allowed 2 lbs. (Races where entered for $10,000 or less not considered.)

Slim Slim Slim	Ch. f. 3 (Apr)			Lifetime Record: 10 2 0 0 $20,815	
Own: Nahem Edward	Sire: Al Mamoon (Believe It) Dam: Quicker Gold (Struck Out)			1993 8 2 0 0 $20,815 Turf 0 0 0 0 1992 2 M 0 0 Wet 0 0 0 0	
ALMEIDA G F (28 1 7 2 .04) $12,500	Br: Nahem Edward (Cal) Tr: Pappalardo John W (3 0 0 0 .00)	L 115	Hol 2 0 0 0 $825 Dist 2 1 0 0 $10,450		

Mollys Concorde
Own: Aguayo Paula A & Vernon E
LONG B (44 1 1 5 .02) $12,500
Dk. b or br f. 3 (Jan)
Sire: King Concorde (Super Concorde)
Dam: Molly Be Good (Gouscinow)
Br: R. E. Fritts & Marie J. Fritts (Cal)
Tr: Aguayo Vernon E (3 0 0 1 .00)
L 115
Lifetime Record: 13 2 1 3 $14,344
1993 13 2 1 3 $14,344 | Turf 0 0 0 0
1992 0 M 0 0 | Wet 1 0 0 0
Hol 5 0 0 1 $1,650 | Dist 1 0 0 0

2Dec93-5Hol fst 6f :214 :444 :57 1:103 ⓕClm 10500 55 7 5 31½ 43½ 44½ 38½ Long B LB 115 b 81.90 78-15 Simply Groovy1138 Queenly118½ Mollys Concorde1151 Inside bid 12
15Oct93-11Fno fst 5f :22 :452 :571 3↑ ⓕClm 10000N2X 47 3 4 4¾ 62¾ 52¼ 55¼ Schvaneveldt C P LB 113 b 3.80 87-11 Adam's Pick1182½ Intersquaw114nk Mezquita113no No factor 6
19Sep93-12Fpx fst 6f :221 :461 :591 1:12 ⓕClm 8000 58 6 4 2½ 2hd 1½ 1no Gomez E A LB 117 b 17.90 87-12 Mollys Concorde117no Inyala Rouge114hd Carla Pockett1161½ Just held 9
3Sep93-8Sac fst 5f :222 :461 :58 3↑ ⓕⓈMd 8000 60 3 1 2hd 1hd 11 12½ Gomez E A LB 116 b 3.30 89-13 Mollys Concorde1162½ Dashing Diane1161½ Freda116½ Clear, driving 10
7Aug93-3LA fst 4½f :211 :44 :503 ⓕMd 5000 48 6 6 46 38 38 Arias J C LB 120 b 13.60 85-10 BrightEyedLady1203½ ThatDuffyGirl1224½ MollysConcorde120nk No match 10
19Jly93-4Sol fst 6f :222 :454 :58 1:111 ⓕMd 8000 55 4 7 42½ 52¾ 31½ 31¼ Gomez E A LB 117 b 5.10 89-12 Gato Go Flow1171 Pocket Trick117nk MollysConcorde1175 Saved ground 9
1Jly93-9Hol fst 6f :214 :452 :574 1:103 3↑ ⓕⓈMd 22500 40 8 8 88½ 76½ 88 814½ Gulas L L5 LB 109 b 45.80 73-13 Toasting Time117½ Blue Eyed Miss1196 Tameo116no Outrun 12
8May93-4Hol fst 6½f :221 :444 1:094 1:16 3↑ ⓕⓈMd Sp Wt 27 3 5 53¾ 78½ 714 726½ Gulas L L5 LB 110 b 61.40 62-09 Andestine1153½ ⒹSanrock1153 Paster's Princess117hd Early trouble 7
Placed 6th through disqualification.
28Apr93-9Hol fst 1 1/16 :224 :461 1:112 1:443 3↑ ⓕMd 32000 31 7 5 64 89½ 817 723¾ Almeida G F LB 115 b 10.30 54-18 Friendly Helen123½ Cheta1166½ Intensly Bold1152¼ 5 Wide stretch 12
22Apr93-6Hol fst 6f :22 :45 :572 1:10 3↑ ⓕMd 32000 55 6 9 54½ 66½ 59 69½ Gulas L L5 B 110 b 74.20 80-11 Gospel Music1222½ Fleet Of Feet117nk Carefree Colleen1152¾ Wide trip 11
WORKOUTS: Nov 30 Fpx 4f gd :494 H 1/1 ●Nov 24 Fpx 5f fst 1:02 H 1/7 Nov 19 Fpx 5f fst 1:034 H 7/9 Oct 6 Fpx 5f fst 1:031 H 3/5 Sep 29 Fpx 5f fst 1:04 H 8/8

Shana Two
Own: Rainbow Stables
GONZALEZ S JR (74 7 7 11 .09) $12,500
Gr. f. 3 (Apr)
Sire: Valsetz (Valdez)
Dam: Rozee Rueez (Don B.)
Br: Joseph H. Cannon (Cal)
Tr: Shoemaker Bill (14 3 1 2 .21)
L 113 5
Lifetime Record: 10 1 4 0 $15,385
1993 10 1 4 0 $15,385 | Turf 0 0 0 0
1992 0 M 0 0 | Wet 1 0 1 0 $880
Hol 1 0 0 0 | Dist 3 1 0 0 $9,350

21Nov93-6Hol fst 6½f :214 :442 1:093 1:161 ⓕClm 16000 38 6 4 2hd 75¾ 812 815 Black C A LB 119 16.90 73-07 Borneastermorn1161½ Jan's Turn1141½ Cool Deal1172 Brief speed 9
22Oct93-4SA fst 6½f :214 :45 1:111 1:18 3↑ ⓕⓈMd 32000 62 10 1 11 1½ 1½ 11¼ Gonzalez S5 LB 112 3.30 81-10 Shana Two1121¼ Point Position117hd Walking Liberty117nk Game win 10
1Oct93-13Fpx fst 6f :221 :461 :591 1:113 3↑ ⓕMd 32000 59 2 1 2½ 21 31½ 24½ Warren R J Jr LB 114 9.90 84-10 Shining Ryder1094½ Shana Two1143 Hillwalker1141 No match 10
15Sep93-4Dmr fst 6½f :223 :461 1:114 1:182 3↑ ⓕⓈMd 32000 24 9 9 105½ 106½ 79¾ 715 Pincay L Jr LB 118 5.80 64-13 Sew Attractive122hd Riviere Miss1182 Other Wise122hd 10
Off slowly, greenly, wide
12Aug93-9Dmr fst 6f :221 :454 :58 1:101 3↑ ⓕMd 32000 53 3 3 3½ 2hd 54½ 511¾ Black C A LB 117 b 4.50 76-14 Kayla's Dream1177½ Miss Fort Worth1222 On Line One117½ Faltered 8
3Jly93-4FP fst 6f :222 :464 1:002 1:143 3↑ ⓕMd Sp Wt 37 2 1 1hd 2hd 21½ 21¾ Gall D L 114 b *.40 70-24 Tilt TheirMinds1141¾ ShanaTwo1143 UnavoidableRisk1143¾ Saved ground 7
20Jun93-6FP my 6f :221 :453 :59 1:122 3↑ ⓕMd Sp Wt 45 4 1 22 23 25 27¾ Bielby J A L 113 b 1.90 75-20 Matagomi1217¾ Shana Two1139 Joy Of Megan121½ Futile chase 9
3Jun93-5AP fst 6f :222 :453 :582 1:114 3↑ ⓕMd 35000 32 7 2 21½ 46½ 613 616¼ Fires E L 114 b 8.40 69-15 Countryo1134 Dixie Dash1141½ Monica Bay1145 Brief speed 7
7May93-3FP gd 5f :223 :473 1:003 ⓕMd Sp Wt 32 6 6 2½ 31 1½ 2¾ Woodley J B 118 b 6.50 85-12 Clarionade118¾ Shana Two1183¾ World Won118¾ Tried hard 8
26Apr93-2Spt fst 6f :231 :472 :593 1:123 3↑ ⓕMd Sp Wt 15 6 5 42 77 715 815 Woodley J B 113 b 18.00 68-12 Lost Silver1141¼ PrettyGoodTime1142 Anaffairtorember113hd Brief speed 8
WORKOUTS: Dec 8 Hol 5f fst 1:021 H 26/40 Dec 1 Hol 4f fst :494 H 27/38 ●Nov 15 SA 4f fst :463 H 1/44 Nov 8 SA 4f fst :473 H 9/50 Nov 1 SA 3f fst :36 H 6/17 Oct 16 SA 4f fst :483 H 2/18

Toasting Time
Own: Altman & Belmonte & Plagman
GRYDER A T (88 12 12 9 .14) $12,500
B. f. 3 (Apr)
Sire: Pass the Glass (Buckpasser)
Dam: Test of Time (Time Tested)
Br: Robert Borick (Cal)
Tr: Mitchell Mike (30 7 10 3 .18)
L 115
Lifetime Record: 6 2 1 0 $21,550
1993 6 2 1 0 $21,550 | Turf 0 0 0 0
1992 0 M 0 0 | Wet 0 0 0 0
Hol 2 1 1 0 $11,650 | Dist 1 0 0 0

4Nov93-1SA fst 6f :212 :443 :57 1:11 ⓕClm c-12500 33 6 12 1210 1110 1011 915 Gryder A T LB 115 5.80 67-14 Simply Groovy1103 Cool Deal1154½ Palace Madame115nk 12
Bumped, steadied start Claimed from Berton & Smith, Monteleone Frank J Trainer
21Oct93-5SA fst 6½f :214 :451 1:10 1:163 ⓕClm 25000 55 7 7 78½ 97½ 89 712 Nakatani C S B 116 10.00 76-14 Jan's Turn1113½ Baby's Got Class1161¾ Ornamental Pirate116¾ No threat 10
26Aug93-1Dmr fst 1 :23 :471 1:114 1:374 ⓕClm 32000 58 6 5 54½ 64¼ 54½ 69 Lopez A D B 115 3.60 69-20 Cheta1161½ Fowler Empire1151¾ How Higher1103½ Wide trip 7
2Aug93-6Dmr fst 6f :222 :46 :582 1:103 ⓕⓈClm c-20000 76 7 4 53½ 53 2hd 1no Delahoussaye E B 116 *2.30 86-10 Toasting Time116no Freedom Reins1151 Flying Vicki108½ Wide trip 8
Claimed from Four Four Forty Farms, Sadler John W Trainer
1Jly93-9Hol fst 6f :214 :452 :574 1:103 3↑ ⓕⓈMd 25000 77 5 3 21½ 2½ 1½ 1½ Valenzuela P A B 117 *2.20 87-13 Toasting Time117½ Blue Eyed Miss1196 Tameo116no Determined 12
19May93-6Hol fst 6f :214 :452 :58 1:113 3↑ ⓕⓈMd 32000 59 10 9 66 53 25 22¼ Gulas L L5 B 110 90.20 80-13 Fleet Of Feet1172¼ Toasting Time1104 Mystical Sky1154 12
Wide early, lugged in lane
WORKOUTS: Dec 8 Hol 4f fst :493 H 30/39 Nov 15 Hol 4f fst :482 H 2/17 Oct 30 SA 4f fst :464 H 2/69 Oct 10 SA 5f fst 1:004 H 28/49 ●Oct 3 SA 3f fst :351 H 1/15 Sep 23 SA 4f fst :473 H 5/43

Irish Anthem
Own: Brown Brothers & Brown
VALENZUELA F H (90 13 10 10 .14) $12,500
B. f. 3 (Mar)
Sire: Kleven (Alydar)
Dam: Ack's Anthem (Ack Ack)
Br: Litman, Miller & Wirtschafter (Cal)
Tr: Dominguez Henry (3 0 0 1 .00)
L 115
Lifetime Record: 10 1 1 2 $35,250
1993 6 0 0 1 $6,450 Turf 0 0 0 0
1992 4 1 1 1 $28,800 Wet 0 0 0 0
Hol 3 0 0 1 $6,450 Dist 2 0 1 1 $11,550

2Dec93-5Hol fst 6f :214 :444 :57 1:103 ⓕClm 12500 — 5 10 — — — — Gryder A T LB 115 b 4.80 — 15 Simply Groovy1138 Queenly118½ Mollys Concorde1151 Lame 12
13Nov93-2SA fst 6f :213 :444 :57 1:094 ⓕClm 20000 60 6 3 31½ 21 22 77¼ Gonzalez S5 LB 110 b 7.30 81-11 WinningStart1154 DecidedlyNatalie115nk Sirenic1131 Bumped hard start 9
6Oct93-1SA fst 6f :22 :451 :572 1:102 ⓕClm c-20000 55 4 4 51½ 52 43 108¼ McCarron C J LB 116 6.80 77-10 Ornamental Pirate116hd Melrose Park1162¼ Winning Start117¾ Wide trip 12
Claimed from Miller & Miller & Wirtschafter, Moreno Henry Trainer
23Aug93-1Dmr fst 7f :223 :454 1:102 1:231 ⓕClm 40000 65 4 6 85¾ 75¾ 76¼ 67½ Stevens G L B 115 8.70 76-12 Angie'sTresure1151½ Jn'sTurn117½ HurryHomeHelen116½ 5 Wide stretch 8
21Jly93-1Hol fst 6½f :214 :444 1:093 1:161 ⓕClm 50000 74 4 3 42 43 38½ 36¼ Delahoussaye E B 116 5.90 82-12 Fast Reward1175 Fibs Galore1171¼ Irish Anthem116¾ 4 Wide stretch 6
24Jun93-7Hol fst 5½f :21 :442 :57 1:033 3↑ ⓕⓈAlw 36000N1X 65 2 6 64½ 53½ 53 57 Garcia J A B 113 15.20 87-07 Sangre Fria1163½ Concords Spirit1131¼ Justin Irish Charm113hd No mishap 7
7Nov92-9SA fst 1 1/16 :224 :464 1:12 1:45 ⓕⓈCa Cp Jv F 100k 61 2 5 86 85½ 88½ 612¼ Nakatani C S B 115 19.70 66-17 Incindress1154 Fast Cruiser1151¾ Fowler Empire115 No mishap 12
16Oct92-8SA fst 6½f :214 :444 1:094 1:163 ⓕAlw 30000 66 7 5 53½ 43 25 25 Nakatani C S B 115 7.50 82-12 Medici Bells1185 Irish Anthem1151¼ Keep Happy118 Wide trip 7
14Sep92-8Dmr fst 6f :213 :45 :58 1:111 ⓕⓈC T B A81k 54 1 9 84¾ 85¾ 67 37 Solis A B 114 17.80 76-12 Mime's Real117no Jamie Nicole117 Irish Anthem114 Improvedposition 9
28Aug92-6Dmr fst 6f :221 :454 :583 1:111 ⓕMd 50000 67 2 6 1½ 1hd 11½ 16 Solis A B 117 5.50 83-13 Irish Anthem1176 Enchanted Beauty1121¾ Yerna117 Ridden out 9
WORKOUTS: Dec 8 SA 5f fst 1:004 H 14/48 Nov 21 SA 4f fst :503 H 38/44 ●Nov 7 SA 4f fst :461 H 1/37 Oct 31 SA 4f fst :493 H 45/59 Oct 24 SA 5f fst 1:021 H 34/48 Oct 17 SA 4f fst :482 H 12/38

Elias Beach
Own: Forebear Farm
CASTANON A L (27 1 3 3 .04) $12,500
Dk. b or br f. 3 (Mar)
Sire: Forebear (Forli)
Dam: Alberta Pie (Vigors)
Br: Pete Cristofi (Cal)
Tr: Perdomo A Pico (8 2 1 2 .25)
L 115
Lifetime Record: 7 1 0 1 $4,290
1993 7 1 0 1 $4,290 Turf 0 0 0 0
1992 0 M 0 0 Wet 0 0 0 0
Hol 5 0 0 1 $1,650 Dist 0 0 0 0

8Dec93-5Hol fst 1 1/16 :23 :462 1:112 1:433 ⓕClm 12500 46 9 2 31 2hd 47 816 Castanon A L LB 116 b 44.40 67-16 PalaceMadame1168 Janet'sDoll1162½ LeadoffPosition111nk Bid, gave way 11
2Dec93-5Hol fst 6f :214 :444 :57 1:103 ⓕClm 12500 41 6 11 96¾ 1013 1115 1114¼ Castanon A L LB 118 b 39.80 73-15 Simply Groovy1138 Queenly118½ Mollys Concorde1151 12
Pinched start, 5 wide turn
17Nov93-7Hol fst 7f :221 :452 1:11 1:24 ⓕClm 12500 60 8 5 41½ 41½ 3½ 33½ Castanon A L LB 118 b 102.50 80-14 DHCorona Chick118 DHQueenly1153½ Elias Beach1182 Outfinished 11
4Nov93-1SA fst 6f :212 :443 :57 1:11 ⓕClm 12500 31 2 5 43 66¼ 1111 1115½ Delahoussaye E LB 116 b 43.40 66-14 Simply Groovy1103 Cool Deal1154½ Palace Madame115nk Brief speed 12
11Oct93-7Fno fst 6f :21 :444 :582 1:112 3↑ ⓕMd 12500 44 7 5 3½ 31 1½ 14 Mercado P LB 116 b *.90 83-15 Elias Beach1164 Fax'n Tricia116nk Guided Dancer1162½ Drew clear 8
13May93-6Hol fst 7f :222 :454 1:112 1:243 3↑ ⓕMd 25000 39 7 2 1hd 1hd 33 611¾ McCarron C J LB 115 b 2.40 69-11 Lovely Mist110½ Be Page1153 Franzen122¾ Dueled, tired 12
22Apr93-9Hol fst 6f :221 :451 :574 1:103 3↑ ⓕMd 32000 37 7 11 95½ 1010 1010 813½ McCarron C J LB 115 16.60 74-11 Indeed A Lady1202¼ Miss Parlay1106 Tavern Maid115hd Troubled trip 11
WORKOUTS: Nov 12 Hol 6f fst 1:142 H 4/17 ●Nov 3 Hol 3f fst :352 H 1/17 Oct 28 Hol 4f fst :473 H 2/17 Oct 21 Hol 5f fst 1:034 H 30/31 Oct 3 Hol 5f fst 1:00 H 5/16 Sep 26 Hol 4f fst :482 H 8/24

Leggy Lisa
Own: McCutcheon & Temple
ATKINSON P (33 4 3 2 .12) $10,500
B. f. 3 (Apr)
Sire: The Irish Lord (Bold Ruler)
Dam: Century Girl (Envoy)
Br: Coelho J & Valenti P (Cal)
Tr: McCutcheon James R (5 0 2 0 .00)
L 113
Lifetime Record: 28 4 2 2 $32,140
1993 18 3 2 2 $14,580 Turf 0 0 0 0
1992 10 1 0 0 $17,560 Wet 4 0 1 0 $2,175
Hol 3 0 0 0 $1,425 Dist 1 0 0 0 $1,750

25Nov93-9Hol fst 6f :22 :45 :572 1:093 3↑ ⓕClm 8000 54 4 6 83 64¾ 55 611¾ Atherton J E LB 114 b 38.80 80-09 Crystal Brown1167½ Whoopon116no Passion For Poker116hd Wide into lane 11
12Nov93-11LA fst 4½f :214 :452 :514 ⓕClm 4000 35 3 8 85¾ 56½ 46¼ Badilla J Jr LB 122 b 4.50 81-14 Swingbala117nk Class N Jazz1184 Emerald Vail1152 Broke slow, wide 8
5Nov93-6LA fst 4½f :214 :453 :52 3↑ ⓕClm 4000 54 6 6 64½ 55 42¼ Badilla J Jr LB 122 b 9.90 84-13 SoThisIsIt1191½ PerfectNumbers117¾ FigurMFbulous110nk Late interest 8
26Sep93-10Fpx fst 6f :222 :461 :584 1:112 ⓕClm 8000 52 1 5 43 32 33½ 66½ Fernandez A L LB 120 b 20.80 83-09 Bolger's Song1173 Delightful Daun1171 Lucky's Baby114½ Weakened 9
19Sep93-12Fpx fst 6f :221 :461 :591 1:12 ⓕClm 8000 28 7 6 55½ 43 88¼ 911¾ Fernandez A L LB 120 b 9.20 75-12 Mollys Concorde117no Inyala Rouge114hd CarlaPockett1161½ Wide 1st turn 9
10Sep93-10LA fst 4½f :22 :454 :52 ⓕClm 5000 61 4 6 51½ 2nk 1¾ Fernandez A L LB 119 b *1.30 86-15 LeggyLis119¾ FigureMeFbulous1182 AskTheAngels1171½ Big wide move 8
29Aug93-7LA fst 4½f :214 :451 :513 3↑ ⓕClm 5000 52 10 5 63 33½ 33 Fernandez A L LB 115 b 16.40 85-12 So This Is It1192½ Figure Me Fabulous116½ Leggy Lisa1153 Raced wide 10
20Aug93-8LA fst 4½f :22 :453 :52 3↑ ⓕClm 4000 48 7 6 41½ 2½ 1½ Fernandez A L LB 117 b 7.80 86-14 LeggyLis117½ FigureMeFbulous117¾ ViolentFemm108½ Big move 4 wide 8
7Aug93-8LA fst 4½f :221 :452 :514 3↑ ⓕClm 5000 40 6 3 52¾ 65½ 53¾ Pfau R K LB 118 b 13.90 83-10 Frozen Fire1141½ Winko De Mayo1171¼ DHSo This Is It117 Raced wide 7
15Jly93-9Sol fst 6f :23 :46 :592 1:121 ⓕClm 6250N2X 50 8 3 63¼ 63¾ 33 34 Hansen R D LB 116 b 3.10 81-13 Visual Magic1181½ Rock N Roll Ballet1152½ Leggy Lisa1162½ Wide late bid 10
WORKOUTS: Dec 11 Fpx 3f fst :361 H 3/18 ●Dec 7 Fpx 4f fst :501 H 1/4 Oct 26 Fpx 4f fst :501 H 4/5

Ornamental Pirate Dk. b or br f. 3 (Jan)
Own: Jeremys Stable
Sire: Pirate's Bounty (Hoist the Flag)
Dam: Lace Pillow (Reflected Glory)
Br: River Edge Farm Inc. & Windy Hill (Cal)
DESORMEAUX K J (51 9 6 7 .18) $12,500 Tr: Hess R B Jr (24 5 5 1 .21) L 115

Lifetime Record:	10 2 0 3	$35,250			
1993	10 2 0 3	$35,250	Turf	0 0 0 0	
1992	0 M 0 0		Wet	0 0 0 0	
Hol	4 0 0 2	$12,600	Dist	2 0 0 1	$2,850

27Nov93-7Hol fst 6f :221 :452 :572 1:102 ⒻClm 25000 57 4 8 72¾ 63½ 55 78¼ Antley C W LB 116 b 5.20 80-11 Melrose Park114½ Ms. Something114¾ Sanrock1172¼ No rally 9
21Oct93-5SA fst 6½f :214 :451 1:10 1:163 ⒻClm c-25000 71 6 2 54½ 3nk 22½ 35¼ Stevens G L LB 116 b 4.20 83-14 Jan'sTurn1113½ Baby'sGotClass1161¾ OrnamentlPirte116¾ Bid, weakened 10
Claimed from Alaska's Great Eagle Inc, Vienna Darrell Trainer
6Oct93-1SA fst 6f :22 :451 :572 1:102 ⒻClm 20000 76 12 3 71½ 42 32 1hd Stevens G L LB 116 b 7.40 85-10 Ornamental Pirate116hd Melrose Park1162¼ Winning Start117¾ Wide trip 12
3Sep93-5Dmr fst 6f :22 :452 :573 1:10 ⒻClm 32000 53 4 12 93½ 95¾ 85¾ 813 Gonzalez S5 LB 110 b 17.20 76-09 Freedom Reins1162¾ StopTheBleeding115no CleverBit1151 6 Wide stretch 12
9Aug93-3Dmr fst 1 :231 :464 1:112 1:363 3+ ⒻClm 40000 69 4 1 22 31½ 34½ 612 Nakatani C S LB 114 14.50 72-14 Saucy Lady B1162¼ Darwolf1175 Cee Xcels116¾ Faltered 7
21Jly93-1Hol fst 6½f :214 :444 1:093 1:161 ⒻClm 50000 58 2 6 52¼ 63¼ 610 613 Solis A LB 116 3.60 75-12 Fast Reward1175 Fibs Galore1171¼ Irish Anthem116¾ Brushed early 6
8Jly93-3Hol fst 7f :231 :461 1:103 1:224 ⒻClm 62500 75 4 2 21½ 21½ 21½ 33½ Nakatani C S LB 116 2.20 86-13 FriendlyBells1163½ Witch'sPower116hd OrnmentlPirte1163½ Edged for 2nd 5
10Jun93-3Hol fst 7f :223 :46 1:102 1:231 ⒻClm 55000 73 1 6 65¾ 62 42½ 32 Nakatani C S LB 114 12.00 86-12 C.C.Overdrive114hd SouthernSwitch1161¾ OrnmntlPirt1141 5 Wide stretch 6
2Apr93-5SA fst 6f :214 :444 :571 1:102 ⒻClm c-40000 64 2 5 41½ 31 43½ 76½ Solis A LB 115 b 5.70 79-13 Melrose Park115½ Tansaui116hd Silky Sand Sammy115no Steadied 5/16 7
Claimed from Wygod Mr & Mrs Martin J, Ellis Ronald W Trainer
12Mar93-2SA fst 6f :214 :451 :574 1:104 ⒻMd 50000 80 8 2 63½ 51¾ 31½ 1nk Solis A LB 117 b 6.50 83-17 Ornamental Pirate117nk Baby Take The Gold1174 Razzi Cat1172 9
Steadied 1/4, bumped late

WORKOUTS: Nov 20 Hol 4f fst :513 H 24/26 Nov 14 Hol 4f fst :503 H 22/28 Nov 8 SA 4f fst :51 H 46/50 Oct 31 SA 4f fst :514 H 58/59 Oct 18 SA 4f fst :492 H 30/48 Oct 13 SA 3f fst :384 B 19/20

ALL-IN-ONE saw the race as follows:

----------------------------------BETTING LINE----------------------------------

Horse name	PEH	H-I	THAAI	P-H	ESP	Rating	Betting Line	Fair Place $	Fair Show $
	--------Rankings--------								
Irish Anthem	2	1	3	3	1	87.75	2-1	3.80	2.80
Mollys Concorde	1	2	2	2	2	79.47	7-2		
Toasting Time	3	3	1	1	4	74.45	5-1		
Elias Beach	4	4	4	4	3	69.86			
Shana Two	5	5	5	5	5	66.54			

The public's line was as follows:

Irish Anthem	7-2
Mollys Concorde	9
Toasting Time	3-2
Slim Slim Slim	6
Shana Two	3
Elias Beach	10
Leggy Lisa	30

According to *ALL-IN-ONE*, there are only two horses that should be considered as win bets: Irish Anthem and Mollys Concorde.

My top two picks were spectacular overlays. Each offered a huge edge.

$$\text{Edge (Irish Anthem)} = .333 \times 3.5 - .667 = .4985$$
$$\text{Edge (Mollys Concorde)} = .222 \times 9 - .778 = 1.220$$

Although Mollys Concorde offered a gigantic edge (122 percent), she wasn't quite as good a win bet as Irish Anthem. Their edge-to-odds ratios were .140 for Irish Anthem (.4985 ÷ 3.5) and .136 for Mollys Concorde (1.22 ÷ 9). Therefore, a win bet on each horse was appropriate. Since their edge-to-odds ratios were practically equal, we would bet the same amount of money on each horse.

Please understand the critical ratio of edge to odds. It's the bet size (optimum ratio) that will maximize your bankoll's growth rate. When you have to decide which choice is the best bet among a number of alternatives, simply compute the edge-to-odds ratio for each alternative. The largest is the correct choice.

I'm a very aggressive bettor. The way I would bet this sample race is to make a win bet on the longest-odds horse and an exacta using my win horse second to the other contender, plus a smaller exacta the other way (providing, of course, that each exacta combination is an overlay). In this case, $100 to win on Mollys Concorde, a $50 exacta Irish Anthem to Mollys Concorde, and a $25 exacta Mollys Concorde to Irish Anthem.

The conservative approach is to bet the same amount on both horses to win and skip the exacta. The reason is that we have a 56 percent chance of winning this bet in the win pool. Why opt for a much riskier situation in the exacta pool?

The exacta prices represented the bargain of the century. The exacta fair prices were:

Irish Anthem–Mollys Concorde	$18	(8.0-to-1)
Mollys Concorde–Irish Anthem	21	(9.5-to-1)

The toteboard prices were:

Irish Anthem–Mollys Concorde	$ 69	(33.5-to-1)
Mollys Concorde–Irish Anthem	116	(57.0-to-1)

Needless to say, these combinations met our minimum 40 percent premium. The Irish Anthem–Mollys Concorde combination only had to pay $25.20 to get our attention. Similarly, the Mollys Concorde–Irish Anthem combination had to pay $29.40 for us to be interested.

The only remaining question is how much we should bet on each combination. The answer, as always, is found by considering the edge-to-odds ratio.

Edge (Irish Anthem-Mollys Concorde) = P(W) × odds − P(L)

= .111 × 33.50 − .889

= 2.83

Edge (Mollys Concorde-Irish Anthem) = .095 × 57.00 − .905

= 4.51

The edge-to-odds ratio on the Irish Anthem–Mollys Concorde combination is .0845 (2.83 ÷ 33.5). On the reverse combination, it's .0791 (4.51 ÷ 57). When we sum these ratios, we get a total of .1636. When we divide each ratio back into this sum, we get the bet-size percentage each combination should have: .5165 on the Irish Anthem–Mollys Concorde combination, .4835 on the Mollys Concorde–Irish Anthem combination. Assuming we bet a total of $100 on the exacta in this race, we'd make a $52 wager on the Irish Anthem–Mollys Concorde combination and a $48 wager on the reverse. (If your total bet was $20 or less, you'd simply bet $10 on each combination.)

We also have to consider the quinella in this race. The Irish Anthem–Mollys Concorde quinella was paying $43. The fair pay for the Irish Anthem–Mollys Concorde quinella is:

$$\text{Fair pay} = \frac{2 \times 3.5 \times 3 \times 4.5}{2 \times 4.5 + 3 \times 3.5} \times 2 = \$9.69$$

Is the quinella on this combination a better bet than the exactas we've considered? Again, we find the answer in edge-to-odds ratios. The odds on the Irish Anthem–Mollys Concorde quinella were 20.5-to-1, a monumental overlay. Our edge on the bet was as follows:

Edge (Irish Anthem–Mollys Concorde quinella) = .206 × 20.5 − .795

= 3.43

The edge-to-odds ratio is .1673 (3.43 ÷ 20.5). Clearly, the quinella represents a wonderful opportunity. But if we play both exactas, $2 on the Irish Anthem–Mollys Concorde combination and $2 on the reverse combination (this was done to make the math a little easier), we actually come out about the same. The total bet was $4. If we consider them as a single bet, the expectation becomes:

$$\text{Expectation (both exactas)} = [P(W) \times \text{gain}] - [P(L) \times \text{loss}]$$
$$= [.111 \times \$65 + .095 \times \$112] - [.794 \times \$4]$$
$$= \$17.86 - 3.18$$
$$= \$14.68$$

This represents an expectation of $14.68 per $4 bet. Therefore, the edge is 367 percent, or 3.67, which is slightly higher than the 343 percent offered by the corresponding quinella. The odds are the weighted sum of $.52 \times (16.25) + .48 \times (28)$, which is 21.89-to-1. The edge-to-odds ratio becomes .1677 $(3.67 \div 21.89)$. Hence the exacta and quinella are basically the same bet.

Whether you're aggressive, moderate, or conservative, you would have made out on this race. The conservative bettor made a modest score. Suppose he invested $100. He would have bet $50 to win on Irish Anthem and $50 to win on Mollys Concorde. His yield was $535, for a $435 profit. The aggressive player would have crushed the exacta, as the higher-paying combination won, returning $117.80 for each $2 ticket. Based on his $100 wager, he had $48 on the winning combination. His gross return was $2,827.20 and his net profit on his exacta bets in this race was $2,727.20. My way to play this race yielded a profit of $2,367.50 on a $175 investment.

If you had bet the quinella instead of both exactas (not the exacta box) you would have come out okay. The quinella paid $43.00 for each deuce. Based on a $100 quinella investment, you would have received a gross return of $2,150 and your net profit on the quinella would have been $2,050.

For the most conservative investor of all, take a guess at what was the very best bet he could have made on this sample race. The answer might surprise you. (Before you read the next paragraph and find out the answer, see if you can figure it out for yourself.)

If you chose the show bet on Irish Anthem, go to the head of the class. It was an epic overlay! Its fair price was $2.80. It paid $4.60. The probability of winning this bet was .667 (a typical 2-to-1 favorite shows about two thirds of the time.) The edge on this bet was:

$$Edge = .667 \times 1.3 - .333 = .5341$$

That's a 53.41 percent edge. The edge-to-odds ratio was .4108! According to the Kelly criterion, this means that we could bet 41.08 percent of our bankroll on this opportunity. This was the absolute safest bet offered on this race. (Again, it's highly recommended that your largest place or show bet not exceed 10 percent of your bankroll.) A $200 show bet would have returned $460, for a profit of $260. Imagine taking a 33 percent risk and getting a 130 percent reward! Nice work if you can get it. You can. This wonderful investment opportunity happens at your local racetrack almost every day. We'll cover how to spot these opportunities in the chapter after the next.

Now let's look at a bet that's not half as lucrative, but just as popular as the exacta and quinella.

The Trifecta

In general, the trifecta is not a good bet. Most of the time it pays an underlay price. The plain and simple fact is that most trifectas are unplayable. The majority of trifectas are won by underlayed combinations. There were 148 trifectas offered at Santa Anita during its 1992–1993 meeting. Payoffs ranged from $115.20 to $36,964.20. Take a guess how many were overlays. If you guessed 67, you're exactly correct. The majority were underlays.

Let me throw some math at you. Please don't be intimidated. It's more important that you understand the general concepts behind these formulas than the specific formulas themselves. This math will lay a solid foundation for my trifecta strategies, which are explained in everyday language.

Let's begin by calculating the fair price for a trifecta combination given the odds in the win pool. The "fair pay" for any bet is the bet size divided by the probability of success. This makes intuitive sense when you think about it. Consider flipping a coin with a friend for a buck a toss. How much should you collect when you win this bet? Your probability of success is .5, and the bet is $1. Dividing $1 by .5, you get the correct answer of $2: your dollar plus your friend's. Consider a 3-to-1 shot at the track. What should this pay to be a fair bet? Well, your probability of success is .25, and your bet size is $2. Dividing $2 by .25, you get $8.

The probability of success is a little tricky to calculate for a trifecta. It's what's called a "dependent-probability" calculation. You're asking for three different things to happen that are not entirely independent. Consider an ABC trifecta. You're asking for a horse A to win, followed by horse B to come in exactly second, followed by horse C coming in exactly third given the AB exacta. The formula to compute this possibility in terms of win odds is:

$$P(ABC) = \frac{1}{[(A \times (B + 1)) - 1] \times (C + 1)}$$

For example: Suppose our top pick (A) was 2-to-1 on our line, our second pick (B) was 3-to-1, and our third pick (C) was 4-to-1. The probability of hitting the ABC trifecta is calculated as follows:

$$P(ABC) = \frac{1}{[(2 \times (3 + 1)) - 1] \times (4 + 1)}$$

$P(ABC) = \frac{1}{35}$, or .029. This is an almost 3 percent chance. In order to calculate the fair price, you take $\frac{1}{35}$ and divide it into the bet size, which we'll assume is $2. The ABC trifecta must pay $70 in order to pay a fair price. But we don't want a fair price. We want a 50 percent premium too. In other words, I would insist upon a price of $105 before I would want to play this trifecta. The problem is, we aren't told how much a trifecta will pay in advance of the bet, as we are when we make an exacta bet.

Let me add another complication. If we use the public odds instead of our own betting-line odds, the calculation changes dramatically depending upon the track take. When a horse is quoted at 2-to-1 at the track, the mutuel takeout is factored in. This horse doesn't have exactly one third of the win pool. It actually has a larger percentage. Each wager in a compound series must be divided by the track payout rate for win bets. If the track take is 17 percent, the track payout rate is 83 percent, or .83. Therefore any exacta payout must be divided by the square of the track payout rate and any trifecta must be divided by the cube of the track payout rate. Our trifecta fair pay equation then becomes:

$$\text{Fair pay} = \frac{\text{Bet size} \times [(A x(B + 1)) - 1] \times (C + 1)}{(\text{Track payout rate})^3}$$

In California the track payout rate is .8467. In New York the rate is .83. In some states it gets as low as .81. In California the multiplier (when you divide by a number less than 1, the effect is multiplication) becomes 1.65, in New York 1.75, and 1.88 in 19 percent takeout states. In the example above, using public odds, the fair pay in California is no longer $70, it's $70 times 1.65, or $115.50.

Before we go any further in our discussion of the trifecta, I want to warn you about low-probability, high-payoff plays. Investing in the trifecta isn't for the risk-averse. You have to plan on long, long losing streaks. Given a relatively high success probability of 20 percent, it wouldn't be at all unusual for you to experience 20 consecutive losses. You'll have to be prepared for an erosion of your bankroll. With a 20 percent success probability, you must be prepared for 24 consecutive losses, hence you should have a substantial trifecta bankroll.

There is some reason to be optimistic about this bet. Do you know about the 2-4-6-8 conjecture? This is an unproven principle stating that the natural odds line for any race is 2-4-6-8. That is, the favorite should be 2-to-1, the second favorite should be 4-to-1, the third favorite should be 6-to-1, and the fourth favorite should be 8-to-1. Whenever practically anybody does a longitudinal study, the results very closely approximate the above. That is, the public favorite wins approximately 33 percent of the time, the second favorite wins approximately 20 percent of the time, the third favorite wins approximately 14 percent of the time, and the fourth favorite wins approximately 11 percent of the time. Let's assume the truth of this conjecture and consider a four-horse trifecta box on the top four public betting choices. Let's bet $48 on each trifecta race (a $2 four-horse box) at Santa Anita in 1993 and see what happens. Let's calculate the probability of hitting this trifecta. The calculations are as follows:

Combination	Fair Odds			Probability
ABC	2	4	6	.015873
ABD	2	4	8	.012345
ACB	2	6	4	.015384
ACD	2	6	8	.008547
ADB	2	8	4	.011764
ADC	2	8	6	.008403
BAC	4	2	6	.012987
BAD	4	2	8	.010101
BCA	4	6	2	.012345
BCD	4	6	8	.004115
BDA	4	8	2	.009523
BDC	4	8	6	.004081
CAB	6	2	4	.011764
CAD	6	2	8	.006535

Combination	Fair Odds			Probability
CBA	6	4	2	.011494
CBD	6	4	8	.003831
CDA	6	8	2	.006289
CDB	6	8	8	.002096
DAB	8	2	4	.008695
DAC	8	2	6	.006211
DBA	8	4	2	.008547
DBC	8	4	6	.003663
DCA	8	6	2	.006060
DCB	8	6	4	.003636
			Total	.204289

Our probability of hitting this trifecta is 20.4 percent. Let's now calculate our expectation on this wager. The actual number of times that three of the public's top four picks completed the trifecta was 24.67 percent. The average payoff was $168.92. If you had played all of these trifectas, your return on the $48 times 148 trifectas ($7,104) was $6,250.10. For every dollar that you invested, you got back 88 cents. So the good news is that you beat the track take. The bad news is that this strategy is a loser.

The only hope of getting a substantial payoff in a trifecta race is for the favorite to be out of the money. With luck, there will be a low-odds false favorite that runs out of the money. The trick to handicapping a trifecta race is to consider all the horses that can run within one second of the final time profile. The pace dynamics of a race tend to eliminate the early speed contenders who go much faster (two ticks for the first call and three ticks for the second call) than the model. When they do, not only don't they tend to win, they tend not to hit the board. Usually this type of false favorite has shown that it can run within five ticks of the winner's profile when given a leisurely pace. Today, it's not going to get an easy pace. It's going to be asked to run faster earlier, which then compromises its adjusted final time. If all the frontrunners go faster than the profile times for the first and second calls, this sets things up for horses that were not involved in the pace (pressers and closers) to pass tiring horses in the stretch. In this situation, one of the pacesetters will sometimes hang on for place or show, but the lead horse usually finishes out of the money.

When we're talking about coming in second or third, adjusted final time is king. Running style and pace considerations are primary when it comes to choosing winners, but not so with place and show horses. (The only exception to this is maiden races. The strongest factor in maiden trifectas is "ability time." Simply use the top five ability times. Ability time is the second fraction plus the second call. The lower the number, the better. Please refer to my *Commonsense Handicapping* for a thorough discussion of this factor.)

The most dangerous trifecta horse is the plodder—the kind of horse that has very little chance to win but completes a trifecta by running second or third at healthy odds. He's the closer on a front-runner's track, a frontrunner on a closer's track, or the even-pace horse on any pace-biased track. Your job as a trifecta handicapper is to consider all the horses that could possibly run second or third. Picking win contenders is easy. You've been doing this all your handicapping life. How much time have you spent studying the place-and-show horses? If you want to master this very challenging bet, you're going to have to keep place profiles and show profiles for your track. If you haven't kept detailed win profiles for your track, I urge you to read Tom Brohamer's classic book *Modern Pace Handicapping*. It's a masterpiece. He shows you how to profile what's winning at your track. Without this vital information, you're trying to play a violin without a bow. If you're going to master trifecta betting, you first must master win betting. If you can't make a profit on win betting, you have no business playing trifectas. Brohamer will teach you how to understand race dynamics. This is the foundation that you'll need to be able to compete in the trifecta arena. The next level of competence is exacta mastery. Until you can make a profit on exacta races, you also have no business betting trifectas.

When you think about it, a trifecta is an exacta plus the show horse. If you've mastered exacta betting, then the trifecta shouldn't be that big a deal. One of the ways I play the trifecta is to play the top two positions in the trifecta as if it were an exacta and then use my win-and-place contenders plus all the horses that can run within one second of the win profile in the third position. If the number of horses becomes too large, I simply pass the trifecta and play the exacta or pass on both. The trick to playing trifectas using this method, as with exactas, is to pick the place horse. You already know that the second-best win horse rarely comes in second. In other words, the place horse is not the second-best win horse. The place horse is usually the horse with the fastest adjusted final time whose running style doesn't match the style that's winning most frequently.

The reason most players lose at trifecta wagering is because they bet too many underlays. (That's in fact the most common reason for losing any type of bet.) The most common trifecta bet is a four-horse box using the handicapper's top four win picks. The problem with this approach is twofold. First, one is betting the same amount of money on the most likely combinations as one is on the least likely combinations. Second, one is not considering the most likely place-and-show horses.

Let's take a look at the 1993 Santa Anita trifecta data. There were 148 trifectas offered. The data are as follows:

ACTUAL	Ow	Op	Os	FAVIN	PARLAY	VALUE
108.20	1.00	8.80	3.60	y	80.96	Overlay
684.80	2.80	16.80	4.40	n	527.47	Overlay
499.80	1.80	14.40	8.90	y	529.06	Underlay
520.80	8.50	1.80	15.30	y	743.28	Underlay
83.00	3.40	1.10	8.80	y	120.34	Underlay
215.20	6.30	1.30	6.20	y	194.26	Overlay
189.80	4.80	4.10	1.80	y	131.49	Overlay
1235.40	4.20	16.20	7.40	n	1196.83	Overlay
6584.40	3.60	36.90	50.50	n	13950.32	Underlay
4816.00	4.70	21.70	20.60	n	4565.81	Overlay
416.00	7.30	3.40	6.10	n	441.90	Underlay
135.40	2.50	5.90	3.30	y	139.75	Underlay
1424.80	11.30	7.40	7.80	n	1652.99	Underlay
74.40	1.90	3.50	6.80	y	117.78	Underlay
8298.60	42.30	17.20	17.60	n	28601.59	Underlay
3538.80	22.50	46.20	7.10	n	17188.20	Underlay
386.80	3.70	7.90	3.70	n	300.14	Overlay
563.20	2.90	19.60	4.40	y	634.39	Underlay
237.00	6.00	0.90	13.50	y	301.60	Underlay
3877.60	6.80	51.20	17.10	n	12813.35	Underlay
806.20	4.10	14.30	9.90	n	1345.71	Underlay
125.20	2.20	4.60	5.50	y	147.16	Underlay
1397.40	9.10	9.80	6.10	n	1381.38	Overlay
571.60	10.30	7.30	3.40	n	743.51	Underlay
2290.40	10.40	3.10	30.10	n	2590.01	Underlay
1041.60	16.00	7.80	3.40	n	1230.24	Underlay
947.20	20.30	3.80	10.80	n	2275.98	Underlay
2542.00	6.20	33.70	2.40	y	1456.15	Overlay
564.20	1.50	13.10	11.20	y	491.66	Overlay
69.60	1.60	4.20	4.50	y	80.52	Underlay

115.20	3.70	1.40	3.30	y	67.77	Overlay
134.80	2.60	5.90	2.10	y	105.03	Overlay
80.20	3.40	0.80	6.30	y	74.75	Overlay
5544.00	7.60	43.20	5.70	n	4487.93	Overlay
306.00	2.90	11.30	3.20	n	291.23	Overlay
1159.40	4.70	7.00	18.70	n	1442.04	Underlay
410.00	2.80	2.60	17.50	y	335.96	Overlay
731.40	3.30	13.80	6.10	n	679.33	Overlay
982.40	11.90	7.10	3.10	n	782.20	Overlay
1176.80	30.00	3.60	2.00	y	822.00	Overlay
274.00	3.40	3.60	5.60	n	193.25	Overlay
367.60	2.00	9.40	10.10	y	439.56	Underlay
36964.20	76.80	54.50	7.30	n	70739.24	Underlay
754.80	9.80	7.30	3.80	n	771.26	Underlay
7439.60	16.30	14.50	12.00	n	6542.90	Overlay
256.60	6.10	5.40	2.60	y	273.89	Underlay
529.80	3.90	3.70	19.50	n	710.53	Underlay
494.40	5.90	2.60	13.30	y	578.86	Underlay
6286.60	11.80	59.20	16.30	n	24543.86	Underlay
219.80	1.20	10.40	8.40	y	238.38	Underlay
1347.40	2.30	14.60	28.00	y	2023.04	Underlay
350.40	2.80	2.20	9.60	y	168.75	Overlay
804.60	3.20	15.10	9.00	y	1010.40	Underlay
798.60	7.00	2.50	11.90	y	606.30	Overlay
431.20	4.30	4.00	7.50	n	348.50	Overlay
888.00	5.70	5.10	17.90	n	1276.51	Underlay
1042.20	4.00	15.30	6.10	n	911.64	Overlay
143.60	1.70	12.60	3.50	y	199.08	Underlay
199.40	3.10	6.90	3.10	y	192.62	Overlay
288.40	7.40	0.80	8.80	y	241.47	Overlay
744.80	6.50	3.80	11.60	n	761.04	Underlay
511.60	3.20	8.60	4.30	n	315.03	Overlay
4523.20	14.30	2.90	59.20	n	6594.31	Underlay
2790.80	15.30	3.40	7.30	y	1100.91	Overlay
303.00	1.30	5.40	31.10	y	469.94	Underlay
134.20	1.90	4.20	9.20	y	181.15	Underlay
154.60	4.10	1.90	7.50	y	185.13	Underlay
341.00	1.50	4.10	28.40	y	391.02	Underlay
118.00	2.80	4.20	2.70	y	100.34	Overlay
895.80	4.00	14.20	4.80	y	693.68	Overlay
99.20	1.50	3.90	9.30	y	130.81	Underlay
66.40	3.00	1.50	3.50	y	58.50	Overlay
82.60	0.50	8.90	15.10	y	127.19	Underlay
2890.40	6.90	9.50	68.00	n	9860.10	Underlay
138.20	2.10	4.60	6.40	y	325.48	Underlay
1260.40	3.80	13.40	12.80	n	2668.39	Underlay
336.40	3.30	6.40	6.40	n	675.87	Underlay
1188.00	5.00	38.90	0.90	y	1906.26	Underlay
339.40	20.80	2.50	1.80	y	911.50	Underlay
1320.60	5.30	2.60	55.20	y	3595.97	Underlay
1491.20	16.80	6.20	4.70	n	2670.29	Underlay
4057.20	9.80	24.90	47.60	n	41480.96	Underlay
7134.20	11.10	17.00	33.60	n	23436.18	Underlay

332.20	7.00	2.50	3.90	y	476.28	Underlay
340.60	3.10	6.20	8.80	n	794.25	Underlay
242.80	5.90	3.10	2.90	n	390.55	Underlay
244.60	1.90	4.00	18.00	y	626.03	Underlay
236.40	2.70	4.50	10.90	n	631.19	Underlay
210.00	3.30	4.40	4.00	n	352.29	Underlay
227.40	3.30	5.60	4.20	n	444.93	Underlay
429.80	5.60	9.90	2.60	n	925.15	Underlay
675.20	2.80	34.70	6.80	n	2898.35	Underlay
231.40	3.30	6.10	3.40	y	416.88	Underlay
883.20	3.20	1.80	91.10	y	2748.52	Underlay
135.80	3.20	4.40	3.80	n	330.23	Underlay
4203.20	10.30	14.70	13.90	n	8471.79	Underlay
4022.00	5.50	45.80	5.00	n	5936.74	Underlay
276.20	4.90	3.70	6.00	y	607.05	Underlay
1396.80	4.40	26.10	3.40	n	2121.57	Underlay
908.20	9.40	26.60	1.40	y	2906.41	Underlay
415.20	6.40	1.30	10.60	y	611.11	Underlay
723.80	6.10	2.10	16.90	y	1177.59	Underlay
387.40	3.20	4.80	9.70	n	715.49	Underlay
77.60	2.00	3.40	4.00	y	173.97	Underlay
318.20	3.50	9.10	2.80	y	559.08	Underlay
69.80	2.30	3.50	2.50	y	153.46	Underlay
459.00	12.60	1.70	4.70	y	751.02	Underlay
1994.40	12.40	20.40	14.60	n	14513.92	Underlay
3322.40	12.60	6.80	25.00	n	8743.20	Underlay
702.00	12.90	5.40	1.80	y	1033.70	Underlay
504.00	5.70	5.60	7.40	n	1165.17	Underlay
2191.40	6.50	3.60	40.40	n	4177.13	Underlay
753.00	17.10	5.40	1.40	y	1226.02	Underlay
505.40	7.40	7.20	3.00	y	999.67	Underlay
653.00	3.30	8.20	14.50	n	1650.54	Underlay
600.00	3.00	8.90	13.10	n	1477.66	Underlay
88.20	1.60	3.10	6.30	y	179.40	Underlay
103.80	4.20	1.60	4.20	y	223.08	Underlay
1299.00	5.30	21.00	2.20	y	1613.58	Underlay
326.40	7.30	2.70	3.40	y	480.57	Underlay
107.00	5.00	2.40	3.80	y	324.88	Underlay
308.20	1.70	9.10	9.60	y	656.25	Underlay
1249.20	7.90	2.40	30.30	n	2858.58	Underlay
122.80	2.40	4.50	3.70	y	247.91	Underlay
216.00	2.60	5.30	6.50	n	458.75	Underlay
1189.80	3.00	10.60	47.30	n	5652.85	Underlay
177.80	5.40	3.10	2.40	y	320.98	Underlay
1038.20	21.90	5.80	0.90	y	1422.96	Underlay
2616.60	10.40	15.00	5.90	n	4331.33	Underlay
1132.00	11.10	3.80	14.50	n	2896.61	Underlay
998.20	2.00	2.90	171.70	y	4464.12	Underlay
6682.20	91.90	10.40	6.30	n	28651.00	Underlay
161.00	2.80	2.70	7.20	y	314.04	Underlay
789.00	2.60	5.80	23.30	n	1473.82	Underlay
559.00	15.00	3.70	1.70	y	859.47	Underlay
1157.00	4.70	18.70	21.00	n	7016.71	Underlay

879.00	14.20	3.00	7.60	n	1796.64	Underlay
59.20	1.10	2.80	4.70	y	92.28	Underlay
532.20	8.60	3.80	7.30	n	1264.92	Underlay
537.60	3.30	15.20	5.80	n	1373.93	Underlay
764.00	9.50	3.30	4.60	n	888.34	Underlay
213.80	1.20	7.20	11.20	y	427.97	Underlay
978.20	2.40	49.50	1.70	y	1477.56	Underlay
191.20	4.20	1.80	8.10	y	391.35	Underlay
208.60	1.40	10.60	5.50	y	401.32	Underlay
60.00	1.80	2.00	7.20	y	163.69	Underlay
169.80	5.10	3.30	1.80	y	274.58	Underlay
359.00	2.60	3.00	17.20	y	657.92	Underlay

Averages
  1416.45   2430.68

The first column represents the actual payoff for the trifecta. The next three columns are the respective win odds for the win, place, and show horses. The next column tells you whether that trifecta contained the favorite or not. The sixth column calculates the fair price using our formula. The final column tells you whether the trifecta was an overlay or an underlay. The bottom part calculates the averages for the columns above.

The range of payoffs was from $59.20 to $36,964.20. The average mutuel was $1,416.45. Let's now look at these data after excluding the 16 trifectas that paid more than 1,000-to-1. You can bet your wedding silver that each trifecta excluded didn't contain a single favorite. We now have a range from $59.20 to $2,890.40 with an average mutuel of $623.79. Let's divide the remaining 132 trifectas into two subsets. The first subset is made up of the 79 trifectas that included the favorite and the second subset is made up of the 53 trifectas that excluded the favorite.

Theoretically, the favorite gets into the trifecta 66 percent of the time. In reality the percentage is usually less because trifecta races are often of dubious quality or have larger-than-average fields. In this sample, at Santa Anita in 1993, only 53.4 percent of favorites managed to get into the trifecta, including the 16 trifectas we discarded. (If you take the subset of maiden trifecta races, you'll find that the public favorite does indeed get into the trifecta its fair share of times. Maiden favorites win more frequently than non-maiden favorites.)

When the favorite did manage to get into the trifecta, the range of payoffs was from $59.20 to $2,790.80. The average mutuel was $449.58. Surprisingly, 43 out of the 79 payoffs were overlays. In other words, the majority of trifectas that included the favorites paid an overlay price. This result is very counter-intuitive. You would expect that the favorite would automatically generate an underlay. Not so.

When the favorite didn't manage to get into the trifecta, the range of payoffs was from $135.80 to $2,890.40. The average mutuel was $883.46. Astonishingly, only 19 out of the 53 payoffs were overlays. In other words, the majority of trifectas that excluded the favorites paid an underlay price. We're in a damned-if-you-do-damned-if-you-don't situation. When we exclude the favorite, we're very likely to get an underlay price. When we include the favorite, we're very likely to get a miserly mutuel.

A little trick is to look at the exacta price on the front part of your trifecta combination. Suppose the AB exacta, which should pay $16, is paying $30. You then have to love all the ABC, ABD, ABE, and ABF trifectas. The reason is because you're getting nice value in the exacta and you'll most likely get good value in the trifecta. On the other hand, if the AB exacta is paying $12, it's best to skip this trifecta because you probably won't get too much value. It's a good idea to check exacta prices before making your trifecta bet. Many times this procedure will save you from betting on underlayed trifectas.

I am very proud of the fact that for every dollar I invest in the trifecta I get back close to $1.75. Unfortunately, I pass a majority of the trifectas offered. That's because I can't eliminate the favorite or because there are too many win contenders. Every now and again I'll play a trifecta using the favorite, providing that I have a monster long shot that figures to be in the money. I'm going to share two strategies with you. The first you'll probably reject because of its complexity. The second you'll love because of its simplicity. I urge you to try both. They both work. The first outperforms the second by a fair margin but is a computational nightmare. It requires the use of a computer. The second is a selection-oriented strategy that requires no math whatsoever. Fortunately, the second strategy shows a respectable profit. Not as good as the first, but acceptable.

A Strategy That You'll Hate

I like to bet approximately the same amount of money on each trifecta. What I do is calculate the probabilities of each of my possible trifecta combinations and add them up to get the total chances of hitting this bet. I then use the ratio of the probability of winning each combination to the total chances. This ratio is the percentage that I will bet on a particular combination. (Please note that this ratio must be rounded to the nearest dollar.) In the Pick-3 I like to bet a total of $200 because my success probability is relatively high. In trifecta races my wager seldom exceeds $100 because my success probability is much lower.

The first thing we must do is make an odds line on the race for our win contenders. All horses that are not win candidates but are show candidates will arbitrarily be assigned win odds of 7-to-1. (The reason for this is to make the probability calculations easier.) Next, we consider the place contenders—we must include all our win contenders as place contenders also. Finally, we consider all the horses that can run within five ticks of the winner's profile for this distance to be show contenders; we must include all our win-and-place contenders as show contenders also.

Suppose my line on a race was:

A (win)	2
B (win)	3
C (place)	5
D (place)	6
E (show)	7
F (show)	7

This is a typical trifecta configuration. A and B are the only horses that match the pace profile for winners. C and D have equal or greater adjusted final times but don't match the pace profile (winner's profile). In addition, there were two horses, E and F, that have demonstrated that they can run within five ticks of the win profile. The way I would construct my trifecta ticket would be to use only A and B on top, A, B, C, and D in the second spot, and A, B, C, D, E, and F in the third spot. The following is my worksheet for this trifecta.

ABC	2	3	5	0.0238	0.0701	7
ABD	2	3	6	0.0204	0.0601	6
ABE	2	3	7	0.0179	0.0525	5
ABF	2	3	7	0.0179	0.0525	5
ACB	2	5	3	0.0227	0.0669	7
ACD	2	5	6	0.0130	0.0382	4
ACE	2	5	7	0.0114	0.0334	3
ACF	2	5	7	0.0114	0.0334	3
ADB	2	6	3	0.0192	0.0566	6
ADC	2	6	5	0.0128	0.0377	4
ADE	2	6	7	0.0096	0.0283	3
ADF	2	6	7	0.0096	0.0283	3
BAC	3	2	5	0.0208	0.0613	6
BAD	3	2	6	0.0179	0.0525	5
BAE	3	2	7	0.0156	0.0460	5
BAF	3	2	7	0.0156	0.0460	5
BCA	3	5	2	0.0196	0.0577	6
BCD	3	5	6	0.0084	0.0247	2
BCE	3	5	7	0.0074	0.0216	2
BCF	3	5	7	0.0074	0.0216	2
BDA	3	6	2	0.0167	0.0490	5
BDC	3	6	5	0.0083	0.0245	2
BDE	3	6	7	0.0063	0.0184	2
BDF	3	6	7	0.0063	0.0184	2
			Totals	0.3400	1.0000	100

The first column represents the trifecta combination. The next three columns are respective win odds for each combination. The fifth column is the probability of that combination hitting. The sixth column is the ratio of the probability of this combination hitting to the total probability of .3400. The seventh column is the amount of money to bet on each combination. Any combination that has less than a 2 percent win probability–to-total chances ratio must be rounded up to $2, the minimum trifecta bet in California. If this were a $3 trifecta, then I would have to bet $3 on all the combinations that had less than a 3 percent win probability–to-total chances ratio.

Using this method, the trifecta is really not that hard to hit. In the above case I had a 34 percent chance of hitting this bet. That's a greater chance than the public has to hit a 2-to-1 favorite! The problem isn't hitting the trifecta, it's getting value for your money. I only play the trifecta when my win contenders are not the public favorite. I like it best when the public makes a false favorite that figures not to hit the board.

I seldom bet on more than 36 combinations. One exception is when I get three win contenders and five place-and-show contenders including the win contenders for place and all the horses that can run within one second of the adjusted final time profile (par) for show. This 3-by-5-by-5 ticket is the largest ticket I would consider. I will not play a trifecta when I have more than three win contenders. When this happens, which is fairly frequently, instead of playing the trifecta I try to crush the exacta by playing the highest-paying exacta combinations involving my contenders.

A wonderful thing happens when you have only one horse that's not the public betting favorite and that can run to the win profile. You can construct a 1-by-6-by-6 ticket that contains 30 trifecta combinations. If you're right about the winner, it's pretty hard not to hit the trifecta.

With exception of the 1-by-6-by-6 play, the major benefit of this "strategy that you'll hate" is the fact that you can hit the trifecta multiple times. It also ensures that you are betting a greater amount of money on the more likely combinations.

A Strategy That You'll Love

I call this the "key-place-all" strategy. It only concerns itself with the horses that can run within one second of the "final time" winner's profile for today's class, distance, and surface at your track. If you don't have a current win profile for your track, I suggest that you start keeping it. This profile tells you the fractional times that you can expect for a given class. If more than six horses can run within one second of the current profile time, skip the race.

To use this strategy, you must make three decisions: First, choose one of these horses as your Key horse; second, choose two to three horses that could possibly beat your Key horse as your Place horses; third, list as your All horses those horses that can run within one second of the winner's profile including your Key horse and your Place horses. A Key horse is the horse that you would be willing to bet your lungs will hit the board. A Place horse has a good adjusted final time but is at a pace disadvantage. All horses are the ones that can run within one second of the winner's profile final time, which includes your Key and Place horses. You then purchase three tri-fecta part-wheels. The first uses the Key horse on top with your Place horses in the second spot and your All horses on the third spot. The second part-wheel has your Place horses on top, your Key horse second, and your All horses on the third spot. Your final part-wheel uses your All horses on top, with your Place horses in the sec-ond spot and your Key horse on the third spot.

The idea behind this strategy is simple. If your Key horse hits the board, you have a good chance of hitting the trifecta. The good news is that you don't have to make a line and you don't have to use a computer to figure things out. There is only one restriction: *Your key horse can't be the betting favorite.*

The trifecta is beaten by a combination of good handicapping and good betting strategy. Most of the time, the trifecta is a sucker bet. It's only when something strange happens, like a big long shot hitting the board, that this bet becomes an overlay. The very best time to play the trifecta is when there is a false favorite who figures not to hit the board.

By the way, the twin trifecta is a wonderful bet. It's your oppor-tunity to make a very big score. You should only play this bet when there is a healthy carry-over. It's a pity that this bet hasn't come to California yet, since I love it. The only time I get to play it is when I'm in Maryland. The idea of the bet is to hit two trifectas in a row, but you can only exchange winning tickets on the first trifecta for live tickets to the second trifecta.

The strategy is to figure out how many tickets you'll need to hit the second trifecta. You then have to buy each combination in the first trifecta that many times. This bet isn't for the faint-hearted. It takes a giant bankroll because you must make a substantial invest-ment in the first part of the bet. It's very much like the Pick-6 in that the little guy gets swallowed up by the big guy. It's much bet-ter to have 10 percent of a $1,000 ticket than to buy your own $100 ticket. It doesn't make much sense to buy a small ticket by yourself, since it's practically certain that the big boys have your ticket cov-ered. Even if you hit, you're not alone. Your goal with the Pick-6 and Twin-Tri is to be the only holder of a winning ticket. This means lots of spreading, which means large-sized tickets. The trou-ble with large sized-tickets is they're expensive. My advice is to join a group of competent handicappers who are willing to invest in the super-exotics.

Let's go from the ridiculous to the sublime. After talking about low-probability bets with the potential for huge scores, let's examine high-probability place-and-show betting.

PLACE-AND-SHOW WAGERING

Place-and-show betting is not a popular form of investment. Many handicappers leave money on the table as a result of not recognizing this wonderful financial opportunity. Before Bill Ziemba and Don Hausch wrote their landmark book, *Beat the Racetrack,* very little was available in the literature of thoroughbred handicapping that addressed the issue. In fact, most of the literature told you to skip place-and-show betting altogether because it was a sucker bet. Authors warned the show bettor that he would have to hit 77 percent at an average price of $2.60 just to break even. Worse yet, he would have to hit 83 percent if his average price were $2.40.

Ziemba and Hausch are college professors and experts in finance. They offered compelling evidence for a system of place-and-show betting that would give the user an advantage when betting at the track.

I used their method in the eighties and did quite well with it. Strictly speaking, I used only a portion of their method. They advocate a system that doesn't require any handicapping whatsoever. They've demonstrated that it's possible to earn profits at the track by simply noting inefficiencies in the place-and-show pools. As a handicapper, I had trouble with the idea of a rigid toteboard system. Therefore, I chose to apply the "Dr. Z System" to only my top handicapped choice that was an underlay in the win pool and was yielding at least a 15 percent "calculated edge" in the place-or-show pool. I used Ziemba and Hausch's formulas to estimate my edge. Here's where the debate begins.

Consider the following table, which is the subject of an enormous controversy. It's the approximate theoretical place-and-show probabilities of horses in California whose win odds are given, according to the Dr. Z System (the source is Ziemba and Hausch, *Betting at the Racetrack*).

Quoted Odds	Place Probability	Show Probability
1-20	99.0	99.5
1-10	98.5	99.0
1-5	96.3	98.5
2-5	89.9	97.5
1-2	86.3	95.9
3-5	82.7	94.3
4-5	77.1	91.1
1-1	72.0	87.7
6-5	67.3	84.3
7-5	62.9	80.8
3-2	61.1	79.3
8-5	59.3	77.7
9-5	56.2	74.9
2-1	51.4	70.2
5-2	45.8	64.4

These values are theoretical. The correct probabilities are stochastic and dependent on the number of contenders and their individual win probabilities in thousands of races. Vince Doyle, Stanford Wong, and Barry Meadow contend that this table is not supported by the empirical data.

When Meadow was writing *Money Secrets at the Racetrack,* he called to ask the results of my place-and-show studies. He was appalled that I didn't have the records of thousands of place-and-show bets. He knew that I was a big Ziemba and Hausch fan and figured that I had zillions of records to justify my support. I told him that I was very perplexed myself about the Dr. Z assumptions, because in the last six years my profit rate was an overall 8 percent on place-and-show bets, yet the absolute minimum Dr. Z computed edge that I ever bet with was 14 percent.

Meadow called every expert he could get in touch with for the results of any place-and-show studies that he could get his hands on. There were none! Just about everyone he talked with offered him studies concerning the efficiency of win bets, but nobody had the data he needed. He then did his own study of 1,000 races in which the favorite was even money or less. His conclusion was that win efficiency doesn't imply place-and-show efficiency to the degree that Ziemba and Hausch predicted. His results are as follows:

Odds	Total	Win	Place	Show	%Win	%Place	%Show
.00–.19	7	6	1	0	85	100	100
.20–.39	80	67	5	3	83	90	93
.40–.49	83	53	13	6	63	79	86
.50–.59	93	55	14	15	59	74	90
.60–.79	304	162	63	32	53	74	84
.80–.99	433	206	109	46	47	72	83
CUMULATIVE	1,000	549	205	102	54	75	85

These data suggest that we are overestimating the place-and-show probabilities. For 3-to-5 shots, Ziemba and Hausch said the the place-and-show probabilities were 82.7 and 94.3 percent, respectively. Meadow's results were 74 and 84 percent. For 4-to-5 shots, Ziemba and Hausch said the the place-and-show probabilities were 77.1 and 91.1 percent, while Meadow's results were 72 and 83 percent. These are rather large discrepancies. An independent study by handicapper Vince Doyle corroborated Meadow's results. This means that we are overestimating our edge when figuring a place-and-show overlay using the Dr. Z method. My experience has been exactly this. This doesn't invalidate the Dr. Z research—it just warns us to be very careful about estimating place-and-show probabilities.

Before I used the Dr. Z System, I used what I called the "long method," which calculated all the place-and-show probabilities for all the horses based upon my computer program's estimate of the win probabilities for all the contenders. I also had a version that would convert the quoted toteboard odds into place-and-show probabilities. Both these methods made money, but they too usually overestimated the expectation. At first I thought this was due to the effect of breakage. (Breakage refers to the amount the pay-off is rounded down to. Ten cents' breakage means that payoffs are rounded down to the nearest ten cents on the dollar, for instance, twenty cents on a $2 bet. If you're fortunate enough to play in a state where the breakage is five cents, then payoffs will be rounded down to the nearest ten cents on a $2 wager.) Breakage can be crucial on a place-or-show payout. Suppose the actual payoff calculated to $2.39—because of ten-cent breakage, the public would be paid $2.20. That's a 95 percent tax! In spite of this outright robbery, I figured that I could accept a smaller edge when place-and-show betting because the likelihood of winning the bet was so great and I was making consistent profits.

When the Dr. Z System came along, it was a gift from the horse-racing gods. At last, a quick method to estimate the edge on a place-or-show bet. Although it overestimated, it was still great. It saved lots of time. Back then I had a state-of-the-art Radio Shack Model 100 computer. It sometimes took three minutes to calculate all the place-and-show probabilities in a large field. Needless to say, there were plenty of nail-biting moments, standing in line and letting people pass, hoping the computer would finish before the bell rang. With the Dr. Z System, the results were instantaneous. I'd push a few buttons and presto—I knew if I had an overlay or not.

It's really interesting that in spite of overestimating my edge, no matter what method I used, I always managed to make a profit on my place-and-show betting. It wasn't the profit rate that I had hoped for, but a profit nevertheless. It's very tough to earn a 20 percent ROI by place-and-show betting—I don't know anybody who has accomplished this. That's not to say it can't be done, I just don't know anyone doing it. What I have done is reduce my requirements to a 10 percent ROI and require a 15 percent minimum Dr. Z edge.

For the moment let's assume that the Dr. Z chart is correct. Did you notice that odds-on favorites have show probabilities greater than 90 percent? Consider a 1-to-2 favorite that pays $2.10 to show. Technically this show price is an overlay.

$$E(x) = .959 \times .05 - .041 = .00695$$

It's amazing that horses going off at even money have a 72 percent chance of placing. This means that any even-money horse paying $2.80 or more to place is an overlay.

Please notice that this table stops at 5-to-2. The reason is that in most cases you shouldn't bet to place or show on any horse whose win odds are greater than 5-to-2. Place-and-show betting should be restricted exclusively to low-priced horses.

As a rule, you should make place-or-show bets on strong favorites only. Place-and-show betting should be reserved for those times when your handicapping selection is going off under your betting-line odds but is an overlay in either the place or show pool. You shouldn't bet long shots to place or show in most cases. The reason is that the place-and-show pools are not divided proportionally to the win odds; they are simply divided by two for place and by three for show. When you bet on long shots to place or show, you're actually subsidizing the favorite.

For example, consider the situation of a 15 percent track take and ten cents breakage. The total place pool is $50,000. A favorite has $20,000 to bet on it and an outsider has $10,000 bet on it to place. They run one-two. Shouldn't the outsider pay twice as much as the favorite to place? The ratio of money bet on each horse is 2-to-1, yet the favorite will pay $2.60 while the outsider pays $3.20.

What's even worse is the situation of a negative pool. You can make a place bet on a 99-to-1 shot, have this horse win or come in second, and you'll only be paid $2.10 if he finishes with the heavy favorite.

How often does it happen that you handicap a race in which one of the contenders stands head and shoulders above the rest? You get to the track only to be disappointed by the fact that most of your fellow citizens are of the same opinion regarding this standout contender. The odds offered are far less than you're comfortable with. What should you do? Most players either go ahead and make the wager anyway regardless of odds, or they pass on the race. The astute player looks for a place-or-show overlay.

We've all seen races in which the favorite won and payoffs were $4.00, $3.20, $3.00, or better, yet where a 3-to-2 favorite ran second and paid $3.80 or $3.40. This most probably was due to spectacular overlays in the place-and-show pools. We'll examine such races in just a little while, but first we must learn to calculate place-and-show probabilities based upon the Harville formulas.

For the moment let's assume we're investing at Philanthropic Downs. At PD there's no track take and programs are free, as they should be. The first at PD has a short field. The toteboard reads as follows:

A	B	C	D	E	Total
4000	1200	1500	500	800	8000
1500	600	1000	300	600	4000
700	300	500	200	300	2000

Using the assumption that the win pool is efficient—in other words, that the amount of money bet on each horse is proportional to the horse's chances—the probability of winning for each horse is as follows:

$$P(A) = 4000 \div 8000 = .5000$$
$$P(B) = 1200 \div 8000 = .1500$$
$$P(C) = 1500 \div 8000 = .1875$$
$$P(D) = 500 \div 8000 = .0625$$
$$P(E) = 800 \div 8000 = .1000$$

There is very little disagreement that the above probabilities reduced by the track take are reliable estimates of each horse's relative chance of winning this race. However, the next part requires an act of faith. The method of computing place-and-show probabilities uses what's known as the Harville formulas. They make the assumption that place-and-show probabilities are dependent upon win probabilities. Here's where Barry Meadow, Stanford Wong, and Vince Doyle disagree. Their research doesn't substantiate these assumptions. Wong said, "I tested them against published results of a thousand races, and found statistically significant differences between actual in-the-money frequencies and what Ziemba's equations predict. Ziemba's books are not worthless; they contain a wealth of information. And his systems probably allow you to approximately break even at the racetrack in the long run, which is 15 percent to 20 percent better than the average horse bettor does."

For the moment let's assume that the Harville formulas are correct. The probability that a horse will place is the probability that it'll win plus the probability that it'll come in second, given that another horse came in first. A place bet is really two bets: You're betting that it'll win or come in second.

Using the Harville formulas, let's now compute the probability that A will place. There are 20 possible finishes involving this field in the first and second positions. The probability that A will place is the ratio of the favorable outcome to total outcomes. Let's enumerate all the possible outcomes and their associated probabilities.

AB	$.5 \times (.15 \div .5)$	$= .15000$
AC	$.5 \times (.1875 \div .5)$	$= .18750$
AD	$.5 \times (.0625 \div .5)$	$= .06250$
AE	$.5 \times (.1 \div .5)$	$= .10000$
BA	$.15 \times (.5 \div .85)$	$= .08824$
BC	$.15 \times (.1875 \div .85)$	$= .03309$
BD	$.15 \times (.0625 \div .85)$	$= .01103$
BE	$.15 \times (.1 \div .85)$	$= .01765$
CA	$.1875 \times (.5 \div .8125)$	$= .11538$
CB	$.1875 \times (.15 \div .8125)$	$= .03462$
CD	$.1875 \times (.0625 \div .8125)$	$= .01442$
CE	$.1875 \times (.1 \div .8125)$	$= .02308$
DA	$.0625 \times (.5 \div .9375)$	$= .03333$
DB	$.0625 \times (.15 \div .9375)$	$= .01000$
DC	$.0625 \times (.1875 \div .9375)$	$= .01250$
DE	$.0625 \times (.1 \div .9375)$	$= .00666$
EA	$.1 \times (.5 \div .9)$	$= .05555$
EB	$.1 \times (.15 \div .9)$	$= .01666$
EC	$.1 \times (.1875 \div .9)$	$= .02083$
ED	$.1 \times (.0625 \div .9)$	$= .00694$

These are the exacta probabilities for all 20 possible two-horse finishes. To compute the probability of the AB finish, you must multiply the probability of A times the probability of B given that A has won. According to this formula, the relative chances of the other horses remain the same once we know that A has won the race. Since we know A has won the race, B's chances are now $.15 \div .50$.

The reason we divide by .50 is because, with A out of the picture, there is only 1-P(A) left, which is .50 or 50 percent. The probability that A will place is the sum of the AB, AC, AD, AE, BA, CA, DA, and EA events divided by the total of all the events. This total must equal 1 because it represents the sum of all the possibilities. Hence the probability of A placing is .1500 + .1875 + .0625 + .1 + .08824 + .11538 + .03333 + .05555, which is .7925. This says that A has a 79.25 percent chance of placing. Did you notice that the probabilities AB, AC, AD, and AE added up to .50? This is as it should be, because we know that A has a 50 percent chance of winning and these are all the possible combinations that contain A as the winner. Therefore, A has a 29.25 percent chance to come in second, which is the sum of BA, CA, DA, and EA.

If you think that the place calculations were nasty, hold on to your hat. To compute show probabilities, we have to enumerate all first, second, and third possible finishes with their associated Harville probabilities. In this example there are 60 possible three-horse finishes of which 36 involve A. Forget about doing these calculations manually or even using a calculator. There are just too damned many of them. That's the beauty of hand-held computers. Here are the results:

Horse	P(Win)	P(Place)	P(Show)
A	.500	.793	.937
B	.150	.361	.615
C	.188	.441	.700
D	.062	.157	.298
E	.100	.247	.451

Did you notice that the sum of the win probabilities equals 1, while the place probabilities add to 2 and the show probabilities add to 3? The reason is because a win bet is a single bet, a place bet is actually two separate bets, and a show bet is three distinct bets.

If you know the probability of an event and want to calculate the mutuel necessary for the selection to be a fair bet, simply divide the probability into the bet size. Horse A has a show probability of .937; in order for this to be an overlay it must pay more than $2 ÷ .937, or $2.13. The following table is the mutuel price necessary for each selection to be an equitable bet.

Horse	Win	Place	Show
A	4.00	2.52	2.13
B	13.33	5.54	3.25
C	10.67	4.53	2.86
D	32.00	12.71	6.71
E	20.00	8.08	4.44

At Philanthropic Downs a win bet is bet by definition an equitable. Unfortunately, PD doesn't exist in the real world. In reality, our payoffs are less than fair due to track take and breakage. Let's consider Reality Downs, whose track take is 17 percent and breakage is ten cents. In spite of the negative expectation due to the take and breakage, win betting is for the most part efficient. The public is a fairly good judge of probabilities and horses generally win in proportion to the amount of money bet on them. Simply put, 2-to-1 horses win more often than 3-to-1 horses. Horses in lower odds groups win more frequently than their higher-odds counterparts. (See Fabricand, Ziemba and Hausch, and Asch and Quandt for a lucid explanation of this phenomenon.) Here are the win prices at Reality Downs for our sample race:

Horse	Win Price
A	3.20
B	11.00
C	8.80
D	26.40
E	16.60

Instead of paying $4.00 to win, Horse A pays only $3.20. Assuming that A's win probability is the ratio of dollars bet on A to total dollars bet to win, the expectation of a bet on A is:

$$E(x) = .50 \times .6 - .50 = -.20$$

Consider for the moment an ABC finish. The payoffs at Reality Downs are as follows:

A	3.20	2.80	2.10
B		4.00	2.20
C			2.20

Notice the place price on horse A. The fair price was $2.52, while he paid $2.80. Let's compute our expectation on this bet.

$$E(x) = .793 \times .4 - .207 = .11$$

In spite of the high track take, including breakage, we managed to get the best of it. At this point we see that it's quite possible for a horse to be an underlay to win and at the same time be an overlay to place or show.

We now know how to calculate the prices we need to guarantee we are wagering on overlays to place and show. What remains is to estimate the actual prices, in advance, that a selection will pay if it places or shows. In reality we can't compute the actual price unless we are the last bettor and have perfect knowledge of all preceding bets—highly unlikely, to understate the case. However, these prices can quickly be figured by a programmable calculator or a hand-held computer. If we bet as close to post time as possible, we shouldn't be too far off. My experience has been that betting at four minutes to post or later is usually adequate.

In our sample race, suppose we like the favorite but it's under-layed in the win pool. Further suppose that we are playing at Not Too Greedy Downs, where the take is 15 percent and breakage is ten cents.

Let's decide if a place-or-show wager on horse A is an overlay or not. When computing place prices, we must either assume the worst or compute the weighted average payoff we can expect. The former is more practical. We must assume that the A horse and the horse with the most money bet on it exclusive of the A horse will finish one-two. We must consider an AC or a CA finish. (It doesn't matter in which order they run—the payoffs are the same.) In this case the total place pool is $4,000. The track takes 15 percent, leaving $3,400 for redistribution. The $2,500 wagered must be returned to the backers of the A and C horses, leaving only $900 to be divided equally between the ticket holders of A and C. Hence the 750 ($2 tickets) backers of A will receive $450 ÷ 750 rounded down to the nearest 20 cents. They'll receive 60 cents plus their original $2 and hence will be paid $2.60. The 500 ($2 tickets) backers of C will receive $450 ÷ 500 rounded down to the nearest 20 cents. They'll receive 80 cents plus their original $2 and hence will be paid $2.80. Therefore the minimum place price we'll receive is $2.60. (Things can only get better if a less heavily bet horse comes in with our choice. For example, if the D horse were to get in with ours, we would receive $3.00.) We've previously calculated that a place bet on A should pay greater than $2.52 to be an overlay, so we'll receive at least 60 ÷ 52 or 15.4 percent more than we deserve. Viewing this from the point of view of expectation—that is, if we made this wager a large number of times—we could on average expect a return of at least $1.03 for every dollar wagered:

$$E(x) = .793 \times .3 - .207 = .0309$$

This isn't anything to get excited about. I will present some actual races that are more worthy objects of enthusiasm.

In this example, a show wager on horse A isn't a good idea. The minimum show price is calculated by considering our horse plus the two horses with the most money bet on them exclusive of our horse. The total show pool is $2,000. Our horse has $700 while the next two have $500 and $300 respectively. There's only $1,700 left after mutuel takeout. In addition, $1,500 must be returned to the backers of A, B, and C. This leaves $200 to be divided three ways. Horse A has 350 ($2 tickets) backers to split the $66.66. This is 19 cents, which rounds down to the minimum $2.10 payoff. We needed at least $2.13 for an overlay.

The toteboard odds are efficient and give us a relatively good idea of a horse's chances. The problem is the toteboard is usually a 120 percent odds line. In order to accept the toteboard as a probability estimator, we must first convert it to a 100 percent odds line.

Consider the eighth race on January 23, 1987, at Santa Anita. It was won by the favorite. The contenders in order of relative probability were:

Horse	Quoted Odds
Corridor Key	2.5
Narghile	3.8
Conquering Hero	4.5
Nugget Point	4.8
Willingness	5.2
Catane	6.0
Avana	26.2

We now convert the odds to probabilities and use them to calculate the place-and-show probabilities.

Horse	Probability
Corridor Key	.2857
Narghile	.2083
Conquering Hero	.1818
Nugget Point	.1724
Willingness	.1613
Catane	.1429
Avana	.0368
	1.1892

Next, we convert to a 100 percent odds line by dividing each probability by 1.1892:

Horse	Probability
Corridor Key	.2402
Narghile	.1752
Conquering Hero	.1529
Nugget Point	.1450
Willingness	.1356
Catane	.1202
Avana	.0309
	1.0000

Let's now calculate the place-and-show probabilities. If we were to do this manually, we would have to calculate each of the 42 possible two-horse finishes (exactas) and each of the 210 possible three-horse finishes (trifectas). We then would have to sum each exacta that contained a particular horse. We would do this for each horse in the race. Of the 42 possible exactas, each horse is involved in 30; of the 210 possible trifectas, each horse is involved in 120.

It should be palpable that this isn't an easy thing to do by hand. For all practical purposes, the only way to accomplish it is with the aid of a programmable calculating device such as a pocket computer. I mentioned before that I wouldn't go near a racetrack without at least one computer in my pocket. Now you see why.

Here are the results with probabilities rounded off to three places:

Horse	P(Win)	P(Place)	P(Show)
Corridor Key	.240	.454	.638
Narghile	.175	.349	.519
Conquering Hero	.153	.309	.469
Nugget Point	.145	.295	.450
Willingness	.136	.278	.427
Catane	.120	.248	.387
Avana	.031	.067	.111

The results of the race were as follows:

Corridor Key	7.00	5.00	3.40
Catane		4.80	3.00
Narghile			3.20

The place-and-show prices on Corridor Key were gifts. The fair place price was $2 ÷ .454, which is $4.41. The fair show price was $2 ÷ .638, which is $3.13.

$$E(\text{Corridor Key} - \text{Place}) = .454 \times 1.5 - .546 = \$.135$$
$$E(\text{Corridor Key} - \text{Show}) = .638 \times .7 - .362 = \$.085$$

The place bet yielded an edge of 13.5 percent, the show bet 8.5 percent. Since we know that our method overestimates the advantage, it's wise to reduce the computed advantage by at least a third. That is, take two thirds of it as your estimate.

Consider the seventh race on January 24, 1987, at Santa Anita. The contenders in order of relative probability were:

Horse	Quoted Odds
High Ace	1.7
Fashion Book	3.7
Clever Edge	3.7
Goldie Hawn	4.6
Kinema	6.2
Gayliole	15.9
Velvet	36.6

The following table represents the theoretical win, place, and show probabilities for each contender.

Horse	P(Win)	P(Place)	P(Show)
High Ace	.301	.560	.752
Fashion Book	.177	.363	.550
Clever Edge	.177	.363	.550
Goldie Hawn	.149	.310	.484
Kinema	.116	.246	.395
Gayliole	.049	.109	.183
Velvet	.022	.050	.085

The mutuel results were as follows:

Fashion Book	9.40	4.80	4.40
High Ace		3.80	3.40
Gayliole			5.20

The show price on High Ace was just wonderful. The fair place price was $2 ÷ .560, which is $3.57. The $3.80 didn't represent a spectacular overlay. However, the fair show price was $2 ÷ .752, which is $2.66.

$$E(\text{High Ace} - \text{Show}) = .752 \times .7 - .248 = \$.278$$

The show bet yielded an edge of 27.8 percent.

One of my all-time favorite races was the 1984 San Luis Rey Stakes. It was a showdown between Interco and the great John Henry. Former Kentucky Derby winner Gato Del Sol also figured as a major threat. The probabilities, according to the public, were as follows:

Horse	P(Win)	P(Place)	P(Show)
Interco	.378	.677	.859
Gato Del Sol	.096	.219	.399
John Henry	.320	.617	.818

The mutuel results were as follows:

Interco	4.40	3.40	2.60
Gato Del Sol		5.00	3.20
John Henry			3.00

Interco had a 67.7 percent chance to place and an 85.9 percent chance to show. Therefore $2.95 to place and $2.33 to show were equitable bets. Needless to say, $3.40 and $2.60 were very generous. Gato Del Sol had to return $9.13 to place or $5.01 to show. He was not a wagering opportunity. The public had little confidence in him. The Old Man, John Henry, would have to pay $3.24 to place and $2.44 to show. He was overlayed in both place and show—fortunately for me, a larger overlay in the latter, as I had bet him to show.

Let's look at our edge-to-odds ratio to see which is the best wager to make on this race.

Interco

$$E/O \text{ (Place)} = .677 \times .7 - .333 = .1409 \div .7 = .20$$
$$E/O \text{ (Show)} = .859 \times .3 - .141 = .1167 \div .3 = .39$$

John Henry

$$E/O \text{ (Place)} = .617 \times .8 - .383 = .1106 \div .8 = .14$$
$$E/O \text{ (Show)} = .818 \times .5 - .182 = .2270 \div .5 = .45$$

Interco offered ratios of .20 and .39 while John Henry offered ratios of .14 and .45. The best bet by far was John Henry to show. (I love John Henry; I never made a bet on him that I didn't cash.)

If we compute all the place-and-show probabilities based on our odds line or the public's perception of our selection and wager when we are offered a calculated edge of 15 percent or more, we indeed have a winning strategy. The price we pay is that we must have a pocket computer and run a bunch of programs. First we must compute the probabilities, then the minimum expected payoffs from the toteboard, then our edge-to-odds ratios, and finally make a wager as close to the bell as possible. This is a lot of work. By doing it this way, our figures are fairly exact but we cannot depend on which horses will get into the money with our selection. It really doesn't matter if we compute our edge on the basis of the worst case. Wouldn't it be nice if we had an approximation technique that saved us from all this drudgery? Well, there is, thanks to Bill Ziemba and Don Hausch in their excellent (and previously mentioned) *Beat the Racetrack*.

The Dr. Z equations for expected return on a $1 place and show wager are as follows:

$$E(\text{Place}) = .319 + .559 \times (Wi \div W) \div (Pi \div P)$$
$$+ (2.2156 - 1.2880 \times (Wi \div W)) \times (Q - .829)$$
$$E(\text{Show}) = .543 + .369 \times (Wi \div W) \div (Si \div S)$$
$$+ (3.6033 - 2.1334 \times (Wi \div W)) \times (Q - .829)$$

W, P, and S represent the totals of the win, place, and show pools. Q represents the track pay, which is the quantity 1 minus the track take. If the track take is 15 percent, then Q is .85. Wi, Pi, and Si represent the amounts bet to win, place, and show, respectively, on the horse we are considering.

There is also a correction factor if your selection is part of a coupled entry. Since you now have an additional chance, your expectation increases by the following:

$$\text{For place add } .867 \times (Wi \div W) - .857 \times (Pi \div P)$$
$$\text{For show add } .842 \times (Wi \div W) - .810 \times (Si \div S)$$

The beauty of these formulas is that the calculations are much easier and the results are instantaneous. When I was testing the Dr. Z method, I had the help of a former student. He was able to get to the track far more often than I. When he shared his results, I would howl. He was betting every race. Without handicapping, he simply played the largest overlay, no matter how small, on the public's top three choices. He said that he had never enjoyed himself so much at the track. He was busy as a beaver between races. It really made going to the track fun. Needless to say, his profits weren't near where they would have been had he used the 15 percent profit edge guideline. In fact it's a miracle that he had any profits at all. He managed to earn almost 3 percent on his investments.

Let's do an example. In our hypothetical race the total win pool was $8,000, the total place pool was $4,000, and the total show pool was $2,000. Horse A had $4,000 bet on it to win, $1,500 to place, and $700 to show. The track take was 15 percent.

The place expectation is calculated as follows:

$$E(\text{Place}) = .319 + .559 \times (4000 \div 8000) \div (1500 \div 4000)$$
$$+ (2.2156 - 1.288 \times (4000 \div 8000)) \times (.85 - .829)$$
$$E(\text{Place}) = .319 + .745 + .033$$
$$E(\text{Place}) = 1.097$$

This means that, on average, a $1 place bet will return $1.097, or a profit of 9.7 percent.

The show expectation is calculated as follows:

$$E(Show) = .543 + .369 \times (4000 \div 8000) \div (700 \div 2000)$$
$$+ (3.6033 - 2.1334 \times (4000 \div 8000)) \times (.85 - .829)$$
$$E(Show) = .543 + .527 + .053$$
$$E(Show) = 1.123$$

You will notice that these figures are different from the ones we calculated. The Dr. Z equations take all possible finishes into consideration. We used worst-case analysis. The Dr. Z formulas are the result of a statistical technique called regression. Hence, they are approximations that correlate reasonably well with the data. The discrepancies between the long way and the Dr. Z method are not large enough to be concerned about, considering the vast time savings. My experience has been that the Dr. Z method usually overstates the long-method expectation, which overstates the empirical results. Ziemba and Hausch recommend that you wager on all opportunities equal to or greater than a 14 percent edge at major tracks and an 18 percent edge at minor ones. These recommendations are excellent, but we'll insist on at least a calculated 15 percent Dr. Z edge. (Major tracks are those where the total mutuel handle is substantial, such as the New York tracks and the southern California tracks.) The following is the place-and-show expectations for the hypothetical race:

Horse	E(Place)	E(Show)
A	1.097	1.123
B	.920	.980
C	.779	.887
D	.829	.846
E	.735	.860

According to the guidelines, this race doesn't offer a betting opportunity. The best bet is A to show. You can expect a 12.3 percent profit, on average, from making such a wager. The worst bet is E to place. You can expect to lose 26.5 percent of your bet on average.

Let's look at some interesting examples of this method. The 1982 Oak Tree Invitational was a classic, a shootout between John Henry and Lemhi Gold. The toteboard at post time read:

	Totals	John Henry	Lemhi Gold
Win	425,976	149,879	183,551
Place	122,847	27,894	48,446
Show	79,645	14,007	29,009

Let's compute the expectations for place and show. The track take was 15 percent.

John Henry

$E(\text{Place}) = .319 + .559\,(149,879 \div 425,976) \div (27,894 \div 122,847)$
$\qquad + (2.2156 - 1.288\,(149,879 \div 425976))(.85 - .829)$
$E(\text{Place}) = .319 + .866 + .037 = 1.222$
$E(\text{Show}) = .543 + .369\,(149,879 \div 425,976) \div (14,007 \div 79,645)$
$\qquad + (3.6033 - 2.1334\,(149,879 \div 425,976))(.85 - .829)$
$E(\text{Show}) = .543 + .786 + .060 = 1.340$

Lemhi Gold

$E(\text{Place}) = .319 + .559\,(183,551 \div 425,976) \div (48,446 \div 122,847)$
$\qquad + (2.2156 - 1.288\,(183,551 \div 425976))(.85 - .829)$
$E(\text{Place}) = .319 + .611 + .035 = .965$
$E(\text{Show}) = .543 + .369\,(183,551 \div 425,976) \div (29,009 \div 79,645)$
$\qquad + (3.6033 - 2.1334\,(183,551 \div 425,976))(.85 - .829)$
$E(\text{Show}) = .543 + .437 + .056 = 1.036$

The best bet was John Henry to show. He won the race and paid $4.80 to win, $4.20 to place, and $3.80 to show. With a 34 percent profit expectation, we have found a wonderful way to invest money.

The 1979 Kentucky Derby saw Spectacular Bid as a 3-to-5 favorite. At post time the toteboard read as follows:

Totals	Spectacular Bid
2,307,288	1,164,220
949,999	339,277
749,274	195,419

$$E(Place) = .319 + .559 \ (1164220 \div 2307288) \div (339277 \div 949999)$$
$$+ \ (2.2156 - 1.288 \ (1164220 \div 2307288)(.85 - .829)$$
$$E(Place) = .319 + .790 + .033 = 1.142$$
$$E(Show) = .543 + .369 \ (1164220 \div 2307288) \div (195419 \div 749274)$$
$$+ \ (3.6033 - 2.1334 \ (1164220 \div 2307288))(.85 - .829)$$
$$E(Show) = .543 + .714 + .053 = 1.310$$

Spectacular Bid won the race and paid $3.20, $3.00, and $2.80.

When Seattle Slew won the 1977 Kentucky Derby, he paid $3.00, $2.80, and $2.80. Do you think that the show betting was somewhat inefficient?

Let's review our place-and-show betting strategy thus far. If our handicapped choice is underlayed in win, we use our odds line or the public's perception of its chances and look for place-or-show wagers that have an acceptable expected profit. The long method uses the ratio of money bet to win on a horse to the total amount bet in the win pool and establishes the probability to win of each contender based on a 100 percent odds line. From these win probabilities we then calculate all the Harville place-and-show probabilities. We then calculate the mutuel necessary for an overlay. Finally, we compute the worst-case payoffs and see if we are offered a calculated positive expectation more than 15 percent. If we're willing to sacrifice a little accuracy, we can enter the quoted odds and develop the probabilities from them. We're absolutely dependent on a pocket computer to do the calculations.

As an alternative, we can use the Dr. Z equations. The advantage is speed. In my own investing I used to use both methods. If I was with a colleague who had a computer, I would use the long method while he computed the mutuel payoffs. If I was alone or with a colleague who didn't have a computer, I would use the Dr. Z equations.

A pocket computer can contain all the programs necessary to rapidly compute the mutuel payoffs, the Dr. Z equations, the place-and-show probabilities, and our edge. (Again, the *Bettor-Handicapper* from Cynthia Publishing is well suited to this task.)

There is another weakness in the Harville formulas: They calculate place-and-show probabilities based on a horse's win probability. But we've all seen horses that either win or run up the track. From a handicapping standpoint, this type of horse is usually a committed frontrunner who's a world-beater when allowed a free and easy lead; when this frontrunner is faced with a little pressure and another horse sticks its nose in front of it early, it quits badly. Here's an example of an all-or-nothing type:

Knight Prospector must have a clear lead at the stretch call or she's doomed. Indeed, all her losses have come when she's relinquished or hasn't made the lead at this point in her races. If she doesn't win, she isn't in (the money). A quick check of her lifetime record indicates this: a win percentage of 58 percent (seven victories in 12 starts), but only one other in-the-money finish aside from that. So if you can predict when the Knight Prospectors of the world will face more heat than usual up front, it's wise to disregard them as logical place-and-show candidates even when they're favored.

Other types of favorites who have a good chance of running out aren't as obvious. I scanned the 1992 Hollywood Park spring-summer meet for even-money or lower favorites that failed to hit the board. I then looked for unifying principles linking these failed favorites.

Of the 674 favorites at the meeting, 165 were sent off at even money or less. Of these 165, 77 (46.7 percent) won and 136 (82.4 percent) were in the money. Very impressive statistics, indeed.

This leaves us with 29 even-money or less favorites that didn't hit the board. If you could have accurately predicted these 29 failed favorites, you'd notice that the public's second-choice became a legitimate favorite: In these 29 races, ten public second choices won while six placed and five showed, good for a 34.5 win percentage and a 72.4 in-the-money percentage.

Even better, if you had bet the public's second choice blindly across the board in these 29 failed-favorite races, you'd have made a nice profit: an ROI of 40.7 percent on win bets, 25.5 percent on place bets, and 75.9 percent on show bets. (The show-bet ROI is larger due to a show payoff that was higher than the win-and-place payoffs in one race.)

What causes favorites to fail? It's not a lack of ability. It's a lack of form and condition. I'll share two form-and-condition angles that can help you predict failed favorites.

Many of the 29 failures in our sample were victims of the infamous "bounce" pattern. Clearly, a lack of ability wasn't the reason for failed favorites. Nearly all the failed odds-on favorites had the best last-race Beyer figure in the field.

But this last-race Beyer was also their career best by a wide margin. The public sees the Beyer domination by itself and bets it accordingly. The public won't even consider that the last race, which was the best of the horse's career, might have exhausted the horse to its detriment today.

As a control, I checked the Beyer figures of all odds-on favorites at Hollywood Park. While many of these also showed the best last-race Beyer in the field, most of these last-race figures were not career bests. This suggests that the animal can duplicate or improve its good figure from last time and run a good-enough number today to hit the board.

There's one type of horse that seems to be immune from this bounce: the lightly raced young horse with fewer than five career starts. These still-developing animals haven't reached their top and can often throw successively higher figures each race. Predict an off-the-board bounce mainly by older experienced horses.

Consider the following race, the first at Hollywood Park on May 31, 1993:

Hollywood Park

1 ***1 3/16 MILES.*** **(1:55^4) CLAIMING. Purse $11,000. 4-year-olds and upward. Weight, 122 lbs. Non-winners of two races at a mile or over since April 11, allowed 3 lbs. Such a race since then, 6 lbs. Claiming Price $10,000; if for $9,000, 2 lbs. (Races when entered for $8,000 or less not considered).**

Mr. Winner
Own: T K A Stables
BLACK C A (133 17 16 11 .13) **$10,000**

B. g. 5
Sire: Raise a Man (Raise a Native)
Dam: Prophecy (Bold Lad)
Br: Mereworth Farm (Ky)
Tr: Villardi Anthony (—)

L 119

Lifetime Record:	27 3 1 5	$51,750			
1993	6 1 0 2	$10,200	Turf	2 0 0 0	$750
1992	10 0 0 3	$11,125	Wet	1 0 0 0	
Hol	5 1 0 1	$12,250	Dist	3 0 0 2	$3,600

2May93-9Hol	fst	1 1/8	:47^2	1:11^2	1:36^2	1:49	Clm 10000	73	2	4	4$^{2\frac{1}{2}}$	4^4	7^8	6$^{8\frac{3}{4}}$	Solis A	LB 119 b	7.40	83-08	Extra Footage117^{nk} Expreso Brazil117$^{1\frac{3}{4}}$ Our Staff116^2	Steadied 1/4	9
15Apr93-1SA	fst	1 1/16	:23^1	:47^3	1:12^3	1:44^2	Clm 10000	78	6	4	5^4	4$^{2\frac{3}{4}}$	2^{hd}	1$^{\frac{1}{2}}$	Solis A	LB 115 b	30.90	82-18	Mr. Winner115$^{\frac{1}{2}}$ Frequent Flyer119$^{2\frac{3}{4}}$ Jamie Jon115$^{\frac{1}{2}}$	Jostled early	12
2Apr93-1SA	fst	1 1/8	:47^3	1:12	1:38	1:51^2	Clm 10000	67	5	5	4^1	3$^{\frac{1}{2}}$	6^5	7$^{5\frac{1}{2}}$	Black C A	LB 115 b	3.60	67-20	Loved And Won115^{hd} Farbet115$^{\frac{1}{2}}$ Waterzip115$^{\frac{3}{4}}$	Boxed in 1/4	9
5Mar93-9SA	fst	1 1/4	:46^1	1:11^2	1:37^1	2:03^2	Clm 10000	90	7	4	4^9	3$^{6\frac{1}{2}}$	3^3	3$^{5\frac{1}{2}}$	Solis A	LB 115 b	9.60	72-22	River Dacer115^5 Loved And Won115$^{\frac{1}{2}}$ Mr. Winner115^6	Not enough late	11
5Feb93-9SA	fst	1 1/16	:23	:47	1:11^3	1:43^3	Clm 10000	78	2	5	5^4	3^4	3^4	3$^{3\frac{1}{2}}$	Black C A	LB 115 b	10.60	82-15	Gentlemen's Style115$^{\frac{1}{2}}$ Siam Ruler118^3 Mr. Winner115^{no}	Battle for 3rd	11
8Jan93-1SA	my	1 1/8	:48^3	1:13	1:38^1	1:51^1	Clm 10000	78	8	4	3^2	8$^{4\frac{3}{4}}$	5$^{2\frac{3}{4}}$	6$^{3\frac{3}{4}}$	Stevens G L	LB 115 b	11.50	70-23	Jet Shuttle110$^{1\frac{1}{2}}$ Cautivador115^{nk} Crack In The Ice115^{nk}	4 Wide stretch	11

13Dec92-4Hol fst 1 1/16 :474 1:124 1:382 1:571 3+ Clm 10000 55 4 6 73¾ 53 610 819½ Black C A LB 115 4.30 73-10 Gold Bally1157 Empty Floor1157½ Ambushed115hd Wide trip 9
22Nov92-6Hol fst 1 1/16 :484 1:131 1:38 1:564 3+ Clm 10000 80 4 3 2hd 1hd 2hd 33½ Black C A LB 115 6.40 91-06 Oh Wow1151½ Gold Bally1152¼ Mr. Winner115 Weakened a bit 9
8Nov92-9SA fst 1 1/16 :232 :472 1:121 1:44 3+ Clm 12500 72 7 9 88½ 77 76¾ 99¼ Sorenson D LB 116 27.70 73-17 Loved And Won1161½ Asterisca's Dance1182 Palmdale116 Outrun 11
16Oct92-1SA fst 1⅛ :482 1:123 1:373 1:504 3+ Clm 12500 73 8 7 74½ 75 74¼ 42½ Sorenson D LB 116 8.90 73-22 Chantasong116no Loved And Won1142¼ Rouvignac-Fr116 4-wide stretch 8
WORKOUTS: May 23 Hol 4f fst :493 H 24/37 May 14 SA 3f fst :372 H 12/16 Apr 29 SA tr.t 3f fst :38 H 2/2 Mar 27 SA 4f gd :504 H 43/51 Mar 21 SA 3f fst :362 H 8/29 Mar 15 SA tr.t 3f fst :362 H 1/2

Latest Release (Ire)

Own: Caine Robert E
GULAS L L (39 0 2 6 .00) **$10,000**
Ch. g. 7
Sire: Kris (Sharpen Up-GB)
Dam: Irish Edition (Alleged)
Br: Moyglare Stud Farm Ltd (Ire)
Tr: Haynes Jack B (1 0 0 0 .00)
L 111 5

Lifetime Record:	39 6 9 11	$204,583			
1993	4 0 0 2	$8,160	Turf	27 4 1 4	$94,378
1992	18 3 3 3	$83,433	Wet	4 1 1 1	$34,995
Hol	7 0 0 2	$5,375	Dist	2 0 0 2	$3,900

12May93-5Hol fst 1 1/16 :234 :472 1:111 1:421 Clm 20000 69 5 10 1014 1012 99¾ 714¾ Stevens G L LB 116 4.60 75-12 Play Ten1164 Loved And Won1163¼ Sir Alex1161½ Wide trip 10
25Apr93-11Alb fst 1⅛ :453 1:092 1:344 1:512 Downs at Alb 40k 87 7 12 1222 1117 77½ 3½ Baze D L 118 9.50e 95-17 Tony'sTriumph122hd Asterisca'sDnce117½ LtestRelese1183¼ 7-Wide 3/16's 12
17Jan93-11TuP sf 1⅛ Ⓣ :481 1:134 1:40 1:524 3+ Turf Prds H 25k 88 4 10 108½ 115 96¼ 42 Patton D B L 116 4.60 89-09 Military Shot119¾ Asterisca'sDance1151 NobleCookie117nk Finished well 12
3Jan93-11TuP my 1 1/16 :241 :483 1:142 1:493 3+ Maricopa C H 15k 84 7 9 87½ 45½ 35½ 36 Patton D B L 118 *2.40 52-50 Fappamoto1175 Asterisca's Dance1151 Latest Release1186 Gaining 9
6Dec92-10TuP yl *1 1/16 Ⓣ :232 :483 1:141 1:474 3+ Cluer H 15k 81 5 9 86¾ 65¼ 66¾ 53 Desilva A J L 120 *1.40 85-20 Cove Dancer114¾ Northern Empire1121 Noble Cookie1171 Mild str. gain 10
Originally scheduled on dirt
21Nov92-10TuP fm *1 Ⓣ :24 :49 1:133 1:391 3+ Alw 10100 77 7 8 86¼ 83¾ 63¾ 42½ Desilva A J L 121 *1.20 97-05 LordPleasant1181 BeyondTheLedge1161 Mr.Ppion116 Some late gain 8
31Oct92-5TuP fm 1 Ⓣ :233 :47 1:114 1:363 3+ Alw 10100 85 2 7 65½ 62¾ 31 12½ Desilva A J L 117 *2.50 96-09 Latest Release-Ir1172½ Regal Billy116½ Fappamoto115 Drove clear 8
4Oct92-9Fpx fst 1⅜ :46 1:112 1:383 2:181 3+ Hcp 25000 82 3 8 822 52½ 2½ 21 Desilva A J LB 117 3.40 85-13 Forest Rain1121 Latest Release-Ir1175 Mind Power114 8
25Sep92-9Fpx fst *1⅛ :48 1:124 1:374 1:51 3+ Alw 25000 88 4 5 53½ 42 31½ 2nk Desilva A J LB 116 9.20 87-17 Eddie Champion114nk Latest Release-Ir1161½ Rouvignac-Fr114 Rallied 5
19Sep92-9Fpx fst 6f :22 :451 :573 1:10 3+ Clm 25000 80 1 7 78 65 65 64 Desilva A J LB 116 11.00 92-11 Imploding116no Frosty Paws119½ Contented116 Outrun 7
WORKOUTS: May 21 SA 1 fst 1:42 H 1/1 Apr 20 TuP 6f fst 1:164 B 5/5 Apr 8 SA 5f fst 1:002 H 6/37 Mar 10 TuP 5f fst 1:01 H 12/27 Mar 6 TuP 4f fst :521 B 34/35 Dec 3 TuP 4f fst :473 H 10/31

Waterzip

Own: Hewit & Young & Young
LOPEZ A D (76 4 10 11 .05) **$10,000**
B. g. 8
Sire: Herb Water (Herbager)
Dam: Northern Zip (Norcliffe)
Br: Paparo Irving (NY)
Tr: Aguirre Paul (5 1 1 0 .20)
L 116

Lifetime Record:	63 11 7 8	$214,730			
1993	8 1 1 2	$14,000	Turf	7 2 0 0	$60,990
1992	15 3 2 2	$40,300	Wet	5 2 1 0	$29,975
Hol	13 2 2 2	$25,725	Dist	3 0 1 0	$2,700

1May93-4GG fst 1¼ :471 1:12 1:362 2:012 Hcp 12500s 76 2 7 710 89¾ 812 712 Baze G LB 116 fb 25.30 90-14 Favorite Norm1145 Super Image114nk Pleasantly Round116nk No threat 9
22Apr93-3Hol fst 1 1/16 :233 :464 1:11 1:421 Clm 12500 64 3 5 76½ 79 69¾ 615 Pedroza M A LB 116 fb 7.00 75-14 Stylish Majesty116nk Loved And Won1166 Please Return116nk No mishap 7
2Apr93-1SA fst 1⅛ :473 1:12 1:38 1:512 Clm 10000 75 8 4 63½ 62 53½ 3½ Pedroza M A LB 115 fb 4.10 72-20 Loved And Won115hd Farbet115½ Waterzip115¾ Boxed in 5/16-3/16 9
27Mar93-1SA gd 1 :223 :463 1:122 1:382 Clm 10000 72 7 9 910 88½ 55½ 36 Pedroza M A LB 115 fb 3.80 72-23 MilkshakeMarty1154 IndinLegend1152 Wterzip1151¼ Bumped start, wide 10
5Mar93-9SA fst 1¼ :461 1:112 1:371 2:032 Clm 10000 80 10 7 610 811 79½ 512½ Pedroza M A L 117 b 3.80 65-22 River Dacer1155 Loved And Won115½ Mr. Winner1156 11
Off slowly, steadied 5/16
19Feb93-9SA sly 1⅛ :463 1:111 1:38 1:51 Clm 10000 82 9 7 75 65½ 21½ 2hd Pedroza M A LB 120 b 3.60 75-19 Roisterous116hd Waterzip120nk Our Staff1162½ Dropped whip 5/16 12
17Jan93-1SA my 1 1/16 :231 :471 1:121 1:433 Clm 16000 51 4 5 66½ 69 512 628½ Pedroza M A LB 115 b 5.50 58-24 Gas Man11511 Portillo115¾ Please Return1159 Showed little 6
2Jan93-1SA my 1 1/16 :223 :454 1:102 1:442 Clm 12500 83 2 7 610 79½ 34 1nk Pedroza M A LB 117 b 5.20 82-14 Waterzip117nk Malibu Parker109¾ Liberty Offiftysix1124½ Got up 8
16Dec92-8BM fst 1 :231 :47 1:112 1:362 3+ Clm 25000 77 3 3 21 53 56½ 58 Meza R Q LB 117 b 5.20 80-23 Bobs Brother Chip1171 Canyon Park117hd Varney1173½ Off slowly 5
24Oct92-9BM fm 1⅜ Ⓣ :482 1:141 1:393 2:191 3+ Hcp 12500 84 4 8 89½ 86½ 31½ 1no Pedroza M A LB 114 b 10.20 93-06 Waterzip114no Lepanto1143 Our Genius117 Drifted out late 10
WORKOUTS: May 25 Hol 5f fst 1:001 H 3/14 May 19 Hol 5f fst 1:014 H 13/29 May 13 Hol 3f fst :382 H 22/23 Feb 27 Hol 4f my :50 H 4/6 Feb 3 Hol 4f fst :492 H 6/10 Jan 27 Hol 4f fst :521 H 19/19

Emperor's Reign

Own: Kerr James R & James Jr & William
DELAHOUSSAYE E (140 20 25 20 .14) **$10,000**
B. g. 5
Sire: Empire Glory (Nijinsky II)
Dam: Early Night Rain (Night Invader)
Br: Kerr & Kerr & Kerr (Cal)
Tr: Stute Warren (18 3 4 3 .17)
116

Lifetime Record:	14 1 2 1	$11,276			
1993	5 0 1 0	$3,226	Turf	3 0 1 0	$1,900
1992	6 1 1 1	$7,225	Wet	0 0 0 0	
Hol	1 0 1 0	$1,800	Dist	0 0 0 0	

21May93-2Hol fst 1 1/16 :231 :461 1:104 1:442 Clm 8000 75 6 5 58 35½ 1½ 2½ Solis A LB 115 b 18.10 78-21 Bear's Pizazz115½ Emperor's Reign1151 Chief Snow1154 5 Wide stretch 8
14May93-6GG fst 1 1/16 :23 :463 1:104 1:431 Clm 10500N2L 63 1 5 66½ 67 610 410 Chapman T M LB 117 22.20 71-22 Royal Dixie1196 Addicted To Run1192½ Winter Warlock1191½ Even try 8
29Apr93-7GG fst 1 :224 :463 1:112 1:37 Clm 12500N2L 72 9 9 89½ 75½ 55½ 46 Chapman T M LB 119 67.10 79-21 Golden Conquest119¾ Mr. Coconuts1194½ Addicted To Run119¾ No rally 10
9Apr93-1GG fst 1 :23 :464 1:12 1:382 Clm 12500N2L 54 6 8 77¾ 76½ 78½ 79 Chapman T M LB 119 7.80 69-20 Good Hunting119nk Chuck'sFirst1193½ Strassel1191¼ Steadied early stages 8
31Mar93-1GG fst 6f :22 :45 :564 1:091 Clm 12500N2L 60 2 5 67 55½ 56½ 69½ Chapman T M LB 119 21.30 84-06 Exceed Speed Limit119nk D. B. Ton'z1195 Ice To Go1171½ Showed little 7
25Jun92-4GG fm 1 1/16 Ⓣ :24 :48 1:12 1:434+ Clm 12500 78 2 4 55 45 32½ 22 Chapman T M LB 119 3.00 91-10 Desert Rumor1192 Emperor's Reign119½ Legal Appeal119 Mild late bid 6
10May92-6GG fm 1 1/16 Ⓣ :23 :461 1:11 1:433+ Clm 16000 81 3 6 711 810 87½ 84 Chapman T M LB 117 28.90 90-10 Bular117½ Strogien1171 Midnight Rocker117 Outrun 9
2May92-8GG fm 1⅛ Ⓣ :484 1:131 1:382 1:504 Alw 23000 78 2 6 77½ 77½ 76¾ 65¾ Kaenel J L LB 119 47.30 85-04 Pride Of Storm1192 T. V. Rebel119hd Hot Date119 No threat 9
8Apr92-1GG fst 1⅛ :47 1:12 1:381 1:512 Ⓢ Md 12500 69 7 4 42½ 31 31 1nk Chapman T M LB 119 *1.50 77-23 Emperor's Reign119nk Alltogethernow119no Lavish Fleet119 Game try 8
20Mar92-1GG fst 6f :221 :452 :572 1:10 Md 18000 68 4 3 67½ 65¾ 66¾ 34½ Chapman T M LB 117 40.90 83-11 Nipsy's Son119no Success Bound1194½ Emperor's Reign117 Wide stretch 6
WORKOUTS: May 28 Hol 5f fst 1:013 H 11/25 May 19 Hol 4f fst :483 Hg 18/37 May 10 GG 5f fst 1:022 H 6/11 Apr 25 GG 4f fst :481 Hg 9/82 Apr 19 GG 4f fst :494 H 30/58 Mar 27 GG 4f gd :52 H 46/50

Roisterous

Own: Scarlett Roger J
SOLIS A (140 18 17 21 .13) **$10,000**
B. g. 5
Sire: His Majesty (Ribot)
Dam: Femme Pleasure (What a Pleasure)
Br: Darby Dan Farms & Liberty Farm (Ky)
Tr: Shulman Sanford (47 11 7 7 .23)
L 116

Lifetime Record:	28 3 4 2	$74,485			
1993	8 1 1 1	$12,425	Turf	4 0 0 0	$3,625
1992	12 0 1 1	$22,510	Wet	1 1 0 0	$6,600
Hol	7 1 1 1	$21,750	Dist	1 0 0 0	$900

6May93-1Hol fst 1 1/16 :224 :46 1:104 1:431 Clm 12500 77 7 7 718 715 59½ 35 Desormeaux K J LB 116 4.40 80-15 Frequent Flyer1163 Cautivador1162 Roisterous1162 Broke slowly 7
24Apr93-5Hol fst 1 1/16 :223 :46 1:103 1:423 Clm c-10000 70 1 10 711 59½ 59 510¾ Black C A LB 116 4.40 77-04 This Time Tony1162¼ Our Staff1165 Current Pleasure109no 4 Wide stretch 11
Claimed from Garber Gary M, Cross David C Jr Trainer
15Apr93-1SA fst 1 1/16 :231 :473 1:123 1:442 Clm 10000 69 1 12 109¾ 98¾ 75½ 55½ Black C A LB 117 10.30 76-18 Mr. Winner115½ Frequent Flyer1192¾ Jamie Jon115½ Broke slowly 12
19Mar93-9SA fst 1 1/16 :232 :471 1:121 1:443 Clm 10000 81 8 9 98½ 52½ 1hd 2nk Black C A LB 119 10.40 81-14 Turbo Trick116nk Roisterous119¾ Mollys Charge115¾ Wide trip 12
5Mar93-9SA fst 1¼ :461 1:112 1:371 2:032 Clm 10000 81 1 11 1120 79½ 57½ 411½ Black C A LB 119 6.00 66-22 River Dacer1155 Loved And Won115½ Mr. Winner1156 Wide trip 11
19Feb93-9SA sly 1⅛ :463 1:111 1:38 1:51 Clm 10000 82 12 12 1215 129½ 63¾ 1hd Black C A LB 116 6.50 75-19 Roisterous116hd Waterzip120nk Our Staff1162½ Very wide trip 12
14Feb93-2SA fst 6½f :22 :45 1:092 1:154 Clm 12500 63 4 12 1215 1211 1213 1113 Black C A LB 116 b 25.30 79-12 Crushed Rock1176 Bering Gifts111nk Indian Legend118no No factor 12
31Jan93-9SA fst 7f :223 :46 1:103 1:231 Clm 16000 60 5 7 810 710 812 811½ Black C A LB 115 b 5.00 76-12 El Toreo1152¾ Classic Case115no Irontree1171 No mishap 10
27Dec92-9SA fst 1 1/16 :231 :472 1:113 1:424 3+ Clm 16000 85 3 4 44½ 22 23 42¾ Stevens G L LB 115 b 7.50 87-13 Majestic Nasr115¾ Skylaunch1152 Portillo115no Nipped for 3rd 9
5Dec92-10Hol fm 1 1/16 Ⓣ :233 :471 1:111 1:422 3+ Alw 33000N1X 73 11 11 1117 813 810 910¾ Black C A LB 117 b 19.60 72-17 Major Launch1171½ Sinag1171¾ First 'n Gold1161 No factor 11
WORKOUTS: May 22 Hol 4f fst :481 H 13/51 May 14 Hol 4f fst :52 H 23/24 May 1 Hol 4f fst :471 H 2/26 Apr 9 SA 5f fst 1:012 H 25/42 Jan 29 SA 4f fst :51 H 46/48 Jan 22 SA 6f gd 1:152 H 6/20

Current Pleasure

Own: Brown Rubin
DESORMEAUX K J (130 34 28 19 .26) **$10,000**
B. h. 5
Sire: Little Current (Sea-Bird)
Dam: Ain't She Adorable (Vertex)
Br: Red Oak Farm Inc (Fla)
Tr: Lewis Craig A (42 9 3 6 .21)
L 116

Lifetime Record:	15 2 1 3	$45,275			
1993	2 0 0 1	$2,475	Turf	0 0 0 0	
1992	3 0 0 0	$825	Wet	1 0 0 0	$825
Hol	6 0 1 2	$10,300	Dist	0 0 0 0	

15May93-9Hol fst 1⅛ :463 1:104 1:362 1:492 Clm 9000 87 8 7 64¾ 63¾ 42½ 41 Gonzalez S5 LB 109 b 17.00 89-13 King Alain116¾ Extra Footage119hd Bear's Pizazz116nk Finished well 10
24Apr93-5Hol fst 1 1/16 :223 :46 1:103 1:423 Clm 9000 76 2 5 47 44½ 44 37¼ Gonzalez S5 LB 109 b 22.50 81-04 This Time Tony1162¼ Our Staff1165 Current Pleasure109no 4 Wide stretch 11
30Jan92-1SA fst 1 1/16 :231 :464 1:111 1:434 Clm 10000 47 9 6 88 914 1018 1022¼ Solis A LB 114 b 11.00 62-22 Tu Eres Mi Heroe1162 Sluki1196 Faixa Ouro-Br115 Wide trip 10
16Jan92-1SA fst 6f :214 :45 :573 1:102 Clm 10000 68 9 7 85½ 109½ 77½ 68¾ Hawley S LB 114 b 5.70e 75-19 Right Rudder115¾ Hajasala1152½ Torchy Wind115 Wide trip 11
5Jan92-1SA sly 6f :221 :454 :581 1:11 Clm 10000 65 8 1 2½ 22 45½ 47 Desormeaux K J LB 114 b 10.80 74-20 Desert Waltz119¾ Tell's End1153½ Torchy Wind110 Weakened 8
19May91-1Hol fst 1 1/16 :231 :464 1:112 1:432 Clm 20000 58 2 6 54½ 59 511 515½ Garcia J A LB 115 b 2.70 69-10 Dr. Fast Love1135 Box Office115nk Buzzywear115 No mishap 8
3May91-5Hol fst 7½f :224 :452 1:11 1:302 Clm 20000 74 7 6 73½ 73¼ 54 35 Garcia J A LB 115 b 2.90 — — Knight's Get Away1155 Screen Tale110no Current Pleasure115 9
Crowded, jostled start, wide trip
22Mar91-7SA fst 1 :224 :461 1:102 1:354 Clm 40000 80 2 6 67½ 65½ 56½ 45½ Santos J A LB 115 3.90 82-13 Black Bark1153 Le Farouche115½ Californian115 5-wide stretch 6
21Feb91-3SA fst 1 :23 :464 1:113 1:38 Clm 40000 73 4 2 21½ 62¾ 62¾ 51½ Santos J A LB 115 *1.70 75-24 Diamond Head Star115no Le Farouche115nk Californian113 Troubled trip 6
24Jan91-3SA fst 1 :231 :472 1:12 1:371 Clm 40000 77 1 5 55½ 47½ 36½ 36 Santos J A LB 115 *1.40 75-17 PrinceOfHoney1152½ Reid'sGold1133½ CurrentPleasure115 Saved ground 6
WORKOUTS: Apr 19 Hol 4f fst :482 H 17/39 Apr 11 Hol 5f fst 1:013 H 17/29 Mar 21 Hol 6f fst 1:153 H 19/21 Mar 14 Hol 4f fst :48 H 3/23 Feb 28 Hol 5f fst 1:01 H 13/33 Feb 21 Hol 6f fst 1:131 H 5/17

Jamie Jon
Own: Amen John B
ALMEIDA G F (85 9 5 12 .11) $10,000
B. g. 6
Sire: Whitesburg (Crimson Satan)
Dam: A Gift of Silver (Mississipian)
Br: Honaker & Wells (Ky)
Tr: Chavez Tony P (9 3 2 1 .33)
L 116

Lifetime Record:	35	3	2	2	$58,925						
1993	6	0	0	1	$4,500	Turf	1	0	0	0	
1992	18	1	1	0	$15,850	Wet	4	0	0	0	$3,350
Hol	12	1	0	1	$17,675	Dist	0	0	0	0	

Entered 30May93- 5 HOL

15May93-9Hol	fst	1⅛	:463 1:104 1:362 1:492	Clm 10000	70	1	1	3nk	53½	65¼	811½	Lopez A D	LB 116 f	18.40	79-13	King Alain116¾ Extra Footage119hd Bear's Pizazz116nk	Speed, tired 10
15Apr93-1SA	fst	1$\frac{1}{16}$	:231 :473 1:123 1:442	Clm 10000	72	2	1	1hd	1hd	3nk	33¼	Nakatani C S	LB 115 f	15.90	79-18	Mr. Winner115½ Frequent Flyer119²¾ Jamie Jon115½	Weakened a bit 12
19Mar93-9SA	fst	1$\frac{1}{16}$	:232 :471 1:121 1:443	Clm 10000	78	3	2	3nk	2hd	4¾	41¾	Torres H	LB 115 f	16.60	79-14	Turbo Trick116nk Roisterous119¾ Mollys Charge115¾	Weakened slightly 12
21Feb93-1SA	gd	1$\frac{1}{16}$	:233 :481 1:124 1:443	Clm 10000	69	5	3	32	34½	37	411	Flores D R	LB 116	6.70	70-20	Supporting1161¾ Gentlemen'sStyl1209 Mdow'sIntrco111hd	Edged for 3rd 7
12Feb93-9SA	fst	1$\frac{1}{16}$	:234 :48 1:123 1:431	Clm 10500	77	2	4	41	53	76¾	710½	Gonzalez S Jr	LB 114	15.30	77-12	Big Paz1166 Standard1162½ Siam Ruler116hd	Boxed in 4 1/4-3/8 9
9Jan93-1SA	my	1$\frac{1}{16}$	:233 :473 1:124 1:453	Clm 10000	74	9	5	52¾	52¼	45½	46	Nakatani C S	LB 117	6.60	70-21	Red X1152½ Keen Line1152½ Hour Finder1161½	Wide trip 9
26Dec92-9SA	fst	7f	:222 :45 1:093 1:23 3↑	Clm 12500	65	4	6	43	65½	911	1010¾	Torres H	LB 115	18.10	77-09	Asterisca's Dance1171¾ Screen Tale115½ Jet Of Gold115hd	Hustled early 11
10Dec92-3Hol	fst	1⅛	:471 1:114 1:371 1:494 3↑	Clm 16000	78	1	4	33	42½	45½	49	Pedroza M A	LB 115	16.80	76-19	Indian Legend1172 Palmdale1164½ Charismatic Con1162½	Not enough late 6
1Nov92-5SA	sl	1$\frac{1}{16}$	:233 :483 1:133 1:47 3↑	Clm 22500	60	5	7	74¾	55	47½	516¾	Torres H	LB 114	11.10	51-34	Shinko Wine118½ Desert Lover1168 PleaseReturn116	Wide backstretch 8
15Oct92-9SA	fst	1$\frac{1}{16}$	:232 :473 1:12 1:431 3↑	Clm 10000	88	4	4	42½	31½	2hd	11½	Torres H	LB 116	23.00	87-17	Jamie Jon1161½ Worthy Rolfe116 Supporting116	Driving 12

WORKOUTS: May 25 Fpx 5f fst 1:024 H 4/12 May 4 Fpx 4f fst :49 H 1/1 Apr 3 Fpx 5f fst 1:024 H 3/8 ●Mar 25 Fpx 5f fst :594 H 1/9 Mar 6 Fpx 5f fst 1:031 H 5/9 Jan 23 Fpx 5f fst 1:023 H 6/12

Current Pleasure boasts the best last-race Beyer in the field; even though it was achieved in a fourth-place finish, this figure was a career best by seven points over his previous best. Current Pleasure went off at 4-to-5 and ran a badly beaten fourth.

The other easily identified cause for failed favorites also has to do with a lack of form and condition: the layoff into a route.

Forget about the old business of a layoff horse being better suited to the slower pace of a route in its comeback race. A layoff horse is more likely to run well in its first race back if that race is a sprint.

Consider the following race, the eighth at Hollywood Park on June 19, 1993:

Hollywood Park

8

1$\frac{1}{16}$ MILES. **(1:40) 28th Running of THE PRINCESS STAKES. GRADE II. Purse $100,000 Added. Fillies 3-year-olds. By subscription of $100 each which shall accompany the nomination, $1,000 additional to start with $100,000 added, of which $20,000 to second, $15,000 to third, $7,500 to fourth and $2,500 to fifth. Weight, 121 lbs. Non-winners of $30,000 twice at one mile or over since December 25, allowed 2 lbs. One such race in 1993 or $50,000 at a mile or over at any time, 4 lbs. $35,000 at any distance in 1993, 6 lbs. Starters to be named through the entry box by closing time of entries. Hollywood Park reserves the right not to divide this race. Should this race not be divided and the number of entries exceed the starting gate capacity preference will be given to high weights based upon weight assigned as prescribed in the above conditions and an also eligible list will be drawn. Total earnings in 1993 will be used in determining the order of preference horses assigned equal weight. Failure to draw into this at scratch time cancels all fees. Trophies will be presentes to the winning Owner, Trainer and Jockey. Closed Wednesday, June 9, with 10 nominations.**

1 1/16 MILES
FINISH START

Eliza
Own: Paulson Allen E
VALENZUELA P A (144 21 17 23 .15)
B. f. 3 (Mar)
Sire: Mt Livermore (Blushing Groom–Fr)
Dam: Daring Bidder (Bold Bidder)
Br: Paulson Allen E (Ky)
Tr: Hassinger Alex L Jr (14 3 0 2 .21)
L 119

Lifetime Record:	8	5	2	1	$1,071,040						
1993	3	1	1	1	$263,040	Turf	0	0	0	0	
1992	5	4	1	0	$808,000	Wet	0	0	0	0	
Hol	0	0	0	0		Dist	3	3	0	0	$771,400

30Apr93-9CD	fst	1⅛	:47 1:122 1:383 1:522	ⒻKy Oaks-G1	91	8	5	54½	31	2hd	21¼	Valenzuela P A	L 121	*.60	81-17	Dispute1211¼ Eliza121nk Quinpool121nk	Made lead, wkend late 11
3Apr93-5SA	fst	1⅛	:464 1:101 1:352 1:49	S A Derby-G1	96	4	2	2½	1½	2hd	31	Valenzuela P A	LB 117	3.20	84-12	Personal Hope122¾ Union City122nk Eliza1171½	Game try 7
7Mar93-8SA	fst	1$\frac{1}{16}$	:23 :471 1:11 1:424	ⒻS A Oaks-G1	99	7	2	2½	12	15	12¼	Valenzuela P A	LB 117	1.80	90-14	Eliza1172¼ Stalcreek1171 Dance For Vanny1171¾	Driving 9
31Oct92-5GP	fst	1$\frac{1}{16}$	:231 :47 1:103 1:424	ⒻBr Cp Juv F-G1	92	9	3	3nk	11	11½	11	Valenzuela P A	L 119	*1.20	98-03	Eliza1191 Educated Risk119 Boots 'n Jackie119	Strong handling 12
17Oct92-8Kee	fst	1$\frac{1}{16}$	:223 :461 1:10 1:431	ⒻAlcibiades-G2	99	3	2	2	11½	17	14	Valenzuela P A	LB 118	*.80	88-23	Eliza1184 Avie's Shadow1185 True Affair1184	Easily 6
19Sep92-10AP	fst	1	:233 :463 1:122 1:392	ⒻArl Lassie-G2	84	2	1	12	13	18	112	Valenzuela P A	L 119	*.90	69-35	Eliza11912 Banshee Winds1193 Tourney119	Stumbled 6
19Aug92-8Dmr	fst	7f	:214 :441 1:092 1:223	ⒻSorrento-G3	80	7	2	1½	11½	1hd	23½	Valenzuela P A	B 117	*1.10	83-12	Zoonaqua1173½ Eliza117 Medici Bells117	Held 2nd 11
9Aug92-6Dmr	fst	5½f	:211 :44 :562 1:03	ⒻMd Sp Wt	87	6	6	3½	1hd	11	12¼	Stevens G L	117	1.90	96-05	Eliza1172¼ Set Them Free1175 Nijivision117	Handily 10

WORKOUTS: ●Jun 12 Hol 5f fst :583 H 1/24 ●Jun 7 SLR tr.t 6f fst 1:113 H 1/9 ●Jun 1 SLR tr.t 5f fst :573 H 1/4 ●May 26 SLR tr.t 4f fst :47 H 1/8 ●Apr 23 CD 5f fst 1:00 H 1/23 Apr 18 CD 5f fst 1:034 B 24/37

Zoonaqua
Own: Moss Mr & Mrs J S
MCCARRON C J (130 22 28 23 .17)
B. f. 3 (Apr)
Sire: Silver Hawk (Roberto)
Dam: Made in America (Explodent)
Br: Heyward James H (Va)
Tr: Mayberry Brian A (39 8 2 7 .21)
L 119

Lifetime Record:	8	3	0	2	$259,525						
1993	1	0	0	0		Turf	1	0	0	1	$37,500
1992	7	3	0	2	$259,525	Wet	0	0	0	0	
Hol	3	1	0	0	$15,400	Dist	3	1	0	0	$120,000

29May93-8Hol	fst	7f	:214 :442 1:091 1:222	ⒻRailbird-G2	50	2	6	65	810	813	819¾	Delahoussaye E	LB 121	4.90	72-12	Afto114hd Fit To Lead121hd Nijivision1132¾	Dull effort 8
19Dec92-7Hol	fst	1$\frac{1}{16}$	:24 :481 1:123 1:433	ⒻHol Starlet-G1	62	4	5	52¼	53	67½	812¼	Solis A	LB 120	2.60	71-17	CrekingBord1208 PssingVic120hd MdmL'njolur1201¼	Wide, brushed early 9
28Nov92-5Hol	fm	1 Ⓣ	:24 :481 1:12 1:353	ⒻMiesque 250k	76	4	3	31	32	43	33	Solis A	LB 121	2.60	84-10	Creaking Board1152¼ Ask Anita117¾ Zoonaqua121¾	Bid, hung 10
31Oct92-5GP	fst	1$\frac{1}{16}$	:231 :47 1:103 1:424	ⒻBr Cp Juv F-G1	75	1	4	53¾	35	35½	79½	McCarron C J	L 119	4.90e	88-03	Eliza1191 Educated Risk119 Boots 'n Jackie119	Svd grnd,gve wy 12
10Oct92-5SA	fst	1$\frac{1}{16}$	:224 :463 1:114 1:434	ⒻOak Leaf-G1	83	1	3	33	2hd	11	1nk	McCarron C J	LB 115	*.60	84-17	Zoonaqua115nk Turkstand1155 MdmeL'Enjoleur115	Gamely came back 10
5Sep92-8Dmr	fst	1	:213 :451 1:111 1:37	ⒻDel Mar Deb-G2	80	4	5	54½	1hd	1½	32¼	Delahoussaye E	B 120	*1.00	80-18	Beal Street Blues1162 Fit N Fappy114nk Zoonaqua120	Wide 3/8 10
19Aug92-8Dmr	fst	7f	:214 :441 1:092 1:223	ⒻSorrento-G3	88	6	7	84½	86¾	42¾	13½	Delahoussaye E	B 117	6.80	87-12	Zoonaqua1173½ Eliza117 Medici Bells117	11
Bumped start, wide, driving																	
25Jly92-3Hol	fst	5½f	:214 :451 :58 1:042	ⒻMd Sp Wt	76	4	1	2hd	2hd	11½	16	Delahoussaye E	B 117	*1.10	91-10	Zoonaqua1176 Voluptuous1173 Aleyna's Love117	Ridden out 6

WORKOUTS: ●Jun 10 Hol 4f fst :463 H 1/32 May 21 Hol 5f fst 1:002 H 3/31 May 13 Hol 5f fst :594 H 5/36 ●May 5 Hol 4f fst :463 H 1/44 Apr 23 Hol 4f fst :492 H 12/37 Apr 16 SA 4f fst :502 H 38/51

Fit To Lead
Own: Colbert & Hubbard & Sczesny

Dk. b or br f. 3 (May)
Sire: Fit to Fight (Chieftain)
Dam: Islands (Forli)
Br: Laura Leigh Stable (Ky)
Tr: Mandella Richard (68 11 14 12 .16)

L 117

Lifetime Record: 11 3 4 1 $174,415

1993	4 1 2 1	$108,790	Turf 0 0 0 0
1992	7 2 2 0	$65,625	Wet 0 0 0 0
Hol	4 1 2 0	$49,350	Dist 3 0 1 0 $15,700

DELAHOUSSAYE E (217 35 34 34 .16)

WORKOUTS: Jun 13 Hol 6f fst 1:113 H 1/17 May 26 Hol 4f fst :482 H 16/42 May 19 Hol 7f fst 1:253 H 1/7 May 13 Hol 5f fst :592 H 2/36 May 6 Hol 4f fst :482 H 16/30 May 2 Hol 4f fst :503 H 34/37

Passing Vice
Own: Iron County Farms Inc

B. f. 3 (Mar)
Sire: Vice Regent (Northern Dancer)
Dam: Passing Look (Buckpasser)
Br: North Ridge Farm (Ky)
Tr: Lewis Craig A (57 13 6 6 .23)

L 119

Lifetime Record: 14 3 3 0 $167,350

1993	5 1 0 0	$60,000	Turf 1 0 0 0 $2,500
1992	9 2 3 0	$107,350	Wet 2 1 0 0 $57,500
Hol	7 1 2 0	$88,650	Dist 5 2 1 0 $126,350

DESORMEAUX K J (291 54 46 22 .27)

WORKOUTS: Jun 13 SA 4f fst :484 H 15/40 May 31 SA 5f fst 1:003 H 4/38 May 25 SA 5f fst 1:01 H 13/45 May 8 SA 7f fst 1:253 H 1/5 Apr 30 SA 6f fst 1:15 H 14/25 Apr 23 SA 6f fst 1:153 H 13/24

Swazi's Moment
Own: Gordy Berry

B. f. 3 (Mar)
Sire: Moment of Hope (Timeless Moment)
Dam: Swazi Girl (Hatcheman)
Br: American Star Corp (Ky)
Tr: Rash Rodney (49 5 6 5 .10)

115

Lifetime Record: 6 3 0 0 $100,655

1993	4 1 0 0	$45,600	Turf 0 0 0 0
1992	2 2 0 0	$55,055	Wet 0 0 0 0
Hol	2 1 0 0	$26,600	Dist 3 1 0 0 $43,100

STEVENS G L (142 34 21 17 .24)

WORKOUTS: Jun 17 Hol 3f fst :352 H 6/33 Jun 12 Hol 5f fst 1:012 H 16/24 Jun 7 Hol 3f fst :383 H 45/51 May 26 Hol 5f fst 1:023 H 36/44 May 20 Hol 5f fst 1:01 H 16/42 May 14 Hol 3f fst :374 H 23/40

The champion Eliza has been away from the races for more than six weeks and was coming back in the mile-and-a-sixteenth Princess Stakes. She's going off at 3-10 (1-5 on the toteboard), and some mad plunger has put $100,000 on her to show, creating a minus pool. (Later, I'll show you how to take advantage of a minus show pool.) But the fact that she's coming off a layoff into a route should make you wary.

EIGHTH RACE

Hollywood
JUNE 19, 1993

1 1/16 MILES. (1.40) 28th Running of THE PRINCESS STAKES. Grade II. Purse $100,000 Added. Fillies, 3–year–olds. By subscription of $100 each which shall accompany the nomination, $1,000 additional to start with $100,000 added, of which $20,000 to second, $15,000 to third, $7,500 to fourth and $2,500 to fifth. Weight, 121 lbs. Non–winners of $30,000 twice at one mile or over since December 25, allowed 2 lbs. One such race in 1993 or $50,000 at a mile or over at any time, 4 lbs. $35,000 at any distance in 1993, 6 lbs. Starters to be named through the entry box by closing time of entries. Hollywood Park reserves the right not to divide this race. Should this race not be divided and the number of entries exceed the starting gate capacity; preference will be given to high weights based upon weight assigned as prescribed in the above conditions and an also eligible list will be drawn. Total earnings in 1993 will be used in determining the order of preference horses assigned equal weight. Failure to draw into this at scratch time cancels all fees. Trophies will be presentes to the winning owner, trainer and jockey. Closed Wednesday, June 9, with 10 nominations.

Value of Race: $106,000 Winner $61,000; second $20,000; third $15,000; fourth $7,500; fifth $2,500. Mutuel Pool $458,233.00 Exacta Pool $343,702.00

Last Raced	Horse	M/Eqt. A.Wt	PP	St	¼	½	¾	Str	Fin	Jockey	Odds $1
29May93 8Hol2	Fit To Lead	LB	3 117	3	3	2hd	22	26	11	1hd	Delahoussaye E	4.20
29May93 8Hol5	Swazi's Moment	B	3 115	5	4	410	48	32½	3hd	2hd	Stevens G L	5.00
5Jun93 8Hol5	Passing Vice	LB	3 119	4	5	5	5	5	425	38	Desormeaux K J	15.30
30Apr93 9CD2	Eliza	LB	3 119	1	1	11	11½	12	23½	431	Valenzuela P A	0.30
29May93 8Hol8	Zoonaqua	LB	3 119	2	2	33½	34	42	5	5	McCarron C J	19.10

OFF AT 5:19 Start Good. Won driving. Time, :223, :452, 1:092, 1:354, 1:422 Track fast.

$2 Mutuel Prices:

3–FIT TO LEAD	10.40	4.60	30.40
5–SWAZI'S MOMENT		5.20	31.80
4–PASSING VICE			51.40

$2 EXACTA 3–5 PAID $44.40

(Please note the epic show prices from this chart. In a few pages, they'll be well within your reach.)

Besides the bounce and layoff-into-a-route factors, surface switches also account for a good number of failed favorites. Knight Prospector, whose past performances we have looked at already, was sent off at 3-5 in her second turf start, even though she had never won on the grass. In that second turf start, she finished out of the money.

As you know, the presence of a legitimate favorite who's likely to finish in the money severely reduces the place-and-show prices on any long shots who run in with the favorite. But if you've identified a favorite who's vulnerable or false and unlikely to run in the money, place-and-show betting on long shots becomes a viable "backup" to your win bets on the long shots.

The first method has been promoted by Mark Cramer and Gordon Pine. Let's quote Pine's work from a recent issue of *The Short Line,* a publication for computer handicappers:

> If you make an accurate Betting Line, you will often encounter horses that you consider to be legitimate contenders who are let go by the public at odds much higher than their fair odds.
>
> Since longshots tend to finish second more often than they finish first, and finish third more often than they finish second, betting these longshot overlays [to win] can, though profitable in the long run, be an exercise in frustration in the short run. When your 3-to-1 fair odds horse goes off at 20-to-1 and finishes third, paying well over 3-to-1 to show, it's a tribute to your handicapping, but it doesn't help your bankroll much.
>
> Mark Cramer, at the urging of one of his students, posed this same question years ago: "If you're willing to take a $10 price on a horse to win, why wouldn't you take the same price in the place or show pools?" Good question!
>
> A rough and conservative estimate of the ratio of the average win/place/show odds might be 6/2/1. Thus, if you're getting three times your fair price in the win pool, it's likely that you'll get your fair price in the place pool. If you're getting six times your fair price in the win pool, it's likely that you'll get your fair price in the show pool, and more than your fair price in the place pool.

It doesn't really matter if this 6/2/1 estimate is completely accurate, since there's a huge built-in advantage because we're only asking for fair win prices for a much more likely event: finishing second or third.

Based on this, here's what I suggest: when any horse goes off at odds three to five times greater than its fair odds, bet it to win and place. When a horse goes off at odds six or more times greater than its fair odds, bet it across the board to win, place and show.

Pine then provides the following chart:

Fair Odds	Bet W/P If Tote Odds	Bet W/P/S If Tote Odds
3-5	9-5 to 7-2	4-1+
4-5	5-2 to 9-2	5-1+
1-1	3-1 to 5-1	6-1+
6-5	4-1 to 7-1	8-1+
7-5	9-2 to 8-1	9-1+
3-2	9-2 to 8-1	9-1+
8-5	5-1 to 9-1	10-1+
9-5	6-1 to 10-1	11-1+
2-1	6-1 to 11-1	12-1+
5-2	8-1 to 14-1	15-1+
3-1	9-1 to 17-1	18-1+
7-2	11-1 to 20-1	21-1+
4-1	12-1 to 23-1	24-1+
9-2	14-1 to 25-1	30-1+
5-1	15-1 to 25-1	30-1+
6-1	18-1 to 35-1	40-1+
7-1	21-1 to 40-1	45-1+

The odds under the "Fair Odds" column represent your betting-line odds for any given horse in the race.

As you can see, Pine's approximation technique isn't reserved exclusively for long shots. For example, suppose you make a horse 3-to-5 on your win betting line. According to Pine's chart, you'll get that same 3-to-5 in the place pool if the horse's actual public win odds are 9-to-5 or higher.

In his *Kinky Handicapping,* Mark Cramer writes, "When the horseplayer discovers a live longshot in a 12-horse field that also includes a false favorite, an unkinky win-place bet is called for. If your longshot wins and the favorite is out, especially in this large field, the place price is going to be significant."

Negative (or minus) show pools sometimes offer a very nice opportunity. There is a strategy that is very safe and profitable. In high-grade races with overwhelming favorites, plungers will bet huge amounts on the favorite to show.

In those races, the strategy is to bet your top pick in the race, exclusive of the overwhelming favorite, to show. Most of the time you'll be paid $2.10; every so often, your horse will run out of the money.

Less frequently, you receive a bonanza. Imagine being paid boxcars on a show bet! This happens with a frequency large enough to make a flat-bet profit, if you're able to detect vulnerable favorites. The Princess Stakes example showed you the vulnerability of Eliza at 1-5. The following race run at Santa Anita on October 28, 1993, provides another example of the minus show pool strategy in action:

Santa Anita Park

8 ***1 MILE.*** **(Turf). (1:32^3) ALLOWANCE. Purse $55,000. Fillies and mares, 3-year-olds and upward which are non-winners of $19,500 other than closed or claiming at one mile or over since July 07. Weights: 3-year-olds, 110 lbs. Older, 122 lbs. Non-winners of such a race since June 1, allowed 3 lbs. Of such a race since April 1, 5 lbs.**

(1 MILE)

Pacific Squall
Own: McCaffery & Toffan
GONZALEZ S JR (60 10 1 6 .17)

Dk. b or br f. 4
Sire: Storm Bird (Northern Dancer)
Dam: Rambolie (Ruffinal)
Br: Folson & Jones & McCombs (Ky)
Tr: Gonzalez J Paco (10 3 1 0 .30)

112^5

Lifetime Record:	8 5 1 1	$360,450			
1993	2 1 1 0	$103,900	Turf	2 1 0 0	$69,600
1992	6 4 0 1	$256,550	Wet	2 1 0 1	$87,900
SA Ⓣ	0 0 0 0		Dist Ⓣ	1 0 0 0	$2,500

30Jan93-8SA fst 1⅛	:47^1 1:11^3 1:37 1:49^4	ⒻLa Canada-G2	98	9	4	2^1	$3^{\frac12}$	1^{hd}	$2^{1\frac12}$	McCarron C J	B 119	*.60	79-19	Alysbelle116$^{1\frac12}$ Pacific Squall119$^{5\frac12}$ Interactive117$^{\frac12}$	Wide early	9
10Jan93-8SA sly 1 1/16	:23^2 :47^2 1:12^1 1:45^3	ⒻEl Encino-G2	96	3	2	2^1	$1^{\frac12}$	$1^{1\frac12}$	$1^{2\frac12}$	McCarron C J	B 119	1.80	76-25	Pacific Squall119$^{2\frac12}$ Avian Assembly118^6 Magical Maiden119^{hd}		7
Drifted out bit 1/16, driving																
15Aug92-8Sar my 1¼	:47^1 1:11^2 1:36^2 2:02^3	ⒻAlabama-G1	96	7	6	$4^{2\frac12}$	5^4	$4^{3\frac12}$	$3^{1\frac34}$	Pincay L Jr	121	*1.60	89-09	November Snow121^{no} Saratoga Dew121$^{1\frac34}$ Pacific Squall121	Wide trip	7
12Jly92-8Hol fst 1⅛	:47 1:11 1:35^2 1:48	ⒻHol Oaks-G1	109	5	3	2^{hd}	2^{hd}	1^{hd}	$1^{1\frac34}$	Desormeaux K J	B 121	2.40	94-09	Pacific Squall121$^{1\frac34}$ Race The Wild Wind121^8 Alysbelle121	Driving	7
6Jun92-8Hol fm 1 1/16 Ⓣ	:23^2 :46^3 1:10^1 1:41	ⒻHoneymoon H-G1	90	6	8	$9^{5\frac34}$	$8^{5\frac14}$	$4^{3\frac14}$	1^1	Desormeaux K J	115	*2.10	90-05	Pacific Squall115^1 Miss Turkana119 Morriston Belle118	Driving	10
16May92-8Hol fm 1 Ⓣ	:23 :46 1:09^2 1:33^3	ⒻSnrta Br Cp-G3	82	12	8	7^6	7^6	4^5	5^3	Desormeaux K J	B 116	3.80	94 —	ChrmAGendrme116$^{\frac12}$ MoonlightElegnc116$^{\frac12}$ MorristonBll118	Wide trip	13
24Apr92-3SA fst 1	:23 :46^2 1:10^3 1:35	ⒻAlw 35000	90	5	2	1^{hd}	$1^{\frac12}$	$1^{1\frac12}$	1^4	Desormeaux K J	B 118	*1.90	92-12	Pacific Squall118^4 Nan's Prospector115^1 Alysbelle118	Ridden out	7
29Feb92-4SA fst 1	:22^3 :46^1 1:10^4 1:37^1	ⒻMd Sp Wt	81	2	1	$1^{\frac12}$	$1^{\frac12}$	1^4	1^4	Pincay L Jr	B 117	2.10	81-12	Pacific Squall117^4 Omjii I117$^{2\frac14}$ Turko Milady112	Ridden out	7

WORKOUTS: ●Oct 17 SA 5f fst :58^4 H *1/41* Oct 12 SA 7f fst 1:25^1 H *1/3* ●Oct 6 SA 5f fst :58^2 H *1/50* Oct 1 SA 7f fst 1:26^3 H *5/18* Sep 25 SA 6f fst 1:13^1 H *11/32* Sep 20 SA 5f fst 1:00^2 B *17/56*

Sacramentada (Chi)
Own: Allred & Hubbard & Shajay Stables
DESORMEAUX K J (51 10 7 7 .20)

Ch. m. 7
Sire: Northair (Northern Dancer)
Dam: Sembrada (El Oriental)
Br: Haras Curiche (Chi)
Tr: Mandella Richard (16 3 3 2 .19)

L 117

Lifetime Record:	25 12 5 1	$213,078			
1993	2 0 1 0	$12,000	Turf	0 0 0 0	
1992	6 1 1 0	$88,600	Wet	0 0 0 0	
SA Ⓣ	0 0 0 0		Dist Ⓣ	0 0 0 0	

11Sep93-3Dmr fst 1	:22 :45^1 1:09^4 1:35^2 3↑	ⒻⓇDesert Trl H 60k	99	4	4	4^2	4^2	$3^{\frac12}$	2^1	Desormeaux K J	LB 116 b	3.40	89-12	Prying117^1 Sacramentada116$^{3\frac12}$ Fowda122^{hd}	Good effort	5
1Jan93-5SA fst 1	:22^2 :46 1:09^4 1:35	ⒻRun Roses 62k	56	8	1	$1^{\frac12}$	$6^{2\frac12}$	$8^{8\frac34}$	$8^{22\frac12}$	Delahoussaye E	LB 116 b	10.20	73-10	Re Toss114$^{1\frac12}$ Exchange117$^{\frac34}$ Lite Light115$^{1\frac12}$	Stopped	9
15Nov92-8Hol fst 1 1/16	:22^2 :45^4 1:10^1 1:42^3 3↑	ⒻSlvr Blls H-G2	88	7	6	6^5	$5^{3\frac12}$	$4^{4\frac12}$	$5^{5\frac14}$	Delahoussaye E	LB 116 b	2.40	83-17	Brought To Mind120^{hd} Re Toss115 Interactive117	6-wide 1st turn	8
6Sep92-8Dmr fst 1 1/16	:23^1 :46^3 1:10^3 1:42 3↑	ⒻChla Vsta H-G2	94	8	6	$6^{3\frac14}$	$6^{2\frac14}$	$5^{2\frac12}$	5^3	Desormeaux K J	LB 117 b	4.80	88-14	Exchange120$^{\frac34}$ Fowda120^{nk} Brought To Mind119	Broke slowly	8
13Jun92-8Hol fst 1 1/16	:22^3 :45^4 1:10 1:41^2 3↑	ⒻMilady H-G1	81	3	5	$6^{3\frac12}$	$7^{4\frac14}$	7^{11}	$7^{11\frac34}$	Desormeaux K J	LB 118 b	6.50	82-12	Paseana125$^{2\frac34}$ Re Toss115 Fowda119	Not urged late	7
23May92-8Hol fst 1 1/16	:23 :46^3 1:10^4 1:43 3↑	ⒻHawthorne H-G2	97	2	4	$4^{1\frac12}$	4^1	2^1	1^{hd}	Desormeaux K J	LB 117 b	1.70	86-16	Sacramentada-Ch117^{hd} Brought To Mind120$^{3\frac12}$ Re Toss-Ar116	Gamely	5
29Apr92-8Hol fst 7f	:21^4 :44^3 1:09^2 1:22 3↑	ⒻA Gleam H-G2	98	8	6	6^3	5^3	3^1	4^{nk}	Desormeaux K J	LB 117	1.90	94-10	ForstFlty116^{no} BroughtToMind120 Dvil'sOrchid120	Wide,bumped late	8
1Jan92-7SA fst 1	:22^3 :46 1:10^1 1:34^4	ⒻⓇRun Roses 61k	104	2	4	$3^{3\frac12}$	3^2	$3^{\frac12}$	2^{nk}	Delahoussaye E	LB 118	*.60	93-11	LunElegnte-Ar116^{nk} Scrmentd-Ch118^4 SlipWithMe-Fr113	Jostled start	6
7Dec91-7Hol fst 1 1/16	:23^2 :46^3 1:11^1 1:42^3 3↑	ⒻHcp 0	105	1	3	$3^{1\frac12}$	$3^{1\frac12}$	$1^{1\frac12}$	$1^{3\frac12}$	Delahoussaye E	LB 118	1.90	88-17	Sacramentada-Ch118$^{3\frac12}$ Luna Elegante-Ar120$^{1\frac14}$ Venturilla114		6
27Apr91♦ Hipodromo(Chi) fst *1⅜	LH 2:17^1 3↑	Stk 40000							$1^{5\frac34}$	Salazar H	126	3.50	— —	Sacramentada126$^{5\frac34}$ Melihual123$^{7\frac12}$ Sombreadero134		11
		Gran Premio Hipodromo Chile-G1												*Led after a half, clear 2f out, handily*		

WORKOUTS: Oct 17 SA 5f fst :59^3 B *5/41* Oct 12 SA 5f fst 1:00 H *11/51* Oct 4 SA 7f fst 1:25^3 H *2/13* Sep 27 SA 5f fst 1:00^2 H *5/64* Sep 23 SA 4f fst :48^2 H *16/43* Sep 5 Dmr 7f fst 1:26^3 B *2/6*

Euphonic
Own: Juddmonte Farms
STEVENS G L (68 10 10 16 .15)
Ch. f. 4
Sire: The Minstrel (Northern Dancer)
Dam: Razyana (His Majesty)
Br: Juddmonte Farm Inc (Ky)
Tr: Frankel Robert (11 2 2 0 .18)
L 117
Lifetime Record: 14 3 1 1 $91,567
1993 6 1 1 0 $36,250 | Turf 11 3 1 1 $84,442
1992 7 1 0 1 $38,471 | Wet 1 0 0 0
SA ⓣ 2 1 1 0 $30,750 | Distⓣ 4 0 0 1 $13,630

18Aug93-7Dmr fm 1 ⓣ :234 :48 1:111 1:351 3+ ⒻAlw 55000N$mY 81 5 3 32 31½ 41¼ 76¾ McCarron C J LB 116 12.50 88-04 Misterioso116½ Frenchman's Cove116nk La Favorita1161¼ 7
In tight, took up 1/16
24Jly93-1Hol fst 7f :221 :45 1:091 1:213 ⒻReminscingH 55k 82 5 1 31½ 32 43 44¼ Desormeaux K J LB 115 6.20 92-08 Interactive1191 Miss Dominique116nk Forest Haven1153 Wide trip 6
9May93-4Hol fm 1$\frac{1}{16}$ ⓣ :232 :464 1:094 1:391 ⒻAlw 55000N$mY 86 5 4 53 55½ 57 58½ Solis A LB 114 b 1.80e 91-04 Bel's Starlet1142 Heart Of Joy1143 Terre Haute1142½ No mishap 9
27Mar93-8GG sly 1$\frac{1}{8}$:234 :471 1:104 1:422 3+ ⒻGldn Ppy H-G3 61 2 5 54½ 57½ 713 717½ Baze R A LB 115 3.20 67-25 Steff Graf1141 Amorously1141 Peterhof's Patea1141½ Dull try 7
14Feb93-7SA fm *6½f ⓣ :211 :434 1:073 1:141 ⒻAlw 41000N3X 92 5 3 55¾ 54½ 43 1½ Delahoussaye E LB 116 *1.30 87-12 Euphonic116½ Melo Melody1181¼ Forest Haven1151 4 Wide stretch 6
30Jan93-7SA fm *6½f ⓣ :222 :444 1:08 1:141 ⒻAlw 41000N3X 92 5 6 63¼ 31 21 21½ Delahoussaye E LB 116 *2.10 85-13 Shes A Sure Bet1161½ Euphonic116¾ Forest Haven1141½ Good effort 7
5Dec92-8Hol fm 1$\frac{1}{16}$ ⓣ :241 :481 1:122 1:423 3+ ⒻAllz Frnc H 75k 91 3 2 31 51¾ 41¾ 53¼ Delahoussaye E B 116 3.20 79-17 Guislaine116nk Explosive Ele1161¼ Alysbelle111½ No late bid 10
31Oct92-2GP fst 7f :222 :444 1:091 1:214 3+ ⒻSfly Kep H 100k 88 5 6 74 43½ 53½ 54 Smith M E 113 15.20 93 — MyOwnTrueLove115½ GenePropp'sDrm112no Nnnrl119 Wide weakened 8
14Jly92♦ Saint-Cloud(Fr) gd *7f ⓣLH 1:25 ⒻStk 42000 13 Eddery Pat 121 *1.70 — — Euphonic1213 Adoryphar1212 Always On Time121½ 6
Tr: Andre Fabre Prix Amandine (Listed) *Tracked in 2nd, led halfway, clear over 2f out, easily*
17Jun92♦ Ascot(GB) gd 7f ⓣStr 1:26 Stk 127000 76¼ Eddery Pat 119 *3.30 — — Prince Ferdinand127½ Pursuit Of Love1271½ Fair Cop1271 12
Jersey Stakes-G3 *Reserved in 7th, ridden without response over 2f out*
WORKOUTS: Oct 18 SA 4f fst :484 H *22/48* Oct 12 SA 5f fst 1:013 H *34/51* Oct 6 SA 7f fst 1:253 H *2/10* Oct 1 SA 5f fst 1:013 H *27/59* ●Sep 25 SA 7f fst 1:244 H *1/14* Sep 19 SA 5f fst 1:003 H *8/46*

Supah Gem
Own: Perez & Stephen
NAKATANI C S (53 8 10 6 .15)
B. f. 3 (Mar)
Sire: Gold Meridian (Seattle Slew)
Dam: Jenny's Nandy (Great Above)
Br: Bush John (Fla)
Tr: Dollase Wallace (5 0 2 1 .00)
L 113
Lifetime Record: 17 5 1 5 $263,499
1993 6 1 0 2 $45,509 | Turf 1 0 0 0 $4,509
1992 11 4 1 3 $217,990 | Wet 1 1 0 0 $7,100
SA ⓣ 0 0 0 0 | Distⓣ 0 0 0 0

15Sep93-3Dmr fst 1$\frac{1}{16}$:23 :463 1:111 1:421 ⒻⓇTorrey Pines 55k 72 7 3 31½ 31½ 79 711¾ Nakatani C S LB 122 7.80 79-15 Adorydar1151 Glass Ceiling115½ Golden Klair116nk 5 Wide stretch 7
15Aug93-10Crc gd *1⅛ ⓣ 1:464 ⒻOffice Qn H 70k 77 2 2 22½ 21½ 41¾ 42¾ Madrid S O L 114 b 2.90 82-14 Urus114nk Courageous Belle111nk Koollanna1112¼ Faded 8
17Jly93-11Crc fst 170 :233 :47 1:121 1:43 ⒻJudys R S H 50k 88 3 1 31 1hd 2hd 32 Lopez R D L 117 b 2.40e 94-05 Kimscountrydiamond1161½ ADemonADay113¾ SuphGem1173 Weakened 8
3Feb93-9GP fst 7f :221 :451 1:101 1:233 ⒻFwd Gal B C-G2 67 3 6 52¾ 57½ 711 813 Madrid S O L 118 b 7.90 72-19 Sum Runner1182½ Boots 'n Jackie121½ Lunar Spook1183½ Faltered 9
17Jan93-10GP fst 1$\frac{1}{16}$ ⊗ :224 :462 1:114 1:453 ⒻHcmsbrde 50k 82 7 3 27 24 2½ 32 Madrid S O L 116 b 2.60 80-21 Sigrun1161½ So Say All Of Us112½ Supah Gem1164 8
Brushed on final turn, brushed top of stretch
1Jan93-10Crc gd 1$\frac{1}{16}$ ⊗ :241 :492 1:15 1:482 ⒻTro Pk Oaks 50k 88 2 1 1½ 11 2hd 1no Madrid S O L 117 b 2.70 79-19 Supah Gem117no Sigrun1174½ Miss Gold Peace1171¾ Fully extended 9
12Dec92-10Crc fst 1$\frac{1}{16}$:234 :49 1:144 1:471 ⒻBoca Raton 50k 79 4 4 43½ 42 31½ 36 Madrid S O L 120 b 2.20 79-13 Sigrun1154 Lunar Spook1202 Supah Gem1201½ 10
Brushed stretch, lacked response
31Oct92-5GP fst 1$\frac{1}{16}$:231 :47 1:103 1:424 ⒻBr Cp Juv F-G1 80 6 6 64¾ 67½ 55¾ 47 Madrid S O L 119 b 75.50 91-03 Eliza1191 Educated Risk119 Boots 'n Jackie119 Lugged in late 12
17Oct92-10Crc fst 1$\frac{1}{16}$:233 :482 1:133 1:464 ⒻⓇFla Stalion 410k 84 11 3 2hd 1½ 12 22½ Madrid S O L 120 b 3.60 90-11 Boots 'n Jackie1202½ Supah Gem120 Sigrun120 2nd best 13
The My Dear Girl Division
27Sep92-10Crc fst 170 :234 :482 1:141 1:45 ⒻGardenia 76k 78 2 2 43½ 42 13½ 12 Madrid S O L 114 b 10.00 88-12 Supah Gem1142 Boots 'n Jackie1166 Near the Edge112 Driving 11
WORKOUTS: ●Oct 17 SA 5f fst :584 H *1/41* Oct 12 SA 5f fst 1:003 H *17/51* Oct 6 SA 4f fst :471 H *3/28* ●Aug 31 Crc 5f fst 1:00 H *1/17* Aug 11 Crc ⓣ 4f fm :462 H *1/1* Aug 4 Crc ⓣ 6f fm 1:141 H (d) *1/1*

Potrichal (Arg)
Own: Hotehama Tadahiro
PINCAY L JR (52 6 7 10 .12)
B. m. 5
Sire: Potrillazo (Ahmad)
Dam: Chaldee (Banner Sport)
Br: Haras La Madrugada (Arg)
Tr: McAnally Ronald (28 3 4 8 .11)
L 117
Lifetime Record: 16 4 1 3 $121,100
1993 5 1 0 1 $35,050 | Turf 10 2 0 2 $62,382
1992 5 0 1 1 $15,800 | Wet 1 1 0 0 $25,300
SA ⓣ 1 0 0 0 | Distⓣ 2 1 0 0 $6,082

6Aug93-8Dmr fm 1⅜ ⓣ :472 1:12 1:373 2:161 3+ ⒻHoney Fox H 60k 72 1 8 814 95¾ 711 612½ Pincay L Jr LB 117 5.90 68-15 Campagnarde1171 Luna Tiniebla1162¾ Liztoane114¾ 9
Took up, impeded 1/4
20Jun93-3Hol fm 1¼ ⓣ :473 1:121 1:361 2:004 ⒻⓇStar Ball 60k 88 3 6 79 78 76 52½ Pincay L Jr LB 117 4.90 88-11 Silvered118hd Miatuschka1131¾ Campagnarde118no 4 Wide stretch 7
3Jun93-8Hol fm 1$\frac{1}{16}$ ⓣ :234 :47 1:101 1:403 ⒻAlw 55000N$mY 95 5 5 66¼ 65¾ 44 3½ Pincay L Jr LB 117 20.60 92-10 MissHighBlade121½ CharmAGendarme116hd Potrichl1171 4 Wide stretch 7
9May93-4Hol fm 1$\frac{1}{16}$ ⓣ :232 :464 1:094 1:391 ⒻAlw 55000N$mY 82 4 9 910 911 911 710½ Pincay L Jr L 117 15.00 89-04 Bel's Starlet1142 Heart Of Joy1143 Terre Haute1142½ 5 Wide stretch 9
6Jan93-8SA sly 1$\frac{1}{16}$ ⊗ :232 :464 1:11 1:422 ⒻAlw 46000N3X 85 2 5 57¾ 57 42 11¾ Pincay L Jr L 117 *2.30 92-05 Potrichal1171¾ Bright Ways1185 Cafe West115hd 4 Wide stretch 5
14Nov92-7Hol fm 1 ⓣ :241 :482 1:121 1:36 3+ ⒻAlw 42000 82 6 7 79 78 76 55½ Pincay L Jr L 117 18.80 80-15 Guiza115¾ Cut Clear-GB1161½ Highland Tide115 Came on 7
15Oct92-8SA fm 1⅛ ⓣ :472 1:114 1:363 1:481 3+ ⒻAlw 42000 81 5 6 63½ 74 96½ 87¼ McCarron C J L 116 8.30 71-22 Fantastic Ways116½ Guiza116 Now Showing116 Lugged out 10
7Sep92-7Dmr fst 1 :231 :464 1:104 1:353 3+ ⒻAlw 43000 92 3 4 42½ 42 42½ 2½ McCarron C J L 116 3.70 88-13 Lovely Habit116½ Potrichal-Ar1162½ Highland Tide116 Good try 7
10Aug92-8Dmr fm 1$\frac{1}{16}$ ⓣ :234 :48 1:114 1:421 3+ ⒻAlw 46000 75 7 6 95½ 94¾ 97¾ 87¼ McCarron C J 122 *2.00 88-07 Border Mate1161½ Ms. Aerosmith116 Fantastic Ways122 No mishap 10
28May92-8Hol fm 1$\frac{1}{16}$ ⓣ :243 :49 1:13 1:42 ⒻAlw 41000 91 3 6 62½ 63½ 3½ 33½ McCarron C J 115 *1.20 81-13 Lady Blessington1161½ Kikala116 Potrichal115 Wide into lane 7
WORKOUTS: Oct 15 SA 7f fst 1:274 H *4/5* Oct 10 SA 6f fst 1:143 H *15/19* Oct 4 SA 5f fst 1:01 H *20/41* Sep 28 SA 7f fst 1:27 H *2/8* ●Sep 22 SA 6f fst 1:134 H *1/20* Sep 15 Dmr 7f fst 1:274 H *2/2*

Like Eliza, Pacific Squall is a prohibitive choice at 2-5. Like Eliza, she is coming off a layoff and racing in a route in her return. Like Eliza, she has a huge amount bet on her to show, creating a minus show pool. Most players say, "Who needs 'em at $2.10 to show?" As was mentioned earlier, in these cases the public's second choice often becomes a legitimate favorite. Let's take a shot and bet the second public choice, Sacramentada, to show.

EIGHTH RACE
Santa Anita
OCTOBER 21, 1993

1 MILE. (Turf)(1.323) ALLOWANCE. Purse $55,000. Fillies and mares, 3-year-olds and upward which are non-winners of $19,500 other than closed or claiming at one mile or over since July 27. Weights: 3-year-olds, 118 lbs. Older, 122 lbs. Non-winners of such a race since June 1, allowed 3 lbs. Of such a race since April 1, 5 lbs.

Value of Race: $55,000 Winner $30,250; second $11,000; third $8,250; fourth $4,125; fifth $1,375. Mutuel Pool $225,401.00 Exacta Pool $199,010.00 Quinella Pool $16,677.00

Last Raced	Horse	M/Eqt.	A.	Wt	PP	St	¼	½	¾	Str	Fin	Jockey	Odds $1
11Sep93 3Dmr2	Sacramentada-Ch	LBb	7	117	2	1	2½	21	2½	2½	1hd	Desormeaux K J	3.40
15Sep93 3Dmr7	Supah Gem	LB	3	113	4	2	11	1½	1½	1hd	21½	Nakatani C S	17.70
18Aug93 7Dmr7	Euphonic	LB	4	117	3	3	31½	32	32	32	32	Stevens G L	4.70
30Jan93 8SA2	Pacific Squall	B	4	112	1	4	4hd	4hd	43	44	45½	Gonzalez S Jr5	0.40
6Aug93 8Dmr6	Potrichal-Ar	LB	5	117	5	5	5	5	5	5	5	Solis A	17.70

OFF AT 4:36 Start Good. Won driving. Time, :233, :472, 1:111, 1:23, 1:35 Course firm.

$2 Mutuel Prices:			
2-SACRAMENTADA-CH	8.80	5.20	11.60
4-SUPAH GEM		11.40	31.60
3-EUPHONIC			14.40

$2 EXACTA 2-4 PAID $97.80 $2 QUINELLA 2-4 PAID $52.60

While the show prices in this race aren't as spectacular as the ones generated when Eliza finished out of the money, they're a good example of the relatively easy pickings available in the event of a minus show pool created by a false or vulnerable favorite.

In a race that features a legitimate favorite who's likely to run in the money, a place or show bet on a long shot in the same race is a bad bet: The long shots subsidize the place and show prices on the favorite. Since betting against legitimate favorites in any pool isn't too smart and since this type of legitimate favorite is often an underlay in the win pool, it's a good idea to check the place and show pools to see if the favorite is overlayed in either one. If it's a place or show overlay, you can then bet with the legitimate favorite.

Vulnerable and false favorites are cause for celebration. Since the favorite has less of a chance of running in the money, place-and-show bets on long shots become much more feasible—and much more lucrative. Look for reasons—such as the bounce, lay-off-into-a-route, and surface-switch factors—that lead to failed favorites. When they are present, exploit nonfavorites in the place and show pools, particularly if a mad plunger has created a minus show pool.

Contrary to popular opinion, place-and-show betting isn't a sissy bet. It's not strictly limited to old ladies who want to cash a ticket. It's for astute investors who are unwilling to leave money on the table. It's the absolute best use of underlays in the win pool. Why shouldn't you get paid for picking an odds-on winner? Who says that you have to get paid from the win pool?

Let's get back to the land of low-probability, high-payoff bets.

ADVANCED EXOTICS

The advanced exotics are the superfecta, the Pick-4, the Pick-6, and the Place-Pick-9. These are very difficult to hit and require a huge bankroll. If your profit goals are lofty, these are the bets that can possibly get you a six-figure income. Let's take a brief look at each of them.

The Superfecta

The superfecta requires you to pick the exact order of the first four finishers in a race. In general it's a horrible bet. Most of the time it pays an underlay price. The plain and simple fact is that most superfectas are lotteries, and the overwhelming majority of them are won by underlayed combinations. There were 99 superfectas offered at Hollywood Park during 1993. Payoffs ranged from $106.80 to $59,487.60. Take a guess how many were overlays. If you guessed 18, you're on the nose. The vast majority (82 percent) were underlays.

Let me throw some more math at you. As usual, please don't be intimidated. It's more important that you understand the general concepts behind them than the formulas themselves. Let's take a closer look at this bet. How do you calculate a fair price for a superfecta combination given the odds in the win pool? (Once more, the "fair pay" for any bet is the bet size divided by the probability of success.)

The probability of success is a little tricky to calculate for a superfecta. It's a dependent-probability calculation. You're asking for four different events to occur, and they're all independent. Consider an ABCD superfecta. You're asking for a horse A to win, followed by horse B to come in exactly second, followed by horse C coming in exactly third, given the AB exacta, and horse D to come in exactly fourth, given the ABC trifecta. The formula to compute this possibility in terms of win odds is:

$$P(ABCD) = \frac{1}{[(A \times (B + 1) - 1) \times (C + 1) - 1] \times (D + 1)}$$

For example, suppose our top pick (A) was 2-to-1 on our line, our second pick (B) was 3-to-1, our third pick (C) was 5-to-1, and our fourth pick (D) was 6-to-1. The probability of hitting the ABCD superfecta is calculated as follows:

$$P(ABC) = \frac{1}{[(2 \times (3 + 1) - 1) \times (5 + 1) - 1] \times (6 + 1)}$$

P(ABC) = $\frac{1}{287}$ or .003. That's three chances in a thousand! In order to calculate the fair price, take $\frac{1}{287}$ and divide it into the bet size, which is $1. The ABCD superfecta must pay $287 in order to pay a fair price. But we want the 50 percent premium. In other words, I would insist upon a price of $431 before I would play this superfecta. The problem is, unlike when we make an exacta bet, we aren't told in advance how much a superfecta will pay.

Let me add another complication. If we use the public odds instead of our own betting-line odds, the calculation changes dramatically because of the track take. When a horse is quoted at 2-to-1 at the track, this reflects the mutuel takeout. This horse doesn't have exactly one third of the win pool. It actually has a larger percentage. Each wager in a compound series must be divided by the track payout rate for win bets. If the track take is 17 percent, the track payout rate is 83 percent or .83. Therefore, any exacta payout must be divided by the square of the track payout rate, and any trifecta must be divided by the cube of the track payout rate. Hence, the superfecta must be divided by the fourth power of the track pay. Our superfecta fair-pay equation thus becomes:

$$\text{Fair pay} = \frac{\text{Bet size} \times [(A \times (B + 1)) - 1 \times (C + 1) - 1] \times (D + 1)}{(\text{Track payout rate})^4}$$

In California the track payout rate is .8467. In New York this rate is .83. In some states, again, it gets as low as .81. In California the multiplier becomes 1.95, in New York 2.11, and 2.32 in 19 percent takeout states. In the example above, using public odds, the fair pay in California is no longer $287, it's $560. Therefore we must insist upon an $840 payoff.

There is very little reason to be optimistic about this bet. Remember the 2-4-6-8 conjecture? Let's assume it's true and consider a four-horse superfecta box on the top four public betting choices. Let's bet $24 on each superfecta race, a $1 four-horse box, at Hollywood Park in 1993 and see what happens. Let's calculate the probability of hitting this superfecta. The calculations are as follows:

Odds 1	Odds 2	Odds 3	Odds 4	Probability
2	4	6	8	.0018
2	4	8	6	.0018
2	6	4	8	.0017
2	6	8	4	.0017
2	8	4	6	.0017
2	8	6	4	.0017
4	2	6	8	.0015
4	2	8	6	.0015
4	6	2	8	.0014
4	6	8	2	.0014
4	8	2	6	.0014
4	8	6	2	.0014
6	2	4	8	.0013
6	2	8	4	.0013
6	4	2	8	.0013
6	4	8	2	.0013
6	8	2	4	.0013
6	8	4	2	.0013
8	2	4	6	.0013
8	2	6	4	.0013
8	4	2	6	.0012
8	4	6	2	.0012
8	6	2	4	.0012
8	6	4	2	.0012
				.0342

Our probability of hitting this superfecta is 3.4 percent. Hence, the fair pay for this superfecta is $705.88. (Our probability of hitting a similar trifecta was 20.4 percent. In other words, this particular bet is six times harder to hit than the corresponding trifecta.)

Let's now calculate our expectation on this wager. The actual number of times that four of the public's top four picks completed the superfecta was seven. The total return was $1,488.30. The average payoff was $212.61. If you had played all of these superfectas, your return on the $24 times 99 superfectas ($2,376) was $1,488.30. For every dollar you invested, you got back 63 cents. If you want to divest yourself of all your worldly goods, I can't think of a faster way.

The following is the summary of all the superfectas offered at Hollywood Park in 1993:

date	odds1	rank1	odds2	rank2	odds3	rank3	odds4	rank4	actual	theory	value
04/21/93	1.40	1	15.90	6	9.60	5	3.10	2	491.30	980.7036	underlay
04/22/93	4.90	3	34.50	9	15.40	6	2.90	2	7037.50	11057.982	underlay
04/23/93	21.10	8	3.80	3	2.60	1	5.10	4	1888.20	2196.0488	underlay
04/24/93	4.60	3	6.60	5	6.20	4	2.80	1	592.50	925.3456	underlay
04/25/93	11.70	6	1.00	1	7.60	4	4.30	2	250.10	1015.692	underlay
04/28/93	1.20	1	3.60	2	18.30	7	73.90	10	1306.10	6459.0764	underlay
04/29/93	1.50	1	2.20	2	61.70	9	38.90	8	1000.30	9466.674	underlay
04/30/93	1.90	1	2.70	2	8.50	5	44.40	9	542.30	2555.339	underlay
05/01/93	10.60	5	1.00	1	16.20	6	16.50	7	2825.70	6062.7	underlay
05/02/93	1.70	1	11.40	8	6.20	3	10.10	5	4308.80	1593.6936	overlay
05/05/93	4.10	3	7.90	5	4.80	4	11.10	6	2652.70	2478.5882	overlay
05/06/93	1.20	1	22.30	7	8.10	5	4.10	2	1751.30	1246.1136	overlay
05/07/93	3.60	2	37.50	7	1.10	1	5.40	3	2142.40	1842.944	overlay
05/08/93	9.80	6	3.50	2	3.50	1	6.80	4	715.90	1505.01	underlay
05/09/93	1.60	1	3.00	2	4.90	3	8.30	5	94.40	286.998	underlay
05/12/93	1.60	1	18.10	7	4.40	3	47.70	8	2644.00	7724.9888	underlay
05/13/93	21.70	6	6.50	3	9.00	4	1.90	2	7463.90	4687.85	overlay
05/14/93	2.90	2	1.00	1	75.40	10	38.80	9	14626.40	14555.656	overlay
05/15/93	7.20	4	1.70	1	3.20	2	17.00	7	977.80	1376.064	underlay
05/16/93	3.20	1	3.40	2	45.50	10	6.90	4	4632.20	4797.038	underlay
05/19/93	38.70	9	1.40	1	5.10	2	14.70	6	8035.50	8783.6476	underlay
05/20/93	6.40	4	4.10	2	36.60	9	1.50	1	1787.70	2971.66	underlay
05/21/93	2.20	1	4.20	3	11.00	5	6.50	4	236.80	932.1	underlay
05/22/93	11.40	6	0.80	1	4.10	2	9.80	5	244.00	1064.3616	underlay
05/23/93	45.70	10	6.10	4	15.60	6	3.00	2	20020.00	21474.408	underlay
05/26/93	2.40	1	4.30	3	10.80	6	157.10	10	8445.20	21706.4976	underlay
05/27/93	1.80	1	2.40	2	3.60	3	34.00	7	218.50	789.32	underlay
05/28/93	12.10	6	24.50	7	110.80	11	59.80	10	38492.30	2090491.872	underlay
05/29/93	3.20	2	11.80	6	5.70	3	14.40	7	2358.90	4107.6728	underlay
05/30/93	1.40	1	30.10	6	1.90	2	3.70	3	188.60	575.1202	underlay
05/31/93	26.00	8	2.20	1	6.10	4	4.50	3	3328.10	3204.41	overlay
06/02/93	3.90	2	4.10	3	1.30	1	30.10	7	583.00	1320.1017	underlay
06/03/93	5.10	2	6.80	4	19.70	8	1.60	1	2218.90	2084.5396	overlay
06/04/93	8.40	4	1.70	1	9.50	5	3.10	2	781.30	929.224	underlay
06/05/93	14.00	6	4.80	3	12.40	5	5.50	4	5957.90	6978.92	underlay
06/06/93	5.20	3	3.00	2	7.00	5	21.80	8	3641.30	3588.72	overlay
06/09/93	2.80	1	4.30	4	65.50	9	3.70	3	2554.20	4320.992	underlay
06/10/93	11.40	5	20.40	6	0.90	1	47.90	8	11343.20	22524.5136	underlay
06/11/93	3.90	2	4.90	3	5.70	5	5.20	4	560.70	908.0954	underlay
06/12/93	15.40	6	1.00	1	2.90	2	51.60	9	4466.00	6060.572	underlay
06/13/93	14.10	7	1.40	1	16.40	8	7.50	4	4078.40	4848.536	underlay
06/16/93	2.60	2	2.10	1	5.80	4	5.10	3	181.90	286.7488	underlay
06/17/93	2.70	1	4.60	3	14.20	7	8.70	5	1138.00	2072.1528	underlay
06/18/93	1.60	1	85.90	8	4.10	3	7.30	4	3687.20	5834.9332	underlay
06/19/93	1.90	1	7.70	5	3.60	2	21.40	9	536.20	1577.8112	underlay
06/20/93	26.40	8	3.20	2	4.90	4	20.40	7	14172.30	13852.0488	overlay
06/23/93	2.10	2	1.90	1	13.40	5	4.60	3	190.10	404.8576	underlay
06/24/93	4.20	3	21.50	6	2.90	2	51.90	9	9561.10	19237.085	underlay
06/25/93	7.40	4	3.40	3	3.20	2	1.40	1	296.40	315.7248	underlay
06/26/93	4.30	3	2.60	2	2.10	1	12.00	6	295.40	570.544	underlay
06/27/93	10.30	7	1.50	1	9.70	6	7.90	3	1839.40	2348.0425	underlay

06/30/93	5.50	3	1.90	1	2.40	2	6.60	4	225.80	378.708	underlay
07/01/93	2.20	1	4.40	3	11.40	6	71.70	8	1131.40	9735.4024	underlay
07/02/93	7.30	4	1.90	1	4.80	3	10.70	5	1573.30	1357.0362	overlay
07/03/93	9.30	5	40.00	12	7.10	4	12.80	6	18110.70	42496.134	underlay
07/04/93	2.20	1	2.60	2	51.00	9	16.30	7	1300.80	6207.932	underlay
07/05/93	12.00	6	13.60	7	7.90	4	16.40	9	3814.90	26959.212	underlay
07/07/93	2.10	2	23.10	7	2.10	1	27.40	9	3135.30	4339.2644	underlay
07/08/93	5.20	3	101.20	8	1.80	1	3.50	2	5811.20	6679.044	underlay
07/09/93	2.50	1	11.50	7	4.30	2	38.20	10	2992.10	6245.54	underlay
07/10/93	3.20	2	2.40	1	26.30	6	9.70	5	438.40	2875.3468	underlay
07/11/93	1.30	1	12.50	5	24.40	7	7.30	3	2261.00	3480.771	underlay
07/14/93	1.00	1	7.40	5	5.80	2	10.80	6	312.10	581.976	underlay
07/15/93	2.00	1	4.50	4	3.80	3	9.40	5	132.80	488.8	underlay
07/16/93	14.30	7	13.20	6	40.10	9	5.50	4	56403.70	53973.829	overlay
07/17/93	3.70	3	2.70	2	2.40	1	95.60	10	1514.00	4071.3036	underlay
07/18/93	2.30	1	5.30	4	45.50	7	11.80	6	2087.60	8016.448	underlay
07/21/93	8.50	5	39.10	9	8.30	4	1.90	1	17839.30	9162.8545	overlay
07/22/93	10.20	6	1.70	1	5.70	4	5.50	3	1173.70	1149.317	overlay
07/23/93	3.70	2	1.30	1	4.30	3	6.20	4	115.80	279.3816	underlay
07/24/93	1.70	1	13.00	6	7.70	4	2.30	2	629.60	651.288	underlay
07/25/93	38.20	8	3.90	2	36.10	7	1.00	1	59487.60	13812.556	overlay
07/26/93	3.90	2	0.80	1	26.60	6	35.60	8	1597.70	6044.5632	underlay
11/17/93	4.10	3	4.10	2	1.60	1	7.30	4	267.90	421.3578	underlay
11/18/93	8.90	5	2.20	1	2.70	2	96.80	8	4372.90	9846.1128	underlay
11/19/93	2.70	2	2.00	1	4.40	3	6.80	4	225.70	291.252	underlay
11/20/93	1.60	1	6.60	3	8.60	4	1.80	2	174.80	297.1808	underlay
11/21/93	2.80	2	1.70	1	4.60	3	8.50	5	106.80	339.492	underlay
11/24/93	5.90	4	3.10	1	16.70	8	4.70	3	2678.20	2333.9391	overlay
11/25/93	2.90	2	4.50	3	7.90	5	33.70	9	895.00	4582.3085	underlay
11/26/93	6.70	4	3.40	2	11.80	6	46.90	9	3805.30	17413.7576	underlay
11/27/93	10.50	5	5.40	3	2.00	2	16.30	7	2977.00	3418.48	underlay
11/28/93	2.60	2	1.20	1	17.50	6	3.80	3	174.90	414.336	underlay
12/01/93	11.80	5	1.00	1	4.80	3	19.50	6	1145.80	2666.64	underlay
12/02/93	4.20	2	0.70	1	22.30	5	43.30	8	832.50	6293.3466	underlay
12/03/93	9.80	5	13.30	7	1.80	1	11.30	8	2316.60	4779.6818	underlay
12/04/93	15.70	6	10.70	5	18.10	8	1.70	1	11011.70	9418.6233	overlay
12/05/93	1.30	1	20.10	9	9.90	4	5.80	3	1669.70	1952.1916	underlay
12/08/93	6.30	3	2.60	2	16.50	6	41.30	10	2387.10	16006.32	underlay
12/09/93	6.20	4	2.70	2	2.70	1	195.20	11	4989.90	15730.9236	underlay
12/10/93	4.20	3	1.90	1	20.90	8	3.00	2	486.90	975.368	underlay
12/11/93	7.20	4	1.50	1	5.30	3	7.80	5	846.70	933.68	underlay
12/12/93	9.30	6	3.70	2	4.50	3	12.90	8	2884.70	3251.2795	underlay
12/15/93	16.10	6	2.40	1	2.60	2	8.30	4	1173.20	1404.9872	underlay
12/16/93	3.70	3	6.40	4	2.40	1	58.90	9	1658.30	5312.6508	underlay
12/17/93	1.40	1	18.60	7	18.50	6	3.10	2	902.50	2109.778	underlay
12/18/93	4.80	4	3.80	3	39.58	10	13.80	7	15408.10	13195.976	overlay
12/19/93	1.00	1	24.00	5	25.30	6	51.70	11	5996.20	33211.54	underlay
12/20/93	3.40	2	4.00	4	8.30	5	22.10	8	1519.20	3414.18	underlay

If we throw out all the payoffs of more than $10,000, there were 88 superfectas to consider. Only 11 of the 88 offered an overlay; 87.5 percent were underlays! The average payoff was $2,107.54. The average should have been $4,579.81. It doesn't take a genius to see that this bet is strictly for suckers. If you want to stay up nights devising winning strategies for the superfecta, you have my fondest wishes.

When you think about it, the superfecta is a trifecta plus the fourth horse. The trifecta is a marginal bet to begin with. My advice is to downgrade these bets (trifecta and superfecta) in favor of bets that are grossly misplayed, such as the exacta and the Pick-3.

But I hate the thought of missing an opportunity. There has to be a strategy that will yield a positive expectation in the superfecta. Damn if I can find it. Of the 11 overlays, 8 contained the favorite, and two contained both the first and second favorites. In the trifecta, I look for races with false favorites. It doesn't seem to do that much good in the superfecta. There were 21 superfectas in which the first and second favorite didn't run either first or second. Only six of these were overlays. It's a damn shame that underlays rule this bet. Again, my advice is to invest your money in those opportunities where you'll get some bang for your buck, such as the daily double, exacta, and Pick-3.

The Pick-4

The Pick-4 is simply an extension of the Pick-3. Unfortunately, this bet isn't offered in California. The trick is to research this bet and find out how often it pays more than the corresponding parlay. If this bet is offered at your track, I suggest that you review the Pick-3 chapter and extend each of the strategies to include the fourth leg. Things will be the same except that the fair pay equation now becomes:

$$\text{Fair Pay} = \text{Bet Size} \times (\text{Odds } 1 + 1) \times (\text{Odds } 2 + 1) \times (\text{Odds } 3 + 1) \times (\text{Odds } 4 + 1)$$

This bet requires a much bigger bankroll than the Pick-3. (I must assume there are carry-overs from time to time. If so, it's always best to play when there is "free money.") I have to apologize for not being able to give too much insight into this bet. On the surface, it looks good.

The Pick-6

The Pick-6 includes the toughest races on the card. There are usually two and sometimes three playable races among the six. Let's assume we can get 50 percent going three deep in unplayable races and 60 percent by going two deep in playable races. If we were to invest in a Pick-6 with two playable races, we would have to invest in 3-3-3-3-2-2, or 324 combinations. The Pick-6 is a $2 bet in southern California, so we would invest $648. The probability of success is $.5 \times .5 \times .5 \times .5 \times .6 \times .6 = .0225$. The average Pick-6 payoff at Hollywood Park in 1993 was $22,366. Our expectation on this wager is:

$$E(x) = .0225 \times \$21,718 - .9775 \times \$648 = -\$144.77$$

That's negative $144.77 on a $648 investment, an edge of negative 22.3 percent. Thanks but no thanks.

Suppose the Pick-6 contained three playable races. We now would purchase a 3-3-3-2-2-2 ticket for $432. Our success probability is .5 × .5 × .5 × .6 × .6 × .6 = .027. Our expectation is:

$$E(x) = .027 \times \$21{,}934 - .973 \times \$432 = \$171.88$$

That's $171.88 on a $432 wager, for an edge of 39.79 percent.

Once again, a strategy suggests itself, if you are willing to invest $432 per day and be prepared for 194 consecutive losses! In order to invest in this strategy you will need a bankroll of at least $84,000.

We can reduce bet size and bankroll size by improving our handicapping. Suppose we could hit 50 percent going three deep on the two most difficult races, hit 50 percent going two deep on the tough races, and 60 percent going two deep on the playable races. We now would have to purchase a 3-3-2-2-2-2 ticket, which costs $288. The success probability is .5 × .5 × .5 × .5 × .6 × .6 = .0225. The expectation is:

$$E(x) = .0225 \times \$22{,}078 - .9775 \times \$288 = \$215.24$$

That's $215.24 on a $288 wager, an edge of 74.73%. In this example, our investment is less, but we must be prepared for 233 consecutive losses and have a bankroll of $67,000.

In playing the Pick-6 we must face a harsh reality: On most days we'll have to go three deep just to get 50 percent on at least two races. Let's accept this as an unavoidable condition. The other four races must be reasonably predictable. We should insist on at least one single. (A single is a race in which our top choice has a 40 percent or better probability of winning.) If this minimum condition isn't present, we pass on the Pick-6 unless there is a carry-over. The boldest Pick-6 we will attempt without a carry-over is a 3-3-2-2-2-1, ticket which costs $144. Our success probability is .5 × .5 × .5 × .5 × .6 × .4 = .0150. Our expectation is:

$$E(x) = .015 \times \$22{,}222 - .985 \times \$144 = \$191.49$$

That's $191.49 on a $144 wager, an edge of 132.98 percent. Even with this large edge we still have to be prepared for 351 consecutive losses and have a bankroll of $51,000.

From our discussion so far it should be apparent that the Pick-6 requires a healthy bankroll. To illustrate just how tough this bet really is, consider the average handicapper whose top pick wins 33 percent of the time. When he buys a single ticket, it has a success probability of .00129. The odds against it are 775 to 1 and he must be prepared to experience a 4,073-day losing streak. If he were to attend the races twice a week, it wouldn't be unreasonable for him to go 39 years between winning Pick-6 tickets.

Let's suppose we have two singles, two tough races, one hard race, and one playable race. Our ticket would be 3-3-2-2-1-1, which costs $72. Our success probability is $.5 \times .5 \times .5 \times .6 \times .4 \times .4 = .0120$. Our expectation is:

$$E(x) = .012 \times \$22,294 - .988 \times \$72 = \$196.39$$

That's $196.39 on a $72 bet, a 272.77 percent edge. We must be prepared for 439 consecutive losses and have a bankroll of $32,000.

The way I used to lose money in the Pick-6 was to insist upon at least two singles and no more than two tough races. The worst case was a 3-3-2-2-1-1 ticket for $72; the best case was a 2-2-2-2-1-1 ticket for $32. My original estimates were 60 percent in tough races (going three deep), 60 percent in playable races (going two deep), and 40 percent on singles. My calculated probability on a $72 ticket was $.6 \times .6 \times .6 \times .6 \times .4 \times .4 = .0207$. I used $20,000 as the average payoff. It's a pity that these estimates were so wildly optimistic and unrealistic. My expectation would have been:

$$E(x) = .0207 \times \$19,928 - .9793 \times \$72 = \$342$$

That's an edge of 475 percent. My original estimates suggested that I should get all six about once every fifty times and get a consolation every nine times. It wouldn't be unusual for 254 losses to intervene between winning wagers.

Needless to say, because of my insistence on at least two singles I didn't play too many Pick-6's. Typically, in a long meeting (70 racing days or more) I would get maybe six plays. Five years ago, during the Hollywood Park meeting, there were 11 days that qualified. In these 11 days, I didn't earn a nickel from the Pick-6, not even a consolation. I spent the eighties as a losing Pick-6 player.

As I reviewed my records, it became apparent that my original estimates were much too high. My singles hit only 34 percent of the time, my doubles 50 percent of the time, and my triples were okay. My strategy was fine—it was my basic assumptions that were wrong. When the Pick-3 came along in the late eighties, I forgot about the Pick-6. It was a nut I couldn't crack.

The first year that I ever make a profit on the Pick-6 was 1993. I'm almost embarrassed to tell you how I accomplished this. (I'll tell you later.)

Barry Meadow advises it's wiser to own 10 percent of a $720 ticket than 100 percent of a $72 ticket. (I can promise you that he's absolutely correct.) From the standpoint of consecutive losses he's definitely right because of the higher probabilities associated with higher-cost tickets. My experience confirms this. Most of the Pick-6 winners I know, including me, belong to syndicates. One of my colleagues is an accountant for one of the larger syndicates in southern California. This syndicate has had only one losing year in the past ten. It's earned profits ranging from $25,000 to almost $400,000 per year.

There's always an exception to every rule. A dear friend of mine is ahead more than $50,000 on the Pick-6. He always buys a share of a relatively inexpensive ticket. One of his scores was on a $288 ticket. He invested a total of $144. His share was worth a little more than $7,000. He continues to perform his magic. The reason he gets away with it is that he's one of the best handicappers in this country.

For most investors it's probably best to join a group. Each group member should have a specialty. The "junk race" specialist is an absolutely vital member. You must have at least one handicapper adept at maiden and low-class claiming races. It doesn't hurt to have a turf specialist if your track offers turf races. A group of four with diverse backgrounds is about ideal. If the group gets any larger, the vociferous members tend to dominate. You'll find to your surprise and amazement that consensus isn't what helps you win. It's the oddball horse you reluctantly put on the ticket because one of the members insisted that gets you the prize. It's also a good experience to have your views challenged. Having to explain yourself to others helps clarify things for yourself. The Pick-6 requires a large bankroll plus superior handicapping in order to effect positive expectation.

The best instructions on the topic of the Pick-6 appear in the works of Barry Meadow and Steven Crist. Please read Barry Meadow's discussion of the Pick-6 in his excellent book *Money Secrets at the Racetrack*. Also, listen to Steven Crist's Pick-6 presentation from *Handicapping EXPO '93*. (This audiotape can be ordered from Lawlor Productions in San Diego. Their toll-free phone number is 800-999-9992.)

I am happy to report that my association with Barry Meadow and his colleagues has been very productive. We play the Pick-6 as a group and play only when there is a carry-over. One year (1993) we hit the Pick-6 five times, plus had numerous consolations. Five out of six gets paid a consolation, albeit a relatively small one. Our group is ahead more than $70,000 for the year.

Meadow and Crist are winning investors when it comes to the Pick-6. Remember the principle of learning to do things from experts. We defined an expert as a person who is doing it. Experts are qualified to teach you how to win this bet. Why try to reinvent the wheel? Why not model yourself on successful practitioners? Meadow and Crist are excellent models. I am a net winner on the Pick-6, but it's due to my association with Barry Meadow.

The Place-Pick-9

I can't decide which is a worse bet, the Place-Pick-9 or the superfecta. Figuring the chances of a horse either winning or placing given its win odds is a bit of a nightmare. Calculate all the possible exacta combinations in the race, then add up the probabilities of the horse being in either the first or second spot. Let's do a very simple example using only a five-horse field. The fair odds line is as follows:

A	1.00-to-1
B	5.67-to-1
C	4.33-to-1
D	15.00-to-1
E	9.00-to-1

The probability line is:

$$P(A) = .5000$$
$$P(B) = .1500$$
$$P(C) = .1875$$
$$P(D) = .0625$$
$$P(E) = .1000$$

Let's enumerate all the exacta probabilities:

AB	$.5 \times (.15 \div .5)$	$= .15000$
AC	$.5 \times (.1875 \div .5)$	$= .18750$
AD	$.5 \times (.0625 \div .5)$	$= .06250$
AE	$.5 \times (.1 \div .5)$	$= .10000$
BA	$.15 \times (.5 \div .85)$	$= .08824$
BC	$.15 \times (.1875 \div .85)$	$= .03309$
BD	$.15 \times (.0625 \div .85)$	$= .01103$
BE	$.15 \times (.1 \div .85)$	$= .01765$
CA	$.1875 \times (.5 \div .8125)$	$= .11538$
CB	$.1875 \times (.15 \div .8125)$	$= .03462$
CD	$.1875 \times (.0625 \div .8125)$	$= .01442$
CE	$.1875 \times (.1 \div .8125)$	$= .02308$
DA	$.0625 \times (.5 \div .9375)$	$= .03333$
DB	$.0625 \times (.15 \div .9375)$	$= .01000$
DC	$.0625 \times (.1875 \div .9375)$	$= .01250$
DE	$.0625 \times (.1 \div .9375)$	$= .00666$
EA	$.1 \times (.5 \div .9)$	$= .05555$
EB	$.1 \times (.15 \div .9)$	$= .01666$
EC	$.1 \times (.1875 \div .9)$	$= .02083$
ED	$.1 \times (.0625 \div .9)$	$= .00694$

To compute the probability that horse A will either win or place, we simply add up all the combinations involving A in either the first or second spot. They are: AB, AC, AD, AE, BA, CA, DA, and EA. They add to .7925.

A little computational short cut you can use is to consider all of your noncontenders as a single horse. For example, suppose your line on a race was:

A   2-to-1

B   3-to-1

C   4-to-1

The probability line is as follows:

$$P(A) = .3333$$
$$P(B) = .2500$$
$$P(C) = \underline{.2000}$$
$$.7833$$

Since your total win line adds to .7833, create a horse that has a .2167 probability of winning. Your new probability line looks like this:

$$P(A) = .3333$$
$$P(B) = .2500$$
$$P(C) = .2000$$
$$P(D) = .2167$$

Now enumerate all the exacta combinations for a four-horse race. There are only 12.

AB	$.3333 \times (.25 \div .6667)$	$= .1250$
AC	$.3333 \times (.2 \div .6667)$	$= .1000$
AD	$.3333 \times (.2167 \div .6667)$	$= .1083$
BA	$.25 \times (.3333 \div .75)$	$= .1111$
BC	$.25 \times (.2 \div .75)$	$= .0667$
BD	$.25 \times (.2167 \div .75)$	$= .0722$
CA	$.2 \times (.3333 \div .8)$	$= .0833$
CB	$.2 \times (.25 \div .8)$	$= .0625$
CD	$.2 \times (.2167 \div .8)$	$= .0542$
DA	$.2167 \times (.3333 \div .7833)$	$= .0922$
DB	$.2167 \times (.25 \div .7833)$	$= .0692$
DC	$.2167 \times (.2 \div .7833)$	$= .0553$

If you were to single A in the Place-Pick-9, this method incorrectly suggests that you would have a 61.99 percent chance of hitting this leg. If you were to use both A and B in the Place-Pick-9, this method says that your chances of hitting are now .8905. (Add up all the combinations that contain A or B in the first or second spot.) You can't go more than two deep because all the combinations contain an A, B, or C. If you want to go more than two deep, your odds line must be more accurate, and you must include the win probability of at least one more horse. The rule is simple: If you want to consider n horses in the Place-Pick-9, you must make a line for at least n + 2 horses.

It should be apparent that this method is very optimistic. We know that 2-to-1 favorites win or place around 52 percent of the time. The reason this method's approximation breaks down is because it assumes that the size of the field is only four! Hence, we must make a correction. Reduce the estimates by 20 percent and you'll have a fairly accurate approximation of the Place-Pick-9 probability for any horse. In this case, horse A had a computed 61.99 percent chance. If we multiply by this number by .8 (which is the same as reducing by 20 percent), we have a conservative estimate of 49.6 percent. Horses A and B had a computed chance of .8905 of getting in the Place-Pick-9. Multiply this number by .8 and you get a 71.2 percent chance of success. We now have a conservative estimate that is supported by my empirical data.

Suppose we bet each Place-Pick-9 by going two deep in each leg using our top two choices. Furthermore, let's say we could hit 70 percent of the time using only two choices (a stretch assumption because of chaos races). Our Place-Pick-9 ticket would have cost us $512. The average Place-Pick-9 payoff at Hollywood Park in 1993 was $5,898.84. We would use two selections per race for nine races. Our chances of hitting the bet were 4.04 percent. Our expectation on the bet was as follows:

$$E(x) = .0404 \times \$5,386.84 - .9596 \times \$512 = -\$273.69$$

Our edge is a negative 53.45 percent return. (We divide negative $273.69 by the $512 bet size.)

This is a sucker bet of the highest order. Let me share some interesting statistics with you. The Place-Pick-9 at Hollywood Park has ranged from $49.10 to $45,274.60. The average payoff was $5,898.84. If we throw out all payoffs more than $20,000, we have a range of $49.10 to $19,378.20 and an average payoff of $3,828.02. More than 33 percent of the time, the Place-Pick-9 paid less than $1,000.

A $3,828.02 average payoff sounds like a generous number. (It's not. It's actually very parsimonious.) This is more than a 3,800-to-1 payoff. The trouble is, you need a much bigger payoff just to break even. On most race days you have three playable races, five contentious races, and at least one chaos race. The minimum ticket would be three singles, five doubles, and one triple. This ticket costs $96. We'll assume that a single has a 52 percent chance of hitting, a double in a contentious race a 60 percent chance, and a triple in a chaos race a 70 percent chance. Therefore, the probability of this $96 ticket hitting is $(.52)^3 \times (.6)^5 \times (.7) = .0077$. This is a less than 1 percent chance, which means that the Place-Pick-9 must pay $131 for each dollar wagered—in this case it must pay $12,543.16 just to be a fair bet. Needless to say, it rarely pays this amount. Leave this one to suckers.

The Place-Pick-9 and the superfecta are terrible bets. The Pick-6 is a wonderful bet if you have a monstrous bankroll or belong to a syndicate. I suspect that the Pick-4 is a good opportunity but lack any experience with it.

The superexotics offer an opportunity to move a lot of money through the mutuels. And that's the name of the game, once you've determined you have a positive edge on a particular type of wager. (I don't think it's easy to get a positive edge in the superfecta or in the Place-Pick-9.) So that leaves the Pick-4 and the Pick-6. Study these opportunities. Do the research for your track. Determine the bankroll size necessary to avoid gambler's ruin. Then decide if you can use these opportunities to move the appropriate amount of money through the mutuels to assure the size income you require.

My vote for best bet at the racetrack goes to the Pick-3. Unlike the Pick-6, it doesn't require a six-digit bankroll, plus it's a lot easier to hit. My next vote goes to the daily double, followed by the exacta. It should be axiomatic that you shouldn't touch an exotic until you can show a flat-bet profit on your win bets.

Please realize that the truth of betting strategy never changes. It's based upon mathematics. The truth of mathematics is as close to certain as you can get on this planet. Study this book as you would a textbook. Also, study Barry Meadow's *Money Secrets at the Racetrack*. Read these books over and over until you get it. Master each type of bet, starting with win wagering. Set very specific profit goals and write yourself a plan to achieve them.

Your betting skills will make all the difference in the world. As I said before, an average handicapper with superior betting skills will outperform a superior handicapper with average betting skills every time. I know. Many of my students and colleagues are much better handicappers than I am, yet they don't make nearly as much money at the track as I do. It always amazes me when I spend time with them, which usually happens at my "Winning Weekend" seminars. I meet players who are really good handicappers but admit that their betting skills need work. Their results are less than optimum. I should be attending their seminars when it comes to picking horses. But, alas, the name of this game is picking bets, not horses.

In the next chapter we'll look at a typical day at the races. Unfortunately, I didn't write down all the possible payoffs. I usually do, but this day was part of our *ALL-IN-ONE* national conference, and I spent most of the time between races chatting with students and going over betting lines.

WORKSHOP

We're now ready to do battle against the odds. What follows is an actual day at the races. Please consider this an opportunity to put what you've learned into practice.

There is one further distinction that I would like to make. Races come in three flavors: orderly, semi-orderly, and chaotic. An orderly race contains at least one contender who can run to the pars and the win profile for the track. A semi-orderly race has at least one contender who can run within two ticks of the par and the win profile. A chaos race has no contenders who can run within two ticks of the par and win profile. Major bets can only be made in orderly races. All non-orderly races demand a reduced bet size because of their unpredictability. Place-and-show bets aren't even considered in chaos races.

Let's now go to the track and apply the principles of proper money management. For each race, you'll be provided with past performances, a fair-odds line, and the actual public win odds. Where appropriate, daily double and exacta probable payoffs will be given. Use this information to make your own betting decisions as if you were actually at the track and had handicapped the races in the exact same manner we did. Please don't get hung up on handicapping considerations. Just make sure that every bet you make carries a positive edge. Then consult our analysis to see which bets we actually made. Please don't think that your analysis must match ours. Betting strategy involves temperament as well as science.

A major point of learning by doing is to make mistakes, then to learn from them. Your only concern should be not learning from the mistakes you might make in this workshop. It's a lot more costly to make a mistake at the track with real money.

The example races consist of the racing program offered at Hollywood Park on Saturday, December 4, 1993. That day at Hollywood Park, my staff and I hosted a large group of *ALL-IN-ONE* users who came from all parts of North America to attend our annual *ALL-IN-ONE* national conference. The betting lines were generated by *ALL-IN-ONE* and were based on the contender and paceline selection of my staff handicapper, Kitts Anderson.

Before we begin, let's take a look at the betting options offered on this 12-race card, which consisted of 10 live races plus two simulcasts from Bay Meadows in Northern California. In addition to win, place, and show betting, we can bet the exacta on every race and the quinella on every live race. These bets require a $2 minimum. In live races with seven or more starters, we can bet the trifecta. (In the day's last live race, the trifecta is replaced by the superfecta.) Both the trifecta and the superfecta have $1 minimums. There are two $2 daily doubles, on the day's first two and last two races. A $3 Pick-3 begins with each live race except, of course, the last two races. Finally, we have a $2 Pick-6 on live races four through nine, plus a "Bet-a-Buck" ($1 Place-Pick-9) on live races one through nine. Quite a full and varied wagering menu. We truly will be able to put everything we've learned into practice.

Now, imagine you're at Hollywood Park about ten minutes before post time for the first race. In your hands you've got the *Daily Racing Form*, *ALL-IN-ONE*'s printouts and betting lines, and the official track program. You take your seat, spread out your information resources, and manage a quick glance at the toteboard. Here are the past performances for the upcoming race:

Hollywood Park

1 **1 1/16 MILES.** (1:40) CLAIMING. Purse $17,000. 3-year-olds and upward. Weights: 3-year-olds, 119 lbs. Older, 122 lbs. Non-winners of two races at a mile or over since October 4, allowed 3 lbs. Such a race since then, 6 lbs. Claiming price $25,000; if for $22,500, 2 lbs. (Races when entered for $20,000 or less not considered.)

1 1/16 MILES
FINISH▲ ▲START

Payand Payand Pay
Own: Litt Brothers
BLACK C A (50 8 8 6 .16) $25,000
Gr. g. 5
Sire: Press The Tab
Dam: Zenica-Fr (Faraway Son)
Br: Margulies David W (NJ)
Tr: Assinesi Paul D (4 1 3 0 .25)
L 119

Lifetime Record: 54 6 6 8 $104,688
1993 15 4 0 6 $54,600 Turf 9 0 0 1 $1,970
1992 14 0 0 1 $2,695 Wet 2 0 1 0 $4,240
Hol 7 1 0 2 $9,700 Dist 6 1 1 0 $17,740

7Nov93-7SA fst 1 :233 :471 1:112 1:364 3+ Clm 35000 85 6 5 44 42½ 2½ 11¼ Black C A LB 114 fb 10.00 86-11 Payand Payand Pay1141¼ Davus116¾ The Cleaners117nk Drifted in late 7
17Oct93-1SA fst 1 :23 :464 1:11 1:361 3+ Clm c-25000 83 6 9 85½ 76 66 43¼ Flores D R LB 116 b 3.40 86-12 Cocooning1161¾ Le Axe A L'ame1171 Ivoreto116½ Wide trip 9
Claimed from Carava & Osterberg, Carava Jack Trainer
3Oct93-4Fpx fst 1 1/16 :224 :462 1:112 1:433 3+ Clm 20000 91 4 5 43½ 3nk 1½ 13 Flores D R LB 116 b *1.50 90-11 PayndPyndPy1163 Bbyitscoldoutside115hd TheDrouller116hd Clearly best 5
1Sep93-5Dmr fst 7f :231 :46 1:104 1:224 3+ Clm 12500 88 1 9 73½ 52¼ 2½ 14 Flores D R LB 117 b 4.10 86-16 Payand Payand Pay1174 Courageous Marine119hd Cesar Eduardo1172 9
Off slowly, boxed in 3 1/2-1/8, handily
16Aug93-1Dmr fst 6f :221 :451 :573 1:094 3+ Clm 12500 88 2 7 711 78¾ 76¼ 3½ Flores D R LB 117 b 19.20 90-11 Sinceriffic117nk El Toreo117hd Payand Payand Pay117½ Off slowly, wide 7
2Aug93-4Dmr fst 7f :224 :453 1:094 1:222 3+ Clm 12500 81 7 6 74½ 75¼ 64¾ 33¼ Flores D R LB 115 b 3.10 85-10 Otay Mesa1152 Terrific Trip1151½ Payand Payand Pay1153¼ Very wide trip 8
24Jly93-9Hol fst 6½f :214 :442 1:084 1:151 Clm 12500 78 3 12 1213 1210 98 46¼ Flores D R LB 117 b 7.90 87-08 To Be A Saros1124 El Toreo117½ Fire Commander1171¾ 7 Wide stretch 12
4Jly93-5Hol fst 6½f :214 :441 1:092 1:16 Clm 12500 86 9 8 88 88 65½ 3nk Delahoussaye E LB 117 b 4.30 89-11 Keep Clear112no Midnight Leader117nk Payand PayandPay117no Wide trip 9
24Jun93-5Hol fst 6f :214 :444 :564 1:092 Clm 12500 78 4 10 108½ 107¾ 97½ 55¼ Delahoussaye E LB 117 fb 11.30 88-07 High Mesa1121½ Dr. Hyde117¾ Earplug1171¾ 7 Wide stretch 10
28May93-5Hol fst 7f :221 :45 1:093 1:224 Clm 14000 69 7 11 118¾ 76¾ 89 79¼ Lopez A D LB 115 fb 26.10 81-14 No Commitment1171½ Turn TheKey1172¾ GallantGuy1171¾ Off slowly, wide 12
WORKOUTS: Nov 27 SA 4f fst :482 B 15/37 Nov 18 SA 4f fst :462 H 2/27 Oct 12 Hol 3f fst :35 H 3/13 Sep 26 Hol 5f fst :593 H 2/40 Sep 19 Hol 5f fst 1:002 H 3/19 Sep 11 Dmr 4f fst :484 H 21/41

Davus
Own: Buss Jerry
NAKATANI C S (60 14 10 13 .23) $25,000
B. g. 5
Sire: Naevus (Mr. Prospector)
Dam: Elegant Beauty (Norcliffe)
Br: Straub Cecilia (Cal)
Tr: Buss Jim (6 0 2 1 .00)
L 116

Lifetime Record: 39 8 7 5 $201,645
1993 18 3 4 2 $88,445 Turf 11 1 1 1 $40,150
1992 10 1 2 2 $46,900 Wet 3 1 0 1 $22,450
Hol 8 2 3 1 $55,600 Dist 6 3 1 0 $58,600

7Nov93-7SA fst 1 :233 :471 1:112 1:364 3+ Clm 40000 83 7 3 31 1hd 1½ 21¼ Nakatani C S LB 116 b 5.80 85-11 Payand Payand Pay1141¼ Davus116¾ The Cleaners117nk Lugged in 1/8 7
24Oct93-9SA fst 1 1/16 :231 :464 1:104 1:422 3+ Clm c-32000 80 7 2 2½ 2hd 22 66½ Delahoussaye E LB 116 b *1.80 85-08 Quintana1164 Lovely One116no Tell Boy1161 Weakened 9
Claimed from Jarvis & Lew, Marshall Robert W Trainer
14Oct93-3SA fst 1 1/16 :24 :472 1:112 1:422 3+ Clm 40000 88 5 2 1½ 1hd 1hd 2½ Delahoussaye E LB 116 b 2.00 91-09 Doulab's Image116½ Davus1161¼ Dixie Venture1161¼ Held well 5
24Sep93-9Fpx fst *1⅛ :46 1:124 1:38 1:504 3+ Alw 25000s 82 3 4 41½ 31 3½ 34 Lopez A D LB 114 b 2.40 84-12 The Cleaners1142 Lil Orphan Moonie1162 Davus1142½ Bid, weakened 6
21Aug93-9Dmr fm 1 Ⓣ :221 :452 1:10 1:352 3+ Clm 50000 61 6 1 1hd 1hd 63½ 815¾ Nakatani C S LB 117 b 8.70 78-04 Eton Lad1171¾ Fantastic Don117no Red Monsoon117no Stopped 9
22Jly93-3Hol fst 1 1/16 :234 :472 1:113 1:421 Alw 32000s 96 2 1 11 11½ 11½ 12 Delahoussaye E LB 116 b *.90 90-19 Davus1162 Coco's Main Man115nk Careening For Paul1153¼ Ridden out 5
15Jly93-8Hol fm 1 Ⓣ :232 :463 1:101 1:343 Alw 26000s 92 5 3 21½ 21 2½ 2nk Nakatani C S LB 115 b *1.30 92-09 Shaynoor115nk Davus115no Qasar122hd Sharp effort 5
4Jly93-1Hol fst 1 1/16 :231 :462 1:102 1:42 Clm 25000 96 6 2 21½ 2hd 1½ 14½ Nakatani C S LB 116 b 3.30 91-13 Davus1164½ No Commitment1175 Lil OrphanMoonie1091 As rider pleased 6
2Jun93-7Hol fst 6½f :22 :443 1:091 1:154 Clm c-25000 77 4 6 1½ 3½ 31½ 65¼ Solis A LB 117 fb 2.90 85-10 Racer Rex1181¾ King Raj117½ Heat1172 Weakened 7
Claimed from Herold Stephen G, Salazar Marco P Trainer
18May93-2Hol fst 7f :223 :451 1:092 1:214 Clm 32000 92 5 3 21 2hd 11 21¼ Solis A LB 117 b 6.30 94-08 Chief Dare1171¼ Davus1171 Sondheimer1175½ Outfinished 8
WORKOUTS: Oct 10 Hol 5f fst 1:01 H 11/14 Oct 4 Hol 4f fst :492 H 4/10 Sep 18 Hol 5f fst :592 H 7/12 Sep 12 Dmr 5f fst 1:001 B 13/44 Sep 6 Dmr 4f fst :48 B 11/40

Lackington (Chi)
Own: Clear Vly Stbl & Scofield & Winner
SOLIS A (67 9 12 12 .13) $25,000
Ch. h. 5
Sire: Laguardia (Lyphard)
Dam: Espinada (Tantoul)
Br: Haras Santa Amelia (Chi)
Tr: Shulman Sanford (24 4 4 2 .17)
L 116

Lifetime Record: 28 5 3 4 $148,841
1993 10 0 1 3 $25,750 Turf 23 5 1 3 $127,191
1992 11 1 2 1 $54,175 Wet 1 0 1 0 $7,600
Hol 2 0 0 0 Dist 2 0 1 0 $8,500

28Nov93-1Hol fst 7f :214 :44 1:091 1:22 3+ Clm 45000 45 6 3 1hd 31 69¼ 720¼ Valenzuela P A LB 117 22.60 74-09 Sharp Bandit117nk Misting Rain1171½ Alta Blue1121¼ Gave way 7
10Nov93-3SA fm *6½f Ⓣ :214 :441 1:074 1:141 3+ Clm 80000 60 3 4 52¼ 75½ 78¼ 713¼ Flores D R LB 116 17.00 74-13 Echo Of Yesterday1163 C. T. Express1081 Regal Groom1172 Outrun 7
11Oct93-5SA fst 6½f ⊗ :214 :442 1:084 1:152 3+ Clm 75000 78 3 7 73 45 36½ 3¾ Flores D R LB 114 23.90 88-11 Bet On The Bay109¾ Regal Groom1175½ Lackington1147½ Best of rest 7
24Jly93-3Hol fm 5½f Ⓣ :22 :443 :562 1:024 Clm 62500 69 1 6 31½ 32 87 89¼ Pedroza M A LB 117 16.90 82-09 Struttin Joey P.112½ Shafouri117½ Zephyr Art1172 Gave way 8
20Jun93-9Hol fm 5½f Ⓣ :214 :44 :554 1:021 3+ Clm 62500 67 1 9 97½ 86½ 88¼ 810 Pincay L Jr LB 117 8.20 84-06 B. G.'s Drone117¾ Blue Tiger116¾ Grover's Mill1192¾ Outrun 10
23May93-7Hol fm 5½f Ⓣ :22 :442 :56 1:02 Clm 62500 90 1 4 31½ 31½ 31½ 3¾ McCarron C J LB 117 15.80 94-05 Grover's Mill117nk Harlem's Boy117½ Lackington1171¾ Sharp try 6
18Apr93-8SA fm 1⅛ Ⓣ :461 1:094 1:343 1:471 Clm 80000 57 5 3 21½ 21½ 811 818 McCarron C J LB 115 17.20 65-12 River Rhythm1161 Scheimer1151¾ Lanner115½ Brushed start 8
13Mar93-5SA fm *6½f Ⓣ :214 :44 1:071 1:131 Clm 80000 78 2 11 51¾ 63¾ 94¼ 128¾ McCarron C J LB 115 8.90 83-08 Exemplary Leader117no Record Boom1142 Blue Tiger116½ Weakened 12
5Mar93-7SA fm *6½f Ⓣ :214 :441 1:08 1:141 Clm 100000 92 2 6 32 33 32½ 31 McCarron C J LB 115 17.10 86-13 Dancing Boy115¾ Shirkee115hd Lackington1151¾ Edged for 2nd 8
14Feb93-5SA fm *6½f Ⓣ :214 :434 1:072 1:134 Clm 75000 92 4 10 64¼ 74¼ 64 21¼ Stevens G L LB 115 43.20 87-12 Rocket Gibralter1164½ Lackington115½ Dancing Boy114½ Good effort 12
WORKOUTS: ●Nov 18 Hol 3f fst :344 H 1/20 Nov 7 SA 4f fst :464 H 3/37 Oct 31 SA 4f fst :472 H 5/59 Oct 24 SA 4f fst :482 H 21/55 Oct 20 SA 3f fst :354 H 6/36 Oct 7 SA 3f fst :352 Hg 2/28

Cocooning
Own: Rehak & Skinner & Weigel
VALENZUELA P A (54 6 10 2 .11) $25,000
Dk. b or br g. 4
Sire: Saros*Fr (Sassafras-Fr)
Dam: Regal Air (Olympiad King)
Br: Shima Mr-Mrs R J (Cal)
Tr: Hess R B Jr (13 3 2 1 .23)
L 119

Lifetime Record: 35 8 5 7 $109,313
1993 17 4 4 0 $56,320 Turf 0 0 0 0
1992 17 4 1 7 $52,825 Wet 1 1 0 0 $7,150
Hol 11 2 0 5 $32,525 Dist 0 0 0 0

7Nov93-4SA fst 1 :23 :463 1:11 1:354 3+ Clm c-20000 95 5 1 1hd 1hd 12 2½ Nakatani C S LB 118 f 4.70 90-11 Potrichan118½ Cocooning1183½ Garmanni1162 Came in start 8
Claimed from Burke Gary W & Timothy R, Mitchell Mike Trainer
17Oct93-1SA fst 1 :23 :464 1:11 1:361 3+ Clm 25000 89 3 1 1½ 12 12½ 11¾ Nakatani C S LB 116 f *2.60 89-12 Cocooning1161¾ Le Axe A L'ame1171 Ivoreto116½ Gamely 9
7Oct93-4SA fst 1 [illegible] 3+ Clm c-20000 83 2 1 11 11½ 11½ 2no Solis A B 116 f 3.10 88-16 Tell Boy117no Cocooning1161¼ Cheyenne Gold110no 9
Stumbled start, bumped late; Claimed from Inside Track Racing, Shulman Sanford Trainer
18Sep93-10Fpx fst 6f :213 :444 :571 1:094 3+ Clm 25000 67 2 7 67½ 65½ 88¾ 69 Lopez A D B 116 f 4.20 89-09 U. S.OfAmerica1162 BriskSailing1162 CandymanBee116nk Wide 1st trurn 10
27Aug93-2Dmr fst 6f :221 :451 :57 1:093 3+ ⓈClm c-16000 79 9 1 12 12½ 11½ 12½ Valenzuela P A B 117 f *2.00 91-11 Cocooning1172½ Evil Wizard117¾ The Drouller1171 9
Wide, driving, jumped mirror reflection finish; Claimed from Aldabbagh Sam H, Aldabbagh Sam H Trainer
18Aug93-1Dmr fst 6½f :221 :451 1:101 1:162 3+ Clm 25000 75 2 5 4¾ 3nk 2½ 56¼ Castaneda M B 117 f 8.90 83-14 Fistylee1172½ Joboc115hd Heat1172 Weakened 8
9Jly93-8Hol fst 6f :221 :451 :571 1:094 Alw 12500s 91 1 4 31½ 4½ 3½ 41¼ Castanon A L B 115 f 12.30 90-15 Wild Tech115nk Screen Tale115½ Book Publisher122½ Inside trip 8
4Jly93-6Hol fst 6½f :222 :45 1:093 1:154 Clm 20000 89 3 1 1hd 1½ 1½ 11¾ Castanon A L B 117 f 16.60 90-11 ⒹCocooning1171¾ Sondheimer117½ Steady Silver117hd 10
Impeded foes lane; Disqualified and placed 4th
6Jun93-4Hol gd 6f :221 :453 :582 1:111 Clm c-16000 64 2 6 52 52¾ 54 47¾ Garcia J A B 119 f 2.80 76-16 Safe To Say117¾ Major Howey1172 Fire Commander1175 5 Wide stretch 6
Claimed from Thompson Chris, Puhich Michael Trainer
27May93-4Hol fst 5½f :221 :451 :571 1:032 Clm 20000 68 6 8 89 88¾ 89¼ 69¼ Sorenson D B 117 f 9.70 86-12 Sinceriffic1171¼ Regalstaff1191¼ Random Brown117no 8
Poor start, lost iron briefly
WORKOUTS: Nov 28 Hol 5f fst 1:022 H 30/36 Nov 21 Hol 4f fst :484 H 20/38 Sep 30 SA 5f fst 1:014 H 20/48 ●Sep 24 SA 3f fst :343 H 1/9 Sep 11 Dmr 5f fst :594 H 4/40

Lovely One (Arg)
Own: Team Green
LOPEZ A D (13 1 2 0 .08) $25,000
B. h. 6
Sire: Un Reitre (Nonoalco)
Dam: Very Lovely (Vervain)
Br: Haras La Borinquena (Arg)
Tr: Stain Roger M (7 1 1 1 .14)
L 116

Lifetime Record: 44 4 7 4 $136,779
1993 13 1 2 2 $42,025 Turf 21 1 3 1 $50,563
1992 10 1 2 0 $40,300 Wet 2 1 0 0 $21,450
Hol 3 0 0 0 $950 Dist 11 1 2 1 $38,600

26Nov93-6Hol fst 1 1/16 :243 :482 1:114 1:413 3+ Clm 32000 74 5 6 66¾ 68¼ 610 613 Antley C W LB 116 7.70 80-09 Skylaunch1167½ Tell Boy117½ Dixie Venture1171¼ Outrun 6
24Oct93-9SA fst 1 1/16 :231 :464 1:104 1:422 3+ Clm 32000 85 2 9 916 913 87½ 24 Lopez A D LB 116 19.00 88-08 Quintana1164 Lovely One116no Tell Boy1161 Finished well 9
14Oct93-3SA fst 1 1/16 :24 :472 1:112 1:422 3+ Clm 40000 75 2 5 57¼ 55 54¾ 58 Gonzalez S5 LB 111 8.10 84-09 Doulab's Image116½ Davus1161¼ Dixie Venture1161¼ No threat 5
2Oct93-4BM fm *1⅛ Ⓣ :473 1:123 1:364 1:454 3+ Bay Mdws H-G2 82 4 6 56½ 65 78¾ 79 Meza R Q LB 112 b 40.60 94-04 Slew Of Damascus1141¼ Fast Cure115no Lissitki112hd No threat 7
18Sep93-11Fpx fst 1 1/16 :23 :462 1:104 1:422 3+ P D Shepherd50k 90 2 7 78 67½ 66 55 Castaneda M B 115 b 23.10 91-11 Southern Wish122¾ Native Boundary1152½ Big Pal1221¼ Mild late bid 7
5Sep93-4Dmr fst 1 1/16 :24 :482 1:122 1:423 3+ Clm c-40000 80 1 8 87½ 86½ 86 75¼ Delahoussaye E B 117 7.40 84-11 His Legacy112½ Crystal Wes1152½ Doulab's Image117½ Wide trip 8
Claimed from Di Nella Enzo Alfredo, Moreno Henry Trainer
22Aug93-7Dmr fst 1 1/16 :231 :471 1:113 1:43 3+ Clm 32000 85 2 5 58 56½ 43½ 21¼ Velasquez C H B 117 13.20 86-16 Moofer1171¼ Lovely One117hd World In My Eyes1172 4 Wide stretch 5
22May93-4Hol fst 1⅛ :482 1:123 1:371 1:492 Alw 40000s 74 1 6 68 67 610 611¼ Lopez A D B 115 27.10 79-09 Treat Tobeatyafeet1172½ Icy Resolution115nk The Cleaners1161 Trailed 6
24Apr93-9Hol fm 1⅛ Ⓣ :473 1:111 1:344 1:463 Clm 50000 82 2 6 76 85¾ 97½ 96 Montano M5 B 111 43.90 85-08 Polar Boy115nk Aromatic1131¾ Military Shot116½ Outrun 12
27Mar93-3SA gd 1 1/16 :233 :472 1:114 1:431 Clm 60000 84 3 7 78¼ 87¾ 79¼ 610¼ Montano M5 B 109 19.10 77-23 IcyResolution1141 PrinceOfHoney115½ Efervescente1172½ Bumped start 8
WORKOUTS: Nov 23 SA 5f fst 1:004 H 17/25 Nov 17 SA 5f fst 1:021 H 19/27 Sep 27 SA 5f fst 1:014 H 32/64 Sep 13 Dmr 4f fst :473 Hg 7/41 Sep 4 Dmr 3f fst :361 H 6/18

ALL-IN-ONE's output for race is as follows:

```
4DEC93                              HOL                    8.5 furlongs dirt
Race #1                                                          6 starters
C25,000                                                   Age: 3+years, Male
--------------------------------------INPUT DATA-----------------------------

                   #  #  #  #  $'S                              1st C  2nd C  Final
Horse name         ST W  P  S  Earned Date     Trk Dist. S     time   time   time
----------------------------------------------------------------------------------
PAYAND PAYAND PAY  15 4  0  6  54600 7NOV93     SA  8.000 D     47.1   111.2  136.4
DAVUS              18 3  4  2  88445 7NOV93     SA  8.000 D     47.1   111.2  136.4
LACKINGTON-CH      10 0  1  3  25750 28NOV93    HOL 7.000 D     21.4   44.0   122.0
COCOONING          17 4  4  0  56320 7NOV93     SA  8.000 D     46.3   111.0  135.4
LOVELY ONE-AR      13 1  2  2  42025 26NOV93    SA  8.500 D     46.4   110.4  142.2


                                1st C  2nd C  Final
Horse name         Class Lvl    B.L.   B.L.   B.L.    SR   Var
----------------------------------------------------------------------
PAYAND PAYAND PAY  C40,000      4.00   2.50   0.00    86   11.0
DAVUS              C40,000      1.00   0.00   1.25    85   11.0
LACKINGTON-CH      C50,000      0.00   1.00   20.25   74   9.0
COCOONING          C20,000      0.00   0.00   0.50    90   11.0
LOVELY ONE-AR      C32,000      16.00  13.75  4.00    88   8.0


-------------------------------------BETTING LINE----------------------------

                   -------Rankings--------          Betting    Fair     Fair
Horse name         PEH H-I THAAI P-H ESP  Rating    Line       Place $  Show $
----------------------------------------------------------------------------------
PAYAND PAYAND PAY  2   2   1    1   4      73.27     4-1
DAVUS              1   3   3    3   3      73.29     4-1
COCOONING          3   4   4    2   5      71.88     9-2
LOVELY ONE-AR      5   1   2    4   2      70.88     5-1
LACKINGTON-CH      4   5   5    5   1      70.04     5-1


-------------------------------------EXACTA GRID-----------------------------

             |PAYAND PAYAND P| DAVUS       | COCOONING    | LOVELY ONE-AR |
-------------+---------------+-------------+--------------+---------------+
PAYAND PAYAND| . . . . . . . |   35    88  |   39    98   |   43    107   |
             | . . . . . . . |             |              |               |
             | . . . . . . . |             |              |               |
-------------+---------------+-------------+--------------+---------------+
DAVUS        |   36    88    | . . . . . . |   40    99   |   43    107   |
             |               | . . . . . . |              |               |
             |               | . . . . . . |              |               |
-------------+---------------+-------------+--------------+---------------+
COCOONING    |   41    101   |   41    101 | . . . . . . .|   49    123   |
             |               |             | . . . . . . .|               |
             |               |             | . . . . . . .|               |
-------------+---------------+-------------+--------------+---------------+
LOVELY ONE-AR|   45    112   |   45    112 |   50    125  | . . . . . . . |
             |               |             |              | . . . . . . . |
             |               |             |              | . . . . . . . |
-------------+---------------+-------------+--------------+---------------+


4DEC93                              HOL                    8.5 furlongs dirt
Race #1                                                          6 starters
C25,000                                                   Age: 3+years, Male
------------------------------------SPEED/PACE SUMMARY-----------------------

Race Type:       Chaos Race
Race Profile:    47.04  110.85  142.41   Winners' Pace Profile: FRONT
Ability Par:     94.66                   Pace Contention Point:  0.59 lengths

Projected Times:                         Ability  Balance  Last  Proj  Con-
                 1st C  2nd C   Fin C     Time     Time     Frac  Pace  tender
----------------------------------------------------------------------------------
PAYAND PAYAND PAY 47.97 111.67* 143.23    95.38    100.11   31.56 REAR  N
DAVUS             47.40 111.21* 143.48    95.01    100.57   32.27 REAR  N
COCOONING         46.62 110.81* 142.33    95.00    99.79    31.52 REAR  N
LOVELY ONE-AR     49.40 112.34* 141.29    95.28    97.43    28.95 REAR  N
LACKINGTON-CH     46.00 109.65  146.33    93.31    103.41   36.68 FRONT N
```

```
------------------------------------PACE GRAPH------------------------------------
        Profile:              47.04              110.85              142.41
     Front Runner:            46.00              109.65              141.29
Horse name                      1C                  2C                    F
PAYAND PAYAND PAY --------X---------+ ---------X--------(+ --------X---------+
DAVUS             -----------X------+ ----------X------(+ -------X---------+
COCOONING         -------------X--+ -----------X----(+ ------------X----+
LOVELY ONE-AR     -X----------------+ ------X----------(+ ------------------X
LACKINGTON-CH     -----------------X ----------------(X -------------------+
```

The morning line for the contenders in this race is:

Payand Payand Pay	3-1
Davus	5-2
Cocooning	2-1
Lovely One	5-1
Lackington	10-1

The toteboard displays the following win odds:

Payand Payand Pay	2-1
Davus	2-1
Cocooning	5-2
Lovely One	7-1
Lackington	15-1

Davus is the slight favorite. He has a few more dollars bet on him to win than Payand Payand Pay does.

The exacta probable pays are as follows:

Payand Payand Pay–Davus	$ 21
Payand Payand Pay–Cocooning	24
Payand Payand Pay–Lovely One	55
Payand Payand Pay–Lackington	110
Davus–Payand Payand Pay	20
Davus-Cocooning	21
Davus-Lovely One	48
Davus-Lackington	96
Cocooning–Payand Payand Pay	25
Cocooning–Davus	22
Cocooning–Lovely One	59
Cocooning–Lackington	118

Lovely One–Payand Payand Pay	65
Lovely One–Davus	59
Lovely One–Cocooning	70
Lovely One–Lackington	320
Lackington–Payand Payand Pay	140
Lackington-Davus	127
Lackington-Cocooning	148
Lackington–Lovely One	338

You now have the necessary information to make betting decisions in the win and exacta pools. Before consulting our analysis, please take a few moments now to construct your bets in these pools.

A quick glance at the toteboard won't be sufficient to examine all the betting opportunities in this race. In addition to win, place, show, and exacta wagering on this race, we have three multiple-race exotics to consider: the first half of the daily double, the first leg of the Pick-3, and the first race of the Place-Pick-9. We'll look at the information for the second and third races shortly.

Let's begin at the beginning. The win pool should be our primary focus.

One of the nice things about having a line is that we can quickly make the decision of which horse(s) to bet to win. In this race, we'd need about ten seconds to realize that our top three picks (Payand Payand Pay, Davus, and Cocooning) were huge underlays. That leaves Lovely One and Lackington as potential win bets. Since both of them have an identical win probability (5-to-1, or 16.67 percent), the one with the higher odds represents the superior win bet. That horse is Lackington. Just to make sure, let's calculate the edge on each of these win bets:

$$Lovely\ One = .167 \times 7 - .833 = .336$$
$$Lackington = .167 \times 15 - .833 = 1.672$$

In terms of positive expectation, it's no contest. The edge-to-odds ratio also points to Lackington, .1148 to .048. An aggressive win bettor who chooses the single win bet with the largest edge-to-odds ratio would bet only on Lackington in this race. A moderate win bettor could bet both horses, since each has an expectation greater than 20 percent.

The single best win bet in this race is on Lackington. Lovely One is an acceptable overlay as well. The aggressive win bettor could bet up to 11 percent of his win-betting bankroll on Lackington. (This would be sheer madness. The aggressive bettor should set a maximum of 5 percent of bankroll on any given win bet.) The moderate win bettor would bet both horses. His win bet would be divided 70 percent on Lackington and 30 percent on Lovely One.

What about the ultra-conservative win bettor? Would he or she be able to bet all five horses in the race using the group overlay method?

Group Estimate:

Payand Payand Pay	20%
Davus	20%
Cocooning	18%
Lovely One	16%
Lackington	16%
	90%

Public Estimate:

Payand Payand Pay	33%
Davus	33%
Cocooning	27%
Lovely One	12%
Lackington	6%
	101%

In this case the public has not underestimated the combined win probability of our five contenders. There's no advantage to using the group overlay method here.

What about place-and-show betting? In a race this contentious (it is a chaos race, no less), we don't even consider betting to place or show. Place-and-show bets are best reserved for orderly races. If we have an orderly race, we insist that the potential place or show bet is the top pick at 5-to-2 or less on our line. The public must confirm our opinion by making the horse its first or second betting choice.

Since the line considers this race quite contentious, a swing-for-the-fences exacta strategy is in order. The Mitchell Matrix asks us to write down the probable pays for each of the 20 exacta combinations involving these five contenders. The five highest-paying exactas are then bet. In this race, the five highest-paying exacta combinations are the two involving Lackington and Lovely One, plus the three combinations having Lackington on top of Payand Payand Pay, Davus, and Cocooning.

Of course, we could apply an overlay approach to the exacta in this race as well. The fair pays in the exacta can be found on the *ALL-IN-ONE* printout under the heading "Exacta." Each win horse is listed in the leftmost column. Each place horse is listed along the top row. For example, the fair pay for the $2 exacta combining Payand Payand Pay to win and Davus to place is $35. (The larger number in each box represents the fair pay for the $5 exacta. Notice that this number is approximately 2.5 times the number to its left.) You'll also notice that there isn't enough space for the combinations involving *ALL-IN-ONE*'s fifth choice, Lackington. However, since Lackington is rated at the same 5-to-1 odds as Lovely One, we can safely accept Lovely One's fair exacta pays for Lackington.

Which exactas are overlayed? With *ALL-IN-ONE*'s exacta grid, we have a neat, painless way to make sense of the 20 combinations:

```
--------------------------------EXACTA GRID---------------------------------- L
                                                                              A
             |PAYAND PAYAND P|    DAVUS     |    COCOONING   | LOVELY ONE-AR | C
                                                                              K
-------------+---------------+--------------+----------------+---------------+----
PAYAND PAYAND| . . . . . . . |   35    88   |   39    98     |   43   107    | 43
             | . . . . . . . |              |                |               |
             | . . . . . . . |              |                |               |
-------------+---------------+--------------+----------------+---------------+----
DAVUS        |   36    88    | . . . . . . .|   40    99     |   43   107    | 43
             |               | . . . . . . .|                |               |
             |               | . . . . . . .|                |               |
-------------+---------------+--------------+----------------+---------------+----
COCOONING    |   41   101    |   41   101   | . . . . . . .  |   49   123    | 49
             |               |              | . . . . . . .  |               |
-------------+---------------+--------------+----------------+---------------+----
LOVELY ONE-AR|   45   112    |   45   112   |   50   125     | . . . . . . . | 60
             |               |              |                | . . . . . . . |
             |               |              |                | . . . . . . . |
-------------+---------------+--------------+----------------+---------------+----
LACKINGTON   |      45       |      45      |      50        |      60       |
             |               |              |                |               | X
```

The first thing we do is write the actual pay for each combination in its corresponding box. This step is depicted in the graphic immediately below:

-----------------------------------EXACTA GRID-----------------------------------

	PAYAND PAYAND P	DAVUS	COCOONING	LOVELY ONE-AR	L A B
PAYAND PAYAND	. . . .	35 88 21	39 98 24	43 107 55	43 110
DAVUS	36 88 20	. . . .	40 99 21	43 107 48	43 96
COCOONING	41 101 25	41 101 22	. . . .	49 123 59	49 118
LOVELY ONE-AR	45 112 65	45 112 59	50 125 70	. . . .	60 320
LACKINGTON	45 140	45 127	50 148	60 338	X

Next, we circle the box for each combination whose actual pay is greater than its fair pay. We put an "X" through the box of each combination whose actual pay is less than or equal to its fair pay, like this:

-----------------------------------EXACTA GRID-----------------------------------

	PAYAND PAYAND P	DAVUS	COCOONING	LOVELY ONE-AR	L A B
PAYAND PAYAND	. . . .	35 88 (X) 21	39 98 (X) 24	43 107 55	43 110
DAVUS	36 88 (X) 20	. . . .	40 99 (X) 21	43 107 48	43 96
COCOONING	41 101 (X) 25	41 101 (X) 22	. . . .	49 123 59	49 118
LOVELY ONE-AR	45 112 65	45 112 59	50 125 70	. . . .	60 320
LACKINGTON	45 140	45 127	50 148	60 338	X

We count up the number of circled combinations. This is the number of combinations we can potentially bet. In this case we have 14 potential exacta combinations to bet. This guarantees at least 13 losing bets. Hence, we must demand a $26 premium on each combination. That is, we must demand that the actual pay of each circled combination is at least $26 greater than its fair pay. Those that satisfy this premium can be considered further. Those that don't are eliminated. After this step, the grid resembles the following:

```
-------------------------------EXACTA GRID-------------------------------
```

	PAYAND PAYAND P	DAVUS	COCOONING	LOVELY ONE-AR	L R
PAYAND PAYAND	. . . .	~~35~~ 88 *21*	~~39~~ 98 *24*	⊘ 43 107 *55*	⟨43⟩ *110*
DAVUS	~~36~~ 88 *26*	. . . .	~~40~~ 99 *21*	⊘ 43 107 *48*	⟨43⟩ *96*
COCOONING	~~41~~ 101 *25*	~~41~~ 101 *22*	. . . .	⊘ 49 123 *59*	⟨49⟩ *118*
LOVELY ONE-AR	⊘ 45 112 *63*	⊘ 45 112 *59*	⊘ 50 125 *70*	. . . .	⟨60⟩ *320*
LACKINGTON	⟨45⟩ *140*	⟨45⟩ *127*	⟨50⟩ *148*	⟨60⟩ *338*	X

We're left with eight circled combinations. The final step is to demand that each circled combination meet our minimum edge requirement. Barry Meadow demands a 50 percent edge, so he multiplies each payoff by 1.5. (Again, I use 1.4 as a multiplier.) In Meadow's case, he'd take the $43 fair pay on the Payand Payand Pay-Lackington combination and multiply it by 1.5. His answer is $64.50. Since that exacta is projected to pay $110, it survives the final cut. Based on my own edge requirement, this combination has to pay only $63. As you can see, all the exacta combinations involving Lackington survived this requirement.

There were no further eliminations. All eight combinations offer value significantly higher than both my minimum edge requirement and Meadow's. In either case, there are eight overlayed exacta bets: Lackington on top of our four other contenders, and Lackington underneath our four other contenders.

There was also a quinella offered on this race; unfortunately, I didn't copy the payoff prices down.

To figure out the daily double, we need to look at the line for the second race. Here are the past performances for that race:

Hollywood Park

2

1¹⁄₁₆ MILES. (1:40) CLAIMING. Purse $11,000. 3-year-olds and upward. Weights: 3-year-olds, 118 lbs. Older, 121 lbs. Non-winners of two races at a mile or over since October 4, allowed 3 lbs. Such a race since then, 6 lbs. Claiming price $10,000; if for $9,000, 2 lbs. (Races when entered for $8,000 or less not considered.)

Royal Dixie		Dk. b or br c. 4			Lifetime Record: 24 3 4 5 $56,645			
Own: Petrosian Brothers Racing Stable		Sire: Dixieland Band (Northern Dancer)			1993 11 3 1 2 $36,750	Turf 1 0 0 0 $350		
		Dam: Fearless Queen (Iron Ruler)			1992 11 M 3 3 $19,895	Wet 1 0 0 0		
ATKINSON P (21 3 1 2 .14)	$10,000	Br: Little Marvin Jr & Brooks R A Jr (Ky)		L 115	Hol 6 1 1 1 $18,750	Dist 8 2 1 1 $23,120		
		Tr: Scolamieri Sam J (3 1 0 0 .33)						

230ct93–4BM fm 1¾ ⓕ :49² 1:15 1:40 2:18⁴ 3↑ Hcp 12500s   76 6 1 1¹⁄₂ 1¹⁄₂ 2¹ 5⁴ Martinez J C   LB 113 b 9.40 90 – 05 Top Reality115⁹⁄₂ Turkish Lord115¹ Yes Me115¹   Weakened 9

25Sep83–11Fpx fst 1¾   :47¹ 1:12 1:38² 2:17² 3↑ Hcp 12500s   85 1 1 1¹ 1¹ 1² 2ⁿᵏ Martinez J C   LB 114 b 3.40 90 – 08 Stylish Majesty115ⁿᵏ Royal Dixie114⁹ Expreso Brazil116¹   Caught late 7

16Sep93-11Fpx fst *1⅛ :472 1:13 1:384 1:512 3+ Alw 12500s 81 3 1 12½ 11½ 2hd 32½ Martinez J C LB 113 b 14.00 82-15 Cannon Man1151 Skylaunch1151½ Royal Dixie1132 Outfinished 10
31Jly93-10SR fst 1 1/16 :214 :444 1:092 1:42 3+ Hcp 12500s 50 5 2 43½ 68½ 919 1022 Martinez J C LB 116 b *3.00 75-14 Yes Me1153½ Turkish Lord115½ Whisk Spree1141 Through early 10
10Jly93-10Pln fst 170 :222 :451 1:102 1:392 3+ Alw 22000N1X 89 8 1 13 13 11½ 12½ Martinez J C LB 117 b 8.50 98-11 Royal Dixie1172½ Le Axe A L'ame1175 Tank's Spirit1171 Steady drive 10
14May93-6GG fst 1 1/16 :23 :463 1:104 1:431 Clm 12500N2L 80 3 1 12 11½ 15 16 Martinez J C LB 119 b *2.00 81-22 RoylDixi1196 AddictdToRun1192½ WntrWrlock1191½ Bumped early stages 8
25Apr93-9Hol fst 1⅛ :473 1:121 1:372 1:501 3+ Md 28000 82 4 1 11 11 12½ 11¼ Atkinson P LB 121 b 11.70 86-10 Royal Dixie1211¼ Mysterious Moon123½ Sean1216 Driving 12
2Apr93-4SA fst 1 :23 :47 1:114 1:371 Md 35000 71 9 4 2½ 2½ 32½ 36¾ Atkinson P LB 118 b 12.70 77-20 Call Me Wild120¾ Mysterious Moon1206 Royal Dixie1182 Wide early 9
18Mar93-6SA fst 1 1/16 :222 :454 1:111 1:44 Md 35000 59 3 1 1hd 2hd 43½ 615 Atkinson P LB 118 b 6.20 69-19 Meditation Walk118no Mysterious Moon1184½ Sean1182¼ Faltered 11
4Feb93-9SA fst 1 1/16 :224 :464 1:113 1:44 Md 35000 75 6 3 2hd 1hd 2½ 55¾ Atkinson P LB 117 b 13.10 78-15 Crystal Wes119¾ Lend The Gold119¾ Buck Tide1204 Weakened 12
WORKOUTS: Nov 27 SLR tr.t 5f fst 1:024 H *11/16* Nov 12 SLR tr.t 4f gd :50 H *9/12* Nov 4 SLR tr.t 4f fst :484 H *5/8* Oct 9 SLR tr.t 4f fst :51 H *15/15* Sep 10 SLR tr.t 4f fst :49 H *4/8*

Royal Torrent

Own: Nadel & Soriano
DELAHOUSSAYE E (27 2 1 3 .07) **$10,000**

B. g. 4
Sire: His Majesty (Ribot)
Dam: Spout (Delta Judge)
Br: Elmendorf Farm (Ky)
Tr: Cassidy James (—)

L 115

Lifetime Record:	15 2 1 0	$42,375			
1993	8 0 1 0	$6,625	Turf	11 2 0 0	$39,175
1992	7 2 0 0	$35,750	Wet	0 0 0 0	
Hol	1 0 0 0		Dist	2 0 0 0	$300

12Nov93-1SA fst 1¼ :474 1:13 1:391 2:053 3+ Clm 10000 73 1 5 42½ 2hd 1½ 23½ Lopez A D LB 116 4.60 63-33 Le Farouche1113½ Royal Torrent1161 Double Agent1162 Led, outfinished 7
10Oct93-1SA fst 1 1/16 :231 :47 1:112 1:43 3+ Clm 10500 71 5 5 44 33½ 34 59¼ Lopez A D LB 114 5.00 80-11 Prime Condition1096½ Notwithstanding116½ Expreso Brazil116no No rally 7
25Sep93-7BM fm 1 1/16 ⓣ :23 :46 1:104 1:423 3+ Clm 22500 70 1 4 48 51½ 58½ 49 Boulanger G LB 115 8.00 88-03 FourFiveTime1174 HandsomeWeed117no WrittenStatement1175 No rally 7
11Sep93-5Dmr fm 1⅜ ⓣ :492 1:143 1:392 2:162 3+ Clm 45000 61 8 5 75 84½ 811 917 Black C A LB 115 64.70 63-12 Shaynoor117hd Tibaldi115¾ Fire Top1172 No mishap 10
15Aug93-5Dmr fm 1⅜ ⓣ :473 1:12 1:372 2:154 3+ Clm 45000 85 8 8 97½ 97¾ 75 66½ Warren R J Jr LB 115 67.20 77-10 Elytis1171½ Mr. P. And Max117nk Go Gremlin Go1171½ Broke slowly 10
18Jun93-4Hol fm 1⅛ ⓣ :463 1:102 1:342 1:463 Clm 50000 67 4 6 610 76½ 79½ 712¼ Garcia J A LB 116 13.20 79-09 Intelligently1141¼ Tibaldi112½ Mr. P. And Max1171½ Wide trip 7
15May93-1Hol fm 1⅛ ⓣ :48 1:112 1:35 1:471 Alw 42000N2X 86 4 6 54 52¾ 63½ 65¼ Almeida G F LB 115 20.70 83-09 Dilatado115½ Spruce Gum118½ Tax Collection1152¼ No late bid 7
16Apr93-4SA fm 1 ⓣ :234 :473 1:112 1:352 Alw 39000N2X 78 4 4 53½ 47 48 410¼ Delahoussaye E LB 116 16.80 78-12 Rainbow Corner114nk Eskay Creek1132 Dilatado1178 No mishap 7
29Aug92-8Dmr fm 1⅛ ⓣ :473 1:114 1:361 1:484 Dmr Dby Inv-G2 81 12 12 129¾ 117½ 99½ 87¾ Lopez A D LB 122 140.20 84-10 Daros1222 Smiling And Dancin122 Major Impact122 Broke slowly 12
10Aug92-5Dmr fm 1 1/16 ⓣ :231 :463 1:11 1:43 Alw 36000 83 1 10 108¾ 86¾ 52½ 1½ Delahoussaye E L 120 6.00 91-07 Royal Torrent120½ Eddie Valient1172 Spruce Gum120 Wide, handily 10
WORKOUTS: Nov 28 SA 5f fst 1:002 H *10/44* Nov 7 SA 6f fst 1:141 H *14/22* Sep 6 Dmr 5f fst 1:004 H *15/57*

Lanky Lord

Own: Kirby & Schow & Schow
BLACK C A (50 8 8 6 .16) **$10,000**

B. g. 4
Sire: Lord Gaylord (Sir Gaylord)
Dam: Cantiniere (Raise a Cup)
Br: Fred M. Allor (Mich)
Tr: Jackson Declan A (1 0 0 0 .00)

L 115

Lifetime Record:	21 3 3 0	$50,460			
1993	7 1 0 0	$12,935	Turf	1 0 0 0	
1992	14 2 3 0	$37,525	Wet	2 1 0 0	$10,625
Hol	5 2 1 0	$24,050	Dist	8 2 2 0	$29,595

11Nov93-5SA gd 1 :222 :481 1:121 1:383 3+ Clm 10000 73 8 5 22 1½ 1½ 44 Black C A LB 116 b 11.40 73-24 King Raj1162½ Days Gone By117½ Jean Pierre S1161½ Led, weakened 10
22Oct93-9SA fst 7f :223 :451 1:10 1:223 3+ Clm 10000 73 6 9 104½ 86½ 67½ 45½ Valenzuela F H LB 116 b 18.90 84-10 Five Sharps1181 Lajara1164½ Fire Commander116hd Mild late bid 12
6Oct93-9SA fst 7f :223 :451 1:10 1:223 3+ Clm 10500 73 9 10 98½ 98½ 84¾ 75 Black C A LB 115 b 17.70 85-10 Gallant Guy1162 Otay Mesa1182¾ Kolbe's Gold118hd Wide trip 12
27Sep93-11Fpx fst 1 1/16 :221 :46 1:111 1:43 3+ Clm 10000 78 7 4 1½ 2hd 31½ 54½ Gulas L L5 LB 111 b 4.00 88-14 Box Office1162 Our Staff1111 Joanie's Prince115½ Weakened 9
16Sep93-9Fpx fst 1 1/16 :23 :461 1:113 1:444 3+ Clm 12500 79 10 5 3nk 2hd 1½ 42½ Lopez A D LB 116 b 16.00 81-15 The Drouller116½ Stylish Majesty1161½ Great Event116½ 10
Lugged in, steadied late
29Aug93-9Dmr fst 1 :23 :464 1:114 1:37 3+ Clm 14000 88 2 4 42 72¾ 61¾ 78¼ Gonzalez S5 LB 110 fb 21.70 73-18 BechLights117hd MysteriousMoon1171½ Roistrous1121¼ Took up hard 3/16 10
13Jan93-5SA sly 1 :224 :471 1:132 1:411 Clm 16000 77 4 6 65 43¼ 32 2hd Black C A LB 118 b 11.30 64-36 [D]Liberty Offiftysix111hd Lanky Lord1182¼ Farbet1163½ Bumped late 10
Placed first through disqualification.
29Dec92-5SA gd 1 1/16 :223 :46 1:104 1:423 Clm 16000 66 6 5 61¾ 3½ 22½ 46½ Black C A LB 117 b 5.50 83-08 Aero Energy1153½ Shabeen115no Jean Pierre S1153 Wide early 9
12Dec92-1Hol fst 1 1/16 :224 :47 1:131 1:464 Clm 16000 68 7 2 2½ 1hd 12 12 Black C A LB 115 b 3.90 67-23 Lanky Lord1152 Haloshine1151¾ Some Call It Jazz1152¼ Ridden out 7
19Nov92-4Hol fst 1 1/16 :231 :462 1:11 1:423 Clm 20000 70 4 6 63¾ 45½ 46½ 510½ Solis A LB 115 b 5.00 77-18 Refuge115½ Devilish Dream119 Bold Patriot115 Rough start 9

Foolhearty

Own: Riggs & Varela
LONG B (23 1 0 3 .04) **$10,000**

Ch. g. 8
Sire: Conduction (Graustark)
Dam: So Fonda Sol (Maggie's Pet)
Br: Riggs Conrad E (Cal)
Tr: Graves Ronald L (1 0 0 0 .00)

L 115

Lifetime Record:	27 1 3 4	$47,840			
1993	9 0 0 1	$2,115	Turf	6 0 2 1	$16,600
1991	2 0 0 0		Wet	1 0 0 0	
Hol	3 0 0 1	$2,400	Dist	9 1 0 1	$20,725

12Nov93-1SA fst 1¼ :474 1:13 1:391 2:053 3+ Clm 10000 66 4 2 31½ 41¾ 63½ 68½ Perez I5 LB 111 39.50 58-33 Le Farouche1113½ Royal Torrent1161 Double Agent1162 Saved ground 7
16Sep93-11Fpx fst *1⅛ :472 1:13 1:384 1:512 3+ Alw 12500s 62 10 4 43¾ 32 910 914½ Torres R V LB 115 173.90 70-15 Cannon Man1151 Skylaunch1151½ Royal Dixie1132 Gave way 10
4Sep93-8Sac fst 1 :234 :464 1:104 1:361 3+ [S]Clm 6250 68 4 3 33 33 44½ 34½ Schvaneveldt C R LB 116 3.50 82-18 Bickers Wager1162 Good Hunting1182½ Foolhearty1162 No late bid 5
20Aug93-9Dmr fst 1⅛ :481 1:121 1:381 2:041 3+ Clm 10500 81 4 3 37½ 68½ 66 48 Perez I5 LB 110 84.80 69-19 Tax Collection1173 Bit Of Petrone1175½ Wretham117½ No mishap 8
26Jly93-9Hol fm 1¼ ⓣ :482 1:13 1:373 2:012 Alw 12500s 61 10 4 64½ 98½ 911 715¼ Gulas L L5 LB 110 198.40 72-13 Polaris Star1153 HandsomeWeed1226 TaxCollection1162 5 Wide stretch 11
28Apr93-2Hol fst 1 1/16 :231 :464 1:112 1:432 [S]Clm 10000 27 2 7 89½ 916 923 932¼ Carvalho M A LB 116 97.00 51-10 Gold Bally114½ Bear's Pizazz1167 Farbet116¾ Early trouble 9
31Mar93-9SA fst 1 1/16 :222 :462 1:111 1:432 [S]Clm 10000 60 5 7 74¾ 107¾ 1112 1115 Garcia R J LB 115 126.90 72-15 Cannon Ho117¾ Bear's Pizazz117no Sky Rider115½ Wide backstretch 12
18Mar93-1SA fst 1 :222 :464 1:11 1:373 [S]Clm 10000 53 7 9 810 911 712 515½ Garcia R J LB 115 62.40 66-19 T. O. Nacho1176½ Chief Snow110½ Courageous Prince1166 5 Wide stretch 10
18Feb93-9SA sly 1 :23 :461 1:103 1:363 [S]Clm 10000 26 1 10 1015 1018 1023 1030½ Sanchez J M LB 116 53.60 56-15 Boldandcayerless1144 River Of Green1142 Sky Rider116hd Took up early 10
5May91-1Hol fst 1 1/16 :471 1:113 1:371 1:501 Clm [illegible] [illegible] Patton D B LB 113 28.70 68-17 RunawayDunwy1151½ Prtnerswnswitch1154½ WellAwre115 Broke slowly 8
WORKOUTS: Oct 22 Fpx 3f fst :372 H *4/5* Oct 11 Fpx 4f fst :471 H *1/7*

Double Agent

Own: Cho Myung Kwon
ALMEIDA G F (14 1 5 1 .07) **$10,000**

Dk. b or br g. 6
Sire: Secretariat (Bold Ruler)
Dam: Privacy (Turn to Reason)
Br: Firestone Mr-Mrs B R (Ky)
Tr: Cho Myung Kwon (2 0 0 0 .00)

L 115

Lifetime Record:	21 1 2 3	$31,775			
1993	2 0 0 1	$1,650	Turf	4 0 1 1	$11,400
1992	4 0 1 0	$3,100	Wet	1 0 0 0	$800
Hol	7 1 1 0	$13,525	Dist	4 0 1 0	$3,850

12Nov93-1SA fst 1¼ :474 1:13 1:391 2:053 3+ Clm 10000 72 2 1 11 1hd 31 34½ Almeida G F LB 116 b 7.80 62-33 Le Farouche1113½ Royal Torrent1161 Double Agent1162 Outfinished 7
31Oct93-9SA fst 6f :213 :442 :563 1:093 3+ Clm 14000 62 9 8 53¼ 66½ 99¼ 912 Almeida G F LB 114 b 42.00 77-12 Diable Rouge1182 Friedlander116½ Sinceriffic1162 Wide, gave way 9
20May92-5Hol fst 1 1/16 :23 :454 1:103 1:431 Clm 12500 80 9 2 22 21½ 3½ 2¾ Martinez F F5 LB 110 b 47.00 84-16 Our Staff115¾ Double Agent110hd Well Aware118 4-wide 1st turn 9
8Apr92-7SA fst 1 1/16 :231 :464 1:111 1:434 Clm 18000 76 4 8 85¾ 85¾ 67½ 59¾ Martinez F F5 LB 108 b 27.20 74-16 J. T.'s Pet115½ [D]Real Affirmed1152 Yes Can Do115 Wide trip 8
14Mar92-2SA fst 6½f :214 :443 1:083 1:151 Clm 25000 73 3 5 74½ 76½ 612 612¾ Castanon A L LB 115 b 75.50 81-13 Abergwaun Lad1152 Diamond Out1174½ Hot Operator115 Outrun 7
1Mar92-1SA fst 6f :212 :434 :562 1:09 Clm 25000 78 4 10 109 1010 108¾ 88 Nakatani C S L 115 b 46.90 83-10 Slew The Surgeon112½ Borscht Ryder1152¾ Sam Who117 6-wide stretch 10
23Jun91-9Hol fst 7½f :214 :441 1:091 1:283 Clm 20000 76 5 6 66½ 78½ 77¾ 88 Santos J A L 116 b 37.80 — — Elikos116no Coningsburgh1162½ Partnerswanaswitch116 Outrun 9
25May91-7Hol fm 1¼ ⓣ :474 1:114 1:353 2:00 3+ Hcp 50000 71 5 2 2hd 89½ 816 819 Mena F LB 112 b 57.20 74-07 Splendid Career1212 Preston-Fr1142 Cool Gold Mood119 Stopped 8
4May91-4Hol fst 7½f :221 :45 1:10 1:292 Clm 50000 70 7 2 42 62¼ 79½ 612 Lovato A J5 LB 112 b 27.60 — — Hot Operator1152 Serious Flight117no Jonathan's Gold117 Wide stretch 7
23Mar91-7SA fst 7f :222 :45 1:10 1:23 Alw 32000 73 9 4 74 97¼ 79 68¼ Meza R Q LB 118 b 65.10 80-11 Maxibob118no Pappy Yokum1184½ Golden Voyager121 Wide early 11
WORKOUTS: Nov 28 SA 5f fst 1:01 H *18/44* Oct 22 SA 1 fst 1:443 H *5/5* Oct 17 SA 7f fst 1:293 H *2/2* Oct 7 Hol 5f fst 1:012 H *11/29* Oct 1 Hol 4f fst :473 H *4/21*

Spruce Navy

Own: Shulman Ina Sue
CASTANON A L (13 0 3 2 .00) **$10,000**

Dk. b or br g. 4
Sire: Polish Navy (Danzig)
Dam: Spruce Song (Verbatim)
Br: Elmendorf Farm (Ky)
Tr: Shulman Sanford (24 4 4 2 .17)

L 115

Lifetime Record:	22 3 3 1	$59,985			
1993	14 1 2 1	$28,675	Turf	1 0 0 0	
1992	8 2 1 0	$31,310	Wet	2 0 0 0	$750
Hol	5 2 1 0	$33,850	Dist	9 2 2 0	$38,760

11Nov93-5SA gd 1 :222 :461 1:121 1:383 3+ Clm 10000 60 7 8 77 64 76 710¾ Castanon A L LB 116 f *3.30 66-24 King Raj1162½ Days Gone By117½ Jean Pierre S1161½ 5 Wide into lane 10
29Oct93-9SA fst 1⅛ :464 1:112 1:37 1:494 3+ Clm 10000 87 8 4 32 2½ 11 2½ Castanon A L LB 116 9.50 80-20 Palmdale116½ Spruce Navy1164 Golden Conquest1171½ Game try 11
15Oct93-9SA fst 1 1/16 :224 :461 1:104 1:432 3+ Clm 10000 70 11 8 88¼ 86½ 98¼ 87¼ Lopez A D LB 116 f 5.90 80-13 Tu Eres Mi Heroe1161 King Drone1162 Cautivador118¾ Very wide trip 12
25Sep93-11Fpx fst 1⅜ :471 1:12 1:382 2:172 3+ Hcp 12500s 76 7 2 21 21 45 56¾ Lopez A D LB 116 3.30 83-08 Stylish Majesty115nk Royal Dixie1143 Expreso Brazil1161 Weakened 7
3Sep93-3Dmr fst 1 1/16 :223 :463 1:111 1:431 3+ Clm 12500 84 2 6 53½ 41½ 21 21¾ Lopez A D LB 117 18.00 84-19 Classic Case1171¾ Spruce Navy1172¾ Our Staff1102½ Good effort 8
12Aug93-5Dmr fst 1 :223 :461 1:11 1:362 3+ Clm c-10000 74 9 7 61¾ 31½ 44½ 47¾ Desormeaux K J LB 117 *1.60 77-19 Classic Case1174½ Our Staff1123 Fappamoto117nk 10
Wide trip, bore out badly 3/4; Claimed from Kellstrom Francis S, Hess R B Jr Trainer
31Jly93-9Dmr fst 1 :223 :454 1:104 1:362 3+ Clm 16000 81 5 6 54 31 45 68 Valenzuela P A LB 118 4.10 77-11 Boldandcayerless120½ Cannon Man1162¾ Bit Of Petrone1112¾ Wide trip 10
4Jly93-1Hol fst 1 1/16 :231 :462 1:102 1:42 Clm 25000 77 1 3 31½ 31½ 35½ 410½ Desormeaux K J LB 119 3.00 80-13 Davus1164½ No Commitment1175 Lil Orphan Moonie1091 Faltered 6
13Jun93-1Hol fst 1 1/16 :224 :454 1:102 1:44 Clm 25000 82 3 5 42 42½ 21½ 1¾ Desormeaux K J LB 116 3.80 81-19 Spruce Navy116¾ Refuge1112¼ Meditation Walk116no Got up 7
8May93-4GG fst 1 :223 :462 1:102 1:353 Alw 23000N1X 70 8 8 710 79½ 711 69½ Chapman T M LB 119 5.60 82-09 Flashy Encore1191½ San Fran's Halo1193 Tank's Spirit1193 Showed little 8
WORKOUTS: Nov 29 Hol 4f fst :48 H *7/28* Nov 20 Hol 4f fst :481 H *10/26* Nov 5 SA 3f fst :364 H *17/41* Oct 24 SA 4f fst :472 H *7/55* Oct 9 SA 4f fst :483 H *23/49* Oct 2 SA 4f fst :471 H *5/34*

Claret (Ire)
Own: Brown G W & C W & Arlene & Barbara
GRYDER A T (46 9 5 6 .20) $10,000
B. g. 5
Sire: Roussillon (Riverman)
Dam: Consolation (Troy)
Br: Lord Rotherwick (Ire)
Tr: Mitchell Mike (22 3 9 2 .14)
L 115

Lifetime Record :	24	4	5	4		$254,388
1993	6	0	0	0	$10,375 Turf 17 4 4 3	$70,013
1992	6	1	2	1	$209,650 Wet 0 0 0 0	
Hol	0	0	0	0	Dist 1 0 0 0	$750

15Nov93–7SA fst 1
4Jun93–5Hol fm 1 ①
Claimed from Pabst Henry, Cross Richard J Trainer
28Mar93–7GG gd 1⅛
3Mar93–8SA gd 1⅛
12Feb93–8SA fst 1
1Jan93–7SA fst 1
7Nov92–5BM fm 1⅛
11Oct92–8SA fst 1⅛
30Aug92–8Dmr fst 1⅛
8Aug92–8Dmr fst 1⅛
WORKOUTS: Nov 27 Hol 4f fst :50 H 19/26   Nov 22 Hol 4f fst :48² H 4/30   ●Nov 12 Hol 7f fst 1:27¹ H 1/7   Nov 5 Hol 6f fst 1:15⁴ H 5/7   Oct 28 Hol 5f fst 1:03² H 21/25   Oct 21 Hol 5f fst 1:02¹ H 20/31

Carrie's Glory
Own: Davis & Davis & Goddard
ATHERTON J E (21 0 0 2 .00) $10,000
Dk. b or br g. 6
Sire: Empire Glory (Nijinsky II)
Dam: Carrie's Angel (Fleet Host)
Br: Popik Richard (Cal)
Tr: Davis William F (2 0 0 0 .00)
L 110⁵

Lifetime Record :	35	3	6	3		$64,500
1993	1	0	0	0	Turf 2 0 0 0	
1992	1	0	0	0	Wet 2 0 1 0	$4,500
Hol	15	2	3	1	$29,725 Dist 7 0 2 0	$11,700

20Nov93–9Hol fst 7½f
25Nov93–9Hol fst 7½f
15Dec91–10Hol fm 1 ①
20Nov91–1Hol fst 1
8Nov91–9SA fst 1⅛
18Oct91–1SA fst 6½f
20ct91–1SA fst 6f
8Sep91–2Dmr fst 6f
2Sep91–2Dmr fst 6f
14Aug91–9Dmr fst 1
WORKOUTS: Dec 2 Hol 4f fst :47 H 2/17   Nov 12 Hol 1 fst 1:42¹ H 2/2   Nov 6 Hol 7f fst 1:27³ H 1/1   Oct 29 Hol 6f fst 1:14 Hg2/7   Oct 24 Hol 5f fst 1:02 H 14/18   ●Oct 10 Hol 4f fst :46⁴ H 1/21

Here's *ALL-IN-ONE*'s analysis and line on the second race:

```
4DEC93                          HOL              8.5 furlongs dirt
Race #2                                               8 starters
C10,000                                      Age: 3+years, Male
----------------------------INPUT DATA----------------------------

              #   #   #   #   $'S                        1st C  2nd C  Final
Horse name    ST  W   P   S  Earned Date    Trk Dist. S  time   time   time
-----------------------------------------------------------------------------
ROYAL DIXIE    0   0   0   0     0 23OCT93 GG  8.500 D  46.3  110.4  143.1
ROYAL TORRENT  0   0   0   0     0 12NOV93 SA  8.500 D  47.0  111.2  143.0
LANKY LORD     0   0   0   0     0 11NOV93 FPX 8.500 D  46.0  111.1  143.0
SPRUCE NAVY    0   0   0   0     0 11NOV93 SA  9.000 D  46.4  111.2  149.4
CLARET-IR      0   0   0   0     0 15NOV93 GG  8.500 D  45.3  109.3  142.2


                          1st C  2nd C  Final
Horse name    Class Lvl   B.L.   B.L.   B.L.   SR   Var
-----------------------------------------------------------
ROYAL DIXIE   C12,500     0.00   0.00   0.00   81   22.0
ROYAL TORRENT C12,500     4.00   3.50   9.25   80   11.0
LANKY LORD    C10,000     0.00   0.10   4.50   88   14.0
SPRUCE NAVY   C10,000     2.00   0.50   0.50   80   20.0
CLARET-IR     STAKES      7.00   5.75   3.25   82   15.0


----------------------------BETTING LINE----------------------------

              -------Rankings--------         Betting   Fair    Fair
Horse name    PEH H-I THAAI P-H ESP  Rating    Line    Place $ Show $
-----------------------------------------------------------------------------
SPRUCE NAVY    1   1    1    1   1   93.89     6-5
CLARET-IR      4   2    2    4   2   70.00     6-1
LANKY LORD     2   5    5    3   3   69.73     6-1
ROYAL TORRENT  3   3    3    2   4   69.44
ROYAL DIXIE    5   4    4    5   5   64.05
```

```
-------------------------------EXACTA GRID----------------------------------
           | SPRUCE NAVY  |  CLARET-IR  |  LANKY LORD  |
-----------+--------------+-------------+--------------+
SPRUCE NAVY| . . . . . . .|   17    43  |   18    44   |
           | . . . . . . .|            |             |
           | . . . . . . .|            |             |
-----------+--------------+-------------+--------------+
CLARET-IR  |   27    68   | . . . . . . .|   91   227   |
           |              | . . . . . . .|             |
           |              | . . . . . . .|             |
-----------+--------------+-------------+--------------+
LANKY LORD |   28    70   |   92   228  | . . . . . . .|
           |              |             | . . . . . . .|
           |              |             | . . . . . . .|
-----------+--------------+-------------+--------------+
```

```
4DEC93                         HOL                    8.5 furlongs dirt
Race #2                                                      8 starters
C10,000                                              Age: 3+years, Male
-------------------------SPEED/PACE SUMMARY---------------------------------

Race Type:          Double Advantage Race
Race Profile:       47.31   111.37   143.25    Winners' Pace Profile: FRONT
Ability Par:        95.42                       Pace Contention Point:  0.59 lengths

Projected Times:                            Ability Balance   Last Proj  Con-
                    1st C   2nd C   Fin C    Time    Time     Frac Pace tender
-----------------------------------------------------------------------------
SPRUCE NAVY         46.41  110.53  141.25   94.65   98.71   30.73 FRONT  Y+
CLARET-IR           47.80  111.40* 142.89   94.99   99.73   31.50 LATE   N
LANKY LORD          46.36  110.64  143.82   94.93  101.32   33.18 FRONT  N
ROYAL TORRENT       47.44  110.64  143.82   95.26   99.88   31.42 LATE   N
ROYAL DIXIE         47.51  111.57* 143.05   95.62  100.22   31.49 REAR   N


-------------------------------PACE GRAPH-----------------------------------

       Profile:              47.31            111.37              143.25
       Front Runner:         46.36            110.53              141.25
Horse name                     1C               2C                   F
SPRUCE NAVY        -------------------X -----------------(X ----------------X
CLARET-IR          -----------X------+ ----------------X--(+ ----------X-------+
LANKY LORD         ===============X   ========X+ =====X============+
ROYAL TORRENT      -----------X----+ ----------------X--(+ ----------X-------+
ROYAL TORRENT      -----------X=====+ ========== X  (I =========X========+
```

We can choose from several daily double strategies. If we're risk-averse, we can play all the combinations involving the contenders who are 6-to-1 or lower on our line. We size these bets proportionally to their probability of winning. That is, we'd bet more money on a combination pairing two 2-to-1 shots (on our line) than we would on a combination pairing two 3-to-1 shots. The reason is that the combination pairing 2-to-1 shots has a 11.11 percent chance of winning, while the combination pairing 3-to-1 shots has a 6.25 percent chance of winning.

We calculate a daily double combination's probability of winning as follows: Multiply the win probability of the win horse in the first half by the win probability of the win horse in the second half. For example, two 2-to-1 shots have an 11.11 percent chance of winning ($\frac{1}{3} \times \frac{1}{3}$ = .1111). Here's the win probability for each of the combinations in our workshop early double:

Payand Payand Pay–Spruce Navy	.0909
Payand Payand Pay–Claret	.0286
Payand Payand Pay–Lanky Lord	.0286
Davus–Spruce Navy	.0909
Davus–Claret	.0286
Davus–Lanky Lord	.0286
Cocooning–Spruce Navy	.0826
Cocooning–Claret	.0260
Cocooning–Lanky Lord	.0260
Lovely One–Spruce Navy	.0758
Lovely One–Claret	.0238
Lovely One–Lanky Lord	.0238
Lackington–Spruce Navy	.0758
Lackington–Claret	.0238
Lackington–Lanky Lord	.0238

The Payand Payand Pay–Spruce Navy and Davus–Spruce Navy double combinations are the most likely to win. Hence, they'll get the largest amount of our double bankroll. Outsider combinations such as Lackington–Lanky Lord will get much less of our bankroll. These probabilities clearly suggest more money should be bet on the Payand Payand Pay–Spruce Navy combination than on the Lackington–Lanky Lord combination.

Remember, we calculate the optimal amount to bet on each combination by adding together the individual probability of winning for each combination, then dividing each combination's probability of winning back into that sum. When we add up the individual probabilities of winning, the sum is .6774. This means we have a 67.74 percent probability of cashing this daily double, based on our contenders and lines. What percentage of our total daily double bet size for these races should we allocate to the Payand Payand Pay–Spruce Navy combination? Divide .0909 by .6774. The answer is .1342, or 13.42 percent. The following represents the optimal bet-size proportion for each combination (the number in the rightmost column is a bet amount):

Payand Payand Pay–Spruce Navy	.1366	$14
Payand Payand Pay–Claret	.0422	4
Payand Payand Pay–Lanky Lord	.0422	4
Davus–Spruce Navy	.1366	14
Davus–Claret	.0422	4
Davus–Lanky Lord	.0422	4
Cocooning–Spruce Navy	.1219	12
Cocooning–Claret	.0384	4
Cocooning–Lanky Lord	.0384	4
Lovely One–Spruce Navy	.1119	11
Lovely One–Claret	.0351	4
Lovely One–Lanky Lord	.0351	4
Lackington–Spruce Navy	.1119	11
Lackington–Claret	.0351	4
Lackington–Lanky Lord	.0351	4

The number on the right is the amount you would bet on that particular combination if your total bet was $102. (Your goal bet was $100, but rounding off causes a small variation.) When we add up these bet-size proportions, we get very close to 1, which is the same thing as 100 percent of bet size. Suppose we wanted to invest a total of $100 in this double. We'd bet $14 on the Payand Payand Pay–Spruce Navy combination and $4 on the Lackington–Lanky Lord pairing. If we bet a sum other than $100, we'd simply multiply that sum by the individual bet-size proportion. The result is the amount we should bet on each individual daily double combination.

The above daily double strategy covers all the possible combinations involving the contenders that are 6-to-1 or lower on our line. Another double strategy is to select a key horse in half of the double and pair it with the contenders in the remaining half, leaving out those combinations that pair two probable favorites.

We know who the actual favorite will be in the first half of the double. By consulting the morning line for the second race, we can get a pretty good idea of who the favorite will be in the second half of the double. (The best way to check is to watch the daily double probable pays. The double combination in the second race with the favorite in the first race that's paying the lowest will usually point to the public favorite in the second race.) Here's the morning line for the second race:

Spruce Navy	4-1
Claret	2-1
Lanky Lord	8-1

We know that Davus is the actual betting favorite in the first race. Claret is the morning-line favorite for the second race. Thus we should avoid betting any doubles that combine Davus and Claret. We can key our top horse in the first race, Payand Payand Pay, to our three contenders in the second. We can also key our top horse in the second race, Spruce Navy, to our top three contenders in the first race.

We also have an overlay method for investing in the daily double. We can compute the fair pay for each combination, then note the probable pays. The combinations that are paying more than their fair pay are the overlays. The fair pay is calculated by dividing probability of winning into the minimum bet size, which at Hollywood Park is $2. For example, the Payand Payand Pay–Spruce Navy combination's probability of winning is .0909. Dividing this probability into $2 equals $22.00, which is the fair pay for this daily double combination. Here are the fair pays for each of the daily double combinations:

Payand Payand Pay–Spruce Navy	$ 22.00
Payand Payand Pay–Claret	70.00
Payand Payand Pay–Lanky Lord	70.00
Davus–Spruce Navy	22.00
Davus–Claret	70.00
Davus–Lanky Lord	70.00
Cocooning–Spruce Navy	24.20
Cocooning–Claret	77.00
Cocooning–Lanky Lord	77.00
Lovely One–Spruce Navy	26.40
Lovely One–Claret	84.00
Lovely One–Lanky Lord	84.00
Lackington–Spruce Navy	26.40
Lackington–Claret	84.00
Lackington–Lanky Lord	84.00

The following are the probable pays (to the nearest dollar) for each of these combinations:

Payand Payand Pay–Spruce Navy	$ 32.00
Payand Payand Pay–Claret	31.00
Payand Payand Pay–Lanky Lord	62.00
Davus–Spruce Navy	31.00
Davus–Claret	28.00
Davus–Lanky Lord	57.00
Cocooning–Spruce Navy	36.00
Cocooning–Claret	33.00
Cocooning–Lanky Lord	66.00
Lovely One–Spruce Navy	76.00
Lovely One–Claret	72.00
Lovely One–Lanky Lord	145.00
Lackington–Spruce Navy	151.00
Lackington–Claret	157.00
Lackington–Lanky Lord	302.00

The technique for betting daily double overlays is identical to the one for betting exacta overlays. First, we compare fair pays to the probable pays. Then we eliminate all the underlayed combinations. We count up the remaining overlayed combinations and demand an additional premium for our guaranteed losing wagers. Finally, we add our minimum edge requirement to the fair pay of the remaining overlayed combinations. We bet the combinations that are still paying more than they should. Here's what our daily double Mitchell Matrix would look like after completing these steps:

Eight combinations survived the first step. If we bet them all, we'd have seven guaranteed losing bets. Hence, we must add a $14 premium to the fair pay of each combination. After doing that we're left with only five overlayed combinations. Based on a 20 percent minimum edge requirement, all five can be bet: Lovely One to Spruce Navy and Lanky Lord, Lackington to Spruce Navy, Claret to and Lanky Lord.

Now for the first Pick-3. Here is the information for the third race:

Hollywood Park

3 5½ Furlongs. (1:02¹) CLAIMING. Purse $13,000. Fillies and mares, 3-year-olds and upward. Weights: 3-year-olds, 120 lbs. Older, 122 lbs. Non-winners of two races since October 4, allowed 3 lbs. A race since then, 5 lbs. Claiming price $20,000, if for $18,000, allowed 2 lbs. (Races when entered for $16,000 or lesss not considered.)

Datsdawayitis
Own: Lewis Beverly J & Robert B

B. f. 4
Sire: Known Fact (In Reality)
Dam: Baton Twirler (Reverse)
Br: Clinkinbeard Mr-Mrs Robert M (Ky)
Tr: Baffert Bob (10 2 1 2 .20)

NAKATANI C S (60 14 10 13 .23) $20,000 L 117

Lifetime Record: 9 3 2 0 $36,850
1993 8 3 2 0 $36,850 Turf 1 0 0 0
1992 1 M 0 0   Wet 0 0 0 0
Hol 3 2 0 0 $15,400 Dist 0 0 0 0

Chicharrones
Own: Conde Raymond J

Gr. m. 6
Sire: Orbit Ruler (Our Rulla)
Dam: Major Attraction (First Balcony)
Br: Cofer Rhys S (Cal)
Tr: Craigmyle Scott J (5 0 0 2 .00)

PINCAY L JR (60 10 9 7 .17) $18,000 L 115

Lifetime Record: 33 5 4 11 $89,090
1993 12 3 2 1 $26,375 Turf 0 0 0 0
1992 13 0 1 8 $20,120 Wet 1 0 1 0 $2,600
Hol 12 1 2 5 $20,725 Dist 1 0 0 1 $2,550

Perky Slew
Own: Kenis Charles

Dk. b or br m. 5
Sire: Slew's Royalty (Seattle Slew)
Dam: Sunny Ridge (Commissioner)
Br: Vicki-Beth Stables Inc (Cal)
Tr: Van Berg Jack C (33 3 5 4 .09)

ANTLEY C W (43 5 5 5 .12) $20,000 L 117

Lifetime Record: 38 5 11 7 $247,625
1993 7 1 2 2 $25,300 Turf 2 0 0 0
1992 8 1 0 2 $48,800 Wet 3 2 1 0 $68,750
Hol 14 2 6 2 $89,900 Dist 3 1 2 0 $20,850

Solda Holme
Own: Dinius John

Ch. m. 7
Sire: Jeff's Companion (Noholme II)
Dam: Broker's Pleasure (Second Pleasure)
Br: Hebard Mr-Mrs K L (Ore)
Tr: Chambers Mike (4 1 0 2 .25)

STEVENS G L (36 4 10 5 .11) $20,000 L 117

Lifetime Record: 36 20 5 2 $146,077
1993 6 1 3 0 $25,324 Turf 0 0 0 0
1992 2 2 0 0 $13,420 Wet 4 3 0 1 $14,995
Hol 0 0 0 0   Dist 4 3 0 1 $29,695

9May93-10YM fst 6f :224 :443 :564 1:084 3+ ⒻRhdndron H25k 73 6 2 2hd 21 21½ 22½ Eide B M LB 118 b *1.30 96-05 I. B. Forty1222½ Solda Holme1182 Money By Choice1182 No match 7
11Apr93-10YM fst 5½f :223 :451 :572 1:033 3+ ⒻFashion H25k 81 2 1 1hd 1hd 1hd 11½ Eide B M LB 116 b 2.40 95-11 Solda Holme1161½ Money By Choice1192½ I. B. Forty1193 Drew clear late 6
9May92-10Lga fst 6½f :222 :45 1:101 1:172 ⒻClm 40000 84 6 1 2hd 1½ 13 14 Doocy T T LB 120 b *.60 84-22 Solda Holme1204 Doin' The Puyallup1141 Azi Lee110 Easily 6
11Apr92- 9Lga fst 5½f :214 :45 :574 1:042 ⒻClm 40000 86 8 1 42½ 23 22½ 1hd Doocy T T LB 114 b 2.00 91-19 Solda Holme114hd Session's Flame1143½ Bidder Trick114 Hard drive 9
25Aug91- 9Lga fst 6f :221 :453 :581 1:111 3+ ⒻAlw 20000 80 5 2 2hd 11 12½ 22 Boulanger G LB 114 b *.60 82-17 Loose Sue1142 Solda Holme1143 Con's Bon Bon120 No match 6
7Aug91- 9Lga fst 6f :22 :444 :57 1:10 3+ ⒻClm 50000 94 5 2 2hd 1hd 13 13½ Boulanger G LB 111 b 2.10 90-19 Solda Holme1113½ Con's Bon Bon1172 Tami's Secret115 Easily 6
WORKOUTS: Nov 28 SA 3f fst :353 H *3/27* Nov 7 SA 4f fst :47 H *4/37* Oct 14 SA 5f fst 1:003 H *18/42* Oct 7 SA 5f fst 1:012 H *23/46* ●Sep 12 YM 5f fst :593 H *1/25*

Old Time Romance
Own: Robiliard Kris S
GONZALEZ S JR (45 3 5 5 .07) **$20,000**

B. m. 5
Sire: Pancho Villa (Secretariat)
Dam: Brian's Babe (Olden Times)
Br: Bacacita Farms (Ky)
Tr: Wells Forrest (—)

L 112[5]

Lifetime Record :	28 5 6 6	$112,225			
1993	14 1 3 4	$37,375	Turf	1 0 0 0	
1992	8 2 0 2	$36,175	Wet	8 1 4 1	$31,400
Hol	1 0 0 1	$2,100	Dist	1 0 1 0	$3,400

14Nov93- 1SA fst 6f :212 :441 :562 1:092 3+ ⒻClm 25000 53 7 2 31 42½ 76½ 712½ Almeida G F LB 116 30.70 77-06 Sal's My Gal117no Class Confirmed116nk Her Elegant Ways1162 Gave way 7
9Oct93- 1SA fst 7f :222 :443 1:093 1:221 3+ ⒻClm c-22500 49 4 5 33 31½ 54 616½ Black C A LB 116 3.80 76-09 PersinSunshine1182¼ HerElegntWys1163½ PssionAndPride1165½ 4 Wide 1/4 8
Claimed from Bethany Investments Inc, Knight Terry Trainer
5Sep93- 9Dmr fst 6½f :22 :444 1:092 1:16 3+ ⒻClm 30000 82 1 4 1½ 1½ 11½ 32¾ Black C A LB 116 6.20 88-08 CottonBloomrs1121¼ LoknAtABlrr1191½ OldTmRmnc116nk Weakened a bit 8
25Aug93- 3Dmr fst 6f :214 :451 :574 1:11 3+ ⒻClm c-22500 78 3 4 53½ 41 1hd 11 Gonzalez S5 LB 110 2.80 84-14 OldTimeRomance1101 Tiaradncer1172 PerkySlew1155½ Wide, ridden out 5
Claimed from Mcbrayer C H Or Susan G, Tinsley J E Jr Trainer
7Aug93- 1Dmr fst 6f :22 :451 :573 1:102 3+ ⒻClm 20000 63 3 6 715 712 711 46½ Pedroza M A LB 115 9.90 81-09 Perky Slew115hd Proangle1153½ No Sacrifice1102¾ 7
Severely impeded early
31Jly93- 5Dmr fst 6f :221 :453 :574 1:103 3+ ⒻClm 16000 83 4 4 42½ 42½ 31½ 41½ Pedroza M A LB 115 20.80 85-10 Brilliant Light115¾ Proangle116no Teri115½ Always close 9
16Apr93- 8GG fst 6f :214 :451 :581 1:11 ⒻClm 20000 54 7 3 3½ 41¾ 33 68¾ Meza R Q LB 116 3.70 76-15 Tolder116½ Labiblica1162½ Dragonetta1163 Wide, gave way 9
10Apr93- 3GG fm 1 1/16 Ⓣ :24 :484 1:131 1:44 + ⒻClm 25000 61 5 1 1½ 21 43½ 1010 Meza R Q LB 116 8.70 76-08 Bel Darling1162 Miss King116hd Campy1181 Stopped 10
27Mar93- 4GG sly 5f :211 :443 :574 ⒻClm 20000 79 2 6 45½ 48 46½ 22 Meza R Q LB 116 3.70 91-09 FoxyBaby1152 OldTimeRomance1161½ ShezaShiningstar1161 Closed well 7
4Mar93- 7GG fst 6f :214 :45 :573 1:104 ⒻClm 25000 70 6 2 41¾ 53½ 32 33 Meza R Q LB 116 4.10 83-17 CandinMischief116hd MndyMck1163 OldTimeRomnce116hd Closed inside 9
WORKOUTS: ●Nov 26 Hol 5f fst :591 H *1/42* Nov 5 Hol 4f fst :493 H *8/16* Nov 1 Hol 5f fst 1:03 H *29/30* Sep 27 Hol 5f fst 1:034 H *15/16* ●Sep 18 Hol 5f fst :584 H *1/12*

Isleo Bebe
Own: Helstrom & Mevorach
GRYDER A T (46 9 5 6 .20) **$20,000**

B. m. 5
Sire: Island Whirl (Pago Pago)
Dam: She Can't Miss (Duck Dance)
Br: Elcee-H Stable (Fla)
Tr: Lewis Craig A (11 2 4 2 .18)

L 117

Lifetime Record :	15 3 3 0	$40,100			
1993	6 1 1 0	$16,050	Turf	1 0 0 0	$900
1992	5 1 2 0	$14,250	Wet	0 0 0 0	
Hol	4 2 1 0	$19,750	Dist	1 1 0 0	$9,900

14Nov93- 1SA fst 6f :212 :441 :562 1:092 3+ ⒻClm 25000 80 6 3 52½ 32½ 21½ 42½ Desormeaux K J LB 116 5.50 88-06 Sal's My Gal117no Class Confirmed116nk HerElegantWays1162 No late bid 7
22Oct93- 5SA fst 6½f :213 :441 1:09 1:153 3+ ⒻClm c-20000 79 2 9 65¼ 89½ 65¾ 26 Delahoussaye E LB 116 5.90 87-10 Class Confirmed1166 Isleo Bebe116½ Tiaradancer1161¾ Wide into lane 12
Claimed from Madison Stewart, Sadler John W Trainer
24Sep93-10Fpx fst 1 1/16 :224 :463 1:12 1:443 3+ ⒻAlw 12500s 60 4 1 1hd 2hd 64½ 911¼ Sorenson D LB 115 2.60 73-12 Sweet J. And J.1187¼ Cheri Creame116no Svclt J114½ Weakened 10
5Sep93- 9Dmr fst 6½f :22 :444 1:092 1:16 3+ ⒻClm 32000 77 2 6 62¾ 32 21½ 55 Desormeaux K J LB 117 *2.10 86-08 CottonBloomrs1121¼ LooknAtABlrr1191½ OldTmRmnc116nk Troubled trip 8
23Aug93- 7Dmr fm 1 Ⓣ :222 :461 1:11 1:36 3+ ⒻAlw 36000N1X 55 4 2 24 3½ 53½ 514¼ Desormeaux K J LB 119 3.10 76-11 Mr. P's Lady122¾ Roau Perrault119nk Happy Wife1221¼ Not urged late 8
10Jly93- 8Hol fst 5½f :22 :45 :574 1:033 ⒻAlw 12500s 91 6 3 53½ 54½ 53¼ 11½ Desormeaux K J LB 115 3.90 94-13 Isleo Bebe1151½ Mittens And Mink117hd Junior Queen1152 Late kick 8
5Sep92- 3Dmr fst 1 :214 :453 1:104 1:37 3+ ⒻClm c-20000 83 4 4 31½ 1hd 1hd 2½ Delahoussaye E LB 116 *1.50 81-10 Cindy Jane116½ Isleo Bebe1168 Heartsafiying116 Good effort 7
Claimed from Granja Vista Del Rio Stable, Palma Hector O Trainer
22Aug92- 2Dmr fst 1 1/16 :223 :461 1:112 1:441 3+ ⒻClm 25000 68 6 3 32½ 42 52½ 54½ Atkinson P LB 116 5.50 76-15 Helen D.116½ Pennblue1162 Ultra Sass114 Blocked 1/2-1/16 7
15Jly92- 5Hol fst 1 1/16 :224 :461 1:104 1:424 ⒻClm 20000 85 6 3 31½ 42 31 21 Atkinson P LB 115 18.80 86-12 Pennblue1161 Isleo Bebe115 Doctor Wendie115 Good try 8
22Jun92- 1Hol fst 7f :221 :451 1:101 1:231 ⒻClm 10000 79 1 4 11½ 11½ 12½ 13 Delahoussaye E LB 116 7.20 88-13 Isleo Bebe1163 Bounty Mane116no Go For Treasure116 Ridden out 9
WORKOUTS: Nov 26 SA 3f fst :372 B *9/16* Nov 8 SA 4f fst :472 H *7/50* Nov 1 SA 4f fst :481 H *19/45* Oct 18 SA 6f fst 1:144 H *11/18* Oct 12 SA 6f fst 1:01 H *27/51* ●Sep 19 SA 4f fst :484 H *1/50*

ALL-IN-ONE's output for race is as follows:

```
4DEC93                              HOL                   5.5 furlongs dirt
Race #3                                                          6 starters
C20,000                                              Age: 3+years, Female
---------------------------------INPUT DATA---------------------------------
```

Horse name	# ST	# W	# P	# S	$'S Earned	Date	Trk	Dist.	S	1st C time	2nd C time	Final time
DATSDAWAYITIS	8	3	2	0	36850	17NOV93	HOL	6.500	D	22.1	45.0	117.1
PERKY SLEW	7	1	2	2	25300	9OCT93	DMR	6.500	D	22.0	44.4	116.3
SOLDA HOLME	6	1	3	0	25324	18SEP93	YM	6.000	D	22.1	44.0	109.0
OLD TIME ROMANCE	14	1	3	4	37375	14NOV93	DMR	6.500	D	22.0	44.4	116.0
ISLEO BEBE	6	1	1	0	16050	14NOV93	SA	6.500	D	21.3	44.1	115.3

Horse name	Class Lvl	1st C B.L.	2nd C B.L.	Final B.L.	SR	Var
DATSDAWAYITIS	C12,500	2.00	1.50	0.00	83	14.0
PERKY SLEW	C20,000	4.00	4.75	6.75	81	10.0
SOLDA HOLME	C20,000	3.50	3.50	1.50	96	9.0
OLD TIME ROMANCE	C32,000	0.00	0.00	2.75	88	8.0
ISLEO BEBE	C20,000	5.25	8.50	6.00	87	10.0

```
--------------------------------BETTING LINE---------------------------------
```

Horse name	PEH	H-I	THAAI	P-H	ESP	Rating	Betting Line	Fair Place $	Fair Show $
	-------Rankings--------								
SOLDA HOLME	1	1	1	1	1	92.12	7-5	3.20	2.60
OLD TIME ROMANCE	2	2	2	3	2	82.14	5-2	4.00	3.20
DATSDAWAYITIS	3	4	3	2	4	67.35			
ISLEO BEBE	4	3	4	4	5	63.80			
PERKY SLEW	5	5	5	5	3	60.66			

```
-----------------------------EXACTA GRID----------------------
                   | SOLDA HOLME  |OLD TIME ROMANC|
         ----------+--------------+---------------+
SOLDA HOLME        | . . . . . . .|     9    22    |
                   | . . . . . . .|                |
                   | . . . . . . .|                |
         ----------+--------------+---------------+
OLD TIME ROMAN     |   11    27    | . . . . . . .  |
                   |               | . . . . . . .  |
                   |               | . . . . . . .  |
         ----------+--------------+---------------+
```

```
4DEC93                          HOL              5.5 furlongs dirt
Race #3                                                 6 starters
C20,000                                       Age: 3+years, Female
---------------------------SPEED/PACE SUMMARY---------------------

Race Type:        Double Advantage Race
Race Profile:     22.17    45.55  104.40   Winners' Pace Profile: FRONT
Ability Par:      68.93                     Pace Contention Point:  1.71 lengths

Projected Times:                           Ability Balance  Last  Proj Con-
                  1st C   2nd C   Fin C      Time    Time   Frac  Pace tender
                  -------------------------------------------------------------
SOLDA HOLME       21.96   44.76  103.90     67.57   62.12  19.14  FRONT  Y+
OLD TIME ROMANCE  21.78   45.04  104.29     68.31   62.55  19.25  FRONT  Y
DATSDAWAYITIS     22.27   45.79* 105.02     69.31   63.24  19.23  REAR   N
ISLEO BEBE        22.21   45.93* 104.54     69.65   62.64  18.61  REAR   N
PERKY SLEW        22.47   45.90* 105.67     69.32   63.83  19.77  REAR   N


------------------------------PACE GRAPH--------------------------
        Profile:                22.17            45.55           104.40
        Front Runner:           21.78            44.76           103.90
Horse name                         1C               2C                F
SOLDA HOLME       -----------------X+ ----------------(-X -------------------X
OLD TIME ROMANCE  -----------------X  ----------------(X+ -----------------X-+
DATSDAWAYITIS     -----------------X-+ ------------X--(-+ ------------X-----+
ISLEO BEBE        -----------------X-+ ------------X---(-+ ----------X--+
PERKY SLEW        -----------------X--+ -----------X---(-+ ---------X--------+
```

The morning line for our contenders in the third race is:

Solda Holme	3-1
Old Time Romance	15-1
Datsdawayitis	5-2
Isleo Bebe	7-5
Perky Slew	10-1

We have two methods for betting the Pick-3. The first is to bet all the combinations involving all the horses that are 6-to-1 or lower on our odds line, with two crucial exceptions. The first exception is the Pick-3 combination that contains three favorites. In the Pick-3 chapter of this book, we showed how the favorite-favorite-favorite combination is always a huge underlay. The second exception is the Pick-3 combination that contains two favorites. This combination is almost always underlayed. Once we remove these underlayed combinations from consideration, the remaining combinations are bet proportionally, with the likelier combinations receiving a bigger percentage of our bankroll. Let's apply this method to the Pick-3 on races 1-2-3. Here are our odds lines for these races:

First Race

Payand Payand Pay	4-1
Davus	4-1
Cocooning	9-2
Lovely One	5-1
Lackington	5-1

Second Race

Spruce Navy	6-5
Claret	6-1
Lanky Lord	6-1

Third Race

Solda Holme	7-5
Old Time Romance	5-2

We can quickly figure the maximum number of Pick-3 combinations we have to consider: We simply multiply the number of contenders in each leg. In this case, we multiply 5 × 3 × 2 and get 30. Hollywood Park's minimum Pick-3 bet size is $3. Hence, we must be prepared to invest more than $90 in this Pick-3. Do you see why? Unless all our combinations have the same probability of winning, we will wind up betting more than the minimum $3 on the likelier combinations. If we can invest only the minimum $90, we won't get the full benefit of this method—namely, to crush the strongest combinations.

The procedure behind this Pick-3 strategy is exactly like the risk-averse strategy for the daily double. We're playing all the possible combinations with the exception of those that have two or more favorites. We know that Davus is the first-race favorite. The morning-line favorites in the second and third races are Claret and Isleo Bebe, respectively. We will not play the combinations that contain two or all three of these horses.

We must first compute the probability of winning for each of our potential Pick-3 combinations. We do this as follows: Multiply the win probability of the win horse in the first leg by the win probability of the win horse in the second leg by the win probability of the win horse in the third leg. For example, a Pick-3 containing three 2-to-1 shots on our odds line would have a win probability of 3.7 percent ($\frac{1}{3} \times \frac{1}{3} \times \frac{1}{3} = .037$). Here is the win probability of each of our early Pick-3 combinations:

Payand Payand Pay–Spruce Navy–Solda Holme	.0379
Payand Payand Pay–Spruce Navy–Old Time Romance	.0260
Payand Payand Pay–Claret–Solda Holme	.0119
Payand Payand Pay–Claret–Old Time Romance	.0082
Payand Payand Pay–Lanky Lord–Solda Holme	.0119
Payand Payand Pay–Lanky Lord–Old Time Romance	.0082
Davus–Spruce Navy–Solda Holme	.0379
Davus–Spruce Navy–Old Time Romance	.0260
Davus–Claret–Solda Holme	.0119
Davus–Claret–Old Time Romance	.0082
Davus–Lanky Lord–Solda Holme	.0119
Davus–Lanky Lord–Old Time Romance	.0082
Cocooning–Spruce Navy–Solda Holme	.0344
Cocooning–Spruce Navy–Old Time Romance	.0236
Cocooning–Claret–Solda Holme	.0108
Cocooning–Claret–Old Time Romance	.0074
Cocooning–Lanky Lord–Solda Holme	.0108
Cocooning–Lanky Lord–Old Time Romance	.0074
Lovely One–Spruce Navy–Solda Holme	.0316
Lovely One–Spruce Navy–Old Time Romance	.0216
Lovely One–Claret–Solda Holme	.0099
Lovely One–Claret–Old Time Romance	.0068
Lovely One–Lanky Lord–Solda Holme	.0099
Lovely One–Lanky Lord–Old Time Romance	.0068
Lackington–Spruce Navy–Solda Holme	.0316
Lackington–Spruce Navy–Old Time Romance	.0216
Lackington–Claret–Solda Holme	.0099
Lackington–Claret–Old Time Romance	.0068
Lackington–Lanky Lord–Solda Holme	.0099
Lackington–Lanky Lord–Old Time Romance	.0068

We see that the most likely combinations involving our contenders each have just a 3.79 percent probability of winning. And the least likely combinations have less than a 1 percent chance of connecting. If we sum these probabilities, we find that our total likelihood of winning the Pick-3 based on these contenders is 47.58 percent.

The next step is to divide each combination's probability of winning by the total probability of winning. The result is the percentage of total bet size we should bet on that combination. In this example, the Payand Payand Pay–Spruce Navy–Solda Holme Pick-3 combination has a win probability of .0379. Dividing .0379 by .4758 we get .0797; .0797 represents the percentage of our total Pick-3 bet we can bet on this combination. When we apply this step to all the combinations, here's what we get:

Payand Payand Pay–Spruce Navy–Solda Holme	.0797	$8
Payand Payand Pay–Spruce Navy–Old Time Romance	.0546	$5
Payand Payand Pay–Claret–Solda Holme	.0250	$3
Payand Payand Pay–Claret–Old Time Romance	.0172	$3
Payand Payand Pay–Lanky Lord–Solda Holme	.0250	$3
Payand Payand Pay–Lanky Lord–Old Time Romance	.0172	$3
Davus–Spruce Navy–Solda Holme	.0796	$8
Davus–Spruce Navy–Old Time Romance	.0546	$5
~~Davus–Claret–Solda Holme~~	~~.0250~~	~~$3~~
~~Davus–Claret–Old Time Romance~~	~~.0172~~	~~$3~~
Davus–Lanky Lord–Solda Holme	.0250	$3
Davus–Lanky Lord–Old Time Romance	.0172	$3
Cocooning–Spruce Navy–Solda Holme	.0724	$7
Cocooning–Spruce Navy–Old Time Romance	.0496	$5
Cocooning–Claret–Solda Holme	.0227	$3
Cocooning–Claret–Old Time Romance	.0156	$3
Cocooning–Lanky Lord–Solda Holme	.0227	$3
Cocooning–Lanky Lord–Old Time Romance	.0156	$3
Lovely One–Spruce Navy–Solda Holme	.0663	$3
Lovely One–Spruce Navy–Old Time Romance	.0455	$5
Lovely One–Claret–Solda Holme	.0208	$3
Lovely One–Claret–Old Time Romance	.0143	$3
Lovely One–Lanky Lord–Solda Holme	.0208	$3
Lovely One–Lanky Lord–Old Time Romance	.0143	$3

Lackington–Spruce Navy–Solda Holme	.0663	$7
Lackington–Spruce Navy–Old Time Romance	.0455	$5
Lackington–Claret–Solda Holme	.0208	$3
Lackington–Claret–Old Time Romance	.0143	$3
Lackington–Lanky Lord–Solda Holme	.0208	$3
Lackington–Lanky Lord–Old Time Romance	.0143	$3
	.9999	$118

The number to the right is the amount you would bet if your total bet was $118. (The reason that the total is greater than $100 is the many combinations that had a probability less than 3 percent.) We multiply each of the numbers following the horses' names by the total amount we're investing in this Pick-3. Each result tells us how much to bet on that particular combination. For example, suppose we have a total of $300 to wager on. How much should we bet on the Payand Payand Pay–Spruce Navy–Solda Holme combination? We bet .0797 × $300, or $23.91 (which rounds to $24). Of course, the amount you bet on each combination would be a function of the total amount you invested in this Pick-3. Regardless of bet size, however, it's apparent that we'll bet more on the Payand Payand Pay–Spruce Navy–Solda Holme combination than we would on the Lackington–Lanky Lord–Old Time Romance combination.

What remains is to eliminate those combinations that contain two or three probable favorites. Davus is the actual first-race favorite. Checking the morning line, we see that Claret is the projected favorite in the second race and Isleo Bebe is the likely favorite in the third race. Isleo Bebe doesn't appear on our line, so the only combinations we need to drop are those that include both Davus and Claret. Let's draw a line through those combinations. Hence, we will no longer consider the Davus–Claret–Solda Holme and Davus–Claret–Old Time Romance combinations.

From a bet-size standpoint, we can eliminate these two combinations entirely and simply bet 5.08 percent less than we originally would have. Or we can preserve our original bet size. We take the money we would have bet on these two combinations and transfer it proportionally to the remaining combinations.

The second Pick-3 method is the "Key-3-3" strategy, which involves much less math. It asks us to designate our top three contenders in each leg. From these contenders, we then choose a "key" horse in each leg. Each key horse is paired to the remaining three contenders in each of the other legs. Hence we have three Pick-3 part-wheels: key horse–three contenders–three contenders, three contenders–key horse–three contenders, three contenders–three contenders–key horse. Each of these part-wheels covers nine combinations, so we are actually playing a total of 27 combinations.

We don't cover each combination equally, however. For example, the combination containing three key horses will be covered three times. The combinations containing two key horses will be covered twice. All other combinations will be covered once. Using this strategy, it's necessary for at least one key horse to win in order for us to have a shot at winning the Pick-3. We then need one of our three contenders in each of the remaining legs to win.

Ideally, the three key horses will be our top pick in each of their respective races. However, we must always protect ourselves from keying three probable favorites, or for that matter two probable favorites. We know who the favorite in the first leg will be. We check the morning line to get a good idea of who the favorites in the other two legs will be. If two or more of our key horses figure to be favored, we choose a different trio of key horses until we have only one key horse who's favored.

Let's construct a Key-3-3 Pick-3 ticket on workshop races one through three. Here are *ALL-IN-ONE*'s top three selections for races two and three:

First Race	Second Race	Third Race
Payand Payand Pay	*Spruce Navy*	*Solda Holme*
Davus	Claret	Old Time Romance
Cocooning	Lanky Lord	Datsdawayitis

We know that Davus is the favorite in the first race. Claret and Isleo Bebe are the morning-line favorites for the second and third races, respectively. Hence, we have no difficulty in making our three top picks, Payand Payand Pay, Spruce Navy, and Solda Holme, our key horses. We buy three Pick-3 part-wheels: The first is Payand Payand Pay with Spruce Navy, Claret, and Lanky Lord with Solda Home, Old Time, and Datsdawayitis; the second is Payand Payand Pay, Davus, and Cocooning with Spruce Navy with

Solda Home, Old Time Romance, and Datsdawayitis; the third is Payand Payand Pay, Davus, and Cocooning with Spruce Navy, Claret, and Lanky Lord with Solda Home.

Let's step back and see just how much work we've done to pick the proper bets before the first race. We've decided on bets in the win, exacta, quinella, daily double, and Pick-3 pools. Here's what we found:

Win Bets

The aggressive bettor bets one horse per race. He calculates his edge on each bet. If a bet offers no edge or a negative edge, it's no longer considered. Any potential win bet must have an edge of at least 20 percent. If more than one bet offers this edge, the edge-to-odds ratio determines the single best bet.

In the first race, the aggressive bettor has only one bet: Lackington. Although the edge-to-odds ratio or Kelly criterion says this bettor could risk up to 11 percent of his bankroll on this bet, it would be much more prudent to invest a considerably smaller sum, no more than 5 percent of bankroll. Since this is a chaos race, it's wise to bet your minimum amount. (You can't trust odds lines in chaos races.) In my case, this amount is $20. Normally, when I like a race I'll bet $200 or more to win.

The moderate bettor can bet more than one horse per race, provided all his bets satisfy his minimum edge requirement. If he has more than one win bet in a race, he uses the edge-to-odds ratio to determine which of his bets deserves the most money.

In the first race, Lackington and Lovely One each offer an edge in excess of 20 percent. Hence the moderate bettor would bet them both. The edge-to-odds ratio favors Lackington .1148 to .048. This suggests that the bet size should be divided 70-30 in favor of Lackington.

The conservative bettor looks for situations in which his contenders are grossly underestimated by the betting public. He seeks a group probability of at least 66 percent among his contenders and demands that these contenders be underestimated by the betting public by 10 percent. When he finds such a situation, he can bet all his contenders in varying amounts so that he approximately gains the same amount of profit no matter which of his contenders wins. In the first race, the conservative bettor's five contenders were not underestimated by the betting public.

Exacta

The Mitchell Matrix is reserved for contentious races in which four or more contenders are considered equal. (It's especially powerful in chaos races because there is no ordering and all the putative contenders are equal.) Since all contenders are equal, each exacta involving these contenders should have the same chance of coming in. Since the risk attached to each combination is the same, the potential reward of each combination should dictate which combinations are played. The highest-paying combinations are played, and the number of combinations played is equal to the number of contenders in the race.

In the first race, there are five evenly matched contenders: Payand Payand Pay, Davus, Cocooning, Lovely One, and Lackington. Based on these contenders, the five highest-paying exacta combinations are Lovely One–Lackington, Lackington–Lovely One, Lackington–Payand Payand Pay, Lackington-Davus, and Lackington-Cocooning. The same amount is bet on each of these combinations.

The exacta overlay strategy assigns a fair pay to each combination. It then compares the fair pay to the probable pay. Any combination whose probable pay is less than its fair pay is dismissed. The probable pay of the remaining combinations must be high enough to compensate for the guaranteed losing bets on the other remaining combinations, plus offer an additional edge of at least 20 percent. In the first race, the exacta overlay strategy uncovers eight combinations: Lackington top and bottom with the other four contenders. The edge-to-odds ratio is used to determined how much to bet on each of these combinations.

Daily Double

The risk-averse bettor will bet all the possible combinations involving contenders that are 6-to-1 or lower on the betting line in races one and two. The combinations that have a greater chance of winning will be bet more heavily.

In the first race, there are five contenders; in the second, three. Hence, there are 15 combinations to bet on. He will bet more money on the combinations that have a greater chance of winning according to his line on both races.

The aggressive daily double player operates much like the exacta overlay player. He calculates each combination's fair pay, then compares it to the probable pays. He eliminates those combinations that are paying less than they should. He then demands two premiums from the remaining combinations: that they pay enough to compensate for the guaranteed losing bets on the other remaining combinations and that they offer an additional edge of at least 20 percent.

In the early double there are five bettable combinations: Lovely One–Spruce Navy, Lovely One–Lanky Lord, Lackington–Spruce Navy, Lackington-Claret, and Lackington–Lanky Lord. He uses the edge-to-odds ratio to determine how much to bet on each combination.

Pick-3

The decision-oriented Pick-3 player bets on nearly all the possible combinations involving the horses that are 6-to-1 or less on his line in the three legs. He leaves out those combinations that contain two or more probable favorites. He bets more money on the remaining combinations that have a higher probability of winning.

In the day's first Pick-3, there are 28 combinations to bet out of a possible 30. The Key-3-3 Pick-3 player selects his top three contenders in each leg of the series. He then selects a key horse from among those three horses in each leg, for a total of three key horses. The trio of key horses should contain not more than one probable favorite. Each key horse is then singled in its leg of the Pick-3 to the three contenders in each of the other legs.

In the day's first Pick-3 the key horses are Payand Payand Pay, Spruce Navy, and Solda Holme.

You're probably getting the idea that these commonsense betting strategies require a huge amount of work. You're also seeing that this work is nearly impossible to do by hand in the few short minutes before each race. Now you see why I wouldn't venture

within 50 feet of a betting window without at least one, and prefer-
ably two (just in case one fails), pocket computers. Let's see what
happened in the first race:

Last Raced	Horse	M/Eqt.A.Wt	PP	St	¼	½	¾	Str	Fin	Jockey	Cl'g Pr	Odds $1
7Nov93 4SA²	Cocooning	LB	4 119	5	1	2¹	2¹½	2ʰᵈ	1ʰᵈ	1ʰᵈ	Valenzuela P A	25000	2.50
10Oct93 8Fpx²	Great Event	LBb	6 117	1	4	3ʰᵈ	3ʰᵈ	31	3ʰᵈ	2ʰᵈ	Pincay L Jr	25000	6.60
7Nov93 7SA²	Davus	LBb	5 116	3	3	42½	41	42	45	3½	Nakatani C S	25000	*2.30
28Nov93 1Hol⁷	Lackington–Ch	LB	5 116	4	2	1½	1½	11	21	41½	Solis A	25000	15.90
26Nov93 6Hol⁶	Lovely One–Ar	LB	6 116	6	6	6	6	6	6	5⁹	Lopez A D	25000	7.10
7Nov93 7SA¹	Payand Payand Pay	LBbf	5 119	2	5	5¹⁰	5¹²	57	5ʰᵈ	6	Black C A	25000	2.30

FIRST RACE 1¹⁄₁₆ MILES. (1.40) CLAIMING. Purse $17,000. 3-year-olds and upward. Weights: 3-year-olds, 119 lbs.
Older, 122 lbs. Non-winners of two races at a mile or over since October 4, allowed 3 lbs. Such a race
Hollywood since then, 6 lbs. Claiming price $25,000; If for $22,500, 2 lbs. (Races when entered for $20,000 or less not
DECEMBER 4, 1993 considered.)(Day 14 of a 26 Day Meet. Clear. 78.)
Value of Race: $17,000 Winner $9,350; second $3,400; third $2,550; fourth $1,275; fifth $425. Mutuel Pool $233,131.00 Exacta Pool
$185,157.00 Quinella Pool $32,493.00

*—Actual Betting Favorite.

OFF AT 12:30 Start Good. Won driving. Time, :23, :46¹, 1:10⁴, 1:36³, 1:42⁴ Track fast.

$2 Mutuel Prices:

5–COCOONING	7.00	4.40	2.80
1–GREAT EVENT		7.00	3.40
3–DAVUS			2.80

$2 EXACTA 5–1 PAID $41.80 $2 QUINELLA 1–5 PAID $23.40

Our win bet on Lackington nearly came out; the horse was
beaten by less than a length in the end. Pity. We also lost our win
wager on Lovely One.

Lackington was an integral part of all our exacta strategies.
Needless to say, we won't be cashing that bet this time. Nor will we
collect on the quinella, since Great Event wasn't included among
our contenders.

The risk-averse daily double player is alive to three horses in the
second. So is the daily double player who chose a key horse in each
half and part-wheeled his key horses to the top three contenders in
the remaining half. The more aggressive daily double overlay
player isn't as fortunate: None of the overlayed combinations he
played shows Cocooning winning the first race.

Finally, both Pick-3 strategies produced tickets that include
Cocooning as the winner of the first leg.

Let's move on to the second race. We don't have a daily double
to worry about. We do have a new Pick-3 to consider. The past performances and *ALL-IN-ONE* printout for the second race ap-
peared earlier. Refer to them to determine how you'd bet this race.

Here are the odds for our contenders in this race as they ap-
peared on the toteboard just before post time:

Spruce Navy	3-1
Claret	3-1
Lanky Lord	7-1

At a glance, we see that Claret is a huge underlay. Lanky Lord offers a slight overlay, but is it enough? Let's find out:

$$E(x) = .1429 \times 7 - .8571 = .1432$$

Our edge on Lanky Lord is 14.32 percent. This indeed is a positive expectation, but it doesn't meet our minimum 20 percent edge requirement on win bets. Regardless of our temperaments as aggressive or moderate win bettors, the only win bet we can consider in this race is Spruce Navy. He's going off at two and a half times his rightful odds. The edge on Spruce Navy is 81.8 percent; the edge-to-odds ratio is .27. This suggests we can bet 27 percent of our total win-betting bankroll on Spruce Navy. As always, betting this percentage of our total stake would be sheer lunacy. We should bet no more than 5 percent of our total.

Does the group overlay method apply here? Our group estimate is 73 percent. The public's estimate of our group is 63 percent. Our group estimate is greater than 66 percent. The public has undervalued our group by at least 10 percent. Hence, we can apply the group overlay method to this race. The ultraconservative group overlay method allows us to win this race nearly three out of four times by betting all three of our contenders: the huge overlay (Spruce Navy), the marginal overlay (Lanky Lord), and the big underlay (Claret).

We notice that *ALL-IN-ONE* considers Spruce Navy a very strong top pick who should be considered in the place-and-show pools. The program doesn't recommend place-and-show bets on a horse unless it has a betting line of 5-to-2 or lower. In the case of Spruce Navy, we can bet him to place if he pays at least $3.20 in the worst-case scenario. Or we can play him to show if he pays at least $2.40, again in the worst-case scenario. These prices represent fair pays, so we should demand slightly higher actual place-and-show prices in order to guarantee a positive-expectation situation.

In terms of exactas, the second race doesn't appear contentious. We have a very strong top pick in Spruce Navy. We can quickly figure that the exactas involving Claret will be serious underlays, since Claret is 6-to-1 on our line and 3-to-1 on the public line. A rough estimate of the exacta overlays would combine Spruce Navy and Lanky Lord, the two overlays on our line.

This race has seven starters, so we're also offered a trifecta. Remember the Key-Place-All strategy. It asks us to designate a "key" horse, which should be our top-figure horse. On paper, the key horse should easily come in first and have almost no chance of finishing worse than second or third. Most important, the key horse must not be the public favorite. In this race, Spruce Navy makes a wonderful key horse. He dominates the field on the numbers and isn't the public favorite.

We next designate the "place" horses. Public favorites who have the top figures make wonderful place horses, since we can't make them key horses. Generally, we'll have two to three place horses. Based on *ALL-IN-ONE*'s line, Claret and Lanky Lord seem to be the place horses in this race. From a handicapping standpoint, however, Claret and Royal Torrent have the second and third-fastest final times in the field. So let's make Claret, Lanky Lord, and Royal Torrent our place horses.

Finally, we designate the "all" horses. The all horses can generally run within five lengths (one second) of the final time par for the race. The all horses should also contain our key and place horses as well. We should end up with around four or five all horses. According to the printout, all five of our contenders can run to within five lengths of the final-time par of 143.25 for this race. This allows us to make Royal Dixie an all horse. So our all horses include all five of our contenders in this race.

We now have our key horse (Spruce Navy), our place horses (Claret, Lanky Lord, and Royal Torrent), and our all horses (our five contenders). We construct the trifecta bets using the following three trifecta part wheels: Key-Place-All, Place-Key-All, All-Place-Key.

A new Pick-3 begins with this race, so let's look ahead to our contenders and line for the fourth race:

Hollywood Park

4

1 1/16 MILES. (1:40) **MAIDEN CLAIMING. Purse $17,000. 2-year-olds. Weight, 119 lbs. Claiming price $32,000; if for $28,000, allowed 2 lbs. (Horses which have not started for a claiming price of $20,000 or less preferred.)**

1 1/16 MILES — FINISH ▲ START

Sierra Real
Own: McCaffery & Toffan
GONZALEZ S JR (45 3 5 5 .07) $32,000
Dk. b or br g. 2 (Mar)
Sire: Cox's Ridge (Best Turn)
Dam: Prove Us Royal (Prove It)
Br: Marian L. Conrad (Ky)
Tr: Gonzalez J Paco (7 1 2 1 .14)
1145

Lifetime Record: 3 M 0 1 $4,125
1993 3 M 0 1 $4,125 | Turf 0 0 0 0
1992 0 M 0 0 | Wet 0 0 0 0
Hol 0 0 0 0 | Dist 0 0 0 0

22Oct93-6SA fst 1 :224 :464 1:123 1:384 Md 32000 60 6 4 41½ 1hd 1½ 33 Gonzalez S5 B 112 b 12.70 73-21 Veracity117hd Prevasive Force1172¾ Sierra Real1123½ 4 Wide 2nd turn 9
3Sep93-9Dmr fst 1 :223 :463 1:112 1:372 Md 40000 57 6 8 85½ 69½ 69 411½ Gonzalez S5 B 113 b 12.60 68-19 Mr Wonder Boy1112½ Set On Cruise1183½ U Dirty Rat1185½ Off slowly, wide 9
28Jly93-6Dmr fst 5f :22 :454 :583 Md Sp Wt 51 4 6 76¾ 79½ 79 78¼ Gonzalez S5 112 b 13.40 96-07 Showdown1172½ Shepherd's Field117hd Drouilly River1172 4 Wide stretch 8
WORKOUTS: Nov 28 SA 6f fst 1:142 H 9/20 Nov 22 SA 6f fst 1:142 H 12/18 Nov 14 SA 4f fst :471 H 4/39 Nov 5 SA 3f fst :354 H 2/41 Oct 31 SA 5f fst 1:012 H 33/67 Oct 16 SA 6f fst 1:17 H 5/7

My Ideal
Own: Gesell & Leimbach & Smith
ANTLEY C W (43 5 5 5 .12) $32,000
Gr. g. 2 (Feb)
Sire: Swing Till Dawn (Grey Dawn II)
Dam: Mapleton (Big Spruce)
Br: Gesell, Leimbach, Smith & Gesell (Cal)
Tr: Ellis Ronald W (6 3 0 0 .50)
119

Lifetime Record: 1 M 0 0 $425
1993 1 M 0 0 $425 | Turf 0 0 0 0
1992 0 M 0 0 | Wet 0 0 0 0
Hol 0 0 0 0 | Dist 0 0 0 0

15Nov93-6SA fst 7f :232 :47 1:114 1:243 SMd 32000 49 8 9 82 62¾ 57 56½ Gonzalez S5 B 112 6.10 74-15 He's Fabulous1171¾ Win The Case115hd Al's Sunshine1173½ 4 Wide trip 10
WORKOUTS: Dec 2 SA 3f fst :361 H 8/19 Nov 25 SA 5f fst 1:012 H 17/39 Nov 4 SA 5f fst 1:03 Hg 33/37 Oct 29 SA 5f fst 1:044 H 46/47 Oct 22 SA 6f fst 1:17 H 17/18 Oct 15 SA 6f fst 1:162 H 21/23

Prevasive Force
Own: Cox Or Rice Or V-K Stable
SOLIS A (67 9 12 12 .13) $32,000
Dk. b or br g. 2 (Apr)
Sire: Banner Bob (Herculean)
Dam: Cabin Home (Cabin)
Br: Arthur B. Hancock III (Ky)
Tr: Dominguez Caesar F (20 4 4 5 .20)
L 119

Lifetime Record: 12 M 4 3 $38,090
1993 12 M 4 3 $38,090 | Turf 1 0 0 0 $2,250
1992 0 M 0 0 | Wet 0 0 0 0
Hol 3 0 0 1 $7,875 | Dist 2 0 1 0 $5,840

17Nov93-4Hol fm 1 Ⓣ :463 1:111 1:361 Md Sp Wt 60 8 7 811 86½ 46 48 Solis A LB 118 b 3.00 76-14 Valiant Nature1183½ Saltgrass1183½ Unrivaled1181 Wide into lane 9
Quarter time unavailable
4Nov93-7SA fst 1 :223 :462 1:113 1:373 Clm 45000 78 7 6 77½ 53 43½ 3½ Solis A LB 113 b 11.30 81-17 TripleThunder115½ CllMeSncho116hd PrevsiveForc1133 Lacked room 1/4 7
22Oct93-6SA fst 1 :224 :464 1:123 1:384 Md 32000 65 3 5 52¾ 51½ 41½ 2hd Solis A LB 117 b 2.70 76-21 Veracity117hd Prevasive Force1172¾ Sierra Real1123½ Game try 9
8Oct93-4SA fst 1 1/16 :23 :48 1:13 1:452 Md 32000 69 6 5 52¾ 53 2½ 2nk Solis A LB 117 *1.80 77-17 SetOnCruise117nk PrevsiveForce11710 WelcomDiscovry1172 Good effort 9
23Sep93-7Fpx fst 1 1/16 :23 :472 1:13 1:45 Md Sp Wt 72 1 6 74½ 64 55½ 43½ Valenzuela F H LB 118 3.10 79-14 SirHrryBright118hd Peter'sPride'njoy1182 SoundsSoLucky1181½ Mild bid 7
10Sep93-6Dmr fst 6f :22 :451 :572 1:102 Md 50000 69 6 6 89¾ 65½ 34 33¼ Solis A LB 118 2.60 84-13 Mkinnhonstbuck1182 Twictonght1181½ PrvsvForc1185½ Wide backstretch 10
27Aug93-6Dmr fst 5½f :22 :452 :573 1:041 Md 50000 71 2 5 65 65½ 43½ 22 Solis A LB 117 3.10 88-11 Mark Ninety1152 Prevasive Force1171½ Ninety Knots1171 5 Wide stretch 8
14Aug93-4Dmr fst 6f :221 :45 :571 1:10 Md Sp Wt 68 2 6 79½ 710 58½ 46 Solis A LB 117 38.60 83-13 Ferrara1171¾ Devil's Mirage117hd Shepherd's Field1174 4 Wide stretch 7
30Jly93-6Dmr fst 5½f :22 :46 :581 1:044 Md 50000 66 10 5 54 54 42 23 Solis A LB 117 5.70 84-13 Puzar1173 Prevasive Force117hd Bursting Point1171½ Wide backstretch 10
10Jly93-2Hol fst 5½f :22 :453 :581 1:044 Md Sp Wt 46 6 1 61¾ 43 46 38½ Flores D R LB 117 16.00 79-12 Prenup117no Gracious Ghost1178½ Prevasive Force1172¾ Wide trip 7

Vinoyhielo
Own: Sides Clay R & Geri & Jill
LOPEZ A D (13 1 2 0 .08) $28,000
Dk. b or br g. 2 (Apr)
Sire: Desert Wine (Damascus)
Dam: Queenly Command (Empery)
Br: Cardiff Stud Farm (Cal)
Tr: Sides Robert C (2 0 0 0 .00)
117

Lifetime Record: 6 M 0 0 $2,175
1993 6 M 0 0 $2,175 | Turf 0 0 0 0
1992 0 M 0 0 | Wet 0 0 0 0
Hol 1 0 0 0 | Dist 0 0 0 0

24Nov93-9Hol fst 6½f :22 :451 1:112 1:18 SMd 28000 24 4 12 1211 1211 1012 1013¼ Silva J G B 117 b 79.20 66-09 StoneCountyRod117nk LordsIrishAngel119¾ MyFltStr119¾ Pinched start 12
13Nov93-9SA fst 6f :22 :45 :573 1:11 SMd 32000 46 4 8 119¾ 109¾ 87½ 66½ Silva J G B 118 b 107.40 76-11 Daily Eagle118no Smooth Shot118no Dash Of Vanilla1162¼ By tired ones 11
29Oct93-4SA fst 7f :221 :451 1:112 1:25 Md 32000 20 10 9 129 1216 1116 1117 Silva J G LB 118 b 226.70 61-19 Ketchum Z's1181½ Win The Case116hd Al Khedive1132¾ Wide, outrun 12
9Sep93-6Dmr fst 6f :22 :451 :57 1:092 SMd 32000 31 10 4 62¾ 109¾ 1114 1121¾ Noguez A M LB 118 b 86.60 70-09 Double The Weather1187½ Still Swingin'118no Golden Explo1135 Wide trip 12
29Aug93-3Dmr fst 6f :223 :46 :58 1:103 SMd Sp Wt 36 3 4 54 57½ 513 416¾ Perez I5 L 112 b 44.70 69-11 Don's Reality1171¾ Teasing Sea1175 Super Half11710 No mishap 6
15Aug93-6Dmr fst 5½f :211 :442 :573 1:044 SMd Sp Wt -0 1 8 1018 1028 1026 1028½ Perez I5 LB 112 b 131.50 59-11 Subtle Trouble117½ Best Year Ever1171½ Don's Reality1173½ Trailed 10
WORKOUTS: Nov 29 SLR tr.t 6f fst 1:162 H 3/3 Nov 5 SLR tr.t 5f fst 1:013 Hg 3/5 Oct 25 SLR tr.t 4f fst :482 H 2/4 Oct 19 SLR tr.t 5f fst 1:02 H 5/6 Oct 14 SLR tr.t 5f fst 1:022 H 4/6 Oct 9 SLR tr.t 4f fst :481 H 4/15

Stage Door Tyler
Own: Chadwick & Park & Sukasian
VALENZUELA F H (49 8 3 3 .16) $32,000
Ch. g. 2 (May)
Sire: Lil Tyler (Halo)
Dam: Cherry Sauce (Stage Door Johnny)
Br: Richard D. Clark & Charles E. Clark (Cal)
Tr: Valenzuela Martin Jr (3 0 0 1 .00)
L 119

Lifetime Record: 11 M 3 2 $9,835
1993 11 M 3 2 $9,835 | Turf 0 0 0 0
1992 0 M 0 0 | Wet 0 0 0 0
Hol 4 0 0 1 $2,550 | Dist 2 0 1 1 $5,610

17Nov93-2Hol fst 1 1/16 :233 :474 1:114 1:431 Md 32000 56 6 7 55½ 56½ 310 318 Valenzuela F H LB 119 b 8.50 67-17 StillSwingin'11914 DnnyTheDemon1194 StgDoorTylr1196½ Stumbled start 8
14Oct93-3BM fst 1 :234 :48 1:132 1:40 Md 12500 56 10 3 31½ 42½ 33½ 33 Chapman T M LB 118 b *2.00 67-26 T. C. Blue1181 Taj Raj1182 Stage Door Tyler1186 Far wide early 10
9Oct93-4BM fst 1 :23 :472 1:124 1:392 Md Sp Wt 29 9 8 73¾ 89½ 916 618½ Meza R Q LB 118 b *1.90 55-20 Night Letter1181½ Zee Bee1186 Barts Demon1182 No rally 10
29Sep93-7Fpx fst 1 1/16 :224 :47 1:123 1:452 Md 32000 72 6 3 4¾ 12 1hd 2no Lopez A D LB 118 b 7.10 81-21 IsidroYMrtine118no StgeDoorTyler1185 TrifectChif1187 4 Wide 2nd turn 9
20Sep93-5Fpx fst 6f :221 :454 :58 1:104 Md 32000 51 1 3 65¾ 47 47½ 57 Valenzuela F H LB 118 b 4.00 86-08 Mindy's Moon1182 Tis Careno1183 Key Mood1181 No late bid 9
31Aug93-7Sac fst 6f :22 :454 :583 1:111 Md 12500 49 3 6 65½ 53½ 2½ 2hd Martinez J C LB 118 b 2.90 83-14 Niners Song118hd Stage Door Tyler11810 Postchopper118½ 8
Steadied 1/8
25Aug93-6Sac fst 6f :221 :461 :59 1:12 Md 12500 42 4 8 74¾ 4½ 2½ 22 Noguez A M LB 118 b 2.20 77-16 HlosPreferred1182 StgeDoorTyler1181½ PrinceSpikedT1191½ Second best 8
29Jly93-4Dmr fst 5½f :223 :464 :594 1:063 SMd 32000 24 10 2 84¾ 85 98½ 99½ Sanchez P N5 LB 112 b 63.00 69-18 Our Blue Michael112½ SlickSurface1173 Skyhook117hd Wide backstretch 11
16Jly93-6Hol fst 5½f :221 :462 :59 1:054 SMd 32000 43 9 8 84¾ 85½ 85½ 85 Sanchez P N5 LB 113 b 72.70 78-13 Mamystere1181½ Cutlass Steal118no Tioga Summit1162¾ Wide early 11
23Jun93-6Hol fst 5f :221 :461 :59 Md 32000 12 4 5 65 78 79 714 Pedroza M A B 118 b 7.30 75-13 King Coping1181½ Key Mood1164½ Umpscious116½ Outrun 8
WORKOUTS: Nov 27 Fpx 5f fst 1:032 H 13/15 ●Nov 15 Fpx 3f fst :364 H 1/5 Nov 9 Fpx 7f fst 1:283 H 1/1 ●Nov 3 Fpx 6f fst 1:16 H 1/4 Oct 27 Fpx 5f fst 1:031 H 2/3 Sep 18 Fpx 3f fst :364 H 9/15

Skagit Chief
Own: Ferguson & Garza
LONG B (23 1 0 3 .04) $32,000
B. c. 2 (Mar)
Sire: Greenough (Prince John)
Dam: Spring Time Lady (Philately)
Br: Mr. & Mrs. Robert Ferguson (WA)
Tr: Dolan John K (3 1 1 0 .33)
119

Lifetime Record: 1 M 0 0 $0
1993 1 M 0 0 | Turf 0 0 0 0
1992 0 M 0 0 | Wet 0 0 0 0
Hol 0 0 0 0 | Dist 0 0 0 0

30Oct93-2SA fst 6f :211 :444 :581 1:112 Md 32000 34 9 7 1011 1115 1212 1212¾ Lopez A D B 118 130.30 67-12 Water Garden118no Decidedly Friendly1182¾ Cajero1182½ Wide, outrun 12
WORKOUTS: Nov 27 Hol 1 fst 1:444 H 3/3 Nov 13 Hol 1 fst 1:434 H 2/2 Nov 7 Hol 4f fst :483 Hg 12/21 Oct 23 Hol 5f fst 1:013 Hg 12/16 Oct 12 Hol 4f fst :474 H 3/13 Oct 6 Hol 5f fst 1:05 H 20/21

Al's Sunshine
Own: J B S Stable
PEDROZA M A (27 1 2 6 .04) $32,000
Ch. g. 2 (Apr)
Sire: Al Mamoon (Believe It)
Dam: Forli's Sunshine (Forli)
Br: Cardiff Stud Farm (Cal)
Tr: Moerman Gerald C (1 0 0 0 .00)
L 119

Lifetime Record: 2 M 0 1 $2,550
1993 2 M 0 1 $2,550 | Turf 0 0 0 0
1992 0 M 0 0 | Wet 0 0 0 0
Hol 0 0 0 0 | Dist 0 0 0 0

15Nov93-6SA fst 7f :232 :47 1:114 1:243 SMd 32000 59 1 4 61¾ 83½ 44 32 Pedroza M A LB 117 16.00 78-15 He's Fabulous1171¾ Win The Case115hd Al's Sunshine1173½ Inside bid 10
6Oct93-6SA fst 1 :23 :464 1:12 1:38 Md Sp Wt 37 6 10 97 97¾ 911 919 Valenzuela F H LB 117 85.40 61-20 Hot Number117½ Devil's Mirage117hd Twicetonight1185 Steadied start 10
WORKOUTS: Nov 26 SA 4f fst :463 H 2/39 Nov 12 SA 5f gd 1:033 H 38/53 Nov 2 SA 6f fst 1:16 H 12/12 Oct 28 SA 5f fst 1:013 H 8/9 Oct 23 SA 3f fst :364 B 13/22 Oct 4 SA 4f fst :471 H 11/38

Rifling Thru
Own: Hoffman Lathrop G
ATKINSON P (21 3 1 2 .14) $28,000
Ro. g. 2 (May)
Sire: Night Mover (Cutlass)
Dam: Bullion (Ack Ack)
Br: Diane C. Kem (WA)
Tr: Fanning Jerry (7 2 0 0 .29)
L 117

Lifetime Record: 2 M 0 0 $425
1993 2 M 0 0 $425 | Turf 0 0 0 0
1992 0 M 0 0 | Wet 0 0 0 0
Hol 0 0 0 0 | Dist 0 0 0 0

11Nov93-4SA gd 6f :214 :454 :59 1:123 Md 32000 52 4 7 86¾ 74¾ 73¾ 53 Atkinson P LB 118 b 14.60 71-21 Viareggio118no Sundays Cream118nk Chuppatti118¾ Mild bid 8
26Sep93-5Fpx fst 6f :214 :464 :584 1:122 Md 32000 38 1 8 917 1014 99½ 96¼ Atkinson P B 118 28.80 79-09 Mob Stage1181½ Suomi Power1181 Gary's Lucky One1181 Outrun 10
WORKOUTS: Dec 1 SA 4f fst :482 H 15/48 Nov 24 SA 6f fst 1:133 H 4/8 ●Nov 18 SA 6f fst 1:124 H 1/13 Nov 5 SA 5f fst 1:013 H 40/93 Oct 30 SA 4f fst :484 H 37/69 Oct 15 SA 6f fst 1:144 H 17/23

Count Con
Own: Hawn W R
GRYDER A T (46 9 5 6 .20) $32,000
Dk. b or br c. 2 (May)
Sire: Fast Account (Private Account)
Dam: Con's Sister (Summer Time Guy)
Br: W. R. Hawn (Cal)
Tr: MacDonald Mark (5 0 0 0 .00)
L 119

Lifetime Record: 1 M 0 0 $0
1993 1 M 0 0 | Turf 0 0 0 0
1992 0 M 0 0 | Wet 0 0 0 0
Hol 0 0 0 0 | Dist 0 0 0 0

15Nov93-6SA fst 7f :232 :47 1:114 1:243 SMd 32000 23 2 10 1010 1010 917 818½ Antley C W B 117 15.60 61-15 He's Fabulous1171¾ Win The Case115hd Al's Sunshine1173½ Off slow, green 10
WORKOUTS: Dec 1 SA 5f fst 1:004 Hg 12/51 Nov 25 SA 5f fst 1:02 H 26/39 Nov 7 SA 4f fst :473 H 14/37 Nov 1 SA 4f fst :484 Hg 24/45 Oct 26 SA 7f fst 1:271 H 9/11 Oct 20 SA 6f fst 1:14 H 15/26

ALL-IN-ONE's output for the race is as follows:

```
4DEC93                          HOL                    8.5 furlongs dirt
Race #4                                                        8 starters
MCL                                                 Age: 2 years, Male
--------------------------------INPUT DATA--------------------------------
```

Horse name	# ST	# W	# P	# S	$'S Earned	Date	Trk	Dist.	S	1st C time	2nd C time	Final time
SIERRA REAL	0	0	0	0	0	22OCT93	SA	8.000	D	46.4	112.3	138.4
MY IDEAL	0	0	0	0	0	15NOV93	SA	7.000	D	23.2	47.0	124.3
STAGE DOOR TYLER	0	0	0	0	0	17NOV93	HOL	8.500	D	47.4	111.4	143.1
AL'S SUNSHINE	0	0	0	0	0	15NOV93	SA	7.000	D	23.2	47.0	124.3
RIFLING THRU	0	0	0	0	0	11NOV93	SA	6.000	D	21.4	45.4	112.3

Horse name	Class Lvl	1st C B.L.	2nd C B.L.	Final B.L.	SR	Var
SIERRA REAL	MCL	1.25	0.00	2.00	73	21.0
MY IDEAL	MCL	3.00	0.75	6.50	74	15.0
STAGE DOOR TYLER	MCL	5.50	6.50	18.00	67	17.0
AL'S SUNSHINE	MCL	1.75	3.50	1.00	78	15.0
RIFLING THRU	MCL	6.75	4.75	3.00	71	21.0

```
-------------------------------BETTING LINE-------------------------------
```

Horse name	PEH	H-I	THAAI	P-H	ESP	Rating	Betting Line	Fair Place $	Fair Show $
SIERRA REAL	1	2	2	1	2	74.58	9-5	3.60	2.80
AL'S SUNSHINE	2	1	1	2	5	69.58	7-2		
MY IDEAL	3	3	3	3	4	64.85	7-1		
STAGE DOOR TYLER	5	4	4	4	1	64.59			
RIFLING THRU	4	5	5	5	3	61.68			

```
-------------------------------EXACTA GRID-------------------------------
```

	STAGE DOOR TYLE		AL'S SUNSHINE		MY IDEAL	
STAGE DOOR TYL	. . . .		15	36	28	69
AL'S SUNSHINE	18	43	. . . .		49	122
MY IDEAL	38	94	57	141	. . . .	

```
4DEC93                          HOL                    8.5 furlongs dirt
Race #4                                                        8 starters
MCL                                                 Age: 2 years, Male
-----------------------------SPEED/PACE SUMMARY---------------------------
```

Race Type:	Chaos Race						
Race Profile:	46.99	111.67	144.48	Winners' Pace Profile: EARLY			
Ability Par:	96.36			Pace Contention Point: 0.79 lengths			

Projected Times:	1st C	2nd C	Fin C	Ability Time	Balance Time	Last Frac	Proj Pace	Con- tender
SIERRA REAL	46.61	112.05	145.76	97.50	103.60	33.70	FRONT	N
AL'S SUNSHINE	47.60	113.25*	145.06	98.90	102.74	31.81	REAR	N
MY IDEAL	47.65	113.10*	146.17	98.56	103.78	33.07	REAR	N
STAGE DOOR TYLER	48.85	112.99*	146.66	97.13	103.59	33.67	LATE	N
RIFLING THRU	47.86	112.99*	147.10	98.12	104.41	34.11	LATE	N

```
----------------------------------PACE GRAPH----------------------------------------
        Profile:                46.99              111.67               144.48
        Front Runner:           46.61              112.05               145.06
Horse name                        1C                 2C                     F
SIERRA REAL        ------------------X -----------------(X ------------------X--+
AL'S SUNSHINE      -------------X----+ -------------X----(+ ------------------X
MY IDEAL           -------------X----+ -------------X---(+ ------------X-----+
STAGE DOOR TYLER   -------X----------+ -------------X---(+ ----------X-------+
RIFLING THRU       -------------X-----+ -------------X---(+ --------X---------+
```

The morning line for our contenders in the fourth race is:

Sierra Real	2-1
Al's Sunshine	4-1
My Ideal	5-2

We can simply add this information for the fourth race to our existing Pick-3 information for races two and three. If we want to play all the possible combinations, we simply reuse our lines for races two and three in addition to our line for race four. And if we prefer to use the Key-3-3 strategy, we can make our top pick in race four our key, since we already know that our key horses in races two and three aren't probable favorites. Even though Sierra Real is the morning-line favorite in race four, we'd still have only one probable favorite among our three key horses.

Let's recap our straight betting for the second race. We have a big overlay to win on Spruce Navy. If we're ultraconservative win bettors, we can instead bet all of our top three contenders to win since the public has underestimated their probability of winning by more than 10 percent. Depending on the actual pays, we can also reduce our risk by betting Spruce Navy to place or show rather than to win.

Our exacta and quinella strategies will eliminate Claret from consideration, since he's grossly overbet in relation to our line. But our trifecta strategy will include all five of our contenders, since they all can run within five lengths of the final-time par.

Our Pick-3 strategies follow the same format as those applied in the first race. Race two turned out as follows:

SECOND RACE	1½ MILES. (1.40) CLAIMING. Purse $11,000. 3-year-olds and upward. Weights: 3-year-olds, 118 lbs.

Hollywood

DECEMBER 4, 1993

Older, 121 lbs. Non-winners of two races at a mile or over since October 4, allowed 3 lbs. Such a race since then, 6 lbs. Claiming price $10,000; if for $9,000, 2 lbs. (Races when entered for $8,000 or less not considered.)

Value of Race: $11,000 Winner $6,050; second $2,200; third $1,650; fourth $825; fifth $275. Mutuel Pool $253,992.00 Exacta Pool $199,850.00 Trifecta Pool $107,574.00 Quinella Pool $36,505.00

Last Raced	Horse	M/Eqt. A.Wt	PP	St	¼	½	¾	Str	Fin	Jockey	Cl'g Pr	Odds $1
11Nov93 5SA7	Spruce Navy	LB	4 115	6	1	3hd	31	22	22	1hd	Castanon A L	10000	3.30
23Oct93 4BM5	Royal Dixie	LBb	4 115	1	4	1½	11	11½	11	23½	Atkinson P	10000	2.30
11Nov93 5SA4	Lanky Lord	LBb	4 115	3	3	53½	53	3hd	32½	31½	Black C A	10000	7.10
12Nov93 1SA2	Royal Torrent	LB	4 116	2	6	7	6hd	62½	43	46½	Delahoussaye E	10000	4.00
12Nov93 1SA3	Double Agent	LBb	6 115	5	2	2½	43	53	53	58	Almeida G F	10000	11.20
12Nov93 1SA6	Foolhearty	LB	8 115	4	7	6hd	7	7	7	6½	Long B	10000	61.20
15Nov93 7SA7	Claret-Ir	LBbf	5 115	7	5	43	2hd	41	61½	7	Gryder A T	10000	3.20

OFF AT 12:59 Start Good. Won driving. Time, :23, :45³, 1:10¹, 1:36², 1:43 Track fast.

$2 Mutuel Prices:

6-SPRUCE NAVY	8.60	4.00	3.00
1-ROYAL DIXIE		3.40	2.60
3-LANKY LORD			3.40

$2 EXACTA 6-1 PAID $30.00 $2 TRIFECTA 6-1-3 PAID $151.20 $2 QUINELLA 1-6 PAID $14.00

$2 Daily Double 5-6 Paid $35.80 Daily Double Pool $189,621.00

Spruce Navy puts us in the win column. All three forms of win betting included this low-priced overlay. The place-and-show prices represented overlays as well. Even with the favorite Royal Dixie running second, Spruce Navy still paid $4.00 to place, much higher than his $3.20 fair-place price. The show price also was a massive overlay, but this may have been due to the fact that a mild long shot ran third.

The exactas and quinellas fell through since Royal Dixie's line was greater than 6-to-1. We also missed the trifecta because we didn't include Royal Dixie among our place horses.

The risk-averse player also managed to collect on the daily double a goodly number of times, since the Cocooning–Spruce Navy combination had the third-highest probability of winning among our 15 possible combinations.

And both our Pick-3 strategies from the first race stay alive. In fact, as long as one of our top three contenders wins the third race, we'll collect. Obviously, the risk-averse strategy has covered all the possible combinations. But if one of our top three contenders wins the third race, the Key-3-3 strategy also will hit since one of our key horses, Spruce Navy, has already won. If a non-key contender wins the third, we collect on one of our part-wheels. If our key horse in the third wins, we hit on two of our part-wheels. With the non-favorite key horse Spruce Navy winning, we're also alive in the Pick-3 on races two through four.

Let's move on to the third race. Here again is *ALL-IN-ONE*'s printout:

```
-------------------------------BETTING LINE----------------------------------
               -------Rankings--------          Betting   Fair     Fair
Horse name     PEH  H-I THAAI P-H  ESP  Rating   Line    Place $  Show $
------------------------------------------------------------------------------
SOLDA HOLME     1    1    1    1    1    92.12    7-5      3.20     2.60
OLD TIME ROMANCE 2   2    2    3    2    82.14    5-2      4.00     3.20
DATSDAWAYITIS   3    4    3    2    4    67.35
ISLEO BEBE      4    3    4    4    5    63.80
PERKY SLEW      5    5    5    5    3    60.66
```

Here are the actual toteboard odds for our contenders in this race a few minutes before post time:

Solda Holme	2-1
Old Time Romance	12-1

From a win-betting standpoint each horse is an overlay. But which is the better bet? The horse with the longer odds, right? Not necessarily. Or is it the horse with the largest edge? Maybe. The overarching criterion for determining the best win bet is edge-to-odds *ratio*. The edge on Solda Holme is 25.01 percent, hence its edge-to-odds ratio is .1251. The edge on Old Time Romance is 271.41 percent, hence its edge-to-odds ratio is .2262. In this case, Old Time Romance represents the better bet. Aggressive win bettors would single her. Moderate bettors would bet both horses, wagering 64 percent of their bet size in this race on Old Time Romance and the remaining 36 percent on Solda Holme. And ultraconservative bettors would bet them both using the Group Overlay Method, since these two horses account for a group probability of more than 69 percent, while the public has estimated their combined chances at 41 percent.

Both horses have a line of 5-to-2 or lower, so place-and-show betting is again an option. However, we must remember that the place-and-show prices offering the biggest edges are found on horses whose win odds are 5-to-2 or lower on the toteboard. Hence, we should limit any place-and-show activity in this race to Solda Holme.

The exacta and quinella both look like no-brainers. Old Time Romance is going off at nearly five times her rightful odds. The two exactas pairing her with Solda Holme will undoubtedly pay much more than the fair prices listed on the exacta grid. So will the quinella. With only six horses in the field, there's no trifecta betting.

The Pick-3 on races three through five also deserve our attention. As always, the risk-averse bettor would cover all the contenders in each leg that were listed at 6-to-1 or lower on their lines. But the Key-3-3 Pick-3 player would find himself in the following situation:

Hollywood Park

5 *1 MILE.* (Turf). (1:324) CLAIMING. Purse $24,000. 3-year-olds and upward. Weights: 3-year-olds, 119 lbs. Older, 122 lbs. Non-winners of two races at a mile or over since October 4, allowed 3 lbs. Such a race since then, 6 lbs. Claiming price $40,000; for each $2,500 to $35,000, allowed 2 lbs. (Races when entered for $32,000 or less not considered.)

TURF COURSE — 1 MILE — FINISH START

Notwithstanding
Own: Alesia Frank & Sharon
SORENSON D (14 0 1 4 .00) $37,500
Ch. g. 5
Sire: Stanstead (Gummo)
Dam: Tepee Time Gal (Any Time Now)
Br: Hinds Thomas F (Cal)
Tr: Eurton Peter (5 0 1 0 .00)
L 114
Lifetime Record: 27 3 8 6 $124,300
1993 6 0 2 1 $9,250 | Turf 13 2 3 4 $85,725
1992 10 1 1 2 $40,450 | Wet 0 0 0 0
Hol (T) 3 1 2 0 $32,500 | Dist (T) 2 0 1 1 $12,100

27Oct93-9SA fst 1 :233 :472 1:112 1:364 3+ [S]Clm 10000 79 3 8 88½ 88¼ 84¼ 44½ Delahoussaye E LB 116 b 3.60 81-20 ThDroullr118nk ElgntBrgin1163½ McclymondsHigh1111 Far wide into lane 10
10Oct93-1SA fst 1 1/16 :231 :47 1:112 1:43 3+ Clm 12500 76 1 4 65¾ 46 45 26½ Stevens G L LB 116 b *1.10 82-11 PrimCondition1096½ Notwithstnding116½ ExprsoBrzil116no Wide into lane 7
15Sep93-9Dmr fst 1 1/16 :231 :471 1:113 1:432 3+ Clm c-10000 79 11 9 95¾ 64½ 42 42 Stevens G L LB 117 b *2.50 83-15 ExpresoBrzil1171¼ WrittenWords119½ LovedAndWon117nk 4 Wide stretch 11
Claimed from Burke Gary W & Timothy R, Mitchell Mike Trainer
9Sep93-5Dmr fst 1 :223 :461 1:111 1:364 3+ Clm 10000 79 7 5 53 53 44½ 2nk Stevens G L LB 117 b *2.20 83-13 Orchard Court117nk Notwithstanding117no TuEresMiHeroe117½ Wide trip 9
25Aug93-1Dmr fst 1 1/16 :231 :47 1:114 1:442 3+ Clm 20000 72 3 7 69 65½ 34 34½ Stevens G L LB 117 b 3.10 75-17 CheyennGold1172¼ Mxibob1172 Notwithstnding1175½ Wide, flattened out 7
31Jly93-9Dmr fst 1 :223 :464 1:104 1:363 3+ Clm c-16000 65 8 3 31½ 53 911 916½ McCarron C J LB 116 b 11.10 68-11 Boldandcayerless120½ Cannon Man1162¾ Bit Of Petrone1112¾ Stopped 10
Claimed from Hinds John D & Thomas F Iii, Robbins Jay M Trainer
25Oct92-9BM fm 1 1/16 (T) :224 :471 1:123 1:442 3+ Alw 23000 81 8 8 63¾ 42 52 54 Baze R A LB 119 b 2.90 84-10 Go Gremlin Go122nk Speak Firm122nk Boldly Excellent117 Far wide 9
17Oct92-6BM fm 1 (T) :233 :474 1:121 1:38 3+ [S]Hrris Fm H30k 94 2 6 65 43 42 3½ Baze R A LB 115 b 3.60 88-12 Journalism117½ Valentine Lad115hd Notwithstanding115 Rallied late 8
12Sep92-4BM fm 1 1/16 (T) :222 :461 1:103 1:424 3+ Alw 23000 84 2 7 711 66 54½ 34 Boulanger G LB 122 b 2.30 92-03 FourFivTim1174 Hro'sWlcom-Ir117hd Notwithstndng122 Steadied, wide 7
26Aug92-8Dmr fm 1 1/16 (T) :231 :46 1:101 1:414 3+ Alw 38000 85 4 7 715 711 56 55¾ Desormeaux K J LB 116 b 5.00 91-06 Ionadi1161½ Barraq-Fr1162 Big Barton116 4-wide stretch 7
WORKOUTS: Nov 30 SA 3f gd :362 H *4/12* Nov 25 SA 1 fst 1:412 H *1/1* Nov 19 SA 6f fst 1:13 H *5/14* Nov 14 SA 4f fst :483 H *18/39* Oct 19 SA 3f fst :352 H *3/18* Oct 1 SA 5f fst 1:01 H *12/59*

Record Boom
Own: K C Stable
SOLIS A (67 9 12 12 .13) $40,000
Ch. g. 7
Sire: Lord Avie (Lord Gaylord)
Dam: Krassata (Nijinsky II)
Br: Moyglare Stud Farm Ltd (Ky)
Tr: Mitchell Mike (22 3 9 2 .14)
L 116
Lifetime Record: 17 9 2 4 $219,325
1993 7 5 1 0 $88,525 | Turf 7 3 2 1 $91,100
1992 2 1 0 1 $33,700 | Wet 0 0 0 0
Hol (T) 7 3 1 2 $94,750 | Dist (T) 0 0 0 0

24Nov93-7Hol fst 7f :22 :443 1:091 1:212 3+ Clm 32000 90 2 4 4½ 1½ 11 14½ Solis A LB 117 *1.10 97-09 Record Boom1174½ Skerry1174 Bet A Bic1173½ Drifted out 1/8 5
4Jun93-7Hol fst 7½f :223 :451 1:093 1:282 Clm 35000 101 1 5 52¼ 4¾ 1½ 11 Solis A LB 118 *1.00 93-12 Record Boom1181 Moscow M D1172 Chief Dare1174 Wide trip 7
14May93-8Hol fm 1 1/16 (T) :25 :49 1:12 1:413 Clm 45000 96 1 2 21 2½ 1hd 1½ Solis A LB 115 3.30 88-12 Record Boom115½ Tatsfield114nk Fire Top117½ Gamely 7
1May93-3Hol fst 1⅛ :483 1:124 1:361 1:484 Alw 25000s 95 1 3 42 3½ 12 12¾ Solis A LB 115 *1.30 93-07 Record Boom1152¾ Eddie Valient1151¼ Book Publisher1222 7
Lugged out lane, ridden out
21Apr93-7Hol fst 1 1/16 :223 :452 1:091 1:404 Clm 62500 95 1 4 57 44½ 54 46½ Stevens G L LB 116 *2.10 90-11 IcyResolution1174½ PrinceOfHoney1161 Bossanova1111 Not enough late 10
4Apr93-9SA fst 7f :222 :444 1:091 1:214 Clm c-25000 94 1 9 96¼ 75½ 1½ 12 Desormeaux K J LB 115 *1.20 94-11 Record Boom1152 Chief Dare1171¼ Ledger1152½ Speed to spare 9
Claimed from Wygod Mr & Mrs Martin J, Hendricks Dan L Trainer
13Mar93-5SA fm *6½f (T) :214 :44 1:071 1:131 Clm 75000 99 3 6 63¼ 53¾ 53 2hd Stevens G L LB 114 *2.50 92-08 Exemplary Leader117hd Record Boom1142 Blue Tiger116½ 4 Wide stretch 12
27Jun92-8Hol fst 7f :221 :443 1:084 1:212 3+ Trp Bend H-G3 98 3 4 62¾ 62¼ 52½ 3¾ Desormeaux K J LB 114 5.80 96-10 SlwThSurgon111hd SoftshoSrShot114¾ RcordBoom114 Boxed 5/16to1/8 8
23May92-9Hol fm 5½f (T) :213 :44 :551 1:012 Clm 60000 99 6 8 63 63¼ 2½ 11 alvarado F T LB 115 12.20 98-02 Record Boom1151 Ruff Hombre1071½ Centurion-NZ117 5-wide stretch 12
23Jly90-8Hol fm 1½ (T) :49 1:134 2:014 2:253 3+ Sunset Hcp-G2 96 2 3 52½ 53½ 65 55¼ Garcia J A L 114 13.60 88-11 Petite Ile115½ Live The Dream1163½ Soft Machine110 4-wide into lane 9
WORKOUTS: Nov 18 Hol 5f fst 1:02 H *25/38* Nov 11 Hol 4f fst :493 H *9/10* Nov 5 Hol 5f fst 1:031 H *23/30* Oct 28 Hol 6f fst 1:194 H *18/18* Oct 21 Hol 6f fst 1:14 H *2/6* Oct 14 Hol 5f fst 1:011 H *12/37*

Character (GB)
Own: Munari Jack J
NAKATANI C S (60 14 10 13 .23) $40,000
Ch. h. 5
Sire: Never So Bold (Bold Lad)
Dam: Ravaro (Raga Navarro)
Br: Cheveley Park Stud Ltd (GB)
Tr: Baffert Bob (10 2 1 2 .20)
L 116
Lifetime Record: 11 2 4 1 $137,420
1993 4 0 2 0 $13,000 | Turf 8 2 4 0 $104,420
1991 4 1 1 1 $115,600 | Wet 0 0 0 0
Hol (T) 2 1 1 0 $82,600 | Dist (T) 4 1 2 0 $31,733

14Nov93-7BM fm 1 (T) :224 :461 1:104 1:361 3+ Clm 40000 94 3 9 98¾ 76 32½ 2nk Belvoir V T LB 117 3.50 98-08 Macho's Issue117nk Character117nk PerfectlyProud1171¼ Rallied well wide 10
30Oct93-5SA fm 1 (T) :222 :45 1:094 1:34 3+ Clm 70000 77 7 4 42½ 2hd 32½ 512¾ Valenzuela F H LB 114 f 5.00 82-09 Bat Eclat1131 Seti I.1186 Dream Of Fame115¾ Bid, weakened 9
11Oct93-5SA fst 6½f ⊗ :214 :442 1:084 1:152 3+ Clm 80000 57 1 6 61½ 35 48 715¼ Nakatani C S LB 116 f 2.90 79-11 Bet On The Bay109¾ Regal Groom1175½ Lackington1147½ Saved ground 7
19Aug93-5Dmr fm 1 1/16 (T) :233 :474 1:122 1:422 3+ Alw 40000N2X 91 1 4 54 52½ 21½ 2nk Nakatani C S LB 117 f 5.00 94-06 SouthrnWish117nk Chrctr1172¼ Triumphl'sBounty114nk Boxed in 5/16-3/16 9
22Jun91-8AP fst 1⅛ :462 1:112 1:364 1:49 A P Clssic-G2 99 8 8 710 73¾ 37 35¾ Stevens G L L 120 4.80 83-29 Whadjathink1205 Freezing Dock114¾ Character-GB120 Mild rally 8
1Jun91-8Hol fm 1⅛ (T) :464 1:103 1:343 1:47 Cinema H-G2 97 3 3 31 41¾ 1hd 12½ Stevens G L LB 114 *2.00 95-07 Character-GB1142½ River Traffic117½ Kalgrey-Fr114 Driving 6
4May91-5Hol fm 1 (T) :233 :47 1:103 1:342 Sptlt B C H-G3 96 4 6 41½ 3½ 2hd 21¾ Garcia J A LB 112 8.50 91-07 Whadjathink1171¾ Character-GB112¾ Soweto-Ir117 10
17Mar91-7SA fst 1 1/16 :231 :471 1:113 1:423 Alw 35000 69 3 8 86¾ 85 811 814½ Flores D R LB 120 19.80 76-10 Excavate1173½ Quintana117½ King's Canyon120 Broke slowly 8
19Sep90♦ Ayr(GB) sf 1 (T)LH 1:452 Maiden 9300 12½ Reid J 126 *2.75 Character1262½ Matahif1262 Wings Of Freedom126nk 22
Tr: Lynda Ramsden Sandgate Maiden Stakes *Tracked in 3rd, rallied to lead 1f out, driving*
27Aug90♦ Newcastle(GB) gd 7f (T)Str 1:274 Maiden 9100 2½ Lowe J 126 5.50 Kashteh121¾ Character1263 Engelaab126nk 17
EBF Hedgehope Maiden Stakes *Angled over to stands side after 1f, bid 2f out, finished well*
WORKOUTS: Nov 29 SA 5f fst :594 H *3/31* Nov 23 SA 4f fst :471 B *7/38* Nov 8 SA 5f fst 1:002 H *10/42* Oct 26 SA 4f fst :474 H *15/48* Oct 20 SA 4f fst :473 B *12/44* Oct 4 SA 4f fst :492 B *27/38*

Robinski (NZ)
Own: Mirage Stable & Sicilia & Tully
GRYDER A T (46 9 5 6 .20) $35,000
Dk. b or br g. 10
Sire: Noble Bijou (Vaguely Noble)
Dam: Robanna (Mellay)
Br: Lalor T W (NZ)
Tr: Lewis Craig A (11 2 4 2 .18)
L 112

Lifetime Record: 102 17 20 16 $555,480										
1993	12	2	4	2	$84,725	Turf	102	17	20	16 $555,480
1992	18	1	3	6	$77,900	Wet	0	0	0	0
Hol Ⓣ	22	2	7	4	$135,875	Dist Ⓣ	18	3	4	3 $116,550

26Nov93-7Hol fm 1 Ⓣ :233 :463 1:102 1:344 3+ Clm 45000 89 1 6 76¼ 55 34 31½ Gryder A T LB 113 b 7.90 90-12 Dream Of Fame116½ Major Moment116¾ Robinski113½ Inside rally 9
13Sep93-4Dmr fm 1 1/16 Ⓣ :241 :484 1:131 1:422 3+ Ⓡ Sandshark H50k 81 5 6 64 64 65 77½ Desormeaux K J LB 116 b 4.90 87-06 Fantastic Don117hd Bossanova1223½ Eton Lad1191¾ No rally 7
21Aug93-9Dmr fm 1 Ⓣ :221 :452 1:10 1:352 3+ Clm 45000 87 2 9 913 97¼ 75 54 Delahoussaye E LB 120 b 4.40 90-04 Eton Lad1171¾ Fantastic Don117no Red Monsoon117no 6 Wide stretch 9
7Aug93-5Dmr fm 1 Ⓣ :22 :452 1:093 1:343 3+ Clm 55000 97 9 7 53½ 22½ 22 1½ Desormeaux K J LB 115 b 5.50 98-03 Robinski115½ Garmanni116½ Seti I.1162¾ Late surge 10
16Jly93-5Hol fm 1 Ⓣ :231 :454 1:094 1:342 Clm 45000 96 2 5 66½ 41½ 2hd 1¾ Desormeaux K J LB 115 b 3.00 93-07 Robinski115¾ Deputy Meister1162¾ Seti I.1163 Inside rally 8
2Jly93-6Hol fm 1 1/16 Ⓣ :241 :48 1:112 1:413 Clm 45000 95 6 5 41½ 41¾ 3½ 2½ Desormeaux K J LB 116 b 4.80 87-11 Scottish Castle116½ Robinski1161½ Fantastic Don116nk 4 Wide stretch 8
18Jun93-8Hol fm 1⅛ Ⓣ :47 1:102 1:344 1:47 Clm 45000 92 8 6 63½ 63½ 41½ 2½ Almeida G F LB 112 b 4.20 88-09 Palos Verdes107½ Robinski112½ Quaglino116nk 4 Wide stretch 8
4Jun93-5Hol fm 1 Ⓣ :232 :472 1:104 1:341 Clm 45000 94 2 8 74½ 64 52½ 2nk Almeida G F LB 112 b 17.90 94-09 Tatsfield116nk Robinski1121½ Bossanova116hd Gained strongly 10
7May93-3Hol fm 1⅛ Ⓣ :483 1:12 1:353 1:473 Clm 55000 92 1 3 31½ 31½ 53½ 43½ Solis A LB 113 b 19.30 83-14 Mr. P. And Max115½ Aromatic1131¾ Military Shot1161 Steadied 1/8 7
12Mar93-5SA fm 1½ Ⓣ :473 1:12 2:014 2:261 Clm 57500 75 4 5 67½ 65 54 711 Pedroza M A LB 113 b 8.40 76-13 Single Dawn1151¼ Intelligently1145½ Lovely One107nk A bit rank 12
WORKOUTS: Nov 20 Hol 6f fst 1:132 H 8/24 Nov 15 Hol 6f fst 1:15 H 4/10 Nov 7 Hol 6f fst 1:154 H 10/11 Oct 30 Hol 5f fst 1:013 H 11/24 Oct 21 Hol 4f fst :48 H 3/21 Oct 15 Hol 3f fst :367 H 7/10

Breakfast Table
Own: Taub Stephen M
STEVENS G L (36 4 10 5 .11) $40,000
B. g. 9
Sire: Never Tabled (Never Bend)
Dam: Briquette (T V Lark)
Br: Windy Hill TBA (Cal)
Tr: Hendricks Dan L (8 2 2 0 .25)
L 116

Lifetime Record: 33 9 4 4 $220,925										
1993	2	0	0	0		Turf	26	8	4	4 $207,400
1992	3	1	1	1	$29,100	Wet	0	0	0	0
Hol Ⓣ	13	7	2	1	$148,050	Dist Ⓣ	9	5	1	1 $104,600

26Nov93-7Hol fm 1 Ⓣ :233 :463 1:102 1:344 3+ Clm 50000 72 4 8 87½ 88 89½ 89 McCarron C J LB 116 3.60 82-12 Dream Of Fame116½ Major Moment116¾ Robinski113½ No threat 9
16Oct93-7SA fm 1 Ⓣ :224 :46 1:094 1:34 3+ Ⓢ CalCupMile H150k 74 3 11 109¾ 109 812 714¾ Stevens G L LB 115 f 10.00 80-05 Megan'sInterco1193½ MoscowChnges1144 Journlism1221¾ Wide into lane 11
10Oct92-2SA fm *6½f Ⓣ :213 :434 1:07 1:13 3+ Clm 80000 101 5 7 810 86½ 73¾ 2hd Solis A LB 116 6.60 94-06 Rocket Gibralter116hd Breakfast Table116hd Bruho116 7-wide stretch 9
24Jly92-8Hol fm 1 1/16 Ⓣ :24 :471 1:104 1:404 Clm 62500 89 1 2 32 32 42½ 35 Stevens G L LB 116 *1.60 86-09 Seti I.116hd Polar Boy1165 Breakfast Table116 No mishap 5
4Jly92-10Hol fm 5½f Ⓣ :214 :442 :561 1:022 3+ Clm 47500 93 8 5 53½ 54½ 21½ 11¼ Stevens G L LB 115 4.80 93-05 Breakfast Table1151¼ Xcaret-Mx1191½ Sam Who113 Strong kick 9
18Aug91-5Dmr fm 1 1/16 Ⓣ :234 :472 1:112 1:423 3+ Clm 80000 101 8 6 58 56 32½ 31½ Stevens G L LB 118 *2.80 92-09 C. Sam Maggio118½ Tatsfield-Ir1161 Breakfast Table118 Came on 8
22Jly91-3Hol fm 1 Ⓣ :24 :472 1:103 1:34 Clm 80000 99 3 3 42½ 42 22 21½ Stevens G L LB 119 *1.40 93-11 Gulf Star-Br1191½ Breakfast Table1193½ CoolGoldMood112 Always close 6
16Jun91-7Hol fm 1½ Ⓣ :483 1:13 2:02 2:261 3+ Hcp 62500 99 5 3 32½ 43½ 42 21¾ Baze R A LB 119 2.10 90-08 Splendid Career1231¾ Breakfast Table119½ Preston-Fr114 2nd best 6
2Jun91-9Hol fm 1 Ⓣ :242 :473 1:103 1:334 Clm 80000 106 5 4 42 53 42 1nk Baze R A LB 116 3.20 96-06 BreakfastTble116nk GulfStr-Br116nk CollegeGreen116 Good kick, got up 7
11May91-9Hol fm 1 Ⓣ :224 :452 1:09 1:34 Clm 62500 103 9 10 106¼ 85½ 62½ 01¾ Baze R A LB 116 2.10 95-10 DH Despatch-Fr1191¾ DH Breakfast Table1161¾ Cannon Man111 Wide trip 11
Dead heat
WORKOUTS: Nov 21 Hol 5f fst 1:013 H 26/40 Nov 14 Hol 5f fst 1:023 H 26/37 Nov 7 Hol 5f fst 1:034 H 22/22 Oct 31 Hol 4f fst :492 H 21/30 Oct 13 Hol 4f fst :502 H 11/14 ●Oct 7 Hol 7f fst 1:272 H 1/5

Aromatic (GB)
Own: Peyton Kari
GONZALEZ S JR (45 3 5 5 .07) $37,500
Dk. B h. 6
Sire: Known Fact (In Reality)
Dam: Mint (Meadow Mint)
Br: Juddmonte Farms (GB)
Tr: Bunn Thomas M Jr (6 0 0 0 .00)
L 109⁵

Lifetime Record: 29 6 4 4 $143,702										
1993	8	2	2	1	$57,300	Turf	28	6	4	4 $139,652
1992	4	1	0	0	$23,000	Wet	1	0	0	0 $4,050
Hol Ⓣ	6	1	2	1	$45,750	Dist Ⓣ	9	3	0	1 $62,300

28Oct93-8BM fm 1 Ⓣ :232 :472 1:114 1:364 3+ Clm 45000 88 1 5 54 53½ 42¼ 43 Baze R A LB 115 *1.40 92-05 MajesticNasr1192 Lee'sTanthem1171 Rolandthemonarch117no Even late 6
18Sep93-8BM fm 1 Ⓣ :224 :462 1:102 1:364 3+ Clm 30000 90 3 8 59½ 21 11½ 1nk Solis A LB 116 *2.20 95-08 Aromatic115nk Sekondi1174 Perfectly Proud117no Held gamely 10
16Jly93-5Hol fm 1 Ⓣ :231 :454 1:094 1:342 Clm 45000 71 7 6 56½ 52½ 44¼ 611¼ Nakatani C S LB 113 *1.70 82-07 Robinski115¾ Deputy Meister1162¾ Seti I.1163 Wide backstretch 8
2Jly93-6Hol fm 1 1/16 Ⓣ :241 :48 1:112 1:413 Clm 50000 85 7 3 51¾ 73½ 64 75 Nakatani C S LB 119 *1.70 83-11 Scottish Castle116½ Robinski1161½ Fantastic Don116nk 8
In tight, shuffled back 5/16
17Jun93-6Hol fm 1 Ⓣ :231 :463 1:101 1:332 Clm 62500 92 5 9 84¾ 74¾ 54¼ 33½ Valenzuela P A LB 117 *1.90 94-05 Bossanova1163 Tatsfield116½ Aromatic1173½ Boxed in 3/8-1/4 9
21May93-5Hol fm 1 Ⓣ :23 :46 1:094 1:334 Clm 50000 99 2 6 65 42 1hd 11½ Nakatani C S LB 116 *1.60 96-09 Aromatic1161½ Greensmith1161 Fantastic Don116hd Ridden out 10
7May93-3Hol fm 1⅛ Ⓣ :483 1:12 1:353 1:473 Clm 55000 98 3 6 74½ 73¾ 2½ 2½ Nakatani C S LB 113 *1.00 85-14 Mr. P. And Max115½ Aromatic1131¾ Military Shot1161 Troubled trip 7
24Apr93-9Hol fm 1⅛ Ⓣ :473 1:111 1:344 1:463 Clm 45000 94 1 5 43 51¾ 1½ 2nk Nakatani C S LB 113 6.60 91-08 Polar Boy115nk Aromatic1131¾ Military Shot116½ Boxed in 3/8-1/4 12
18Apr92-7SA fm 1 Ⓣ :223 :46 1:10 1:351 Clm 70000 95 7 7 77 4¾ 11 1hd Berrio O A LB 111 8.30 87-23 Aromatic-GB111hd River Dacer115½ Robinski-NZ115 Off slowly, wide 7
9Apr92-5SA fm 1 Ⓣ :233 :47 1:102 1:342 Clm 100000 89 6 3 31 3½ 32 76½ Alvarado F T LB 114 39.10 85-09 HollywoodRportr1152½ DoublFound110 Trbizond117 Wide, bumped 1/8 10
WORKOUTS: Nov 15 Hol 6f fst 1:14 H 2/10 Oct 18 Hol 7f fst 1:271 H 1/2 Oct 7 Hol 5f fst 1:05 H 29/29 Sep 28 Hol 4f fst :512 H 6/7 Sep 14 Hol 6f fst 1:132 H 1/3 Sep 7 Dmr 5f fst 1:003 H 14/45

Purdue Prince
Own: Valpredo John
PINCAY L JR (60 10 9 7 .17) $40,000
Dk. b or br g. 4
Sire: Dimaggio (Bold Hitter)
Dam: Purdue Princess (Truxton Fair)
Br: Valpredo John (Cal)
Tr: Caganich Barbara (5 1 0 0 .20)
L 116

Lifetime Record: 20 1 1 4 $38,270										
1993	6	1	0	1	$15,400	Turf	4	0	1	0 $6,000
1992	11	M	1	2	$19,150	Wet	1	0	0	1 $3,000
Hol Ⓣ	2	0	1	0	$6,000	Dist Ⓣ	0	0	0	0

19Nov93-4Hol fst 7½f :223 :453 1:103 1:30 3+ Md 28000 69 5 1 12½ 12½ 11½ 12¼ Pincay L Jr LB 119 b 12.70 85-12 Purdue Prince1192¼ Sky Bryn119hd Bettys Big Boy121½ Driving 10
3Nov93-2SA fst 6f :214 :451 :572 1:10 3+ Ⓢ Md 35000 57 10 2 93 76½ 68½ 512 Pincay L Jr LB 118 b 33.50 75-14 Singapore Boy118nk Kool Kelly1206 Megawing1185½ No rally 12
21Oct93-6SA fst 6½f :214 :442 1:092 1:16 3+ Md Sp Wt 56 6 10 97¾ 99¾ 98½ 914½ Almeida G F LB 120 b 126.30 76-14 GettingEnough112hd ForeignMerger1202 CrimsonLef1201½ Steadied start 11
4Oct93-3Fpx fst 7f :213 :451 1:111 1:241 3+ Md Sp Wt 63 5 4 35 33 31½ 34 Castro J M LB 118 b 6.50 93-10 Don'tTellFrnk1142 GoodPresenttion1162 PurduPrinc1181½ Saved ground 7
20Sep93-9Fpx fst 6f :221 :453 :582 1:11 3+ Md Sp Wt 66 8 5 87¾ 67½ 64 45¼ Castaneda M LB 118 b 9.50 87-08 Phoenician1151½ Good Presentation1143 Summer Lord1141 Wide trip 9
9Sep93-9Dmr fst 6f :22 :45 :57 1:091 3+ Md 35000 63 11 2 74¾ 73 75¾ 510¾ Pincay L Jr LB 120 b 13.00 82-09 Lakota Brave1226½ Bettys Big Boy122nk Super Randy1173½ Wide trip 12
19Nov92-5Hol fm 1 1/16 Ⓣ :233 :472 1:122 1:44 Md 45000 68 6 1 11½ 1½ 63 68½ Berrio O A LB 113 b 41.40 67-22 Bright Day Bob116½ Rare Cat116 Kings On Top114 Full of run early 7
30Oct92-2SA sly 6½f :221 :451 1:104 1:174 3+ Md 45000 76 7 6 32½ 33½ 33½ 32½ Berrio O A LB 115 b 3.10 78-19 Mint Jubilee117¾ Milkshake Marty118 Purdue Prince115 8
Bobbled start, wide, zig-zagged lane
16Oct92-3BM fm 1 1/16 Ⓣ :233 :472 1:124 1:454 3+ Md Sp Wt 59 1 1 11½ 1½ 53 77½ Kaenel J L LB 118 b 9.70 73-19 Swiss Mirage1181 Hurricane Express118 El Nisir122 Falktered 11
3Oct92-12Fpx fst 6½f :22 :46 1:104 1:171 3+ Md Sp Wt 75 5 4 32 32½ 34 47 Pedroza M A LB 114 b 4.50 83-15 Sean Thomas1151 Please Pause Paul1143 Rathsallah118 Weakened 9
WORKOUTS: Nov 26 Hol 5f fst 1:001 H 6/42 Nov 12 Hol 4f fst :471 H 2/23 Oct 28 Hol 5f fst :594 H 2/25 Oct 18 Hol 4f fst :472 H 2/16 Oct 12 Hol 5f fst :593 H 2/8 ●Sep 28 Fpx 4f fst :473 H 1/6

Impact
Own: Fischer & Kjelstrom & Reyes
VALENZUELA P A (54 6 10 2 .11) $40,000
B. g. 5
Sire: Pocket Park (Verbatim)
Dam: Gypsie Sister (War Helmet)
Br: Fischer Cal (Cal)
Tr: Jory Ian P D (8 0 0 0 .00)
L 116

Lifetime Record: 32 4 2 7 $127,865										
1993	12	0	0	2	$26,950	Turf	24	3	1	5 $103,665
1992	9	1	1	3	$57,015	Wet	2	0	0	0 $4,500
Hol Ⓣ	6	0	0	0	$6,000	Dist Ⓣ	11	1	1	2 $57,015

26Sep93-6BM fm 1 Ⓣ :231 :463 1:11 1:361 3+ Ⓢ Harris Frm H30k 78 5 7 710 65½ 56 57¾ Hansen R D LB 115 7.70 90-10 Struttin Joey P.116nk His Legacy1155 Icy Kevin114½ No rally 7
13Sep93-4Dmr fm 1 1/16 Ⓣ :241 :484 1:131 1:422 3+ Ⓡ Sandshark H50k 85 3 2 21 42 42½ 45½ Valenzuela P A LB 116 20.70 89-06 Fantastic Don117hd Bossanova1223½ Eton Lad1191¾ Not enough late 7
27Aug93-7Dmr fm 1 Ⓣ :224 :464 1:104 1:343 3+ Clm 55000 86 7 8 84¾ 64½ 54 45 Solis A LB 114 51.10 93-05 Seti I.117nk Struttin Joey P.1173 I Will Reign1171¾ 4 Wide stretch 8
25Jun93-7Hol fm 1 Ⓣ :223 :451 1:091 1:34 3+ Ⓢ Khaled H55k 77 4 6 78 77 79½ 611¼ Castaneda M LB 114 42.40 84-09 Patriotaki114¾ Bossanova1161¼ C. Sam Maggio1192½ 4 Wide stretch 8
4Jun93-5Hol fm 1 Ⓣ :232 :472 1:104 1:341 Clm 50000 91 1 3 42½ 32 31 41½ Castaneda M LB 116 18.00 92-09 Tatsfield116nk Robinski1121¼ Bossanova116hd Always close 10
14May93-8Hol fm 1 1/16 Ⓣ :25 :49 1:12 1:413 Clm 50000 93 6 7 64 43½ 41¾ 41½ Almeida G F LB 116 20.80 87-12 Record Boom115½ Tatsfield114nk Fire Top117½ Finished well 7
2May93-10GG fm 1 1/16 Ⓣ :23 :47 1:112 1:433+ Clm 50000 87 1 4 43½ 44½ 43½ 53½ Hansen R D LB 117 b 3.20 84-10 Hoofer1172 Music Machine115no Valentine Lad1151 Even late 7
10Apr93-2GG fm 1 1/16 Ⓣ :23 :464 1:102 1:414+ 3+ Ⓢ Tiburon H40k 94 2 4 52¾ 64 53 32¼ Hansen R D LB 115 b 12.40 95-08 Journalism1162 Arvada115nk Impact115nk Mild late bid 7
4Mar93-7SA fm 1⅛ Ⓣ :484 1:124 1:371 1:493 Clm 75000 76 6 2 22 21½ 65¾ 89½ Munro A LB 114 b 48.50 61-27 Lord Charmer1141 Coco's Main Man115¾ Robinski113no Faltered 10
13Feb93-7SA fm 1 Ⓣ :24 :48 1:112 1:36 Ⓢ Dbl Dscnt55k 77 6 6 65¾ 65 66 77¾ Black C A LB 114 b 15.70 77-20 Fax News117¾ Mystery's Edge121½ J. F. Williams1162½ Outrun 7
WORKOUTS: Nov 26 Hol 6f fst 1:131 H 4/23 Nov 20 Hol 5f fst 1:01 H 28/63 Oct 25 Hol 5f fst 1:002 H 5/24 ●Oct 20 Hol 5f fst 1:00 H 1/18 Sep 6 Dmr 6f fst 1:133 H 9/24

Shtick
Own: McCullough James A
LONG B (23 1 0 3 .04) $40,000
Ch. c. 4
Sire: Chivalry (Nijinsky II)
Dam: Teste Sespe (Test Market)
Br: James Allen McCullough (Cal)
Tr: Verret Clegg (1 0 0 0 .00)
L 116

Lifetime Record: 7 1 0 0 $10,800										
1993	7	1	0	0	$10,800	Turf	2	0	0	0
1992	0	M	0	0		Wet	0	0	0	0
Hol Ⓣ	0	0	0	0		Dist Ⓣ	0	0	0	0

29Oct93-8SA fm 1⅛ Ⓣ :464 1:112 1:361 1:48 3+ Alw 34000N1X 67 8 1 1hd 2hd 41½ 810½ Long B LB 119 126.40 69-21 Only Alpha118no Cherokee Tribute1131¼ Memento Mori1191¾ Dueled, tired 8
2Oct93-7Fpx fst 1 1/16 :23 :464 1:121 1:45 3+ Md 32000 77 5 3 32 31 21 13 Long B LB 118 4.00 83-16 Shtick1183 Again Tonight1153½ Gentle Shepherd1143 Perfect trip 10
24Sep93-7Fpx fst 1 1/16 :23 :47 1:122 1:443 3+ Ⓢ Md 32000 63 3 2 31½ 33½ 33½ 54 Valenzuela F H LB 118 10.40 81-12 Faxitover1183 Just N Allen118½ Native Bearing113nk Steadied 1st turn 9
8Sep93-2Dmr fm 1 1/16 Ⓣ :241 :484 1:132 1:441 3+ Md Sp Wt 54 2 3 32 63 68½ 612 Sanchez P N Jr B 122 97.10 73-11 Daskiyawar1221¾ Slew Supreme118½ Schoendienst1221¾ 7
Returned bleeding from mouth
19Aug93-2Dmr fst 6½f :222 :453 1:102 1:164 3+ Ⓢ Md 32000 27 1 10 74½ 811 1114 1124½ Castanon A L B 122 99.40 63-14 Ke Express1175 Both Guns Blazing1172 Simply SnowChief1172 Stopped 11
2Aug93-2Dmr fst 6f :221 :452 :581 1:112 3+ Md 32000 38 2 12 1115 917 810 810½ Castaneda M B 121 b 56.50 72-10 Lucky Rival117nk DedicatedDon115no Bolger'sLead1151¾ Broke awkwardly 12
14Jly93-6Hol fst 6f :221 :452 :574 1:103 3+ Md 32000 46 5 11 1013 912 715 813½ Castaneda M 122 b 161.70 73-10 Niner Bush1171 Cutting Deep1171¾ Barton1175 Dwelt start 11
WORKOUTS: Nov 28 Hol 5f fst 1:02 H 26/36 Nov 19 Hol 5f fst 1:024 H 25/33 Nov 13 Hol 4f fst :494 H 19/29 Oct 20 Fpx 5f fst 1:01 H 3/8

ALL-IN-ONE's output for the race is as follows:

```
4DEC93                          HOL                    8 furlongs turf
Race #5                                                      9 starters
C40,000                                            Age: 3+years, Male
-------------------------------INPUT DATA------------------------------

              #  #  #  #  $'S                        1st C  2nd C  Final
Horse name    ST W  P  S  Earned Date    Trk Dist. S time   time   time
-----------------------------------------------------------------------
RECORD BOOM    7  5  1  0  88525 24NOV93 HOL 8.500 T 49.0  112.0  141.3
CHARACTER-GB   4  0  2  0  13000 14NOV93 BM  8.000 T 46.1  110.4  136.1
ROBINSKI-NZ   12  2  4  2  84725 26NOV93 HOL 8.000 T 46.3  110.2  134.4
BREAKFAST TABLE 5 1  1  1  29100 26NOV93 HOL 8.000 T 46.3  110.2  134.4
AROMATIC-GB    8  2  2  1  57300 28OCT93 BM  8.000 T 47.2  111.4  136.4


                          1st C  2nd C  Final
Horse name     Class Lvl  B.L.   B.L.   B.L.   SR   Var
-----------------------------------------------------------------------
RECORD BOOM    C50,000    1.00   0.50   0.00   99   12.0
CHARACTER-GB   C40,000    8.75   6.00   6.00   98    8.0
ROBINSKI-NZ    C50,000    6.25   5.00   1.25   90   12.0
BREAKFAST TABLE C50,000   7.25   8.00   9.00   82   12.0
AROMATIC-GB    C50,000    4.00   3.50   3.00   92    5.0


-----------------------------BETTING LINE------------------------------

              -------Rankings--------      Betting  Fair    Fair
Horse name    PEH H-I THAAI P-H ESP Rating Line   Place $ Show $
-----------------------------------------------------------------------
RECORD BOOM    1   2   1   1   3   80.00    3-1
CHARACTER-GB   3   1   2   2   1   85.67    7-2
ROBINSKI-NZ    2   3   3   3   2   83.00    4-1
AROMATIC-GB    4   4   4   4   4   68.83
BREAKFAST TABLE 5  5   5   5   5   61.41


-----------------------------EXACTA GRID-------------------------------

              | RECORD BOOM | CHARACTER-GB | ROBINSKI-NZ |
--------------+-------------+--------------+-------------+
RECORD BOOM   | . . . . . . |    22    55  |   25    61  |
              | . . . . . . |              |             |
              | . . . . . . |              |             |
--------------+-------------+--------------+-------------+
CHARACTER-GB  |   23    57  | . . . . . .  |   29    72  |
              |             | . . . . . .  |             |
              |             | . . . . . .  |             |
--------------+-------------+--------------+-------------+
ROBINSKI-NZ   |   27    66  |   30    74   | . . . . . . |
              |             |              | . . . . . . |
              |             |              | . . . . . . |
--------------+-------------+--------------+-------------+


4DEC93                          HOL                    8 furlongs turf
Race #5                                                      9 starters
C40,000                                            Age: 3+years, Male
---------------------------SPEED/PACE SUMMARY--------------------------

Race Type:       Orderly Race
Race Profile:    47.16  110.88  135.00  Winners' Pace Profile: EARLY
Ability Par:     71.28                   Pace Contention Point: 2.93 lengths

Projected Times:                    Ability Balance  Last  Proj  Con-
                 1st C  2nd C  Fin C  Time    Time   Frac  Pace  tender
-----------------------------------------------------------------------
RECORD BOOM      48.45 111.26 134.48  71.67  90.80  23.23 EARLY  Y
CHARACTER-GB     47.57 110.97 134.49  71.09  91.46  23.52 FRONT  Y
ROBINSKI-NZ      47.76 111.30 135.03  71.49  92.01  23.73 FRONT  Y
AROMATIC-GB      47.92 111.55 135.62  71.99  92.64  24.07 MID    N
BREAKFAST TABLE  47.94 111.83* 136.44 72.56  93.70  24.62 LATE   N
```

```
-------------------------------PACE GRAPH------------------------------------
        Profile:              47.16              110.88              135.00
     Front Runner:            47.57              110.97              134.48
Horse name                     1C                  2C                     F
RECORD BOOM        ---------------X---+ ----------------(-X+ -------------------X
CHARACTER-GB       ---------------X ----------------(--X -----------------------X
ROBINSKI-NZ        ---------------X+ ----------------(X-+ -----------------X--+
AROMATIC-GB        ---------------X-+ --------------X-+ -------------X-----+
BREAKFAST TABLE    ---------------X-+ --------------X(--+ --------X---------+
```

The morning line for these contenders in the fifth race is as follows:

Record Boom	9-5
Character	6-1
Robinski	3-1

In races three and four, the top picks are Solda Holme and Sierra Real, respectively. Sierra Real, like Record Boom, is the morning-line favorite. If we automatically make the top in each leg our key horse, we find that we have two probable favorites, Sierra Real and Record Boom, among our trio of key horses. This is a highly undesirable development. Hence, we must juggle our trio of key horses until only one of them is a probable favorite.

Solda Holme is neither the morning-line nor actual favorite as the third race approaches. She can be our key horse in the first leg. But we cannot have both Sierra Real and Record Boom as the two other key horses. We must decide on one or the other.

A practical way around this dilemma is to compare the line odds between the two conflicting horses and make the horse with the lower odds a key horse. In the remaining leg, the second-ranked horse on the line becomes the third key horse.

In this instance, Sierra Real is 9-5 on our line. Record Boom is 3-1. We therefore make Sierra Real our key horse for the second leg. And we make Character, our second-ranked horse in the final leg, our third key horse. After this juggling, only one of our key horses, Sierra Real, is a probable favorite. So the Key-3-3 Pick-3 part-wheels for races three through five are Solda Holme–three contenders–three contenders, three contenders–Sierra Real–three contenders, and three contenders–three contenders–Character.

With that, we've figured out our bets on the third race. Let's see what happened:

THIRD RACE	5½ FURLONGS. (1.021) CLAIMING. Purse $13,000. Fillies and mares, 3–year–olds and upward.
Hollywood	Weights: 3–year–olds, 120 lbs. Older, 122 lbs. Non–winners of two races since October 4, allowed 3 lbs. A race since then, 5 lbs. Claiming price $20,000, if for $18,000, allowed 2 lbs. (Races when entered for $16,000
DECEMBER 4, 1993	or less not considered.)

Value of Race: $13,000 Winner $7,150; second $2,600; third $1,950; fourth $975; fifth $325. Mutuel Pool $300,520.00 Exacta Pool $295,061.00 Quinella Pool $50,204.00

Last Raced	Horse	M/Eqt. A.Wt PP St	¼	¾	Str	Fin	Jockey	Cl'g Pr	Odds $1
9Oct93 9SA10	Perky Slew	LBbf 5 117 3 3	2½	32½	21	1no	Antley C W	20000	8.40
17Nov93 3Hol1	Datsdawayitis	LB 4 117 1 5	31	1hd	1hd	22	Nakatani C S	20000	4.90
18Sep93 9YM2	Solda Holme	LBb 7 117 4 6	6	6	41	32½	Stevens G L	20000	2.20
14Nov93 1SA7	Old Time Romance	LB 5 112 5 2	4½	4hd	51½	45	Gonzalez S Jr5	20000	12.00
17Nov93 3Hol5	Chicharrones	LB 6 117 2 4	1hd	2hd	31½	52¾	Pincay L Jr	18000	8.10
14Nov93 1SA4	Isleo Bebe	LB 5 117 6 1	51	5¼	6	6	Gryder A T	20000	1.40

OFF AT 1:29 Start Good. Won driving. Time, :221, :452, :574, 1:04 Track fast.

$2 Mutuel Prices:	3–PERKY SLEW	18.80	7.40	4.20
	1–DATSDAWAYITIS		6.20	3.40
	4–SOLDA HOLME			3.00

$2 EXACTA 3–1 PAID $104.20 $2 QUINELLA 1–3 PAID $42.80

$3 Triple 5–6–3 Paid $1,102.80 Triple Pool $120,068.00

Perky Slew jumps up and ruins all of our best-laid plans. At higher than 6-to-1 on our line, Perky Slew doesn't figure in any of our bets. She effectively takes us out of the win, exacta, and quinella pools. Even worse, the Pick-3s we were alive to from race one have all lost. The Pick-3s we started in races two and three are also history. The only bet we could have possibly cashed was the show bet on Solda Holme, who paid an overlayed $3.00 to show. However, this show price was the result of the 6-to-5 favorite, Isleo Bebe, finishing out of the money.

Here is the betting-line information for the fourth race:

```
-----------------------------BETTING LINE-----------------------------
                -------Rankings--------       Betting  Fair    Fair
Horse name      PEH  H-I THAAI P-H ESP Rating  Line    Place $ Show $
----------------------------------------------------------------------
SIERRA REAL      1    2   2    1   2   74.58   9-5     3.60    2.80
AL'S SUNSHINE    2    1   1    2   5   69.58   7-2
MY IDEAL         3    3   3    3   4   64.85   7-1
STAGE DOOR TYLER 5    4   4    4   1   64.59
RIFLING THRU     4    5   5    5   3   61.68
```

Since this is a maiden race, it would be a wise idea to check the entire morning line in order to identify any bet-down horses that aren't included among our contenders:

Sierra Real	2-1
My Ideal	5-2
Vinoyhielo	30-1

Stage Door Tyler	6-1
Skagit Chief	20-1
Al's Sunshine	4-1
Rifling Thru	6-1
Count Con	10-1

Here are the toteboard odds a few moments before post time:

Sierra Real	9-5
My Ideal	3-1
Vinoyhielo	80-1
Stage Door Tyler	7-1
Skagit Chief	50-1
Al's Sunshine	4-1
Rifling Thru	4-1
Count Con	17-1

Let's look first at our potential win bets. Sierra Real is going off at 9-5, the same odds we've given him in our line. If we are aggressive or moderate win bettors, can we play him? Absolutely not. Remember—no edge, no bet. But Sierra Real does represent a quasi-legitimate favorite: He's less than 5-2 on our line and he's bet down from his morning line in this maiden race. The trouble is, this is a chaos race. Sierra Real rightfully merits some respect, but not too much.

At 4-to-1, Al's Sunshine is a slight overlay from our betting-line odds of 7-to-2. The edge is a modest 11 percent, not enough to warrant a bet. While he's not a bet-down, he does offer a positive expectation.

My Ideal is a win bet we should avoid at all costs: He's an underlay based on our line and he hasn't been bet down by the public.

It looks like a washout in the win pool. Sierra Real is a quasi-legitimate, bet-down maiden favorite who offers no edge. Al's Sunshine offers an edge but isn't bet down. My Ideal offers none of the advantages of his fellow contenders. A real lesser-of-evils race in the win pool. Best to pass.

Even the ultraconservative win bettors among us are left without a bet. Our group estimate of these three contenders is 70.4 percent. The public's estimate is 80.1 percent. Regardless of our wagering temperament, there is no way we can make any win bets in this race.

We continue our search for overlays in the place-and-show pools. We see that we have a fair place price of $3.60 and a fair show price of $2.80 on Sierra Real. If Sierra Real's actual place-and-show prices are higher than these fair prices, we'll have a place or show overlay. But we won't bet it because the race is a chaos race. Fortunately, Sierra Real's actual place price is bouncing between $3.40 and $3.20 in the worst-case scenario (teaming him with the second most popular place horse, My Ideal). And Sierra Real's actual show price is hovering around $2.40 with the second and third most popular show horses, My Ideal and Al's Sunshine. No advantage in the place-and-show pools.

Is there an overlay lurking in the exacta pool? We can obviously eliminate any exacta involving My Ideal, who's overbet in relation to our line. If he's an underlay in the win pool, he'll most likely be an underlay in both slots of the exacta as well. Sierra Real and Al's Sunshine have been bet pretty close to their betting-line odds. This suggests that the exactas combining them will be right around the fair pays listed on ALL-IN-ONE's exacta grid. However, when we add our minimum 40 percent edge to the fair pays, we effectively eliminate any potential exacta bet we may have considered.

There is a trifecta as well. Sierra Real is our top pick and should be our key horse in the Key-Place-All strategy. However, he is the public favorite, and we know that the favorite cannot be our key horse. But Sierra Real is a quasi-legitimate favorite. Our numbers, the bet-down factor, and the public-favorite-in-a-maiden-race factor are just a few of the signals pointing to Sierra Real. If we are desperate enough to key against Sierra Real, then Al's Sunshine becomes our horse. But it looks like we'd be best off in abstaining from this trifecta.

At this point, we haven't found a single positive-expectation wager in the win, place, show, exacta, quinella, or trifecta pools in this race. This isn't cause for despair. Remember: no edge, no bet. We bet only when we have the odds in our favor, not because we're dying for action or think we have a small chance of making a big score on an impossible combination. The toteboard and actual pay matrices are our best friends. They give us a calm, cool, rational approach for betting the races. Compare this to most racegoers. In their urge to gamble, the nonsensical bettors will force themselves into negative-expectation bets when positive-expectation bets don't exist. As commonsense bettors, we bet for financial reasons, not emotional or psychological ones. We watch the fourth race for academic purposes:

FOURTH RACE

Hollywood

DECEMBER 4, 1993

1 1/16 MILES. (1.40) MAIDEN CLAIMING. Purse $17,000. 2–year–olds. Weight, 119 lbs. Claiming price $32,000; if for $28,000, allowed 2 lbs. (Horses which have not started for a claiming price of $20,0000 or less preferred.)

Value of Race: $17,000 Winner $9,350; second $3,400; third $2,550; fourth $1,275; fifth $425. Mutuel Pool $275,433.00 Exacta Pool $224,593.00 Trifecta Pool $190,580.00 Quinella Pool $36,077.00

Last Raced	Horse	M/Eqt. A.Wt	PP	St	¼	½	¾	Str	Fin	Jockey	Cl'g Pr	Odds $1
22Oct93 6SA3	Sierra Real	Bb 2 114	1	3	1hd	1hd	1hd	1hd	11	Gonzalez S Jr5	32000	1.80
15Nov93 6SA5	My Ideal	L 2 119	2	4	2½	21	21½	23	22	Antley C W	32000	3.10
17Nov93 2Hol3	Stage Door Tyler	Lb 2 119	4	7	6½	73	5hd	3½	31	Valenzuela F H	32000	7.40
11Nov93 4SA5	Rifling Thru	LBb 2 117	7	2	4½	4hd	63	41	47½	Atkinson P	28000	4.30
15Nov93 6SA3	Al's Sunshine	LB 2 119	6	1	51	52	31	54	5no	Pedroza M A	32000	4.00
24Nov93 9Hol10	Vinoyhielo	Bb 2 117	3	8	8	8	8	62	68½	Lopez A D	28000	80.50
15Nov93 6SA8	Count Con	LBb 2 119	8	5	3hd	31	41	72	71	Gryder A T	32000	17.60
30Oct93 2SA12	Skagit Chief	Bb 2 119	5	6	73½	6hd	7hd	8	8	Long B	32000	57.40

OFF AT 1:58 Start Good. Won driving. Time, :23³, :47², 1:12¹, 1:38¹, 1:45 Track fast.

$2 Mutuel Prices:

1–SIERRA REAL	5.60	3.20	2.60	
2–MY IDEAL		3.80	2.80	
4–STAGE DOOR TYLER			3.60	

$2 EXACTA 1–2 PAID $20.20 $2 TRIFECTA 1–2–4 PAID $100.60 $2 QUINELLA 1–2 PAID $10.40

$3 Triple 6–3–1 Paid $600.60 Triple Pool $81,698.00

The public and *ALL-IN-ONE* were right on the money. Sierra Real gamely held his frontrunning position throughout to score. The win, place, and show prices on this quasi-legitimate favorite offered little or no value. The exacta should have paid at least $28.00 in order to be an equitable bet. It paid a miserly $20.20.

Let's look at the fifth race:

```
------------------------------BETTING LINE-----------------------------

                   -------Rankings--------          Betting   Fair    Fair
Horse name         PEH  H-I THAAI P-H  ESP  Rating   Line    Place $  Show $
----------------------------------------------------------------------
RECORD BOOM         1    2    1    1    3   80.00    3-1
CHARACTER-GB        3    1    2    2    1   85.67    7-2
ROBINSKI-NZ         2    3    3    3    2   83.00    4-1
AROMATIC-GB         4    4    4    4    4   68.83
BREAKFAST TABLE     5    5    5    5    5   61.41
```

Here are the toteboard win odds on our contenders just before the race:

Record Boom	1-1 (even money)
Character	5-2
Robinski	5-1

At a glance, we see that Record Boom and Character are big underlays. Robinski is a nominal overlay whose edge rests right at our minimum requirement: 20 percent. For aggressive and moderate bettors, the only bet is Robinski.

As a group, our three contenders account for 75 percent of the probability of winning this race. The public's estimate of the same contenders' probability of winning is more than 90 percent. Robinski remains the only possible win bet.

As win underlays, Record Boom and Character will probably be overbet in the exacta pools as well. We can safely eliminate the two exactas pairing these two horses. The exactas from these two to Robinski also are underlayed.

However, we can also play the exacta in a strategic, defensive sense. Since we'll bet Robinski to win, we can "insure" this win bet with the exacta as a place bet. As long as Record Boom is a legitimate favorite, we can put him on top of Robinski in the exacta. This bet serves as a high-yield place bet. It saves us from doing something drastic if Robinski gets beaten by a narrow margin. Instead of collecting nothing and feeling the sting of defeat if Robinski gets nosed at the wire, we can cash a healthy exacta. We do this by putting Robinski in the place spot of the exacta behind the horse most likely to beat him: the legitimate favorite. In this case, the public favorite, Record Boom, is our top pick and a legitimate favorite. This gives us a cushion of psychological comfort and rewards us for "good handicapping, bad outcome."

Since Record Boom is the public favorite, the Key-Place-All trifecta strategy in this race suggests using another horse as a key. Character seems to be the most likely candidate for key horse. His projected final time is just $\frac{1}{100}$ of a second slower than Record Boom's. Record Boom becomes a place horse, along with Robinski. And Aromatic would join Record Boom and Robinski as the all horses. (Breakfast Table can't run within five lengths of the final-time race par of 1:35.)

Here is the result of the fifth race:

FIFTH RACE
Hollywood
DECEMBER 4, 1993

1 MILE. (Turf)(1.324) CLAIMING. Purse $24,000. 3-year-olds and upward. Weights: 3-year-olds, 119 lbs. Older, 122 lbs. Non-winners of two races at a mile or over since October 4, allowed 3 lbs. Such a race since then, 6 lbs. Claiming price $40,000; for each $2,500 to $35,000, allowed 2 lbs. (Races when entered for $32,000 or less not considered.)

Value of Race: $24,000 Winner $13,200; second $4,800; third $3,600; fourth $1,800; fifth $600. Mutuel Pool $423,582.00 Exacta Pool $370,475.00 Trifecta Pool $306,018.00 Quinella Pool $42,757.00

Last Raced	Horse	M/Eqt.	A.	Wt	PP	St	¼	½	¾	Str	Fin	Jockey	Cl'g Pr	Odds $1
24Nov93 7Hol1	Record Boom	LB	7	116	2	3	1hd	21	21½	1hd	1hd	Solis A	40000	1.10
26Nov93 7Hol3	Robinski-NZ	LBb	10	113	4	9	7½	71	62	62	21	Gryder A T	35000	5.10
14Nov93 7BM2	Character-GB	LBf	5	116	3	5	51	5½	51½	5½	31	Nakatani C S	40000	2.60
26Nov93 7Hol8	Breakfast Table	LBf	9	116	5	4	41	41	3hd	4hd	42	Stevens G L	40000	10.50
26Sep93 6BM5	Impact	LB	5	116	8	1	3hd	3hd	4½	3½	51¾	Valenzuela P A	40000	23.50
27Oct93 9SA4	Notwithstanding	LBb	5	115	1	7	9	9	72½	710	62	Sorenson D	37500	58.20
28Oct93 8BM4	Aromatic-GB	LB	6	109	6	2	21½	1hd	1hd	2½	714	Gonzalez S Jr5	37500	8.30
29Oct93 8SA8	Shtick	LB	4	116	9	8	82	81	9	8½	81	Long B	40000	131.90
19Nov93 4Hol1	Purdue Prince	LBb	4	117	7	6	61½	61	81	9	9	Pincay L Jr	40000	46.20

OFF AT 2:27 Start Good. Won driving. Time, :241, :481, 1:122, 1:363 Course firm.

$2 Mutuel Prices:			
2–RECORD BOOM	4.20	3.00	2.20
4–ROBINSKI-NZ		4.20	2.60
3–CHARACTER-GB			2.40

$2 EXACTA 2–4 PAID $15.80 $2 TRIFECTA 2–4–3 PAID $44.00 $2 QUINELLA 2–4 PAID $11.00

$3 Triple 3–1–2 Paid $306.30 Triple Pool $115,207.00

Record Boom barely beats Robinski for the win. Our win bet on Robinski fails, but the exacta as a place bet has connected for a modest $15.80 score. The trifecta with our key horse Character running third behind place horse Record Boom and place/all horse Robinski also hits for a $44 return.

In between live races five and six at Hollywood Park was a simulcast of race six from Bay Meadows. This race isn't part of any serial bets, and neither quinella nor trifecta wagering is offered on it. Here are the past performances and line for the race:

Bay Meadows

6

1 MILE. (Turf). (1:343) **ALLOWANCE. Purse $20,000. Fillies, 2-year-olds, which have not won $3,000 other than maiden, claiming, starter or classified handicap. Weight: 118 lbs. Non-winners of a race other than claiming, starter or classified handicap at one mile or over since October 1, allowed 3 lbs. One such race since September 1, 5 lbs.**

TURF COURSE — 1 MILE — START — FINISH

Lucky Jo B.
Own: Swenson Vernon
ESPINOZA V (69 6 5 8 .09)
Ch. f. 2 (Jan)
Sire: Synastry (Seattle Slew)
Dam: This Ole Queen (Princely Native)
Br: WH/BCR Joint Venture (Idaho)
Tr: Battles Olen (15 2 0 2 .13)
L 1135

Lifetime Record:	4 1 0 1	$11,525			
1993	4 1 0 1	$11,525	Turf	0 0 0 0	
1992	0 M 0 0		Wet	1 0 0 0	$1,250
BM ①	0 0 0 0		Dist ①	0 0 0 0	

28Nov93- 8BM sly 1 ⊗ :223 :471 1:121 1:38 ⓕWoodside50k 40 4 2 44½ 510 519 523½ Miranda V LB 111 21.30 56-23 WorkTheCrowd1153½ PrivtePrsusion1179 BurningDsir1155 Overmatched 5
14Nov93- 3BM fst 1 :234 :482 1:133 1:392 ⓕMd Sp Wt 56 1 1 11 11½ 11½ 1nk Miranda V LB 117 4.80 73-18 Lucky Jo B.117nk Vanilla Wafer1175 Sonata Sky11710 Held gamely 5
31Oct93- 1BM fst 6f :223 :461 :59 1:121 ⓕMd 20000 40 4 2 33 43 59½ 38¾ Chapman T M B 117 6.40 67-17 Double Jewel1177 Baroness V Ullmann1171¼ Lucky Jo B.117hd Even try 7
7Oct93- 2BM fst 6f :23 :461 :583 1:112 ⓕMd 20000 42 1 4 1hd 2hd 25 47¾ Chapman T M B 117 4.50 71-15 Olive H.1177 Skeptic Lady Lee117hd Call Me The Star118½ Weakened 7
WORKOUTS: Nov 8 BM 7f fst 1:25 H *1/1* ●Nov 5 BM 3f fst :344 H *1/23* Oct 28 BM 4f fst :481 H *4/26* Oct 21 BM 6f fst 1:151 H *2/3* Oct 5 BM 4f fst :482 H *5/24* Oct 1 BM 4f fst :484 H *12/24*

Bubble Dance
Own: Thatcher Frank R
JAUREGUI L H (117 3 7 17 .03)
B. f. 2 (Jan)
Sire: Moscow Ballet (Nijinsky II)
Dam: Bubble Bite (Poleax)
Br: Harris Farm, Inc. (Cal)
Tr: Grudziewski Bob (7 1 1 3 .14)
L 113

Lifetime Record:	4 1 2 0	$8,875		
1993	4 1 2 0	$8,875	Turf	0 0 0 0
1992	0 M 0 0		Wet	0 0 0 0
BM ①	0 0 0 0		Dist ①	0 0 0 0

7Nov93-10BM fst 1 :224 :464 1:112 1:364 ⓕBurlingame50k 41 3 8 87¼ 911 1018 1019¾ Boulanger G LB 111 16.20 66-15 Work The Crowd1151 Choobloo11510 Vegas Sis1153 Far back 10
4Oct93- 7BM fst 5½f :221 :461 :583 1:05 ⓕAlw 20000N1X 73 4 3 1hd 11 1hd 2no Gonzalez R M LB 115 14.60 86-19 Work The Crowd115no Bubble Dance115nk Dancing Fir1132 Wide early 7
5Sep93- 5BM fst 5½f :213 :454 :584 1:051 ⓕMd c-12500 54 6 4 56¼ 32 11 11¼ Kaenel J L LB 117 *1.80 85-15 Bubble Dance1171¼ Bev1171½ Hub City Dancer1173 Wide trip 9
Claimed from Harris Farms Inc, Gaines Carla Trainer
14Aug93- 6Bmf fst 5½f :214 :454 :584 1:053 ⓕMd 12500 51 5 8 107½ 78 36 24 Kaenel J L LB 118 12.10 83-10 Royal Boutique1174 Bubble Dance1181 Septembrist1173 Good late bid 12
WORKOUTS: Nov 27 BM 3f fst :372 H *19/29* Nov 19 BM 5f fst 1:022 H *18/24* Oct 27 BM 5f fst 1:011 H *9/22* Oct 16 BM 3f fst :381 H *2/3* Sep 27 BM 5f fst 1:013 H *43/74* Sep 20 BM 3f fst :354 H *4/21*

```
Jilly's Halo                               Ch. f. 2 (Mar)                                    Lifetime Record :  7 1 0 1   $14,030
Own: Heerensperger David & Jill            Sire: Sunny's Halo (Halo)                         1993  7 1 0 1   $14,030  Turf    0 0 0 0
                                           Dam: Gray Tab (Zulu Tom)                          1992  0 M 0 0            Wet     0 0 0 0
                                           Br:  Grousemont Farm (Ky)                 L 118   BM ⓣ  0 0 0 0            Distⓣ   0 0 0 0
BELVOIR V T (420 78 78 50 .19)             Tr:  Roberts Craig (65 12 8 9 .18)
7Nov93-10BM fst 1    :224 :464 1:112 1:364 ⒻBurlingame50k  50 9 9 9¾ 7¾ 713 515 Jauregui L H   B 111 b 28.70 71-15 Work The Crowd1151 Choobloo11510 Vegas Sis1153   Showed little 10
17Oct93- 1BM gd 1    :224 :474 1:133 1:401 ⒻMd Sp Wt       60 1 3 22 2½ 11 16    Baze R A       B 117 b  2.40 69-28 Jilly's Halo1176 Vanilla Wafer1171½ Day Rate1175   Drifted in midstretch 5
2Sep93- 2Dmr fst 1   :222 :463 1:12 1:38   ⒻMd 40000       50 3 6 52¾ 4¾ 3½ 4½  McCarron C J   B 118 b  6.20 68-18 BurningDesire1163 AvSingstheblues1135½ CloudyLin118no   4 Wide stretch 8
8Aug93- 6Dmr fst 6½f :223 :46 1:103 1:17   ⒻMd Sp Wt       49 10 6 62¾ 73¾ 107½ 1012½ Warren R J Jr B 117 b 41.30 74-11 Top Of The Sky117nk Tin117¾ Malibu Light117no   Wide trip 11
31Jly93- 2Dmr fst 5f :214 :453 :58          ⒻMd Sp Wt       52 3 10 1012 98¾ 87½ 510¼ Warren R J Jr B 117 b 50.80 97-10 Noassemblyrequired1173½ StrongColors1172¾ Terakt1173   Stumbled start 10
29Jun93- 9Pln fst 5½f :213 :46 :573 1:042  ⒻMd Sp Wt       56 2 6 58 68 39 35½   Warren R J Jr    117 b 11.50 85-09 Saucy Trick1173 Gentle Rainfall1172½ Jilly's Halo1171½   Even late 10
11Jun93- 6GG fst 5f  :212 :45 :573         ⒻMd Sp Wt       31 10 10 1111 118 9¾ 711½ Warren R J Jr B 117 b 6.90 82-08 Tan Line1174 Yearly Tour117¾ Fits Best1174   Brushed start, wide 12
WORKOUTS: Nov 28 BM 4f fst :491 H 18/44  Nov 17 BM ⓣ 5f fm 1:054 H (d)4/5  Oct 30 BM 7f fst 1:30 H 4/4  Oct 7 BM 4f fst :502 H 21/32  Sep 27 BM 3f fst :37 H 11/28  Sep 17 BM 4f fst :50 H 15/22

Skeptic Lady Lee                           Dk. b or br f. 2 (Jan)                            Lifetime Record :  5 2 3 0   $15,625
Own: John H Deeter Trust                   Sire: Our Michael (Bolero)                        1993  5 2 3 0   $15,625  Turf    0 0 0 0
                                           Dam: Skeptic Lady (Olden Times)                   1992  0 M 0 0            Wet     0 0 0 0
                                           Br:  Rancho Jonata (Cal)                  L 113   BM ⓣ  0 0 0 0            Distⓣ   0 0 0 0
SCHACHT R (114 9 16 9 .08)                 Tr:  Benedict Jim (70 13 13 8 .19)
17Nov93- 6BM fst 6f  :222 :46 :584 1:12    ⒻClm 16000      62 1 6 79½ 76¼ 43 1no  Boulanger G   LB 113 b 11.40 76-17 Skeptic Lady Lee113no January Hussy1151 Olive H.1132½   Rallied far wide 7
28Oct93- 5BM fst 6f  :223 :46 :584 1:12    ⒻMd 12500       53 1 6 52¼ 32½ 21 1nk  Baze R A      LB 117 b *1.30 76-17 SkepticLdyLee117nk DesertMystique1173½ K.L.'sImgene117nk   Rallied wide 12
7Oct93- 2BM fst 6f   :23 :461 :583 1:112   ⒻMd 20000       43 5 7 76¼ 65½ 36 27   Tohill K S    LB 117 b  3.10 72-15 OliveH.1177 SkepticLadyLee117hd CllMeTheStr118½   Shuffled back start 7
23Sep93- 6BM fst 6f  :222 :46 :591 1:121   ⒻMd 20000       60 5 6 56½ 46 3½ 2½   Tohill K S    LB 117 b  8.70 74-17 My Blue Genes117½ Skeptic Lady Lee117no Olive H.1173   Wide late bid 8
29Aug93- 5BM fst 5f  :22 :46 :59           ⒻⓈMd 12500      56 4 8 66 55½ 44 2¾   Tohill K S    LB 117 b 24.40 88-17 Hazy Star117¾ Skeptic Lady Lee1172 La Campesina117nk   Wide late run 9
WORKOUTS: Nov 28 BM 3f fst :39 H 11/12  Nov 13 BM 3f fst :36 H 3/27  Oct 21 BM 5f fst 1:054 H 28/29  Oct 3 BM 3f fst :38 H 9/12  Sep 18 BM 5f fst 1:041 H 31/36  Sep 9 BM 5f fst 1:03 H 18/23

Princess Mitterand                         B. f. 2 (Mar)                                     Lifetime Record :  4 1 1 1   $22,870
Own: Cowan Irving & Marge                  Sire: Seattle Slew (Bold Reasoning)               1993  4 1 1 1   $22,870  Turf    0 0 0 0
                                           Dam: Mitterand (Hold Your Peace)                  1992  0 M 0 0            Wet     0 0 0 0
                                           Br:  Irving Cowan (Ky)                    L 113   BM ⓣ  0 0 0 0            Distⓣ   0 0 0 0
CHAPMAN T M (321 34 30 49 .11)             Tr:  Drysdale Neil (9 1 1 0 .11)
31Oct93- 4SA fst 6f  :213 :444 :572 1:10   ⒻMd Sp Wt       87 9 1 63¾ 31½ 2½ 1hd  Delahoussaye E LB 117 *1.20 87-12 Princess Mitterand117hd Whatawoman1174 GlidingLark1174½   4 Wide turn 9
10Oct93- 7SA fst 6f  :213 :45 :572 1:10    ⒻMd Sp Wt       75 7 1 54½ 51¼ 34½ 24¼ Delahoussaye E B 117  6.20 85-16 SophisticatedCielo1174¼ PrincessMittrnd1172 WovnGold112½   Second best 10
8Jly93- 7AP gd 5f    :222 :454 :58         ⒻMd Sp Wt       54 3 5 77 74¼ 48 37    Sibille R        118  7.70 92-09 Candleberry1182½ GraciousGrnny1184½ PrincessMitternd118nk   Mild rail bid 10
13Jun93- 4CD fst 5½f :221 :463 :524 1:054  ⒻMd Sp Wt       56 11 11 86 87½ 65¾ 55 Romero R P      118  5.50 88-10 Tier118hd Brook Blues118¾ Cherokee Crossing1184   No late threat 12
WORKOUTS: Nov 23 Hol 7f fst 1:254 H 2/2  Nov 18 Hol ⓣ 7f fm 1:291 H (d)2/3  Nov 13 SA 6f fst 1:134 H 15/31  Nov 5 SA 3f fst :373 B 23/41  Oct 27 SA 4f fst :472 H 5/54  Oct 22 SA 6f fst 1:13 H 3/18

Royal Boutique                             Dk. b or br f. 2 (May)                            Lifetime Record :  4 1 2 0   $18,735
Own: Fessler & Pagan & Zafran              Sire: Forceten (Forli)                            1993  4 1 2 0   $18,735  Turf    0 0 0 0
                                           Dam: Escada (Cormorant)                           1992  0 M 0 0            Wet     0 0 0 0
                                           Br:  Dean-Chris Partnership (Cal)         L 113   BM ⓣ  0 0 0 0            Distⓣ   0 0 0 0
FLORES D R (1 0 0 0 .00)                   Tr:  Vince James J (24 3 4 1 .13)
18Nov93- 8BM fst 6f  :221 :453 :582 1:12   ⒻPrsd Nth Cal25k 60 4 5 57 46 35 2½    Boulanger G   LB 115   *.70 75-21 Nellie'sBargain115½ RoyalBoutique1155 Sarah'sBoop1151½   Bumped early 7
17Oct93- 8BM gd 5½f :213 :451 :581 1:05    ⒻDomnt Dancer40k 72 6 6 57½ 54½ 43 41½ Boulanger G    B 111   3.00 84-21 Work TheCrowd115½ Choobloo1171 Kasi'sCashQueen113hd   Wide late bid 6
25Sep93- 8BM fst 6f  :22 :451 :574 1:104   ⒻⓈCourtship35k  78 3 4 55½ 64¼ 44½ 21  Boulanger G    B 111  13.00 81-14 Canyon Winds1131 Royal Boutique1112½ Tan Line1151   Rallied inside 6
14Aug93- 6Bmf fst 5½f :214 :454 :584 1:053 ⒻMd 12500       62 4 3 2½ 2½ 12 14    Doocy T T      B 117  *2.30 87-10 Royal Boutique1174 Bubble Dance1181 Septembrist1173   Ridden out 12
WORKOUTS: Nov 13 BM 4f fst :48 H 16/59  Nov 4 BM 4f fst :473 H 4/31  Oct 28 BM 3f fst :373 H 10/21  Oct 13 BM 3f fst :352 H 2/12  Oct 6 BM 3f fst :371 H 7/21  Sep 20 BM 4f fst :474 H 10/59

Little Brass                               B. f. 2 (Apr)                                     Lifetime Record :  1 1 0 0   $8,250
Own: Green Valley Ranch & Arterburn & Co   Sire: Dixieland Brass (Dixieland Band)            1993  1 1 0 0   $8,250   Turf    0 0 0 0
                                           Dam: Little Ferrous (Iron Ruler)                  1992  0 M 0 0            Wet     0 0 0 0
                                           Br:  Eaton Farms Inc., Red Bull Stable, et al. (Ky)  L 113  BM ⓣ  0 0 0 0     Distⓣ   0 0 0 0
BAZE R A (438 113 81 57 .26)               Tr:  Arterburn Lonnie (73 20 20 7 .27)
7Nov93- 1BM fst 6f   :222 :454 :584 1:122  ⒻMd Sp Wt       60 4 5 56½ 57½ 34½ 13  Baze R A      LB 117   4.90 74-18 Little Brass1173 Day Rate117nk Boz Connection117½   Rallied wide 6
WORKOUTS: Nov 23 BM 7f fst 1:29 H 2/2  Nov 16 BM 7f fst 1:263 H 1/2  Nov 3 BM 4f fst :491 H 19/30  Oct 28 BM 6f fst 1:164 H 6/7  Oct 21 BM 5f fst 1:024 Hg 19/29  Oct 14 BM 4f fst :51 H 25/28

Princess In Charge                         Ro. f. 2 (Mar)                                    Lifetime Record :  5 3 0 0   $17,290
Own: Jones Reginald C                      Sire: Prince Card (Prince John)                   1993  5 3 0 0   $17,290  Turf    1 1 0 0   $8,800
                                           Dam: Saint in Charge (The Big Boss)               1992  0 M 0 0            Wet     0 0 0 0
                                           Br:  Laveen Farms (Idaho)                 L 113   BM ⓣ  1 1 0 0   $8,800   Distⓣ   1 1 0 0   $8,800
WARREN R J JR (318 24 45 59 .08)           Tr:  Elordi Donna R (37 5 4 5 .14)
25Nov93- 6BM fm 1 ⓣ :223 :471 1:13 1:394   ⒻClm 25000      62 8 8 89¾ 55½ 42¼ 1hd Warren R J Jr LB 114   4.20 80-13 Princess In Charge114hd MyBlueGenes1172 CleverCovers1151¼   Wide rally 9
28Oct93- 4BM fst 6f  :222 :452 :574 1:104  ⒻAlw 20000N1X   61 1 6 67½ 53½ 54 53½ Warren R J Jr LB 115  32.00 79-17 Dancing Fir115¾ Alconnie116hd Clever Covers1152½   Steadied early stages 7
10Oct93- 1BM fst 6f  :223 :454 :583 1:12   ⒻClm 16000      62 3 5 53½ 55 32 1hd   Belvoir V T   LB 115   4.10 76-15 PrncssInChrg115hd Phnmntt1151 Eghtstndnt1142½   Angled out midstretch 6
4Sep93- 6BM fst 5½f  :211 :452 :58 1:043   ⒻClm 22500      50 1 7 714 712 79¾ 68  Hansen R D     B 114   9.90 80-14 Road Buddy1142½ Clever Covers116½ Jetting Trip1161   Off slowly 7
31Jly93- 3Boi fst 5f :234 :474 1:004       ⒻMd Sp Wt       32 1 2 513 33 2½ 1½    Ayers L        B 120   3.00 80-17 Princess In Charge120½ Lassaroo1203 Casual Outing1225½   Driving 7
WORKOUTS: Nov 19 BM 7f fst 1:261 H 1/3  Nov 14 BM 5f fst 1:011 H 22/63  Oct 22 BM 5f fst 1:002 H 10/24  Oct 7 BM 4f fst :491 H 13/32  Oct 1 BM 5f fst 1:012 H 10/30  Sep 16 BM 6f fst 1:021 H 8/18
```

ALL-IN-ONE's output for the race is as follows:

```
4DEC93                              BM                         8 furlongs turf
Race #6                                                             8 starters
NW1                                                      Age: 2 years, Female
--------------------------------INPUT DATA----------------------------------
                     #  #  #  #   $'S                          1st C   2nd C  Final
Horse name          ST  W  P  S  Earned Date     Trk Dist.  S  time    time   time
----------------------------------------------------------------------------
LUCKY JO B.          0  0  0  0       0 28NOV93  BM  8.000 D  48.2    113.3  139.2
JILLY'S HALO         0  0  0  0       0 7NOV93   BM  8.000 D  47.4    113.3  140.1
SKEPTIC LADY LEE     0  0  0  0       0 17NOV93  BM  6.000 D  22.2     46.0  112.0
PRINCESS MITTERAND   0  0  0  0       0 31OCT93  SA  6.000 D  21.3     44.4  110.0
ROYAL BOUTIQUE       0  0  0  0       0 18NOV93  BM  6.000 D  22.1     45.3  112.0

                                   1st C   2nd C   Final
Horse name          Class Lvl      B.L.    B.L.    B.L.     SR    Var
--------------------------------------------------------------------
LUCKY JO B.         MSW            0.00    0.00    0.00     73   18.0
JILLY'S HALO        MSW            2.00    1.50    0.00     69   28.0
SKEPTIC LADY LEE    C16,000        9.25    6.25    0.00     76   17.0
PRINCESS MITTERAND  MSW            3.75    1.50    0.00     87   12.0
ROYAL BOUTIQUE      STAKES         7.00    6.00    0.50     75   21.0
```

```
-----------------------------------BETTING LINE-----------------------------------
                      -------Rankings--------           Betting   Fair    Fair
Horse name            PEH H-I THAAI P-H  ESP  Rating    Line      Place $ Show $
---------------------------------------------------------------------------------
PRINCESS MITTERAND     1   1   1    1    1    90.49     9-5
LUCKY JO B.            2   2   2    3    3    73.47     5-1
ROYAL BOUTIQUE         3   4   4    4    2    71.70     6-1
SKEPTIC LADY LEE       5   3   3    2    4    70.23
JILLY'S HALO           4   5   5    5    5    65.86
```

```
-----------------------------------EXACTA GRID-----------------------------------
                |PRINCESS MITTER| LUCKY JO B.  | ROYAL BOUTIQUE|
----------------+---------------+--------------+---------------+
PRINCESS MITTE  | . . . . . . . |   20     48  |   22     55   |
                | . . . . . . . |              |               |
                | . . . . . . . |              |               |
----------------+---------------+--------------+---------------+
LUCKY JO B.     |   26     64   | . . . . . . .|   66    163   |
                |               | . . . . . . .|               |
                |               | . . . . . . .|               |
----------------+---------------+--------------+---------------+
ROYAL BOUTIQUE  |   31     76   |   67    168  | . . . . . . . |
                |               |              | . . . . . . . |
                |               |              | . . . . . . . |
----------------+---------------+--------------+---------------+
```

```
4DEC93                            BM                     8 furlongs turf
Race #6                                                        8 starters
NW1                                                 Age: 2 years, Female
-----------------------------SPEED/PACE SUMMARY-----------------------------

Race Type:        Semi-Orderly Race
Race Profile:     47.93  112.50  138.18   Winners' Pace Profile: EARLY
Ability Par:      73.61                    Pace Contention Point:  3.42 lengths

Projected Times:                   Ability  Balance  Last  Proj  Con-
                  1st C  2nd C  Fin C  Time    Time   Frac  Pace  tender
                 ----------------------------------------------------------
PRINCESS MITTERAND 48.41 112.75 138.25 73.91  95.67  25.50 FRONT  Y
LUCKY JO B.        48.79 113.34 138.73 74.18  96.08  25.39 MID    N
ROYAL BOUTIQUE     48.82 113.50* 138.89 74.21 96.23  25.39 LATE   N
SKEPTIC LADY LEE   49.46 113.98* 138.87 74.36 95.87  24.90 REAR   N
JILLY'S HALO       48.52 113.51* 139.31 74.32 96.96  25.80 LATE   N
```

```
-----------------------------------PACE GRAPH-----------------------------------
      Profile:                47.93              112.50              138.18
      Front Runner:           48.41              112.75              138.25
Horse name                     1C                  2C                  F
PRINCESS MITTERAND------------------X --------------(---X ------------------X
LUCKY JO B.         ----------------X-+ --------------(X--+ ----------------X-+
ROYAL BOUTIQUE      ----------------X-+ --------------X---+ ----------------X--+
SKEPTIC LADY LEE    --------------X---+ --------------X-(---+ ------------X--+
JILLY'S HALO        ----------------X+ --------------X---+ ------------X----+
```

The betting from Hollywood Park goes directly into the Bay Meadows pools. The win odds are the same at both tracks:

Princess Mitterand	3-5
Lucky Jo B.	50-1
Royal Boutique	4-1

The win betting in this race is a no-brainer. Lucky Jo B. is going off at ten times the price she should. The group won't be underestimated by the public since Princess Mitterand is listed as 3-5 on the toteboard.

As for place-and-show betting on this race, don't. Turf racing is full of blanket finishes, like "fourth beaten a neck" and "seventh beaten a length." When less than a neck can, and often does, separate the second-place horse from the fourth-place horse in a turf race, we'll probably lose as many place and show bets as we hit. And the whole point of place-and-show betting is to cash more often than we lose. Reserve place-and-show betting for orderly dirt races, where there's a greater margin separating the horses at the wire. We should totally disregard the fair place and show prices listed for Princess Mitterand.

As for the exacta, it's apparent that any combination including Lucky Jo B. will be a terrific overlay, even the combinations with the odds-on Princess Mitterand. It's also apparent that the two exacta combinations pairing the win underlays Princess Mitterand and Royal Boutique will be underlays in the exacta, too. The combination linking Princess Mitterand on top of Lucky Jo B. represents the best of all possible worlds: an overlay exacta that's also a worthy exacta as a place bet.

SIXTH RACE 1 MILE. (Turf)(1.34³) ALLOWANCE. Purse $20,000. Fillies, 2-year-olds, which have not won $3,000 other than maiden, claiming, starter or classified handicap. Weight: 118 lbs. Non-winners of a race other

Bay Meadows than claiming, starter or classified handicap at one mile or over since October 1, allowed 3 lbs. One such race since September 1, 5 lbs.

DECEMBER 4, 1993

Value of Race: $20,000 Winner $11,000; second $4,000; third $3,000; fourth $1,500; fifth $500. Mutuel Pool $237,333.00 Exacta Pool $283,002.00

Last Raced	Horse	M/Eqt.	A.Wt	PP	St	¼	½	¾	Str	Fin	Jockey	Odds $1
31Oct93 4SA¹	Princess Mitterand	LB	2 114	5	3	4³	1½	1hd	1³	1¹½	Chapman T M	0.70
25Nov93 6B M¹	Princess In Charge	LB	2 114	8	8	7¹½	7³	6⁵	3¹	2²½	Warren R J Jr	6.10
18Nov93 8B M²	Royal Boutique	LB	2 113	6	6	6²	5¹½	4²	4½	3¹	Meza R Q	4.40
28Nov93 8B M⁵	Lucky Jo B.	LB	2 113	1	1	1½	2²	2²	2½	4nk	Espinoza V⁵	51.90
7Nov93 10B M¹⁰	Bubble Dance	LB	2 113	2	4	2²	3¹½	3hd	5hd	5hd	Jauregui L H	51.80
7Nov93 10B M⁵	Jilly's Halo	LBb	2 118	3	5	3hd	4hd	5¹	6⁶	6⁵	Belvoir V T	18.70
17Nov93 6B M¹	Skeptic Lady Lee	LBb	2 114	4	2	5hd	6²	7⁶	7	7	Schacht R	22.10
7Nov93 1B M¹	Little Brass	LB	2 115	7	7	8	8	8	—	—	Baze R A	5.20

Little Brass:Eased

OFF AT 2:48 Start Good. Won driving. Time, :23³, :48, 1:13², 1:26³, 1:39⁴ Course firm.

$2 Mutuel Prices:

5–PRINCESS MITTERAND	3.40	2.60	2.20
8–PRINCESS IN CHARGE		3.80	2.60
6–ROYAL BOUTIQUE			2.40

$2 EXACTA 5–8 PAID $15.40

The parade of chalk continues. Princess Mitterand wins and pays $3.40. Of the six winners so far today, five have paid single digits to win, and three consecutive favorites have won. Lucky Jo B. outruns her odds by finishing fourth, but we can't collect unless she finishes second or better.

Hollywood Park

6 $1\frac{1}{16}$ *MILES.* (1:40) MAIDEN CLAIMING. Purse $17,000. Fillies and mares, 3–year–olds and upward . Weights: 3–year–olds, 118 lbs. Older, 121 lbs. Claiming price $32,000; if for $28,000, allowed 2 lbs. (Horses which have not started for a claiming price of $20,000 or less preferred.)

Pantalona
Own: Adams & Maestro Jr
Dk. b or br f. 4
Sire: Private Account (Damascus)
Dam: Corselette (Hoist the Flag)
Br: Keck Howard B (Ky)
Tr: Adams Craig (4 0 1 0 .00)

SOLIS A (67 9 12 12 .13) **$32,000** **L 121**

Lifetime Record:	11 M 0 2	$18,640	
1993	6 M 0 2	$8,015	Turf	2 0 0 0	$2,250
1992	5 M 0 0	$10,625	Wet	0 0 0 0	
Hol	3 0 0 1	$4,900	Dist	2 0 0 0	$3,015

Point Position
Own: Allen Byron
Ch. f. 3 (May)
Sire: Pencil Point – IR (Sharpen Up – GB)
Dam: Executive Position (Lines of Power)
Br: Joseph A. Duffel (Cal)
Tr: Allen Byron (5 0 0 1 .00)

TORRES R V (4 0 0 1 .00) **$28,000** **L 116**

Lifetime Record:	7 M 2 2	$14,265	
1993	7 M 2 2	$14,265	Turf	1 0 0 0	$750
1992	0 M 0 0		Wet	0 0 0 0	
Hol	0 0 0 0		Dist	0 0 0 0	

Soheather
Own: Pitti Carl C
Ch. f. 4
Sire: So Talented (Herbager)
Dam: Panocha (T V Minstral)
Br: Carl C. Pitti (Cal)
Tr: Needham Lloyd B (1 0 0 0 .00)

CASTRO J M (19 1 0 4 .05) **$32,000** **L 121**

Lifetime Record:	3 M 0 0	$0	
1993	3 M 0 0		Turf	0 0 0 0	
1992	0 M 0 0		Wet	0 0 0 0	
Hol	0 0 0 0		Dist	0 0 0 0	

Starlings Darling
Own: Coppess S J & Carolyn
Dk. b or br f. 3 (Feb)
Sire: Maxistar (Pia Star)
Dam: Lord's Lassie (The Irish Lord)
Br: Bud Coppess (Cal)
Tr: Nettles Kenneth (1 0 0 0 .00)

LONG B (23 1 0 3 .04) **$32,000** **L 118**

Lifetime Record:	4 M 0 0	$490	
1993	4 M 0 0	$490	Turf	0 0 0 0	$320
1992	0 M 0 0		Wet	0 0 0 0	
Hol	0 0 0 0		Dist	0 0 0 0	

Boom Boom Barbara
Own: Chambers Thomas L
Gr. f. 3 (May)
Sire: Swing Till Dawn (Grey Dawn II)
Dam: Our Lincinsue (Reflected Glory)
Br: Tom Chambers (Cal)
Tr: Fanning Jerry (7 2 0 0 .29)

ATKINSON P (21 3 1 2 .14) **$32,000** **L 118**

Lifetime Record:	2 M 0 0	$425	
1993	2 M 0 0	$425	Turf	0 0 0 0	
1992	0 M 0 0		Wet	0 0 0 0	
Hol	0 0 0 0		Dist	0 0 0 0	

Yesternight
Own: Ridder Thoroughbred Stable
B. f. 3 (May)
Sire: Skywalker (Relaunch)
Dam: Past Pleasures (Pleasure Seeker)
Br: Ridder Thoroughbred Stable (Cal)
Tr: Hofmans David (11 2 1 1 .18)

STEVENS G L (36 4 10 5 .11) **$32,000** **L 118**

Lifetime Record:	1 M 0 1	$3,000	
1993	1 M 0 1	$3,000	Turf	0 0 0 0	
1992	0 M 0 0		Wet	0 0 0 0	
Hol	0 0 0 0		Dist	0 0 0 0	

Raise the Runway
Own: Jackson Bruce L
B. f. 3 (Apr)
Sire: Raise a Man (Raise a Native)
Dam: Runaway Lady (Caucasus)
Br: Vanier Mr–Mrs H & Varney Mr–Mrs L (Ky)
Tr: Jackson Bruce L (2 0 1 0 .00)

PEDROZA M A (27 1 2 6 .04) **$28,000** **L 116**

Lifetime Record:	11 M 1 4	$16,700	
1993	5 M 0 2	$6,200	Turf	0 0 0 0	
1992	6 M 1 2	$10,500	Wet	1 0 0 0	
Hol	2 0 0 0		Dist	3 0 0 1	$4,050

Sweet Lady Czar
Own: Masada Keiichi

SOTO J F (1 0 0 0 .00) $32,000

B. f. 3 (Mar)
Sire: Czaravich (Nijinsky II)
Dam: Wind Capers (Mr Prospector)
Br: Dorothy M. Turner Trust (Ky)
Tr: Masada Gary (—)

L 118

					Lifetime Record :	2 M 0 0	$500
	1993	2 M 0 0	$500	Turf	0 0 0 0
	1992	0 M 0 0		Wet	0 0 0 0
	Hol	0 0 0 0		Dist	0 0 0 0

10Nov93-2SA fst 6½f :22 :45 1:10⁴ 1:17⁴ 3+ ⓜMd 32000   49 9 11 10⁵½ 9⁸½ 9⁹½ 9⁵ Soto J F   L 118 f 36.50 77 – 12 Right Smart Girl118¾ Best Berry112½ Dances With Wolves120ʰᵈ   Wide trip 12
21Oct93-3SA fst 6f :21² :44⁴ :57 1:10³ 3+ ⓜMd 50000   51 1 8 8⁸½ 6¹⁰ 6⁹ 5¹⁰½ Soto J F   B 117 f 64.50 73 – 14 Liver Pate'117½ Morning Showers117¾ Yesternight117⁴   Off slow 8
WORKOUTS: Nov 28 Hol 6f fst 1:14² Hg5/9   Nov 4 Hol 5f fst 1:05 H 26/26   Oct 16 Hol 5f fst :59⁴ H 3/25   Oct 3 Hol 6f fst 1:15¹ H 7/9   Sep 27 Hol 5f fst 1:01¹ H 5/16   Sep 11 SA 5f fst 1:01¹ H 10/16

Hagley's Lass
Own: Kellstrom Francis S

GRYDER A T (46 9 5 6 .20) $28,000

Gr. f. 3 (Feb)
Sire: Hagley (Olden Times)
Dam: Watanga Miss (Drone)
Br: Walnut Green & Jones Bros. Ltd. (Pa)
Tr: Machowsky Michael (3 0 0 0 .00)

116

					Lifetime Record :	2 M 0 0	$0
	1993	2 M 0 0		Turf	0 0 0 0
	1992	0 M 0 0		Wet	0 0 0 0
	Hol	1 0 0 0		Dist	0 0 0 0

17Nov93-5Hol fst 6f :22 :45¹ :57² 1:10³ 3+ ⓜMd 32000   43 7 4 7⁴½ 5⁸½ 6¹¹ 6¹³½ Gryder A T   B 119 17.90 73 – 14 Wild N Super119² Enchanted Beauty119⁵½ Native Ridge119⁴   No rally 10
27Oct93-4SA fst 6f :21⁴ :45² :57⁴ 1:10³ 3+ ⓜMd 32000   52 10 8 7⁵ 8⁵ 5⁷½ 6¹⁰½ Gryder A T   117 24.20 74 – 14 Naskras Rapture117½ Native Ridge117⁴¾ NeverQuicker117²½   Wide into lane 12
WORKOUTS: Dec 1 Hol 4f fst :48¹ H 8/38   Nov 12 Hol 4f fst :47⁴ H 5/23   Oct 24 Hol 4f fst :48² Hg7/18   Oct 13 SLR tr.t 6f fst 1:15¹ H 1/1   Oct 7 SLR tr.t 5f fst 1:01³ H 2/3   ●Sep 30 SLR tr.t 6f fst 1:13 H 1/4

ALL-IN-ONE's output for the race is as follows:

```
4DEC93                          HOL                 8.5 furlongs dirt
Race #6                                                    9 starters
MCL                                         Age: 3+years, Female
-------------------------------INPUT DATA-------------------------------

                 #   #   #   #   $'S                              1st C  2nd C  Final
Horse name       ST  W   P   S  Earned Date     Trk Dist.  S     time   time   time
-----------------------------------------------------------------------------------
PANTALONA        0   0   0   0     0  12NOV93 FPX 8.500  D     46.2  111.3  144.2
POINT POSITION   0   0   0   0     0  25NOV93 SA  6.500  D     21.4   45.0  118.0
YESTERNIGHT      0   0   0   0     0  21OCT93 SA  6.000  D     21.2   44.4  110.3
RAISE THE RUNWAY 0   0   0   0     0   3NOV93 SA  8.500  D     47.0  112.1  144.2
SWEET LADY CZAR  0   0   0   0     0  10NOV93 SA  6.500  D     22.0   45.0  117.4


                             1st C  2nd C  Final
Horse name       Class Lvl   B.L.   B.L.   B.L.    SR    Var
-----------------------------------------------------------------
PANTALONA        MSW         4.50   7.00  13.50    72   10.0
POINT POSITION   MCL         6.50   5.00   1.25    80   10.0
YESTERNIGHT      MCL         4.50   3.00   2.25    82   14.0
RAISE THE RUNWAY MCL         6.25   3.50   3.25    79   20.0
SWEET LADY CZAR  MCL         9.50   8.75   4.00    77   12.0


-----------------------------BETTING LINE-----------------------------

                 -------Rankings--------              Betting   Fair   Fair
Horse name       PEH  H-I THAAI P-H  ESP    Rating     Line   Place $ Show $
----------------------------------------------------------------------------
RAISE THE RUNWAY  2    1    1    1    1     82.20      5-2
YESTERNIGHT       3    2    2    2    2     75.58      4-1
PANTALONA         1    5    5    3    4     71.22      6-1
POINT POSITION    4    4    4    4    3     70.22      6-1
SWEET LADY CZAR   5    3    3    5    5     65.08
```

```
-----------------------------EXACTA GRID-----------------------------

                 | RAISE THE RUNWA | YESTERNIGHT  | PANTALONA    | POINT POSITION |
-----------------+-----------------+--------------+--------------+----------------+
RAISE THE RUNW   | . . . . . . .   |   24    59   |   33    81   |   36    89     |
                 | . . . . . . .   |              |              |                |
                 | . . . . . . .   |              |              |                |
-----------------+-----------------+--------------+--------------+----------------+
YESTERNIGHT      |   27    66      | . . . . . .  |   52   129   |   57   141     |
                 |                 | . . . . . .  |              |                |
                 |                 | . . . . . .  |              |                |
-----------------+-----------------+--------------+--------------+----------------+
PANTALONA        |   39    98      |   55   138   | . . . . . .  |   83   207     |
                 |                 |              | . . . . . .  |                |
                 |                 |              | . . . . . .  |                |
-----------------+-----------------+--------------+--------------+----------------+
POINT POSITION   |   44   108      |   62   153   |   84   210   | . . . . . .    |
                 |                 |              |              | . . . . . .    |
                 |                 |              |              | . . . . . .    |
```

```
4DEC93                              HOL                        8.5 furlongs dirt
Race #6                                                               9 starters
MCL                                                           Age: 3+years, Female
-------------------------------SPEED/PACE SUMMARY-------------------------------

Race Type:       Chaos Race
Race Profile:    47.28   112.16   144.93   Winners' Pace Profile: EARLY
Ability Par:     97.04                      Pace Contention Point:  1.07 lengths

Projected Times:                          Ability  Balance   Last  Proj  Con-
                 1st C    2nd C    Fin C    Time     Time     Frac  Pace  tender
                 ------------------------------------------------------------------
RAISE THE RUNWAY 48.11   112.33*  144.40   96.54   101.42   32.07  MID    N
YESTERNIGHT      47.58   112.26*  145.06   96.95   102.38   32.80  EARLY  N
PANTALONA        46.92   111.89   146.00   96.85   103.54   34.12  FRONT  N
POINT POSITION   48.15   112.69*  145.75   97.23   102.85   33.06  LATE   N
SWEET LADY CZAR  48.91   113.32*  146.07   97.74   102.90   32.74  REAR   N


------------------------------------PACE GRAPH----------------------------------
       Profile:               47.28              112.16                 144.93
   Front Runner:              46.92              111.89                 144.40
Horse name                      1C                 2C                       F
RAISE THE RUNWAY -------------X-----+ ----------------X-+ --------------------X
YESTERNIGHT      -------------X--+ ----------------X-+ ---------------X--+
PANTALONA        ----------------X ----------------(-X ----------X-------+
POINT POSITION   -------------X-----+ ----------------X-(-+ ----------X------+
SWEET LADY CZAR  ---------X---------+ ----------X----(-+ ----------X-------+
```

Race six is also a maiden race, so let's look at the entire morning line. Pantalona was a late scratch:

Point Position	3-1
Soheather	30-1
Starlings Darling	30-1
Boom Boom Barbara	8-1
Yesternight	6-5
Raise The Runway	6-1
Sweet Lady Czar	20-1
Hagley's Lass	20-1

Here are the toteboard odds just before the race:

Point Position	7-1
Soheather	99-1
Starlings Darling	99-1
Boom Boom Barbara	6-1
Yesternight	1-2
Raise The Runway	7-2
Sweet Lady Czar	25-1
Hagley's Lass	35-1

We have three bet downs: Boom Boom Barbara, Raise The Runway, and the prohibitive 1-to-2 favorite Yesternight. According to our line, Raise The Runway also is an overlay offering an edge of 31 percent. Raise The Runway gives us what we want: a bet-down maiden who's also an overlay on our line. Boom Boom Barbara isn't among our contenders, and Yesternight is a big underlay. Point Position is a marginal overlay with a 14 percent edge, but isn't bet down.

Yesternight must be respected. As Sierra Real demonstrated in the fourth race, maiden favorites who are bet down from their morning line are usually legitimate favorites. We're in a dilemma. A win bet on Raise The Runway wouldn't be incorrect, but we should also respect the crowd's keen sense of judgment in maiden races. Is there a way to combine Yesternight and Raise The Runway?

According to our betting line and exacta grid, the exacta with Yesternight on top of Raise The Runway should pay $27. The actual pay is hovering around $8. Needless to say, we can't play this exacta combination. The quinella with these two horses should pay $13.20 to be a fair bet. It's paying approximately $6.00. That's also an underlay.

But what if our 4-to-1 line on Yesternight is incorrectly high and our line on Raise The Runway is too low? If we take the public's odds line as gospel, the fair quinella price on the Yesternight–Raise The Runway combination becomes $3.15. Now the actual quinella price of $6.00 on this combination represents close to a 100 percent overlay.

SIXTH RACE
Hollywood
DECEMBER 4, 1993

1¹⁄₁₆ MILES. (1.40) MAIDEN CLAIMING. Purse $17,000. Fillies and mares, 3-year-olds and upward. Weights: 3-year-olds, 118 lbs. Older, 121 lbs. Claiming price $32,000; if for $28,000, allowed 2 lbs. (Horses which have not started for a claiming price of $20,000 or less preferred.)

Value of Race: $17,000 Winner $9,350; second $3,400; third $2,550; fourth $1,275; fifth $425. Mutuel Pool $271,580.00 Exacta Pool $249,810.00 Trifecta Pool $244,895.00 Quinella Pool $32,065.00

Last Raced	Horse	M/Eqt.A.Wt	PP	St	¼	½	¾	Str	Fin	Jockey	Cl'g Pr	Odds $1
21Oct93 3SA³	Yesternight	LBb 3 118	5	7	3²	2hd	1hd	12½	16½	Stevens G L	32000	0.50
3Nov93 4SA³	Raise the Runway	LB 3 116	6	6	6½	6hd	4hd	42	23½	Pedroza M A	28000	3.60
10Nov93 2SA⁹	Sweet Lady Czar	LBbf 3 118	7	1	2hd	34½	24	21	3¾	Soto J F	32000	25.90
10Nov93 2SA⁵	Boom Boom Barbara	LB 3 118	4	5	73½	51½	51½	56	4½	Atkinson P	32000	6.90
25Nov93 4Hol⁵	Point Position	L 3 116	1	3	42½	41	31½	31	58½	Torres R V	28000	7.70
17Nov93 5Hol⁹	Starlings Darling	LB 3 118	3	4	5hd	76	76	66	6¹⁹	Long B	32000	133.90
12Nov93 4SA⁸	Soheather	LB 4 121	2	8	8	8	8	8	7⁹	Castro J M	32000	144.70
17Nov93 5Hol⁶	Hagley's Lass	LBb 3 116	8	2	11	1hd	6²	73	8	Gryder A T	28000	35.80

OFF AT 3:10 Start Good. Won driving. Time, :23, :46¹, 1:11, 1:38², 1:45¹ Track fast.

$2 Mutuel Prices:

6-YESTERNIGHT	3.00	2.40	2.20
7-RAISE THE RUNWAY		2.80	2.40
8-SWEET LADY CZAR			4.20

$2 EXACTA 6-7 PAID $8.00 $2 TRIFECTA 6-7-8 PAID $62.00 $2 QUINELLA 6-7 PAID $5.60

$3 Triple 1-2-1 or 6 Paid $27.30 Triple Pool $85,361.00

The crowd was absolutely correct. Yesternight ran like a 1-to-2 shot. Raise The Runway bested the rest of the field. We lost the win bet on Raise The Runway, but if we were wise enough to accept the public's view of things, the $5.60 quinella price was more than fair. The favorite has now won four races in a row and it appears that short prices are the order of the day.

Hollywood Park

7 — **1⅛ MILES.** (Turf). (1:44⁴) ALLOWANCE. Purse $34,000. Fillies and mares, 3-year-olds and upward which have not won $3,000 twice other than maiden, claiming or starter. Weights: 3-year-olds, 118 lbs. Older, 121 lbs. Non-winners of two races other than claiming at a mile or over since September 15, allowed 3 lbs. Such a race other than maiden or claiming since then, 6 lbs.

TURF COURSE · 1⅛ MILES · START · FINISH

Alyshena
Own: Hilaski & Hilaski & Sahl
B. f. 3 (Mar)
Sire: Alysheba (Alydar)
Dam: Shukey (Key to the Mint)
Br: Petelain Stables (Fla)
Tr: Van Berg Jack C (33 3 5 4 .09)
L 112
NAKATANI C S (60 14 10 13 .23)

Lifetime Record: 14 2 5 3 $91,300
1993 10 2 3 2 $74,800 Turf 2 1 0 0 $21,450
1992 4 M 2 1 $16,500 Wet 1 0 1 0 $6,000
Hol ① 1 1 0 0 $21,450 Dist ① 0 0 0 0

Sheer Quality
Own: Hotehama Tadahiro
Ch. m. 5
Sire: Irish River–Fr (Riverman)
Dam: Hire a Brain (Seattle Slew)
Br: Moyglare Stud Farm Ltd (Ky)
Tr: Sweeney Brian (—)
L 115
LONG B (23 1 0 3 .04)

Lifetime Record: 33 2 6 4 $94,100
1993 12 0 4 3 $46,090 Turf 21 2 1 1 $40,750
1992 9 1 0 1 $22,350 Wet 0 0 0 0
Hol ① 5 0 1 0 $7,000 Dist ① 0 0 0 0

Onesta
Own: Keck Howard B
Ro. f. 4
Sire: Relaunch (In Reality)
Dam: Courtney's Day (Roberto)
Br: R. A. Brooks, Jr. (Ky)
Tr: Whittingham Charles (13 4 1 1 .31)
L 118
DELAHOUSSAYE E (27 2 1 3 .07)

Lifetime Record: 17 2 0 1 $50,950
1993 7 1 0 0 $24,850 Turf 11 2 0 1 $47,300
1992 10 1 0 1 $26,100 Wet 1 0 0 0
Hol ① 5 0 0 1 $5,950 Dist ① 4 2 0 0 $37,750

Eminere (NZ)
Own: Stein Richard Douglas
B. m. 6
Sire: Cocky Golfer (Sir Ivor)
Dam: Neti (Indian Order)
Br: P W Ryan (NZ)
Tr: Stein Roger M (7 1 1 1 .14)
L 118
GRYDER A T (46 9 5 6 .20)

Lifetime Record: 25 4 4 2 $28,768
1993 13 4 3 1 $27,665 Turf 25 4 4 2 $28,768
1992 6 M 1 0 $564 Wet 0 0 0 0
Hol ① 5 0 0 1 $18,150 Dist ① 1 1 0 0 $18,150

Lady Member (Fr)

B. m. 5
Sire: Saint Estephe (Top Ville)
Dam: Brave Lass (Ridan)
Br: Acton Robert & Houyvet Mrs Yan (Fr)
Tr: Frankel Robert (13 1 3 1 .06)

Own: Engelson Dale & Morley

ANTLEY C W (43 5 5 5 .12)

L 115

Lifetime Record :	25 2 5 4	$112,677
1993	8 1 2 1	$52,225	Turf	25 2 5 4	$112,677
1992	8 0 3 1	$28,825	Wet	0 0 0 0	
Hol ①	6 1 2 2	$49,225	Dist ①	5 0 2 0	$13,600

WORKOUTS: Nov 28 Hol 5f fst 1:00⅔ H 11/36   Nov 12 Hol 5f fst 1:15 H 13/17   Nov 7 Hol 5f fst 1:01² H 10/22   Oct 31 Hol 4f fst :50⁴ H 27/30   Oct 17 Hol 5f fst 1:01² H 11/21   Oct 11 Hol 7f fst 1:27² H 2/2

Assert Oneself

B. f. 3 (Feb)
Sire: Affirmed (Exclusive Native)
Dam: Rosey Ramble (Chieftain)
Br: Huntington Interests, Inc. & Robert (Ky)
Tr: Chambers Mike (4 1 0 2 .25)

Own: Three Sisters Stable

STEVENS G L (36 4 10 5 .11)

L 112

Lifetime Record :	11 2 0 4	$49,625
1993	11 2 0 4	$49,625	Turf	5 1 0 3	$30,500
1992	0 M 0 0		Wet	2 1 0 0	$12,775
Hol ①	1 0 0 1	$5,250	Dist ①	1 0 0 1	$6,000

Entered 2Dec93- 7 HOL

Fractious prior to start

Disqualified and placed third

WORKOUTS: Nov 25 SA 4f fst :51 H 26/28   Nov 15 SA 4f fst :51⁴ H 43/44   Nov 9 SA 5f fst 1:01³ H 21/42   Nov 3 SA 4f fst :52² H (d) 35/36   Oct 24 SA 5f fst 1:02³ H 44/46   ●Oct 11 SA fr 1 5f fst 1:01³ H 1/4

Island Orchid

B. f. 3 (Apr)
Sire: Aggravatin' (Silent Screen)
Dam: Granizada (Wohigemuth)
Br: Patricia R. Lopez (Cal)
Tr: Tinsley J E Jr (4 0 0 0 .00)

Own: Champagne & Davidson & Ordonez

VALENZUELA F H (49 8 3 3 .16)

L 115

Lifetime Record :	6 2 0 1	$35,400
1993	6 2 0 1	$35,400	Turf	0 0 0 0	
1992	0 M 0 0		Wet	0 0 0 0	
Hol ①	0 0 0 0		Dist ①	0 0 0 0	

WORKOUTS: Nov 25 SA 6f fst 1:14³ H 4/8   Nov 18 SA 5f fst 1:01⁴ H 25/37   Oct 31 SA 5f fst 1:01 H 27/67   Oct 24 SA 5f fst 1:01² H 24/48   Oct 3 SA 6f fst 1:14² H 28/28   Sep 27 SA 5f fst 1:03⁴ H 57/64

Chipeta Springs

B. f. 4
Sire: Alydar (Raise a Native)
Dam: Salt Spring (Salt Marsh)
Br: Gayno Stables (Ky)
Tr: Bunn Thomas M Jr (6 0 0 0 .00)

Own: Gayno Stable

PINCAY L JR (60 10 9 7 .17)

L 115

Lifetime Record :	14 2 4 2	$602,000
1993	6 0 1 1	$21,525	Turf	3 0 0 0	$3,500
1992	8 2 3 1	$380,475	Wet	1 0 0 1	$5,400
Hol ①	2 0 0 0	$2,625	Dist ①	0 0 0 0	

WORKOUTS: Nov 26 Hol 5f fst 1:02³ H 30/42   Oct 29 Hol 5f fst 1:01² H 8/18   Oct 15 SA ① 3f fm :37² B (d) 1/1   Oct 7 Hol 7f fst 1:28 H 3/5   Oct 1 Hol 7f fst 1:28² H 2/7   Sep 19 Hol 5f fst 1:00² H 3/19

ALL-IN-ONE's output for the race is as follows:

```
4DEC93                        HOL                    9 furlongs turf
Race #7                                                   8 starters
NW2                                              Age: 3+years, Female
--------------------------------INPUT DATA---------------------------
                     #   #   #   #   $'S                  1st C  2nd C  Final
Horse name           ST  W   P   S   Earned  Date  Trk Dist.  S  time   time   time
--------------------------------------------------------------------------------
ALYSHENA             10  2   3   2   74800  13NOV93 DMR 8.000  T  46.0   110.0  135.0
SHEER QUALITY        12  0   4   3   46090  4NOV93  GG  9.000  T  47.3   111.4  150.1
ONESTA                7  1   0   0   24850  3NOV93  SA  9.000  T  48.2   113.1  150.1
LADY MEMBER-FR        8  1   2   1   52225  17NOV93 HOL 8.500  T  46.1   110.0  141.2
ASSERT ONESELF       11  2   0   4   49625  17NOV93 HOL 8.500  T  46.0   110.2  141.4
```

Horse name	Class Lvl	1st C B.L.	2nd C B.L.	Final B.L.	SR	Var
ALYSHENA	NW2	9.00	9.50	5.25	91	9.0
SHEER QUALITY	NW2	6.00	4.00	4.00	86	14.0
ONESTA	NW1	2.00	1.50	0.00	68	32.0
LADY MEMBER-FR	NW1	4.75	4.75	0.00	89	7.0
ASSERT ONESELF	NW2	7.25	2.25	2.25	85	14.0

------------------------------BETTING LINE------------------------------

	-------Rankings--------						Betting	Fair	Fair
Horse name	PEH	H-I	THAAI	P-H	ESP	Rating	Line	Place $	Show $
LADY MEMBER-FR	1	1	2	2	1	91.09	2-1	3.80	2.80
ALYSHENA	2	2	1	1	2	81.81	7-2		
SHEER QUALITY	4	3	3	3	3	72.92	6-1		
ASSERT ONESELF	3	5	4	4	5	72.17			
ONESTA	5	4	5	5	4	66.76			

------------------------------EXACTA GRID------------------------------

	LADY MEMBER-FR		ALYSHENA		SHEER QUALITY	
LADY MEMBER-FR	. . . .		16	39	26	65
ALYSHENA	18	45	. . . .		43	107
SHEER QUALITY	34	85	48	120	. . . .	

4DEC93   HOL   9 furlongs turf
Race #7   8 starters
NW2   Age: 3+years, Female
------------------------------SPEED/PACE SUMMARY------------------------------

Race Type:	Double Advantage Race						
Race Profile:	48.03	111.96	148.11	Winners' Pace Profile: EARLY			
Ability Par:	84.18			Pace Contention Point: 2.47 lengths			

Projected Times:				Ability	Balance	Last	Proj	Con-
	1st C	2nd C	Fin C	Time	Time	Frac	Pace	tender
LADY MEMBER-FR	47.65	111.60	148.02	84.06	104.80	36.42	FRONT	Y+
ALYSHENA	48.27	112.27*	148.30	84.29	104.98	36.03	LATE	N
SHEER QUALITY	48.56	112.29*	148.46	84.73	104.92	36.17	LATE	N
ASSERT ONESELF	47.91	111.55	148.86	85.22	105.36	37.31	EARLY	N
ONESTA	48.78	113.14*	149.14	84.78	105.83	36.00	REAR	N

------------------------------PACE GRAPH------------------------------

```
    Profile:              48.03            111.96              148.11
    Front Runner:         47.65            111.55              140.02
Horse name                  1C               2C                   F
LADY MEMBER-FR     ------------------X ---------------(--X ------------------X
ALYSHENA           -------------X--+ ---------------X(--+ -----------------X+
SHEER QUALITY      -------------X----+ ---------------X(--+ ----------------X-+
ASSERT ONESELF     ------------------X+ ---------------(--X ---------------X---+
ONESTA             -----------X-----+ ----------X----(--+ -----------X-----+
```

Here are the public odds on our contenders a few minutes before post time:

Lady Member	5-2
Alyshena	5-2
Sheer Quality	70-1

The actual betting favorite is Alyshena, who has a few more dollars to win than Lady Member does.

It doesn't take a genius to figure out that we should bet Sheer Quality to win and forsake Alyshena. However, the situation with Lady Member requires a bit more judgment. She's an overlay by definition, but the 16.3 percent edge she offers isn't all that tempting. Our group estimate for these three horses is 69.8 percent. The public's estimate is 58.6 percent. We could apply the group overlay method in this race, since our group estimate exceeds 66 percent and the public has underestimated our group by more than 10 percent.

This race is on turf, so place-and-show betting are out, even though *ALL-IN-ONE* lists fair place and show prices for Lady Member.

As for the exacta, any combination containing Sheer Quality will be a huge overlay, way over our 40 percent minimum edge. The combinations involving Lady Member and Alyshena will probably pay somewhere around fair value but won't offer anything near a 40 percent edge.

Our top pick, Lady Member, isn't the favorite. Hence, we can make her our key horse in the Key-Place-All trifecta strategy. The other contenders that are 6-to-1 or below on our line, Alyshena and Sheer Quality, make sensible place horses. And Assert Oneself and Onesta show sufficient final-time capabilities to join the ranks of our all horses.

This time we're done in by a non-contender. All our bets (win, exactas, quinellas, and trifectas) have lost. Even the ultraconservative group overlay method failed us. Sad.

This race serves as a good example of how our betting decisions are only as good as the lines on which they're based. If we have too many non-contenders winning, we're going to take a serious beat-

SEVENTH RACE
Hollywood
DECEMBER 4, 1993

1½ MILES. (Turf)(1.44⁴) ALLOWANCE. Purse $34,000. Fillies and mares, 3-year-olds and upward which have not won $3,000 twice other than maiden, claiming or starter. Weights: 3-year-olds, 118 lbs. Older, 121 lbs. Non-winners of two races other than claiming at a mile or over since September 15, allowed 3 lbs. Such a race other than maiden or claiming since then, 6 lbs.

Value of Race: $34,000 Winner $18,700; second $6,800; third $5,100; fourth $2,550; fifth $850. Mutuel Pool $449,294.00 Exacta Pool $380,200.00 Trifecta Pool $248,607.00 Quinella Pool $44,989.00

Last Raced	Horse	M/Eqt. A.Wt	PP	St	¼	½	¾	Str	Fin	Jockey	Odds $1
4Nov93 8SA⁵	Island Orchid	LB	3 115	7	6	1hd	11	11	11	12½	Valenzuela F H	3.80
17Nov93 8Hol³	Assert Oneself	LBb	3 114	6	5	2¹	3½	2hd	2½	2hd	Stevens G L	5.90
25Nov93 7Hol¹	Eminere-NZ	LB	6 118	4	2	4¹½	5¹	3¹½	3¹	3nk	Gryder A T	12.00
13Nov93 8SA⁵	Alyshena	LBbf	3 113	1	4	6½	7³	5hd	4¹½	4³½	Nakatani C S	2.60
17Nov93 8Hol²	Lady Member-Fr	LB	5 115	5	8	7³	6hd	4hd	5²	5³½	Antley C W	2.70
4Nov93 8SA⁸	Sheer Quality	LBb	5 115	2	3	8	8	8	7½	6no	Long B	73.20
17Nov93 8Hol⁴	Chipeta Springs	LBb	4 117	8	7	3¹	2hd	7¹	8	7½	Pincay L Jr	10.60
3Nov93 8SA¹	Onesta	LB	4 118	3	1	5¹½	4½	6½	6¹	8	Delahoussaye E	7.90

OFF AT 3:38 Start Good. Won driving. Time, :24³, :49⁴, 1:14¹, 1:38, 1:50² Course firm.

$2 Mutuel Prices:	7-ISLAND ORCHID	9.60	5.80	4.60
	6-ASSERT ONESELF		6.20	4.00
	4-EMINERE-NZ			8.60

$2 EXACTA 7-6 PAID $74.40 $2 TRIFECTA 7-6-4 PAID $854.40 $2 QUINELLA 6-7 PAID $35.20

$3 Triple 2-1 or 6-7 Paid $43.50 Triple Pool $96,992.00

ing in the win, daily double, and Pick-3 pools. And even if we pick our win contenders with a fair degree of accuracy, we still may get hammered on exacta, quinella, and trifecta bets if we fail to include the place-and-show horses among our betting-line contenders.

Bay Meadows

8

1⅛ MILES. (Turf). (1:40³) 14th Running of THE BROWN BESS BREEDERS' CUP HANDICAP. Purse $50,000 Added. *$25,000 Added, plus $25,000 from Breeders' Cup Fund. Fillies and mares 3-year-olds and upward. By subscription of $25 each, to accompany the nomination, $125 to pass the entry box and $125 additional to start, with $25,000 added and an additional $25,000 from Breeders' Cup Fund for Breeders' Cup eligibles only. The $25,000 added, of which $5,000 to second, $3,750 to third, $1,8775 to fourth and $6,25 to fifth. The Breeders' Cup Fund monies will be divided 55% to the winner, 20% to second, 15% to third, 7.5% to fourth and 2.5% to fifth provided a Breeders' cup nominee has finished in an awarded position. Any Breeders' Cup Fund monies not awarded will revert back to the fund. Preference will be given to (1) high weights Breeders' Cup nominees, (2) Breeders' Cup nominees and (3) high weights. Weights, Sunday, November 28, 1993. Starters to be named through the entry box by the closing time of entries. A trophy will be presented to the owner of the winner. Closed Thursday, November 25, with nominations.

Don't Touch Lil
Dk. b or br. f. 4
Own: Clark & Silver & Simon
Sire: Caveat (Cannonade)
Dam: Lil Stable (NJ)
Br: Lil Stable (NJ)
Tr: Sumja Brent (22 4 4 6 .18)

L 114

Lifetime Record: 19 5 2 3 $117,200
1993 6 2 0 0 $58,500 Turf 10 4 0 1 $88,500
1992 11 3 2 3 $58,700 Wet 1 0 0 0 $3,000
BM ① ⑥ 6 3 0 1 $60,350 Dist ① 6 2 0 1 $45,650

Splashing Wave
Gr. f. 4
Own: Crook John B
Sire: Icecapade (Nearctic)
Dam: Moving Waters (Ambehaving)
Br: Crook Investment Co (Ky)
Tr: Hollendorfer Jerry (221 42 48 37 .19)

L 113

Lifetime Record: 18 6 3 2 $124,360
1993 10 4 1 2 $88,885 Turf 10 3 3 0 $57,020
1992 8 2 2 0 $35,475 Wet 1 0 0 1 $16,995
BM ① ⑥ 6 2 3 0 $35,350 Dist ① 6 3 2 0 $47,520

Misspitch

Own: Baer Sidney M

VERGARA O (22 3 1 2 .14)

B. f. 3 (Feb)
Sire: Waquoit (Relaunch)
Dam: Duo Disco (Spring Double)
Br: Farish W S (Ky)
Tr: Devereux Joe (—)

113

Lifetime Record: 22 6 2 4 $131,548											
1993	14	5	1	3	$117,103	Turf	12	3	1	2	$65,833
1992	8	1	1	1	$14,445	Wet	4	1	1	1	$24,880
BM Ⓣ	0	0	0	0		Dist Ⓣ	7	2	0	1	$36,313

11Oct93-9Lrl	fm	1 1/16	Ⓣ	:224 :47 1:12 1:424	ⒻMartha WashiG3	84	8	12	1213	1210	99¾	75	Prado E S	L 113 b	11.20	83-12	Tennis Lady113no Putthepowdertoit113no Missymooiloveyou1132¾	Outrun	12
26Sep93-9Pim	my	1 1/16	⊗	:24 :473 1:121 1:451	3↑ ⒻSensational50k	74	1	3	33	32	32½	21	Turner T G	L 110 b	2.00	78-22	Logan's Mist1161 Misspitch1101½ Amber Princess1146	Wide, closed	4
6Sep93-7Med	fm	1 1/16	Ⓣ	:241 :484 1:122 1:423	ⒻBoiling Sp HG3	80	10	4	31½	2½	53	75½	Santagata N	L 118 b	14.70	80-13	Tribulation1102¾ Exotic Sea114nk Bright Penny1151½	Gave way	11
22Aug93-10Mth	gd	1 1/16	Ⓣ	:241 :494 1:141 1:454+	ⒻLittle Slvr35k	91	3	6	41¾	41¾	31	1½	Santagata N	L 121 b	6.80	72-29	Misspitch121½ Artful Minister1142 Shananie's Dancer114nk	Driving	8
7Aug93-8Mth	fst	1 1/16	⊗	:24 :481 1:124 1:453	ⒻTwin Lghts35k	88	5	5	32½	11	15	16¾	Santagata N	L 121 b	*1.30	77-26	Misspitch1216¾ R M's Girl11413 Punkin Pie112nk	Ridden out	5
24Jly93-9Lrl	fm	1⅛	Ⓣ	:47 1:114 1:364 1:484	ⒻBold Queen35k	70	1	5	32	33	89¼	810¾	Rocco J	L 117 b	8.80	75-21	La Turka115nk Eloquent Silver1201¾ Tennis Lady1152	Fell back	8
26Jun93-10Mth	fst	170		:231 :474 1:114 1:414	ⒻPost-Deb-G2	82	5	7	74½	56	57	512¼	Santagata N	L 117 b	55.00	79-25	Jacody1195¼ Sheila's Revenge1132¼ Future Pretense1131	Tired drive	9
12Jun93-10Mth	fm	1	Ⓣ	:224 :461 1:103 1:354	3↑ ⒻRevidere35k	84	5	8	74¾	21½	2½	1½	Santagata N	L 116 b	2.70	87-08	Misspitch116½ Artful Pleasure112hd Sharp Tracy11210	Hung wide, driving	8
31May93-9Pim	fm	1 1/16	Ⓣ	:23 :462 1:111 1:422	ⒻHilltop50k	60	7	4	36½	32	48	412	Rocco J	L 116	*1.20	77-15	Open Toe1134½ Exotic Sea1137½ Perkins Star118nk	Gave way	7
10Apr93-7Hia	fm	*1 1/16	Ⓣ	1:421	ⒻBal Harbour25k	88	4	8	62½	53¼	31½	31	Ramos W S	112	4.40	95-07	Track Gossip116no O. P. Cat1181 Misspitch1121½	Lacked response	11

WORKOUTS: Nov 29 SA 5f fst 1:004 H 11/31 Nov 24 SA 5f fst :593 H 4/50 Nov 9 Lrl 4f fst :491 B 5/20 Sep 23 Lrl 5f fst 1:012 B 3/16

Peterhof's Patea

Own: Strait Patty & Williams Roger

KAENEL J L (288 48 30 37 .17)

Gr. m. 5
Sire: Peterhof (The Minstrel)
Dam: Tea At Ten (Drone)
Br: Oak Crest Farm (Wash)
Tr: Klokstad Bud (76 21 14 8 .28)

L 117

Lifetime Record: 39 15 8 6 $538,467											
1993	13	3	3	5	$166,730	Turf	9	1	1	2	$80,255
1992	9	5	1	0	$100,730	Wet	2	0	1	1	$23,000
BM Ⓣ	7	0	1	2	$51,875	Dist Ⓣ	5	1	1	2	$62,130

14Nov93-8BM	fst	1		:222 :462 1:11 1:36	3↑ ⒻLos Altos H40k	91	7	3	33	31	21½	11	Kaenel J L	LB 116	*1.90	90-18	Peterhof'sPatea1161 RunAwyStevie1165 SplshingWve1152½	Rallied wide	7
9Oct93-3BM	fm	*1⅛	Ⓣ	:471 1:104 1:352 1:454	3↑ ⒻCal J C H-G3	83	3	3	43	43½	55½	56¾	Baze R A	LB 115	3.40	96-03	Gravieres114¾ Miss Turkana1184 Alta's Princess112½	Came wide stretch	6
4Sep93-5BM	gd	1 1/16	Ⓣ	:24 :472 1:11 1:42	3↑ ⒻHillsbrgh H-G3	94	9	4	43	43½	42½	31	Baze R A	LB 115	11.50	99-03	MissTurkana117no BorderMate1151 Peterhof'sPate115¾	Raced well wide	9
21Aug93-11Bmf	fm	1 1/16	Ⓣ	:241 :481 1:114 1:421	3↑ ⒻLady Mvch H50k	92	5	4	31	31½	21	31	Baze R A	LB 116	1.60	102 —	Don't Touch Lil114¾ Sun And Shade119hd Peterhof'sPatea1162	Wide trip	6
~~24Jly93-11Sol~~	~~fst~~	~~1~~		~~:233 :472 1:12 1:374~~	~~3↑ ⒻWiggins BC H45k~~	~~86~~	~~6~~	~~6~~	~~42½~~	~~42~~	~~43~~	~~31½~~	~~Warren R J Jr~~	~~LB 115~~	~~2.50~~	~~91-11~~	~~DrlingDme115hd CdetteStevens1201½ Petrhof'sPt1151½~~	~~Angled out stretch~~	~~7~~
4Jly93-11Pln	fst	1 1/16		:23 :461 1:10 1:424	3↑ ⒻHandicap50k	85	4	5	55½	34	35	28	Warren R J Jr	LB 119	*.80	86-13	Cadette Stevens1168 Peterhof's Patea1191½ Catlina1154	Wide late bid	5
22May93-8GG	gd	1 1/16	Ⓣ	:231 :471 1:11 1:422+	3↑ ⒻⓇPcfc Hgts H40k	92	2	6	65½	63¾	21	12	Warren R J Jr	LB 115	5.60	94-09	Peterhof'sPatea1152 LoveAvie117hd RunAwyStevie115hd	Rallied far wide	8
24Apr93-8GG	fm	1⅛	Ⓣ	:481 1:12 1:364 1:49	3↑ ⒻCntes Fgr H-G3	92	5	4	45½	54	64¼	53½	Boulanger G	L 113	11.10	92-10	MissHighBlade115hd Silvered1151½ Frenchmn'sCove1141	Raced well wide	8
27Mar93-8GG	sly	1 1/16		:234 :471 1:104 1:422	3↑ ⒻGldn Ppy H-G3	88	6	4	44	43½	33½	32	Boulanger G	L 114	*2.40	83-25	Steff Graf1141 Amorously1141 Peterhof's Patea1141½	Wide trip	7
13Mar93-8GG	fst	1 1/16		:234 :474 1:113 1:424	3↑ ⒻMiss Amrca HG3	91	1	3	32	32½	34½	32¼	Boulanger G	L 115	4.10	83-11	SouthernTruce120nk Apreciada1122 Peterhof'sPate115½	Wide stetch run	4

WORKOUTS: ●Nov 26 BM 6f fst 1:13 H 1/10 ●Nov 9 BM 5f fst :584 H 1/21 Nov 1 BM 7f fst 1:25 H 1/3 ●Oct 24 BM 5f fst :591 H 1/33 Oct 4 BM 6f fst 1:142 H 4/15 ●Sep 24 BM 6f fst 1:14 H 1/6

Cappucino Bay

Own: Bell Joyce

FLORES D R (1 0 0 0 .00)

B. f. 4
Sire: Balljumper (Damascus)
Dam: Dubbed In (Silent Screen)
Br: Bell A & Joyce (Wash)
Tr: Blincoe Thomas H (—)

L 112

Lifetime Record: 18 5 0 5 $155,681											
1993	7	3	0	1	$83,575	Turf	8	4	0	1	$97,000
1992	6	1	0	2	$33,300	Wet	1	0	0	1	$1,305
BM Ⓣ	0	0	0	0		Dist Ⓣ	2	1	0	0	$30,950

19Nov93-8Hol	fm	1	Ⓣ	:231 :47 1:104 1:351	3↑ ⒻAlw 39000N3X	92	5	2	22	22½	21½	31	Flores D R	LB 115 f	5.40	88-14	QueensCourtQueen115¾ MmselleBbtt113hd CppucinoBy1151½	Good effort	5
23Oct93-4SA	fm	*6½f	Ⓣ	:214 :433 1:072 1:132	3↑ ⒻAlw 40000N3X	80	5	1	2hd	2½	31	46½	Flores D R	LB 116 f	*1.80	84-09	Badarma113¾ Shir Dar1165½ Melo Melody116nk	Weakened	7
31Jly93-3Dmr	fm	1 1/16	Ⓣ	:241 :474 1:114 1:422	3↑ ⒻAlw 46000N3X	92	7	1	11½	11	1½	41½	Flores D R	LB 116 f	4.70	92-04	La Sarcelle118½ Queens Court Queen1181 Freewheel116no	Nipped for 3rd	8
18Jun93-2Hol	fm	1 1/16	Ⓣ	:233 :471 1:103 1:403	ⒻClm 80000	92	5	1	11	11½	11½	11	Flores D R	LB 116 f	6.90	93-09	Cappucino Bay1161 Paula Revere1161½ Run Away Stevie1162½	Ridden out	7
9Apr93-2SA	fm	*6½f	Ⓣ	:212 :433 1:074 1:14	ⒻClm 80000	91	6	7	51¾	31½	3½	1nk	Flores D R	LB 119	6.50	88-15	CappucinoBay119nk ShelteredView115hd ThirstForPeace1151	Boxed in 1/2	12
28Mar93-5SA	gd	6½f	⊗	:22 :444 1:094 1:161	ⒻAlw 41000N3X	76	4	1	1½	2½	44½	411	Flores D R	LB 119	2.90	79-14	Prying117nk Captivant1151¾ Snow Forest1169	Faltered	4
3Mar93-5SA	gd	*6½f	Ⓣ	:214 :442 1:081 1:143	ⒻAlw 36000N2X	95	9	1	11½	11½	1½	1½	Flores D R	LB 115	6.10	85-17	Cappucino Bay115½ Yousefia1156 Chimmy Rock1151	Ridden out	11
20Dec92-5Hol	fm	5½f	Ⓣ	:222 :451 :572 1:034	3↑ ⒻClm 62500	91	5	2	2hd	11	1½	11	Flores D R	LB 116	5.70	86-14	Cappucino Bay1161 Nat's Sallie114¾ Rejoice1143½	Driving	9
12Dec92-3Hol	fst	5½f		:22 :453 :574 1:041	3↑ ⒻAlw 34000N2X	85	1	4	42¼	41¾	31½	32¾	Delahoussaye E	LB 116	10.80	89-15	Walk Of Fame117no Beverly Z.1152¾ Cappucino Bay1161	Always close	6
18Nov92-8Hol	fst	6½f		:213 :44 1:082 1:15	3↑ ⒻAlw 34000	80	7	2	31½	31½	35	47½	Flores D R	LB 113	34.40	89-09	Nannetta1163½ Looie Capote116 Beverly Z.118	Wide,jostled 1/2	7

WORKOUTS: ●Nov 17 SA 3f fst :352 B 1/13 Nov 12 SA 6f gd 1:151 H 15/32 Nov 5 SA 5f fst 1:013 H 40/93 Oct 15 SA 5f fst :592 B 8/55 Oct 8 SA 5f fst 1:00 H 5/45 Sep 30 SA 5f fst 1:002 H 7/48

Let's Sgor (NZ)

Own: Allred & Hubbard & Sczesny

WARREN R J JR (318 24 45 59 .08)

Ch. m. 6
Sire: Crag-an-Sgor (Rash Prince)
Dam: Alycide (Oncidium)
Br: Osborn Arthur & Son Pty Ltd (NZ)
Tr: Josephson Jedd B (32 5 9 3 .16)

L 111

Lifetime Record: 23 6 4 3 $200,164											
1993	3	0	0	1	$10,125	Turf	23	6	4	3	$200,164
1992	3	0	0	0	$8,000	Wet	0	0	0	0	
BM Ⓣ	0	0	0	0		Dist Ⓣ	1	0	0	1	$4,500

15May93-8GG	fm	1⅜	Ⓣ	:482 1:14 1:38 2:15	3↑ ⒻYba Buena H-G3	70	3	2	21	2hd	612	618	Meza R Q	LB 112	20.50	76-12	Party Cited1173 Silvered1156 Rougeur1153	Stopped	8
23Apr93-6GG	fm	1 1/16	Ⓣ	:232 :471 1:112 1:422+	ⒻSoft Copy30k	87	1	4	33	21	2½	32	Chapman T M	LB 115	3.60	92-08	Splashing Wave1151½ Paula Revere118½ Let's Sgor1157		5
Steadied early while rank																			
3Apr93-7SA	fm	*6½f	Ⓣ	:212 :431 1:062 1:123	ⒻL Cngs B C HG3	87	5	5	66½	68	56	46	Flores D R	LB 113	57.30	89-04	Glen Kate121hd Heart Of Joy121¾ Worldly Possession1155	No mishap	6
25Nov92-8Hol	fm	1	Ⓣ	:234 :471 1:112 1:352	3↑ ⒻAlw 50000	68	8	6	52½	52½	86¾	1013¼	Pincay L Jr	LB 117	32.50	75-16	Guiza114¾ Kenbu111 Elegance116		10
1Nov92-8SA	fm	1	Ⓣ	:223 :463 1:092 1:343	3↑ ⒻRowan H81k	81	3	5	59	36½	35	57½	Flores D R	B 116	6.00	83-10	Visible Gold117¾ Vijaya1163 Fortissima-Ch116	Rank early	7
9Sep92-8Dmr	fm	1	Ⓣ	:241 :481 1:12 1:361	3↑ ⒻAlw 55000	80	5	5	43½	31½	42½	45	Delahoussaye E	B 122	*1.60	85-10	Fortissima-Ch120¾ CarCrissim116nk Number'sGme120	Off poorly, rank	5
4Dec91♦Te Rapa(NZ)	fm	*1	ⓉLH	1:341	3↑ ⒻStk 26000							55½	Cassidy L V	120	-		Kiss1221½ Fun On The Run1222¼ Penny Royal120		15
					Lion Red Dulcie Stakes-G2														
27Nov91♦Otago(NZ)	fm	*7f	ⓉLH	1:214	3↑ Stk 13000							2nk	Cassidy L V	120	-		Plume120nk Let's Sgor1202½ Just Willi108		11
					Levin Stakes (Listed)														
23Oct91♦Hawera(NZ)	fm	*7f	ⓉLH	1:23	3↑ ⒻStk 16000							2½	Phillips B A	120	-		Fun On The Run122½ Let's Sgor1203 On The Beat120		13
					Evergreen Stakes (Listed)														
3Apr91♦Randwick(Aus)	gd	*1½	ⓉLH	2:30	ⒻStk 50000							107½	Paine N	119	10.00		Triscay119hd Lee's Bid119hd Mannerism119		12
					AJC Oaks-G1														

Darling Dame

Own: Golden Eagle Farm

BAZE R A (438 113 81 57 .26)

B. f. 4
Sire: Lyphard (Northern Dancer)
Dam: Darling Lady (Alleged)
Br: Mabee Mr-Mrs John C (Ky)
Tr: Fierce Fordell (65 12 15 8 .18)

L 113

Lifetime Record: 17 5 6 1 $142,675											
1993	6	1	3	0	$47,750	Turf	4	1	1	0	$23,225
1992	10	4	3	1	$94,925	Wet	1	0	1	0	$4,600
BM Ⓣ	2	0	1	0	$10,000	Dist Ⓣ	3	1	0	0	$13,225

24Oct93-8BM	fst	1 1/16		:23 :464 1:11 1:424	3↑ ⒻRunning Luck25k	84	4	2	1hd	11	2hd	22	Campbell B C	LB 116	2.30	87-18	Run Away Stevie1142 Darling Dame116hd Becky'sQueen1157	Held gamely	5
4Sep93-11Sac	fst	1 1/16		:222 :451 1:092 1:412	3↑ ⒻMthr Lde BCH40k	84	5	6	66¾	42½	42½	52¾	Campbell B C	LB 118	*.70e	92-18	Alta's Princess116no My True Lady1152 Sheer Quality116½	Mild late bid	8
7Aug93-11SR	fst	1 1/16		:223 :462 1:102 1:421	3↑ ⒻL Burbank H40k	86	2	3	32	31½	23	43	Campbell B C	LB 115	4.00	93-10	CdetteStvns1192 ShrQulity113hd Alt'sPrincss1151	Very wide second turn	7
24Jly93-11Sol	fst	1		:233 :472 1:12 1:374	3↑ ⒻWiggins BC H45k	89	3	1	1hd	1½	1½	1hd	Campbell B C	LB 115	6.20	93-11	DrlingDme115hd CdetteStevens1201½ Peterhof'sPt1151½	Drifted wide drive	7
20Jun93-11Stk	fst	1 1/16		:23 :46 1:101 1:411	3↑ ⒻDotson B C H40k	87	3	3	31	1hd	1hd	21½	Campbell B C	LB 115	2.00	94-12	Cadette Stevens1151½ Darling Dame1152 Autumn Mood1149	Game try	5
21May93-8GG	fst	1		:23 :462 1:10 1:351	ⒻWatch Wndy H30k	86	3	2	21	21	21½	23	Warren R J Jr	LB 115	6.20	91-18	Catlina1153 Darling Dame115½ Amorously116nk	Second best	6
8Nov92-6BM	fm	1 1/16	Ⓣ	:232 :464 1:11 1:422	ⒻPlo Alto H100k	65	4	3	36½	33½	67¼	813½	Baze R A	LB 115	6.90	84-05	Skimble1174 Petite Sonnerie115 Royal Jelly114		8
10Oct92-8BM	fst	1		:234 :48 1:12 1:37	ⒻⓇS Clara Inv53k	79	6	3	31½	2½	1hd	1nk	Baze R A	LB 115	3.00	85-18	Darling Dame115nk S Maxine117½ Las Leader115	Wide trip	7
30Aug92-8BM	fm	1	Ⓣ	:241 :482 1:121 1:373	ⒻThe San Jose51k	83	5	1	1½	1hd	2hd	2nk	Boulanger G	LB 114	4.80	91-11	Charm A Gendarme120nk Darling Dame114½ S Maxine115	Held well	5
31Jly92-11SR	fst	1		:23 :461 1:104 1:371	ⒻFair Dir H 32k	78	6	3	34	32	1½	1½	Boulanger G	LB 115	*2.40	91-13	Darling Dame115½ Sweet Pair A Dice1161 S. Maxine113	Game win	6

WORKOUTS: Nov 26 BM 4f fst :49 H 16/26 Nov 19 BM 4f fst :481 H 6/27 Nov 13 BM 5f fst 1:022 H 45/62 Nov 7 BM 4f fst :482 H 15/72 ●Oct 18 BM 4f fst :464 H 1/68 Oct 9 BM 4f fst :48 H 7/32

ALL-IN-ONE's output for the race is as follows:

```
4DEC93                           BM                    8.5 furlongs turf
Race #8                                                         7 starters
CLF                                                  Age: 3+years, Female
-------------------------------INPUT DATA-------------------------------
                  #  #  #  #                              1st C  2nd C  Final
Horse name        ST W  P  S  Earned Date    Trk Dist. S  time   time   time
----------------------------------------------------------------------------
DON'T TOUCH LIL    6  2  0  0  58500 15SEP93 HOL 8.000 T  46.3  110.3  135.2
SPLASHING WAVE    10  4  1  2  88885 14NOV93 BM  8.500 T  48.3  112.3  144.2
PETERHOF'S PATEA  13  3  3  5 166730 14NOV93 BM  8.500 T  47.2  111.0  142.0
CAPPUCINO BAY      7  3  0  1  83575 19NOV93 HOL 8.000 T  47.0  110.4  135.1
LET'S SGOR-NZ      6  0  0  1  16125 15MAY93 GG  8.500 T  47.1  111.2  142.2
DARLING DAME       6  1  3  0  47750 24OCT93 BM  8.500 D  46.4  111.0  142.4


                             1st C  2nd C  Final
Horse name        Class Lvl  B.L.   B.L.   B.L.   SR   Var
-----------------------------------------------------------
DON'T TOUCH LIL   C50,000    8.25   4.75   0.00   88  13.0
SPLASHING WAVE    C40,000    0.00   0.00   0.00   88  13.0
PETERHOF'S PATEA  STAKES     3.00   3.50   1.00   99   3.0
CAPPUCINO BAY     NW3        2.00   2.50   1.25   88  14.0
LET'S SGOR-NZ     STAKES     3.00   1.00   2.00   92   8.0
DARLING DAME      STAKES     0.00   0.00   2.00   87  18.0



-------------------------------BETTING LINE-----------------------------
                  -------Rankings--------            Betting   Fair    Fair
Horse name        PEH H-I THAAI P-H ESP   Rating     Line    Place $  Show $
----------------------------------------------------------------------------
PETERHOF'S PATEA   1   1   1    1   1     98.27      7-5      3.20     2.40
DARLING DAME       2   2   2    2   3     74.01      5-1
SPLASHING WAVE     3   4   3    3   4     71.16      6-1
LET'S SGOR-NZ      6   3   4    5   2     68.12
CAPPUCINO BAY      4   6   5    4   5     68.08
DON'T TOUCH LIL    5   5   6    6   6     64.65



-------------------------------EXACTA GRID------------------------------
              |PETERHOF'S PATE| DARLING DAME  | SPLASHING WAVE|
--------------+---------------+---------------+---------------+
PETERHOF'S PAT| . . . . . . . |   15     37   |   19     46   |
              | . . . . . . . |               |               |
              | . . . . . . . |               |               |
--------------+---------------+---------------+---------------+
DARLING DAME  |   23     56   | . . . . . . . |   75    186   |
              |               | . . . . . . . |               |
              |               | . . . . . . . |               |
--------------+---------------+---------------+---------------+
SPLASHING WAVE|   29     72   |   78    193   | . . . . . . . |
              |               |               | . . . . . . . |
              |               |               | . . . . . . . |
--------------+---------------+---------------+---------------+


4DEC93                           BM                    8.5 furlongs turf
Race #8                                                         7 starters
CLF                                                  Age: 3+years, Female
-------------------------SPEED/PACE SUMMARY-----------------------------

Race Type:        Double Advantage Race
Race Profile:     48.06   112.03  143.49   Winners' Pace Profile: EARLY
Ability Par:      79.51                     Pace Contention Point:  2.65 lengths

Projected Times:                           Ability Balance  Last Proj  Con-
                  1st C   2nd C   Fin C      Time    Time    Frac Pace  tender
----------------------------------------------------------------------------
PETERHOF'S PATEA  47.97   111.64  142.19     78.52   99.02  30.55 FRONT  Y+
DARLING DAME      47.88   111.61  144.03     80.30  100.94  32.42 FRONT  N
SPLASHING WAVE    48.60   112.60* 144.40     80.40  101.24  31.80 LATE   N
LET'S SGOR-NZ     48.63   112.62* 143.88     79.89  100.68  31.26 REAR   N
CAPPUCINO BAY     48.50   112.95* 144.99     80.54  102.02  32.04 REAR   N
DON'T TOUCH LIL   49.30   113.18* 145.00     81.12  101.59  31.82 REAR   N
```

```
-------------------------------PACE GRAPH------------------------------------
     Profile:            48.06              112.03             143.49
     Front Runner:       47.88              111.61             142.19
Horse name                 1C                 2C                    F
PETERHOF'S PATEA   -------------------X ----------------(--X -------------------X
DARLING DAME       -------------------X ----------------(--X ---------X--------+
SPLASHING WAVE     --------------X---+ ---------------X-(--+ -------X----------+
LET'S SGOR-NZ      --------------X--+ --------------X-(--+ ----------X--------+
CAPPUCINO BAY      --------------X--+ -----------X---(--+ ----X------------+
DON'T TOUCH LIL    -----------X------+ -----------X----(--+ ----X-------------+
```

This race is the second and last simulcast of the day from Bay Meadows. We have no Pick-3, quinella, or trifecta to deal with. Here are the win odds on our contenders:

Peterhof's Patea	2-1
Darling Dame	6-1
Splashing Wave	17-1

At a glance we see that all three of our contenders are win over-lays by definition. A closer look reveals that Splashing Wave offers the biggest edge: 157 percent. By comparison, the edge on Peterhof's Patea is a respectable 25 percent and the edge on Darling Dame is a modest 16.7 percent.

With such a large edge, it appears that the absolute best win bet in the race is Splashing Wave. But looks can be deceiving. Edge-to-odds ratio, not edge, determines the worth of each bet. The edge-to-odds ratios are as follows:

Edge-to-odds (Peterhof's Patea)	$= .25 \div 2 = .125$
Edge-to-odds (Splashing Wave)	$= 1.57 \div 17 = .092$
Edge-to-odds (Darling Dame)	$= .167 \div 6 = .028$

Closer inspection shows that Peterhof's Patea represents the single-best win bet in this race, even though the edge offered on Splashing Wave is much larger. Aggressive win bettors would make a lone win bet on Peterhof's Patea.

If we are moderate win bettors, we can bet Peterhof's Patea and Splashing Wave, since each offers an edge of greater than 20 percent. According to the edge-to-odds ratios we calculated, more money would be bet on Peterhof's Patea than on Splashing Wave, 58 to 42 percent.

And ultraconservative win bettors could use the group overlay method. Our group estimate is 72.63 percent. The public's estimate is 53.18 percent. The public has underestimated our three contenders by a substantial 19 percent margin.

We skip the place-and-show pools since this is a turf race.

The exacta figures prove to be juicy as well. Any combination containing Splashing Wave is bound to be a nice overlay. In this case, even the exacta with 2-to-1 favorite Peterhof's Patea on top of Splashing Wave is returning more than $60.00. Our exacta grid tells us the fair pay on this combination is $19.00. Splashing Wave smacks of value, not only in the win pool, but on both sides of the exacta with our lower-priced contenders (Peterhof's Patea and Darling Dame).

EIGHTH RACE
Bay Meadows
DECEMBER 4, 1993

1$\frac{1}{16}$ MILES. (Turf)(1.40³) 14th Running of THE BROWN BESS BREEDERS' CUP HANDICAP. Purse $50,000 Added. *$25,000 Added, plus $25,000 from Breeders' Cup Fund. Fillies and mares 3–year–olds and upward. By subscription of $25 each, to accompany the nomination, $125 to pass the entry box and $125 additional to start, with $25,000 added and an additional $25,000 from Breeders' Cup Fund for Breeders' Cup eligibles only. The $25,000 added, of which $5,000 to second, $3,750 to third, $1,8775 to fourth and $6,25 to fifth. The Breeders' Cup Fund monies will be divided 55% to the winner, 20% to second, 15% to third, 7.5% to fourth and 2.5% to fifth provided a Breeders' cup nominee has finished in an awarded position. Any Breeders' Cup Fund monies not awarded will revert back to the fund. Preference will be given to (1) high weights Breeders' Cup nominees, (2) Breeders' cup nominees and (3) high weights. Weights, Sunday, November 28, 1993. Starters to be named through the entry box by the closing time of entries. A trophy will be presented to the owner of the winner. Closed Thursday, November 25, with nominations.

Value of Race: $51,500 Winner $29,625; second $10,000; third $7,500; fourth $3,750; fifth $625. Mutuel Pool $257,086.00 Exacta Pool $284,901.00

Last Raced	Horse	M/Eqt.	A.Wt	PP	St	¼	½	¾	Str	Fin	Jockey	Odds $1
14Nov93 8BM³	Splashing Wave	Lb	4 113	2	1	1½	1½	11	1½	1½	Meza R Q	17.10
14Nov93 8BM¹	Peterhof's Patea	LB	5 117	4	5	3½	3hd	2hd	2¹	2²	Kaenel J L	2.10
24Oct93 8BM²	Darling Dame	LB	4 115	7	4	4½	42	3½	3½	3nk	Baze R A	6.40
15Sep93 5Dmr¹⁰	Don't Touch Lil	LB	4 115	1	3	7	7	7	5³	42	Belvoir V T	5.30
15May93 8GG⁶	Let's Sgor-NZ	LB	6 114	6	7	5hd	5½	53	43	54	Warren R J Jr	33.50
11Oct93 9Lrl⁷	Misspitch	LBb	3 114	3	6	63	64	61	64	65	Chapman T M	7.30
19Nov93 8Hol³	Cappucino Bay	LBf	4 114	5	2	2¹	2½	4hd	7	7	Flores D R	1.60

OFF AT 3:58 Start Good. Won driving. Time, :23², :47³, 1:12¹, 1:38, 1:44⁴ Course firm.

$2 Mutuel Prices:				
	2–SPLASHING WAVE	36.20	10.40	6.20
	4–PETERHOF'S PATEA		3.80	2.80
	7–DARLING DAME			4.60

$2 EXACTA 2–4 PAID $119.20

Splashing Wave is our first boxcar overlay of the day. Moderate and ultraconservative win bettors connected on the $36.20 mutuel she returned. Aggressive bettors bit the bullet and got hurt, but that's the nature of their game: trading the safety and comfort of multiple win bets for the superior return offered by single-horse betting.

Exacta players also collected big. According to our exacta grid, the fair pay for the Splashing Wave–Peterhof's Patea combination is $29.00. It paid nearly $120.00. Even if we demanded an outrageous 400 percent minimum edge on our exactas, we would have been able to bet this wonderfully undervalued combination. If only there had been a trifecta on this race.

Hollywood Park

8

1⅛ MILES. (1:46⁴) 15th Running of THE NATIVE DIVER HANDICAP. $100,000 Added Grade III. 3-year-olds and upward. By subscription of $100 each, which shall accompany the nomination, $1,000 additional to start, with $100,000 added, of which $20,000 to second, $15,000 to third, $7,500 to fourth and $2,500 to fifth. Weights, Monday, November 29. Starters to be named through the entry box by closing time of entries. Hollywood Park reserves the right not to divide this race. Should this race not be divided and the number of entries exceed the starting gate capacity, high weights on the scale will be preferred and an also eligible list will be drawn. Total earnings in 1993 will be used in determining the order of preference for horses assigned equal weight on the scale. Failure to draw into this race at scratch time cancels all fees. Trophies will be presented to the winning owner, trainer and jockey. Closed Wednesday, November 17, with 13 nominations.

Casual Lies
Own: Riley Shelley L

BOULANGER G (—)   L 115

B. o. 4
Sire: Lear Fan (Roberto)
Dam: Morna–GB (Blakeney)
Br: Meadowhill (Ky)
Tr: Riley Shelley L (—)

Lifetime Record: 17 6 1 3 $788,491
1993 2 1 0 0 $83,383 Turf 2 0 0 0 $15,530
1992 9 2 1 2 $544,480 Wet 0 0 0 0
Hol 7 0 0 1 $91,440 Dist 2 0 0 1 $90,000

Have Fun
Own: Gann Edmund A

ANTLEY C W (43 5 5 5 .12)   112

B. n. 4
Sire: Topsider (Northern Dancer)
Dam: Arewehavingfunyet (Sham)
Br: Juddmonte Farms Inc (Ky)
Tr: Frankel Robert (13 1 3 1 .08)

Lifetime Record: 16 5 3 0 $106,666
1993 8 1 2 0 $57,375 Turf 11 4 3 0 $70,800
1992 7 3 1 0 $42,931 Wet 2 0 0 0 $5,616
Hol 1 0 0 0 Dist 4 0 0 0 $5,516

Originally scheduled on turf
9Aug92◆ Deauville(Fr) sf *1¼ ⑫RH 2:14¹ Hcp 63500 ... 4¹½ Eddery Pat 130 6.20 Bella Mimosa118½ Hatch Princess115½ Raider115½ 17
Tr: Christiane Head Prix du Casino de Deauville Unhurried to stretch 3f out, wide rally into 3rd, evenly late
WORKOUTS: Nov 24 Hol 3f fst 1:00⁴ H 14/42 Nov 18 Hol 5f fst 1:00⁴ H 11/38 Nov 12 Hol 5f fst 1:14² H 4/17 Nov 5 SA 5f fst 1:02² H 61/93 Oct 26 SA 4f fst :47² H 21/48 Sep 26 SA 7f fst 1:26¹ H 3/8

Ravenwood
Own: Oak Crest Farm

DELAHOUSSAYE E (27 2 1 3 .07)   L 113

B. h. 5
Sire: Woodman (Mr. Prospector)
Dam: Blue Claret (Tom Rolfe)
Br: Oak Crest Farm (Ky)
Tr: Mandella Richard (11 1 2 4 .09)

Lifetime Record: 14 4 0 2 $109,325
1993 2 0 0 0 $7,875 Turf 3 0 0 0 $6,525
1992 5 2 0 2 $49,500 Dist 2 0 0 0 $1,500
Hol 5 2 0 2 Dist 2 0 0 0 $1,500

WORKOUTS: Dec 1 Hol 5f fst 1:02⁴ H 20/41 Nov 27 Hol 5f fst 1:43³ H 1/3 ... Nov 21 Hol 7f fst 1:26⁴ H 1/4 Nov 15 SA 5f fst 1:00² B 13/29 Nov 10 SA 7f fst 1:28³ H 5/10 Oct 19 SA 5f fst :59¹ H 6/48

L'Express (Chi)
Own: Hirsch & Mathewson

SOLIS A (67 9 12 12 .13)   L 115

B. c. 4
Sire: Gallantsky (Nijinsky II)
Dam: Pachita Game (Saratoga Game)
Br: Haras Santa Olga (Chi)
Tr: Stute Warren (6 1 0 1 .17)

Lifetime Record: 13 5 2 1 $151,164
1993 7 1 2 1 $101,625 Turf 1 0 0 0
1992 6 4 0 0 $49,539 Wet 2 0 0 0
Hol 3 2 0 0 $53,650 Dist 3 0 1 0 $44,375

Wide, jogged out badly final 3/8
27Jun92◆ Hipodromo(Chi) fst *7¼f LH 1:29³ Stk 30000 ... 17½ Rivera P 123 1.80 L'Express123¹²½ Saint Honore123¹½ Newbery123 11
Tanteo de Potrillos-G1 Close up, bid 2f out, soon led, quickly clear
WORKOUTS: Nov 29 Hol 5f fst 1:00⁴ H 8/27 Nov 24 Hol 1 fst 1:40⁴ H 1/1 Nov 18 Hol ① fm 1:41⁴ H (d) 1/1 Nov 12 SA 4f gd :48¹ H 6/52 Nov 3 SA 4f fst :47² H (d)6/36 Oct 29 SA 1 fst 1:39² H 2/5

Slew of Damascus

Own: Harbeston & Losh & Maccaroto

NAKATANI C S (60 14 10 13 .23)

Ch. g. 5
Sire: Siewacide (Seattle Slew)
Dam: Damascus Isle (Accipiter)
Br: Fulmer Farms (Tenn)
Tr: Roberts Craig (—)

L 118

		Lifetime Record:	25 10 4 3	$365,750
1993	13 7 2 2	$344,545	Turf	7 4 1 1	$257,385
1992	8 2 2 0	$16,755	Wet	1 0 1 0	$5,000
Hol	1 0 0 0	$7,500	Dist	0 0 0 0	

Bossanova

Own: Kenis & 3 Plus U Stable

GRYDER A T (46 9 5 6 .20)

Ch. g. 4
Sire: Romeo (T. V. Lark)
Dam: Patella (Jungle Cove)
Br: Rancho Jonata (Cal)
Tr: Van Berg Jack C (33 3 5 4 .09)

L 112

		Lifetime Record:	31 5 4 8	$242,950
1993	13 2 2 4	$149,850	Turf	13 3 4 1	$115,525
1992	12 1 2 2	$55,525	Wet	2 0 0 0	$7,500
Hol	4 1 0 2	$35,500	Dist	4 0 0 2	$60,750

Claimed from Sss Stable, Dominguez Caesar F Trainer

Juliannus

Own: Darley Stud Management

STEVENS G L (34 4 10 5 .11)

Dk. b or br c. 4
Sire: Alydar (Raise a Native)
Dam: Princess Juliet (Gallant Romeo)
Br: Calumet Farm (Ky)
Tr: Drysdale Neil (2 0 0 2 .00)

114

		Lifetime Record:	7 3 2 1	$75,950
1993	7 3 2 1	$75,950	Turf	0 0 0 0	
1992	0 M 0 0		Wet	0 0 0 0	
Hol	2 2 0 0	$39,050	Dist	0 0 0 0	

Lottery Winner

Own: Auerbach Ernest

BLACK C A (50 8 8 6 .16)

B. g. 4
Sire: Apalachee (Round Table)
Dam: Dr Penny Bian (Seat of Power)
Br: Bion Moreton (Ky)
Tr: Robbins Jay M (5 0 0 1 .00)

L 117

		Lifetime Record:	25 6 6 3	$356,225
1993	11 3 1 1	$253,325	Turf	0 0 0 0	
1992	12 3 4 2	$97,300	Wet	1 0 1 0	$6,000
Hol	7 1 1 3	$78,750	Dist	5 1 0 1	$168,950

ALL-IN-ONE's output for the race is as follows:

```
4DEC93                            HOL                        9 furlongs dirt
Race #8                                                         8 starters
STAKES                                                  Age: 3+years, Male
------------------------------INPUT DATA------------------------------
```

Horse name	# ST	# W	# P	# S	$'s Earned	Date	Trk	Dist.	S	1st C time	2nd C time	Final time
CASUAL LIES	11	3	1	2	637863	6NOV93	GG	8.500	D	46.2	109.4	140.4
HAVE FUN	8	1	2	0	57375	17OCT93	DMR	9.000	T	47.3	112.1	148.4
SLEW OF DAMASCUS	13	7	2	2	344545	30OCT93	BM	8.500	T	47.4	111.3	143.0
JULIANNUS	7	3	2	1	75950	13OCT93	SA	8.000	D	45.2	109.3	135.3
LOTTERY WINNER	11	3	1	1	253325	6NOV93	SA	9.000	D	45.4	110.0	147.4

Horse name	Class Lvl	1st C B.L.	2nd C B.L.	Final B.L.	SR	Var
CASUAL LIES	STAKES	2.50	1.00	0.00	93	15.0
HAVE FUN	CLF	4.00	1.50	3.25	89	13.0
SLEW OF DAMASCUS	STAKES	0.00	0.00	0.00	95	12.0
JULIANNUS	NW2	8.50	4.00	0.00	92	12.0
LOTTERY WINNER	STAKES	13.50	6.50	2.75	88	10.0

---------------------------------BETTING LINE---------------------------------

Horse name		Rankings				Rating	Betting Line	Fair Place $	Fair Show $
	PEH	H-I	THAAI	P-H	ESP				
SLEW OF DAMASCUS	1	3	3	1	2	86.62	2-1	3.60	2.80
CASUAL LIES	2	2	1	2	4	74.42	9-2		
LOTTERY WINNER	3	1	2	3	1	74.38	9-2		
JULIANNUS	5	4	4	4	5	66.09			
HAVE FUN	4	5	5	5	3	65.88			

-------------------------------EXACTA GRID-------------------------------

	SLEW OF DAMASCU	CASUAL LIES	LOTTERY WINNER
SLEW OF DAMASC	. . . .	20 49	20 49
CASUAL LIES	24 60	. . . .	44 110
LOTTERY WINNER	25 61	44 110	. . . .

4DEC93   HOL   9 furlongs dirt
Race #8   8 starters
STAKES   Age: 3+years, Male
------------------------------SPEED/PACE SUMMARY------------------------------

Race Type: Orderly Race
Race Profile: 47.34   110.80   147.30   Winners' Pace Profile: EARLY
Ability Par: 94.26   Pace Contention Point: 2.44 lengths

Projected Times:

	1st C	2nd C	Fin C	Ability Time	Balance Time	Last Frac	Proj Pace	Con- tender
SLEW OF DAMASCUS	47.10	110.55	147.09	94.00	103.76	36.54	EARLY	Y
CASUAL LIES	48.42	111.38*	147.30	94.34	103.43	35.92	REAR	N
LOTTERY WINNER	48.18	111.06*	147.04	93.94	103.26	35.98	LATE	N
JULIANNUS	47.80	111.25*	148.27	94.70	104.75	37.02	LATE	N
HAVE FUN	46.47	110.33	147.96	94.19	104.84	37.63	FRONT	N

-------------------------------PACE GRAPH-------------------------------

Profile:	47.34	110.80	147.30
Front Runner:	46.47	110.33	147.04
Horse name	1C	2C	F
SLEW OF DAMASCUS	---------------X--+	---------------(-X+	-----------------F
CASUAL LIES	--------X---------+	-------------X-(--+	-----------------X+
LOTTERY WINNER	---------X--------+	-------------X--(+	-----------------X
JULIANNUS	-----------X------+	-------------X-(--+	-------------X-----+
HAVE FUN	----------------X	---------------(-X+	-----------X---+

Here are the public win odds on our contenders:

Slew Of Damascus	3-1
Casual Lies	9-5
Lottery Winner	4-1

Casual Lies is a decided underlay. Lottery Winner offers no edge. Slew Of Damascus sticks out as the only playable overlay. His edge is 33 percent.

The group overlay method attaches a 69.7 percent probability of winning to our three contenders. The public's estimate of these contenders is greater than 80 percent. Slew Of Damascus is the only possible win bet in this race.

We might also consider a place-or-show bet on this strong top pick. We need a place price of $3.60 or a show price of $2.80 in order to be fairly compensated for our risk in these pools. Incredibly, the *minimum* place price on Slew Of Damascus was hovering around $4.60 for nearly the entire betting period. Believe it or not, the maximum place price on Slew Of Damascus was returning $6.80! The show price on Slew Of Damascus was also overlayed in the worst-case scenario.

With Casual Lies a big underlay, our exacta overlays will probably be found in the combinations pairing Slew Of Damascus and Lottery Winner. Indeed, the Casual Lies–Slew Of Damascus exacta combination is returning approximately $20, well below our $24 fair pay. By comparison, the Slew Of Damascus–Lottery Winner combination is paying around $32, 60 percent more than it should.

Based on our odds line, the Slew Of Damascus–Lottery Winner quinella should pay $12.12 to be a fair bet. It's returning around $18. This quinella combination offers outstanding value as well.

Slew Of Damascus gives win bettors of all persuasions a modest $8-and-change mutuel. On the surface, this doesn't seem too glamorous. But a 33 percent overlay is a 33 percent overlay whether it pays $8 or $18. We'll gladly accept the proceeds of our win bet on Slew Of Damascus.

EIGHTH RACE
Hollywood
DECEMBER 4, 1993

1⅛ MILES. (1.46⁴) 15th Running of THE NATIVE DIVER HANDICAP. $100,000 Added Grade III. 3-year-olds and upward. By subscription of $100 each, which shall accompany the nomination, $1,000 additional to start, with $100,000 added, of which $20,000 to second, $15,000 to third, $7,500 to fourth and $2,500 to fifth. Weights, Monday, November 29. Starters to be named through the entry box by closing time of entries. Hollywood Park reserves the right not to divide this race. Should this race not be divided and the number of entries exceed the starting gate capacity, high weights on the scale will be preferred and an also eligible list will be drawn. Total earnings in 1993 will be used in determining the order of preference of horses assigned equal weight on the scale. Failure to draw into this race at scratch time cancels all fees. Trophies will be presented to the winning owner, trainer and jockey. Closed Wednesday, November 17, with 13 nominations.

Value of Race: $108,300 Winner $63,300; second $20,000; third $15,000; fourth $7,500; fifth $2,500. Mutuel Pool $562,982.00 Exacta Pool $437,469.00 Trifecta Pool $209,610.00 Quinella Pool $46,224.00

Last Raced	Horse	M/Eqt.	A.Wt	PP	St	¼	½	¾	Str	Fin	Jockey	Odds $1
30Oct93 6BM1	Slew of Damascus	LBb	5 118	5	1	1½	1½	1½	12½	13	Nakatani C S	3.10
6Nov93 10SA4	Lottery Winner	LB	4 117	7	4	21	21½	21	21½	2¾	Black C A	4.30
6Nov93 10SA2	L'Express-Ch	LB	4 115	4	7	7	7	61	41½	3nk	Solis A	4.40
6Nov93 9SA4	Casual Lies	LB	4 115	1	3	43	43½	4hd	31	43½	Boulanger G	1.80
13Oct93 8SA1	Juliannus	B	4 114	6	5	64	62½	7	7	52	Stevens G L	11.00
24Oct93 3SA4	Ravenwood	LBb	5 116	3	6	3hd	31	32	5hd	6nk	Delahoussaye E	9.70
17Oct93 8SA6	Have Fun	B	4 114	2	2	51	51½	53	6½	7	Antley C W	26.30

OFF AT 4:21 Start Good. Won ridden out. Time, :23³, :47¹, 1:11, 1:35², 1:47² Track fast.

$2 Mutuel Prices:				
	5-SLEW OF DAMASCUS	8.20	4.60	3.20
	8-LOTTERY WINNER		4.60	3.00
	4-L'EXPRESS-CH			3.20

$2 EXACTA 5-8 PAID $32.80 $2 TRIFECTA 5-8-4 PAID $107.20 $2 QUINELLA 5-8 PAID $17.80

$3 Triple 1 or 6-7-5 Paid $118.80 Triple Pool $110,965.00

With favored Casual Lies running out of the money, Slew Of Damascus returned a very generous $4.60 to place. Had Casual Lies run second to Slew Of Damascus, the place price on the latter still would have been an overlayed $3.80.

The exacta and quinella both were overlays. The exacta paid $32.80 from a fair price of $20. The quinella yielded $17.80 from a fair price of $12.12. For a change, the public favorite runs out, and we get excellent value in all the mutuel pools: win, place, show, exacta, and quinella.

Hollywood Park

9 *6 Furlongs.* (1:08) CLAIMING. Purse $11,500. 3-year-olds and upward. Weights: 3-year-olds, 120 lbs. Older, 122 lbs. Non-winners of two races since October 4, allowed 3 lbs. A race since then, 5 lbs. Claiming price $16,000; if for $14,000, allowed 2 lbs. (Races when entered for $12,500 or less not considered.)

START / 6 FURLONGS / FINISH

Contented
Own: Marckesano & Marckesano & Rodas III
GUTIERREZ G R (—) $16,000

B. g. 6
Sire: Key to Content (Forli)
Dam: In Absentia (Believe It)
Br: White Fox Farm (Ky)
Tr: Koriner Brian (1 0 0 0 .00)

L 117

Lifetime Record:	25 7 6 3	$80,640			
1993	8 0 3 2	$12,970	Turf	0 0 0 0	
1992	7 2 1 1	$25,460	Wet	1 0 1 0	$3,600
Hol	6 1 0 1	$12,125	Dist	17 4 3 3	$46,740

18Nov93-7Hol	fst	5½f	:214	:45	:57	1:031	3↑ Clm 22500	60	7	1	2hd	2½	65	613½	Pedroza M A	LB 115 b	6.60	82-11	Candyman Bee1191¼ Lord Byron1171½ Ocean Native1121½	Dueled, tired	7
23Oct93-1SA	fst	7f	:224	:453	1:10	1:222	3↑ Clm 20000	87	2	2	11½	11½	11	22½	Pedroza M A	LB 116 b	7.00	88-14	Perfect Prankster1162½ [D]Contented116½ Heat116nk	Lugged in 1/8	7
Disqualified and placed 6th																					
3Oct93-7Fpx	fst	6f	:221	:451	:573	1:10	3↑ Clm 22500	89	1	1	1½	12	11	2nk	Perez I5	LB 109 b	7.30	97-09	Candyman Bee116nk Contented1092 Susan's Corsair114½	Held well	8
18Sep93-5Fpx	fst	6f	:224	:46	:58	1:103	3↑ Clm 16000	84	3	3	12	1½	1½	2no	Gulas L L5	LB 111 b	4.70	94-09	Susan's Corsair116no Contented1111 Orthos116½	Game try	9
27Aug93-5Dmr	fst	6½f	:222	:452	1:10	1:162	3↑ Clm 10000	84	6	1	11	11½	11	2hd	Pedroza M A	LB 117 b	5.20	89-11	Anonymouslew117hd Contented1171¼ Five Sharps1173	Sharp effort	11
8Aug93-10SR	fst	6f	:22	:443	:57	1:092	3↑ Clm 16000	84	4	5	11½	11	2hd	32¼	Martinez O A Jr	LB 117 b	8.20	95-08	Moscow's Pretense1171½ Great Decision117¾ Contented117½	Tired late	10
9Jly93-8Hol	fst	6f	:221	:451	:571	1:094	Alw 12500s	53	6	1	11½	51¾	79	716	Lopez A D	LB 115 b	22.30	75-15	Wild Tech115nk Screen Tale115½ Book Publisher122½	Took up 1/4	8
13Jun93-6Hol	fst	6f	:221	:451	:572	1:101	Clm c-10000	82	2	4	11½	12	14	31	Lopez A D	LB 117 b	*1.70	88-09	High Mesa114hd Dr. Hyde1171 Contented1171	Weakened	8
Claimed from Clear Valley Stables, Shulman Sanford Trainer																					
22Nov92-10Hol	fst	6f	:221	:452	:574	1:102	3↑ Clm 10000	58	8	1	22½	32	33½	98½	Pedroza M A	LB 118 b	*1.70	79-12	Spell Victorious115½ Kurrajong-GB115½ Don Miguel115	Gave way	12
31Oct92-2SA	my	6f	:214	:444	:571	1:102	3↑ Clm 22500	86	1	6	1½	1½	2hd	22½	Cedeno E A	LB 114 b	3.40	81-18	Father Six To Five1162½ Contented114hd Marlar112	Held 2nd	6

WORKOUTS: Nov 4 LA 5f fst 1:011 H *2/2*

King of the Bayou

Own: Doyle John Earl

MARTINEZ F F (3 0 0 0 .00) $14,000

B. g. 7
Sire: Cajun Prince (Ack Ack)
Dam: Speed Queen (Tyrant)
Br: Bernheim Alain P (Cal)
Tr: Keller Sherman W Jr (4 0 0 0 .00)

L 115

	Lifetime Record :	26	8	1	4	$99,875	
1993	1 0 0 0		Turf	0 0 0 0			
1991	8 1 0 2	$23,950	Wet	1 0 0 0			
Hol	3 2 0 0	$13,475	Dist	22 7 1 4	$91,075		

18Nov93–7Hol fst 5½f .214 .45 .57 1:03¼ 3+ Clm 22500 35 5 4 6¾ 7¾ 7¹¹ 7²² Berrio O A LB 115 fb 40.80 74–11 Candyman Bee115¾ Lord Byron117¼ Ocean Native112½ Lugged out turn 7
40ec91–7BM fst 6f .22 .443 .563 1:09 3+ Clm 32000 79 5 3 5⁴ 4¹¾ 4²¾ 54½ Hansen R D LB 119 b 3.20 85–16 Happy In Space117⁹ We're Just Bluff117¾ Express Me115 Evenly late 7
11Nov91–6BM fst 6f .223 .451 .571 1:09¾ 3+ Clm 32000 82 1 1 1½ 1½ 2¹ 33½ Hansen R D LB 119 b 3.30 86–16 Dr. Hart119¾ Martini To Tango112¾ King Of The Bayou119 Set pace 7
20Oct91–8BM fst 6f .221 .463 .563 1:09 3+ Van Mar Fm H 69 2 2 2½ 2² 43½ 66½ Doocy T T LB 119 b 9.70 84–14 Dominated Debut115¾ Burn Annie122¾ Crystal Run114 Faltered 6
50ct91–6BM fst 6f .224 .452 .571 1:09³ 3+ Alw 22000 82 6 1 1¼ 14 1⁵ 16 Baze R A LB 117 b *1.50 89–13 KingOfTheBayou117⁶ SangerBrve118½ ObiesQusr115 Ridden out, wide 6
20Sep91–8BM fst 6f .22 .444 .571 1:10 3+ Alw 22000 78 2 4 1½ 1hd 2hd 52¼ Miller D A Jr LB 117 b 5.40 83–16 Dr. Hart122ⁿᵏ Crystal Sir117² Rippling Deal116 Drifted out late 7
6Sep91–7BM fst 6f .22 .444 .571 1:10¼ 3+ Alw 22000 78 4 2 1hd 1hd 3¼ 33½ Miller D A Jr LB 117 b *1.30 84–17 Toney Tony119¾ Crystal Sir117³ King Of The Bayou117 Weakened 7
27Jly91–11SR fst 6f .213 .441 .563 1:09¾ 3+ Ernst Fnly H 83 2 2 11½ 11 2hd 42½ Lozoya D A LB 117 b 7.40 93–10 Ambessa120¹½ Magic Prospect114¹ Variety Road120 Game to late 6
14Jly91–11Sol fst 6f .22 .434 .56 1:09¹ 3+ Carquinez H 79 6 1 1½ 11 2¼ 53½ Lozoya D A LB 112 b 4.00 91–08 Ambessa119¹½ Spectacularphantom114¹ Harrow Whip116 Speed tired 9
8Oct90–7SA fst 6f .212 .434 .564 1:09² 3+ Alw 32000 105 2 3 1½ 1² 14 15 Desormeaux K J LB 120 b 5.60 92–17 King Of The Bayou120⁵ Blaze O'Brien117½ Intercup120 Easily 9

WORKOUTS: Nov 13 Hol 4f fst :48³ H 10/29 Nov 5 Hol 5f fst 1:02¹ H 13/30 Oct 30 Hol 5f fst 1:01⁴ H 14/24 Oct 24 Hol 5f fst 1:00⁴ H 7/10 Oct 18 Hol 4f fst :51¹ H 13/16 Oct 12 Hol 4f fst :48³ H 4/13

Dr. Augusta

Own: Whaley Don & Betty

NAKATANI C S (60 14 10 13 .23) $16,000

Dk. b or br g. 4
Sire: Shanekite (Hoist Bar)
Dam: Fun Finder (Pleasure Seeker)
Br: Halo Farms (Cal)
Tr: Baffert Bob (10 2 1 2 .20)

L 117

	Lifetime Record :	14	2	2	3	$82,625	
1993	3 0 1 1	$4,550	Turf	0 0 0 0			
1992	8 1 1 1	$34,975	Wet	0 0 0 0			
Hol	2 0 0 1	$11,050	Dist	9 2 1 2	$79,850		

14Nov93–4SA fst 6½f .214 .441 1:08⁴ 1:15 3+ Clm 16000 80 11 5 42 31½ 21 2¹½ Pedroza M A LB 116 b 49.50 90–06 Cool Chili118¹½ Dr. Augusta116ⁿᵏ Precise Cut117½ Good effort 11
11Oct93–1SA fst 6f .221 .45 .57 1:09³ 3+ Clm 16000 83 6 1 2½ 2hd 2¹ 31¼ Pedroza M A LB 116 b 4.80 88–11 Cool Chili116ⁿᵏ Sinceriffic116½ Dr. Augusta116¾ Bid, outfinished 7
13Sep93–5Dmr fst 6f .221 .452 .573 1:10 3+ Clm c–12500 42 7 2 3½ 41½ 97½ 815 Castaneda M LB 117 fb 8.40 74–10 Kolbe's Gold119ⁿᵏ Peach Boy112¹⁸ Sinceriffic119¹½ 10
Acted up gate, wide; Claimed from Halo Farms & Ward, Sise Clifford Jr Trainer
20Dec92–10BM gd 6f .223 .443 .572 1:04 3+ Clm 16000 59 3 6 6⁴ 7⁷½ 7⁸ 11⁹½ Hansen R D LB 117 b 4.30 72–22 Sure To Run117ʰᵈ Timely Encore117ⁿᵏ Favorite Norm117¹ Through early 11
40ec92–7BM gd 6f .221 .451 .574 5:11 3+ Clm 20000 74 4 5 53½ 5¹½ 41½ Baze R A LB 117 b *2.00 79–19 Whoa Dude119ⁿᵒ Carrie's Style117¹¾ It's Blind Justice117ⁿᵏ Raced far wide 7
13Nov92–8BM fst 6f .221 .461 1:09¹ Van Mar Fm H 25k 67 5 2 63½ 45 3⁵ 48¼ Baze R A LB 118 b 4.80 84–15 Crafty Dude116⁶ Senor A. H. Wasu113¾ Western Man118 No rally 6
30Oct92–3BM fst 1 .223 .461 1:11 1:36¾ ⒶVinehill H 30k 68 4 3 3¼ 2hd 24 41¼ Solis A LB 118 b 4.90 75–14 Never Round117¾ Mt. Lapin114¹³ Boundary Ridge115 Ducked out late 6
17Sep92–12Fpx fst 6f .212 .444 .562 1:09² 3+ Clm 32000 79 9 7 3¹ 42½ 53¾ 76½ Pedroza M A LB 122 b 9.90 87–12 Prospect For Four117¾ Tormeric117¼ Aro122 Gave way 10
21Aug92–11Bmf fst 6f .22 .44 .563 1:09² S M Co Soph 31k 86 1 5 2¼ 2² 2hd 1² Baze R A LB 118 b *.70 89–13 Dr. Augusta118² Fly Fast116½ Zopilote118 Closed gamely 5
9Aug92–7Dmr fst 6½f .214 .44 1:074 1:14¹ 3+ Alw 33000 88 1 4 3² 2² 2⁴½ 37 McCarron C J LB 116 2.60 95–05 Trick Me121⁵ Double O' Slew116⁴ Dr. Augusta116 Weakened 7

WORKOUTS: ●Nov 30 SA 5f gd 1:00 H 1/12 Nov 24 SA 4f fst :48⁴ H 24/41 ●Nov 9 SA 6f fst 1:12 H 1/9 Nov 2 SA 4f fst :48³ B 16/38 ●Oct 8 SA 3f fst :34² H 1/20 Oct 3 SA 5f fst 1:01 H 17/41

Baraonet

Own: Carey John J

VALENZUELA P A (54 6 10 2 .11) $16,000

B. g. 6
Sire: Chivalry (Nijinsky II)
Dam: Ambica (Red Fox)
Br: Rigg Wilfred C (Cal)
Tr: Hronec Philip (1 0 1 0 .00)

L 117

	Lifetime Record :	38	7	5	1	$160,046	
1993	14 2 2 0	$38,522	Turf	9 2 2 0	$52,624		
1992	7 3 1 0	$61,774	Wet	4 0 1 0	$6,762		
Hol	1 1 1 0	$21,837	Dist	13 2 2 1	$41,210		

14Nov93–4SA fst 6½f .214 .441 1:08⁴ 1:15 3+ Clm 16000 78 4 3 2hd 1hd 3¹ 63½ Pincay L Jr LB 117 6.70 89–06 Cool Chili118¹½ Dr. Augusta116ⁿᵏ Precise Cut117½ Weakened 11
7Nov93–1SA fst 6f .214 .441 .562 1:09 3+ Clm 16000 70 1 4 3ⁿᵏ 3½ 1hd 32¼ Valenzuela P A LB 117 12.70 81–11 Dr. Hyde116ⁿᵏ Candyman Bee116¾ Moscow M D118½ Inside duel 7
18Sep93–10Fpx fst 6f .213 .444 .571 1:09⁴ 3+ Clm 25000 66 8 6 42½ 2² 55 78½ Atkinson P LB 115 14.70 68–09 U. S. Of America116² BriskSailing116² CandymanBee116¾ Wide 1st turn 10
5Sep93–2Dmr fst 5½f .213 .444 .571 1:04⁴ 3+ Clm 35000 76 4 5 33½ 3¹ 42½ 53 Almeida G F LB 117 23.10 90–08 Ocean Native112¹½ Candyman Bee117ⁿᵒ Pancho's Cup112½ 4 Wide stretch 9
21Aug93–5Dmr fst 6f .214 .443 1:08⁴ 3+ Clm 35000 80 9 6 7²¾ 63¼ 73½ 54½ Almeida G F LB 115 39.10 87–09 Davy Be Good117²¾ Viva El Capitan117²¾ Phone Talk117¹½ Wide trip 10
7Aug93–4Dmr fst 6f .22 .45 1:09³ 3+ Clm 32000 76 6 1 1½ 1½ 4½ 51¹ McCarron C J LB 115 3.70 85–09 Roo Tale117ⁿᵈ Moscow M D119½ Won On Appeal108¹ Gave way 7
5Jun93–4Hol my 5f ⊗ .221 .46 .582 1:04⁴ 3+ Clm 47500 75 2 8 4³ 43 5¹¹¼ McCarron C J LB 115 8.10 77–22 Susan's Corsair109ⁿᵈ Xcaret119⁸ Friedlander117¾ Broke slowly 8
19Mag93–7Hol fst 6f .213 .444 .57 1:03³ 3+ Clm 40000 80 2 5 2½ 2hd 2¼ 43½ McCarron C J LB 117 5.20 90–13 Davy Be Good117hd CandymanBee117¾ RuffHombre117¹ Weakened a bit 6
16Apr93–7SA fst 5½f .214 .443 .57 1:03¹ 3+ Clm c–32000 87 6 4 45 41½ 4½ 42½ Flores D R LB 115 *1.90 91–13 Ruff Hombre119¼ Davy Be Good115³ Pancho's Cup115⁹ Bumped start 7
Claimed from Hogate Howard, Spawr Bill Trainer
28Mar93–9SA gd 6f .22 .451 .573 1:10¹ Clm 32000 92 5 3 1hd 1¹ 1¼ 2² Stevens G L LB 115 *3.40 84–14 Tide Is High116² Baraonet115hd Regional115ⁿᵏ Good effort 10

WORKOUTS: ●Oct 31 SA 5f fst :58ʰ H 1/67 Oct 19 SA 5f fst 1:00³ H 3/48 Oct 13 SA 5r.t 4f fst :48² H 1/7

He's Like the Wind

Own: Sprague Pansy & Ronald

DELAHOUSSAYE E (27 2 1 3 .07) $16,000

Gr. g. 6
Sire: Navajo (Grey Dawn II)
Dam: Anny Rooney (Misty Day)
Br: Kuster Mr–Mrs T (Ky)
Tr: Carava Jack (7 2 1 0 .29)

L 117

	Lifetime Record :	20	1	5	2	$52,010	
1992	1 0 0 1	$1,920	Turf	0 0 0 0			
1991	8 0 2 1	$12,900	Wet	1 0 0 0	$16,500		
Hol	4 0 0 0	$4,100	Dist	10 0 2 1	$16,845		

19Sep92–6Fpx fst 6f .213 .444 .572 1:09⁴ 3+ Clm 16000 80 3 5 6⁶ 77 67¾ 34 Lopez A D LB 116 4.70 93–11 Shining Prince116² Father Six To Five116² He's Like The Wind116 8
27Nov91–1Hol fst 6f .22 .45 .573 1:10 3+ Clm c–16000 79 6 5 5³ 4² 53½ 43½ Desormeaux K J LB 115 7.80 85–14 Over The Pole116½ Hajasala115¾ Sport Grip116 Wide backstretch 9
Claimed from , Hronec Philip Trainer
10Nov91–1SA fst 6f .221 .452 .582 1:09⁴ 3+ Clm 16000 79 3 8 66¾ 77½ 54½ 24½ Desormeaux K J LB 115 8.90 81–13 Loaded Juan118⁴¾ He's Like The Wind115ⁿᵒ Intercup115 Split rivals 1/8 9
19Oct91–9SA fst 1¼ .224 .454 1:10¹ 1:43⁴ 3+ Clm 16000 76 1 3 66⁵ 55 4³½ 24½ Valenzuela P A LB 115 8.40 81–14 Zaleucus115ⁿᵏ Bassman115⁴¼ Lyphing Dancer115 Wide trip 10
29Sep91–12Fpx fst 6f .221 .452 1:11¹ 1:17⁴ 3+ Clm c–12500 76 8 4 52½ 5³ 2¹½ 2ⁿᵏ Torres H S LB 111 2.60 87–14 Sergeant Jay Tee116ⁿᵏ He's LikeTheWind111¹¾ MajorBuper116 Wide trip 10
Claimed from , Garcia Juan Trainer
14Sep91–12Fpx fst 6f .221 .452 .582 1:09⁴ 3+ Clm 20000 81 8 5 5⁵ 4² 43½ Castanon A L LB 116 4.30 88–12 Santa Tecla–En114ⁿᵒ Lyphard's Fan116½ OverThePole119 Edged for 3rd 9
6Sep91–5Dmr gd 6f .221 .452 .574 1:10 3+ Clm 20000 75 2 8 10⁴½ 96½ 76¼ 44½ Nakatani C S LB 115 7.50 81–14 CndymnBee121ⁿᵒ DrweeProspector115¹ Rconnoitring115 Broke slowly 10
18Aug91–2Dmr fst 6f .221 .45 .571 1:09¾ 3+ Clm 20000 90 8 4 63½ 62¼ 52½ 44ⁿᵏ Solis A LB 115 21.00 90–11 Over The Pole117ⁿᵒ B. A. Believer115ⁿᵒ Roman Avie116 Bumped, wide 10
8Aug91–10LA fst 6f .221 .45 1:10³ 1:17¹ 3+ Clm 20000 75 1 5 45 4⁴ 3² 32 Castanon J L LB 117 4.00 87–11 Contented115¹½ Miami Dan117⅓ He's Like The Wind117 Well placed trip 10
25Sep90–11Fpx fst 6f .221 .45 .571 1:10 Clm 25000 96 8 8 5⁵ 45 2² 2⅓ Garcia J A LB 116 4.30 95–07 Viaggio111½ He's Like The Wind116⁴¾ Stan's Boy116 Late bid 8

WORKOUTS: Nov 26 Hol 5f fst :59⁴ H 4/42 Nov 19 Hol 5f fst 1:14 H 9/20 Nov 13 Hol 5f fst 1:00⁴ H 6/25 Nov 7 Hol 5f fst 1:00² H 4/22 Nov 1 Hol 4f fst :48² H 8/32 Oct 26 Hol 4f fst :48² H 4/17

Wild Tech

Own: Tons Of Fun Stable

LOPEZ A D (13 1 2 0 .08) $16,000

B. g. 5
Sire: Wild Again (Icecapade)
Dam: Letechav (Dust Commander)
Br: Millison Larry (Fla)
Tr: Passey Blake (—)

L 117

	Lifetime Record :	20	8	4	0	$119,915	
1993	9 3 1 0	$34,865	Turf	1 0 0 0			
1992	4 2 1 0	$37,250	Wet	0 0 0 0			
Hol	5 2 2 0	$25,250	Dist	5 1 1 0	$17,340		

13Oct93–3SA fst 6f .214 .441 1:08⁴ 1:15² 3+ Clm 25000 75 2 7 7¾ 7⁴ 64½ 57¼ Lopez A D LB 116 fb 8.60 87–11 Moscow M D118¹¼ Talent Connection116½ Candyman Bee118³ Wide trip 7
30ct93–7Fpx fst 6f .221 .451 .573 1:10 3+ Clm 25000 83 6 5 5⁵ 44½ 42½ 43½ Castanon A L LB 116 fb 3.60 94–09 Candyman Bee116ⁿᵏ Candyman Bee116² Susan's Corsair116¾ Wide into lane 8
18Sep93–8Hol fst 6f .221 .451 .571 1:09⁴ 3+ Clm 25000 79 7 0 7ⁿ 3⁴ 44⅓ Sorenson D LB 116 fb 6.90 94–09 U. S. Of America116² Brisk Sailing116² Candyman Bee116ⁿᵏ Even finish 10
9Jly93–8Hol fst 6f .221 .452 .571 1:09⁴ Alw 1250Os 94 8 3 5²¼ 1hd 1½ 1ⁿᵏ Nakatani C S LB 115 fb 2.30 91–15 Wild Tech115ⁿᵏ Screen Tale115½ Book Publisher122½ Wide trip 8
11Jun93–9Hol fst 6f .223 .452 1:09³ 1:15⁴ Clm 20000 95 8 3 2hd 2hd 1½ 1ⁿᵏ Nakatani C S LB 115 fb 6.10 87–14 Wild Tech117¾ Turn The Key117ⁿᵒ King Raj117¼ Ridden out 10
19May93–3Hol fst 6½f .463 1:124 1:36¹ Alw 25000s 83 3 4 1½ 1² 1hd 2¼ Nakatani C S LB 115 fb *1.40 90–11 Heat117¾ Wild Tech117ⁿᵒ Dog Gate115¾ Overtaken early 11
1May93–3Hol fst 1¼ .463 1:124 1:36¹ Alw 2500Os 82 7 4 3² 41½ 5⁴ 59½ Lopez A D LB 115 fb 23.10 85–07 Record Boom115²¼ Eddie Valient115¹½ Book Publisher122² Wide trip 6
27Mar93–4SA gd 6½f .22 .45 1:09¹ 1:15³ 3+ Clm c–20000 58 4 4 43½ 44 5²½ 61⁵½ Atkinson P LB 115 fb *1.10 73–09 Agiotage115²¼ Kelly G.108¼ Maxibob115⁴½ Wide trip 6
Claimed from Gaines & Rodas, Koriner Brian Trainer
11Mar93–5SA fst 6f .22 .452 .571 1:09¹ 3+ Clm c–12500 87 11 2 4½ 1³ 1⁵ 1² Atkinson P LB J 121 b 2.80 89–14 Wild Tech115² Jet Of Gold115ⁿᵏ Payand Payand Pay116⁴ Wide, handily 12
Claimed from Campbell Toni E, Hronec Philip Trainer
14Mar92–2SA fst 6½f .214 .441 1:08³ 1:15¹ Clm 25000 — 5 3 43 54½ 713 — Desormeaux K J LB 121 b 2.60 —3 Abergwaun Lad115² Diamond Out117²¾ Hot Operator115 Eased, lame 7

WORKOUTS: Nov 28 Hol 5f fst 1:02³ H 32/36 Nov 15 Hol 4f fst :48³ H 6/17 Nov 8 Hol 5f fst 1:00⁴ H 6/13 Sep 27 Hol 3f fst :36² H 4/7 Sep 13 SA 4f fst :51³ H 19/19

San Berdou

Own: Three Sisters Stable

STEVENS G L (36 4 10 5 .11) $16,000

Dk. b or br g. 4
Sire: Superoyale (Raise a Native)
Dam: Tibouchina (Nodouble)
Br: Verne H. Winchell (Ky)
Tr: Chambers Mike (4 1 0 2 .25)

117

	Lifetime Record :	10	1	4	2	$29,325	
1993	10 1 4 2	$29,325	Turf	0 0 0 0			
1992	0 M 0 0		Wet	0 0 0 0			
Hol	4 1 1 2	$17,850	Dist	3 0 1 1	$7,725		

7Nov93–1SA fst 6f .213 .441 .562 1:09 3+ Clm 25000 79 4 2 2hd 2hd 3¼ 5¾ Stevens G L B 116 4.30 85–11 Dr. Hyde116ⁿᵏ Candyman Bee116¾ Moscow M D118¹½ Dueled between 7
15Oct93–6BM fst 5½f .213 .45 .573 1:04¹ 3+ Clm 25000 90 2 2 1ⁿᵈ 1hd 1½ 2ⁿᵒ Boulanger G B 117 4.50 90–19 Sharp Event115ⁿᵒ San Berdou117¼ Dr George B115hd Just missed 7
18Aug93–10mr fst 6f .221 .45 .573 1:041 3+ Clm c–25000 69 4 3 2hd 1hd 3¼ 69 Gonzalez S⁵ B 112 *1.30 80–14 Fistylee117¾ Joboc119hd Heat117² Gave way 8
Claimed from V H H Stables, McAnally Ronald Trainer
28Jly93–4Dmr fst 6f .22 .451 .563 1:09 3+ Clm 25000 102 10 1 1½ 1hd 1hd 2½ Gonzalez S⁵ B 110 5.00 90–07 Moscow M D119¾ San Berdou110¾ Racer Rex117½ Good effort 10
30Jun93–6Hol fst 5½f .222 .452 .57 1:03 3+ Md 25000 101 8 2 2½ 1hd 1¼ 1½ Gonzalez S⁵ B 117 *.60 97–12 San Berdou117² Cutting Deep117¹² Noble Year117⁶ 12
Drifted out late, ridden out

```
10Jun93-6Hol fst 5½f  :22  :451 :571 1:033 3+ Md 32000   79 4 4 32 32½ 31½ 32   Delahoussaye E B 122  *1.60 92-12 Icy Tactics116½ Moon Dream1161½ San Berdou1222½          Always close 11
26May93-2Hol fst 6f   :214 :45  :571 1:101 3+ Md 40000   70 3 3 2hd 2½ 21½ 34¾  Black C A      B 122   3.40 84-11 Madeira Wine1152 Seattle Tudor1222¾ San Berdou1225          Weakened 7
21Apr93-3Hol fst 6½f  :22  :444 1:094 1:16 3+ Md 45000   80 3 3 1½ 1½ 1½ 22½    Black C A      B 120   2.50 86-11 Starlight Excess1202½ San Berdou120hd Seattle Tudor1155     Shown whip 9
17Mar93-6SA  fst 6½f  :22  :45  1:094 1:162   Md 40000   77 3 2 1hd 1hd 2½ 25   Black C A      B 120   5.80 84-15 Collirio1205 San Berdou120½ Centennial Axe1186½        Battle for 2nd 12
17Feb93-9SA  fst 6½f  :22  :444 1:10 1:17     Md 40000   42 2 1 11 11 11½ 615½  Black C A      B 119   9.10 71-14 Big Gate117½ Starlight Excess1181¼ Collirio119hd     Bolted midstretch 11
WORKOUTS: Nov 27 SA 5f fst 1:022 B 40/45  Nov 21 SA 4f fst :48 B 6/44  Oct 31 SA 5f fst 1:001 H 8/67  Oct 24 SA 4f fst :48 H 15/55  Oct 10 SA 5f fst 1:003 H 22/48  Sep 29 SA 6f fst 1:154 H 27/32
```

```
Burn and Turn                                  B. g. 5                                          Lifetime Record :  18 5 1 3   $39,735
Own: Campochiaro & Chema & Epstein             Sire: Tilt Up (Olden Times)                     1993   2 1 0 1   $7,300  Turf  0 0 0 0
                                               Dam: Blaze a Trail (Nantequos)                  1992  11 3 0 2  $19,885  Wet   0 0 0 0
                                               Br:  Mamakos James L (Ky)
PINCAY L JR (60 10 9 7 .17)          $16,000   Tr:  Mitchell Mike (22 3 9 2 .14)      L 117    Hol    9 4 0 1  $28,900  Dist 10 3 0 1  $17,750

27Nov93-9Hol fst 6f   :213 :443 :57  1:093 3+ Clm c-10000   90 8 10 76¾ 55¼ 21½ 12¾ Pincay L Jr  LB 117 fb  2.90 92-11 Burn And Turn1172¾ Lord Stevan1141¾ Knight Teller116nk            12
   Bumped hard, took up start; Claimed from Mamakos James L, Mamakos Jason Trainer
25Mar93-5SA  gd  6f   :212 :434 :56  1:09     Clm 12500     83 2 5 56½ 46½ 44½ 31½  Pincay L Jr  LB 117 b   5.10 91-11 Takeagiantstep115hd Zee Maestro1151½ Burn And Turn117hd  Up for 3rd 6
24Dec92-6Hol fst 6½f  :212 :441 1:092 1:16 3+ Clm 10000     72 5 6 54 33½ 55 67½    Pedroza M A  LB 118 b  *2.60 85-11 Slew Man Slew117½ No Doubles Match116½ Oh Dat Fox1162¼   Gave way 11
13Dec92-3Hol fst 7f   :222 :454 1:10 1:223 3+ Clm 16000     75 8 3 3½ 11½ 2½ 36½    Pedroza M A  LB 116 b  *1.70 84-13 Intercup1163½ Skylaunch1163 Burn And Turn116½          Steadied 3/8 8
 4Dec92-7Hol fst 6f   :214 :442 :563 1:091 3+ Alw 31000N1X  67 5 8 86¼ 78¾ 86¼ 78   Berrio O A   LB 117 b  13.60 86-09 Sharp Bandit1182¼ Father Six To Five1171¾ Won On Appeal116½          10
   Bumped start, carried out late
14Nov92-9Hol fst 6f   :22  :45  :57  1:092 3+ Clm 10000     98 12 3 42 1hd 11½ 16   Pincay L Jr  LB 117 b   4.50 93-11 Burn And Turn1176 Kelly G.118 Scorpio Twenty116      Wide, ridden out 12
16Oct92-6BM  fst 5f   :214 :453      :574 3+ Hcp 6250       79 7 5 33½ 54¾ 63¼ 31   Meza R Q     LB 113 b   6.70 94-17 BarryChancy1161 FantsticHope116hd BurnAndTurn113      Raced well wide 7
 4Oct92-5Fpx fst 6f   :22  :46  :584 1:113 3+ Clm 6250      73 7 7 41¼ 31 1hd 11½   Pedroza M A  LB 116 b   6.90 88-12 Burn And Turn1161½ Nino's Chance1161 Valid Remark116       Driving 10
24Sep92-6Fpx fst 6½f  :22  :453 1:112 1:174 3+ Clm 8000      61 5 4 21 21 53 77½    Lopez A D    LB 116 b   3.60 79-13 Northern Stevens1162 Rull Me In116 Nino's Chance116        Gave way 8
27Aug92-9Dmr fst 6f   :214 :442 :571 1:101 3+ Clm 10000     69 1 11 63¼ 55 74¾ 86¼  Lopez A D    LB 120 b  12.70 81-11 Early Returns116nk Going Easy1162¼ Redneck Ways116      Broke slowly 12
WORKOUTS: ●Nov 19 Hol 6f fst 1:13 H 1/20  Oct 27 Hol 5f fst 1:01 H 3/25  Oct 20 Hol 5f fst 1:012 H 4/18  Oct 13 Hol 4f fst :491 H 6/14  ●Oct 7 Hol 3f fst :351 H 1/11  Oct 1 Hol 3f fst :35 H 2/5
```

```
Cool Chili (GB)                                Gr. g. 5                                         Lifetime Record :  42 9 9 6  $164,064
Own: Tarheel Stable                            Sire: Formidable (Forli)                        1993  14 4 4 2  $44,885  Turf 15 1 2 2  $26,601
                                               Dam: Chili Girl (Skymaster)                     1992  14 4 2 2  $93,628  Wet   2 0 1 0   $6,200
                                               Br:  Heinz Mrs H J III (GB)
BLACK C A (50 8 8 6 .16)             $16,000   Tr:  Assinesi Paul D (4 1 3 0 .25)     L 122    Hol    3 0 2 0   $6,925  Dist 22 7 5 2 $112,730

14Nov93-4SA  fst 6½f  :214 :441 1:084 1:154 3+ Clm 16000    84 2 2 1hd 2hd 11 11¾   Black C A    LB 118 b   4.90 92-06 Cool Chili1181½ Dr. Augusta116hd Precise Cut117½         Inside duel 11
11Oct93-1SA  fst 6f   :221 :45  :57  1:093 3+ Clm c-16000  86 4 2 1½ 1hd 1hd 1nk   Sorenson D   LB 116 b [illegible] 89-11 Cool Chili116nk Sincerific116½ Dr. Augusta116½      Very game 7
   Claimed from Pattan Dick Van, Accrino John Trainer
26Sep93-7Fpx fst 6½f  :222 :453 1:094 1:161 3+ Clm 16000    90 4 1 1hd 1hd 1hd 2hd  Sorenson D   LB 116 b   2.70 95-09 Orthos116hd Cool Chili1165 Cove Way1161½                Game try 7
18Sep93-5Fpx fst 6f   :224 :46  :58  1:103 3+ Clm 16000     80 7 5 32½ 3½ 32 41½    Atkinson P   LB 116 b   4.60 92-09 Susan's Corsair116no Contented1111 Orthos116½          Outfinished 9
29Aug93-7Dmr fst 6½f  :222 :45  1:09 1:152 3+ Clm 16000     83 4 4 2½ 23 33½ 37     Flores D R   LB 117 b   5.90 87-11 El Toreo1173½ Dr. Hyde1143½ Cool Chili1172           Bumped start 8
 1Aug93-2Dmr fst 6f   :22  :45  :573 1:10 3+ Clm 16000      81 1 3 21 21½ 3½ 33¼    Gonzalez S5  LB 110 b   9.30 88-05 Fistylee115½ Ocean Native1152¼ Cool Chili110hd          Weakened 9
20Jun93-9GG  fst 6f   :213 :434 :582 1:092    Clm 16000     84 7 2 21 2hd 1hd 21    Meza R Q     LB 117 b   3.60 92-06 Desert Victor1191 Cool Chili117½ Timely Encore117nk                8
   Drifted in early stages
14May93-1Hol fst 6f   :22  :45  :57  1:093    Clm 16000     78 1 6 1hd 2½ 31 45¾    Sorenson D   LB 117 b  10.00 86-10 Screen Tale1172¾ Racer Rex1173 Machote117no            Inside duel 7
23Apr93-2Hol fst 6f   :214 :442 :57  1:10     Clm c-12500   83 7 1 3½ 3½ 21½ 21¾    Sorenson D   LB 117 b   2.20 88-12 Ebonair1171¾ Cool Chili1172 El Toreo110no             Good effort 8
   Claimed from Smith Nannette, Monteleone Frank J Trainer
 7Apr93-1SA  fst 6f   :214 :444 :57  1:101    Clm c-10000   89 1 3 1hd 1hd 12½ 12   Sorenson D   LB 119 b   2.50 86-14 Cool Chili1192 Classic Case1162 Power Slyde1151¼             Driving 8
   Claimed from Dye Gil V Jr, Harte Michael G Trainer
WORKOUTS: Nov 27 SA 3f fst :373 H 15/17  Nov 5 SA 5f fst 1:05 H 92/93  Oct 25 SA 4f fst :502 H 44/47  Sep 13 SA 4f fst :50 H 9/19
```

ALL-IN-ONE's output for the race is as follows:

```
4DEC93                                HOL                      6 furlongs dirt
Race #9                                                              9 starters
C16,000                                                   Age: 3+years, Male
----------------------------------INPUT DATA----------------------------------

                     #   #   #   #   $'S                        1st C   2nd C   Final
Horse name           ST  W   P   S   Earned Date     Trk Dist. S time    time    time
-------------------------------------------------------------------------------------
BARAONET             14  2   2   0   38522 14NOV93  SA  6.500 D  21.4    44.1    115.4
HE'S LIKE THE WIND    9  0   2   2   14820 19SEP92  FPX 6.000 D  21.3    44.4    109.4
SAN BERDOU           10  1   4   2   29325 7NOV93   SA  6.000 D  21.2    44.1    109.0
BURN AND TURN        13  4   0   3   27185 27NOV93  HOL 6.000 D  21.3    44.3    109.3
COOL CHILI-GB        14  4   4   2   44885 14NOV93  SA  6.000 D  22.1    45.0    109.3


                                  1st C   2nd C   Final
Horse name           Class Lvl    B.L.    B.L.    B.L.     SR    Var
--------------------------------------------------------------------
BARAONET             C16,000      0.10    0.00    2.75     89    6.0
HE'S LIKE THE WIND   C16,000      6.00    7.00    4.00     93   11.0
SAN BERDOU           C25,000      0.10    0.10    6.75     85   11.0
BURN AND TURN        C10,000      6.75    5.25    0.00     92   11.0
COOL CHILI-GB        C16,000      0.00    0.00    0.00     89   11.0


---------------------------------BETTING LINE---------------------------------

                    -------Rankings--------         Betting    Fair     Fair
Horse name          PEH  H-I  THAAI  P-H  ESP  Rating   Line    Place $  Show $
-------------------------------------------------------------------------------
BARAONET             3    1     1     4    1    77.75    7-2
SAN BERDOU           1    3     3     3    2    75.00    4-1
COOL CHILI-GB        2    4     2     1    3    73.05    5-1
BURN AND TURN        4    2     4     2    4    71.83    5-1
HE'S LIKE THE WIND   5    5     5     5    5    62.22
```

```
--------------------------------EXACTA GRID-------------------------------
          |   BARAONET   |  SAN BERDOU  | COOL CHILI-GB | BURN AND TURN |
----------+--------------+--------------+---------------+---------------+
BARAONET  | . . . . . .  |   31    78   |   36    89    |   39    98    |
          | . . . . . .  |              |               |               |
          | . . . . . .  |              |               |               |
----------+--------------+--------------+---------------+---------------+
SAN BERDOU|   33    82   | . . . . . .  |   44   110    |   49   121    |
          |              | . . . . . .  |               |               |
          |              | . . . . . .  |               |               |
----------+--------------+--------------+---------------+---------------+
COOL CHILI-GB| 39    96  |   46   113   | . . . . . .   |   57   143    |
          |              |              | . . . . . .   |               |
          |              |              | . . . . . .   |               |
----------+--------------+--------------+---------------+---------------+
BURN AND TURN| 43   108  |   51   127   |   58   145    | . . . . . .   |
          |              |              |               | . . . . . .   |
          |              |              |               | . . . . . .   |
----------+--------------+--------------+---------------+---------------+
```

```
4DEC93                         HOL                     6 furlongs dirt
Race #9                                                     9 starters
C16,000                                           Age: 3+years, Male
---------------------------SPEED/PACE SUMMARY-----------------------------

Race Type:      Chaos Race
Race Profile:   22.23   45.17  110.04   Winners' Pace Profile: EARLY
Ability Par:    68.10                   Pace Contention Point:  0.99 lengths

Projected Times:                     Ability Balance  Last  Proj Con-
                1st C   2nd C   Fin C   Time    Time   Frac  Pace tender
----------------------------------------------------------------------
BARAONET        21.99   44.50  110.57  67.01   68.03  26.07 FRONT  N
SAN BERDOU      21.80   44.57  110.85  67.33   68.27  26.29 FRONT  N
COOL CHILI-GB   22.59   45.35* 110.11  68.11   67.87  24.77 LATE   N
BURN AND TURN   22.76   45.51* 109.60  68.26   67.40  24.09 REAR   N
HE'S LIKE THE WIND 22.84 45.79* 109.85 68.75   67.63  24.06 REAR   N


---------------------------------PACE GRAPH-------------------------------
        Profile:            22.23            45.17           110.04
     Front Runner:          21.80            44.50           109.60
Horse name                    1C               2C                   F
BARAONET          --------------------X+ ----------------(X ------------X----+
SAN BERDOU        --------------------X  ----------------(X ------------X-----+
COOL CHILI-GB     --------------------X--+ ------------X--(+ -----------X--+
BURN AND TURN     -----------------X---+ ------------X---(+ ------------------X
HE'S LIKE THE WIND-----------X----+ ------------X----(+ ------------------X+
```

The public win odds on our contenders in this race were as follows:

Baraonet	15-1
San Berdou	6-1
Cool Chili	5-2
Burn And Turn	2-1

Burn And Turn is the favorite in this race, which shapes up as contentious. We cannot tolerate low-priced horses such as Cool Chili and Burn And Turn. Our focus should rightly be on Baraonet and San Berdou.

Our group estimate on the four contenders is 75.6 percent. The public's estimate is 82.4 percent. That leaves us with win bets on Baraonet and San Berdou. Our edge on Baraonet is 255 percent. On San Berdou it's 40 percent.

We obviously avoid place-and-show betting in this chaos race. As for the exacta, we could go any number of ways. The Mitchell Matrix wouldn't be a bad idea. It's likely that the three exactas with Baraonet on top and the exacta of San Berdou on top of Baraonet would represent the four highest-paying combinations.

Overlayed exactas would certainly key Baraonet and San Berdou top and bottom. And the quinellas involving these two with the other contenders should offer some value.

At public odds of 15-to-1, Baraonet, our top pick, makes an ideal key horse for our Key-Place-All trifecta. The place horses would include the other three horses that are 6-to-1 or less on our line. And the all horses would be the place horses, plus He's Like The Wind, that can run to within five lengths of the race par.

We also have the late daily double to consider. If we're risk-averse, we can play all the combinations involving the contenders that are 6-to-1 or less on our line for each race. A look ahead shows that we have four contenders in race 10. Hence, we'd be covering 16 combinations.

We might also choose a key horse in each half of the double and wheel it to all the contenders in the remaining half, eliminating the favorite-probable-favorite combination if it appears.

Or we could narrow our focus to the overlayed double combinations, demand our minimum edge and a premium for our guaranteed losing combinations, and bet the combinations that will still pay more than their fair price after these bonuses.

NINTH RACE

Hollywood

DECEMBER 4, 1993

6 FURLONGS. (1.08) CLAIMING. Purse $11,500. 3-year-olds and upward. Weights: 3-year-olds, 120 lbs. Older, 122 lbs. Non-winners of two races since October 4, allowed 3 lbs. A race since then, 5 lbs. Claiming price $16,000; if for $14,000, allowed 2 lbs. (Races when entered for $12,500 or less not considered.)

Value of Race: $11,500 Winner $6,325; second $2,300; third $1,725; fourth $863; fifth $287. Mutuel Pool $312,698.00 Exacta Pool $241,073.00 Trifecta Pool $245,322.00 Quinella Pool $34,456.00

Last Raced	Horse	M/Eqt. A.Wt	PP	St	¼	½	Str	Fin	Jockey	Cl'g Pr	Odds $1
13Oct93 3SA5	Wild Tech	LBbf 5 117	5	8	8	5¹	3¹	1¹½	Lopez A D	16000	6.90
19Sep92 6Fpx3	He's Like the Wind	LB 6 117	4	3	6hd	6hd	5¹	2¹	Delahoussaye E	16000	11.50
14Nov93 4SA2	Dr. Augusta	LBb 4 117	2	6	2hd	2¹	1hd	3¼	Nakatani C S	16000	4.40
18Nov93 7Hol6	Contented	LBb 6 117	1	5	1½	1¹½	2½	4nk	Gutierrez G R	16000	29.10
27Nov93 9Hol1	Burn and Turn	LBb 5 117	7	7	7½	7hd	6hd	5nk	Pincay L Jr	16000	2.30
7Nov93 1SA5	San Berdou	B 4 117	6	2	4½	4½	4¹½	6¼	Stevens G L	16000	6.10
14Nov93 4SA1	Cool Chili-GB	LBb 5 122	8	1	5⁴	8	7⁴	7	Black C A	16000	2.80
14Nov93 4SA6	Baraonet	LBb 6 117	3	4	3¹	3hd	8	—	Valenzuela P A	16000	15.80

Baraonet: Pulled up

OFF AT 4:50 Start Good. Won driving. Time, :21⅘, :44⅕, :56⅖, 1:09⅕ Track fast.

$2 Mutuel Prices:				
	6–WILD TECH	15.80	8.80	4.80
	5–HE'S LIKE THE WIND		14.60	7.20
	3–DR. AUGUSTA			4.20

$2 EXACTA 6–5 PAID $180.00 $2 TRIFECTA 6–5–3 PAID $1,086.20 $2 QUINELLA 5–6 PAID $103.00

$3 Triple 7–5–6 Paid $451.80 $2 Pick Six (1–2–1,6–7–5–6) 6 Correct 51 Tickets Paid $1,824.60 5 Correct 1105 Tickets Paid $84.20 $1 Place Pick 9 — 7 tickets with 9 Paid $4,581.70 P9 No.(1,5—1,6,8—1,3—1,2—2,4—1,6,7—6,7—5,8—5, 6) Triple Pool $105,153.00 Pick Six Pool $232,889.00 Place Pick Nine Pool $40,130.00

A non-contender wins. There go our win bets. So do our exactas, quinellas, trifectas, daily doubles, and Pick-3s, for that matter. Wild Tech is nowhere to be found on our line. We haven't included him in any of our bets for this race or in the double.

Hollywood Park

10

5½ Furlongs. **(Turf). (1:01) ALLOWANCE. Purse $30,000. 3-year-olds and upward which have never won two races. Weights: 3-year-olds, 119 lbs. Older, 121 lbs. Non-winners of a race other than claiming, allowed 3 lbs.**

Pricelessly
Own: Harbor View Farm
SOLIS A (67 9 12 12 .13)

B. c. 3 (Mar)
Sire: Affirmed (Exclusive Native)
Dam: La Confidence (Nijinsky II)
Br: Harbor View Farm (Ky)
Tr: Whittingham Charles (13 4 1 1 .31)

L 119

Lifetime Record: 4 1 0 1 $21,150
1993 2 1 0 0 $16,500 | Turf 1 0 0 0
1992 2 M 0 1 $4,650 | Wet 0 0 0 0
Hol Ⓣ 1 0 0 0 | Dist Ⓣ 1 0 0 0

7May93-8Hol fm 5½f Ⓣ :212 :44 :554 1:022 Tsnmi Siew H50k 69 3 8 8⁵½ 10¹¹ 10⁹ 10⁸¾ McCarron C J LB 115 b 12.20 84–07 Silver Picea116½ Dale's Best116nk D'hallevant116½ Steadied 3/8 11
31Jan93-6SA fst 1 :23 :47 1:113 1:371 Md Sp Wt 87 8 3 3¹½ 1hd 1½ 1⁴ McCarron C J B 117 b 4.20 84–17 Pricelessly1174 Hapsburg1172 Big Way1171¾ Ridden out 8
27Dec92-6SA fst 1 :23 :471 1:12 1:371 Md Sp Wt 71 2 4 4²½ 3²½ 3³½ 3⁴¾ McCarron C J B 117 5.60 76–13 ArtOfLiving1174 Pleasedontexplin117¾ Pricelessly117nk Not enough late 8
6Dec92-6Hol fst 6f :213 :443 :572 1:103 Md Sp Wt 61 7 11 12¹⁷ 12¹⁴ 12⁷ 8⁸ McCarron C J B 118 9.20 79–11 D'hallevant1183 Real Hit118hd Whosthepurplecomet1182 Outrun 12

WORKOUTS: Nov 22 Hol 7f fst 1:262 H 1/1 Nov 17 Hol 7f fst 1:263 H 1/1 Nov 12 SA 6f gd 1:194 H 32/32 Nov 7 SA 6f fst 1:163 H 20/22 Nov 1 SA 6f fst 1:134 H 8/26 Oct 27 SA 5f fst 1:012 H 27/49

Known Approach
Own: Kirkwood Al & Sandee
STEVENS G L (36 4 10 5 .11)

Dk. B c. 3 (Apr)
Sire: Known Fact (In Reality)
Dam: Low Approach (Artaius)
Br: Anthoney Warrender (Ky)
Tr: Puhich Michael (4 0 0 2 .00)

119

Lifetime Record: 5 1 2 0 $9,291
1993 1 0 0 0 | Turf 4 1 1 0 $7,795
1992 4 1 2 0 $9,291 | Wet 0 0 0 0
Hol Ⓣ 0 0 0 0 | Dist Ⓣ 0 0 0 0

15Nov93-8SA fm *6½f Ⓣ :222 :443 1:08 1:142 3↑ Alw 32000N1X 61 1 7 3½ 5⁴¼ 7⁸½ 7¹¹ Flores D R B 119 8.80 75–14 Giant Asset119hd Duke Dust116hd Barton116hd Steadied down hill 7
27Aug92 ♦ Lingfield(GB) fst 1 LH 1:404 Alw 7600 Cranleigh Stakes 2¹½ Quinn T 130 *1.00 Foolish Heart125 1½ Known Approach1308 Balustrade Boy1234 8
Tr: Paul Cole — *Tracked pacesetting winner, pushed along 3f out, no match*
30Jly92 ♦ Goodwood(GB) gd 7f ⓉRH 1:26 Stk 59600 Lanson Champagne Vintage Stks-G3 9⁹¼ Quinn T 123 12.00 Maroof123 1½ Humam1261 Shebl123nk 10
Pushed along to track leaders, 4th 2-1/2f out, quickly weakened
10Jly92 ♦ Chester(GB) gd *7f ⓉLH 1:29 Alw 12600 Cardinal Puff Graduation Stks 2¹ Quinn T 130 *1.75 Marillette1251 Known Approach130 1½ Totally Unique1233 5
Tracked leading pair, pushed along turn 2-1/2f out, finished well
24Jun92 ♦ Salisbury(GB) fm *7f ⓉStr 1:282 Maiden 7300 EBF Southampton Maiden Stakes 1² Quinn T 126 *.70 Known Approach1262 Woodhaunter1266 Sharro126no 6
Chased leader, led after 3f, ridden out

WORKOUTS: Nov 25 SA 3f fst :362 H 8/16 Nov 8 SA 6f fst 1:134 H 11/22 Nov 3 SA 5f fst 1:024 H (d)33/38 Oct 27 SA 6f fst 1:15 H 13/17 Oct 21 SA 5f fst 1:00 Hg8/49 Oct 13 SA 5f fst 1:004 H 13/40

Irish Adventurer
Own: Anson & Augustmoon Farm & Sloan
GRYDER A T (46 9 5 6 .20)

Dk. b or br c. 4
Sire: Irish River (Riverman)
Dam: Fast Trick (Northfields)
Br: Delahaye Jeanna (Ky)
Tr: Hess R B Jr (13 3 2 1 .23)

L 121

Lifetime Record: 16 1 4 4 $63,064
1993 2 0 1 0 $7,200 | Turf 16 1 4 4 $63,064
1992 12 1 2 4 $51,115 | Wet 0 0 0 0
Hol Ⓣ 2 0 1 1 $12,150 | Dist Ⓣ 0 0 0 0

14Mar93-7SA fm *6½f Ⓣ :214 :44 1:071 1:133 Alw 36000N2X 82 6 7 8⁶½ 8⁸ 5⁸ 6⁶½ Desormeaux K J LB 115 4.20 84–10 Sinag117¾ Monarch's Pride115 1½ Bahatur1192 4 Wide stretch 9
6Feb93-7SA fm *6½f Ⓣ :212 :443 1:081 1:143 Alw 36000N2X 91 3 6 6⁶ 6⁵¾ 3¹ 3¹¾ Stevens G L LB 115 b 3.50 83–15 Auriga114 1½ ⒹGreat117½ Irish Adventurer115nk 8
Took up, impeded 1/16; Placed second through disqualification.
27Dec92-7SA fm 1⅛ Ⓣ :47 1:112 1:362 1:492 3↑ Alw 37000N2L 83 7 2 2½ 1hd 1hd 3²½ Stevens G L LB 118 b 2.60 69–28 Royal Upset118¾ Seth121 1¾ ⒹIrish Adventurer118hd 8
Bumped, impeded foe drive; Disqualified and placed 4th
6Dec92-5Hol fm 1⅛ Ⓣ :481 1:122 1:364 1:492 3↑ Alw 37000N2X 87 5 4 3³ 3¹½ 3¹ 3³½ Desormeaux K J LB 115 b 4.10 73–21 Desert Sun116 3½ Misty Valley115hd Irish Adventurer115 1¼ 10
Hard to settled 1st 1/2
13Nov92-8Hol fm 1⅛ Ⓣ :472 1:111 1:36 1:492 3↑ Alw 33000 86 1 2 2¹ 1hd 1hd 2½ Desormeaux K J LB 118 *.40e 76–24 Eddie Valient115½ Irish Adventurer118 Saveneli115 A bit rank early 8
23Oct92-8SA fm 1 Ⓣ :234 :481 1:123 1:363 3↑ Alw 36000 87 7 6 6⁴½ 6²½ 6⁴ 5³½ Delahoussaye E LB 116 4.10 77–20 Fax News112hd Southern Wish115 1¾ Mojave Gold115 7
Hopped start, boxed in far turn
8Sep92 ♦ Longchamp(Fr) gd *1⅜ Ⓣ 2:061 PrixSainteCroixHcp 5¹½ Jeanpierre N 123 9.50 Voglio129nk April Shower121 1½ Premonitor122 Prom,led 18
9Aug92 ♦ Deauville(Fr) yl *1¼ Ⓣ 2:141 Pr Casino deDeauvilleHcp 10⁷½ Jeanpierre N 122 b *3.25 Bella Mimosa118½ Hatch Princess115¾ Raider119 Led to str 17
14Jly92 ♦ StCloud(Fr) gd *1⅜ Ⓣ 2:123 Prix de Lizy Hcp 3nk Jeanpierre N 120 b 5.25 Seattle Savour130nk Voglio124hd Irish Adve120 Game fin 18
27Jun92 ♦ Longchamp(Fr) gd *1⅜ Ⓣ 2:184 PrixGrandeDameHcp 3¹ Jeanpierre N 122 b 4.00 Seattle Savour126no Extreme Dream1241 Irish Adve122 Led 10f 16

WORKOUTS: Dec 1 Hol 3f fst :364 H 13/27 Nov 26 Hol 6f fst 1:12 H 2/23 Nov 18 Hol 5f fst 1:001 H 5/38 Nov 10 Hol 5f fst 1:01 H 11/24 Nov 3 Hol 4f fst :481 H 5/16 Oct 27 Hol 4f fst :513 H 14/15

Lady of the Opera

Own: Bleomer Robert L
GONZALEZ S JR (45 3 5 5 .07)
B. f. 3 (Mar)
Sire: The Minstrel (Northern Dancer)
Dam: Bodecia (Green Dancer)
Br: Sterlingbrook Farm & Elfie Ninneman (NJ)
Tr: Cross Richard J (3 0 0 1 .00)
108⁵

Lifetime Record :	6 1 1 0	$12,945			
1993	6 1 1 0	$12,945	Turf	1 0 0 0	
1992	0 M 0 0		Wet	0 0 0 0	
Hol ⓣ	1 0 0 0		Dist ⓣ	1 0 0 0	

12Nov93- 4SA fst 6f :214 :451 :574 1:11 3↑ ⒻMd 32000 70 1 5 2hd 1½ 12½ 13 Valenzuela P A B 118 9.70 82-16 Lady Of The Opera1183 Never Quicker118½ Miss Fort Worth120nk Driving 8
7Oct93- 9SA fst 1 1/16 :223 :462 1:113 1:441 3↑ ⒻMd 32000 56 7 5 31½ 61¾ 58 512¼ Lopez A D B 117 22.40 71-16 Ms. Jiles1171¾ Uncanny Ann119½ Charlierusse1172¼ Gave way 11
17Sep93- 5Fpx fst 6½f :214 :461 1:122 1:19 3↑ ⒻMd 32000 49 6 1 21½ 32 43 25 Lopez A D B 116 8.60 76-13 Queenly1165 Lady Of The Opera116½ Rullababy111½ Steadied 1/8 9
27Aug93- 9Dmr fst 6½f :214 :444 1:104 1:174 3↑ ⒻMd 32000 46 12 1 62¾ 62½ 107½ 88¾ Flores D R B 117 47.10 73-11 Treva1172¼ Watercolourtwo115½ Native Ridge117hd Very wide trip 12
25Jly93- 6Hol fm 5½f ⓣ :221 :451 :562 1:024 3↑ ⒻMd Sp Wt 46 10 1 41¾ 41¼ 78 714 Flores D R B 116 51.40 77-09 Malojen1162¼ Catch1174 Amity Ar1212¼ Wide trip 10
16Jly93- 2Hol fst 6f :221 :46 :584 1:114 3↑ ⒻMd 32000 37 6 9 99¼ 84¾ 74¾ 511¼ Ishibashi M B 117 75.20 70-13 Phoenician Miss117½ Shining Ryder1174¼ AlmostIce1152¾ Ducked in start 9
WORKOUTS: Nov 29 SA 5f fst :593 H 2/31 Nov 22 SA 3f fst :35 H 2/19 Nov 5 SA 5f fst 1:022 H 61/93 Oct 28 SA 3f fst :371 H 8/13 Oct 22 SA 5f fst 1:001 H 6/37 Oct 16 SA 3f fst :363 H 3/10

Duane

Own: Paulson Allen E
PINCAY L JR (60 10 9 7 .17)
Ch. c. 3 (Apr)
Sire: Naskra (Nasram)
Dam: Wood Elf (Syncopate)
Br: Allen E. Paulson (Ky)
Tr: Shoemaker Bill (7 1 0 0 .14)
119

Lifetime Record :	4 1 0 1	$20,325			
1993	3 1 0 0	$16,125	Turf	0 0 0 0	
1992	1 M 0 1	$4,200	Wet	1 0 0 0	$730
Hol ⓣ	0 0 0 0		Dist ⓣ	0 0 0 0	

6Mar93- 2SA fst 1 :22 :452 1:104 1:362 Alw 36000N1X 15 4 4 43 810 921 940½ Valenzuela P A B 117 8.50 48-13 Gavel Gate1178 Lucky's First One117hd Zignew117no Not urged late 9
30Jan93- 6SA fst 5½f :213 :45 :573 1:042 Md Sp Wt 76 9 7 64¼ 51¾ 41¾ 1¾ Pincay L Jr B 118 5.40 88-11 Duane118¾ Sir Hutch118¾ Lucky Navajo118no Wide trip 11
17Jan93- 4SA sly 6f :214 :453 :584 1:123 Md Sp Wt 53 3 3 3½ 43¾ 55 56 Stevens G L B 118 *.60 68-19 Rio De La Plata1182¼ Believe Anything118½ Niner Bush1181¼ Steadied 1/2 6
19Dec92- 4Hol fst 6f :221 :451 :573 1:102 Md Sp Wt 69 5 4 53 52¾ 44 33¾ Walls M K B 118 4.70 84-10 Personal Hope1183¼ Ballet Aly118nk Duane118no 4 Wide stretch 8
WORKOUTS: Dec 1 Hol 4f fst :464 H 3/38 Nov 26 Hol 6f fst 1:143 H 10/23 Nov 20 Hol 6f fst 1:144 H 17/24 Nov 12 SA 5f gd 1:02 H 18/53 Nov 5 SA 5f fst 1:004 H 16/93 Oct 31 SA 3f fst :364 B 14/23

Bettor Every Day

Own: Fallowfield Ranch
BLACK C A (50 8 8 6 .16)
B. g. 3 (Feb)
Sire: Big Leaguer (Bold Bidder)
Dam: Eastern Bettor (Out of the East)
Br: Hanson Stock Farm (Cal)
Tr: Aiello Leeanne (2 1 0 0 .50)
116

Lifetime Record :	5 1 0 1	$14,520		
1993	2 0 0 0	$2,470	Turf	0 0 0 0
1992	3 1 0 1	$12,050	Wet	0 0 0 0
Hol ⓣ	0 0 0 0		Dist ⓣ	0 0 0 0

30Oct93- 1SA fst 6f :211 :441 :562 1:092 Clm 40000 83 7 4 43½ 43¼ 63¾ 53¼ Delahoussaye E B 116 b 5.40 87-12 Westcot1181 Western Scout1111½ Starlifter116¼ Mild bid 7
28Sep93-11Fpx fst 6f :22 :452 :582 1:11 Clm 25000 79 5 8 810 75 43 4nk Black C A B 116 b 5.30 92-09 Choices119no Sir Taikow116hd Sugar Syrup116no Stumbled badly start 8
16Jly92- 6Hol fst 5f :221 :453 :574 ⓈMd 32000 71 2 4 31½ 31 21 2no Pincay L Jr B 117 b 6.50 93-07 ⒹNever Cancelled117no Bettor Every Day1179 Pencil's Dream117 10
Placed first through disqualification
29Jun92- 4Hol fst 5½f :221 :461 :582 1:043 ⓈMd 40000 60 4 6 31½ 31 43½ 34¾ Pincay L Jr B 117 b 14.50 85-09 Just Sid1174¾ Quite By Chance117nk Bettor Every Day117 5-Wide stretch 10
11Jun92 4Hol fst 5f :22 :48 :584 Md 32000 45 4 7 65½ 54½ 65½ 66¼ Pincay L Jr B 117 b 42.90 82-13 Weyburn1171¾ Dale's Best117¾ Loville Slew117 5-wide stretch 10
WORKOUTS: Nov 29 Hol 5f fst 1:013 H 19/27 Nov 22 Hol 5f fst 1:002 H 8/31 Nov 16 Hol 5f fst 1:002 H 2/19 Oct 24 Hol 5f fst :591 H 2/18 Oct 10 Hol 3f fst :382 H 8/13 ●Sep 24 Hol 5f fst 1:002 H 1/15

Camouflage Pirate

Own: Rowe & Ward
VALENZUELA P A (54 6 10 2 .11)
B. c. 3 (Feb)
Sire: Pirate's Bounty (Hoist the Flag)
Dam: Sun Charm (Solazo)
Br: Martin J. Wygod & James R. Buell (Cal)
Tr: Sadler John W (12 2 4 1 .17)
L 119

Lifetime Record :	9 1 2 3	$45,645		
1993	9 1 2 3	$45,645	Turf	0 0 0 0
1992	0 M 0 0		Wet	0 0 0 0
Hol ⓣ	0 0 0 0		Dist ⓣ	0 0 0 0

24Oct93- 5SA fst 6f :212 :441 :562 1:093 Clm 25000 85 7 1 11 12 12 2nk Valenzuela P A LB 117 *2.30 89-12 Azul YBlanca116nk CamouflagePirate117½ HolidayPoint116no Caught late 10
2Oct93- 8Fpx fst 6½f :214 :452 1:094 1:161 3↑ Alw 36000N1X 67 2 5 44½ 33 35½ 610¾ Flores D R LB 114 5.30 84-09 Quotion1146 Rubin's Champion1143 Video Alert1131 Knocked off stride 8
3Sep93- 7Dmr fst 6f :213 :442 :563 1:092 3↑ ⓈAlw 33000N1X 77 5 4 1hd 1½ 31½ 57¼ Flores D R LB 118 3.00 85-09 Outlawed119½ Doc Mccoy1192¼ Ke Express1172¼ Gave way 7
18Aug93- 8Dmr fst 7f :22 :444 1:094 1:23 ⓈReal Gd Deal60k 84 9 2 11½ 11½ 1hd 32 Flores D R LB 115 9.70 83-14 CantuaCreek115¾ TownCaper1151½ CamouflgePirte1152¾ Weakened a bit 9
2May93- 7Hol fst 7f :221 :444 1:091 1:221 3↑ ⓈAlw 36000N1X 62 1 2 11 1½ 21½ 99½ Desormeaux K J B 116 *2.40 84-08 Careening For Paul114hd Rubin'sChampion1131¾ Triumphal'sBounty116¾ 11
Lugged out badly, unmanageable lane
4Apr93- 3SA fst 6½f :221 :45 1:09 1:152 Alw 33000N2L 83 1 1 11½ 11½ 2hd 25 Valenzuela P A B 120 2.90 89-11 Chayim1205 Camouflage Pirate1201¼ Demigod1205 Held 2nd 5
12Mar93 7SA fst 6½f :214 :443 1:101 1:171 Alw 33000N2L 78 6 1 1hd 1hd 1hd 31 Flores D R B 120 4.30 84-17 Boyo120hd Real Hit120¾ Camouflage Pirate1201¼ Good effort 8
6Feb93- 4SA fst 6½f :22 :451 1:094 1:163 ⓈMd Sp Wt 85 7 1 11 1½ 11½ 13 Valenzuela P A B 118 2.70 88-11 Camouflage Pirate1183 Be Sum Interco1182 Westcot1181¾ All out 8
23Jan93- 5SA fst 6f :214 :444 :57 1:092 ⓈMd Sp Wt 78 1 4 2½ 21 32 38¾ Solis A B 118 4.40 81-15 All Slewped Up1187 Westcot1181¾ Camouflage Pirate1181 Weakened 10
WORKOUTS: Nov 30 Hol 5f fst :593 H 4/8 Nov 26 Hol 4f fst :493 H 25/35 ●Nov 18 Hol 6f fst 1:13 H 1/10 Nov 12 SA 5f gd 1:003 H 3/53 Nov 5 SA 4f fst :484 H 36/88 Oct 19 SA 3f fst :362 H 9/18

Bold And Lacey

Own: Sides Clay R & Robert C
VALENZUELA F H (49 8 3 3 .16)
B. c. 3 (Jun)
Sire: Bold Badgett (Damascus)
Dam: Wyola Lace (Ace of Aces)
Br: Ullmann Larry & Sheila (Cal)
Tr: Sides Robert C (2 0 0 0 .00)
L 119

Lifetime Record :	12 1 0 2	$33,500			
1993	6 1 0 1	$26,550	Turf	0 0 0 0	
1992	6 M 0 1	$6,950	Wet	2 1 0 0	$20,950
Hol ⓣ	0 0 0 0		Dist ⓣ	0 0 0 0	

13Nov93- 3SA fst 6f :22 :444 :563 1:084 3↑ ⓈAlw 32000N1X 82 3 2 31½ 21 22 34¼ Valenzuela F H LB 118 f 18.70 89-11 Special Task1182¼ Long Gone Jules1182 Bold And Lacey1183¼ No late bid 7
3Nov93- 3SA fst 6½f :221 :444 1:093 1:161 3↑ Alw 32000N1X 77 2 2 21 21 31½ 65¼ Valenzuela F H LB 118 f 54.60 84-14 Spartan Order110nk Nevada Range1182 Private Isle1161¼ Stumbled start 6
20Oct93- 8SA fst 6f :213 :441 :563 1:091 3↑ Alw 32000N1X 88 3 5 55 54½ 55½ 59¾ Valenzuela F H LB 118 f 79.00 82-13 Super Trax117nk Sir Hutch1182¾ Private Isle1161¾ Brief speed 6
10Feb93- 8SA fst 1 ⊗ :233 :474 1:121 1:364 Alw 39000N2X 56 7 1 1½ 2hd 56½ 616¼ Alvarado F T LB 117 31.90 69-17 Corby1175 Elkhart1172¼ The Real Vaslav115no Stopped 7
23Jan93- 3BM my 1 1/16 :232 :471 1:121 1:433 Cmno Rl Dby-G3 72 6 4 43 42 66 57¾ Alvarado F T LB 117 83.00 77-14 El Atroz1171 Offshore Pirate1173½ Lykatill Hil119nk Steadied upper str 9
7Jan93- 6SA sly 6½f :22 :452 1:104 1:173 ⓈMd Sp Wt 78 5 1 22½ 21½ 2hd 11 Alvarado F T LB 118 18.90 83-13 Bold And Lacey1181 Eldorado Pete1185 I'm Ruined1182 Brushed 1/16 8
24Dec92- 4Hol fst 7f :221 :45 1:091 1:214 ⓈMd Sp Wt 60 3 4 3½ 31 36½ 616 Alvarado F T LB 118 10.50 79-11 Glowing Crown1184½ Goldigger's Dream11810 Clever Wheatly118¾ 8
Bumped start, steadied a bit 1/4
13Dec92- 6Hol fst 7½f :223 :461 1:112 1:304 Md Sp Wt 58 4 5 1hd 1hd 42½ 45¾ Alvarado F T LB 119 5.10 75-13 Blazing Aura119¾ Respectable Rascal1191 Jaltipan1194 Weakened 9
28Nov92- 6Hol fst 7f :221 :45 1:093 1:222 Md Sp Wt 74 3 2 3½ 1hd 21 33 Alvarado F T LB 118 128.10 89-06 Brinkstone1182¾ Hapsburg118hd Bold And Lacey118no Inside speed 11
9Nov92- 6SA fst 6½f :213 :45 1:10 1:164 ⓈMd Sp Wt 61 8 7 1111 119¾ 811 513 Sorenson D LB 118 149.70 73-17 Powrofthnintys1185 GlowingCrown118 KingdomFound118 No mishap 12
WORKOUTS: Nov 29 SLR tr.t 5f fst 1:01 H 1/1 Oct 30 SLR tr.t 4f fst :481 H 3/11 Oct 14 SLR tr.t 6f fst 1:163 H 1/1 Oct 7 SLR tr.t 6f fst 1:13 Hg 1/3 Sep 30 SLR tr.t 6f fst 1:132 H 2/4 ●Sep 23 SLR tr.t 5f fst :593 H 1/5

Grand Millesime

Own: Loughran & Richie
LOPEZ A D (13 1 2 0 .08)
B. g. 4
Sire: Sovereign Dancer (Northern Dancer)
Dam: Guadery (Golden Act)
Br: Carrion Jaime S (Ky)
Tr: Hess R B Jr (13 3 2 1 .23)
L 121

Lifetime Record :	8 1 1 0	$26,993			
1992	5 0 1 0	$12,296	Turf	8 1 1 0	$26,993
1991	3 1 0 0	$14,697	Wet	0 0 0 0	
Hol ⓣ	0 0 0 0		Dist ⓣ	0 0 0 0	

5Nov92- 8SA fm 1 ⓣ :231 :464 1:11 1:351 3↑ Alw 32000 78 3 7 75 65½ 66½ 46¼ Delahoussaye E LB 116 b 4.90 80-13 Lissitki-Fr116½ PhiladelphiaDave1151½ BadBoyButch115 4-wide stretch 9
10Sep92- 8Dmr fm 1 1/16 ⓣ :241 :501 1:144 1:451 3↑ Alw 35000 80 2 3 41½ 53½ 43½ 43¼ Desormeaux K J LB 115 b *1.00 76-20 Plus Perfect119¾ Allawinir1222½ Duxster118 Not enough late 7
8Jly92 ♦ Longchamp(Fr) gd *1¼ ⓣRH 2:064 Alw 33500 52¼ Legrix E 123 b 10.00 Petit Loup123¼ Sakura Bering128hd Luazur128¾ 7
Tr: Pascal Bary Prix de Bougival *Led for 9 furlongs, outfinished*
6May92 ♦ Evry(Fr) gd *1⅛ ⓣLH 1:524 Stk 47500 65¼ Legrix E 121 b 6.50 Kitwood1212¼ Stormnight121½ Star Beam1211 6
Prix Matchem (Listed Race) *Tracked in 2nd, dueled for lead 4f out, weakened 2f out*
21Apr92 ♦ Saint-Cloud(Fr) gd *1⅝ ⓣLH 2:15 Alw 24500 21½ Legrix E 123 b 6.00 Shamawna1241½ Grand Millesime1232 Olanthe1232 8
Prix Rodosto *Led for 9-1/2f, no answer to winner, second best*
4Sep91 ♦ Evry(Fr) gd *1 ⓣLH 1:413 Stk 35578 63 Lequeux A 123 10.00 Mendocino123½ Tyramisou118nk Gold Dust121no 9
Prix Herod (Listed) *Trailed behind slow pace, mild late gain*
20Jly91 ♦ Evry(Fr) gd *7f ⓣLH 1:27 Alw 23400 1nk Lequeux A 128 2.90 Grand Millesime128nk Martial du Berlais128hd Daskiyawar1283 8
Prix Presidents Fosse *Rallied to lead 1-1/2f out, soon clear, just held*
19Jun91 ♦ Evry(Fr) yl *6f ⓣStr 1:153 Alw 23000 42¼ Jarnet T 123 2.70 Hundredfold1231 Mio Robertino1281 Martial du Berlais123nk 11
Prix Saint-Crespin *Raced in mid-pack, evenly late*
WORKOUTS: Dec 1 Hol 4f fst :481 Hg 8/38 Nov 18 Hol 7f fst 1:274 H 2/2 Nov 12 Hol 7f fst 1:273 H 5/7 Nov 5 Hol 7f fst 1:292 H 3/4 Oct 30 Hol 7f fst 1:291 H 4/5 Oct 24 Hol 6f fst 1:144 H 5/9

Canaska Star (GB)
Own: Sifton June M

DELAHOUSSAYE E (27 2 1 3 .07)

B. c. 3 (Apr)
Sire: Doyoun (Mill Reef)
Dam: North Telstar (Sallust)
Br: M L Page (GB)
Tr: Russell John W (3 1 0 1 .33)

119

Lifetime Record:	13 1 3 1	$68,958			
1993	7 1 0 1	$7,556	Turf	13 1 3 1	$68,958
1992	6 M 3 0	$61,402	Wet	0 0 0 0	
Hol①	0 0 0 0		Dist①	0 0 0 0	

17Oct93-8WO sf 1½ ① :48¹ 1:13⁴ 2:10 2:36² 3+ Rothmn Int-G1C — 4 2 11⁵⁰ 11³⁰ 11⁵¹ Walls M K 119 54.20 — 51 Husband119⁵ Cozzene's Prince126½ Regency119³ 11
Broke slowly, press outside early, faded badly

31Aug93-Epsom(GB) gd 7f ①LH 1:22¹ 3+ Maiden 8300 1² Quinn T 126 *1.25 Canaska Star126² Resist The Force126½ Frinedly Brave126³ 6
Sherwood Maiden Stakes — Led after first 16th, soon well clear, roused over 1f out, driving

19Jun93-Ascot(GB) sf 1 ①RH 1:45⁴ Maiden 24100 3⁴ Munro A 126 5.00 Western Cape126²¼ Tochar Ban121½ Canaska Star126⁸ 5
Tr: Paul Kelleway — Southern Comfort Maiden Stakes — Chased leader, led halfway, headed 1-1/2f out, faded

2Jun93-Epsom(GB) gd *1½ ①LH 2:34³ Stk 1219000 14²⁸½ Munro A 126 200.00 Commander In Chief126³¼ Blue Judge126½ Blues Traveller126³ 16
Epsom Derby-G1 — Always towards rear

18May93-Goodwood(GB) gd 1¼ ①RH 2:13¹ Stk 51700 5²¾ Quinn T 124 b 33.00 Geisway124ⁿᵒ Beneficial127² Visto Si Stampi124½ 6
Predominate Stakes (Listed) — Reserved in 6th, mild progress 2f out, one-paced final furlong

1May93-Newmarket(GB) gd gd ①RH 1:13 Maiden 10400 6³½ Eddery Pat 126 *1.75 Big Sky126½ Putout121½ Robleu119ⁿᵒ 9
Chippenham Maiden Stakes — Away slowly, bid over 1f out, lacked room, angled right, unlucky

15Apr93-Newmarket(GB) gd 1 ①Str 1:37⁴ Stk 71300 9⁹¼ Dettori L 121 25.00 Emperor Jones121ⁿᵒ Wharf124½ Ventiquattrofogli121ⁿᵒ 9
Craven Stakes-G3 — Sluggish start, pushed along to keep pace halfway, faded

30Oct92-Longchamp(Fr) sf *1 ①RH 1:46⁴ Stk 428000 7¹⁰½ Kinane M J 123 42.00 Tenby123²¾ Blush Rambler123ⁿᵈ Basim123²¼ 11
Grand Criterium-G1 — Slowly into stride, trailed halfway, beaten 2f out. Kingmambo 5th

13Sep92-Longchamp(Fr) gd *7f ①RH 1:23¹ Stk 172000 4⁵ Cauthen S 123 11.20 Zafonic123³ Kingmambo123½ Splendent123½ 6
Prix de la Salamandre-G1 — One-paced throughout, never a factor

29Jly92-Goodwood(GB) gd 6f ①Str 1:11¹ Stk 164000 2¹ Eddery Pat 123 2.50 Son Pardo123¹ Canaska Star123¼ Green's Bid123² 6
Richmond Stakes-G2 — Steadied start, bid for lead halfway, outfinished

WORKOUTS: Nov 27 SA 7f fst 1:26 H 4/8 Nov 22 SA 6f fst 1:19⁴ H 18/18 Nov 16 SA 7f fst 1:31¹ H 5/5 .Nov 8 SA 6f fst 1:14³ H 13/22 Oct 16 WO ① 4f fm :47³ B (d) 1/3 Oct 15 WO ① 5f fm 1:07¹ B (d) 1/1

ALL-IN-ONE's output for the race is as follows:

```
4DEC93                          HOL              5.5 furlongs turf
Race #10                                          11 starters
NW1                                          Age: 3+years, Male
```

-----INPUT DATA-----

Horse name	# ST	# W	# P	# S	$'s Earned	Date	Trk	Dist.	S	1st C time	2nd C time	Final time
PRICELESSLY	4	1	0	1	21150	7MAY93	HOL	5.500	T	21.2	44.0	102.2
DUANE	4	1	0	1	20325	6MAR93	SA	5.500	D	21.3	45.0	104.2
CAMOUFLAGE PIRATE	9	1	2	3	45645	24OCT93	SA	6.000	D	22.3	44.1	109.3
BOLD AND LACEY	6	1	0	1	26550	13NOV93	SA	6.000	D	22.0	44.4	108.4
GRAND MILLESIME	5	0	1	0	12296	5NOV92	SA	8.000	T	46.4	111.0	135.1

Horse name	Class Lvl	1st C B.L.	2nd C B.L.	Final B.L.	SR	Var
PRICELESSLY	STAKES	5.25	11.50	8.75	84	7.0
DUANE	MSW	4.25	1.75	0.00	88	11.0
CAMOUFLAGE PIRATE	C25,000	0.00	0.00	0.20	89	12.0
BOLD AND LACEY	NW1	1.50	1.00	4.25	89	11.0
GRAND MILLESIME	NW1	5.00	5.50	6.50	80	13.0

-----BETTING LINE-----

Horse name	PEH	H-I	THAAI	P-H	ESP	Rating	Betting Line	Fair Place $	Fair Show $
DUANE	2	3	2	1	5	82.61	7-2		
GRAND MILLESIME	5	1	4	3	1	81.76	7-2		
CAMOUFLAGE PIRATE	1	2	1	2	3	76.14	5-1		
PRICELESSLY	3	4	3	5	2	73.09	6-1		
BOLD AND LACEY	4	5	5	4	4	69.52			

-----EXACTA GRID-----

	DUANE	GRAND MILLESIME	CAMOUFLAGE PIRA	PRICELESSLY
DUANE	. . . .	28 69	37 92	45 113
GRAND MILLESIM	28 70	. . . .	39 97	48 118

```
+------------+----------------+----------------+---------------+--------------+
| CAMOUFLAGE PIR|   40  100   |    42  104    | . . . . . . . |   69   171   |
|            |                |                | . . . . . . . |              |
+------------+----------------+----------------+---------------+--------------+
| PRICELESSLY|   51  127   |    53  132    |    71  177    | . . . . . . . |
|            |                |                |               | . . . . . . .|
|            |                |                |               | . . . . . . .|
+------------+----------------+----------------+---------------+--------------+
```

```
4DEC93                         HOL                      5.5 furlongs turf
Race #10                                                       11 starters
NW1                                              Age: 3+years, Male
------------------------------SPEED/PACE SUMMARY------------------------------

Race Type:       Orderly Race
Race Profile:    22.53   45.29   103.03   Winners' Pace Profile: MID
Ability Par:     40.28             Pace Contention Point:  5.05 lengths

Projected Times:                    Ability Balance   Last Proj  Con-
                 1st C  2nd C  Fin C   Time    Time    Frac Pace tender
---------------------------------------------------------------
DUANE            22.86  45.17  103.19  40.99  61.45  18.02  EARLY   Y
GRAND MILLESIME  22.66  45.48  102.84  40.02  61.00  17.37  MID     Y
CAMOUFLAGE PIRATE 22.16 44.98  103.55  40.73  61.86  18.57  FRONT   N
PRICELESSLY      22.29  45.99  103.92  40.23  62.06  17.94  REAR    N
BOLD AND LACEY   23.03  45.76  103.48  40.75  61.65  17.72  LATE    N


----------------------------PACE GRAPH----------------------------

        Profile:              22.53            45.29              103.03
   Front Runner:              22.16            44.98              102.84
Horse name                      1C               2C                     F
DUANE             ------------------X--+ ------------(----X+ ----------------X-+
GRAND MILLESIME   ----------------X-+ ------------(---X+ ----------------X
CAMOUFLAGE PIRATE ------------------X ------------(-----X ----------------X---+
PRICELESSLY       ----------------X+ ------------(X----+ ------------X---+
BOLD AND LACEY    ------------X---+ ------------(-X---+ ----------------X-+
```

Here are the public win odds for our contenders in this race:

Duane	7-2
Grand Millesime	35-1
Camouflage Pirate	8-5
Pricelessly	18-1

We must approach this race with caution. *ALL-IN-ONE* does a wonderful job assessing the win probability of horses that have already run and proved themselves under conditions like those of today's race. The field for this race includes Pricelessly, whose turf ability will be measured off his lone turf start, which was dismal. The race also includes Canaska's Star, whose only start in North America was a horrible effort at a mile-and-a-half over soft turf and whose ability to win this race also will be questioned by *ALL-IN-ONE*. In addition, four horses in this field have never even raced on dirt.

Here we must weigh *ALL-IN-ONE*'s line against a valid handicapping argument: A horse's previous dirt performance has absolutely no bearing on how well that horse will perform in its first start on turf. Breeding (specifically, the horse's sire) is the major factor in predicting how well the horse will run in its first on turf. If a horse runs outstanding races on dirt, it's usually a bad idea to assume he'll transfer that stellar form to the turf in his grass debut.

For example, Duane is listed at 7-to-2 on our line. This line is based on one of Duane's good dirt races. It would be unwise to expect that he'll be able to duplicate that dirt race for today's turf race unless he also shows positive turf breeding.

That's not to say you can't make an accurate line on the race. You can. But that line must take into account all the factors that your computer program or handicapping routine might miss. Another example involves first-time starters. *ALL-IN-ONE* accurately measures the ability of experienced horses. But it can't assign a line to a single first-time starter. Hence, if a race contains four or five experienced maidens and four or five first-time starters, we tend to take *ALL-IN-ONE*'s line with a grain of salt. We may ignore the line altogether or assign our own odds line to the first-time starters that have the best chance to win. The moral of the story? Whenever we have reason to question the accuracy of *ALL-IN-ONE*'s line, we tend to bet much less than usual.

That's the case in this race, where Duane, Grand Millesime, and Pricelessly all are overlays in the win pool. They offer individual edges of 55.5, 722, and 171 percent, respectively. The aggressive win bettor finds his best edge-to-odds ratio on Grand Millesime: .2006. The moderate win bettor would bet all three. And the ultra-conservative win bettor could bet all three overlays, plus the underlayed Camouflage Pirate. The group estimate on these four horses is 75 percent. The public's estimate is 59 percent.

As always in contentious races, the Mitchell Matrix exacta strategy is a fine option. Based on our four contenders, it's probable that the four highest-paying exactas will be the two combinations involving Grand Millesime and Pricelessly and the two combinations with Grand Millesime and Pricelessly both on top of Duane.

For the exacta overlay players, the nine combinations involving the long shots Grand Millesime, Pricelessly, and Duane should all offer more than fair value, even after adjusting for the eight guaranteed losing wagers and our minimum 40 percent edge.

TENTH RACE	5½ FURLONGS. (Turf)(1.01) ALLOWANCE. Purse $30,000. 3-year-olds and upward which have never

Hollywood
DECEMBER 4, 1993

won two races. Weights: 3-year-olds, 119 lbs. Older, 121 lbs. Non-winners of a race other than claiming, allowed 3 lbs.

Value of Race: $30,000 Winner $16,500; second $6,000; third $4,500; fourth $2,250; fifth $750. Mutuel Pool $381,934.00 Exacta Pool $360,081.00 Superfecta Pool $275,570.00 Quinella Pool $43,167.00

Last Raced	Horse	M/Eqt.	A.Wt	PP	St	¼	⅜	Str	Fin	Jockey	Odds $1
30Oct93 1SA5	Bettor Every Day	LBb	3 116	6	3	2hd	2½	22½	12	Black C A	15.70
15Nov93 8SA7	Known Approach	LB	3 119	2	8	72	5hd	52	2nk	Stevens G L	10.70
7May93 8Hol10	Pricelessly	LBb	3 119	1	10	10	10	6hd	3hd	Solis A	18.10
24Oct93 5SA2	Camouflage Pirate	LB	3 119	7	1	11	11½	1hd	4½	Valenzuela P A	1.70
13Nov93 3SA3	Bold And Lacey	LB	3 119	8	2	31½	32	31½	51	Valenzuela F H	16.20
17Oct93 8WO11	Canaska Star-GB	B	3 119	10	9	96	83	73	61½	Delahoussaye E	4.20
14Mar93 7SA6	Irish Adventurer	LBb	4 121	3	7	4½	41½	4hd	73	Gryder A T	4.50
12Nov93 4SA1	Lady of the Opera	B	3 109	4	5	5hd	61	8½	81½	Gonzalez S Jr5	26.50
5Nov92 8SA4	Grand Millesime	LB	4 121	9	6	8hd	91	93	96	Lopez A D	36.40
6Mar93 2SA9	Duane	B	3 119	5	4	61	7½	10	10	Pincay L Jr	6.40

OFF AT 5:20 Start Good For All But PRICELESSLY. Won driving. Time, :22², :45¹, :57³, 1:04¹ Course firm.

$2 Mutuel Prices:

6-BETTOR EVERY DAY	33.40	13.20	7.60
2-KNOWN APPROACH		10.80	6.40
1-PRICELESSLY			8.40

$2 EXACTA 6-2 PAID $369.00 $1 SUPERFECTA 6-2-1-7 PAID $11,011.70
$2 QUINELLA 2-6 PAID $148.00

$2 Daily Double 6-6 Paid $164.40 $3 Triple 5-6-6 Paid $2,012.10
Daily Double Pool $126,876.00 Triple Pool $118,346.00

Hollywood Park Attendance: 12,232 Total Mutuel Pool: $2,767,041 Off Track Attendance: 19,392
Total Mutuel Pool: $7,392,303 Total Attendance: 31,624 Total Mutuel Pool: $10,059,344

Yet another non-contender wins, but this long shot outcome wasn't that surprising. After all, the 10-horse field contained no fewer than eight horses whose turf-sprinting ability was unknown.

Let's recap the day's activity:

Win bets

Three overlays won outright: Spruce Navy, Splashing Wave, and Slew Of Damascus. Based on the $2 minimum, we collected a total of $53.00 on these winners. Let's assume that we bet only on horses that offered at least an edge of 20 percent. Over the day's 11 races, we had 17 win bets that offered an edge of at least that. Hence, our investment on win bets totals $34. Our return adds up to $53. Our profit is $19 and our return on investment on win bets is 55.9 percent. Not bad.

Place-and-show bets

In the day's second race, Spruce Navy's fair place and show prices were $3.20 and $2.40, respectively. Spruce Navy won the race and the favorite finished second. Spruce Navy still paid $4 to place and $3.00 to show. In the third race, only Solda Holme could be considered as a place or show bet. She ran third and paid $3.00 to show. In the fourth race, which was a chaos race, favored Sierra Real was an underlay in both the place and show pools. It didn't matter—we never make a back-hole bet in a chaos race. In the eighth race, Slew Of Damascus was a big overlay in both the place and show pools. (I personally bet this one to place because he was paying more than 2-to-1 in the place pool. My win line on him was 2-to-1! Hence, I bet him to both win and place.) We usually skip place-and-show betting in the turf races.

We had a total of three horses that were overlayed in the place-and-show pools today. Based on the $2 minimums, our total investment to place was $6, as was our investment to show. We got back $8.60 to place and $9.20 to show. Our return on investment to place was 43 percent; to show, it was 53 percent.

Exacta bets

With so many short-priced favorites winning today, most of the exactas were decided underlays. In addition, we failed to include a few place horses among our betting-line contenders.

Nonetheless, the exacta on race eight at Bay Meadows and the one on race eight at Hollywood were both well within our reach. Based on the $2 minimum, these exactas returned $152.00. As long as we averaged no more than six exacta combinations ($12) per race, we managed a modest profit with this type of bet.

Quinella bets

Based on our lines, most of the day's quinellas were underlays. But the sixth-race quinella was a fine overlay based on the public's perception of the win odds. On this day, only the race eight quinella was within our grasp.

Trifecta bets

Here's a bet we got skunked on. The only possible trifecta we could have connected on (live race five) paid a miserly $44. The other trifectas were sabotaged by non-contenders who finished in the money.

Daily double bets

The risk-averse double player connected on the early double for a $35.80 payout based on the $2 minimum. Both halves of the late double were won by non-contenders that we didn't include on our line.

Pick-3 bets

Again, too many non-contenders ruined our sequences. In the third race, a horse that was higher than 6-to-1 on our line won. In the seventh, eighth, and ninth races, non-contenders won. The only uninterrupted Pick-3 sequence we had was on races four through six. And even then, those races were won by three hot favorites that we wouldn't have covered anyway. (By the way, that favorite-favorite-favorite triple paid a regrettable $27.30 per $3 ticket.)

• • •

So there you have it. These results are typical of a day at the races. High-probability wagers such as win, place, and show betting will be the most dependable performers in your racetrack portfolio. Low-probability/high-payoff bets like the exacta, daily double, trifecta, and Pick-3 will connect less often. When you do connect on these home runs, your returns will make for handsome profits in the long run. That is, if you haven't previously gone overboard by purchasing too many combinations in a desperate attempt to chase these monster payouts. As always, let the laws of mathematics dictate your betting. If you're patient enough to bet only when you have a sufficient edge, you'll bet less often. But you'll collect at a large enough mutuel to make up for all your losing bets, and still have a handsome chunk of profit left over.

I had a wonderful day, thanks to the Splashing Wave race. I had a $100 win bet and a $20 ticket on the winning exacta combination. In spite of the fact that my $200 win bet on Peterhof's Patea went south, I still managed a $1,986 profit on this race. It was a key race for me, as I had spent most of the day nursing my betting wounds. I wound up more than $1,500 ahead for the day.

There is one final race that I would like to share with you. It's my way to exercise "bragging rights." It was the biggest score of my career to date. Tom Brohamer and *ALL-IN-ONE* correctly predicted the order of finish for the first three horses. My top pick was Prospector's Ghost. Here's the *ALL-IN-ONE* printout for the race:

Santa Anita Park

9 $1\frac{1}{16}$ **MILES.** (1:39) CLAIMING. Purse $24,000. 4-year-olds and upward. Weights: 4-year-olds, 120 lbs. Older, 121 lbs. Non-winners of two races at one mile or over since December 1, allowed 3 lbs. Of such a race since January 1, 5 lbs. Claiming price $25,000; if for $22,500, 2 lbs. (Maiden or races when entered for $20,000 or less not considered.)

Runaway Dunaway
Own: Hoffman Betty
ATKINSON P (47 6 1 4 .13) $25,000

Ro. g. 8
Sire: Vigers (Grey Dawn II)
Dam: Oval Room (Bold Commander)
Br: Mereworth Farm (Ky)
Tr: McAnally Ronald (50 7 5 10 .14)

L 116

Lifetime Record: 56 7 8 7 $219,335
1994	1 0 0 0		Turf	10 0 0 2	$13,600
1993	10 0 2 0	$22,175	Wet	3 1 0 0	$19,125
SA	25 3 2 3	$91,100	Dist	29 4 7 2	$126,035

Border Run
Own: Clear Valley Stables
VALENZUELA P A (83 7 10 16 .08) $25,000

Ch. g. 6
Sire: Secretariat (Bold Ruler)
Dam: Crimson Saint (Crimson Satan)
Br: Gentry Olin B (Ky)
Tr: Shulman Sanford (42 8 5 5 .19)

L 116

Lifetime Record: 23 3 6 2 $117,125
1994	2 0 0 0	$3,000	Turf	3 0 1 0	$6,500
1993	4 1 0 1	$22,750	Wet	2 0 1 0	$8,675
SA	11 1 3 1	$49,625	Dist	5 0 0 1	$10,775

Crystal Wes
Own: Jones Richard M
NAKATANI C S (136 10 17 21 .07) $25,000

Dk. b or br g. 5
Sire: Crystal Water (Windy Sands)
Dam: Queenie B (Don B)
Br: Richard M. Jones (Cal)
Tr: Luby Donn (17 2 0 0 .12)

L 116

Lifetime Record: 28 2 6 7 $98,575
1993	16 2 1 4	$69,550	Turf	6 0 0 2	$16,025
1992	12 M 5 3	$29,025	Wet	1 0 0 0	
SA	6 1 2 1	$25,650	Dist	10 2 4 1	$57,000

Prospector's Ghost
Own: Syndicate Stable
DELAHOUSSAYE E (104 14 15 13 .13) $25,000

B. g. 4
Sire: Silver Ghost (Mr. Prospector)
Dam: Fille Du Nord (Tentam)
Br: West Mr & Mrs R Smiser (Ky)
Tr: Sterling Patty (3 1 0 0 .33)

L 117

Lifetime Record: 14 4 0 2 $49,050
1994	1 1 0 0	$15,400	Turf	3 0 0 1	$3,300
1993	12 3 0 1	$31,700	Wet	1 0 0 0	
SA	2 0 0 0	$15,400	Dist	1 0 0 0	$8,050

Son Of A Bronze

Own: Freed & Wilmot & Zamora
PEDROZA M A (86 7 11 8 .08) $25,000
B. g. 5
Sire: To-Agori-Mou (Tudor Music)
Dam: Cindy Bronze (Tobin Bronze)
Br: Zamora John (Cal)
Tr: Wilmot William B (6 1 2 0 .17)
L 116

Lifetime Record: 14 2 2 4 $39,755
1994 1 1 0 0 $9,350 | Turf 1 0 0 0 $1,500
1993 13 1 2 4 $30,405 | Wet 0 0 0 0
SA 5 1 1 1 $16,100 | Dist 4 2 0 2 $23,150

13Jan94-5SA fst 1 1/16 :224 :464 1:11 1:423 Clm 16000 89 8 8 86¾ 53¾ 2hd 13½ Pedroza M A LB 116 6.20 82-21 Son Of A Bronze1163½ Cape Royale111hd Royal Torrent116½ Clearly best 10
17Dec93-7Hol fst 1 1/16 :233 :464 1:103 1:424 3↑ Clm 18000 76 4 8 712 77½ 44½ 310 Gryder A T LB 114 25.30 77-18 Great Event1174½ World In My Eyes1165½ SonOfABronze1141¾ Best of rest 8
27Nov93-3BM fm 1 1/16 Ⓣ :232 :474 1:123 1:44 3↑ Alw 20000N1X 76 4 4 46½ 42 46 46½ Chapman T M LB 117 7.40 83-12 Explosive Blast1155 Fabulous Pole1181 I'm Huge117½ No rally 6
3Nov93-9SA fst 1 1/16 :232 :472 1:113 1:434 3↑ Clm 12500 83 9 9 84½ 77½ 54½ 32½ Solis A LB 116 35.20 82-20 Midnight Leader1172 Material Eyes116½ Son Of A Bronze1161 Wide trip 10
18Sep93-5Fpx fst 6f :224 :46 :58 1:103 3↑ Clm 16000 76 8 8 911 88¾ 66½ 63¼ Valenzuela F H LB 116 20.80 91-09 Susan's Corsair116no Contented1111 Orthos116½ Mild bid 9
15Aug93-9Dmr fst 1 :23 :461 1:104 1:354 3↑ Clm 25000 66 4 4 47½ 88¾ 810 716 Black C A LB 117 56.50 72-12 Queen's Page1174½ Lil Orphan Moonie110hd Le Axe AL'ame117¾ Wide trip 10
25Jly93-2Hol fst 1 1/16 :231 :47 1:114 1:444 3↑ Md 32000 68 3 5 4¾ 11 13 1¾ Gonzalez S5 LB 117 3.10 77-19 Son Of A Bronze117¾ Cugar117hd Imperial Kid1164 Ridden out 10
5Jly93-10Hol fst 7½f :223 :453 1:104 1:294 3↑ Md 28000 72 10 8 107¼ 96¼ 33 32½ Gonzalez S5 LB 115 7.90 83-11 Saros' Triumph1171¼ Cap Haitien1151¼ Son Of A Bronze1154½ Wide trip 12
3Jun93-6Hol fst 7½f :223 :451 1:102 1:294 3↑ Md 28000 69 5 4 64½ 76½ 56½ 43¾ Dominguez R E LB 120 2.50 82-12 Dr. Chocolate115hd Sit Look And Hope1163½ Valor116no Wide trip 8
20May93-2Hol fst 7½f :222 :45 1:101 1:292 3↑ [S]Md 28000 70 6 8 85¾ 75¼ 45 26½ Dominguez R E LB 120 3.70 81-11 Radical Phase1156½ Son Of A Bronze1204½ Point Zoot117hd 5 Wide stretch 12

WORKOUTS: ●Dec 31 Fpx 5f fst 1:001 H 1/17 ●Dec 11 Fpx 4f fst :472 H 1/13 Nov 21 Fpx 6f fst 1:122 H 1/2 Nov 15 Fpx 6f fst 1:121 H 1/3

The Cleaners

Own: Far Fellow Farms
PINCAY L JR (130 19 15 16 .15) $25,000
Ch. g. 6
Sire: Lines of Power (Raise a Native)
Dam: Truly Do (Vigors)
Br: Green & White Syndicate (Ky)
Tr: Spawr Bill (47 6 5 12 .13)
L 116

Lifetime Record: 38 11 3 8 $222,225
1994 1 0 0 0 $2,100 | Turf 2 0 0 0 $1,000
1993 13 2 1 4 $66,975 | Wet 2 0 1 1 $9,850
SA 19 7 3 3 $129,875 | Dist 16 5 2 2 $95,250

16Jan94-1SA fst 1 1/16 :23 :46 1:101 1:42 Clm 32000 86 3 6 714 614 67½ 46½ Pincay L Jr LB 117 6.90 79-11 Misting Rain1166 Record Boom118nk Bucking Bird116hd Mild late bid 8
7Nov93-7SA fst 1 :233 :471 1:112 1:364 3↑ Clm 40000 81 4 7 76 65¼ 53 32 Pincay L Jr LB 117 3.00 84-11 Payand Payand Pay1141¼ Davus116¾ The Cleaners117nk Finished well 7
30Oct93-9Fpx fst 1⅜ :472 1:133 1:391 2:174 3↑ Hcp 25000s 82 2 5 515 43½ 44½ 34½ Flores D R LB 120 f *.90 83-11 Evil Wizard1163½ Cannon Man1151 The Cleaners1203 No late bid 7
24Sep93-9Fpx fst *1⅛ :46 1:124 1:38 1:504 3↑ Alw 25000s 88 6 6 65¾ 54½ 1hd 12 Flores D R LB 114 2.90 88-12 TheCleaners1142 LilOrphanMoonie1162 Dvus1142½ Stumbled badly start 6
5Sep93-4Dmr fst 1 1/16 :24 :482 1:122 1:423 3↑ Clm 40000 80 4 4 52½ 72½ 63½ 85½ Pincay L Jr LB 117 4.90 84-11 His Legacy112½ Crystal Wes1152½ Doulab's Image117½ Boxed in 3/8-1/8 8
8Aug93-9Dmr fst 1 :23 :464 1:11 1:353 3↑ Clm 40000 89 4 9 96½ 93½ 73½ 33½ Pincay L Jr LB 117 7.70 85-11 Shaynoor116hd Skylaunch1163½ The Cleaners117nk 4 Wide stretch 10
22Jly93-3Hol fst 1 1/16 :234 :473 1:113 1:421 Alw 32000s 86 5 5 56½ 56 55 45¾ Pincay L Jr LB 117 4.20 84-19 Davus1162 Coco's Main Man115nk Careening ForPaul1163½ 4 Wide stretch 5
18Jun93-8Hol fm 1⅛ Ⓣ :47 1:102 1:344 1:47 Clm 50000 83 4 8 86¾ 88¾ 65 54¾ Pincay L Jr LB 117 8.20 84-09 Palos Verdes107½ Robinski112½ Quaglino116nk Wide backstretch 8
22May93-4Hol fst 1⅛ :482 1:123 1:371 1:492 Alw 40000s 88 4 4 56½ 56½ 54½ 32¾ Delahoussaye E LB 116 9.60 87-09 Treat Tobeatyafeet1172½ Icy Resolution116nk The Cleaners1161 Wide trip 6
1May93-3Hol fst 1⅛ :483 1:124 1:361 1:484 Alw 25000s 81 2 7 73¾ 74½ 68½ 68½ Nakatani C S LB 115 3.10 84-07 Record Boom1152¾ Eddie Valient1151¼ Book Publisher1222 No threat 7

WORKOUTS: Jan 9 SA 7f fst 1:272 H 7/11 Dec 29 SA 5f fst 1:002 H 15/52 Dec 23 SA 6f fst 1:142 H 28/28 Dec 16 SA 5f fst 1:033 H 49/53 Dec 10 SA 5f fst 1:013 H 30/66 Dec 4 SA 3f fst :374 B 27/38

Big Barton

Own: Barton & Green
VALENZUELA F H (137 15 6 15 .11) $22,500
B. g. 6
Sire: Key to the Kingdom (Bold Ruler)
Dam: Ruana (Ruritania)
Br: Pineau Mr & Mrs A Leonard (Mass)
Tr: Garcia Victor L (1 1 0 0 1.00)
L 114

Lifetime Record: 28 6 1 3 $105,625
1994 1 1 0 0 $6,600 | Turf 11 2 0 2 $56,775
1993 8 1 0 0 $10,575 | Wet 2 0 0 1 $5,700
SA 9 3 1 1 $35,350 | Dist 10 3 1 0 $35,275

7Jan94-1SA fst 1⅛ :463 1:111 1:362 1:492 Clm 10000 84 9 4 31 1½ 15 13½ Antley C W LB 116 b 20.10 86-11 Big Barton1163½ Palmdale1162¾ Jean Pierre S1161¼ Driving 12
11Dec93-11Hol sly 1 1/16 ⊗ :23 :462 1:12 1:464 3↑ Hcp 10000s 23 7 2 22 410 517 735½ Wyatt T LB 143 fb 12.30 31-23 Whisk Spree143nk Cielozar143¼ Cannon Man14315 Gave way 8
Amateur race
18Nov93-5Hol fst 1 1/16 :23 :462 1:111 1:432 3↑ Clm 8000 75 5 1 1hd 1hd 32 46 Pedroza M A LB 118 fb 5.70 78-23 Cautivador118hd For Brentton1151¼ Cielozar1154½ Used up 11
11Nov93-5SA gd 1 :222 :461 1:121 1:383 3↑ Clm 10000 49 10 4 53 86½ 910 917 Valenzuela F H LB 116 fb 5.10 60-24 King Raj1162¾ Days Gone By117½ Jean Pierre S1161¼ Wide trip 10
30Oct93-5SA fm 1 Ⓣ :222 :45 1:094 1:34 3↑ Clm 75000 46 9 3 3½ 97¼ 911 927 Atherton J E5 LB 110 fb 62.30 68-09 Bat Eclat1131 Seti I.1186 Dream Of Fame115¾ Dueled, stopped 9
10Oct93-8Fpx fst 1 1/16 :224 :46 1:114 1:433 3↑ Clm 10500 94 5 1 11 11 11 12 Valenzuela F H LB 114 fb 11.70 90-11 Big Barton1142 Great Event1163 Terrific Trip1113½ Driving 7
16Sep93-9Fpx fst 1 1/16 :23 :461 1:113 1:444 3↑ Clm 12500 62 6 1 1hd 31½ 1010 1012 Sorenson D LB 116 fb 9.60 72-15 The Drouller116½ Stylish Majesty1161½ Great Event116½ Dueled, tired 10
29Aug93-9Dmr fst 1 :23 :464 1:114 1:37 3↑ Clm 16000 74 3 1 2hd 2⅓ 2¼ 64 Sorenson D LB 117 fb 20.50 78-10 Beach Lights117hd Mysterious Moon1171½ Roisterous1121¼ Weakened 10
7Aug93-5Dmr fm 1 Ⓣ :22 :452 1:093 1:343 3↑ Clm 55000 60 7 1 11½ 44 1012 1017 Flores D R LB 113 fb 52.20 81-03 Robinski115½ Garmanni116½ Seti I.1162¾ Faltered 10
14Nov92-10Hol fm 1 1/16 Ⓣ :231 :464 1:104 1:421 3↑ Clm 50000 67 7 1 1⅓ 3⅓ 62¾ 911⅓ Torres H LB 115 b 17.30 72-15 Boldly Excellent1152½ Robinski114 Top Bob115 Gave way 10

WORKOUTS: Jan 27 Hol 5f fst :594 H 5/23 Jan 18 Hol 4f fst :49 H 3/21 Jan 3 Hol 5f fst 1:001 H 5/18 Dec 28 Hol 5f fst 1:01 H 7/31 Dec 22 Hol 5f fst 1:022 H 12/25 Dec 8 Hol 4f fst :483 H 19/40

Cape Royale

Own: 505 Farms
GONZALEZ S JR (117 17 10 13 .15) $25,000
Dk. b or br g. 5
Sire: Capote (Seattle Slew)
Dam: Regal Realm (Majestic Prince)
Br: Sexton & Walden Jr (Ky)
Tr: MacDonald Norman S (4 0 1 0 .00)
L 111^5

Lifetime Record: 13 1 1 2 $124,155
1994 2 0 1 0 $3,400 | Turf 0 0 0 0
1993 4 0 0 0 $475 | Wet 0 0 0 0
SA 8 1 1 2 $119,555 | Dist 4 0 1 0 $6,025

13Jan94-5SA fst 1 1/16 :224 :464 1:11 1:423 Clm 16000 83 7 4 3½ 2hd 1hd 23½ Gonzalez S5 LB 111 11.50 78-21 Son Of A Bronze1163½ Cape Royale111hd Royal Torrent116½ Outfinished 10
1Jan94-9SA fst 1 1/16 :223 :464 1:11 1:414 Clm 25000 70 1 4 61¾ 73¾ 86½ 79½ Esposito M LB 117 37.20 76-11 Impact1162 Lovely One111½ Western Man116nk Gave way 10
19Dec93-3Hol fst 6½f :214 :442 1:092 1:154 3↑ Clm 32000 70 4 1 1hd 2½ 42 56½ Gonzalez S5 LB 112 b 20.90 83-13 Bengal Bay117¾ Talent Connection117nk Cheyenne Gold1151 Checked 1/8 6
4Jly93-1Hol fst 1 1/16 :231 :462 1:102 1:42 Clm 25000 42 5 6 64¼ 68 619 630¾ Flores D R LB 116 fb 15.80 60-13 Davus1164½ No Commitment1175 Lil Orphan Moonie1091 Wide early 6
20Jun93-4GG fst 6f :214 :44 :56 1:084 3↑ Alw 25000N2X 66 3 4 55½ 58 69½ 69¼ Boulanger G LB 119 17.60 87-06 Cup O'huddle1171 Fly Fast119nk Agiotage1193 No threat 6
18Apr93-5SA fst 7f :223 :454 1:094 1:221 Alw 36000N2X 63 1 4 32 42½ 610 714¼ Pincay L Jr LB 117 9.70 78-09 Supermec1141 Ackler1181½ Rathsallah118¾ Faltered 7
6Jly92-8Hol fst 6f :221 :45 :57 1:092 Alw 32000 66 2 5 31 53¼ 66½ 712 Solis A LB 119 b 4.30 81-13 Bet On The Bay119¾ Dr. Augusta1191 Dodsworth119 Faltered 8
13Jun92-3Hol fst 7f :221 :442 1:084 1:212 Handicap 75 4 3 2hd 2½ 55 58¾ Solis A LB 117 b 11.50 88-05 Dolly's Fortune116½ [D]Never Round120¾ WildHarmony115 Took up 3/16 5
Placed fourth through disqualification
23Feb92-7SA fst 1 1/16 :232 :47 1:11 1:432 Alw 35000 80 2 2 31½ 32 32 44½ Solis A L 115 *1.70 81-15 Bold Assert118nk Spudabaker1184 Bright Day Bob115 Weakened 6
9Feb92-5SA fst 7f :22 :442 1:084 1:211 Sn Vcnt B C-G3 82 4 1 2½ 42 54½ 510 Solis A L 120 11.20 87-06 Mineral Wells116no Star Of The Crop1165 Prince Wild118 Faltered 7

WORKOUTS: Jan 24 SA 6f fst 1:122 H 5/23 Dec 28 SA 4f fst :474 H 16/50 Dec 14 SA 4f fst :472 H 3/42 Nov 22 SA 5f fst 1:004 H 22/35 Nov 14 SA 7f fst 1:252 H 2/8 ●Nov 8 SA 6f fst 1:124 H 1/22

Cool Chili (GB)

Own: Lee China
BLACK C A (125 10 10 9 .08) $25,000
Gr. g. 6
Sire: Formidable (Forli)
Dam: Chili Girl (Skymaster)
Br: Heinz Mrs H J III (GB)
Tr: Van Berg Jack C (62 10 14 5 .16)
L 116

Lifetime Record: 46 10 9 7 $173,914
1994 2 0 0 1 $2,700 | Turf 15 1 2 2 $26,601
1993 16 5 4 2 $52,035 | Wet 2 0 1 0 $6,200
SA 13 4 2 2 $44,925 | Dist 1 0 0 0

16Jan94-1SA fst 1 1/16 :23 :46 1:101 1:42 Clm 28000 83 7 4 49½ 45¼ 24 68¼ Valenzuela F H LB 114 b 9.50 77-11 Misting Rain1166 Record Boom118nk Bucking Bird116hd 4 wide 2nd turn 8
7Jan94-2SA fst 6½f :22 :45 1:084 1:151 Clm c-20000 86 7 1 31½ 32 32 32 Nakatani C S LB 118 b 4.00 94-08 Bet A Bic1161 Star Of Greenwood1161 Cool Chili1181½ No late bid 8
Claimed from Glassman Richard M, Spawr Bill Trainer
16Dec93-1Hol fst 5½f :221 :453 :58 1:044 3↑ Clm 20000 80 4 2 21 31½ 3nk 1no Nakatani C S LB 117 b *.90 88-15 Cool Chili117no Pancho's Cup115¾ Lil Orphan Moonie117½ Split rivals 6
4Dec93-9Hol fst 6f :214 :441 :562 1:091 3↑ Clm c-16000 85 8 1 52 84½ 74¼ 73¾ Black C A LB 122 b 2.80 90-07 Wild Tech1171¼ He's Like The Wind1171 Dr. Augusta117½ Gave way 8
Claimed from Tarheel Stable, Assinesi Paul D Trainer
14Nov93-4SA fst 6½f :214 :441 1:084 1:154 3↑ Clm 16000 84 2 2 1hd 2hd 11 11¾ Black C A LB 118 b 4.90 92-06 Cool Chili1181¾ Dr. Augusta116hd Precise Cut117½ Inside duel 11
11Oct93-1SA fst 6f :221 :45 :57 1:093 3↑ Clm c-16000 86 4 2 1½ 1hd 1hd 1nk Sorenson D LB 116 b 2.90 89-11 Cool Chili116nk Sinceriffic116¾ Dr. Augusta1161¾ Very game 7
Claimed from Patten Dick Van, Acerno John Trainer
26Sep93-7Fpx fst 6½f :222 :453 1:094 1:161 3↑ Clm 16000 90 4 1 1hd 1hd 1hd 2hd Sorenson D LB 116 b 2.70 95-09 Orthos116hd Cool Chili1165 Cove Way1161½ Game try 7
18Sep93-5Fpx fst 6f :224 :46 :58 1:103 3↑ Clm 16000 80 7 5 32½ 3½ 32 41½ Atkinson P LB 116 b 4.60 92-09 Susan's Corsair116no Contented1111 Orthos116½ Outfinished 9
29Aug93-7Dmr fst 6½f :222 :45 1:09 1:152 3↑ Clm 16000 83 4 4 2½ 23 33½ 37 Flores D R LB 117 b 5.90 87-11 El Toreo1173½ Dr. Hyde1143½ Cool Chili1172 Bumped start 8
1Aug93-2Dmr fst 6f :22 :45 :573 1:10 3↑ Clm 16000 81 1 3 21 21½ 3½ 33¼ Gonzalez S5 LB 110 b 9.30 86-05 Fistylee115¾ Ocean Native1152½ Cool Chili110hd Weakened 9

WORKOUTS: Nov 27 SA 3f fst :373 H 15/17 Nov 5 SA 5f fst 1:05 H 92/93

```
Tidy Colony                              B. g. 6                                          Lifetime Record :  28 1 0 10   $76,625
Own: Savaglio Joseph E Jr                Sire: Pleasant Colony (His Majesty)              1994   2 0 0 1   $4,275 | Turf 24 1 0 10 $75,925
                                         Dam: Trim and Tidy (Sea-Bird II)                 1993  14 1 0 5  $49,650 | Wet   0 0 0 0
                                         Br:  Evans T M (Ky)
FLORES D R (57 2 12 7 .04)     $22,500   Tr:  O'Hara John (6 0 2 2 .00)          L 114    SA     1 0 0 0     $700 | Dist  1 0 0 0

8Jan94-6BM   fm 1 1/16 Ⓣ :233 :473 1:114 1:452    Alw 22000N1X     77 4 4 43 22 32 42½          Judice J C       LB 117 b  6.20 78-19 Top Reality1171½ Imperial Kid116hd Cuantalacaro1161           No rally 6
1Jan94-7BM   fm 1      Ⓣ :224 :47  1:121 1:383    Clm 25000        84 6 5 52½ 21½ 2½ 31½        Judice J C       LB 117 b  4.30 78-20 Tres Rios1171½ Air Fury115no Tidy Colony117nk                  Closed wide 9
5Dec93-3Hol  fm 1¼     Ⓣ :473 1:122 1:363 2:012 3↑ Alw 32000N2L     75 6 2 3½ 32½ 34½ 49¾        Gryder A T       LB 121    8.40 77-14 Alex The Great1216½ Wise Words1182½ Don't Tell Frank115¾    Weakened 7
13Nov93-7SA  fm 1      Ⓣ :231 :464 1:11  1:371 3↑ Alw 34000N1X     80 6 7 77½ 55¾ 44½ 44        Gryder A T       LB 122   34.40 75-21 Savinio1181¾ Wise Words118nk Daskiyawar1222                No late bid 8
29Oct93-8SA  fm 1⅛     Ⓣ :464 1:112 1:361 1:48  3↑ Alw 34000N1X     81 7 5 58½ 64½ 31 54½        Gryder A T       L 122    22.40 75-21 Only Alpha118no Cherokee Tribute1131½ Memento Mori1191¾    No late bid 8
9Oct93-8BM   fm 1 1/16 Ⓣ :234 :473 1:121 1:434 3↑ Clm 40000        68 3 4 33½ 32½ 98¾ 1012½     Meza R Q         LB 117   14.80 78-03 Sekondi1172 San Fran's Halo1192 Garmanni1172                Stopped 10
1Sep93-8Dmr  fm 1⅛     Ⓣ :482 1:123 1:363 1:49  3↑ Alw 36000N2L     76 7 4 45 31½ 65½ 66½        Black C A        LB 122   15.00 84-09 Passo Geno119¾ Arinthod118hd Alex The Great1222½           Gave way 7
18Aug93-5Dmr fm 1 1/16 Ⓣ :231 :472 1:111 1:414 3↑ Alw 36000N1X     66 7 10 1013 910 79¾ 712½    Pincay L Jr      LB 122    5.30 84-04 Cigar1152¾ Our Motion Granted122hd The Berkeley Man1142½   Dwelt start 10
4Aug93-5Dmr  fm 1⅛     Ⓣ :493 1:141 1:382 1:50  3↑ Alw 36000N2L     89 6 7 62½ 51½ 31 3¾         Pincay L Jr      LB 122   10.80 85-07 Kingdom Of Spain122½ Passo Geno119nk Tidy Colony122½       Wide trip 10
18Jly93-5Hol fm 1      Ⓣ :232 :464 1:104 1:354 3↑ Alw 39000N1X     80 7 3 32 41½ 43½ 35         Valenzuela P A   LB 121 b  3.20 81-13 Taylor Quigley118no Passo Geno1185 Tidy Colony121hd                   8
    Balked gate, carried out early
WORKOUTS:  ●Jan 23 SA 5f fst :584 H 1/41   ●Dec 28 SA 3f fst :342 H 1/29   Dec 21 SA 5f fst :584 H 4/51   Dec 1 SA 4f fst :49 H 25/48   Nov 24 SA 4f fst :474 H 12/40
```

```
Hoedown's Lifter                         Dk. b or br g. 5                                 Lifetime Record :  17 1 2 3   $11,850
Own: Dunn Claudia M                      Sire: Hoedown's Day (Bargain Day)                1993   5 0 0 1   $2,500 | Turf  2 0 0 0   $825
                                         Dam: Golden Lifter (Wallet Lifter)               1992  12 1 2 2   $9,350 | Wet   0 0 0 0
                                         Br:  Kidd Mardee H (Cal)
MARTINEZ F F (7 0 2 1 .00)     $25,000   Tr:  Knight Gerald L (1 0 0 0 .00)       L 116   SA     0 0 0 0          | Dist  6 1 2 1 $7,312

17Dec93-8Hol  fst 7f        :22  :442 1:091 1:214 3↑ Clm 50000        36 1 5 41½ 43 513 528¾      Dorochenko G     LB 117 b 72.70 66-16 Outlawed119¾ His Legacy1172 Misting Rain1175                            6
    Jumped shadow, broke stride 1/4
5Dec93-3Hol   fm 1¼ Ⓣ     :473 1:122 1:363 2:012 3↑ Alw 32000N2L     40 2 3 44½ 710 715 725¼     Dorochenko G     L 118 b  41.20 62-14 Alex The Great1216½ Wise Words1182½ Don't Tell Frank115¾      Brief speed 7
26Nov93-13Hol fm 1 1/16 Ⓣ :224 :461 1:103 1:423 3↑ [S]Alw 33000N1X 68 9 5 42 41¾ 42¾ 54¾       Scott J M        LB 118 b 104.90 78-12 Sky Marine115¾ Natural Fifty Six115½ Special Comic1152¾   Brushed 7/8 10
29Oct93-9BM   fst 1         :221 :454 1:103 1:371 3↑ Clm 8000N2X      74 8 6 44½ 54 24 32½        Harvey B         L 117 b  77.10 81-21 Mandon1172 Luisillo117½ Hoedown's Lifter117½              Saved ground 8
8Oct93-6BM    fst 1 1/16    :231 :47  1:112 1:424 3↑ Clm 8000N2X      47 1 5 41¾ 23 68½ 617½      Harvey B         L 117 b  33.10 71-21 Patdancer1174½ Little Reeves117no Divided Country1158         Gave way 8
12Nov92-9BM   fst 1 1/16    :232 :47  1:121 1:433 3↑ Clm 6250         72 12 2 23 12 21 24½        Meza R Q         LB 118 b  8.70 76-21 Reason To Fight1224½ Hoedown's Lifter1181 Great Finale118      2nd best 12
28Oct92-9BM   fst 1 1/16    :23  :461 1:102 1:442 3↑ Clm 6250         62 10 3 21½ 21½ 24 54½      Meza R Q         LB 118 b  3.20 72-27 Prospector's Ridge1222½ Rafting118nk Reason To Fight122  Pressed pace 11
8Oct92-9BM    fst 1⅛        :461 1:112 1:374 1:511 3↑ Clm 6250         66 6 4 42½ 31 2½ 41¼        Yerena J A5      LB 113 b  4.10 79-25 Attila The Bold122nk Executivo122no Stand Erect118           Hung late 10
23Sep92-9BM   fst 1 1/16    :223 :46  1:11  1:441 3↑ Clm 6250         72 4 8 76½ 51¾ 2½ 22        Yerena J A5      LB 113 b 21.90 76-24 InMmoryOfMom1222 Hodown'sLiftr113½ AttilThBold122        Rallied wide 11
5Sep92-10Sac  fst 1         :224 :461 1:104 1:371 3↑ Clm 8000         67 6 2 1hd 1½ 1½ 74½        Yerena J A5      LB 109 b 18.80 77-19 Lavish Fleet116½ Licorice Breeze1161 On Line UnderFire121      Weakened 10
WORKOUTS:  Jan 22 Hol 5f fst 1:022 H 20/30   Jan 18 Hol 4f fst :491 H 7/21   Jan 3 Hol 5f fst 1:004 H 10/18   ●Dec 23 Hol 4f fst :462 H 1/15   Dec 1 Hol 3f fst :384 H 21/23   Nov 21 Hol 5f fst :594 H 5/40
```

```
Mr. C I Prospector                       Dk. b or br c. 4                                 Lifetime Record :  8 2 2 1   $27,525
Own: Mirage Stable                       Sire: Native Prospector (Mr. Prospector)         1994   1 0 0 0   $1,350 | Turf  0 0 0 0
                                         Dam: Ninky's Rullah (Great Career)               1993   7 2 2 1  $26,175 | Wet   0 0 0 0
                                         Br:  Carmelo Ieraci (Cal)
STEVENS G L (142 17 27 21 .12) $25,000   Tr:  Lewis Craig A (23 3 3 1 .13)        L 115   SA     3 1 0 0  $10,700 | Dist  0 0 0 0

14Jan94-4SA  fst 6f   :212 :442 :562 1:09        Clm c-20000        67 6 6 63½ 64¼ 75¾ 47¼      Valenzuela P A   LB 117  *2.20 85-09 ForestJoy1153½ GoodbyeToYou1153½ Jericho'sProspect110nk  Mild late bid 8
    Claimed from Ieraci Carmelo, Sadler John W Trainer
20Dec93-3Hol fst 6f   :214 :444 :562 1:092       Clm 25000          79 1 4 31½ 1hd 2hd 22½      Valenzuela P A   LB 116   7.80 90-09 Buyimback1162½ Mr. C I Prospector116½ Forest Joy116no          Inside duel 8
25Nov93-5Hol fst 7f   :223 :453 1:094 1:222      Clm 16000          80 2 2 2hd 1hd 13½ 1½       Valenzuela P A   LB 119   6.40 92-09 Mr. C I Prospector119½ Cuepredictive116½ Mr B Cool1161¾       Inside duel 9
13Nov93-3SA  fst 6f   :22  :444 :563 1:084 3↑ [S]Alw 32000N1X   42 7 3 41¾ 42 77¾ 719½      Desormeaux K J   LB 116   6.10 73-11 SpecilTsk1182¼ LongGoneJuls1182 BoldAndLcy1183½   Bobbled start, wide 7
8Oct93-2SA   fst 6f   :221 :452 :58  1:102 3↑ [S]Md 32000       80 9 1 31 43½ 21 1½         Desormeaux K J   LB 117   *.60 85-14 Mr. C I Prospector117½ Singapore Boy1176½ Tasso's Boy1151¼   Stiff drive 9
8Sep93-9Dmr  fst 6f   :221 :452 :572 1:101 3↑ [S]Md 32000       75 2 5 1hd 1hd 2hd 21       Delahoussaye E   LB 118   2.30 87-10 Tell Fred1201 Mr. C I Prospector1184½ Sky Bryn1162          Good effort 10
28Jly93-2Dmr fst 6f   :22  :454 :581 1:11       [S]Md 32000       68 9 5 63½ 64¼ 45½ 36       Valenzuela P A   LB 116   2.40 78-07 Irrefutable116no Ke Express1156 Mr. C IProspector1163½  Not enough late 11
25Jun93-6Hol fst 6½f  :214 :444 1:094 1:162 3↑ [S]Md 32000       79 5 5 1½ 11 2hd 43¼        Valenzuela P A   B 117    7.00 84-13 SitLookAndHope1162 Tony'sPirte1151 LongGonJuls122nk     Edged for 3rd 12
WORKOUTS:  Jan 26 SA tr.t 4f gd :50 H 2/4   Jan 7 SA 6f fst 1:123 H 5/30   Dec 31 SA 5f fst 1:00 H 14/66   Dec 15 Hol 5f my 1:02 H 3/9   Dec 9 Hol 5f fst 1:023 H 33/38   Dec 3 Hol 4f fst :513 H 19/20
```

ALL-IN-ONE's output for race is as follows:

30JAN94　　SA　　8.5 furlongs dirt
Race #9　　10 starters
C25,000　　Age: 4+years, Male

---BETTING LINE---

	-------Rankings--------								
Horse name	PEH	H-I	THAAI	P-H	ESP	Rating	Betting Line	Fair Place $	Fair Show $
Big Barton	5	1	4	3	6	86.79	7-2		
Prospector's Ghost	2	2	1	2	1	79.72	9-2		
The Cleaners	1	3	2	1	10	77.34	5-1		
Son Of A Bronze	6	4	3	5	3	77.08	5-1		
Mr. C I Prospector	4	7	6	4	7	76.06			
Border Run	3	9	7	7	2	75.05			
Crystal Wes	7	5	5	6	9	71.67			
Runaway Dunaway	9	6	8	8	8	70.00			
Cape Royale	8	8	9	9	5	69.91			
Hoedown's Lifter	10	10	10	10	4	68.41			

---SPEED/PACE SUMMARY---

Race Type: Orderly Race
Race Profile: 47.14　111.17　141.87　　Winners' Pace Profile: EARLY
Ability Par: 95.20　　Pace Contention Point: 3.22 lengths

Projected Times:

	1st C	2nd C	Fin C	Ability Time	Balance Time	Last Frac	Proj Pace	Con-tender
Big Barton	46.10	110.72	141.37	95.33	99.07	30.65	FRONT	Y
Prospector's Ghost	47.24	111.12*	142.09	94.99	99.25	30.98	MID	N
The Cleaners	45.92	111.48*	141.63	97.05	99.52	30.14	REAR	N

```
Son Of A Bronze      48.06  111.68* 142.60    95.31   99.42  30.92  REAR    N
Mr. C I Prospector   47.15  111.55* 142.92    95.95  100.26  31.37  REAR    N
Border Run           46.02  110.42  143.41    94.82  101.05  32.99  FRONT   N
Crystal Wes          49.04  113.21* 143.13    97.39   99.84  29.91  REAR    N
Runaway Dunaway      47.68  112.07* 142.94    96.45  100.11  30.87  REAR    N
Cape Royale          46.94  111.17* 143.23    95.39  100.60  32.06  LATE    N
Hoedown's Lifter     46.74  110.94  143.88    95.15  101.31  32.93  MID     N


--------------------------------PACE GRAPH------------------------------------
        Profile:                47.14              111.17              141.87
        Front Runner:           45.92              110.42              141.37
Horse name                        1C                  2C                    F
Big Barton         -----------------X+ --------------(--X+ ----------------X
Prospector's Ghost-----------X------+ --------------(X--+ --------------X---+
The Cleaners       -----------------X --------------X(---+ ----------------X+
Son Of A Bronze    -------X----------+ --------------X-(---+ ------------X-----+
Mr. C I Prospector-----------X------+ --------------X-(---+ ----------X-------+
Border Run         -----------------X+ --------------(---X --------X-------+
Crystal Wes        --X--------------+ ----X---------(---+ --------X--------+
Runaway Dunaway    -----------X------+ ----------X---(---+ --------X--------+
Cape Royale        -------------X---+ --------------X(--+ --------X--------+
Hoedown's Lifter   -------------X---+ --------------(X--+ -----X-----------+
```

Here are the public win odds for our contenders in this race:

Big Barton	18-1
Prospector's Ghost	5-2
The Cleaners	2-1
Son Of A Bronze	6-1

I didn't exactly agree with *ALL-IN-ONE*. (Silly me). My line on this race was:

Prospector's Ghost	2-1
Big Barton	3-1
The Cleaners	6-1
Son Of A Bronze	6-1

I bought the following tickets on this race:

—$100 to win on Prospector's Ghost
—$50 to win on Big Barton
—$50 exacta box, Prospector's Ghost to Big Barton
—$20 exacta part-wheel, Big Barton and Prospector's Ghost with Big Barton, Prospector's Ghost, The Cleaners, and Son Of A Bronze.
—$20 exacta part-wheel, Big Barton and Prospector's Ghost, The Cleaners, and Son Of A Bronze with Big Barton and Prospector's Ghost.

—$20 exacta, Big Barton on top of Prospector's Ghost

—$1 Trifecta part-wheel, Big Barton and Prospector's Ghost with Big Barton, Prospectors Ghost, The Cleaners, and Son Of A Bronze with Big Barton, Prospectors Ghost, The Cleaners, and Son Of A Bronze. I bought this ticket six times.

—$1 Trifecta part-wheel, Big Barton, Prospector's Ghost, The Cleaners, and Son Of A Bronze with Big Barton and Prospector's Ghost with Big Barton, Prospectors Ghost, The Cleaners, and Son Of A Bronze. I bought this ticket three times.

NINTH RACE

Santa Anita

JANUARY 30, 1994

1 1/16 MILES. (1.39) CLAIMING. Purse $24,000. 4–year–olds and upward. Weights: 4–year–olds, 120 lbs. Older, 121 lbs. Non–winners of two races at one mile or over since December 1, allowed 3 lbs. Of such a race since January 1, 5 lbs. Claiming price $25,000; if for $22,500, 2 lbs. (Maiden or races when entered for $20,000 or less not considered.)

Value of Race: $24,000 Winner $13,200; second $4,800; third $3,600; fourth $1,800; fifth $600. Mutuel Pool $302,782.00 Exacta Pool $235,080.00 Trifecta Pool $398,092.00 Quinella Pool $37,802.00

Last Raced	Horse	M/Eqt. A.Wt	PP	St	1/4	1/2	3/4	Str	Fin	Jockey	Cl'g Pr	Odds $1
7Jan94 1SA1	Big Barton	LBb 6 114	7	6	2½	2½	2½	22½	11	Valenzuela F H	22500	18.20
8Jan94 9SA1	Prospector's Ghost	LBb 4 117	4	1	11½	14	12	12½	22	Delahoussaye E	25000	2.90
16Jan94 1SA4	The Cleaners	LBb 6 117	6	9	81½	8½	7½	31½	35½	Pincay L Jr	25000	2.30
23Jan94 9SA4	Border Run	LBb 6 117	2	3	32½	3hd	31	42½	42½	Valenzuela P A	25000	7.80
14Jan94 4SA4	Mr. C I Prospector	LB 4 115	10	5	5½	73	82	6½	5½	Stevens G L	25000	14.70
1Jan94 9SA6	Runaway Dunaway	LB 8 116	1	10	10	92	94	72	6½	Atkinson P	25000	10.10
13Jan94 5SA1	Son Of A Bronze	LB 5 116	5	2	6½	61	5hd	53	76½	Pedroza M A	25000	6.70
19Dec93 9Hol7	Crystal Wes	LBb 5 116	3	4	9hd	10	10	10	8nk	Nakatani C S	25000	8.10
17Dec93 8Hol5	Hoedown's Lifter	Lb 5 116	9	8	4hd	45	42½	82½	99	Martinez F F	25000	73.10
13Jan94 5SA2	Cape Royale	LB 5 111	8	7	73½	5½	61½	9½	10	Gonzalez S Jr5	25000	15.70

OFF AT 4:41 Start Good. Won driving. Time, :22⁴, :46, 1:10, 1:34⁴, 1:41¹ Track fast.

$2 Mutuel Prices:

7–BIG BARTON	38.40	14.40	8.00
4–PROSPECTOR'S GHOST		4.40	3.20
6–THE CLEANERS			3.40

$2 EXACTA 7–4 PAID $167.40 $2 TRIFECTA 7–4–6 PAID $793.40 $2 QUINELLA 4–7 PAID $70.40

When the race was over there was an eerie silence from most of the other racegoers. They were stunned. Our group was whooping and hollering and dancing in the streets. Just about everybody in the group had the win bet and exacta. A bunch of us had the trifecta, too. We crushed this race.

The only ticket that I didn't cash was the $100 win bet on Prospector's Ghost. My total investment in this race was $618. My total return was $13,737.30. My profit was $13,119.30. It was great fun to hand the clerk 14 winning tickets and watch his face as the total got bigger and bigger. I won more than $15,000. It was a great day.

Let's now talk about winning the biggest horse race of all.

Winning the Biggest
Horse Race of All

According to the U.S. Census Bureau, 87 percent of Americans of retirement age retire on annual incomes of $10,000 or less. That's below the poverty level.

According to the Internal Revenue Service, 85 percent of the people reaching age sixty-five don't even have $200 in the bank. Think about that, 85 percent of our senior citizens can't write a check for $200.

According to a study by the United States Department of Health and Human Services, 96 percent of Americans don't achieve financial independence at the end of their working life. They end up depending upon charity or family or government handouts.

As we have seen before, the number-one reason cited by the Internal Revenue Service for financial failure among Americans is the failure to make a plan to get more income and the failure to take action on that plan. The IRS is wrong. That's not the reason. The real reason is the inability to delay gratification. I call this the "Polaroid Syndrome." Most people would rather have things now than have to sacrifice in the short term. They choose short-term gain at the expense of long-term pain. It's the American Way. Spend now and mortgage our future.

Most Americans are on a financial road to misery and deprivation. They feel constant financial pressure. It doesn't matter if they make $25,000 or $250,000 a year. No matter how much they make, they manage to spend a little more, hoping for a wave of prosperity that will solve all their financial problems. Not only do they end up flat broke, they rarely enjoy life along the way because of continual financial pressure. They live from paycheck to paycheck with little or nothing building in investments. Most of their dreams have all but completely faded away. They've surrendered to circumstances, and have come to feel that life happens to them instead of exercising their birthright, which is freedom and prosperity.

I often ask this question to my students: "If you made twice as much money as you're now making, would you be financially secure?" The answer is a resounding yes. However, when I confront my audience with the fact that they are now making at least twice as much as they made eight years ago and aren't financially secure, they start to realize that making more money is not the answer.

The solution is to spend less than you earn and invest the difference. If a person saves $8.62 per week and invests it at 12 percent per year compounded monthly from the time she is 18 until she reaches age 65, she would retire a millionaire and have a retirement income of more than $100,000 per year and never touch a single dollar of her million-dollar estate. (A drugged monkey should be able to earn an average of 12 percent per year.) Becoming a millionaire is actually easy once you have a plan. The problem is that it takes discipline to create the plan and stick to it, and wisdom to change the plan if it's not working or could be made better.

If you are now in debt, take heart. The government itself is in the same dire financial straits. If we continue at our 1993 pace, by the year 2000 the yearly interest on our national debt will be more than a trillion dollars! That's just the interest. What about the principal? The interest alone represents $3,571 for every man, woman and child in America. Needless to say, if you're thinking about Social Security after the turn of the millennium, you may have to think again.

How did things get this bad? Why is it that most people fail when it comes to handling money? How could it be that a doctor making $200,000 a year feels financial pressure? Better yet, how could a movie producer or corporate executive earning more than a million dollars a year, with an unlimited expense account, manage to wind up broke at the age of 65? How could Sammy Davis Jr. die broke when he made millions? How could Wayne Newton de-clare bankruptcy when he has never made less than a million dollars every year since he was a teenager? How could Willie Nelson end up owing the government more than $17,000,000?

The answer is simple. Lack of knowledge of handling finances. Were you ever taught how to manage your financial resources throughout your life? Were you instructed, anywhere in the educational system, about how to grow your money, how to handle credit, how to buy and sell a home, how to buy insurance, how to develop a spending plan to match your family's goals, how to find super bargains for most things you want to own, how to buy a car without being ripped off, how to invest, how to stay out of debt, how to end up with a lot of money and the time to enjoy it? Probably not.

This chapter will give you the necessary strategies (or refer you to where you can learn them) to master your financial destiny. Rather than suffer the fate of 96 percent of your fellow citizens, you'll own a house on Easy Street.

When people are asked what they want for their children, the most prevalent response is for them to live the "American Dream." The American Dream is to get an education, then get a good job, work in a secure occupation, buy a house, and have good credit so you can purchase whatever you want when you need it. Work until age 65 and then retire. After retirement, take it easy, travel and live a reasonably comfortable life. How many Americans have achieved this ideal? Answer: Damn few—less than 4 percent! Talk about lies, big lies, and gross lies (including statistics). The American Dream makes prevarication look like puppy dogs and lollipops. Imagine—our nation's vision available to less than one in 25 of us.

The reason this dream isn't accomplished for 96 percent of us is that we bought into a system that is rigged against us. We actually volunteer to give a large majority of our wealth to giant financial institutions because we refuse to be denied the instant gratification of our immediate wants. Notice I said wants, not needs. The average family earns between one million and two million (1993 dollars) in its working lifetime. How is it that most of us will wind up broke?

Let's consider a couple who earn approximately a million dollars in their working lifetime. Suppose they purchase a $100,000 home and take a 30-year mortgage. Over the 30 years they'll pay over

$375,000 in payments. They'll pay more than $250,000 in interest. They must earn $333,000 to net $250,000 to give it to the mortgage company. That's 33 percent of their wealth! Add to that the $330,000 lifetime of taxes, and now you know where most of it goes. $663,000 is spoken for. That leaves $337,000 for all other expenses. That is $216 a week to pay for all the family food, clothing, utilities, education, automobiles, gifts, credit card payments, and every other expense the family will encounter during these 30 years.

It's no wonder the statistics are so abysmal. Almost two thirds of their wealth is taken by government and the mortgage company. It's damn near impossible to achieve financial independence when the government and big business siphon two thirds to three fourths of their wealth. It's also interesting to note that the government itself is burdened with debt—so much debt, again, that by the year 2000 the interest alone will be more than a trillion dollars per year! To give you an idea of the magnitude of this number, a trillion seconds is 31,709 years. If a trillion dollars, in hundred-dollar bills, were stacked up and counted around the clock, it would take more than 2,000 man-years just to count it.

Let's reverse the above situation. The payment on a $100,000 mortgage exclusive of taxes is approximately $870 per month. Suppose our American Dream couple could invest this each month for 30 years at only 8% interest. This would amount to $1,296,612.72. At 12 percent per year compounded monthly, which is a much more realistic return, it would amount to more than three million dollars. This would provide for a retirement income of more than $300,000 a year and they would never have to touch the principal. They would have financial freedom and would get to keep their wealth instead of giving most of it away.

Back to harsh reality. Let's see what happens instead. Our American Dream couple will most likely fix up their dream house. Suppose they purchase $4,000 worth of furniture, appliances, and improvements. Suppose they use their MasterCard and make only the suggested minimum payments (which banks encourage). It'll take them longer to pay for the improvements than it will to pay off the house. If they listen to the bank and make only minimum payments, it'll take more than 30 years to pay off this debt and they'll have forked out more than $20,000 in total payments. That's more than $16,000 in interest! They must earn $24,000 just to pay the finance company. By not delaying gratification, they gave away $24,000 of their future wealth for the sake of having $4,000 worth of improvements now. Lousy deal.

Let's do this another way. Let's delay gratification and instead invest this money in paying down the mortgage. The first credit card payment would have been $100. If they added this amount to their mortgage payment each month, their house would be paid off in less than 20 years. They then could invest the $970 per month in mutual funds. Assuming an average return of 12 percent per year and tax-free compounding, they would have a paid house and $223,137.53 in investments. If they did what everybody else does, they would have a paid-off house in thirty years and no investments.

Are you starting to see how insidious credit really is? It's like robbing you without a gun. You volunteer for this. How? By listening to the prevailing wisdom. By insisting on having things now instead of when you can afford to pay cash for them. This seems okay because everybody else is doing it. *But you don't want to do what everybody else is doing.* If you do, you'll get the same results. You want to do the very opposite. You must develop the proper attitudes and strategies that build wealth, not a ball and chain of debt.

Let's look at what the average guy does. He loads himself down with monthly payments. House payments, car payments, gasoline credit card payments, department-store credit card payments, MasterCard, Visa, American Express payments, and in some cases supermarket credit card payments. The average number of credit cards per family is 12! Every month he does all the work, yet others receive the benefits of his labor. About 75 percent of his lifetime wealth winds up in the hands of the government, mortgage companies, and credit card companies. It's no wonder 96 percent of Americans reach their golden years broke! Do you realize that a majority of our citizens are living on the financial edge? They are two paychecks away from being homeless. Why? Because they bought somebody else's program. They bought the American Dream. Instant gratification. It's a big lie!

Do you know what most people worry about all the time? Money. Do you know what they think the solution is? Increase their income. In their desperate attempt to get ahead, they sacrifice the two most important things in life, time and their health. Anxiety about money is a killer. Financial stress is real. You feel it, members of your family feel it, and your neighbor feels it. The sense that you just can't seem to get out of your present financial morass. A majority of marital and family problems originate from financial pressures. Spouses become frustrated by unrealized dreams, unpaid bills, and a sense that there's no way out; their irritation focuses on their partner. Worse yet, they react by using drugs and alcohol. Many people come home feeling the squeeze of too many bills and not enough money. Their solution: Take a brief chemical vacation from their unpleasant reality. I'll bet that we each know someone who has succumbed to financial pressures. Sickness or death was the result. My friend Lloyd White committed suicide because he had too many bills and didn't see how he could possibly earn enough money to pay them off. Lloyd took the ultimate vacation.

Thoreau was precisely correct when he wrote, "Most men live lives of quiet desperation." And they do so because of ignorance of the principles of wealth. Instead of sitting down with a few good books on the subject of investing and wealth accumulation, they listen to their accountant, their friends, and, worst of all, their stockbroker. They refuse to accept responsibility for their financial destiny. It doesn't matter how much they earn. The more they earn, the more irresponsible they tend to get. Most high-income earners have a tendency to ask, "Where do I sign?" Rather than try to understand the details, they simply trust the salesperson to have their best interests in mind. This is a big mistake. Most of the time, the salesperson has the salesperson's interest in mind. High earners who are very busy, such as medical doctors and corporate executives, are usually the world's worst investors. The larger the income, the more irresponsible they become. It's no wonder that many of them wind up broke or having to continue to work instead of retiring and enjoying their golden years.

Here's a wonderful example of well-meaning but bad advice: A good friend of mine pays over $25,000 a year for tax and money-management advice. He owns a beautiful house that he intends to live in for the rest of his life. He owes $450,000 on his mortgage. His monthly payment is $3,768.28. Needless to say, he makes a good income. The mortgage has 36 years remaining. His accountant advises that he not prepay his mortgage in order to preserve his one large tax deduction. I told him to fire his accountant. Unless the tax rate is 100 percent, it doesn't make any sense to give away 69 cents in order to save 31 cents. If he pays off this present mortgage, as the bank suggests, he will pay them $1,627,896.96, $1,177,896.96 of which is strictly interest payment. After I pointed this out to him, you can bet your most precious organ that he won't allow the bank to take over one million dollars of his wealth. Instead, the mortgage company will receive 180 payments of $4,768.28, totaling $858,290.40. It really can't complain—it will make more than $400,000 on the deal. My friend pulls in a very good income. He can easily afford to add $1,000 to his mortgage payment. He has a private pension into which he's been depositing $1,000 per month for his retirement. Instead, he'll accelerate his mortgage and invest the entire amount after the house is fully paid off.

Using my plan, his house will be paid off in 15 years. From then on, he'll accrue wealth at the rate of $4,768.28 per month. This will amount to $5,375,759.87 in the 21 years after he's free of mortgage debt. If he listens to his accountant and continues his present plan, in 36 years he'll have a paid house and $2,496,723.53 in investments. The difference between plans is more than $2.8 million! It's a pity that he actually had to pay his accountant for such bad advice.

Please notice that all throughout this discussion you'll be urged to consider strategies using your present income. That's not to discourage you from increasing your income, far from it. My purpose is to show you that you can accomplish amazing financial results within your present means.

Let me give you some magic numbers: $286.45, $1,686.49, and $5,466.09. These are the amounts of money you have to save each month to accumulate $1,000,000 ($286.45 a month for 40 years at 8 percent amounts to $1,000,000; $1,697.73 a month for 20 years at 8 percent amounts to $1,000,000; $5,466.09 a month for 10 years at 8 percent amounts to $1,000,000).

These numbers assume a return of only 8 percent. Remember our friend, the drugged monkey—he can earn 12 percent. A more realistic return is at least that. The new magic numbers become: $85.00 a month for 40 years at 12 percent amounts to $1,000,000; $1,010.86 a month for 20 years at 12 percent amounts to $1,000,000; $4,347.09 a month for 10 years at 12 percent amounts to $1,000,000.

The most insidious wealth-drainer in this life is the monthly payment trap. When you go to buy a new car, the first thing the salesman asks is, "How much you can afford per month"? Don't answer this question! Instead, mentally bend him over and stick his suggested monthly payment plan as far into his posterior as possible. Learn to reframe this situation. Always negotiate total price, not monthly payment. Don't go for the monthly payment crap. That salesman has a siphon hose ready to suck your wealth right into the dealership's pocket. Don't do it. Mentally, rectally examine the salesman. Or else simply avoid this situation altogether. In fact, why bother with an automobile dealer? The best automobile strategy is to purchase a two-year-old car from its original owner. Let the previous owner take it in the shorts. You'll get 80 percent of the useful life of the car for 50 percent of the purchase price. He'll get 20 percent of the useful life of the car for 50 percent of the of the purchase price. When you're financially independent and can pay for a car with cash, then and only then should you bother with new-car dealers.

Did you notice how seldom the total price of an item is ever mentioned when you shop for relatively large items? Have you noticed the recent Cadillac campaign? Lease a brand-new Seville for $499 per month. They conveniently forget to mention that the total purchase price is more than $35,000 and the lease payments have no chance to overcome the depreciation. In other words, it's going to cost you part of your rear end to get out of that lease. Many major appliance stores ticket their goods with monthly payment amounts. A washing machine will be priced at $600. The ticket will proclaim, "Only $29.95 per month!" (The small print tells you the duration is 24 months.) Multiply this out—you're not paying $600, you're paying $718.80 for a $600 washing machine. There's only one way to pay exactly what an item is worth. Cash.

You have to get monthly payments out of your life. If you can't afford something, don't buy it. If it's a need as opposed to a want, buy a used one. Every time you purchase something that you can't afford, you're letting other people dip into your wealth. You're mortgaging your future for immediate gratification. You're letting the destructive principle of exchanging short-term gain for long-term pain steal your wealth. You want to do the very opposite. You want to experience short-term pain for long-term gain. Resist the urge for immediate gratification.

The American Dream teaches us that financial security is a paycheck. You go to work for a big solid company and manage not to get fired and that assures you financial security. Tell that to the 20,000 people laid off at General Motors in 1991. Tell that to the 19,000 people laid off by IBM in 1991. People are taught that when they reach age 65, Social Security will provide for them. Talk about a big lie! The maximum benefit (in 1993) is around $900 per month. Imagine having to have to live on less than $225 per week in your golden years. This is true for 87 percent of Social Security recipients. Forget the American Dream. It's a lie. A big one. A monstrous one.

The IRS says the reason for most people's deplorable financial condition is the failure to make a plan to get more income. That's not the reason. You don't have to increase your income. With your present resources, it's more than likely that you can get out of installment debt in less than five years and turn the system around so it works for you. You don't have to increase your income in order to start building real wealth. What you need is a strategy that accomplishes the following three things:

1. Get out of debt.
2. Operate strictly on cash.
3. Focus all available cash on wealth building.

The prevailing financial strategies don't work. Think about it. If they did, would 96 percent of American still be ending up broke? Where do you turn for help? You'd think that your accountant or lawyer would have the answers. They have answers, but not the correct ones. Most of them are in debt up to their bippies. Please don't mistake driving a Mercedes for true wealth. If your accountant is driving a fancy car, it just means that he or she is making

bigger payments and giving more of his or her wealth to the finance company faster than you are. Most accountants will tell you
to continue to pay mortgage interest because of the tax deduction.
How stupid. Think about that for a moment—do you really believe
that it's prudent to keep paying a dollar in interest so you can save
from 15 to 31 cents in taxes? Or how about the advice to keep paying credit card interest at close to 20 percent while saving 10 percent of your income in a savings account that pays around 3
percent. It doesn't take a genius to see that you're much better off
paying off your credit card debt: 17 percent better off. The danger
of conventional financial wisdom is that it sounds plausible, so we
all just nod and follow one another around in wealth-draining cir-
cles. Make no mistake about it—conventional financial wisdom
leads to poverty. Your goal should be financial independence.

Financial independence means not being financially dependent
upon anyone. It means you don't need a job, because you have a
permanent source of income. Work is optional. It means you don't
have any bills. You read this right. You don't owe a penny on anything, including your house, your car, credit cards, or anything
else. The only things you have to pay for each month are food, utilities, transportation, insurance, and taxes. No one can threaten
you financially because there's nothing they can take away from
you. They can't threaten you with taking away your job, because
you don't need it. They can't threaten you with taking away your
house, because you own it. They can't threaten you with inflation
because it just makes your investments appreciate faster.

When it comes to reaching this kind of independence, most accountants, lawyers, and financial planners don't have a clue how
the system really works. They still believe that mortgage debt is a
good tax shelter. They don't see it for the insidious monster that it
really is. Do you realize that when you take a 30-year mortgage
you'll end up paying the mortgage company more than three
times the amount of the mortgage in total payments? Two thirds of
your total payments are interest payments that drain your wealth.
Better yet, because of taxes, you must earn close to three times
your mortgage to net the total interest payments that you volun-
tarily give to the mortgage company. If you could turn this around
and save the same amount per month, you would be a multimil-
lionaire in less time than the 30-year mortgage term.

Do you realize that we are all millionaires? Let me explain. The average family earns between $25,000 and $50,000 per year. The average working lifetime is 40 years. This means that they'll earn between one million and two million dollars in their lifetimes. If we're typical, almost 70 percent of our wealth will be surrendered to the government, the mortgage company, banks, and credit grantors. If this sounds a little like slavery, that's because it is. Listen to Publilius Syrus: "Debt is the slavery of the free." He knows from whence he speaks, and he said this more than 2,000 years ago!

The purpose of this discussion is to show you how to attain wealth by reallocating your present resources. If you never read another book, please read George Clason's *The Richest Man in Babylon.* In it, he gives the five laws of gold:

1. Gold cometh gladly and in increasing quantity to any man who will put by not less than one tenth of his earnings to create an estate for his future and that of his family.
2. Gold laboreth diligently and contentedly for the wise owner who finds for it profitable employment, multiplying even as flocks of the fields.
3. Gold clingeth to the protection of the cautious owner who invests it under the advice of men wise in its handling.
4. Gold slippeth away from the man who invests it in businesses or purposes with which he is not familiar or which are not improved by those skilled in its keep.
5. Gold flees the man who would force it to impossible earnings or who followeth the alluring advice of tricksters and schemers or who trusts it to his own inexperience and romantic desires in investment.

These laws sum up the principles of wealth rather well. The whole trick to getting rich is to get on the right side of the compounding principle. Getting on the right side of the compounding principle means several things. It means having money in the bank, rather than owing the bank money. But if you're saving by putting money in the bank, you're making a big mistake, as you will see. Getting on the right side of compounding means positioning yourself so that time works for you rather than against you.

When you're positioned properly, each passing hour, day, month, and year should add to your net wealth. If time is not making you rich, you're on the wrong side of the compounding principle. If you'll spend less than you earn and invest the difference, your next address will be Easy Street. You'll be surprised at how quickly you'll get there. Here are some comments on each of these principles, put into a more modern context.

Law #1: Pay yourself first.

Take at least 10 percent of your net earnings and invest it. First fill your security bucket. Build a critical mass of investment dollars so the interest each month is enough to pay all your monthly needs (food, rent, utilities, transportation, insurance, and taxes). The very best investments for your security bucket are tax-deferred cash-accumulating vehicles such as company pension plans, universal life insurance, and variable annuities. These investments should be self-directed, if possible. When the security bucket is full, you've achieved financial security.

Next, fill your growth bucket. Build a critical mass of investment dollars so that the interest each month is enough to pay all your present monthly expenses. That is, fully support your present lifestyle. The best investments for your growth bucket are mutual funds. Invest in a family of mutual funds. (Read Bill Donoghue's *The Donoghue Strategies* and Charles Givens's *Wealth Without Risk*. Use the Donoghue or Givens money-movement strategies.) When your growth bucket is full, you've achieved financial independence. If you haven't already done so, accelerate your mortgage payments. When your mortgage is paid, use the payments for aggressive investing into the bucket you're now working on.

The final bucket is the home-run bucket. Now is the time to invest directly in stocks, commercial real estate, art, precious metals, collectors' items, and any speculative investment that you know something about. Remember, if you don't know how to value an investment, don't buy it. Your ultimate goal is financial freedom. It's to be able to have anything you want, in any quantity you want, anytime you want.

Law #2: Use the law of compound interest.

Saving is not investing even though you're receiving compound interest. Savings accounts and money market accounts offered by

banks are a losing proposition when you consider taxes and inflation. When you have a cash reserve, you'll be able to take advantage of wonderful opportunities. The very best accounts for the
purpose of storing money temporarily are asset-management accounts. Many money market mutual funds allow you to write
checks against your balance. You're much better off in a money
market mutual fund than you are in a money market account or a
CD. Money market funds pay a higher rate of interest and are
safer. Your job is to pick investments that will compound at the
fastest rate with the greatest margin of safety. Your goal should be
to double your net worth every five to six years.

Law #3: Get a good financial coach.

Don't listen to investment salespeople, especially stockbrokers.
Don't purchase an investment over the telephone, no matter how
good it sounds. If you work with financial planners, make sure that
they're fee-based and don't earn commissions on their recommendations. It's best to find a good CPA who understands investments,
taxes, insurance, and estate planning. Make sure that your CPA
has a net worth of at least one million dollars and isn't in debt.
Please don't listen to your neighbors or relatives when it comes to
investments unless they're millionaires. Even if they are, check
things out for yourself. It's not a bad idea to join an investment
club. Invest in books that contain the information relevant to your
present situation. Model a successful investor. Attend financial
seminars in which the presenters are millionaires who have made
the bulk of their fortune from investments: "Wise, indeed is he
who investeth his treasures under the advice of men skilled in the
ways of gold."

Law #4: Don't invest in things you're not qualified to evaluate.

You must understand that you're ultimately responsible for
your investment decisions. If you don't know how to value an investment in which you're interested, you must hire an impartial
advisor who's an expert in his field. For example, if you're considering a piece of investment property and aren't fully knowledge-
able about the property values in the neighborhood you're
considering, you must hire an appraiser. It's always best to get a
second opinion. If you're considering investing in a particular mutual fund, check out its performance in Morningstar or a similar

rating service. Whenever you make an investment of any kind, check out the track record of the company in which you're investing. Also, check out the credentials of your salesperson. Most of the time, you should purchase investments yourself and not involve a salesperson. My personal rule is that I never invest with anyone who has a lesser net worth than mine. In fact, I never even consult with anyone who has a lesser net worth than mine. Whenever I need advice on any subject, I always check out the credentials of a potential advisor before I contact him or her.

Law #5: Don't let your greed get in the way of your good judgment.

If something sounds too good to be true, it usually is. Always ask the question, "What's in it for him?" In every negotiation you enter, make sure that there are two winners. Don't ever try to take advantage of your fellow man. If a deal sounds too one-sided, avoid it. Any proposition that offers immense returns without any risk should be avoided. Remember the aphorism "A fool and his money are soon parted." The world is full of con men and scam artists who are quite convincing in their appeal to your greed. Always check things out for yourself. Don't bother to check the references given to you by a salesperson. Do you think you will be given names of unhappy customers? Professional con men hire "singers"—fellow unethical sleazebags who are paid to give a glowing reference. Exercise due diligence. Don't take unnecessary risks. If things don't check out, pass on them. Opportunities are like streetcars—they come along on a regular basis. If you miss one today, so what. There'll be another one along real soon. If you're ever told that an investment must be made today or you'll miss a golden opportunity, don't walk away—run away!

In order to win the financial game, it's necessary to master five separate aspects of handling money. They are personal spending, insurance, investments, taxes, and estate planning. Your job is to learn and practice the strategies that apply to you. In addition, read biographies of very successful people. This is to prove to yourself that ordinary people can achieve extraordinary things by applying the principles of wealth. Ideally, they'll save you a lot of time and effort by being models for you.

If I seem to be very enthusiastic about the subject of modeling, it's because this technique is so damn powerful. Whatever you want to do, have, or be in this life is yours if you'll simply find the appropriate model(s). If you want to quit smoking, find an ex-smoker and learn her strategies. If you want to lose weight and keep it off, find an ex–fat person and learn his strategies. If you want to be the top salesman in your company, spend a week with the current top salesperson and learn her strategies. If you want to be a master investor, find the appropriate model. In many cases it's not necessary to even make a phone call because your model has written a book detailing his strategies. Such is the case with Peter Lynch. He's the most successful mutual fund manager in history. He details his strategies in his excellent book *One Up on Wall Street*. He followed it with a gem titled *Beating the Street*. Please read and study both books. They contain the key to the mint. Please insist that every author that you've chosen to model has actually accomplished the thing that you want to achieve. In other words, don't read books by college professors who haven't actually accomplished what they are writing about. This is especially the case for investments. You can read all sorts of theoretical stuff that purports to teach winning strategies but is written by authors who don't have two nickels to rub together. By the way, there are excellent books written by genuine achievers on the subjects of quitting smoking, weight management, and acquiring wealth. You must be very careful when choosing your models. Check them out.

Please don't listen to advice from anybody less than an expert. The reason most people don't win the financial game is that they listen to the wrong people. The purpose of this discussion is to make sure that you listen to the right people. Unfortunately, even the right people are wrong some of the time. A good example of this is the advice that Charles Givens gives about life insurance. He states in no uncertain terms that you should "buy term insurance and invest the difference." This isn't the worst advice in the world, but you must consider the fact that universal life insurance allows for tax-deferred accumulation of dividends. There are also some very powerful estate-planning strategies that use life insurance proceeds to guarantee that your heirs pay the minimum estate tax. In general, Charles Givens is a guy you'll want to listen to. He's worth more than $100 million and has mastered the game of life. He's a happy man. He travels the world in style for more than half the year. He's figured out how to accumulate a staggering amount of money by working part-time.

One of the most basic principles of wealth is to spend less than you earn and invest the rest. Donald Gloisten, author of the *Gloisten Investment Letter,* states this principle in a very interesting way. He says, "At some point in your life you must decide to become a creditor as opposed to a debtor if you want to win the financial game." What an elegant thought. It's true that most people spend their lives in debt.

If you perform the following experiment, you'll learn the answer to the question, "Where does it all go?" For the next three months keep track of every penny you spend. The only way to learn about your spending behavior is to keep track of every cent that moves through your life. Go to your local stationery store and purchase an inexpensive expense diary. Write down every single transaction that involves money. Total up all your income. Use this spending log to categorize your expenditures. Be very specific about these categories. For example, don't use very broad categories such as food. Break this spending down to restaurant spending, groceries, snack items at work, lunches at work, etc.

This exercise will blow your mind. You'll be amazed how much money you spend on trivial things. This process of self-discovery will lead you to construct a much more intelligent spending plan. (Notice that I don't use the word "budget.") Let's face it—if you want to become secure financially, you must learn to live within your means. In fact, you must learn to pay yourself first. Your investment money must be a line item in your spending plan.

If you are now in debt, use your investment money to accelerate your debt paydown. Almost everybody thinks that the solution to his financial problems is to increase his income. As usual, almost everybody is wrong. The trick is to learn to live within your means. Increased income then becomes a bonus. It should be used for investments only. (Remember: When you're in debt, your best investment is to pay down your debt as fast as possible.) This technique of developing a spending plan will get you to financial security in the quickest time possible.

Once you've developed your detailed categories, you'll know where to go to save money. One of the first places you can save a bunch of money each month is on insurance. Most people are either underinsured or overinsured. Most people overpay on insurance because they listen to their insurance agent, who's a commissioned sales representative. His goal is to get you to purchase the insurance that yields the highest possible commission for him. Your interests aren't mutual. Learn the facts about insurance. The simplest and best book I can recommend is *Wealth Without Risk* by Charles Givens.

The next place most people can save a bunch of money each month is on their taxes. The IRS has bullied and intimidated us with the threat of a tax audit. Most people are pussycats when it comes to taking allowable tax deductions. The fear of an audit combined with their inadequate record-keeping guarantees they'll pay far more than they actually have to. Now that you'll have an exact record of your spending, you'll have nothing to fear from an IRS tax audit. This should be enough motivation to get you to keep an expense log and develop an intelligent spending plan. Your job is to learn the tax strategies that will put a lot more money in your pocket. Again, *Wealth Without Risk* is an excellent reference.

Here's a simple money-saving technique that the distaff member of the family may not appreciate: Don't go shopping. Did you know that 70 percent of the adult population visits a regional mall weekly? Only 25 percent are actually looking for a specific item. More than half the retail purchases are spur-of-the-moment items that are really not needed! Wait until you have both the need and the money before you purchase anything. When you have both, then you can go. It's best to comparison shop by phone or in discount mail order catalogs. You'll be amazed at the range of prices quoted for the exact same item. Your local merchant will usually honor any lower-advertised price rather than lose the deal. Bargaining has become a way of life in America. To boost sales in a sluggish economy, many retailers are willing to shave substantial amounts off asking prices. Learn to negotiate. Ask for discounts. Use your savings for your investments. The more you invest, the quicker your address will be Easy Street.

It's been stated that 80 percent of what people believe to be true is false. I don't know how to verify the truth of this statement in general. In particular regarding investments, especially stocks, bonds, and money-market instruments, I can assure you beyond a shadow of a doubt that this statement is true. The bond market and the money market dwarf the stock market. Most investors believe that bonds are safe and offer an adequate return, that T-bills are the safest investments, and that stocks are risky and unpredictable and usually result in a loss of principal. As usual, what most people believe turns out to be false.

Listen to what Peter Lynch says:

Historically, investing in stocks is undeniably more profitable than investing in bonds. In fact, since 1927, common stocks have recorded gains of 9.8 percent a year on average, as compared to 5 percent for corporate bonds, 4.4 percent for government bonds, and 3.4 percent for Treasury bills.

The long-term inflation rate, as measured by the Consumer Price Index, is 3 percent a year, which gives common stocks a real return of 6.8 percent a year. The real return on Treasury bills, known as the most conservative and sensible of all places to put money, has been nil. That's right. Zippo.

The advantage of a 9.8 percent return from stocks over a 5 percent return from bonds may sound piddling to some, but consider this financial fable. If at the end of 1927 a modern Rip Van Winkle had gone to sleep for 60 years on $20,000 worth of corporate bonds, paying 5 percent compounded, he would have awakened with $373,584—enough for him to afford a nice condo, a Volvo, and a haircut; whereas if he'd invested in stocks, which returned 9.8 percent a year, he'd have $5,459,720. (Since Rip was asleep, neither the Crash of '29 nor the ripple of '87 would have scared him out of the market.)

In 1927, if you had put $1,000 in each of the four investments listed below, and the money had compounded tax-free, then 60 years later you'd have had these amounts:

Treasury bills	$ 7,400
Government bonds	13,200
Corporate bonds	17,600
Common stocks	272,000

"In spite of crashes, depressions, wars, recessions, ten different presidential administrations, and numerous changes in skirt lengths, stocks in general have paid off fifteen times as well as corporate bonds, and well over thirty times better than Treasury bills!

There's a logical explanation for this. In stocks you've got the company's growth on your side. You're a partner in a prosperous and expanding business. In bonds, you're nothing more than the nearest source of spare change. When you lend money to somebody, the best you can hope for is to get it back, plus interest.

Think of the people who've owned McDonald's bonds over the years. The relationship between them and McDonald's begins and ends with the payoff of the debt, and that's not the exciting part of McDonald's. Sure, the original bondholders have gotten their money back, the same as they would have with a bank CD, but the original stockholders have gotten rich. They own the company. You'll never get a tenbagger (ten times your original investment) in a bond—unless you're a debt sleuth who specializes in bonds in default."

It's interesting to note that 90 percent of all investment dollars are parked in bonds, CDs, and the money market. Nine out of ten invested dollars are invested in the wrong place! The stock market is the absolute best place for you to invest your money. Within the stock market itself there lies a group of companies known as "small caps," which warrant your serious attention.

If, at the end of 1940, you had invested $1,000 in the stocks of the *Standard and Poor's 500*, you would now have $382,001. If, however, you had invested the same $1,000 in smaller companies, you would now have $2,170,000! (These figures exclude taxes and assume you reinvest all dividends.)

There is overwhelming evidence that small cap stocks, those not recommended by institutions and not covered by more than a dozen analysts, outperform the market by a wide margin.

If you want a powerhouse strategy that returns better than 20 percent per year, restrict yourself to small cap stocks that show high book-value-to-price ratios and are not covered by the institutions.

The very best small cap stocks to purchase are the ones that you know something about. Think about the companies that you do business with. Think about the companies that your company does business with. When you're at your local mall, take notice of which shops are crowded.

Once you find a suitable prospect, find out where the company is located. You're a phone call away from all the information that you need to make a judicious investment decision. Call the company and ask for the director of investor relations. Let her tell you about the company. Don't get caught up in her enthusiasm. Have her send you a copy of the company's 10K (the quarterly report filed with the SEC). This document contains the crucial information that you need to make a decision.

We're trying to catch companies in their growth phase. We look for a company that's making a profit and has a PE (price-to-earnings ratio) less than its growth rate. As I write this, the PE of the market is 16.3. That is, the average investor is willing to pay 16.3 times one year's earnings for one share of stock. As value investors, we don't want to pay this much unless there are mitigating circumstances, such as a tremendous growth rate. (My personal investment rule is to never invest in a company whose PE is larger than its growth rate.) Ideally, we would like the PE of the company we invest in to be about half the PE of the market. In addition, we want the book-value-to-price ratio to be greater than one. That is, we are looking for stocks that are selling for less than their fair market value. We actually have the best of both worlds. We own stocks that have not yet been discovered by the institutions and are worth much more than they are selling for.

It sounds like it would be very difficult to find opportunities where the PE of the company is much lower than the PE of the market and the stock sells for less than its book value. It's not. You can find values like this every day. Just keep your eyes open. Ask questions. Make a bunch of phone calls to receive 10Ks from companies that you're interested in.

You can make this a very valuable tax-deductible hobby. On your next vacation, stop and visit a number of companies whose stock you're interested in buying. One or two good picks can put a huge bulge in your retirement account. Master small cap stocks and your address will be Easy Street.

There is plenty of worry and concern around Wall Street these days (late December 1993). Some money mavens are warning that we are on the brink of disaster. They point to the fact that the Dow Jones average is at or near an all-time high, average price/earnings ratios are greater than 20 times earnings, and dividends are at an all-time low. In addition, interest rates are rising and corporate earnings are much lower than expected. If that's not enough, there are new fears of inflation because our president is seen as Don Quixote tilting at windmills when it comes to solving the problem of the budget deficit. All these sentiments taken together seem to suggest a huge downside movement in the stock market. This may or may not happen. (Odds are that it eventually will, but when?) The trick is to be prepared.

When things start coming down, that's the exact time to buy. At the same time all the overvalued behemoths come crashing down, the value stocks will also fall because of investor panic. Historically, investors who purchased good solid companies and kept them for a very long time make very substantial profits on Wall Street. To prove my point, if you had purchased $10,000 worth of stock (using the S&P index) at the exact market tops in the years 1968, 1972, 1980, and 1987 (the worst years in the last quarter century), that $40,000 investment would be worth almost $250,000 today.

Value is value, regardless of the DJ or S&P averages. It's not important when you buy. It's important *what* you buy. If you restrict yourself to stocks that have long-term potential and are not concerned with day-to-day fluctuations, you'll hit a home run in the stock market. A hundred shares of Coca-Cola purchased in 1919 at $40 per share are worth more than $8 million dollars today. (Most shareholders bailed out in 1929.) An investment of $10,000 Boeing Aircraft twenty years ago is now worth $800,000. The same amount invested in Philip Morris and McDonald's is now worth $600,000 and $200,000 respectively. The reason that a vast majority of investors don't cash in on these bonanzas is because they read the newspapers and watch television. They constantly read about gloom and doom. "AEROSPACE TO LOSE 30,000 JOBS THIS YEAR." "IBM TO LAY OFF ANOTHER 5,000 WORKERS." "UNEMPLOYMENT CONTINUES AT DANGEROUS RATE." Do these recent headlines sound familiar? Why would you want to hold on to shares of stock in such horrible economic times? *Because it's so damn profitable, that's why.*

History repeats itself. Things go in cycles. We have boom and bust and everything in between during any 20-year period. In fact, let's shorten our view to ten years. Suppose you invested $10,000 in Philip Morris just ten years ago. Today that investment is worth $63,000. Same is true for PepsiCo. My point is simple: Patience is rewarded.

Greed is a capital sin. (It relieves you of your capital.) You don't have to wait until you die to be punished for yielding to the temptation of greed. You'll get your reward right here on earth. It's an empty pocketbook. Whenever you buy a stock, buy it because it's a good long-term investment. Don't buy it because you think it's going to double or triple in a short time. The stock market isn't a casino. You must remember that you are purchasing ownership in a company. Look at the fundamentals. Is the company earning a profit? Will it continue to do so? Is a share of this company's stock the very best value you can get at this time?

Your portfolio should contain at least one or two stalwarts that have the potential to be tenbaggers over the next ten to 20 years. These stocks should be bought and put away. Don't look at them for at least five years. My votes go to Intel and Microsoft. Both of these companies have virtual monopolies in their respective fields, computer hardware and software. It's no secret that computer microprocessors are here to stay. Ditto for computer software. Some other candidates are Merck, Abbott Labs, General Electric, Bristol-Myers, Boeing, McDonald's, PepsiCo, Syntex, Nordstrom, Rubbermaid, Lockheed, and IBM. (Please realize that these recommendations are being given in December 1993. Things change.)

If you want to make it to Easy Street, you're going to have to get aggressive about your investments. By aggressive I don't mean getting involved with risky, ultra-bold speculations such as commodity trading. I'm talking about using a very large part of your disposable income to purchase investments. You should be paying yourself first. A minimum of 10 percent of any net income should be used to purchase investments. If you are in debt, the best investment that you can purchase is debt service. The sooner that you are out of debt, the sooner you can begin your wealth-building program. Ordinarily I would include mortgage debt in the debt-service equation. However, if you can achieve a larger rate of return on your investments than your mortgage rate, it would be foolish to pay off your mortgage and lose the tax benefits.

The secret to financial success is the same as the secret to success in any endeavor: Know your outcome in advance. Have a desired outcome (goal) and a plan to get there. Instead of reinventing the wheel and devising a super-complicated plan, simply model the already productive plans of financially successful people. Study them. Find out what they did to make it to the top. Do the same things. You'll get the same results.

Develop a personal-wealth plan. Make it realistic, achievable, and entirely within your capacity. You'll then know the exact month in which you'll achieve financial security. Can you imagine life without financial pressure? It's not only probable, it's practically certain. It's simply a matter of executing your plan. Financial worries will become a thing of the past.

Wealth is not a state reserved for certain fortunate individuals. It's a set of skills. Once you learn and practice these skills, wealth is yours. You have a choice. You can choose to continue doing what you've been doing and get the same results you've been getting or you can choose to take action now and move yourself to a new level.

I want to take this opportunity to thank you for giving me the chance to share my ideas with you. My best wishes go with you. Let me conclude with an Irish blessing: "May the road rise to meet you. May the wind be forever at your back. And may the Lord hold you in the hollow of the palm of His hand."

INDEX